Neighboring Faiths

Neighboring
FAITHS

Christianity, Islam, and Judaism in the Middle Ages and Today

DAVID NIRENBERG

The University of Chicago Press | Chicago and London

DAVID NIRENBERG is the Deborah R. and Edgar D. Jannotta Professor of Medieval History and Social Thought and the Roman Family Director of the Neubauer Collegium for Culture and Society, both at the University of Chicago.

The University of Chicago Press, Chicago 60637
The University of Chicago Press, Ltd., London
© 2014 by The University of Chicago
All rights reserved. Published 2014.
Printed in the United States of America

23 22 21 20 19 18 17 16 15 14   1 2 3 4 5

ISBN-13: 978-0-226-16893-7 (cloth)
ISBN-13: 978-0-226-16909-5 (e-book)
DOI: 10.7208/chicago/9780226169095.001.0001

The University of Chicago Press gratefully acknowledges the generous support of the Humanities Visiting Committee at the University of Chicago toward the publication of this book.

Library of Congress Cataloging-in-Publication Data

Nirenberg, David, 1964– author.
    Neighboring faiths : Christianity, Islam, and Judaism in the Middle Ages and today / David Nirenberg.
        pages cm
    Includes bibliographical references and index.
    ISBN 978-0-226-16893-7 (cloth : alkaline paper) — ISBN 978-0-226-16909-5 (e-book) 1. Religions—Relations—History—To 1500. 2. Religious adherents—History—To 1500. 3. Islam—Relations—Christianity—History—To 1500. 4. Islam—Relations—Judaism—History—To 1500. 5. Judaism—Relations—Christianity—History—To 1500. 6. Judaism—Relations—Islam—History—To 1500. 7. Christianity and other religions—To 1500. I. Title.
BL410.N57 2014
201'.50902—dc23

                                                                    2014004370

♾ This paper meets the requirements of ANSI/NISO Z39.48–1992 (Permanence of Paper).

CONTENTS

Introduction: Neighboring Faiths   *1*

1   Christendom and Islam   *15*

2   Love between Muslim and Jew   *35*

3   Deviant Politics and Jewish Love: Alfonso VIII and the Jewess of Toledo   *55*

4   Massacre or Miracle? Valencia, 1391   *75*

5   Conversion, Sex, and Segregation   *89*

6   Figures of Thought and Figures of Flesh   *117*

7   Mass Conversion and Genealogical Mentalities   *143*

8   Was There Race before Modernity? The Example of "Jewish" Blood in Late Medieval Spain   *169*

9   Islam and the West: Two Dialectical Fantasies   *191*

Acknowledgments   *213*
Notes   *215*
Bibliography of Works Cited   *289*
Index   *321*

Neighboring Faiths

"The neighbor of a Jew will never be a good Christian." The words are those of a medieval holy man, Saint Vincent Ferrer, whose massive campaign of religious segregation and conversion in the early fifteenth century forever altered the confessional landscape of Europe. They express a powerful view of the world, simultaneously sociological and theological: right faith requires distance from wrong faith, which otherwise threatens the believer.

Saint Vincent was a brilliant impresario of this view—just how brilliant we will see in chapter 5 of this book—but he certainly did not invent it. Neighboring peoples and faiths occupy a place at the heart of each of the very diverse religious traditions we call Judaism, Christianity, and Islam. The scriptures of each of these faiths contain many, sometimes quite contradictory, teachings about both the dangers and the virtues of "neighborliness."

The Hebrew Bible, for example, enjoined the extirpation of the "seven nations" living in the "Promised Land," lest their presence lead to intermarriage and idolatry (Deut. 7:1–5). But it also decreed "the stranger that dwells with you shall be to you as one born among you, and you shall love him as yourself, for you were strangers in the land of Egypt" (Lev. 19:34, Deut. 10:19). It frequently condemned certain kinds of intermarriage but did not hesitate to start the messianic line of King David with the union of a Moabite woman and a Hebrew man (on which see the Book of Ruth). And it can in one and the same prophecy envision an apocalypse in which Israel's mighty and aggressive neighbors are utterly and vengefully destroyed and one in which they are saved and sanctified: "Blessed be my people Egypt, Assyria my creation, and Israel my heritage" (Isa. 19:25).

The New Testament, too, contains many passages that could be and have been read as commanding love of the neighbor, the stranger, and even the enemy, such as Luke 10:27, Matthew 5:43, and Hebrews 13:1. But it also preserves some that have been understood to enjoin quite the opposite. "He that is not with me is against me"; "Do you suppose that I am here to bring peace on earth? No, I tell you, but rather division"; "As for my enemies who did not want me for their king, bring them here and execute them in my presence" (Luke 11:23, 12:51, 19:27).

Similarly in the Qur'an, we can find many different injunctions about how to treat neighbors of other faiths. Some seem to encourage extermination: "Fight and slay the pagans wherever you find them, and seize them, beleaguer them, lie in wait for them with every stratagem of war" (Surah 9:5). Others might trend toward tolerance: "It is part of the mercy of Allah that you deal gently with them [Unbelievers]. If you were severe or harsh-hearted, they would have broken away from about you: so pass over [their faults], and ask for [Allah's] forgiveness for them; and consult them in affairs" (Surah 3:159).[1] Still others suggest that some pluralism is possible but segregation necessary: "O you who believe, take not Jews and Christians as friends. . . . Who of you takes them as friends is one of them"; "O believers, do not accept into your intimacy those outside your ranks: they will not fail to corrupt you" (Surah 5:56, 3:118).[2]

This is not a book about the scriptures of the three religions that claim descent from Abraham. It is a book about how Muslims, Christians, and Jews lived with and thought about each other in the Middle Ages and about what that medieval past can tell us about how they do so today. But we must start with scripture, because all later periods, including our own, often look to it for instruction about the sorts of neighborliness God has in mind. It is through their reading and rereading of its pages that later Christians, Jews, and Muslims alike debated how (in the words of the greatest medieval rabbi) "the Omnipresent one has sanctified us and separated us from the heathens."[3] So it is crucial to acknowledge from the outset of our studies that the scriptures upon which all three religions are founded can themselves sustain any number of potential attitudes toward "neighbors," ranging from love and toleration to total extermination.

Even this sharp distinction between love and extermination is a bit misleading: many communities of believers have read their scriptures in ways that identify and equate the two. In medieval Catholic canon law, for example, crusading could be considered an act of love toward the Muslim enemy, for whom an early death was considered more charitable than a long life spent in mortal sin. And as late as the mid-twentieth century, the Vatican's lawyers underwent what might seem to us considerable contortions in order to classify the Nazi embargo and segregation of Jews in Germany as legitimate expressions of love of neighbor.[4]

One may choose, from one's own time and perspective, to disagree with these previous interpretations of God's will, and indeed it is important that we do so. Critical scholars of a given scripture, for example, can argue that the authors of the text could not have intended a given interpretation at the time in which it was written. Believers can cleave to the interpretations of their own particular religious community, rather than paying attention or lending credence to those of others. But as historians, at least, we have to concede that for millions of believers in other times and places, these cruel loves and "sharp mercies" (the phrase is Martin Luther's) could be perfectly consonant with God's written word, even demanded by it. Among the many potential truths that scripture teaches on the subject of neighbors, the interpretations that moved these believers must count every bit as much as our own.[5]

That concession alone can protect us from two forms of fantasy as prevalent in our age as in any other. The first is that *my* scripture is loving while that of the other is cruel; that *my* faith community is capable of tolerance and neighborliness while that of the other is not. (Chap. 9 will focus on a few modern manifestations of this type of fantasy.) And the second is that we have scripture right: that our interpretations have recovered its original and true intent, and that all other interpretations are misreadings whose study can provide, at best, only a history of error.

The book before you is premised on a very different conviction. It pays close attention to how Muslim, Jewish, and Christian neighbors loved, tolerated, massacred, and expelled each other—all in the name of God—in periods and places both long ago and far away. And it insists that, no matter how wrongheaded or bizarre these ways of a distant past may seem, they have something to teach us about how we think and act today. "Teach" not by way of example, whether positive or negative: I am not proposing that the past serve us as a model to emulate or avoid. I mean teach rather in the sense of cultivating within us a sensibility that can discover in the past a stimulus to critical awareness about the workings of our own assumptions, hopes, and habits of thought.

Among those habits is the conviction that our religious traditions are independent of one another, that they are stable, and that one contains the capacity for truth and tolerance while the others do not. And among the hopes is the sense that greater knowledge of the neighbor leads to greater tolerance, that if only we understood better the history of our faiths, we would succeed in separating love from violence, choosing proximity over distance, and becoming better neighbors. As a stimulus to critique of these convictions, this book proposes a world in which the three religions are interdependent, constantly transforming themselves by thinking about each other in a fundamentally ambivalent form of neighborliness.

Again, this is not a book about scripture, but we do need to remember that this ambivalent neighborliness, with all its power to produce both proximity and distance, is encoded in the scriptures themselves. Consider just this one example from the Qur'an, a verse focused on the founding moment of scriptural revelation itself:

> And remember we took your covenant and we raised above you (the towering height) of Mount (Sinai) (saying): 'Hold firmly to what we have given you and hearken (to the Law)!' They said: 'We hear, and we disobey.' And they had to drink into their hearts (of the taint) of the calf because of their faithlessness. (2:93; cf. 2:60, 4:153)

In this passage we see the Prophet and his community of believers creating their place in sacred history by looking toward the Hebrew Bible and the people to whom the earlier prophecies were given. They do so in ways that suggest deep familiarity not just with those earlier scriptures (the Hebrew Bible), but also with the religious culture of their contemporary neighbors, the Jews of the Arabian Peninsula circa 600 CE.

That familiarity surfaces even in the geographic vocabulary of the Qur'an, which names the mount of revelation not in Arabic but in Aramaic, the language of the Jews: Ṭūr Sīnīn.[6] Even more remarkable is the cultural interplay that emerges in the strange citation with which the verse begins: "We raised above you the towering height of Mount Sinai." The passage is not a citation from the Hebrew Bible, but rather from the Talmud, the "oral Torah" of the rabbis. Commenting on Exodus 19:17, the Talmud's tractate Shabbat reports the following discussion:

> "And they stood beneath the mount": Rabbi Abdimi the son of Hama son of Hasa said: This teaches that the Holy One, blessed be he, overturned the mountain upon them like an inverted cask, and said to them, "If

you take upon yourselves the Law, good. If not, here you will find your grave."[7]

The stunning familiarity of the early Muslim community with their Jewish neighbors does not end there. Even the devastating line "we hear and we disobey" is an example of multicultural play. In Deuteronomy 5:24 the Israelites declare to Moses, "We hear, and obey." (Compare Exod. 24:7.) The Qur'an's transformation of that phrase is a multilingual pun, playing on the homophony between Hebrew *shama'nu v-'asinu* (we heard and obeyed/we will hear and obey) and Arabic *sami'inā wa-'aṣaynā* (we hear and disobey).[8] The play on words reveals a shared scriptural and linguistic space of neighborliness at the same time that it shatters it.

In this particular example we can see how familiarity with the Jewish neighbor is deployed in early Islam in order to claim continuity with that neighbor's religious tradition (the teachings of the Hebrew prophets) and appropriate its authority while simultaneously distancing the believers from the truth claims of those neighbors themselves (that is, the Jewish people and children of Israel).[9] I take the ambivalence of this gesture to be constitutional of Christian, Jewish, and Muslim scriptural communities, which take shape through a process of simultaneous identification and dis-identification with their rival "siblings" and neighbors.

We might call this process, in all of its ambivalence, the "coproduction" of religious communities.[10] That coproduction does not end with its codification in scripture: on the contrary, precisely because it is modeled in scripture, it continues to shape communities to come. And conversely, each and all of these later communities bring their own experiences and worries of neighborliness to bear upon their interpretation of scripture, transforming how that scripture can be read in the future. The dynamic ambivalence of this process cannot be purged: it lies at the foundations of all of our scriptural communities.

But the study of this process nevertheless offers us its own principle of hope. That principle is different from the dangerous fantasy that if only all converted to the truth we could live together in peace. Nor is it the blandly liberal (and demonstrably false) hope that if only we all knew more about each other we would love each other more. The principle on offer here is much more modest, but perhaps much more realistic. It is the hope that we can become a bit more self-aware, more critical of the ways in which we have learned to think with and about our neighbors, and that this critical awareness can have an impact on how we then act in the world.

One necessary step toward greater self-consciousness of how our thinking about neighbors shapes our world is the realization that "neighborliness"
between the three religions can take many different forms. Among them is
our everyday sense of the word: at some times and in some places, Muslims,
Jews, and Christians occupied houses next to each other. Those times and
places were relatively rare. The lands of Islam contained large populations
of Christians and Jews throughout much of their history, yet it remains the
case that, in the later medieval as in the modern period, most Muslims living
in those lands probably never met a living Christian or a Jew. All the more
so in medieval western Europe, which was—with the exception of the Iberian Peninsula—the least religiously diverse of the regions clustered around
the Mediterranean, harboring vanishingly small communities of Jews and
Muslims.

Many of the pages in this book focus on the lands we now call Spain: the
one extraordinary region of western Europe in which Muslims, Christians,
and Jews did indeed live in close proximity.[11] But we will also dwell on less local types of neighborliness, with their attendant anxieties. After all, the entire
Mediterranean can be thought of metaphorically as a neighborhood, as when
Plato wrote of the many peoples inhabiting the shores of that sea that they
lived "like ants or frogs about a pond" (*Phaedo* 109b). Even at a global level,
the geopolitical "proximity" of the three religions could generate a great deal
of power. A priest in twelfth-century Paris did not have to meet any Muslims
in order to preach about the relationship of "Christendom" to Islam, any
more than it is today necessary for a citizen of the Islamic Republic of Iran
to know an inhabitant of Tel Aviv, or a voter in Boston a resident of Baghdad,
in order for them to learn to think of the perils and opportunities of their
world in terms of the interactions between Islam, Christianity, and Judaism.

Finally, the book introduces yet another kind of neighborliness between
the three religions: not in space and time but in thought. This sense of neighborliness is less obvious than the others but perhaps more expandable, and
so it deserves some explanation. By neighbors in thought I mean that believers in all three faiths defined (and define) themselves and their place in this
world and the one to come by thinking in terms of the other faiths.

Another scriptural example might help to clarify this fundamental point.
We all know that the early followers of Jesus emerged within or in close
proximity to various types of Judaism and that for them determining the appropriate relationship between these communities became an urgent question. There were many different answers to that question, some of which are

preserved in the New Testament scriptures that became canonical. Consider, for example, just one sentence from Saint Paul's Epistle to the Galatians, one of the earliest writings produced by a follower of Jesus, circa 50 CE. In chapter 2, verse 14, Paul upbraids Peter for refusing to eat with Gentile converts who do not observe Jewish dietary laws, and he does so in striking terms: "Since you, though you are a Jew, live like the gentiles and not like the Jews, how can you compel the gentiles to Judaize?"

Early Christians were shocked by Paul's harsh criticism of Peter (in 2:13, he even used the word "hypocrisy"). But for us what is more noteworthy is the logic encoded in this (previously rare) verb "to Judaize." The verb is applied to Gentiles, not Jews. Neither a Jew nor a Jewish follower of Jesus "Judaized" by observing dietary laws or being circumcised. For Paul, "Judaizing" designated the damning displacement of a *Gentile* believer's attention away from Jesus's spiritual message and toward the literal commandments of the Jewish tradition within which Jesus was born and taught. By analogy it came to signify the Christian's erroneous orientation of attention away from the spirit and toward the flesh, the letter of scripture, and the material things of this world: all things that came to be associated with Judaism in Christian thought.[12]

Over time, the repeated application of this type of analogy turned thinking about Judaism and Judaizing into a basic resource for Christian self-definition and self-critique, an important part of the conceptual tool kit with which Christians could make sense of their world, and this even in times and places where there were no "real" Jews to be found. In this sense, the "neighborliness" between Christian and Jew is not simply spatial. A potential "Jew" exists within every Christian no matter how "Gentile," for "Judaism" threatens all of us as we pick our hesitant way through this transitory world of flesh.

Over the course of this book we will see how variants of this Pauline logic were put to work in various Christian societies, work that transformed the possibilities of existence for Christians, Muslims, and Jews alike. But this "neighborliness in thought" is an Islamic and Jewish phenomenon as much as a Christian one. Like Christianity, Islam faced questions about its relations to previous prophetic traditions, questions not so different from the ones Paul and Peter had been trying to address.

In Islam, as in Christianity, this process of coproduction did not end with the establishment of the new religion. According to tradition, Muhammad himself predicted its ongoing power: "Those who were before you of the People of the Book [i.e., Christians and Jews] became divided into 72 sects,

and this community will be divided into 73: 72 in Hell, and one in Paradise."
Across the Islamic centuries charges of "Judaizing" helped to drive this sectarian productivity. It would be difficult to find a medieval Muslim sectarian
community that was not at some time or other accused of being "Jewish" by
its opponents ("the Shi'is are the Jews of our community," as an ancient Sunni
saying has it). [13] As in Christianity, "Jewishness" became a danger to which
every Muslim was potentially subject, and excessive proximity exacerbated
the danger.[14]

For a good example we can turn to the eleventh-century Iberian poet,
polemicist, politician and scholar Ibn Ḥazm, one of the most prolific and
original pens of the Islamic Middle Ages:

> God will treat those who befriend the Jews and take them into their confi-
> dence as He treated the Jews themselves. For whosoever amongst Muslim
> princes has listened to all this and still continues to befriend Jews . . . well
> deserves to be overtaken by the same humiliation and to suffer in this world
> the same griefs which God has meted out to the Jews. . . . Let any prince
> upon whom God has bestowed some of his bounty take heed . . . let him
> get away from this filthy, stinking, dirty crew beset with God's anger and
> malediction, with humiliation and wretchedness, misfortune, filth and dirt,
> as no other people has ever been. Let him know that the garments in which
> God has enwrapped them are more obnoxious than war, and more conta-
> gious than elephantiasis.[15]

Following a logic and a diction very similar to that of Surah 5:56 ("Who of
you takes them as friends is one of them") or 3:118 ("they will not fail to corrupt you"), Ibn Ḥazm produces the "Judaism" of Muslim princes. Perhaps we
could speak of a similar "coproduction" in modern Islamic political discourse,
with its tendency to criticize Muslim politicians as "Jewish" hypocrites, materialists, and agents of Zionism.

What was true of medieval Muslims and Christians was true of Jews as
well: the rabbis, too, understood godliness as produced and maintained in
interaction with and distinction from one's neighbors, both real and imagined. A rabbinic text called Lamentations Rabbah, dating roughly to the fifth
century CE, provides a parable on the subject:

> It is like a king who married a woman and wrote her a large marriage settle-
> ment [ketubbah]. . . . Then he left her for many years and journeyed to

the provinces. Her neighbors used to taunt her and say to her: hasn't your husband abandoned you? Go! Marry another man! She would weep and sigh, and afterward she would enter her bridal chamber and read her marriage settlement and sigh [with relief]. Many years and days later the king returned. He said to her: I am amazed that you have waited for me all these years! She replied: my master the king, if not for the large wedding settlement you wrote me, my neighbors would long ago have led me astray.[16]

Parables permit play, so I will interpret this one provocatively, as recognition of the "neighborly coproductions" I am attempting to describe. Jews in the Diaspora, whether in pagan, Christian, or later in Islamic lands, lived in societies deeply structured by cosmologies and theologies different from their own. Often they adopted aspects of their neighbors' cultures. The study of those adoptions and adaptations has of late become an important field in Jewish studies. The influence of Arabic grammar and verse on Hebrew; of Islamic law on Karaite thought or on the redaction of the Talmud; of Christian mysticism and Neoplatonism on Jewish Kabbalah: these are just a few of the countless coproductions that scholars of Jewish culture have explored.

Each of these borrowings and adaptations could be (and was) attacked from within Judaism as illegitimate, as idolatrous, "Christianizing," or "Islamizing." The Kabbalah, for example, seemed to many medieval (and modern) Jewish critics a Christianizing turn away from the unitary God of Israel. But to continue with my interpretation of the parable, each of these borrowings and transformations could also be authorized (as occurred in the case of the Kabbalah) by returning to the bridal chamber and rereading the "founding contract" in such a way that the new is discovered already within it and appears eternal.[17]

The parable's authors may well have believed in the impermeability of their scriptural interpretations and religious practices, as well as in the stability and continuity of those interpretations and practices across space and time. But I prefer to understand it as pointing toward a more dynamic interaction between authoritative scripture and the many contexts of its reading. In my reading, the marriage contract—that is, scripture—appears both as a historical record of neighborliness and as a living one.

Scripture is a historical record, in that the Hebrew and Christian Bibles, the Islamic Qur'an and Sunnah, and the writings of the Rabbis all provide us with a window into how the communities that came to be called Christian, Muslim, and Jewish produced themselves with and through each other. But these scriptures are also a living record, in that they have been (and continue to be) read and interpreted by believers in all times and places. They provided (and continue to provide) later communities with an archive of ancient worries about neighborliness. The authority of that archive shaped (and continues to shape) some of the ways in which these communities created their own possibilities of neighborliness, reimagining themselves by thinking about their proximity to and distance from the others, and authorizing their fresh visions of the world in the name of God.

How Muslim, Jewish, and Christian communities have imagined and reimagined themselves by thinking about and (sometimes) living with each other: that is the subject of this book. The topic is important to our understanding of the past, but it is also vital to the present, for we too are engaged in similar coproductions, making sense of our own world by thinking about ourselves and our neighbors. Indeed very often, the study of past interactions between these three faiths is undertaken with an eye on the present, in the hope that history might provide us counsel and comfort for the future.

The resulting advice is diverse and often contradictory. For some, the history of neighborliness between the three faiths is one of inevitable conflict. The political scientist Samuel Huntington provided an influential synthesis of this view in his essay and later book "The Clash of Civilizations," where he argued that contemporary geopolitical conflict is structured along the fault lines between competing civilizational blocks. The cohesion of these blocks is determined by a shared religious and cultural history (Buddhist China, Western Civilization, and the Islamic World were his main categories) that puts them at odds with their neighbors. According to Huntington, the most aggressive of these blocks is Islam (in his words: "Islam has bloody borders").[18]

Huntington's vision of an asymmetrically violent neighborliness may well have influenced U.S. foreign policy, but more irenic views have had their geopolitical influence as well. There are, for example, those who believe that the long history of neighborliness shared by the three "Abrahamic" religions provides an exemplary paradigm for the pursuit of peace and mutual prosperity. This is the historical logic behind political initiatives such as the United Nation's "Secretariat for the Alliance of Civilizations" (established in 2005 upon the initiative of the prime ministers of Spain and Turkey) and the "Union for the Mediterranean," championed by French President Nikolas Sarkozy. Sarkozy's "Union" was based on a geographic definition of neighborhood: it was meant as an alliance of all nations—whether Christian, Jewish, or Muslim—whose shores are lapped by the Mediterranean's waters, including both Israel and the Occupied Palestinian Territories. (By the time *The Joint*

Declaration of the Union for the Mediterranean was signed on July 13, 2008, it included the entire European Union and Arab League, embracing such "Mediterranean neighbors" as Iceland and Yemen.)[19]

The last chapter of this book will explore some of these contemporary imaginings, interrogating their invocations of historical examples of neighborliness in order to expose the fantastic underpinnings of their resulting visions of current Muslim-Jewish-Christian relations. Here I'd like merely to reiterate the more general point: our communities continue to constitute themselves by thinking about the long history of relations with their neighbors. The resulting representations of the world are "coproductions" not only of Judaism, Christianity, and Islam but also of past and present. Visions of the past are deployed to do work in the present, and visions of the present transform how we interpret the past.

This interdependence of what-has-been and what-may-yet-be means that history and historians may have a role in shaping the possibilities for how we relate to others in our world. But what should that role be? The question is important, because the pressure of present politics is great. Today even the most technical arguments about, for example, the role of Arabic manuscripts in the medieval transmission history of Aristotle can become touchstones in bitter battles over Muslim immigration to France or the entrance of Turkey into the European Union.[20] How should we write history, knowing that the possibilities for life in the present may be affected by the ways in which we choose to reconstruct the past? And in making these choices, what responsibility do we as self-identified historians (rather than, say, novelists or politicians)[21] owe to the past and its inhabitants? Are we free to work over the past until it resembles our hopes or fears for the future? If not, what commitments should discipline or limit the historian's interpretive freedom?

The chapters that follow approach these questions in different ways, but they all share the goal of demonstrating that the questions themselves are difficult and do not admit any one answer. That modest goal is more ambitious and important than it may seem, for every present tends to seize upon "the manifestations of past or distant spiritual worlds, in order to take possession of them and unfeelingly incorporate them into its own self-absorbed fantasizing."[22] If the past is to provide us with a perspective from which to criticize our dearest certainties, we need to develop strategies for distinguishing between the fantastic and the critical.

Careful attention to the available sources, knowledge of the necessary languages, deployment of relevant methodologies, recognition of divergent interpretations: these are all necessary, but not sufficient protections against self-absorption. After all, the categories of thought through which we approach the past, the methodologies we bring to it, the types of information we recognize as meaningful and significant: these are not independent of our experience in our own time and place. Similarly, the questions about the past that strike us as urgent in the present have a great deal to do with our own fears for the future and with our own sense of what that future should be.

This means that historians must be both critics and prophets if they wish, without impiety or disrespect, to make the dead instructive for the living: critics so as to become conscious of the many gaps and frictions that exist between their own thought-worlds and those of the shades they invoke; and prophets in order to divine the best future in whose service this friction between past and present should be put to work.[23]

Like most historians, I am a poor prophet. So although my account of the past is animated by a sense of what is to come, I've attempted as best I can to keep these chapters free of a particular politics or vision of a future. My goal in them is simply to convince you that Islam, Christianity, and Judaism have never been independent of each other: that it is as neighbors, in close relation to one another, that they have constantly transformed themselves, reinterpreting both their scriptures and their histories. Their pasts are not discrete, independent, or stable, and neither are their presents or their futures.

The Qur'an speaks hauntingly of its own inexhaustible capacity to generate meaning: "If the ocean were ink (wherewith to write out) the words of my Lord, sooner would the ocean be exhausted than would the words of my Lord" (18:109).[24] What is true of prophecy is also true of history. The countless ways in which previous communities have reenvisioned the world through their neighbors constitute an endless archive that future communities will draw upon to imagine, legitimate, and contest untold potential futures. Perhaps it is by making the workings of this process more visible that historians can best serve those communities to come, showing them how their ancestors, too, discovered in the past the seeming eternity of their now long vanished convictions.

Though many a place or period could serve the purpose for this pedagogy, the chapters of this book will almost all focus on medieval and early modern Spain, sometimes called the "land of the three religions." (The exceptions are the first chapter, on how medieval "Christendom" defined itself against "Islam," and the last, on similar strategies today.) In that land we can witness Jews, Muslims, and Christians interacting not only as abstractions or categories in each other's theologies and ideologies but also as neighbors forced to jostle together on narrow streets, figures of thought elbowing figures of flesh and in the process transforming both.

We will, for example, watch them simultaneously theorizing the dangerous attractions of their neighbors and also embracing those neighbors in full carnality, not only in the whorehouse but also in the household, and even in the marriage bed (chaps. 2, 3, and 5). We will explore how the interaction of the two—of thought and of flesh, to hold onto our admittedly inadequate metaphor—produced radically new ways of thinking about the nature of inter-religious relations, some of them horrifically violent, even exterminatory (chap. 4), others segregationist (chap. 5); some playful and poetic (chap. 6), still others (chaps. 7 and 8) giving rise to new theories and vocabularies of what we have learned to call race (from the Spanish word *raza*). And we will see how each of these new ways of thinking about world and neighbor rewrote the ways in which people read their scriptures and their history, so that the new and the particular could be understood as universal and eternal.

These chapters offer new ways of explaining the religious pluralism, massacre and mass conversion, assimilation, segregation, and expulsion that marked the extraordinarily rich history of interaction between the three religions in the medieval Iberian Peninsula. But in their insistence on the dynamic and interdependent ways in which religious communities constantly re-create their reality and their history, they offer us something more. The past of this "land of the three religions" is too often mined for exemplary histories, for models of tolerance or of persecution, Golden Ages or Black Legends. I offer instead a history that resists the exemplarity and stability of the past, in the hope that it might serve as a stimulus to reflection about the ways in which Judaism, Christianity, Islam, and their many heirs continue to coproduce the realities of the world today.

[1]

Christendom and Islam

Given the great variety of Christian and Muslim cultures in the Middle Ages, it should not be surprising that relations between the two defy synthesis. The relationships to Islam of the many Christians who lived in Muslim lands, for example, were very different from those of Christians living in orthodox Christian Byzantium or Catholic Latin Europe. The word "Christendom" in this chapter's title therefore reflects a sharp but necessary abridgment of the topic, a focus only on those lands that came to think of themselves as "Christendom": that is, Catholic western Europe, from the Iberian to the Hungarian kingdoms. I will ask three interrelated questions. First, what did Christians know about Islam? Second, how did their thinking about Islam affect the formation of the concept of Christendom itself? And third, how did Islam experience Christendom? For throughout our period there were not only numerous Christian incursions into the lands of Islam (via pilgrimage, trade, crusade, and mission) but also many Muslims living *within* Christendom.

The first two questions, of course, are quite different from the third, for they have less to do with the study of historical contacts and relations between Christianity and Islam in the Middle Ages and more to do with the study of the role that Christian ideas about Islam play in the formation of Christian conceptualizations of the world and Christianity's place in it. The third question, on the other hand, is about historically specific encounters between Christians and Muslims. I will touch briefly upon the best-known forms of these encounters, namely trade and crusade. But I will give more space to the less well-known phenomenon of the practice of Islam in Christian lands. We tend to think of medieval Catholic Europe as a region largely devoid of Islam, "Muslimrein." Even when we acknowledge the presence of Islam in Christendom, we rarely pause to think about how the Christian context might affect the type of Islam practiced within it. But in fact throughout our period Europe contained Islamic communities whose experience of "being Muslim" was quite different from the experience of Muslims living in more heavily Islamic lands.

1

My first question, "What did medieval Christians know about Islam and when did they learn it?" is often asked by scholars, but it is in at least one sense much less interesting than it seems. Christians knew most of what they felt they needed to know about Islam from the moment it began its muscular journey from the Arabian Peninsula in the mid-seventh century: Islam was not Christianity, and it was mighty in war. From a Christian point of view, the victories of these non-Christians could mean only two things. Either Christianity was an incorrect religion that should be abandoned in favor of Islam or Christians were indeed correct in their religious choice but were being punished by an angry God. The first option was taken by the countless Christians who chose to convert to the Islam of their conquerors. Christian writing about Islam, of course, was generally produced by those who opted for theodicy. Preaching on Christmas day 634 in the midst of the invasions, the patriarch of Jerusalem explained to his trembling flock that God had sent "the godless Saracens" as punishment for "countless sins and very serious faults." "Let us correct ourselves," he exhorted. "If we constrain ourselves . . . we would see their final destruction."[1]

The actual content of the Saracens' faith was irrelevant to Sophronios, who was interested only in elucidating the Muslims' role in Christian sacred history. Nor did penance's failure to stem the invasions incline him more seriously toward ethnography. As the Caliph 'Umar triumphantly entered Jerusalem, the patriarch is said to have proclaimed, "Verily, this is the abomination of desolation standing in a holy place, as has been spoken through the prophet Daniel."[2] Maximus the Confessor, writing from Alexandria at much the same time, put it more bluntly. The invaders were "wild and untamed beasts who have merely the shape of human form." They were, he added,

Jews and followers of the Antichrist.[3] Muslims, in short, were either Christ's scourge for the improvement of Christendom or the shock troops of apocalypse, related one way or another to other enemies of God (such as Jews, idol worshipers and heretics). In either case, contemporaries saw no point in studying their religious beliefs or cultural practices except to condemn them or prove them wrong.

As a very general rule, this one holds true throughout the Middle Ages. From the seventh century to the end of the fifteenth, Christian understanding of Islam was predicated on two basic axioms. First, Islam was a false religion. Second, it was a carnal one, glorying in violence and sexuality. It is striking how early these positions crystallized. Already in 634, for example, a Christian author treated Islam's conquests as a sign of its falsity: "Do prophets come with swords and chariots?" (The same author would, of course, doubtless have interpreted Christian military victories as signs of that religion's truth.)[4] Sexuality too rose immediately to the polemical forefront, with Christians asserting that the religion of Islam had been founded by Muhammad in order to help him satisfy his lusts and that the afterlife he promised to those who died following him was entirely carnal. Increasing familiarity with Islam did not alter the tone of these polemics but only sharpened it. John of Damascus (Yuhanna b. Mansur b. Sarjun), for example, was fluent in Arabic (in fact Greek was for him a second language) and an important financial administrator at the court of the Umayyad caliphs 'Abd al-Malik and Walid I (685–715). His obvious knowledge of Islam did not, however, alter the general lines of the polemic he wrote against it. The Ishmaelites, he wrote, were precursors of the Antichrist. Worshipers of Aphrodite, they were seduced by "a false prophet Mamed . . . who, having casually been exposed to the Old and the New Testament, and supposedly encountered an Arian monk, formed a heresy of his own." According to John, Muhammad's motives were primarily sexual: hence he dwelt extensively on the Qur'anic treatment of polygamy and divorce, and on Muhammad's many wives.[5]

* * *

These are among the earliest Christian accounts of Islam. They predate our period and are from outside the borders of the region with which we are concerned. But they do not differ substantially from what Christians said about Islam centuries later and further west. All of these themes, from heretical monks to idol worship and rampant sexuality, can be found in Christian writings of every century from the eleventh to the sixteenth. (Even today, these tropes are often deployed in anti-Muslim polemics.) This is not to say that available knowledge about Islam in the West was unchanging. On the contrary, if twelfth-century vernacular poets (like the author of the Song of Roland) and Latinate clerics (like the canon lawyers of the Decretals) alike continued to present Muslims as worshipers of Apollo or Aphrodite, it was not for lack of sources that knew better. But even in the best-informed sources, new learning was only intended to give well-worn polemics a sharper edge. For instance, the author of the *Liber denudationis*, a work written in Arabic by an Iberian Christian in the twelfth century, knew a great deal about Islam and was clearly familiar with Arabic commentaries on the Qur'an. But he read these sources in order to solidify rather than challenge his prejudices, mining them for evidence to support the ancient topoi of Muslim materialism and hypersexuality. Thus he trumpeted with great glee a marginal and esoteric (not to say fantastic) Islamic tradition that in paradise each virtuous Muslim believer will be rewarded by the growth of his penis to such a length that he will need seventy Christians and seventy Jews to carry it before him.[6]

Engagement with Islamic texts did not alter Christian understandings of Islam because—like Islamic engagement with Christian and Jewish texts or Jewish engagement with Islamic and Christian texts—this engagement was largely structured by polemic. Of course "largely" does not mean "completely," and there were exceptions in all three faiths. In the twelfth century, for example, the Jewish sage Maimonides insisted that "by no means are Muslims idolaters . . . they recognize God's unity. Just because they falsely accuse us . . . we cannot also lie by saying that they are idolaters. . . . If someone were to argue that the House [in Mecca] where they praise Him is an idolatrous temple that conceals inside the idol their ancestors worshipped [the Kaaba], [they should know that] those who bow to him now have only God in mind. The rabbis have already explained in Sanhedrin that if one bows in an idolatrous temple but believes it is a synagogue, his heart is dedicated to God."[7]

Such exceptions are attractive to us as historians because they seem to suggest that with greater historical knowledge comes greater understanding and even tolerance. But it is just as important to realize that medieval efforts to study the religions of others were more often oriented toward providing more solid footings for the batteries of polemic. The marginal notes in medieval translations of the Qur'an, for example, told Christian readers exactly what they should be taking from it, as in this example: "Note that he everywhere promises a paradise of earthly delights, as other heresies had done before."[8] Indeed these translations were undertaken not to increase knowledge of Islam but simply to reaffirm what every Christian already knew. Peter the Venerable of Cluny, the most powerful churchman of his age and the organizer in the mid-twelfth century of the first translation of the Qur'an and a number of other Arabic texts into Latin, put the point simply in his anti-Islamic manifesto: "I translated from Arabic into Latin the whole of this sect, along with the execrable life of its evil inventor, and exposed it to scrutiny of our people, so that it be known what a filthy and frivolous heresy it is."[9]

Modern historians often stress the importance of subtle differences in medieval Christian characterizations of Islam and are very much on the lookout for evidence of real knowledge about Islamic practice, which they often valorize positively as a sign of cultural engagement and exchange. For the modern critic it makes a great deal of difference whether a medieval Christian author characterized the Muslims as idol worshipers, as Judaizers, or as monotheistic heretics. (In fact most medieval commentators on Islam presented it as a blend of paganism, Judaism, and Christian heresies such as Arianism.) But these subtle distinctions miss a basic point: the vast majority of medieval Christians (at least of those whose opinions have reached us) were certain that Islam was a false and dangerous belief, and, with very few exceptions, their study of it was aimed entirely at its condemnation and defeat.

This did not stop them from developing a body of knowledge, a "science of Islam" involving a great deal of gathering and translation of information. The science they developed remained standard into the early modern period and even transmitted a little of its ideological content to the "Orientalist" learning of French and British scholars in the eighteenth and nineteenth centuries. Yet the truth value of this science was measured by the extent to which it conformed to and reinforced Christian theology, not by its consonance with the historical and religious experience of Muslims. When a medieval chronicler like Otto of Friesing points out that Muslims revere Muhammad as a prophet, not as a god, he is trying to show how well read he is, not trying to educate his readers about Islam or soften their antipathy toward it. There is no real point, he and his contemporaries would have agreed, in worrying too much about details when writing the history of an error. As Gautier de Compiègne put it in his twelfth-century life of Muhammad, "One may safely speak ill of a man whose malignity transcends and surpasses whatever evil can be said about him."[10]

2

The sharp increase in the information about Islam available in Latin Europe across the period from 1000 to 1500 did not substantially redirect the polemical channels through which that knowledge flowed. One reason for this is the increasing importance of the work to which these channels were put over the course of the Middle Ages. Curiously enough, that importance is inversely proportional to the military threat posed by Islam to Latin Europe itself. Before the eleventh century, when the military reach of Islam was longest (the Muslims sacked Genoa as late as 993, for example, and captured Abbot Maiolus of Cluny in the Alps in 972), the polemic with Islam remained relatively unimportant in the core areas of western Europe.[11] After the year 1000, at precisely the point that Latin Christian power began to extend itself once more into the Mediterranean, that polemic began to become ideologically central. We can see one important example of this centrality in the new role assigned to Islam in Christian thinking about violence and war. The same decades that saw the Christian conquest of southern Italy, Sardinia, and Sicily, and of large parts of Muslim al-Andalus, produced the proclamation of Pope Alexander II that, although the shedding of human blood is forbidden to the Christian, it was "just to fight" against the Saracens, "who persecute Christians and expel them from their towns and dwelling places."[12] This is not a coincidence: in the eleventh and twelfth centuries, ideas about Islam played an important role in the creation of a muscular version of European Christianity, one that increasingly saw itself as united by a common destiny to conquer a wider world imagined as Muslim.[13]

What we today call the crusades are, of course, the most famous example of this process. Though western warriors, merchants, and pilgrims had long been present in the eastern Mediterranean, the unruly progress of French, Norman, Occitan, German, and Italian crusaders on their long march to Jerusalem during the First Crusade in 1096 struck observers as something new. The Byzantine princess Anna Comnena described it as the northern forests suddenly emptying themselves into the Mediterranean. For Muslim rulers in the East, the entry of the crusading armies into their domains was indeed the first significant intrusion of western Europe into their political consciousness, and the shape of that first impression is interesting. Muslim rulers did not think of the first few crusades as part of a coherent and ongoing Christian attack on Islam: that consciousness took more than a century to emerge. But they did think of the heterogeneous crusading armies as a unified people, and this from the very beginning. Muslims would for centuries call all the members of these armies "firandj," "Franks," regardless of their actual provenance. The term came to signify "European" in Arabic, Chinese, and a good many other languages of Asia and its subcontinent well into the modern age. If the people Columbus famously mistook for "Indians" in 1492 had in fact been that, they would have doubtless called this Genoese sailing under the flag of Castile a "Frank."[14]

Though entirely the product of too crude an ethnography, the Muslim homogenization of crusading Europe did parallel an explicit goal of the crusade's organizers themselves. For Pope Urban II, the first crusade was as much about establishing peace and unity in the West as it was about giving aid to Byzantium or conquering Jerusalem from Islam. Every report we have of his preaching stresses the same thing: war against Muslims was an antidote to civil war amongst Christians. The summary of Baldric of Bourgueil, archbishop of Dol, is representative:

> Listen and understand. You have strapped on the belt of soldiery and strut around with pride in your eye. You butcher your brothers and create factions amongst yourselves. This, which scatters the sheepfold of the Redeemer, is not the army of Christ. . . . You must either cast off as quickly as possible the belt of this sort of soldiery or go forward boldly as soldiers of Christ, hurrying swiftly to defend the Eastern Church. . . . You may restrain your murderous hands from the destruction of your brothers, and on behalf of your relatives in the faith oppose yourself to the Gentiles. . . . You should shudder, brethren, you should shudder at raising a violent hand against Christians; it is less wicked to brandish your sword against Saracens. It is the only warfare that is righteous.[15]

Robert the Monk assigned to Urban slightly different words but the same argument:

> This land which you inhabit is too narrow for your large population; nor does it abound in wealth; and it furnishes scarcely enough food for its cultivators. Hence it is that you murder one another, that you wage war, and that frequently you perish by mutual wounds. . . . Let therefore hatred depart from among you, let your quarrels end, let wars cease, and let all dissensions and controversies slumber. Enter upon the road to the Holy Sepulcher, wrest that land from the wicked race, and subject it to yourselves.[16]

The consequences of such preaching, according to Otto of Friesing, were dramatic: "And so, as countless peoples and nations . . . were moved to take the cross, suddenly almost the entire West became so still that not only the waging of war but even the carrying of arms in public was considered wrong."[17] Urban, Bernard, Peter the Venerable, all were able students of Durkheim and Frederick Jackson Turner. They promoted peace and unity at home in Christendom by projecting discord outward toward the "Gentile frontier": *Intus pax, foris terrores*, "Peace inside, terror outside."[18]

The crusades were designed to give western Christendom a common project and a shared sense of purpose, as well as to pacify it. They were not the task of just one king, noble, or nation, but a *negotium christianum*, a Christian business. The notion of *christianitas* was expanded through the crusade preaching of popes like Innocent III into the idea of a *populus christianus*, "a Christian people," and thence into the concept of a "Christendom" defined collectively by its struggle against all unfaithful foreign nations. Of course from the papal point of view a single entity needs a single leader, and that leader was to be the pope, the vicar of Christ. It is not a coincidence that the same theologians who championed crusade developed this title "vicar of Christ" (rather than, for example, the older papal title "vicar of Peter"). Bernard of Clairvaux was the first to apply it to the pope alone (rather than including all bishops and even lay princes), and Innocent III was the first pope to use the title publicly.[19]

In other words, Urban, Bernard, Innocent, and other architects of papal power were political theorists as much as sociologists, readers of Carl Schmitt as well as of Durkheim. By emphasizing the danger posed by an external enemy and declaring war upon it they sought not only to pacify Latin Europe but also to strengthen a newly emerging form of sovereignty over it, the sovereignty of the papacy, known among medievalists as "papal monarchy." This sovereignty was not simply a matter of struggle over titles like "vicar of Christ." It was also a matter of building pan-European institutions and wielding pan-European power, and in this construction the crusade against the Muslim "enemies of God and holy Christendom" played a vital role. As a prominent historian put it in the mid-twentieth century, "Crusade and Christendom were made together, in a reciprocal creation."[20]

The history of taxation provides a good example of this process. The need to raise money for crusades (and the possibility of using the crusade to justify the raising of money) put the papacy in the position of establishing the first regular taxation system in the West. Crusading taxes (or tithes) were raised at the level of the locality (parish church, bishopric, etc.), then passed on to the pope as leader of the crusading movement. The pope in turn distributed the money to those kings or nobles who had entered into an agreement with him to carry out a crusade. It was Innocent III who obtained at least theoretical consensus that all benefices should contribute a percentage of their revenues to the support of papally sanctioned crusades. Later popes refined the system. Gregory X (1271–76), for example, divided all of Christendom into a system of twenty-six collectorates, or tax districts, for the collection of a truly universal tithe. And of course once the system was in place its exactions became regular, so that taxes were collected even when no crusade was being fought, as preparation for the next one. (Indeed in Spain, the tax continued to be collected well into the modern period.)[21]

The tax is one example of what would today be called a "transnational European institution." The term is anachronistic for the Middle Ages. But the important point here is simply that the crusades furthered the project of creating pan-European institutions centered about papal authority and control. Another example of such an institution, perhaps the most important one in terms of its implications for the future of European expansion and colonization, is the very idea of crusade itself, that is, of holy war authorized by papal sanction.

In all these ways, the idea of Christian war against Islam gave medieval Europe a much more unified and self-conscious sense of historical mission.[22] But it would be wrong to exaggerate the dependence of this awakening of an expansionary western European notion of Christendom on a confrontation with Islam or on the creation of a "Muslim enemy," although the tendency is understandable in the light of current, twenty-first-century events. It is certainly true that the Muslim strongholds in southern Italy particularly influenced early papal efforts to sanction or directly control warfare, because they threatened papal territorial interests. It is also true that the earliest justifications of crusading did take aim against Islam. This had, however, as much to do with the geography of the sacred as with Islam. It was only because Muslims were occupying "Christ's birthplace," "the land in which his feet had stood," God's "inheritance," that they needed to be defeated, a defeat that need not extend beyond the Holy Land.[23]

If the crusades began as a project to recuperate God's fief and birthplace in the Holy Land, they quickly came to be understood more generally, as "God's war for the expansion of Christendom," "bella Domini . . . ad dilationem Christianitatis."[24] This broader expansionary ideology, however, was no longer particularly motivated by confrontation with Islam. It could take aim at any non-Christian or heretic and in fact over time it ceased to be (with very significant exceptions) aimed primarily at Muslim lands. Indeed, many theological treatises on crusade do not even mention Islam. Saint Thomas Aquinas, for example, codified an influential justification of crusade in his *Summa Theologica*: "Christ's faithful often wage war against the unbelievers, not indeed for the purpose of forcing them to believe (for even if they were to conquer them and take them prisoners, they should still leave them free to believe, if they will), but in order to prevent them from hindering the Christian faith" (II-IIae, Q. X, art. 8). He went on to argue that crusaders had the right to destroy non-Christian governments even when these were sanctioned by human law. Such governments could be "justly done away with by the sentence or ordination of the Church that has the authority of God: since unbelievers in virtue of their unbelief deserve to forfeit power over the faithful who are converted into children of God" (art. 10). Arguments like these would be of tremendous utility to European expansionists precisely because they were not specifically concerned with Muslims but spoke rather more generally of *gentiles* and *infideles*.

In short, Islam was only the first, and an increasingly infrequent, target of an expansionary Christendom. Far more land was added to Europe through the German conquests in eastern Europe that began with the second crusade than in all the wars against Islam put together, Iberian "reconquest" included. Indeed, perhaps the most horrific achievement of the crusades took place not in the Old World but in the New, where logic like that articulated by Saint Thomas justified the destruction of the Aztec, Inca, and other native polities, as well as the subjugation and evangelization of their peoples.

Nor did the crusades produce a monolithic image of the Muslim as "enemy" in the Middle Ages. It is true, as Tomaž Mastnak points out, that crusade preaching and propaganda made "Saracen" an important negative term in the Christian imagination, one that could sometimes be generically applied: Normans, Slavs, east Europeans in general, Saxons, Danes, Scots, Irishmen, Vikings, all are at one point or other in the twelfth century called "Saraceni," "Agareni," and so on.[25] Such usage was, however, rare. Unlike "Jew," "Saracen" did not become a common insult among medieval Christians. Nor, outside of areas like the Iberian Peninsula or the short-lived Crusader States, can we really detect a widespread sense that Islam posed an existential threat to the Christian order itself. For that we must wait until the very end of the medieval period, with the fall of Constantinople (1453) and the beginnings of westward Ottoman expansion.

Moreover, although crusade propaganda could present the Muslim as an almost inhuman foe to be destroyed (the *Song of Roland* provides a good example), such representations were scarcely hegemonic within Christendom. More pragmatically ethnographic views could be found in those regions where interaction with Muslim powers was a fact of life (compare the *Song of the Cid* to that of Roland). For Christians living in Iberia and the Crusader States, or for anyone desiring to participate in the vast economic networks of the Mediterranean and the Black Sea, the point was not (or rather, not only) to demonize Islam and fantasize its destruction but also and often simultaneously to engage with it in constructive and profitable ways.[26] For example, among the earliest compendia of Islamic law translated into European vernaculars is a Catalan handbook produced for a Christian lord so that he could maximize his judicial profits from his Muslim subjects, whose transgressions had to be judged by Muslim law.[27] The considerable knowledge produced by such endeavors had no perceptible effect on the representations of Islam articulated by polemicists or preachers of crusade because the two projects took place in different registers of a complex Christian culture.

Another example of a cultural register that yields very different views of Muslims from those of polemicists or preachers is that of the military elites themselves. Despite the harsh polarization we find in a *chanson de geste* like the *Song of Roland*, already in the twelfth century new genres of lay literature were emerging in which the crusading ideal could coexist with and even foment the recognition of a common culture uniting Christian knights with their Muslim counterparts. Sometimes this sense of commonality was the product of direct military engagement: thirteenth-century crusaders like Joinville did not hesitate to note the dignity, courage, and suffering of their rivals, as well as those of their own coreligionists. But even in regions very far from real Muslims, the image of the Muslim soldier was shaped by an emerging chivalric ideal whose valorization of violence was predicated on the proper treatment of a worthy foe. The result was that, by the late twelfth century and far beyond the end of the period, readers throughout northern Europe expected to find Muslim knights roaming the landscapes of their courtly romances. In *Parzival* we even find one (Feirefiz Angevin) who is the piebald offspring of a Christian and a Muslim, his skin mottled white and brown. Such stories betray no real knowledge about Islam. But they do suggest that in courtly literature Islam was not a category of pure enmity and posed no impediment to an imagined solidarity of military elites. It is this solidarity, both imagined and also (in the late medieval world of mercenary armies) quite real, that Chaucer represents and criticizes through the Knight of his *Canterbury Tales*, a soldier of "sovereign price" to Christian and Muslim employers alike.[28]

Even at the level of political ideology itself, medieval Christian Europe was capable of imagining pluralist polities: "A kingdom of one people and one custom is weak and fragile," as a Hungarian cleric put it in the eleventh or twelfth century. In regions like Hungary or the Iberian Peninsula, Christian kingship, and even Christendom itself, could be self-consciously understood as depending on the services of non-Christian peoples, and this despite papal objection. As King Béla IV wrote to Innocent IV circa 1250, "For the good of Christendom . . . we defend our kingdom today by pagans . . . and we tread the enemies of the church underfoot with the aid of pagans." Similarly, in 1266 King James the Conqueror of Aragon ignored (as his successors would do for centuries) the command of Clement IV that he expel all Jews and Muslims from his kingdoms: to have done otherwise would have meant the destruction of his prosperity and his realms.[29]

Such convictions obviously weakened over the course of the period, but they never disappeared, even with the conquest of Granada and the expulsion of the Jews from Spain in 1492. In that very year, for example, an anonymous chronicler completed a "brief summary" of the history of Spain's kings, beginning with Hercules, addressed to the king of Naples. The chronicler understands Spain's successive incorporation of many peoples as the basis of its strength. And though he everywhere stresses that the reconquest of the Iberian Peninsula from Islam is the most glorious task of a Christian monarch, he also insists that the mistreatment of Muslims or Jews weakens both kingdom and monarchy. The supposed cruelty King Pedro displayed toward his Muslim neighbors in the fourteenth century, for example, helps the chronicler to explain his subsequent downfall in a bloody civil war. Similarly, the unprecedented expulsion of Jews in his own day, the chronicler discreetly but clearly implies, is a mistake that can only weaken the kingdom.[30] The point, in short, is that even in those regions most constantly engaged in armed conflict with Islam, and even at a culminating moment of Christian victory in that conflict, Christendom's relation to both Muslims and Islam remains much more than merely one of enmity. For all its current political importance, the critical study of these relations is still a young field. One of its greatest challenges, as it matures, will be to have its account of those relations reflect that complexity.

3

The self-definition of Christendom vis-à-vis Islam that we have focused on thus far has little to do with the presence of real Islam in Latin Europe, though there were in fact populations of Muslims living within Christendom throughout the Middle Ages. Muslims constituted a minority in Hungary, a few parts of southern Italy, and above all in the Iberian Peninsula. (There were no Muslims yet in the Balkans, since until the very end of the Middle Ages Byzantium still stood between Islam and the West.) By far the largest of these communities, and the only one to survive throughout the entirety of our period, was the Iberian one, and its example can give us a sense of the peculiarities involved in being Muslim in medieval Europe.[31]

Iberian Muslims living under Christian rule were called "Mudejars," and they represented a novel and important phenomenon in Islamic history: "diaspora" communities of Muslims living willingly in the "House of War," that is, in a non-Muslim polity. Today millions of Muslims live in non-Muslim countries. Some of these, like the Mudejars of old, live in areas "reconquered" by Christians from their ancestors (e.g., the Muslims of the former Yugoslavia or the former Soviet Union). Others are emigrants to more prosperous lands. These are all very different historical contexts from the medieval Iberian one. Nevertheless, the questions of acculturation, assimilation, and the maintenance of group identity that these Muslim populations face today bear more than a passing resemblance to those confronted by the Mudejars. Mudejars were Muslims *de pacis*, that is, Muslims who had agreed, or more usually whose ancestors had so agreed, to be at peace with Christians and subject to them. In this fundamental way they differed from Muslims *de guerra*, who remained at war with Christians and could therefore legally be killed or enslaved by them. In principle, the rights of Mudejars were stipulated by treaty signed at the time of conquest. Given that the conquest of the Iberian Peninsula spanned half a millennium and a number of realms, it is not surprising that these treaties varied. The most important concessions, however, were fairly standard across time and are easily listed. In exchange for their labor and their taxes, Mudejars were to receive: (1) safety and confirmation of property rights; (2) guarantee of the free practice of religion, including the right to pray in their mosques, to teach Islam to their children, and to go on pilgrimage; (3) the right to rule themselves according to Muslim law (Sharīʿa), to be judged under it in any case involving only Muslims, and to

name their own religious and judicial officials; (4) the confirmation of exist-
ing pious endowments in perpetuity; and (5) a limitation on taxes, which
were to be roughly similar to those paid under Muslim rule.[32]

These privileges are the foundation stones of Mudejar existence, which is
not to say that they could not be violated or ignored. Mudejars were not naive
on this score: they were aware that, even when they wanted to, Christian
kings could not always force their violent subjects to comply with the provi-
sions of treaties they had signed.[33] Nevertheless, these treaties articulated
the contractual basis for the continued existence of Muslims in Christian
Iberia in formal legal terms that were remarkably stable. The treaty signed
at the surrender of Granada in 1492 would have been completely intelligible
to those Muslims of Toledo who had surrendered their similarly magnificent
city to the Christians some four hundred years before.

Such willing submission by Muslims to Christian jurisdiction was controversial among Islamic jurists, who associated it with cultural vulnerability, corruption, and decline. The most often cited of these writers is the
fifteenth-century North African jurist al-Wansharīsī, whose opinion of the
Mudejar was not ambivalent: "His residence is manifest proof of his vile and
base spirit." "To exalt Christian and diminish Muslim authority is a great and
disastrous ruination . . . and he who does this is on the border of infidelity."
The late fourteenth-century mufti (and emigrant from Christian Iberia?) Ibn
Miqlash illustrated this cultural vulnerability in an unusual passage which
depicts the fate of Islam under Christian rule in sexual terms. The Mudejar,
he claimed, mingled with worshipers of idols and lost his zeal. His wife depended upon (and was therefore sexually vulnerable to) his Christian lord.
What fate could be worse, he asked, than that of one without zeal, either for
his religion or for his wife![34]

Most jurists were less vivid. They stressed, not the debasement of the
Mudejar's wife, but that of his religious and legal culture. By demonstrating
that Mudejars were deficient in legal culture as defined by the Maliki scholars, these jurists argued that they were less than full Muslims. As early as
the twelfth century no less an authority than Ibn Rushd ruled that Mudejars
were of "suspect credibility, their testimony in court cannot be accepted and
they cannot be allowed to lead prayer." The legal authority of the Mudejar
scholars was doubtful, the jurists asserted, because Mudejar judges were
appointed by infidels and because they were ignorant, an ignorance which
became something of a topos in the writings of North African and Granadan
jurists.

There were, of course, less severe opinions on the Mudejar question among Maliki jurists than the ones just quoted, but these provide a clear example of how a jurisdictional classification could translate into a cultural identity.[35] The problem of Muslims who willingly and permanently resided in the lands of Christian enemies, and who by their labors directly supported these enemies in their long and successful war against Islamic polities, forced jurists to confront the question of what constituted a Muslim and to use the ensuing characteristics, which they presented as normative, to distinguish the particular, corrupt nature of Islam under Christian rule.

These jurists approached the corrupting effects of mudejarism through two quite different logics. The first was strictly jurisdictional: the Islamic life could not be fulfilled under Christian rule. How could one follow Muslim law if the scholars, judges, and officials were appointed by Christian authorities? How, without a Muslim head of state to pay it to, could one fulfill the obligation to pay *zakāt*? The second approach was more explicitly cultural. As Al-Wansharīsī put it:

One has to beware of the pervasive effect of their [the Christians'] way of life, their language, their dress, their objectionable habits, and influence on people living with them over a long period of time, as has occurred in the case of the inhabitants of Ávila and other places, for they have lost their Arabic, and when the Arabic language dies out, so does devotion to it, and there is a consequential neglect of worship as expressed in words in all its richness and outstanding virtues.[36]

According to this model, the vital Islamic nature of Mudejar culture could be evaluated by measuring it against certain cultural markers drawn from the normative Islam of more central Muslim lands: language, legal procedure, dress, ritual, and custom. Ridicule of Mudejar Arabic was one very common strategy within this framework. Criticism of Mudejar legal knowledge was another, as when a Mudejar emigrant to Oran claimed, toward the end of the fourteenth century, that among Mudejars innovation (*al-bida'*) has "extinguished the light of Muslim law."[37] We might sum up by saying that for medieval Muslims living in Islamic lands, the idea of "Islam within Christendom" was something of an oxymoron.

Medieval Muslims living in Christian lands, however, clearly felt otherwise. Certainly most Mudejar scholars felt that theirs was a culture in decline. "Because of the distance of our dwelling places and our separation from our coreligionists, no one is studying or writing": such laments were common coin among Mudejar scholars and marked an awareness of the gap they perceived between their textual practice and what they took to be normative. Nor was textual practice the only marker of Islamic identity that required defense and translation in a world ruled by Christians. We have already seen how the Maliki faqihs insisted that Christian domination led to the degradation of a number of specific and indispensable markers of Muslim identity: Arabic, adherence to Qur'anic punishments (ḥudūd), inaccessibility of Muslim women to non-Muslim men. To these we might add, as North African muftis did, the inability to identify the start of Ramaḍān, to leave Christian lands on pilgrimage, or to fulfill the obligation of paying zakāt, all crucial obligations of the believer according to Muslim law. Yet for all their strong sense of cultural decline, Mudejars worked constantly to maintain the boundaries they thought crucial to the expression of Muslim identity, and in the process forged what we today might call a diasporic Islam.

In the case of some obligations this work was relatively straightforward. Mudejars, for example, tended to replace zakāt (which required a Muslim polity) with ṣadaqa, charity, and specifically with alms for the redemption of enslaved or captive Muslims. By the Morisco period we find even some North African muftis advocating this solution. Other boundaries required more than reclassification to remain recognizable. Perhaps the one whose defense exacted the heaviest toll was that between Muslim women and non-Muslim men. The argument that under Christian lords Mudejars could not protect Muslim women from sexual advances by non-Muslims was often made by Granadan and North African jurists (like Ibn Miqlash above). Without the power to enforce Islamic legal prohibitions on intercourse between Muslim women and non-Muslim men, or to punish transgression with Qur'anic punishments, how could Muslims in the diaspora maintain this essential boundary?

This was not a theoretical issue. Christian archives contain references to thousands of Muslim women engaged in sexual relations with Christians and Jews. But these references are the result less of cultural erosion than of new ways of maintaining boundaries deemed essential. Again and again Mudejar communities purchased privileges allowing them to put to death Muslim women accused of adultery or interfaith sex, though the ḥudūd punishment was necessarily commuted to the social death of enslavement to the Crown. Again and again Mudejar fathers accused their own and their neighbors' wives and daughters with transgressing these boundaries and delivered them up for punishment. The Christian nature of the records that document the legal consequences of these actions should not obscure the fact that behind them lie Muslim communities and Muslim individuals translating Islamic legal prescriptions into Mudejar idioms.[38] Just as the risk to Muslim women in the House of War stimulated a heightened awareness of the boundary-marking role of women on the part of Mudejars, so the possibility of conversion prompted a heightened sensitivity to markers of religious identity. We might even say that, in the diaspora, the responsibility for recognizing Islam and maintaining its boundaries devolved more heavily upon the individual Muslim. This process was crucial to the production of an identity that simultaneously recognized its "decline" yet resolutely insisted on its Islam. Consider as an example the rise among Iberian Muslims of Aljamiado, that is, of romance languages written in Arabic characters. The increasing use of Aljamiado has often been cited as a sign of cultural decline, a consequence of the erosion of Arabic. But it could equally well be studied as an example of the expansion of Islamic learning among Mudejars as of its contraction. The fact that the peculiar conditions of Christian domination on the Iberian Peninsula made it possible for Muslims to justify an extensive practice of glossing and translation may have meant that knowledge which was increasingly restricted to the "learned class," the *ulama*, in more central Islamic lands penetrated further into the "popular" or "ignorant" classes in the peninsula.[39]

The point is movingly illustrated by a recently discovered fatwa written by al-Muwwaq, chief qadi of Granada in its final years. Responding to a question about how a Muslim should behave in the House of War, he replied by fusing, rather than opposing, the status of one learned in authoritative Islamic tradition with that of the individual struggling to make the discriminations necessary to maintain a Muslim identity among infidels. The individual Mudejar, he wrote, should "be a faqih of himself " (*faqīh al-nafs*). "He teaches himself, and he should distinguish the good deed which presents itself from the bad one which befalls."[40] This devolution of the responsibility for the recognition of the boundaries between Islam and other faiths from the learned elite onto embattled individual believers is one of the more remarkable cultural consequences of the Islamic diaspora in medieval Christian Europe.

Judging from manuscript evidence, one of the more important ways in which this devolution was achieved was through religious polemic. Beginning with Ibn Ḥazm (994–1064), who wrote in the wake of the collapse of the Caliphate of Cordoba and the beginnings of Christian expansion, Iberian

Muslims seem much more concerned with polemic against Christianity and Judaism than Muslims in more central lands, and this becomes increasingly true as the so-called reconquest continues. Mudejars came to depend on an expanding corpus of polemical texts that they produced, circulated, glossed, and translated. The case of the North African Muhammad al-Qaysī (MS 1557 in the National Library of Algiers) provides a good example. A captive in the Crown of Aragon in the early fourteenth century, Al-Qaysī offers a moving description of the cultural effects of living among Christians, including the claim that his soul had betrayed him, and his interior and exterior had become un-Arabic. But al-Qaysī also provides the text of what he claims was his disputation with a priest in the presence of the king of Aragon. Entitled "the Key of Religion [Kitāb Miftāḥ al-Dīn], or the Disputation between Christians and Muslims," the text was promptly translated in the first half of the fourteenth century into versions which survive in some four Aljamiado manuscripts.[41]

Al-Qaysī is not unique, nor is the Muslim–Christian frontier the only one polemically policed. A mid-fourteenth-century Arabic polemic written by a Mudejar against the Jews, the "Defense of the Faith" (Ta'yīd al-millah), exists in multiple Arabic manuscripts, some of which contain extensive interlinear glosses in Aljamiado and others of which are complete translations and adaptations.[42] The multiple survivals of these polemics are very unusual for so fragmentary a record and attest to their popularity. Moreover, of all genres, these were among the first to be glossed and translated, a process that was well under way already in the early fourteenth century. These translations were not for the learned but for the broader audience of Mudejars, enabling each to become, in this "land of polytheism," a defender of his or her own faith.

The importance of polemics to Muslims living within Christendom reminds us of the conclusions earlier in this chapter about Christian encounters with Islam. Contrary to the expectations of the more naively progressive strands of modernity, increased proximity to and knowledge of other religious communities is as capable of heightening the power of polemical forms as it is of effacing it. Like Mozarabic Christians living under Iberian Islam, Mudejar Muslims living in Christendom learned a great deal more about the religions against which they defined themselves than did their coreligionists in more homogeneous lands. But as we saw already in the Christian cases we touched upon, that knowledge was (with very few exceptions) not oriented toward the understanding and accommodation of religious difference in heterogeneous societies. Rather, it was used to buttress the structures of one's faith against the claims of others.

Yet in the process, that faith was also transformed. Medieval Christendom was in some important senses produced by Christians thinking with and about Islam (and Judaism), just as Mudejar Islam was produced by engagements with Christianity (and Judaism). This coproduction certainly did not require the living presence of other faiths and could take powerful form without it. Very few of the inhabitants of Christendom, for example, ever saw a living Muslim or a Jew, even as their culture was shaped by constant thought about Islam and Judaism. But coproduction could also take place in close proximity: Mudejar Islam emerged in conversation with Christian and Jewish neighbors. The chapters to come will focus largely on the cultural work done among neighbors, in order to show how Christians, Muslims, and Jews jostling with and thinking about each other produced new ways of living in and understanding all three faiths.

[**2**]

Love between Muslim and Jew

Since the rise of Islam and until modern times, the great majority of interaction between Jew and Muslim has taken place in lands ruled by Muslims and under Islamic rules of engagement. The most significant exception to this is the Iberian Peninsula. As large populations of Muslims were absorbed into Christian polities in the course of the so-called reconquest, there emerged in the peninsula what might be termed an Islamic diaspora of Muslim communities under Christian rule. This status, called Mudejar by modern scholars, had many interesting consequences. One, of little importance to the history of Islam but quite relevant to the history of Jewish-Muslim relations, is that for the first time since the Jews' encounter with Muhammad in Medina we have Jewish and Muslim populations living side-by-side, engaged in relations that are openly competitive because mediated by Christian and not Muslim power.

Here I propose to study only one small aspect of these relations, namely love (or more accurately, not love but its bureaucratic traces, found in disputes over interfaith adultery, conversion, and marriage). The choice needs some justification, since the number of examples of such relations is vanishingly small when compared with, for example, economic exchange. But in all three of the religions we are studying love and marriage were foundational metaphors, ruling allegories capable of expressing "deep truths" about other relationships and forms of exchange.[1] I say all three religions because we will soon find that, in affairs of love as in so many others, Muslims and Jews in Christian Spain were not in an exclusive dialogue. Theirs was a triangular relationship, in which the Christian suitor, though sometimes silent, was never absent. Nevertheless, it is worth pausing to review the long traditions of Jewish and Muslim legal thought on the topic of sex and marriage with members of other religions. For Jews in particular, problems of sexual interaction with non-Jews have been (and still are) a constant concern in a long history of living among other peoples. Their authoritative texts, like sedimentary strata, preserve varied opinions on the subject, opinions reflecting particular historical situations and very much tied to questions of power and hierarchy. It was one thing to be exogamous in a position of power, quite another in a position of weakness, yet another when the situation was genuinely competitive. The sex of the Jew involved mattered as well: being a receiver of "brides" was different from being a giver. The rabbis who compiled the Mishnah and the Talmud were quite aware of these differences. A passage in the Babylonian Talmud, for example, asks how Jewish restrictions on intermarriage could be based on a biblical passage that applied explicitly only to intermarriage with people from seven tribes that had ceased to exist shortly after the conquest by the Israelites of the Holy Land, more than a thousand years before.[2] The passage is remarkable in that it treats the evolution of sexual boundaries within historical time (a lesson we will attempt to emulate here). Nevertheless, the rabbis tended to level all such distinctions. Living in exile among more powerful peoples, acutely aware of the dangers of assimilation, acculturation, and conversion, the rabbis systematically prohibited nearly all types of sexual relations with non-Jews, often by generalizing quite specific biblical prohibitions.[3]

The sociological and theological importance of these prohibitions was quite evident to medieval rabbis. As Maimonides put it, "It is in these matters that the Omnipresent one has sanctified us and separated us from the heathens, namely in matters of forbidden unions and forbidden foods."[4] Like the rabbis whose discussions are preserved in the Talmud, Maimonides understood the elaboration of the Torah's prohibitions on intermarriage to many other forms of intercourse as something of a historical process, and he approved of that elaboration "as a precaution, lest such intercourse should lead to intermarriage."[5] He approved as well of zealots who, like Pinehas, kill Jews engaged in public miscegenation, though his equation of "public" with ten or more Israelite witnesses rendered the approval more theoretical than practical.[6] Later Iberian rabbis, such as Yehuda ben Asher ben Yehiel of Toledo and Nahmanides, continued to inveigh against Jewish men who practiced "harlotry with the daughter of a foreign God" and invoked the zealots against them.[7]

Muslim men enjoyed a good deal more freedom within their tradition than Jewish men did, at least in theory. According to classical Islamic jurisprudence, Muslim men could have intercourse with and even marry Christian or Jewish (as well as Zoroastrian) women. All children issuing from such relationships were considered Muslim. Muslim women, on the other hand, could not marry or have intercourse with non-Muslim men.[8] This law was predicated first on the assumption that the male was the dominant force within a "mixed" relationship and, second, on Muslim political superiority, for it depended on the power of Muslim courts to enforce certain hierarchical relations between Muslims and non-Muslims. Nevertheless, it continued to be stipulated as normative by Mudejar law codes in Christian Spain, even though it could clearly not be observed.[9] Only in handbooks of religious instruction like the so-called *Breviario Sunni*, written by Yçe de Gebir, a Segovian Muslim, in 1462, did Muslim authorities recognize that the situation had changed: "Whether men or women, they shall not sleep with nor marry infidels."[10]

This unruffled continuity of legal norms masks the profound shift that Christian conquest produced in the possibilities for interfaith sexual relations in Iberia. Normative halakhic texts might insist on endogamy, Sharīʿa ones on the permissibility of Muslim male exogamy, but in fact new configurations of power encouraged some forms of sexual interaction and discouraged others. The opinion of Yehuda ben Asher ben Yehiel quoted above, for instance, was issued in a context (Toledo ca. 1280) that also produced poems like this one by Todros Abulafia:

> . . .Yea, one should love an Arab girl
> Even if she's not beautiful and pure.
> But stay far away from a Spanish girl
> Even if she's radiant as the sun!
> . . . .
> Her clothes are filled with crap and crud,
> Her hems are blotted with her uncleanness.
> Her harlotry is not taken to heart; she is
> So ignorant of intercourse she knows nothing.
> But every Arab girl has charm and beauty
> . . . .
> She knows all about fornication and is adept at lechery.[11]

I quote this well-known poem to make two fairly obvious points. First, whatever the normative position of rabbis, interfaith intercourse was a very real possibility for Jews living under Christian rule in medieval Spain. Second, that intercourse was most likely to occur between Muslims and Jews, and not only because of Todros's claim that in the art of "harlotry" Arabs were erudite and Christians rustic.[12] Probably equally important was the fact that Christians ruled Todros's Toledo and Christian laws forbidding the sexual mixing of Jew (or Muslim) with Christian were vehemently enforced.[13] With regard to sex between members of minority groups the law was much less clear, the outcome more subject to negotiation. Todros's aesthetic judgments were therefore informed by a taste for safety as well as by a literate eroticism.

Thin though our evidence is, it does allow us to trace across some two centuries (from ca. 1280 until 1492) the negotiations triggered by sexual intercourse, and especially by marriage and conversion, between Muslims and Jews in Christian Iberia. The result is less a single harmonious composition than a diptych, marked by a sharp stylistic transformation at midpoint, that is to say circa 1400. Before the fifteenth century, Muslim and Jewish communities appear to have been comparatively free to compete in the sphere of love, with their competition mediated by Christian fiscal rather than spiritual interests, and the outcome generally dependent on the relative economic and political power of the two communities. For a number of reasons, that balance of power initially favored Jewish access to Muslim women rather than the other way around.

Partly, this was due to the Muslims' status as a conquered people, a conquest that was not only political but also sexual.[14] Muslims were themselves aware of this: in the previous chapter we saw the late fourteenth-century mufti Ibn Miqlash exhorting Mudejars to emigrate to Muslim lands, since under Christian lords they could not protect the chastity of their women.[15] Partly, too, it was due to the fact that the Muslim communities remaining in Christian lands were predominantly rural and agricultural, their political influence fragmented among a multiplicity of Christian lords, whereas Jews depended largely on the king. Third, and perhaps most important, the significant role that war played in justifying slavery meant that Iberian Muslims were much more susceptible to enslavement than either Christians or Jews. Even native Mudejars, though protected by law, could legally be enslaved as punishment for a great variety of crimes.[16] One of these crimes was, in fact, interfaith adultery, and Muslim communities insisted on the punishment as a way of disciplining the sexuality of Muslim women.[17] Since Muslim slaves were commonly owned by Christians and Jews, and since sexual intercourse with one's slaves was a common practice throughout the medieval Christian and Islamic world, these circumstances virtually guaranteed that most cases of interfaith sexuality would involve Muslim women and Christian or Jewish men.[18]

The Jews were not, of course, the conquerors of the Muslims, and their status vis-à-vis their Mudejar neighbors was much less clear, and consequently much more competitive, than that of Christians.[19] But Jews did have several advantages in this competition, especially in the twelfth, thirteenth, and fourteenth centuries. First, the Jews were not a conquered people subject to enslavement, except in the theoretical sense that they were in perpetual "servitude" to the monarchy. Second, Jews were frequently owners of Muslim slaves. And finally, because of their service to the monarchy, they could sometimes exercise a good deal of financial and political power over Muslims living in the peninsula's Christian kingdoms.

This last point deserves some elaboration. In order to exploit their conquests, the conquerors needed trustworthy and bilingual officials. For this they might draw upon Muslim elites in the lands they had conquered, but they could also call upon the Jews. Fluent in both Romance (Spanish, Catalan, Aragonese) and Arabic, without any loyalty to the Islamic polities across the frontier, completely at the mercy of their Christian lords, the Jews were both qualified and dependable (because dependent). Hence we find them in the vanguard of Christian reconquest. The Muslim chronicler Ibn 'Idhārī provided an early example when he complained (somewhat improbably) that in the 1090s the Cid Rodrigo Díaz appointed a Jewish minister to govern the city of Valencia after its conquest:

> The Jew—God curse him—caused the Muslims to suffer the most cruel vexations, and others of his coreligionists became enraged against the [Muslim] Valencians, who attained the heights of the greatest humiliation. Jews also were the tax collectors, officials, scribes of the chancery, and those employed in land and sea services. A Jew acted as magistrate, and as such sentenced [Muslims] to punishment of whipping or lashes.[20]

Ibn 'Idhārī presented the Jews' behavior as the product of Jewish enmity toward Muslims, but it was rather a symptom of a new political reality, one in which the Jews returned to Muslim lands as allies of and sometimes administrators for the Christian conquerors. In such a capacity Jews could come to occupy positions of authority over Muslims. When James I conquered the kingdom of Valencia in the mid-thirteenth century, for example, he did not hesitate to grant some of its lands to Jews or to utilize their services as bailiffs and tax officials over his Muslim (and Christian) subjects in the kingdom.[21] At much the same time Fernando III and Alfonso X of Castile settled Jews in their newly conquered city of Seville, giving them three mosques to convert into synagogues: a grant whose symbolism would, I suspect, have been particularly galling to Muslim observers (though so far as I know none commented upon it).[22]

In short, Muslims sometimes found Jews in positions of authority over their own communities. Even when such authority was indirect (as it most often was), it could be formidable. No medieval Muslim or Jew would have been surprised by the advice of Queen Elionor of Catalonia-Aragon to her son Prince Martí in 1374, when she told him to ignore the complaints of several Muslim *aljamas* about the weight of their debts to the Valencian Jew Jafuda Alatzar. After all, Jafuda alone paid more taxes to the Crown than virtually all the Muslim communities of the kingdom of Valencia combined.[23]

Of course these asymmetries (in affluence, political influence, and the prevalence of slavery) are only a few of the many that differentiated Muslim and Jewish communities. (Contemporaries, for example, often noted that the Mudejars had powerful external Muslim polities capable of negotiating on their behalf, whereas the Jews did not.) They are, however, the ones that seem to me most important in explaining the prevalent direction of sexual traffic between the two communities in the period before 1400. In the relatively frequent cases where Jewish men had intercourse with Muslim women (most often slaves), their exogamy was generally risk-free. On the other hand, we very rarely find documentation of Jewish women having intercourse with Muslim men. Rabbi ben Asher ben Yehiel wrote of a young woman named Leah who had been captured by raiders and taken to Muslim lands, where she converted to Islam and married a Muslim. Other than attempt to ransom the captive before such events occurred, there was little that the Jewish community could do about a case like this one, occurring in Muslim jurisdiction. (In fact the dispute submitted to Asher was about the ransom money that had already been collected, now rendered superfluous by Leah's apostasy).[24] Within the Christian kingdoms, however, the community could and did bring considerable power to bear, as they did in the case of the Zaragozan Jewess Oro de Par, threatened with disfigurement and exile for her transgression with Muslims and Christians.[25] Jewish communities were quite successful in using their resources and influence to restrict Christian male access to Jewish women in the thirteenth and fourteenth centuries.[26] As far as Muslim men were concerned, their victory was total.

There was, however, a good deal of sexual intercourse between Jewish men and Muslim women. I have written about some of these cases elsewhere, but it is worth revisiting them so as to heighten the contrast with the fifteenth-century material that follows. Such intercourse was, of course, bitterly opposed by Muslim communities. We have already seen how the Muslim aljama of Valencia, for example, purchased King Pere's confirmation of its privilege that whenever a Muslim woman was found guilty of adultery (here defined as any sexual intercourse outside of marriage) with a non-Muslim the death penalty would be imposed without possibility of monetary remission.[27] In individual cases, action was often taken by the families and communities of the women involved. A Muslim woman of Zaragoza named Amiri was twice caught in intercourse with Christians and Jews. Both times her community intervened on her behalf, preventing her sale into slavery in exchange for her promise to cease committing adultery with non-Muslims. When she was again found yet again in the Jewish quarter committing adultery with Jews, the two communities came to blows, "wishing to kill each other over her." This time she was convicted, and sold to a Christian for 120 sous, with the proceeds divided between the Crown and the informant who had denounced her.[28]

Amiri's case touches on two disadvantages that Muslim communities faced in their struggle to maintain sexual boundaries vis-à-vis the Jews. The first was the prevalence of Mudejar prostitutes. The relatively large number of Muslim women involved in prostitution had nothing to do with asymmetries of power between Muslims and Jews. It was rather a complex by-product of the interaction between Christian exploitation of Muslim women and Mudejar concerns with the honor of kin-group and community.[29] But once these women became "public females," there was little Muslims could do to prevent their intercourse with Jewish men. Occasionally one finds cases like the one reported in Huesca in 1444, where a group of Muslims seized a Jew they found visiting a brothel in the Muslim quarter, stripped him, and left him naked in the street.[30] Such violence was relatively rare, in part because it was severely punished (the Muslims of Huesca paid a heavy fine); and in part because the activities of Muslim prostitutes did not raise serious reproductive challenges for the community, since the offspring of a prostitute seem to have followed the mother's religion *faut de mieux*. I know of no specific cases, but there is indirect evidence. Saint Vincent Ferrer, for example, criticized Christian patrons of Muslim prostitutes for leaving the souls of the children whom they engendered to languish in the damnation of their mother's religion.[31]

Amiri's enslavement points to a second difficulty: the prevalence of unfree Muslim women in non-Muslim households. For Muslim women like Amiri who were enslaved as punishment for sexual crimes, sexual exploitation by their new owners was probably a matter of course. Occasionally they might even be made to work as prostitutes, with their earnings going to their owners. But the preservation of sexual boundaries was difficult even for the many Muslim women who came to the slave markets from abroad or by the fortunes of war (as Leah had done in the opposite direction), since owners' intercourse with slaves was a common practice in the Mediterranean.[32] Again there was little specific to Muslim-Jewish relations here, but since Christian law did not allow Jews to own Christian slaves, slaves in the few Jewish households wealthy enough to afford them would have been Muslim or pagan (e.g., Tartars).

Most of the surviving cases of interfaith sex, conversion, and marriage arise from this setting of servitude within Jewish households. Though sharply hierarchical, these relationships could produce strong passions. In one convoluted case from Zaragoza, for example, a Jew was accused of poisoning his son because they were both in love with one of their Muslim slaves. The son, it was said, had threatened to convert to Christianity if the father did not stop sleeping with the slave.[33] Nevertheless, we moderns should remind ourselves that there were steep differences of status within medieval households, and that these differences were significant. The inclusiveness suggested by the medieval term *familia* (household) is certainly meaningful, but importance disparities of status (e.g., slavery and freedom) and religion (in this case Judaism and Islam) could separate members of the same household. These divisions could, but need not, be overcome through intercourse. Jewish sex with Muslim slaves could lead to concubinage, conversion, the integration of offspring, even marriage. It could also remain a starkly asymmetrical relationship.

For an example of "integration," we can look to Chresches de Turri and his kinsmen, Jews of Girona, who purchased a license from King James II in 1321 permitting them to circumcise a Muslim boy who was the child of Chresches by a Muslim slave and convert him to the Jewish religion. Chresches's Gironese ancestor Abraham de Turri made a much more horrible choice some forty years earlier, suffocating his two children by one of his Muslim slaves.[34]

At about the same time, in Huesca, the Jew Cecrim Abraham seems to have attempted to maintain something of an intermediate position. His female Muslim slave had converted to Judaism after bearing him a child. Cecrim was trying to establish ownership over the child, that is, to keep him in the status of slave. He argued that "according to the custom of the city" the children born from the union of a Jewish master and Muslim slave belonged to the master. The convert claimed that her conversion retroactively enfranchised her offspring. Cecrim, on the other hand, insisted on the priority of her servile and non-Jewish status at the time of delivery.[35] Assimilation, murderous exclusion, the maintenance of the status quo: all were potential outcomes of these relationships between master and slave.

Nonetheless, some outcomes were more normative than others. Wherever contemporary evidence penetrates the timeless condemnations of a Rabbi Yehuda or a Nahmanides, it is apparent that rabbinic authorities favored the regularization of sexual relationships between Jewish men and Muslim women through conversion and through the granting of full legal rights to the concubine/bride. Such arrangements need not have been rare. We know, for example, that some Jewish communities pronounced bans upon Jews who had Muslim concubines but did not marry them "with betrothal and *ketubah* (marriage contract)." In one *responsum*, a Jew argued that he should be allowed to continue living with a concubine he had converted from Islam to Judaism and married, even though he had not given her a *ketubah*. Shelomo ben Adret disagreed.[36] But despite such attempts at systematization, it seems likely that the majority of these relationships remained unformalized because (as in the case of sex with slaves) they were customary and unremarkable or because they fell between jurisdictional cracks. When Abulfacem, a Jew of Mula [Murcia], and his Muslim concubine, Axona, were arrested by the king's brother and procurator in Murcia, the couple jointly appealed to the king. He ruled that they should be allowed to cohabit unmolested, since neither was a Christian, a ruling which makes explicit the relatively unregulated nature of Muslim-Jewish sexual relations.[37]

When such relations led to conversion, however, they came up against more structured barriers. We have already seen how Chresches de Turri thought it prudent to purchase a royal license before converting his son by a Muslim slave.[38] When the conversion involved a free Muslim woman with roots in a Mudejar community it could be much more conflictual. The case of María is the best documented.[39] She surfaces anonymously on the twelfth of August, 1356, when, at the request of the Jews of Lleida, King Peter ordered his bailiff there to release a Muslim woman arrested for converting to Judaism. The conversion, according to the king, was not a crime punishable by imprisonment.[40] Two weeks later, the king issued the following privilege to Martí Eiximin:

> We hereby grant and concede to you, the said Martius, all rights which
> we do hold, or might or should hold over María, a Jewess who had been
> a Muslim, both for her having recently abandoned the religion of perfidi-
> ous Muhammad and embraced the law of the Hebrews, and for the crime
> of adultery which she is alleged to have committed with Jews while still a
> Muslim. . . . And we accord and allot to you, the said Martius, full power
> and authority to settle with the said Muslim on that amount of money upon
> which you shall be best able to agree with her, . . . as well as [authority for]
> absolving and sentencing this Jewess for the aforesaid and whatever other
> crimes may have been committed by her.[41]

The privilege itself makes no effort to prioritize the two charges, conversion/ apostasy and interfaith sexual contact, or to fix the convert's identity ("said Muslim"/"this Jewess"). But in its two-year effort to repeal the lenient treatment accorded María the Muslim aljama of Lleida proved to be quite aware of where the legal advantages lay. In a document issued in May 1358, the Muslims asked King Pere to intervene against any Christian who attempted to obstruct the punishment of a Muslim convert to Judaism, as had presumably occurred in María's case. They argued that according to a "general constitution of Catalonia recently published and enacted at Tarragona, no Muslim man or woman should dare in any manner to convert to the law of the Jews, and that if any Muslim violates this he shall incur both corporal and financial punishment." According to the Muslims, the license accorded by the king to a recent conversion (María's?) harmed the aljama by encouraging others who might be thinking of converting.[42]

By focusing on Muslim-Jewish apostasy, where the law was relatively clear, rather than on Muslim-Jewish miscegenation, where it was not, the Mudejars hoped to raise the barriers between Muslim women and Jewish men. The Muslims of Lleida might have found support for their arguments in the opinions of distinguished lawyers like Oldradus de Ponte (d. 1337?), who may himself have spent some time teaching in Lleida, and who asked the following question in a *consilium*: "A Jew went over to the sect of the Saracens. The Question is put, should he be punished?" In the first instance, the question seemed as trivial to Oldradus as Abulfacem's case had seemed to James II: "Evidently not, since we tolerate both sects. If each is in a state of damnation it does not matter to which sect he belongs because there is no distinction between equivalents." Oldradus did not stop there, however, and his second argument was much less symmetrical. If apostasy is a turning back, a movement from the better to the worse, then Jewish conversion to Islam was not apostasy, since "the Saracen sect is not as bad as that of the Jews, according to the word of the Lord.": "The Church makes sufficiently clear that they are worse, for when it prays on Good Friday for all people there is no genuflection for Jews, though there is for pagans [i.e., Muslims]." In the case of Jewish conversions to Islam, Oldradus's reasoning is clear: they are not to be punished. He left the question of conversions in the other direction ambiguous, since they were not at issue in this case.[43]

A hundred years later, that ambiguity would be definitively eliminated and in favor of Islam. But it is interesting that before 1400, Muslim efforts to criminalize conversion to Judaism were largely in vain, despite the existence of rulings like Oldradus's and of quite explicit civil laws like the "constitutions of Tarragona" mentioned above. Even in the most conflictual cases, where we know that Mudejar communities worked very hard to have the convert punished, they rarely succeeded, both because the Jews might pay even more to have the Muslims' privilege overturned and because influential Christians might intervene to defend the convert. By the late fourteenth century we find Muslim women like Jamila and Simfa, who converted to Judaism in 1386, facing only the inconvenience of having to pay a fine.[44] In the long run, however, the Muslim strategy proved prescient, in that it gave their communities access to an emerging Christian clerical anti-Judaism, with its attendant desire to circumscribe the spheres of Jewish activity in Christian society.

In fact within little more than a generation of Jamila and Simfa's conversion, the situation was completely reversed. After 1400, a Muslim woman's conversion to Judaism and marriage to a Jew, far from going unremarked or occasioning a mere fine, was certain to become a *cause célèbre*. The fifteenth-century cases I have found are few, but they achieved much notoriety and occupied the attention of some of the greatest theological minds of the age. In them the scope of the transformation is amply clear. By the end of the century it was the right of Jewish women to convert to Islam that Christian authorities were defending, not the reverse.

The first case, from sometime in the first half of the century, involves the affair of a young Muslim woman from Talavera with a Jew from that town and her eventual conversion to Judaism, an event which apparently provoked a "great and scandalous discord."[45] The document contains few details of the conversion itself. The Muslim woman is not named, and we are told only that Yuda, a Jew from Talavera, "took a young moorish woman from her father's house and converted her to Judaism" and that he had been "mixing" sexually with the young woman for some time before the conversion.[46] Instead, the two sides (Christian clerics on behalf of the Muslims on the one hand, the Jews and their Christian lawyer on the other) concentrate entirely on the legal and theological question of whether or not the conversion is permissible. (I will return to the substance of the arguments in a moment.)[47]

Probably at much the same time as the Talavera disputation, the famous canonist and bishop of Avila Alfonso de Madrigal "el Tostado," (1410–55) wrote an opinion (*responsio*) on the following subject: "A woman of Sarracen lineage and of the Sarracen faith, at the instigation of a Jewish man with whom she was sexually involved, professed the Jewish faith . . . and was solemnly received into the Jewish congregation or synagogue by Jewish rabbis." Is such a conversion permissible, and if not, who is to be punished for it? The bishop's answer occupies twenty-five double-columned folios and is definitive (as well as repetitive) in its conclusions: the conversion is not to be allowed, and the Jews are to be punished.[48]

Together, these two treatises make clear that Christian attitudes toward Muslim conversions to Judaism had changed dramatically, and that the very highest echelons of the peninsular church were now militantly arrayed against them. How should we explain this shift? The answer is not, I think, to be found in the sociology of power I invoked in order to explain the pre-1400 situation. Despite a series of disasters such as the massacres and mass conversions of 1391 and the proselytizing and segregationist campaigns of the early fifteenth century (on which see chaps. 4 and 5), many of the economic and social conditions that had facilitated the conversion of Muslims to Judaism in the earlier period still existed. Even in the latter half of the fifteenth century, the Jews of Castile (where these two cases took place) were still more active than Muslims in royal administration. The Muslims of Granada obviously took Jewish power seriously as late as 1491, for they included in their surrender treaty with the Catholic monarchs the clause that "their highnesses would not permit the Jews to have power or command over the Moors, or to be collectors of any tax."[49] Moreover, throughout the century Jews continued to own Muslim slaves, and to wield the power necessary to enforce their rights over these slaves. In 1469, for example, armed Jews conducted a house-to-house search of the Muslim quarter of Murcia looking for fugitive slaves.[50]

Without multiplying such examples, let me assert that the changed possibilities for Muslim-Jewish love, conversion, and marriage were not primarily a product of a shift in the relative power of Muslims and Jews. Rather, they reflected changes in the role these two religious communities (or rather, theological categories) played in the Christian theological imagination and the increasing importance of these theological considerations in the Christian mediation of Jewish-Muslim relations.

A simple comparison of Oldradus de Ponte's position with those of Alfonso de Madrigal and the Talavera lawyers a century later makes the change clear. Oldradus had considered the problem of marriage and conversion in some sense trivial: "If each is in a state of damnation it does not matter to which sect he belongs because there is no distinction between equivalents." But between Oldradus and the mid-fifteenth century there intervened the massacre and forced baptism of thousands of Jews in 1391; the segregations, disputations, and mass conversions of 1412–16. These waves of violence and evangelization brought a number of conflicting Christian anxieties in their wake. On the one hand, Christians could and did take joy in the fact that through their efforts the ranks of Iberian Jewry had been halved. The disappearance of the Jews through conversion and massacre had long been anticipated as a marker of the advent of messianic time, and there were many who felt that such a time was close to hand. On the other, many Christians were becoming increasingly convinced that, rather than being defeated, Judaism had in fact triumphed. Through the nefarious actions of converts to Christianity who remained Jewish at heart, Christian Spain was being "conquered," corrupted, and judaized. (These concerns broke violently into public discourse during the civil wars of the 1440s, and particularly during the Toledan revolt and massacre of converts in 1449.)[51] Either way, a long-standing equilibrium had been broken. In most of the chapters that follow we will be focusing on some of the many consequences of this breakage, which would eventually include the establishment of the Inquisition, the expulsion of the Jews, and the creation of purity of blood statutes, to mention only a few of the more significant. But it is one of the less significant consequences that is my subject here: conversion and marriage between Muslims and Jews now took on a heightened theological significance. If the Jews were believed to be disappearing as the world slouched toward its final battle, then a Muslim conversion to Judaism assumed apocalyptic meaning. And if, to the contrary,

Jewish power was thought to be gaining through the conversos an increasing hold on Iberian society, then a Muslim conversion became confirmation of that suspicion.

So far as I know (his writings are voluminous), Alfonso de Madrigal did not engage actively in any of the many debates about Jews and conversos that agitated his age. For example, unlike some of his illustrious episcopal contemporaries (e.g., Alonso de Cartagena and Lope de Barrientos), he does not seem to have ruled on the legality of the anticonverso violence and discriminatory legislation issuing from Toledo in 1449. Nevertheless, his "Responsio in quaestione de muliere sarracena transeunte ad statum et ritum Iudaicum" is very much marked by the times.

I should note that Alfonso was quite capable of taking love seriously as an explanation for religious *mesaliance*, at least when it occurred far away and long ago. In his commentary on *Judges*, for example, he lingered over Sampson's transgressive predilection for Philistine women. His conclusions were exculpatory, even empathetic. Sampson suffered from lovesickness, a disease that overwhelms volitions, and should not therefore be harshly adjudged for his actions.[52] He was not responsible. Confronted by the power of love in his own time, however, Alfonso took a very different approach indeed.

His treatise begins with the affair: a Muslim woman, at the suggestion of a Jewish man with whom she had "mixed carnally," was solemnly converted by rabbis in the synagogue, the conversion attested by a Christian notary. Should this be tolerated, or should the woman, the Jewish lover, the rabbis and synagogue, even the Christian notary, be punished (and if so, how)? Alfonso's answer is unambiguous: the conversion is not to be tolerated [86rb]. Just as the Jews are not allowed to build new synagogues, so they cannot create new "temples in the spirit," i.e., new converts [86va]. Indeed it is worse to create new converts than to build new synagogues, for it is the observance of the Jewish cult that is damnable, not the place in which the observance is found. If law restricts the place of cultic observance, so much more should the person who carries out that observance be restricted [87rb, 87va]. Moreover the convert to Judaism is embracing a "detestable observance," a "lethal sect that leads to eternal damnation. . . . And a cruel sect, . . . for those who observe it are cruel to their own souls" [87va]. It cannot be said that the convert is adopting a valid law (the term was used in medieval Spain for what today we call religion) or rite (*ritus*), for the Jews' so-called law has been abrogated [88ra]. Through its observance you cannot be saved, and in fact all who participate in it are damned.

Alfonso repeatedly recognizes that there are some who would object, first that no crime has been committed, since as a Muslim the woman was already damned and in a state of mortal sin; and second, that the "status of Muslim was more detestable than that of Jew," so that "in going over to the Jewish rite she did not sin" [88ra-rb, 93va-vb]. His response to these objections is threefold. First, it is the act of choosing damnation that is here condemned, not the state of damnation itself. Those who are born into Islam or Judaism, though damned, are not so contemptible as those who choose such a religion of their own free will [88va]. Moreover, the act of choice itself entails an act of mortal sin that cannot be allowed. "It is like the case of a man who has his sister in concubinage. Then he relinquishes her and takes as concubine a woman to whom he is not related. . . . It is certain that the second status is less detestable than the first," but nevertheless, "by accepting once more such a woman in concubinage he commits once more a mortal sin," and such an action cannot be permitted [88rb, 93vb]. Or as Alfonso puts it later, we are commanded to choose the good, not the lesser evil. Stealing is a lesser crime than killing, yet we are not permitted to choose theft; homosexual sodomy may be worse than heterosexual rape, but Lot still sinned in handing over his daughters to the men of Sodom [100ra]. It does not matter here whether Judaism is superior to Islam or not. The sin lies in choosing damnation, and damnation cannot be hierarchicalized [93vb].

Alfonso's second response is perhaps more revealing: regardless of the relative merits of the two "damned" religions, the conversion constitutes blasphemy against the "true" one, Christianity. By converting to Judaism the Muslim woman explicitly manifests her belief that salvation can be found in Jewish faith and through Jewish ritual, and she implicitly suggests that the Jewish faith is better than the Christian one, that Jewish works are better than the Christian word. These two terrible blasphemies produced by her conversion are "a detestable sin, and this is the reason that is most pressing" [88va-89ra]. Moreover through the conversion Judaism, a "status reprobatus," would come to seem "approbatus," and Judaism would triumph over Christianity. To allow such blasphemy is to invite God's angry retribution upon princes, prelates, and entire congregations [89rb-89vb].

Thus far Alfonso's logic seems oriented toward convincing those who are inclined to accept the superiority of Judaism over Islam that such considerations are irrelevant. He even goes so far as to respond to those who say that Islamic conversion to Judaism should be encouraged, since the latter is a religion closer to the true faith of Christianity. This argument is dangerous, according to Alfonso, because there is no salvation in Judaism. Would not converts be damned if they died in the intermediate state of Jewishness [89va]? Even if we were all agreed that Judaism was better than Islam, he repeats again and again [e.g., 94rb], nevertheless the act of conversion from Islam to Judaism should be prohibited, with infractions vigorously punished.

But of course Alfonso is far from convinced of such superiority himself. He reminds his readers that previous authorities, particularly Oldradus de Ponte and Ludovicus Pontanus of Rome, ranked Islam ahead of Judaism.[53] He repeats a number of their arguments and adds an interesting one himself. The plight of the Jews, he asserts, is due to their murder of Jesus. It is because they crucified the lord that they are condemned by law to be slaves ("seruos") forever. It is as a consequence of this status that they are oppressed in special ways reserved for themselves alone, "that they be recognized and known as slaves" ("ut se seruos agnoscant et sciant") [90rb]. The badge they are forced to wear; their segregation during Holy Week; the ban on their owning Christian slaves, employing Christian wet nurses, receiving testamentary bequests from Christians, holding public office: all these are opprobria reserved for the Jews as marks of the servitude they incurred through deicide. Alfonso's conclusion from these theological commonplaces is novel: how can we allow Muslims, who did not participate in the killing of the Lord, to be brought by the Jews into this status [91ra]?

While Alfonso chose to focus on the problematics of conversion itself, his contemporaries in the Talavera disputation took a different approach, one that highlights the second key change affecting Christian attitudes toward Muslim conversions to Judaism: the heightened tenor of Christian anti-Judaism in fifteenth-century Spain. At Talavera, the central issue is not so much about theological principles (e.g., is it permitted to posit a hierarchy of mortal sin?) as about the relative merits of the two minority religions. Here, the arguments made by the clerics of Talavera on behalf of the Muslims are instructive: "The Jews, in the rites of their religion as they currently practice it, are to a great degree of worse condition and more damnable and more abhorred by the Lord, and more corrupting . . . of us, than are the Moors who live among us."[54] The Jews have rejected their prophets and become a synagogue of Satan, losing all title to Mosaic law and to the name of "Jews."[55] They are blasphemous, blind, and obstinate, willing followers of the Antichrist. The Muslims' "evil way of life," however, "is only a manner of bestial superstition and blind ignorance." Moreover, rather than blaspheme as the Jews do, the Muslims accept Christ. In fact, if the Church teaches that Muslims are to be avoided as much as Jews are, it is only because Muslims have been contaminated by Jewish ways, such as circumcision.[56] Muslim opposition to Christianity, in the past (Muhammad) as in the future (the Antichrist) is the result of Jewish deceit. Being imitative, it is not as deeply rooted as that of the Jews, who are serpents seeking to poison Christendom [108ra]. Hence the Muslims are more easily converted to Christianity than are the Jews, and once baptized, make more sincere converts.

This last argument is revealing, marking as it does the power of new Christian ideologies to transform Jewish-Muslim relations. In making it, the Muslims' lawyers show themselves to be well informed about the key claims and proof-texts of the anticonverso and anti-Jewish circles writing around Toledo in the 1440s. Converts from Judaism, they allege, are known to be especially prone to "return to their own vomit," and even once converted many are "empty talkers and deceivers." "We do not say this in order to introduce division among the sons of the Church, unitary and immaculate . . . for all are, after conversion, of equal condition and value . . . except insofar as the personal virtue and nobility of some raises them, and the error and malice and villainy of others draws them down." Such baseness and error among converts is the "fruit produced by this damned synagogue of Satan," and of all this converts from Islam are innocent.[57]

These claims were radical but chic, very much the latest in anticonverso polemic. The Muslims' lawyers were clearly taking pains to protect themselves against the charge (championed by Alonso de Cartagena, at whose request this transcript of the Talavera trial was probably copied) that such arguments introduced heretical division into the Body of Christ. They did so by insisting, as a number of Toledan writers had begun to do in the 1430s, that the problem was not one of sacramental theology but one of lineage, that is of villainy versus nobility. This is not the place to explore the history of those claims: we will do so in chapters 7 and 8. It is enough to note that the most up-to-date tools of anti-Jewish polemic were here being deployed on the Muslims' behalf.[58]

Of course not all aspects of the lawyers' argument were as novel or as radical as the comparison of Jewish and Muslim converts. Claims about Muslim spiritual superiority to Jews had long been made, not only in learned treatises by churchmen like Oldradus but also in vernacular works like the thirteenth-century *Cantigas de Santa María*, where the Virgin works miracles for Muslims and makes clear her preference for Muslims over Jews.[59] These comparisons often revolved, as at Talavera, around the well-known fact that

Islam accepted Mary's virginity after conception and considered Christ a
prophet.[60] (The Qur'an itself stressed that the Jews had been damned because, among other reasons, they defamed Mary and refused to believe her,
rejecting the prophecies of her son.)[61] But these arguments had not previously been brought to bear effectively on questions of Muslim-Jewish sex and
conversion. In the earlier period, as we have seen, other discourses had dominated, for example the fiscal one. The Talavera disputation is particularly
revealing because it helps us to see how increasing anxiety about the place
of conversos in Christian society transformed an aspect of relations between
Muslims and Jews. As the place of Jews in Christian religiosity changed, so
did the meaning of Muslim-Jewish love and conversion in Christian eyes.
Such relationships were no longer mere "minority affairs." They were now
part of a triangular relationship in which the desires of Christian theologians
played the dominant role.

In the context of the new religious anxieties and shifting hierarchies of
the fifteenth century, powerful Christians had come to question the extent
to which Jewish sex with Muslim women was a "natural" and therefore tol-
erable consequence of social and economic hierarchies. Over the course of
little more than a generation, the sexual boundaries between Muslims and
Jews had been redrawn, and by the end of the century, the direction of traffic across those boundaries would be reversed. In 1489, the Jewish aljama of
Soria complained that a Jewish woman had converted to Islam and adopted
the name Marien in order to marry Abrahén Caballete, a Muslim from Burgos.[62] Christian officials hastened to the defense of the newly married couple
and the Muslim aljama. The following year, at the complaint of a Jew from
Guadalajara, the Catholic monarchs dispatched an official to arrest a Muslim
faqih together with a number of Jews he was said to have converted to Islam.
The investigation confirmed that a Jew named Salamo Çeano had indeed
converted to Islam at the urging of Çide Açan, "alfaquí." But the Muslims
produced documentation in order to support their argument that the conversion was not punishable according to either criminal or civil law. Their claim
deserves citation in full: "The said Jew could turn Moor, and the said *alfaquí*
and the other moors who solicited him could do so, and that this had been
customary in these our kingdoms, and that many Jews had become moors
and had not been arrested for it, as it appeared from the said rulings and
documents, and that never until now had it been forbidden to them."[63] The
actual number of conversions is as debatable as it is unknowable. The point
here, however, is that the Muslims' arguments convinced the monarchs, who

allowed the conversion to stand and absolved the Muslims of any liability, even though they expressly forbade that henceforth any Jew convert to Islam, "under the same penalties as those incurred by moors who become Jewish."

These conversions are the last I know of before the expulsions of 1492 put an end to such spiritual migrations between Judaism and Islam on Iberian soil. There are many questions one would like to put to the converts themselves, questions about motivation (they did not, so far as we know, involve love or marriage), conviction, belief. What worlds of struggle lie concealed beneath the limpid phrase "many Jews had become moors"? The decision to move between two oppressed communities, each so obviously *in extremis* by 1489, is surely overflowing with meaning. Here we must let much of that meaning escape us in order to keep hold of a simpler point. The conversions make clear just how thoroughly the possibilities for movement across the two communities had been altered over the course of a century.

This transformation had many causes, some of them internal to the Jewish and Muslim communities. But the most important of these causes had nothing to do with how Jews and Muslims thought of each other and everything to do with how Christians thought about themselves. By the mid-fifteenth century Spanish Christendom imagined itself engaged in a mortal struggle with Judaism, threatened from without by the Jews themselves, endangered from within by the conversos. In the context of this struggle and the torrent of anti-Jewish theological arguments it produced, conversion between Judaism and Islam took on new meanings and new dangers. Muslims were themselves quick to realize the polemical opportunities of this new world, and they (or in the case at Talavera their Christian lawyers) adopted a strategy of invoking Christ and the Virgin in their competitions with the Jews. Of course such invocations were not completely alien to more traditional Muslim criticisms of Judaism. But classical Islam tended to play down the role of the Jews as killers of Jesus, since according to Islamic tradition God had frustrated the Jews in their designs so that they had not actually killed him. As the Qur'an puts it, "[The Jews] schemed against Jesus, but God also schemed, and God is the best of schemers" [Surah 3:54].

Spanish Muslims were not so reticent. They went far beyond traditional Islam both in their devotion to the Virgin Mary and in their expansion and embroidery of the Jewish role in the killing of Jesus. Numerous Mudejar and Morisco manuscripts survive that detail stories of Jewish conspiracies with the Devil to eliminate Jesus and dwell on the vengeance that would befall the Jews for this perfidy. By the mid-fifteenth century, we can even say that

Iberian Muslim polemicists had adopted all the central tenets of Christian anti-Judaism: (1) that the Jews crucified Jesus; (2) that the siege and destruction of Jerusalem were punishment for this act; (3) that the Diaspora and "servitude" of the Jews was evidence of their infidelity; and (4) that these unfaithful Jews would all be slaughtered at the end of Days.[64]

It is easy to see why, in Christian Iberia, Muslims in situations of competition and conflict with Jews might adopt Christian anti-Jewish themes that were relatively rare in regions under Islamic rule. We should not, however, forget the obvious. The Muslim deployment of these "Christocentric" arguments was effective only insofar as it coincided with the dominant concerns of Christian society and its rulers. In the fourteenth century the coincidence had been slight, with Christian rulers largely indifferent to Mudejar concerns about conversion and intermarriage. In the fifteenth century, however, such issues had migrated to the forefront of Christian consciousness and now resonated strongly with Muslim arguments. The transformation of the sexual boundaries between Muslim and Jew was only one result of this change in Christian consciousness, and numerically it was not a very important one. Its significance lies not in numbers but in the intimate way it reminds us that relationships between subordinate groups can rarely be viewed in isolation from the ideologies of the dominant.

But the ideologies of the dominant Christians were themselves produced by thinking about Muslims and Jews, both real and imagined. In this chapter, we've seen how the changing theological work done by Judaism in the Christian imagination transformed the possibilities of love for Muslims and Jews of flesh and blood. The next chapter is also about love affairs, this time between Jews and Christians. But that love will be more of fiction than of flesh, and it is the dominant themselves who will feel the brunt of the ideologies erected in its name.

[3]

Deviant Politics and Jewish Love
Alfonso VIII and the Jewess of Toledo

"Love" of Jews was a frequent accusation against Christian princes in medieval Christendom. In the words of Ramón Martí, "What do you think that the devil can accomplish through the Jews . . . , so loved by our princes on account of the services they provide and the flatteries they spew forth?" Less often, this accusation took the form of carnal love, fleshy and physical. Guibert of Nogent, for example, excoriated the count of Soissons for his affair with a Jewess. Count Thibault of Blois is said to have had relationship with a Jewess called Pucellina, which ended with his burning a number of her coreligionists alive on charges of ritual murder in 1171. According to Polish legend, King Casimir the Great (1310–70) so loved the Jewess "Estherke" (Esther) that in 1334 he granted the Jews his "Golden Bull" of privileges in her honor and after her death kept her eyes and heart in a box by his bed.[1] But of all of these love stories, perhaps the most interesting, as well as the most long-lived, is told by a king himself, King Sancho IV of Castile (r. 1284–95).

Sancho was a dutiful parent, if not a faithful son. At some point not long after bringing the civil war against his father, Alfonso X, to its successful conclusion, he (or his ghostwriters) began to draft a manual of proper conduct

This chapter began as "Alfonso VIII and the Jewess of Toledo: A Political Affair," in *Essays in Honor of Denah Lida*, ed. Mary Berg and Lanin A. Gyurko (Potomac, MD: Scripta Humanistica, 2005), 27–43. Like its precursor, it is dedicated with love to my great aunt.

for his own heir, Fernando. Among the many moral and political lessons that Sancho hoped to impart to his child through *The Punishments* (*Castigos*) was a strong sense of the value God attributes to royal chastity. The lesson was often repeated, but in chapter 21 it took on a curious shape:

> My son . . . consider the punishment that happened to king don Alfonso of Castile, the victor in the battle of [Las Navas de Tolosa, 1212]. For the seven years that he lived the bad life with a Jewess of Toledo, God punished and beat him in the battle of Alarcos (1195), in which he was defeated and fled, and it went badly for him and for all the subjects of his realms. . . . God also killed all his sons, so that his grandson Ferdinand, son of his daughter, inherited the kingdom. He repented of such a bad sin as this one that he had committed, and later built the monastery of Las Huelgas in Burgos . . . as penance, and God gave him afterward victory against the Muslims in battle. But whatever good fortune he had, it would have been much better if he had not been first defeated at the Battle of Alarcos, in which bad fortune he fell because of his sin.[2]

Here, anonymous and cramped into a handful of humble words ("he lived a bad life with a Jewess of Toledo"), we first encounter the most famous Jewish woman of Iberian letters. Her story would be written and rewritten for the benefit of audiences, early modern and modern, moved by *mésalliances*: Lope de Vega's *Las paces de los reyes y judía de Toledo*, Franz Grillparzer's *Die Jüdin von Toledo*, and Lion Feuchtwanger's *Spanische Ballade/Die Jüdin von Toledo*, these are only a few of the later works of fiction that animate our skeletal Jewess in order to explore the furthest reaches of star-crossed love.[3]

Historians, too, have been attracted by the story. Most insistently they have asked of the Jewess, is her story true? Modern scholars have usually approached this question by scrutinizing the troubling century of silence that separates the Jewess's alleged existence (sometime prior to 1195) in the early part of Alfonso VIII's reign (1158–1214) from her first appearance in the histories (ca. 1292).[4] Why did her story begin to be told only in the late thirteenth century? This silence apparently concerned the early chroniclers as well. Already in the *Crónica de Castilla* (whose surviving Galician-Portuguese version dates to 1295–1312) the story is attributed to the early thirteenth-century historian Rodrigo Jiménez de Rada (ca. 1170–1247). Later chroniclers deleted the attribution, perhaps aware that this august archbishop of Toledo never mentioned the Jewess in any of his known writings.[5] Rodrigo's *De re-*

bus Hispaniae was one of the pillars for the great historical edifice built by Sancho's father, Alfonso X, whose pinnacle was the *Primera Crónica General*. That chronicle too ignored the Jewess, even though it happily embellished other accounts of interfaith affection, such as that of Alfonso VI's marriage with the Muslim princess Zaida. In any event, its chapter on Alfonso VIII was probably redacted shortly after 1289: that is, well after Alfonso X's death and at much the same time as the *Castigos*.[6]

Scholars also find reason for worry in the story's rapid expansion: in the few years that intervene between the composition of the *Castigos* and the *Crónica de Castilla* the tale had spread across three chapters. Chapter 502 of the *Crónica* blames Alfonso VIII's defeat at Alarcos on the factionalism and tepid loyalty of his vassals but attributes that disloyalty to God's punishment of the king's youthful sin. Chapter 503 describes the expiation of that sin through the founding of Santa María de las Huelgas at Burgos. And Chapter 491 records the sin itself:

> After the king Alfonso was married, as you've already heard, he departed to Toledo with his wife. And while there he saw a very beautiful Jewess, and he became so attached to her that he left the queen his wife and shut himself up with the Jewess for a very long time, in such wise that he could not part from her for any reason, and occupied himself with nothing else. And as the Archbishop Rodrigo tells it, he was shut up with her for seven months, so that he paid no heed to himself, nor to his kingdom, nor to anything else. And they say that this great love that he had for the Jewess was caused by spells and love magic that she knew how to make. But the counts and barons and rich men, seeing that the kingdom was in such danger because of this, agreed together on how they would resolve this terrible and unconscionable deed. And the agreement was that they would kill her. And with this intention they entered to where the king was, pretending that they wished to speak to him. And after all had gone in before the king, while some spoke to him the others entered to where the Jewess was and . . . they cut her throat and did the same to the others who were with her. . . . And when the king learned this he was so unhappy that he did not know what to do, for he loved her so much that he wanted to die with her. And then some of his vassals took him and transported him to a place called Illescas. . . . And as he lay one night preoccupied by the affair of this damned Jewess there appeared to him an angel who said to him: how now, Alfonso, are you dwelling on the evil you have done, from which God received great disser-

vice? You do ill, for know that He will charge you dearly for it, you and your kingdom, for it consented to your sin. . . . And then the angel disappeared, filling the room with a great odor, clear and good.[7]

Here we have at last the drama that would attract the likes of Lope de Vega. The Jewess remains anonymous and undescribed, but the power of her beauty is amply reflected in the king's lovesickness: his distraction during her life, his melancholy after her death. We even catch a glimpse of her in a richly furnished chamber, surrounded by unnamed companions who share her fate. The cast of characters, too, has grown, first by a band of nobles so concerned about the state of the realm that they agree to deceive the king and murder the Jewess in his court; and then by a sweet-smelling angel who visits and upbraids the disconsolate monarch.

Historians are generally suspicious of expansion, and this case is no exception. Diego de Colmenares in the seventeenth century, the Marqués de Mondéjar and the Padre Flórez in the eighteenth, in the nineteenth Fidel Fita, all decried the affair as implausible legend. Others defend love but protest the details.[8] Strangely enough it is not the angel who attracts scholarly ire, but the barons. In words penned by Marcelino Menéndez y Pelayo, "What is most unlikely and most insulting in the story is not that the king should be taken by a very beautiful Jewess, but that the great men of Castile should plot together to assassinate a miserable woman." The Jewess's most recent student concurs: Historical material underpins Sancho's account. But the betrayal of the king and the murder of his lover, these must be the embroidery of overheated imaginations.[9]

Of course a great deal has changed over the centuries of critical engagement with the Jewess. Over the past generation of literary studies alone, focus has shifted from questions of truth and transmission to questions of representation. "Even if the tales are not real, they are true in the sense that they mirror and heighten situations, perceptions, and tensions inherent in a society," as Edna Aizenberg put it in her study of the Jewess some twenty years ago. The Jewess's story now serves to illustrate, not the ideal of chastity, but the compulsion of the powerful to sexually objectify the weak. Like so many other peoples ravished in histories, she becomes a "tool for asserting in-group values and dominance, all the while affirming male supremacy." For Aizenberg, as for many of the scholars working on literary representations of gender and sexuality in the Iberian Middle Ages, the challenge is to demonstrate how, in Foucault's famous words, "power . . . dictates its law to sex."[10]

Such readings are productive and liberating, in that they move from "event" to "discourse" and "representation." They are also ethically attractive, in that they seem to turn our attention from the powerful to the oppressed. But premodern power did not speak with one voice, and premodern sex took poor dictation. Because claims about love were the terms in which conflict, both political and hermeneutic, was expressed and negotiated in the Christian Middle Ages, the relationship between politics and sex was one of codependence, not one of tyranny. Our story is a product of this codependence. How to discriminate between political and textual practices that are the products of legitimate love between sovereigns and subjects and those that are not? This is the basic constitutional question posed (though certainly not answered) by the Jewess of Toledo. Her romance, it turns out, can teach us a great deal, not only about conflicts over new forms of governance (such as royal favorites, ministers, and bureaucracies) in late medieval political orders but also about the roles played by figures of Judaism (and of women) in enacting and representing these conflicts within Christian political theology.

"You shall be free to set a king over yourselves, one chosen by the Lord your God," grants Deuteronomy 17, but "he shall not have many wives, lest his heart go astray" (vv. 15–17). Within the context of the ancient Near Eastern polities of Egypt or Mesopotamia, where uxorial expansion was a basic instrument of political incorporation, this restriction of the Israelite sovereign's sexual alliances was remarkable and came to form a distinctive theme of Israelite manuals on kingship. Thus the Book of Proverbs (which, like Sancho's *Punishments,* takes the form of admonitions addressed by the author to his son) represents right rule as resistance to the seduction of "forbidden women."[11] This representation, which permeates the entire book, sometimes takes dramatic form: "My son, heed my words; and store up my commandments. . . . From the window of my house, through my lattice, I looked out and saw . . . a woman. She lurks at every corner. She lays hold of him and kisses him. . . . She sways him with her eloquence, turns him aside with her smooth talk. Thoughtlessly he follows, her, like an ox going to slaughter. . . . Now my sons, listen to me, pay attention to my words; Let your mind not wander down her ways. . . . Her house is a highway . . . leading down to Death's inner chambers."[12] We cannot explore the relationships between these stagings of sovereign seductions in the Hebrew Bible and medieval Christian ones. Suffice it to say that the dangers posed to Christian monarchs by deviant love have a pedigree rooted in Hebrew scripture and that the ways in which biblical kingship "manuals" like Proverbs imagined those dangers influenced the literary imagination of medieval ones.

Given the long shadow of these sexual dangers, it is unsurprising that Alfonso VIII and his Jewess are not alone in the *Punishments*. They appear in the midst of three chapters (19–21) devoted to describing correct political order in terms of the proper sexual relationship to the sacred. Chapter 19, entitled "How man should not grieve God [by having sex] with women with whom he ought not or where he ought not" ("Commo non deue omne fazer pesar a Dios con mugeres con que non deue e o non deue"), introduces the general topic. God takes special offense, the chapter begins by explaining, at sins committed with women in religious orders, married women, virgins, Jews, and Muslims.[13]

In the case of religious women (who form the specific subject of chap. 19), this is because a nun is "married to God." "He who wants to take the wife of God, his lord, commits great treason." Just as it would obviously constitute "great madness" for a poor man to fight with his rich lord, so it is folly to offend God by stealing his brides. The point is made through a political proverb: "Whether in jest or in earnest, never take liberties with your lord." It is brought home (as are all moral claims in the *Castigos*) by a vivid example. A nun is sneaking out of her monastery to meet a would-be lover. Passing the main altar she genuflects and whispers a furtive Ave Maria. The Virgin's statue begins to scream, the crucified Jesus jumps from his crucifix to give chase. Just as the nun reaches the gate he clubs her with his arm, driving through her jawbones the nail that had fixed his hand to the cross. Then he returns to his crucifix, leaving the nun impaled on the floor, nail sticking out of chin.

The denouement is predictable: the nun is revived and repentant, the knight becomes a monk, the crucifix displays henceforth a crooked arm. The moral, too, is near: if mute images, made of wood by the hands of man, take umbrage at such sexual treason against God, how much greater must be the anger of God and Virgin herself? Because in the *Castigos* divine anger so often has military consequences, the chapter concludes with an account (and in Manuscript C an illustration) of a contemporary battle in which Pedro Coronel defeats Juan Corualan thanks to the intervention of a (now spectral?) nun with whom the latter had once sinned.[14]

Sancho's Muslim and Jewish women moved in the same moral, political, and narrative landscape as these erotic nuns and their married (chap. 20) and virgin (chap. 21) Christian sisters. Of course sex with non-Christians offends

God not because, as is the case with nuns, their love is pledged to him, but because they are His enemies. In the case of Jews, who rejected Jesus's kingship and tormented him in the flesh, Sancho emphasized the disparity between religious enmity and physical love through a graphic image: "Moreover, you should not in intimacy bring your face close to that of the Jewess, for she is of the lineage of those who spat in the face of Jesus Christ, your Lord."[15] This imagination of disloyalty to God in terms of sexual intercourse with unbelieving women is part of an ancient sensibility: Jewish and Christian scripture often made claims about the exclusive nature of religious loyalties through stories of inappropriate love.[16] Sancho chose only one scriptural proof-text, the popular Old Testament example of King Solomon, "who was such a wise man, [but] women of another faith drew him from his law and made him abandon the God of David" ["que fue tan sabio omne, mugeres de otra creençia le tiraron de la su ley e le fizieron que dexase el al dios de Dauid," p. 133], but he could have chosen many others. Seen from this discursive distance, the rejection of the Jewess in Sancho's story becomes a performance of religious loyalty, an assertion of "in-group values and dominance" and an account of the boundaries between competing monotheisms. Hence it is at this point in the *Castigos*, in a chapter ostensibly devoted to constraining princely libidos, that the reader is provided an account of the messianic errors of the Jews as well as a polemical history of Muhammad and the origins of Islam.

Though Sancho presents his tale as an account of the transcendent loyalties owed by earthly monarch to heavenly king, one of the most powerful features of this sexual model of religious order and loyalty was its ability to be mapped onto a more explicitly political order. As Sancho himself explains in the case of Alfonso VIII, God punishes the transgressions of the ruler in the bodies of the ruled. The piety of the ruler is therefore reflected in the political order of his kingdom. This ancient theme, central to much medieval Christian political theology, emerges from the very beginning of the work: Adam rebelled against God, hence his own flesh and all of creation rebelled against Adam—"por tal commo fue rebelde a Dios, por tal se le rebello su carne propria, e todas las bestias le fueron rebeldes." The sexual foundations of these political disorders appear just as early. Adam's error began by wanting to please Eve. In yielding sovereignty to his wife he sowed the seeds of the first, and paradigmatic, rebellion: "And as punishment for this our Lord God has ordained that whenever man gives woman lordship over himself, she will always be contrary to him."[17]

This gendered political history of Eden serves as a template for the political history of Spain. Thus Sancho concludes the prologue, "I wrote this book in the year that with the help of God I won Tarifa from the Moors to whom she belonged, and who had held her in their power for more than six hundred years since the King Rodrigo lost her, who was the last king of the Goths, because of the evil and the abominable treason of the bad count Don Julian, and I gave her to the faith of Jesus Christ, and there are in [the book] fifty chapters." The political and moral claim is clear. Spain had been lost because of treason and rebellion awakened by Rodrigo's sexual sin and could be regained only by monarchs both pious and chaste.[18] Sancho was not an obvious candidate. He had, after all, not only usurped the throne but also abandoned his promised bride in favor of "marriage" with María de Molina, a woman he first met when she acted as godmother at the baptism of his illegitimate daughter. (Their union was never sanctioned during his lifetime, nor their children legitimated, despite efforts that included the forging of papal bulls.)[19] According to the logic of the text, however, Sancho's victory over the Muslims at Tarifa, like his authorship of the *Castigos*, proved him to be such a sovereign.

Alfonso's Jewess operates within this moral economy and this political project, but she does a specific type of work that other textual women, Muslim or Christian, could not do. Compare, for example, the often-told story of Alfonso VI's relationship with the Muslim princess Zaida. That love, which resulted in Zaida's conversion and concubinage with the king, served not to reproach Alfonso but to praise him. Insofar as royal intercourse with Muslim women implied (at least in the Castilian literary tradition) a domination of Islam, it expressed positive values of conquering Christian virility. The *Primera Crónica General* even uses the story of Zaida as the frame within which to narrate the arrival from North Africa of Almoravid armies toward the end of Alfonso's reign, representing his encounter with these armies as victorious vengeance for their murder of Zaida's father, al-Mu'tamid, the emir of Seville. The inconvenient fact that the Almoravids halted Christian expansion for a generation did not prevent the use of Alfonso VI's relationship with Zaida to represent the culmination, rather than the reversal, of his conquests.[20]

As for kings and Christian women, there were plenty of stories in which defeat was attributed to inappropriate sex. Jaume I of Catalonia-Aragon, for example, explained the support of his father, Pere, for the Languedocian nobility during the Albigensian crusade as a result of his desire for their wives and daughters, and his death in 1213 on the battlefield of Muret as the consequence of exhaustion from too much intercourse with a courtesan the night before.[21] But at the same time that they criticized royal sexual energy, contemporaries also understood it as a natural manifestation of power and assigned unmarried sexual partners of the king an honorable and legally defined space.[22] Alfonso's relationship with the Jewess of Toledo evoked no such understanding. Its consequences were not only defeat but, even more pointedly, rebellion.

The word is sharp but deliberate. Sancho himself had stressed defeat and disorder, not rebellion, in his telling of the tale. Notwithstanding his precautions, the political and moral implications of Alfonso and his Jewess could not be easily denied, and within a few years the *Crónica de Castilla* had articulated what the *Castigos* left unspoken: Alfonso's errant love must have been punished by baronial revolt. Not only did the king's vassals fail in their duty to fight for him against the Muslims at the battle of Alarcos, they also violated his court, murdered his mistress, and dragged him to Ilescas. In other words, the king's Jewish affair fomented treason, and that treason brought about the kingdom's defeat at the hands of Islam. In the *Crónica de Castilla* and the *Crónica de 1344* the angel articulated the operative constitutional logic. The kingdom was punished, not merely because the king had sinned, but because the kingdom "had consented" to his sin: "Et el angel le dixo sed çierto que tan gran saña a Dios de ti por este pecado que telo demandara y al tu rreyno porque lo consintio."[23] Kingdoms that indulge the deviant loves of their kings will suffer. The barons' only error was in not having rebelled earlier.

This linkage of "Jew love" and rebellion was not incidental: rebellion was peculiarly "Jewish" territory in late thirteenth-century Castile. This "Jewishness" emerges strongly in the accusations made against Sancho's own father, Alfonso X, by those who resisted his rule. The aristocratic uprisings of 1270–75, for example, complained of royal taxes (*servicios*) and of the use of Jewish administrators to collect them. Rebellious grandees claimed the revenues farmed on behalf of the king by his Jews and even took some of these Jews hostage. With the suppression of the rebellion in 1275, however, Alfonso entered once more into arrangements with his Jewish administrators, granting extensive control of his financial administration to Isaac ibn Zadok (aka Çag de la Maleha) in 1276. By 1279, when a council of bishops met to complain about Alfonso's rule, "Alfonso X's accusers represented him as a barely Christian tyrant manipulated by Jewish counselors, intent upon subjecting churchmen to an intolerable yoke of persecution and servitude." It is in this context of these criticisms, and of increasing tension between the king and Prince Sancho, that Alfonso ordered the imprisonment of Jewish tax farmers and the hanging of Isaac/Çag. Sancho himself, unwilling to see the throne pass to the young children of his deceased elder brother, first flirted with and then espoused revolt. He married into the aristocratic party (quite literally: María de Molina came from a powerful clan of magnates) and made himself the champion of their complaints, attacking the Jews and their royal protector.[24]

We could therefore interpret Sancho's use of the story of Alfonso and the Jewess as an oblique legitimation of his own rebellion, one that condenses the political anti-Judaism used against his father, retells it as a gentle tale of sexual rather than fiscal love, and projects it onto safely heroic ancestors. Yet the story describes Sancho's reign just as well as his father's. Consider Sancho's infamous relationship with Lope Díaz de Haro. Lope was head of a lineage that had sided with Sancho in his war against Alfonso X and those lineages (most notably that of the Laras) that supported him.[25] Sancho rewarded Lope with the title of count, with his own sister in marriage, and in June 1287 with the role of "privado," or "governing favorite," granting him complete authority over chancery, treasury, and government. Lope in turn granted the Jew Abraham de Barchillon centralized responsibility for much of the crown's income, and Abraham immediately began recuperating for the Crown revenues alienated during the civil war to nobility and clergy. Resistance was just as immediate. Convinced by his magnates (and by the queen) to reverse course, the king rescinded Abraham's actions in the Cortes of July and August 1288. A ban was declared on the use of Jewish tax collectors, and the magnates were rewarded with a distribution of royal revenues. Don Lope himself, however, suffered a more striking reversal, one that burned itself deeply into historical memory. Like Alfonso's Jewess, he was stabbed to death in the king's court at Alfaro on June 8, 1288.[26]

Of course the Castigos attempted to tell the story of Alfonso's Jewess in such a way as to strengthen Sancho's claims to sovereignty, while at the same time repressing the potential for rebellious violence which accusations of royal philo-Semitism authorized in his father's reign and his own. In his telling, Alfonso VIII's error was characterized as infatuation and lovesickness, not corrupt materialism or tyranny; God, not the barons, punished the wayward king; and Alfonso (like Sancho, are we meant to conclude?) went on to great victories despite early sin. But despite Sancho's narrative efforts, it is clear that the sharp edge of the Jewess cut as deeply into his own reign as it did into his father's and that other authors (like those of the Chroni-

cle of Castile or that of 1344) were quite willing to turn her blade against
their king.

In a handful of years, we have seen the humble Jewish concubine of the
Castigos transformed from a representation of the sovereign's special relationship with God into an exemplary tale of monstrous monarchical affection
justifying revolt. One way to explain this growth is to understand her figure
as a precocious part of a political discourse that criticizes certain aspects of
royal governance, and particularly financial administration, as "Jew loving."
This representation drew its power from (at least) three interrelated phenomena. The first was the increasing weight of the fiscal and administrative
practices that supported the expansion of royal power beginning with the
reign of Alfonso X. The proportionality of the role played by Jewish administrators in this expansion is a matter of irresolvable (given the nature of the
evidence) debate: to my mind it has been much exaggerated.[27] The negative
association of royal fiscal power with Judaism seems to me to be as much the
product of the tools available to Christian theology for the representation of
materialism and its dangers as it was of the functions real Jews carried out in
medieval taxation and administration. As Sancho put it in the *Castigos*, the
greatest enemies of good Christian kingship were the devil, the world, and
the flesh: three things Christians had long associated with and represented
through Jews.[28] But regardless of whether the "Jewishness" of fiscality was
the product of real Jews in royal service, of Christian political theology, or
of some combination thereof, what is clear is that complaints about Jewish
influence and charges of royal philo-Semitism became a preferred weapon in
the increasingly sharp debates over taxation and administration that marked
the late thirteenth, fourteenth, and fifteenth centuries.

We have already seen this charge deployed in the reigns of Alfonso and
Sancho. The idiom became routine in those that followed, with the ac-
cent sometimes thickening in open rebellion. The aristocratic factions that
deposed and murdered King Pedro I "the Cruel" (1350–69) in the mid-
fourteenth century justified their actions by portraying him as a favorer of
Jews and even claimed that he was a cuckoo, the son of a Jewess adopted by
the queen mother to conceal her inability to provide an heir. Much as Sancho
had done a century and a half earlier, Prince Enrique (IV) rebelled against
his father Juan II and his "Jew-loving" minister Álvaro de Luna, charging that
they empowered Jews over Christians. He himself would later be ritually
deposed in the "farsa de Avila," accused of sodomy, favoring Jews, and living
like a Muslim. Even the "Catholic monarchs" Fernando and Isabel, conquer-

ors of Granada, founders of the Inquisition, expellers of the Jews, were said by some of their subjects to be descended from Jews and to benefit them in their policies.[29]

The utility of this linkage between "Judaism" and fiscal power grew with the increasing weight of taxation and administration in an era of what has sometimes been called "state formation." It is this expanding utility that accounts, in part, for the sudden appearance of our "Jewess" in the late thirteenth century and for her rapid discursive transformation into a legitimation of revolt. Her figure was animated, however, not only by the increasing weight of government but also by conflict between monarchs and magnates over control of that government and its profits. Through hereditary office and countless other devices, the great nobles sought to retain as much control over royal administration as possible. Kings, on the other hand, beginning especially with the reign of Alfonso X "the Wise," developed strategies to maintain and increase the autonomy of that administration from the nobility. Alfonso's Jewish concubine combines in one figure both a defense and a critique of some of these practices and is therefore an interesting character in the history of medieval governance.

One of these practices, already touched upon, was the use of Jews as administrators. A second is the expanding administrative importance of queens and concubines in the same period as the story of our Jewess was growing. Sancho himself had solidified his leadership of the aristocratic factions arrayed against his father through his union with María de Molina. Her maneuvers to maintain her position in spite of the legal flimsiness of her "marriage" contributed to the fall of Lope de Haro and to that of the *privado* who had preceded him, the abbot Gomez García.[30] Later she served as regent during the minority of her son Fernando IV (from 1295–1301), defending his rights to the throne against a series of well-armed rivals alleging the illegitimate nature of Sancho's own accession. After the deaths of Fernando and his wife (in 1312), she again exercised guardianship of her grandson Alfonso XI (1311–50), while a swirl of competing aristocratic factions contested the regency and divided among themselves the spoils of government.

Queens as regents were not news. More innovative was the politics of concubinage developed by Alfonso XI (and later his son Pedro I) during the decades that the story of our Jewess was growing. *Barraganas* had long been part of the sexual lives of kings: nearly every monarch of Castile from Alfonso X until Isabel made provision in his testament for the maintenance of his concubines and their children.[31] Alfonso XI and Pedro, however, confronted a particular dilemma: their emancipation as rulers required that they dislodge the rival factions that had gained control of the resources of government during their minorities. Marriage was here a tool of limited utility. Kings, if they wished to increase their autonomy from the great nobility, could not marry into that nobility as the rebellious Sancho IV had done. Not surprisingly, both our later monarchs were betrothed to foreign princesses: Alfonso XI to Maria of Portugal, Pedro I to Blanche of France. But such marriages did not bring with them what kings most needed: a loyal faction of one's own. From 1329 until his death the young Alfonso XI depended not just on the advice of his mistress Leonor de Guzmán but also on the service of members of her family, whom he placed in positions of authority and power. Like his father, Pedro was eighteen years old when he met a young woman from the lesser nobility, named María de Padilla. Like his father (though less successfully), he ennobled and enriched her relatives, assigning to them the most sensitive posts of his administration.[32]

The moral valence accorded to this politics of concubinage in literary representations depended, of course, on its outcome. Chroniclers looking back upon the reign of Alfonso XI, for example, explained Leonor de Guzmán's influence over him in the traditional terms of beauty and virtue: her children, after all, were eventually victorious in founding a new dynasty. The posterity of Pedro's affair was quite different, left as it was to the tender mercy of the triumphant Trastamaran propagandists. According to them, María de Padilla gained her ascendancy over the king by commissioning a Jewish necromancer to enchant the jeweled belt Queen Blanche had given Pedro on his wedding night, so that it turned into a serpent and frightened him away from the marriage bed.[33]

The critical power of our Jewess owes something to this sexual politics of queens and concubines, but it is even more closely intertwined with the rise of another form of "governing affection," that of the *privado*, or beloved councilor, who enjoyed the special favor and intimacy (*privanza*) of his lord. In the political vocabulary of our period, love and intimacy were understood as powerful inspiration for and representations of political confidence: hence kings and princes were well advised to depend upon *amor* and *privanza* in choosing the administrators of their and the kingdom's affairs.[34] But as we have already seen, the power of love was dangerously ambivalent: on the one hand the basis of a well-ordered republic oriented toward the divine; on the other seduction of the monarch, as Sancho repeatedly warned in the *Castigos*, into an excess of carnality and materialism.

This danger was encoded in the word *privanza* from its very earliest usage. We first encounter the word in a text that precedes the appearance of our Jewess by only a generation and that comes, like hers, from the genre of exemplary admonitions about Judaism's dangers: I mean the famous story of Theophilus, as told by Gonzalo de Berceo in his *Milagros de Nuestra Señora*. Gonzalo's Theophilus is the chief administrator, chief judge, and chief accountant of his lord the bishop: all that remains for the worthy pontiff are his devotions. In Gonzalo's words, Theophilus had "with the bishop great love and *privanza*" ("con el bispo amor e grand privança").[35] It is when, under a succeeding bishop, Theophilus loses that "amor e grand privança" that he turns to a Jew, who brokers the sale of his soul to the devil in exchange for renewed favor. The story of Theophilus's miraculous redemption by the Virgin Mary was a favored one in the Middle Ages, told and retold (by Alfonso X in his *Cantigas de Santa María*, for example) to make many different points. Ours is a simple one: already here, at the birth of *privanza*, the Jew stands at the crossroads of administrative love, ready to lead it in the direction of damnation.

Theophilus's administrative love (*amor*) was the product of a clerical court, normatively celibate and childless. Perhaps for this reason Gonzalo de Berceo threatened *privanza* with Judaism, but not with sex.[36] In secular courts where political love was more explicitly carnal, the combination of sex and Judaism was more potent. In the case of royal love for ministers in particular, the union of the two was brokered by scriptural example. I am referring, of course, to the explicit representation of ministerial power as sexual, female, and Jewish in the Book of Esther.[37]

The biblical account of how the Jewish concubine and queen Esther called upon the love of King Xerxes/Ahasueros in order to prevent the destruction of her people was well known to medieval Christian and Jew alike. Jewish communities throughout the Diaspora reenacted the story each year at the festival of Purim: it served them as a political allegory and a source of hope. For Christians the story also encoded love and sexual union as metaphors for political alliance, inclusion, and protection, but that encoding was much more ambivalent. At the level of a purely Christian political typology, Esther served as an example of the ideal queen, putting herself in danger for her people. Hence, for example, the exhortation to emulate Esther in queenly coronation ceremonies, or the prominence of the French queen's coat of arms in the Esther window at the Ste. Chapelle. (The French Queen was Blanche of Castile, who was Alfonso VIII's daughter.)[38]

From another point of view, however, the story was much less comforting. Like Don Sancho's *Castigos*, the Scroll of Esther begins with the general principle that political perils arise whenever woman refuses to be ruled by man. Queen Vashti is condemned for disobeying the king's order to dance in front of his court: "The queen's conduct will soon become known to all the women, who will adopt a contemptuous attitude towards their own husbands. . . . And that will mean contempt and anger all around [1.16–18]." Yet the book concludes with the Jewess Esther and her uncle Mordechai effectively ruling the entire kingdom as queen and minister of Ahasueros and indeed expanding its boundaries. In this book, the only one in the Bible that depends explicitly on female authority, God clearly authorizes the deviant power of a woman over a man and of a Jewish minister over a non-Jewish king: precisely the kind of inversion that Sancho warned against constantly in his *Castigos*.

The manifold medieval readings of the Book of Esther still await their historian.[39] What is evident within the Christian and Castilian context that we have been describing, however, is the book's power to underwrite a broad political critique in which Ahasueros is a bad king, too easily swayed by self-interested councilors, erotic desires, and Jewish ministers; while Esther becomes a negative example of wide-ranging political power obtained not through lineage but through deviant royal love: in short, of *privanza*.[40] Such a reading of Esther could be used to Judaize and feminize the power of kings and their confidants, whether concubines or counts, in order that this power might be resisted as un-Christian and immoral. Precisely such a Judaization and feminization became a preferred weapon against monarchs and their ministers in the tumultuous history of Castilian politics. But before the story of Esther could be put to the hard work not just of criticizing monarchy but of rebelling against "Jew-loving kings," it needed first to be freed from its plain "philo-Semitic" and "philo-ministerial" meaning. The story of "How the King Alfonso Remained Secluded with a Jewess" achieved this liberation. It restaged the drama of Esther as one in which not the Jewish but the Christian nation was in danger, and then exorcised that danger by reversing the biblical ending: the aristocrats triumph, the concubine dies.[41]

This conclusion begs to be understood as merely a reaffirmation of right rule, masculine and Christian, but it is much more than that. The story of Alfonso and his Jewess proved useful precisely because it represented political conflict in terms of consensus, translating the outcome of sharp struggle between sovereign and subject into gendered and religious terms seemingly sanctioned by nature and divinity. These terms, however, masked their origins in crisis and rebellion, both political and exegetical. The story of Alfonso and his Jewess challenged both monarchical authority and scriptural narrative. That challenge left its marks not only in the fractured strata of the chronicle tradition but also in the dramatis personae of the story itself. It is never easy to fly directly in the face of scripture or of sovereigns: hence the angel, who reveals, so to speak, divine approval of assassination and revolt. Angel and Jewess alike were the overdetermined products of political crisis. In the light of such overdetermination it is probably pointless to ask whether Alfonso VIII really had a Jewish concubine, or whether it was the biblical figure of "Queen Esther" and the ministerial powers she authorized who fell under the barons' bloody blades.

Regardless of the reality of our Jewess, real people, both Christians and Jews, felt the consequences of her death. Since it is relatively easy to see how Jews might be at risk from the circulation of an exemplary tale advocating so violent a prophylaxis to the dangers posed by Jewish power, we will focus on the Christian victims. Among the first of these may well have been King Sancho's own *privado*, Lope de Haro, murdered at court in Alfaro. Was the tale of Alfonso VIII's misguided love for his Jewess meant as an apologetic allegory of Sancho's own love for Lope de Haro? It seems plausible. Because the competition for power between the rival aristocratic lineages of Haro and Lara generated a great deal of the politics of late thirteenth-century Castile, chronicles produced in this period drew on the theme of conflict between the two houses in order to explain tensions between monarchical and aristocratic power. These explanations were sometimes set (like the Jewess) in the heroic past of Alfonso VIII's reign, the reign in which the house of Haro rose to prominence.[42] But we need not insist on allegory. The general point is more important: it is no coincidence that the story of Alfonso VIII appeared and flourished when it did and not before. It throve in the loam of a half-century marked by struggle between aristocratic factions and a monarchy increasingly associated in the political imagination with the power of women, financial administrators, favorites, and Jews, powers here conflated in the figure of a Jewish concubine. The tale was very much a product of the period that told it.

It was also, however, productive of that period, providing as it did a powerful new literary form for political pursuits.[43] It would be too much to say that the killing of "Esther" authorized the killing of *privados*, but certainly the Jewess's story gave flesh to a critique of the relationship between monarchs and ministers, a critique that proceeded by characterizing ministerial power in terms of deviant love and "Jewishness." In his "Rimado de Palacio," for example, Pero López de Ayala portrayed the Castilian court as a hotbed of intrigue for royal affection, in which the honeyed words of the Jews united king and favorite in a materialist love triangle.[44] For López de Ayala, as for Gonzalo de Berceo in Theophilus's tale, it was a Jew who lurked near the court waiting to mislead love into a carnal and corrupt *privanza*.

Lust did not always require a "Jewish" face in order to do its critical work. Inés de Torres, confidante of the widowed queen and regent Catherine of Lancaster, "had such great *privanza* with the queen that all things were set free by her hand, so that affairs were not conducted as was required by the service of God, nor the good of her kingdoms." Inés's downfall came in 1416, when she was driven out of the court by accusations of sexual intercourse with a knight of the Royal Guard. Female sovereignty made the gender dynamics of the case extraordinary, but the logic is familiar: sexual access and political influence are mapped onto each other, with deviant love producing corrupt governance.[45] Indeed the very exceptionality of the case makes clear the degree to which *amor* and *privanza* were eroticized in the politics of the day. A male *privado* posed grave sexual danger for a queen. A female favorite did not castrate the danger, but it did displace it, channeling the discourse of sexual access to the sovereign through the body of the *privada*.

Inés was not charged with "Judaism," perhaps because in the case of queens and their *privadas* politico-erotic transgression could be directly represented in terms of heterosexual adultery. Male monarchs and male ministers were more balefully bonded by the twin stars of Judaism and sexual seduction. We might almost say that, over time, *privados* became "Jewish concubines." The *privanza* of Álvaro de Luna under Catherine's son Juan II (r. 1405–54) was loudly denounced as Judaizing (most markedly during the rebellion of 1449 with its attendant massacres of conversos), and the king's affection for him portrayed as unnatural. After decades of *privanza* Luna was executed at the king's command in 1453, but not before (according to the unfriendly chronicle of Alfonso de Palencia) he had taught sodomy to Juan Pacheco, who used it in turn to seduce Juan II's son Enrique IV (r. 1454–74) and become his *privado*.

Unlike Luna, Pacheco survived the many plots of his rivals and died a natural death.[46] But even if the discursive dangers of Judaism and sodomy were not always lethal, they continued to stalk power and its agents. Late fifteenth-century poets (like the anonymous author of the "Coplas del Provincial") treated sodomite and Jew as standard terms of protest, aimed at magnates and high clergy alike. Late fifteenth-century chroniclers converted similar polemics into history. Writing triumphantly after the pacification of the kingdom under Isabel and Fernando, for example, Diego Rodríguez de Almela treated the theme of Jewish *privanza* not as a product of political conflict, but as a historical description of power and its exercise in the troubled centuries that had come before.[47]

Alfonso VIII's affair was pregnant with this politics of ministerial power and its critique: his Jewess was midwife to its birth. I am not claiming that her role was instrumental, or even that it was recognized during the long life span of the politics she delivered.[48] My point is only that her figure redeployed a basic tension in Christian politics, the tension between "love of God" and "love of (wo)man," in such a way as to simultaneously enable and criticize new forms of governance. Writing his immensely influential "On the Government of Princes" at roughly the same time as King Sancho was composing his *Punishments*, the Aristotelian theologian Giles of Rome put my assertion in slightly different terms: "In every ethical affair the way of proceeding, according to the Philosopher, is figural and gross."[49] Our beautiful Jewess was just such a negotiation, "figural and gross," of political (hence also, in pre-Machiavellian terms, moral) crisis and transformation.

It is important to insist, however, that neither love, nor Jews, nor lovely Jews can be understood merely as products of this "figural" negotiation: they were also its arbiters. Though this claim is too large to be honored here, we can turn for down payment to Saint Augustine's hermeneutical handbook "On Christian Doctrine" (III.4–10), which presents, in good Pauline fashion, the confusion of "killing letter" with "quickening spirit," of literal meanings with figurative ones, as the most basic danger of language. This error, which slays the soul and turns man into carnal beast, is (according to Augustine and many other Christian theologians) the error of the Jews. Augustine proposed a simple rule to help Christians avoid the danger and "find out whether a phrase is literal or figurative": whichever reading leads to love of God is to be preferred, whichever leads to lust for the world is false, for "scripture enjoins nothing but love, and condemns nothing but lust."

Augustine's notion of the "figural" was itself already the incarnation of a Christian hermeneutics of love and spirit that articulated and defined itself against an imagined "Jewish" hermeneutics of lust and flesh.[50] In this sense it is a foundational example of the "coproductions" this book is about, although from a much earlier period, and much more the product of a system of thought than of any social encounter. (Though he wrote about Jews often, so far as we know Saint Augustine met only one living exemplar in his career: a plaintiff in his court, seeking to recover property seized by another Christian bishop.) At the level of scriptural interpretation, the friction caused by this intimate dependence could remain reasonably contained for readers (at least until Luther), since their subject and their text were axiomatically grounded in divine love. But for readers of worldly politics, the tension was greater from the beginning. Augustine himself put the problem starkly. Like Cain, who sinned by subjecting his reasoning soul to the desires of his flesh, every earthly city "has its good in this world, and rejoices in [the material world] with such joy as such things can afford," so that it will at the end of time be "committed to the extreme penalty." Just as (according to Augustine) secular power can never escape Cain's conjoined significations as both "founder of the earthly city" and "a figure of the Jews,"[51] neither can political love free itself entirely from lust for the material world. Political love was the foundation of sovereign power in the Christian republic, but it was a foundation built upon lust for "Jewish" flesh. It is within these foundations that Alfonso's Jewess was immured, and it is within them that the constitutional implications of her courtship become clear.

[**4**]

Massacre or Miracle?

Valencia, 1391

Over the previous chapters we have witnessed the intimate embrace between Christian politics, "Judaism," and "Islam." We have seen how that embrace could give shape, more or less simultaneously, both to the possibilities of Christian politics and to the possibilities for Jewish and Muslim life in a Christian polity. Those chapters each ranged over a swathe of time and space in order to demonstrate just how generative these interactions—imagined and real, hermeneutic as well as social, figural as well as in the flesh—were for medieval Christians, Muslims, and Jews, and how central to their interpretations of the world. But although this coproduction was constant, it was by no means continuous or smooth: sometimes the work done with and through the other could completely transform the possibilities of thought and of existence.

One such moment took place in 1391, when massacres and mass conversions swept through several of the Iberian polities (Castile, Valencia, Mallorca, Catalonia) in what counts among the most massive attack upon Jews in the Middle Ages. Aimed as they were at the "royal treasure" (as the Jews were sometimes called), these attacks can tell us a great deal about the work done by Jews in Christian politics (and here I mean not only the work done by living Jews in the polities of medieval Iberia but, even more, the political work done by Christians thinking about "Judaism" and acting upon Jews). In the case of 1391 that work began a process that would eventually result in the elimination of the Jews from the Iberian Peninsula and produce a revolution in the social and theological understanding of what it meant to be Christian. The next four chapters will explore some of the consequences of this revolution. But in this one we will focus on the massacres themselves, as they unfolded in the city of Valencia. I choose the example of Valencia because it is well documented and therefore gives us vivid entry into events elsewhere reduced (as they were in much of Castile) to the perfunctory paragraphs of chronicles.

But my goal is not simply to provide a detailed historical narrative—one of very few available in English or any other language—of a medieval massacre. I would also like to offer a study of the "constitutional" implications of that massacre. For although we have little access to the feelings and motives of the participants in the violence, we can say a great deal about meanings they attributed to that violence and the ways in which they sought to justify it. Those meanings and justifications were above all about the proper foundations of power in a Christian polity. In this sense the massacres of 1391 were, among other things, a constitutional crisis, a moment in which competing Christian visions of sovereignty and subjecthood were posed upon the bodies of the Jews. The constitutional implications of this crisis are not confined to the Middle Ages. They are also instructive for us today, as so many refugees from secularism—Muslim, Christian, and Jewish—look once more toward theology in their quest for transcendent norms that might ground the values of a polity.

But let us begin in the Middle Ages, and specifically in the twelfth century, when princely claims to powers of decision over Jews became a common feature of the medieval political landscape. In all of the emerging monarchies of western Europe, Jews began to be thought of as especially subject to royal power: "serfs (or slaves) of the king's chamber" (*servi regie camerae*), according to a common legal formulation, or even the king's "private thing."[1] Kings increasingly claimed powers of protection, exploitation, and jurisdiction over all Jews, even those residing in the lands of magnates who otherwise minimally recognized their overlordship and used those claims to extend the reach of their sovereignty.[2]

By the late fourteenth century, a long history of such claims had made the Jews figures of supreme subjection to the sovereign's will. Joan I, king of the condominium Crown of Aragon (Catalonia, Aragon, Valencia, etc.), put it well in early 1391, when asked whether the Jews of his realm of Sardinia should be judged under Catalan or Aragonese law: "It is our intention that the

Jews, who are our patrimony and have no specific nation, may and should be judged according to our own will."[3] The Jews' utter subjection to royal will, and the protection it implied, was carved upon the new gates of Valencia in 1390, in the form of the king and queen's coat of arms. Conversely, precisely because Jews represented royal power at its most absolute, they could be used to represent that power, as when Jews were assigned the care of the royal lions displayed in each of the Crown of Aragon's principal cities: a pairing in which both the lion and its keeper were equally symbolic.[4]

In this sense, royal power defined itself through the exceptional status of the Jews. Such claims were useful, but also dangerous, in that they encouraged a tendency to criticize terrestrial sovereignty as itself "Jewish" or Judaizing. That tendency was already latent in a patristic authors like Saint Augustine, who went so far as to place all earthly politics under the sign of the exiled Cain,—the same figure he used to characterize the Jews after the death of Christ—because it "has its good in this world, and rejoices in [the material world] with such joy as such things can afford."[5] Few medieval theorists drew the more radical implications of this position, preferring to develop theologies that aligned the governor's interests with God's.[6] But royal exploitation of Jews did provide an obvious point of purchase for those who wished to associate royal claims to fiscal and legal power with "Judaism." Such associations occurred throughout western Europe, but I will limit my examples here to the fourteenth-century Crown of Aragon. When King Joan's father, Pere IV, demanded services from the town council of Valencia that they viewed as extraordinary, they responded that the demand "is nothing other than to make a Jewry of each of his municipalities. . . . We will not give in to such a demand, for we would rather die than be similar to Jews."[7] Similarly, Christian subjects learned to contest the claims of sovereigns by attacking "their" Jews, and kings learned to expect such attacks. King Pere, for example, urged his son Joan to be skeptical of a host desecration accusation in 1377. Such accusations were often false, he explained, propagated by people who wished to harm the royal patrimony.[8]

In short, in the Crown of Aragon as elsewhere in western Europe, Jews were a focal point for the expression of sovereignty and for its resistance or critique. The tension inherent in this ambivalence was sometimes ritualized in ways that contributed to the containment of the tension itself. (I am thinking here of the annual stoning of Jews and the officials guarding them by children and lower clergy during Holy Week.)[9] Yet even in the more ritualized expressions of this tension there remained a potential for antinomian explosion. This potential was actualized—or so I propose—in the Christian massacres and mass conversions of Jews that took place across much of the Iberian Peninsula in 1391. The following pages will treat the massacres of 1391, approached through the example of Valencia, as a crisis of sovereignty, a suspension of the law expressed in terms of competing claims to the right of deciding the fate of Jews. I will conclude with some of the strategies of re-ritualization through which the tension between these competing claims was once again contained and the performance of royal sovereignty reconstituted.

The explosion itself began not in the Crown of Aragon but in Castile, a throne already weakened by royal minority. A few days before Holy Week, a group of Christians inspired by Ferrant Martínez, archdeacon of Ecija, attempted to attack Seville's Jews.[10] The crowd was disbanded, the movement repressed by representatives of royal authority, but on the sixth of June—allegedly provoked by the judicial whipping of a Christian convicted of attacking a Jew—Seville's Jewish quarter was successfully assaulted, its inhabitants killed or forcibly converted. The violence spread quickly. By the end of August Jews had been attacked or converted in more than seventy other towns and cities of the peninsula. Of these, Valencia was among the first and most important in the Crown of Aragon.[11]

Already on the twenty-eighth of June, Queen Violant had written to officials in Valencia and other cities ordering special vigor in defense of the Jews. By the beginning of July the situation was so grave that King Joan placed his brother, Prince Martí, in charge of the defense. The prince and town council took various measures, among them heightened vigilance around the Jewish quarter, the circulation of town criers announcing that the Jews were under special protection, and the erection of gallows on the periphery of the Jewish quarter as a reminder of sovereign justice and "to induce terror in the people." We hear of these from exculpatory letters written after the event, so it is difficult to know how effectively they were applied. An exception gives rise to pessimism: we know that on July 6 the prince revoked the text he had ordered the town criers to proclaim because of complaints that it violated city privileges. The Jewish quarter was assaulted on Sunday, July 9.[12]

We have multiple accounts of the assault: from Jewish witnesses, from Prince Martí, and from the town council of Valencia.[13] The latter agree that it began with a throng of youths (*fadrins*) chanting that the Jews should convert or die. The gates to the quarter were closed, and the Christians began stoning the defenders. Called from lunch to the fray, the prince rode from gate to gate dispersing the rioters, but as soon as he cleared one location the crowd would reform in another. In the meantime the attackers used drain-pipes and openings in the walls of neighboring houses in order to penetrate the Jewish quarter and began killing, raping, and looting its inhabitants. At some point the gates opened and the prince sought to enter, but a hail of stones and knife thrusts convinced him to withdraw. He then summoned a host of chaplains, in the hope that conversion might calm the crowd. By the time the prince wrote his report at sunset he did not yet know the death toll, but he did know that the pillaging was near total, that almost no Jews ("fort pochs") remained to be baptized, and that the looting was still going on. (The prince would later put the death toll at close to three hundred Jews and a few Christians, while the town council would prefer the number of one hundred Jewish dead.) "Therefore, lord," the prince concluded his first report, "you should correctly understand that this could only be the judgment of God, and nothing else."[14]

"Solament juhi de Deu": there is a constitutional argument latent in this phrase, one that proceeds by shifting jurisdiction from earthly to heavenly king. King Pere, Joan and Martí's father, had been wont to say that the king is "sovereign lord after God."[15] Martí is hinting that in this case God has made his decision known. But King Joan refuses to concede jurisdiction. His response to his brother stresses that this insult to his sovereignty (all the worse for taking place in direct defiance of the prince's presence) must be met with a "punishment so cruel" that it will serve as "sovereign example, for we and you and other princes and officials must . . . punish such incitements and riots . . . in such a way that your punishment be divulged and renown, not only throughout our kingdoms and lands but also through all the others, passing beyond all justice." If the prince does not punish "with sovereign diligence" the temerity will grow "incorrigible" and spread.[16] A few days later the king writes again, marveling at the minimal punishment carried out by the prince and council—one man hung for inciting a (failed) attack on the Muslim quarter, five or six imprisoned for attacking the Jews. He stresses that such brazen belittling of his power of punishment and his royal person (in the form of his brother) should have been met with the immediate execution of three or four hundred people. The prince and the city must now punish the guilty, without "regard to trials, privileges, legalities, or other solemnities customarily observed in judicial acts."[17]

Joan is here insisting that the king—like God—can suspend the normal processes of law in the exercise of his justice. The Crown had been building such claims out of Roman law for more than a century, and municipalities

had been resisting them for just as long. The Valencians might have replied
to the king by citing Thomas Aquinas: "But in order that the volition of what
is commanded may have the nature of law, it needs to be in accord with some
rule of reason. And in this sense is to be understood the saying that the will
of the sovereign has the force of law; otherwise the sovereign's will would
savor of lawlessness rather than of law" (ST II.I.90.1). But such a response
would not quite have accounted for the nature of the king's claim, which
was, after all, that he had the power to suspend the normal working of the
law, the power to impose a temporary lawlessness. They might better have
deployed the words of their fellow citizen and informal "constitutional theorist," the prominent theologian Francesc Eiximenis, and explicitly subjected
the sovereign to the law: "How can a prince grant anyone license to kill
another without a judicial process intervening, since the prince is not lord
of the law but its servant, executor, and minister?"[18] It is perhaps a symptom
of the severity of the crisis that they chose not to make the point so explicit.
Instead, they adopted the prince's strategy and pushed it further, presenting
the assaults as a moment of divine antinomianism, a miraculous suspension
of law for the elimination of the Jews: an assertion, in other words, of God's
supreme sovereignty.

The Valencians begin by stressing the "many and good" preventive measures they had taken. "But," they add, using an apt biblical citation to point
toward the absolute power of divinity, "unless God guards a city, he guards
in vain who watches it" (Psalm 126:1). Their account of the massacre itself,
like that of the prince, begins with youths, this time fifty children (*minyones*)
carrying crosses of cane and a banner (white cross on a blue background),
processing about the Jewish quarter, chanting that the archdeacon of Castile
was coming to convert the Jews. When the Jews closed the gates, the rumor
arose that a child had been hurt and that others were trapped inside, being killed by the Jews. Since the recruiting station for the upcoming naval
campaign against Sicily was nearby, many strangers, out-of-town recruits,
vagabonds, and "people of little and poor condition" responded to the rumor,
and the riot began.[19]

There certainly were foreigners and vagabonds in Valencia, and among
the participants in the riot, but the attempt to blame them for the violence
seems a transparent attempt to protect the town's citizens from the king's
wrath.[20] Similarly, by emphasizing the children's role the council sought to
demonstrate that this was not an organized rebellion by its citizens. (The
council later conceded that the children had been instructed by adult persons

unknown, but insisted that it was nevertheless "true . . . that the deed began with children.") Equally important, it sought to transform the assault into a quasi-liturgical event, presenting it as a ritual—like a Holy Week riot—that had ruptured its restraints. Henceforth the council's efforts would be devoted to the demonstration that this rupture was itself an act of God, an outpouring of the Holy Spirit everywhere evident in prophecy and miracle, a "divine mystery" beyond the judgment of man.[21]

The first miracle they described was the Jews' refusal to open their gates during the riots, so that royal officials could not enter to defend the quarter from within. If this first alleged miracle scarcely seems much of a "mystery" to us, the others have better right to the term. For example, one Jew had dreamt three times of Jesus being crucified. He consulted his rabbi, who told him to go home and tell no one, that God would help him. A few days before the riots the (same?) rabbi had prophesied to other anxious congregants that if they could make it past Tuesday they would be safe. And during the riots themselves another Jew saw a towering figure standing on the roof of the main synagogue, carrying a child on his shoulders "in the fashion that one paints St. Christopher." A mere five days after the riot the synagogue had already been cleaned and a portrait of Saint Christopher placed within it, producing a constant pilgrimage and so large a kindling of candles that "you would not believe."

Even more notable was the mysterious abundance of chrism. So many Jews had sought baptism the day of the riot that the clergy feared a shortage. Instead there was surplus, achieved by a number of miracles. The most dramatic occurred in the parish of Sant Andreu, where a vessel left empty before supper was displayed overflowing after the meal. A foreign chaplain who was present said mockingly that he knew well how this had been achieved, at which point the vessel was found once again to be empty. The chaplain, moved by contrition, threw himself to the floor while all the others prayed, and the vessel filled once more. The councilors sent four notaries to collect evidence of these miracles, all "seen with the eyes, proven, and experienced." As for the final miracle, it was the scale of the conversions themselves. Not only in the city of Valencia, but also in Xàtiva, Algezira, Gandía, nearly all the Jews had converted. (As the Jewish leader Ḥasdai Crescas put it, no Jew remained in the entire kingdom of Valencia except in the town of Morvedre.) "Consider for yourself whether these things can have a natural cause. We believe that they cannot, but can only be the work of the Almighty."[22]

Of course the Valencians had done their best to help that work along. We know, for example, that the bishop of Valencia's officers had threatened with excommunication any Christian found hiding or helping a Jew, and though we have no explicit document from the town council (as we do have in the case of Barcelona), it is likely that it too had taken measures to minimize the number of Jews concealed and unconverted in the homes of Christian neighbors.[23] Valencia's council quickly devised a strategy to prevent the reestablishment of a Jewish community within its walls (see below), and Valencia's citizens trooped to other towns so as to force conversions there and confront the monarch with a realm free of synagogues.[24] In addition to collecting their miracles, the Valencians also circulated "negative miracles" about Morvedre, the one town in the kingdom that successfully protected its Jews, spreading stories in which the town's chrism dried up when a Jew asked for baptism. And they repeatedly reminded the king that, no matter how reprehensible the crimes committed, no Christian could be unhappy about the conversions. Even the converts, according to the council, "understand and say that the robbery was the cause of the cleansing of their sins."[25]

The Valencians' simultaneous profession of their willingness to punish the attack on the king's Jews, and insistence on the wonders that accompanied those attacks, heightened the confrontation between two claims to the sovereign suspension of the law: divine miracle versus royal justice. Some of the king's councilors believed this heightening was deliberate. According to them, the council invented the miracle of the chrism in order to "excuse the event or even approve it in order to alleviate the punishment of the guilty."[26] The council responded by comparing its critics to those who spread discord over biblical interpretation. They were fomenters of faction, enemies of Valencia, and the king should ignore their slanders. As for the miracle of the chrism, "we believe that if we had been quiet about it the stones would have cried it out." Besides, there were now infinitely more miracles to report, among them the lighting, without the aid of human hands, of the new lamps in the church of Saint Christopher (formerly the main synagogue); the miraculous multiplication of the lamp oil; and that oil's healing power, which was every day curing the sick and infirm who came from all parts of the kingdom to be anointed with it. "Now let every slanderer see if the divine virtues should be silenced!" If, as the council conceded, "no justice had really been done," this was not because of their reluctance but because of the political influence of the powerful among the accused and the populace's opposition to the councilors' efforts. The council therefore urged the king to come in person to Valencia: his presence would overcome all resistance and enable the necessary punishment.[27]

The council's request seems in perfect harmony with the king's will. On the sixteenth, for example, he had assured the Jews of Morvedre that if the prince failed to punish their persecutors so severely ("without waiting for any trial") that no one would dare to attack them again, he would ride personally to Valencia and do it himself.[28] The prince confessed failure less than a week later (July 21). Upon the advice of the town's councilors as well as his own, he wrote, he had suspended his attempts to execute justice "because of the great commotion among the populace here" ("per la gran comoció del poble qui ací era"). The prince urged the king to come and carry out the punishment himself.[29] The king repeatedly proclaimed himself ready to do so. On the twenty-sixth, for example, he refused a request from the city of Barcelona that he hurry there to prevent an attack on the Jews, responding that the best prevention he could provide would be to travel to Valencia and punish the perpetrators there. He promised to do so after August 15, giving two reasons for delay: his desire to give the prince a chance to carry out the mission and the summer heat.[30]

Barcelona soon erupted against its Jews, forcing Joan to travel despite the heat, and postponing his visit to Valencia by more than a year.[31] Given the king's clear conviction that the attacks on his Jews and his sovereignty would spread without a display of exemplary justice, and his brother's earlier admission of failure and request for his presence, why had the king not hurried earlier to Valencia?[32] Numerous historians have answered this obvious question by invoking the king's indolence, his preference for hunting over governance, his failure to understand the severity of the situation, or his disinterest in protecting his Jews. But I would suggest that the answer to this question has less to do with Joan's personal shortcomings as monarch and more to do with the peculiar constitutional dilemma that Jews posed to all Christian sovereigns.

Medieval kings had expanded their sovereignty (in part) by assigning the Jews to a status outside normative law and claiming exceptional power to decide their fate. Sovereign power was thus (in part) performed through the protection of those who had themselves denied God's sovereignty, his "enemies" and "killers." According to some medieval theologians—in a tradition we sometimes call Augustinian—God himself had authorized this royal power over the Jews, decreeing that the enemies who had killed him should not themselves be slain but rather protected by princes in a miserable yet deathless exile that would testify to Christ's victory over them.[33] But what if, as other theologians maintained, God was angered by the toleration of his

Jewish enemies within Christian society? Augustine's teacher Saint Ambrose defended monks who had torched a synagogue by claiming that "the synagogue began to burn by the judgment of God" and that the emperor's attempts to maintain his jurisdictional and protect the Jews were not a performance of Christian sovereignty, but rather a "Judaizing" herald of its collapse.[34] In the thirteenth and fourteenth centuries, this type of critique gained resonance as a counterpoint to the expansion of royal power over Jews.

Confronted with this critique, many western European princes chose to maintain their claims to sovereignty over the Jews by expelling rather than protecting them. Charles of Anjou provides a good example. The Jews, according to his edict expelling them from Anjou and Maine in 1289, were enemies of all Christianity and committed any number of "crimes odious to God." He was expelling them because he preferred "to provide for the peace of our subjects rather than to fill our coffers with the mammon of iniquity." He filled those coffers instead with a perpetual capitation tax of six deniers and a hearth tax of three sous, granted by his subjects in exchange for the expulsion.[35] Similarly when Edward expelled the Jews from England in 1290, he received in return from his parliament the largest tax it ever granted to a medieval English monarch.[36]

As these non-Iberian examples show, a prince's decision to persecute Jews could strengthen his sovereignty as much as his decision to protect them could. But Iberian princes depended more on their Jews than others did, and although many of them had endured rebellions prosecuted (at least in part) as critiques of royal relations with Jews, none had ever opted for expulsion. In the previous chapter we saw how, in the 1270s, a civil war had forced Alfonso X "the Wise" of Castile to reverse what his opponents called tyrannical Jewish policies and execute his Jewish minister of finance. In the 1280s the rebellious unions of Aragon and Valencia compelled the Catalan count-kings to promise that they would no longer appoint Jews to positions—such as bailiff—with judicial power over Christians. In the 1360s Enrique of Trastámara (r. 1369–79) went so far as to overthrow and murder his half brother King Pedro, achieving the coup in part by portraying his rival not only as a lover of Jews but as a "Jewish cuckoo," the son of a Jewess secretly adopted by the queen mother to conceal her inability to provide an heir. During the civil war Enrique encouraged his forces to attack Jewish communities loyal to his brother. His attempts to seduce Pedro's subjects included repeated promises to bar Jews from any role in royal administration. But once in power, Enrique would take no such decision. The Jews were, as he told his subjects when they complained that he had not fulfilled his promise, useful to the king and his to do with as he pleased.

In 1391, however, Joan found himself confronted not with a decision but with an event: a seemingly "miraculous" suspension of his jurisdiction. Of course miracles were just as subject to processes of political negotiation and consensus formation as any other claim to authority in the Middle Ages.[37] Joan's difficulty was that—as the prince his brother had already discovered—in this case the claim was proving powerful.

We have seen how the prince's efforts to meet that claim with force had failed. Joan initially chose not to escalate those attempts, perhaps because he knew that the cost of escalation would be high.[38] But neither could he enter Valencia without a performance of his sovereign justice, and that performance depended on the recognition of his power of decision over the Jews. In other words, until the conflict between God's and Joan's claims to jurisdiction in this case was decided, royal justice was at a standstill.[39] So, for that matter, was royal mercy. When Prince Martí asked Violant to use her queenly powers of intercession with King Joan on behalf of a participant in the assault on the Jews of Lleida, she replied that "it is clear to us that the lord king would not condescend to such a supplication on our part, and we would be very humiliated to begin something that we clearly see could not be successfully concluded."[40] In this sense we should say that Joan's inaction in 1391 was not personal, but what I am calling, somewhat loosely, constitutional.

Joan finally visited Valencia on November 23, 1392. His entry was carefully prenegotiated to represent the reestablishment of concord between sovereign and city: "At the intercession and most humble supplication of our very dear companion the queen, who desires that we and she, who have not yet entered as king and queen the city toward which with God's help we are directing our way, enter peaceful and benign," the king forgave all involved in the massacre, with the exception of a "very few" held in the city's jail and twenty of the many who had fled the city, those twenty to be chosen by the council as the most culpable. Cloaked in queenly intercession, the king abandoned any performance of extraordinary justice.[41]

In its place, however, he gained some jurisdiction over antinomian miracle. In 1391, as we have seen, the main synagogue had been at the epicenter of that miracle: "The instant the invasion was over," the city council declared on July 28, "the main synagogue was named Church of St. Christopher." Initially the king had opposed the city's attempt to "make a church out of the synagogue": "Do not suffer the said synagogue to be unmade," the king had written the prince on the sixteenth, "for we wish and intend to rebuild the said Jewish community." Now, as he prepared to direct his footsteps toward Valencia in November 1392, he could not admit defeat by oleous mysteries or by popular will. Instead he endowed the church in his own name and claimed its patronage for himself.[42]

With the exception of Morvedre, Judaism had been exterminated from the kingdom of Valencia. The king had been deprived of his Jews, and his powerlessness to defend them had threatened to reveal, if only for a moment, the emptiness of his claims to stand simultaneously within and outside the law, as a creature between God and man. Unable to defend the claim through justice, he defended it instead through liturgy, celebrating a daily mass at Saint Christopher's in the name of king and queen. Like the city council (albeit in reverse), he found in miracle a zone of indistinction capable of rendering undecidable the conflict between earthly monarch and divine. Valencia's Jews would no longer keep the royal lions.[43] But in the relic of their synagogue we can still hear the echoes of the shattered claim that pairing represented: the claim of the sovereign to decide the exception.

These debates about miracles and quarrels about jurisdiction may seem very far from our modernity. It was in part to narrow that gap that I chose the words in which I formulated the penultimate sentence of the previous paragraph. Sovereignty, decision, exception: this vocabulary is deliberately evocative of a peculiar modern debate about the nature of politics. That debate, which began in Weimar Germany, can be encapsulated within one sentence from each of two prominent participants: Carl Schmitt, who declared in his *Political Theology* of 1922 that "Souverän ist, wer über den Ausnahmezustand entscheidet" (Sovereign is he who decides the exception);[44] and Walter Benjamin, who counter-quipped, in his "Origins of German Tragic Drama" of 1928, that " Der Fürst, bei dem die Entscheidung über den Ausnahmezustand ruht, erweist in der erstbesten Situation, daß ein Entschluß ihm fast unmöglich ist." (The prince, upon whom the decision over the exception rests, discovers in the best of situations that a decision is impossible for him.)[45] The space between these two positions, and the place of Jews and Judaism within that space, is today once more the subject of much attention, thanks in large part to two books by Giorgio Agamben—*Homo Sacer* and *Stato di Eccezione*—whose analysis centers on the twentieth-century extermination of the Jews as an example of how modern sovereignty articulates itself through the "exception."[46] Agamben and many other thinkers inspired by these Weimar debates seek to present our contemporary politics as one in which exception has become the norm, the routine state is the state of emergency, and every citizen faces the biopolitical threat—best exemplified by the Jewish Muselmänner, the weakest inmates of the concentration camps—of being reduced to "bare life." Agamben's own vision of this politics is grim, but a number of other contemporary cultural critics, such as Slavoj Žižek, Alain Badiou, and Eric Santner, are more optimistic. According to them, political theology itself offers us an escape from the state of exception that it creates, and the means of that escape is precisely the one we saw so powerfully deployed in 1391, namely: miracle.

A starting point for this line of argument is Carl Schmitt's analogy, in *Politische Theologie*, between the "state of exception" in jurisprudence and the miracle in theology: "Der Ausnahmezustand hat für die Jurisprudenz eine analoge Bedeutung wie das Wunder für die Theologie" (43: The state of exception has for jurisprudence a meaning analogous to that of the miracle for theology).[47] Though this analogy might seem to promise only a more thorough tyranny in the name of transcendence, some contemporary thinkers find relief in it. Thus Eric Santner suggests (through an elegant reading of Walter Benjamin, Franz Rosenzweig, and Alain Badiou) that the relationship between miracle and sovereign exception is strict but inverse: "A miracle signifies not the state of exception, but rather its suspension, an intervention into this peculiar topological knot—the outlaw dimension internal to law—that serves to sustain the symbolic function of sovereignty."[48] Seen in this light, political theology seems to offer the basis for a revolution and redemption, and the miracle becomes (to quote Žižek) the "moment in which eternal Justice momentarily appears in the temporal sphere of empirical reality." (The "miracle" Žižek is here describing—the refusal of certain Israeli soldiers to serve in the occupied territories—also involves an overcoming of "Judaism," but that is a subject for a different sermon.)[49]

Without pretending to do justice to these ideas, let me just suggest briefly—and by way of conclusion—that the events of 1391 are relevant to these contemporary recuperations of political theology. They can serve as a test case in which sovereign exception and miracle confront each other explicitly, undistorted by any of the secularizations of modernity. It is surely noteworthy that the conflict in Valencia was not about the "suspension" of the "state of exception"—the Jews remained in that state throughout the confrontation—but over which sovereign, the king or God (or rather, human representations of God's actions), was empowered to decide the Jews' fate. And that conflict was not settled outside the sphere of temporal politics but rather within it. "Eternal justice" did not "momentarily appear in the temporal sphere." The claims of miracle were made good only by temporal political processes of conflict, negotiation, and reconciliation.[50] It is through such processes that the competing claims of the earthly sovereign and the divine, of law and of miracle, have always been kept in the inescapable but functional tension that is the hallmark of Christian politics in the pre-apocalyptic world.[51]

In brief, if we call "politics" the aggregate of the countless conflicts across multiple registers of society that decide the outcome of every claim to power, then it would seem that neither the state of exception in the juridical order nor the miracle in the theological suspends politics. To put it another way, even if we concede that there may be an "Ausnahmezustand" in the juridical order as Schmitt would have it, this does not mean that there is one in the political.[52] Miracles and exceptions are as multiple as any other claims to power. If a sovereign's claim to decide the state of exception succeeds in suspending the law (as it did not in 1391), it is not because the claim is grounded in constitutional logic (or aporia), but because political processes have granted the claim that power. And if a community chooses to designate this or that suspension of sovereignty as a miracle revealing "eternal Justice" (as it did in 1391), it is not because transcendent truth has become evidently albeit momentarily visible in the world, but because, within a historical framework, one among many competing claims to transcendence has emerged temporarily victorious. This is as true today as it was in the Middle Ages: Žižek's protesting soldiers constitute a miracle only within a specific consensus about the politics of the Israeli-Palestinian question.

From this medieval point of view it becomes easier to resist some of the choices that contemporary political theology seeks to thrust upon us with its emphasis on the "state of exception." As a polity we are not forced to choose between decisionism (Schmitt) and indecision (Benjamin), between law and miracle, or for that matter, between what we think of as secular politics and theology. All of these are equally subject to the sum of practices and processes that make collective human life possible in an imperfect world, the practices and processes that in aggregate we call politics. From this there was no escape in 1391, and I see none today.[53]

[5]

Conversion, Sex, and Segregation

The previous chapter introduced us to the massacres and mass conversions of 1391 in one particular city and explored some of their political implications, but it scarcely began the task of describing what was after all a wave of violence that swept over much of the Iberian Penninsula, let alone attempting to explain its causes or to give an account of their consequences. We should want to know about what happened, not only in Valencia but also in many other cities and towns across Iberia. And we should want to ask how structures of religious pluralism—structures that had made room over long centuries for large populations of non-Christians in these Christian realms— could collapse so suddenly. Unfortunately the events of 1391, among the most momentous in the history of Judaism and in the history of Spanish Christianity, have not yet received their monograph. I hope someday to provide one, but in this chapter and the ones that follow, I will focus not on description or cause, but on consequences. How did the massacres and mass conversions of 1391 affect the ways in which diverse communities of Christians, Muslims, and Jews drew on each other in order to imagine themselves?

In this chapter the imaginings we will address are sexual. Sex is a popular topic among my generation of professors. Whether because of changing methodologies (social history, the anthropological and the postcolonial turns, gender and queer theory) or the shifting desires of popular audiences, scholars are finding more meaning in the sexual interaction of their subjects than ever before. Some interactions, of course, are more interesting than others. Above all, historians seek sex that destabilizes categories and violates taboos. There is no doubt that the approach has been fruitful. The historiographies of colonial Latin America, of British, French, and German imperialism, and especially of race relations in the United States have all been enriched by studies too numerous to footnote, studies that explore sexual fears in order to understand how societies imagine their boundaries.

But sex has its dangers as well. The first of these is its universality, and the near universality of the many prohibitions that attend it. If, as Borges put it, "universal history is the history of a few metaphors," many of those metaphors are sexual. It is perhaps because so many societies have defined themselves through such similar strictures on sexuality that anthropologists and not historians were the first to explore their mysteries. Insofar as the sexual metaphors and rules through which societies describe themselves are widely dispersed in space and time, they seem a clumsy barometer for the transformations with which historians are often occupied. A second danger is closely related: we moderns tend to project backward our world-weary certainties, making sex pregnant with anachronism. Thus, for example, our experience of sex as the site at which nature and culture meet to produce "race" is often elevated to a general rule.[1] Rarely do we let ourselves be moved to wonder about our own certainties by the scandals of a distant age.

These dangers are precisely what makes sex particularly interesting for us, as we begin to explore a period of rapid change in the way Christians, Muslims, and Jews living in the medieval Iberian Peninsula thought about religious classification. Sex was one of the primary languages through which that classification was articulated, and we will follow its inflection from the late thirteenth century, through 1391, and into the fifteenth century. Our fulcrum, 1391, was from a Jewish point of view a cataclysmic year that witnessed the greatest loss of Jewish souls in the Middle Ages and (in retrospect) marked the beginning of the end for Spanish Jewry. It would become a cataclysm of a different sort for Christians as well, the origins of a crisis of classification ("Who is a Jew?") that has seemed to many Spanish historians a "principal cause of the decadence of the Peninsula."[2] The crisis will be less familiar to most readers than those that accompanied, for example, the emancipation of African Americans in the U.S. South, the emancipation of Jews in modern Europe, or colonialism's (de)stabilization of racial categories. It was, however, every bit as sharp and every bit as productive. In fact, one of its products, according to some historians, was the birth of racism itself, specifically of racial anti-Semitism.[3] But we will not begin with that position. Let us instead approach the subject of sex with an adolescent innocence, in the hope that we might yet be surprised by the past.

We will start with the universal. Medieval people, like their predecessors and successors, had a number of common metaphors to hand with which to imagine themselves as a sexual community. Probably the most familiar is the image of society as a human (generally male) body, as in Saint Paul's "body of Christ" (1 Cor. 12) or John of Salisbury's "body politic."[4] But this corporatist image, so important in medieval politics and theology, was seldom sexualized for the purpose of delineating religious difference. Perhaps this is because the logic of the imagery (organic diversity as a functional aspect of vitality) militated against the automatic exclusion of groups like Jews and Muslims who played recognizable roles in the social order. Or perhaps it is because the image was autonomous, lacking an "other" body capable of producing sexual danger.[5] Whatever the reason, a second corporal image for the Christian community was more widespread in Christian thought and art, and more central to the sexual imagination of society. This was *Ecclesia*, that is, the church personified as a woman. The image provided a strong foundation for a discourse of anxiety about interfaith sex, and this for two reasons. First, unlike with the more political corporatism described above, the non-Christian was firmly excluded from *Ecclesia*. A long tradition of artistic and textual production presented *Ecclesia* as the positive antipode to *Synagoga*, the personification of Judaism.[6] Second, *Ecclesia* was understood in sexualized terms as the bride of Christ. In this sense as in so many others she was the heir of Jerusalem/Israel, whom the prophets had so often characterized as God's beloved spouse. Sentimental readers will think immediately of the Song of Songs, whose erotic imagery has been commented upon by Jew, Christian, and Muslim alike. The more puritanical might recall Hosea, commanded by God to marry a harlot so that he might better empathize with God's wrath over the infidelity of Israel, His chosen bride. Both the bitter and the sweet make amply clear the power of sexual and marital metaphors to describe the exclusive relationship that a monotheistic God expected to have with his people. Monotheism was best imagined as monogamy, idolatry as promiscuity.[7]

But *Ecclesia* was a collective representation. Her erotic charge needed to be fragmented if it was to compel fidelity at the level of the individual. That fragmentation was achieved early. Paul's Epistle to the Ephesians, for example, urged every (male) Christian to care for his wife's body and to guard her purity, just as Jesus guarded his own wife, Ecclesia.[8] It was an analogy well suited to sustaining the vast interpretive edifice necessary for the linking of collective religious identities to the sexual body of the individual. Perhaps for this reason the many medieval Iberian texts concerning sex between Christian and non-Christian rarely invoked the collective corporatist metaphors. Instead they took as their point of departure the (much less studied) individualized analogies. As in Ephesians, these analogies treated the patriarchal family, not the body, as the foundational metaphor for Christian community. The metaphors were common throughout the Christian Middle Ages, but I will restrict myself to a few Iberian examples. King Alfonso the Wise of Castile put it this way: "Since Christians who commit adultery with married women deserve death, how much more so do Jews who lie with Christian women, for these are spiritually espoused to Our Lord Jesus Christ by virtue of the faith and baptism they received in His name."[9] Every Christian woman, wed or unwed, was the bride of Christ through baptism. God had a sexual interest in all Christian women. As His wives, their bodies represented the extension of His authority and community, the point at which His honor as Father and husband was at risk. Because of this, women's bodies could become the site of fears concerning God's honor and that of His Church.

Christian women were not just God's wives. They were also His daughters. Imagine—Saint Vincent exhorted Christians in a sermon against prostitution—that the king had a daughter. Even if she consents with pleasure to have sex with you, do you not betray the king in lying with her? Would you not deserve to be drawn and quartered? The king is Jesus Christ: are prostitutes not His daughters? "Yes, surely, for he has engendered them in baptism, just as he has engendered you and all other [Christians]."[10] God's "engendering" of the Christian family was of course central to the metaphor, and it too was understood in explicitly sexual terms. "Jesus every day impregnates the Church, and the womb is the baptismal font, and he sends there his semen from heaven." It is therefore the obligation of every Christian woman to honor father and mother, Jesus Christ and Holy Mother Church.[11] It is also their spousal duty to honor Him as husband, a duty all the greater because of the immense disparity of status between divine groom and human bride. "If a king takes the daughter of a poor laborer as wife, and she leaves him and goes off with villains, she would be considered a great whore."[12]

In all of these analogies the emphasis is on a sexualized God. Occasionally, this sexuality is gendered feminine.[13] Much more often, however, God is a paterfamilias, whether as husband or as father, with rights over His "family."

The violation of those rights diminishes His honor and constitutes an insult both to Him and to his "household," that is, to the entire Christian community. Of course God's rights and His honor extend far beyond the sexual, and Saint Vincent, like many other medieval preachers, talked frequently of the obligation to honor God in every action.[14] Judging from the space allotted to it in his sermons, however, sex played as large a role in the divine economy of honor as it did in the human one.

These metaphors of marriage and reproduction define the Christian community in a number of related ways. They represent the Christian community as a family of brothers and sisters tied to God through overlapping bonds of marriage and paternity. The limits of the community are marked by strict endogamy. Muslims and Jews are not God's children, since they have not undergone God's engendering baptism.[15] They are explicitly excluded from the kin group and should therefore (as Alfonso put it) have no sexual contact with it, lest such contact establish a kinship in the flesh that dishonored the more vital kinship in the spirit.

The analogy of sexual honor had an additional virtue, for it described the Christian community's claims to privilege and allegiance in the same terms that individual Christians used to describe the claims of their own families. In this sense, the analogy served to bridge the gap between the individual and the collective.[16] In sociological terms (I am adapting Georg Simmel), the discourse of honor functioned to stabilize "the cohesion, standing, regularity, and furtherance of the life processes" of a social group and to isolate it from other groups or classes. It did so by appealing to the individual's "conviction that the maintenance of his honor constitutes his most intrinsic, most profound and most personal self-interest." This is what made honor, according to Simmel, "one of the most marvelous, instinctively developed expediencies for the maintenance of group existence."[17]

There were a number of other ways in which the theology of Christian sexual honor reinforced the Christian community's sense of a coherent and cohesive identity. One of these was as object of collective punishment. Within the economy of honor in which God and medieval Christians functioned, insult required vengeance. A late fourteenth-century altar painting (retable) from Santa María de Sixena reminded worshipers that this vengeance could be aimed at the individual transgressor. It depicted a woman kneeling at Communion, her throat gushing blood where the Eucharist had slit it. In the neighboring panel we see the reason for the wafer's aggression: the communicant had just taken leave of her Muslim lover.[18]

Much more often, however, punishment was aimed not merely at the sin-
ner but at the totality of the collective that was dishonored and corrupted by
the sin. The instruments of God's discipline were plague, famine, civil war,
and other horrors.[19] Again, Saint Vincent was a systematic exponent of this
logic. In a number of his sermons, he listed six particularly dishonorable sins
that provoke God's punishing anger: reliance on witches and fortune-tellers;
blasphemy; ignoring God's feasts (Sundays and holidays); failing to bring
gamblers, usurers, and other thieves of God's goods to justice. The fifth sin
(and the one that often received the most space) was negligence in the repression of prostitution. If the populace wished to avoid divine punishment,
it must locate any brothel outside the town. It must allow no concubines or
public women in its midst, for if even just one man should have a concubine,
"it is something very dangerous for the community." Had not Saint Paul explained that on account of one concubine alone an entire "city was corrupted,
and suffered great plagues"? "Do you not know that a little leaven corrupts
the entire dough?" "Therefore, eject the prostitute into the street, for on her
account so many plagues have come upon you."[20] Finally, the sixth point:
segregate Jews and Muslims and have nothing to do with them. Do not even
light their fires, for it was in just such a seemingly innocent transaction that
"a young Christian girl was raped by a Jew." Proper attention to these six issues, according to Saint Vincent, would guarantee the health of the city and
allow its inhabitants to say, "In the holy dwelling I ministered before Him."[21]

It is not so much the content of this catalog of vice that concerns us here
as the images that were called upon in this and other sermons in order to
express the dangers that sexual sins posed to the community. A little yeast
in a large mass of dough, one sick sheep infecting the flock, a spoiled apple
rotting the entire bin: all these analogies supported models of corruption and
contagion that raised the consequences of individual sin to the level of the
community. In this sense, anxieties about sexual honor helped to define the
Christian community as a collective with "natural" boundaries whose integrity needed to be maintained if disease was to be avoided. Here too, then, the
language of sexual honor worked "to express both the exclusive nature of the
allegiance and the confused social experience."[22]

In other words, the sexualized boundaries inscribed on the bodies of
women in order to demarcate familial honor could be generalized to heighten
the cohesion of larger units of society. This resulted in something of a hierarchy of sexual sins. Moral reformers like Saint Vincent seldom ranked
systematically the sins they preached against, but they clearly feared some

adulteries more than others. For example, because priests touched Christ's Eucharistic body in the Mass, the clerical concubines whose bodies corrupted those hands dishonored Christ doubly: "You, woman, who grant your body to a cleric . . . commit a greater sin by lying just once with him than if you granted it to all the other men in Aragon *in specie*."[23] And of course, forms of sexual activity that might normally be tolerated could be perceived as dangerous at specific times, such as during plagues or Lent. But the type of sexual sin that elicited by far the most sustained and extensive concern, and that was considered to be the greatest "dishonor to God and to the Catholic faith," is the one that concerns us here: intercourse between God's friends and His enemies, that is, in this case, between Christians and Muslims or Jews.

It was largely (but not exclusively) to prevent such intercourse that throughout the Middle Ages Christian theologians (as well as Muslim jurists and Jewish rabbis) emphasized the importance of maintaining sexual boundaries between the three religious groups. These boundaries might be said to constitute the "skin" of the sexualized body social. But it is important to remember that, unlike skin, these boundaries did not have a fixed location, meaning, or function in society. Rather, they were dynamic, displaceable, and highly responsive to the changing needs of the societies that produced them.

At some level, ancient and medieval legislators, whether Christian or Jew, were well aware of this. The Babylonian Talmud wrestled with the fact that the biblical passage on which Jewish restrictions on intermarriage were based applied explicitly only to intermarriage with people from seven nations that had ceased to exist shortly after the conquest by the Israelites of the Holy Land, more than a thousand years before:

> The biblical ordinance [against intermarriage] is restricted to the seven nations [of Canaan] and does not include other heathen peoples; and [the schools of Hillel and Shamai] came and decreed against these also. . . . Perhaps the biblical ordinance refers to an Israelite woman in intercourse with a heathen since she would be drawn after him, but not against an Israelite man having intercourse with a heathen woman, and they [court of the Hasmoneans] came and decreed even against the latter. . . .The decree of the Hasmoneans was against intercourse but not against private association, so they came and decreed even against this.[24]

The Talmudic passage treated the evolution of sexual boundaries in historical time and showed a full awareness that the sexual boundary can be extended to all kinds of nonsexual interaction. The passage even articulated the logic by which such movement occurs. Because sex and marriage can be positioned along a continuum of social and cultural relations and types of exchange, prohibitions on sex and marriage can be moved along that continuum as well: private association may lead to sex, hence association is forbidden. And of course, all these sexual boundaries were related to the more fundamental religious one: "With all the things against which they decreed the purpose was to safeguard against idolatry. . . . [They made a decree] against their bread and oil on account of their wine; against their wine on account of their daughters; against their daughters on account of another matter."[25] The medieval Jewish scholar Maimonides put it more bluntly when he wrote that prohibitions on exchange and social interaction between Jews and non-Jews were established as a "precaution, lest such [social] intercourse should lead to intermarriage." The logic is strikingly similar to that of a formulation famous in anthropology: "A continuous transition exists from war to exchange, and from exchange to intermarriage, and the exchange of brides is merely the conclusion to an uninterrupted process of reciprocal gifts, which effects the transition from hostility to alliance, from anxiety to confidence, and from fear to friendship."[26]

Medieval Christians read little Talmud and less anthropology, but they would have recognized this logic as their own. They, too, shared the sense that seemingly innocent forms of exchange might lead to the effacement of difference and thereby to more dangerous exchanges. The canon lawyer Johannes Teutonicus made the point quite wittily when asked: Why are Christians allowed to talk to Jews but forbidden to eat with them? The reply: talking is one thing, but eating? Who knows what can happen between courses.[27] And they, too, used anxiety about the integrity of sexual boundaries to underwrite any number of practices of discrimination and identification.[28] When, for example, the "Jewish badge" was imposed at the Fourth Lateran Council in 1215, the distinction was justified as necessary in order that easy identification might prevent sexual intercourse across religious lines. The same logic was repeated later in the century by King Alfonso, and it is frequent in Iberian legislation: "Many errors and offensive acts occur between Christian men and Jewish women and between Christian women and Jewish men as a consequence of their living together in cities and dressing alike. In order to obviate the errors and evils that might result from this situation, we consider it proper and decree that all Jewish men and women living in our kingdom wear some sort of mark upon their heads so that all may clearly discern who is a Jew or a Jewess."[29]

In short, many medieval Christians believed, as so many other societies have done, that the transition from "other" to "self" (in this case from infidel and alien to Christian and kin) would culminate in sexual union. Because of this, the entire process of spiritual identification and integration could be most powerfully represented in terms of the sexual act, a process bluntly described by Saint Paul: "You surely know that anyone who links himself with a harlot becomes physically one with her (for Scripture says, 'the pair shall become one flesh'); but he who links himself with Christ is one with Him, spiritually."[30] This is why medieval Christian anxieties about identification and, ultimately, about the integrity of the self were so often expressed in sexual terms. It is also why, for Christian, Jew, and Muslim alike, the question was always where to draw the line to best interrupt this continuum. No matter where these boundaries were drawn, they were sexual in the sense that they justified themselves as safeguards against sexual danger. But they could be constructed in all kinds of places, and the place chosen could have a tremendous effect on intergroup relations. If, as in the Talmudic example, any and all associations were thought to lead to sex, then total segregation was necessary; if only wine drinking were dangerous, then anxiety could focus there.

Thus far, I have been outlining the common logics and enduring metaphors of sex that medieval Christian (as well as Jewish and Muslim) communities used to help define and identify themselves as a collective and to heighten the barriers of honor with which that collective surrounded itself. But the specific outcome of these logics within a given society was highly variable, always dependent on the peculiar shape and physiological needs of that social body. So let us now focus on the sexual vanities and vulnerabilities of Christian Spain in concrete time, namely before 1391 and after. Where did our subjects imagine their society to be sexually most at risk? How did they seek to defend that society from the sexual dangers that assailed it? It is through such questions that the sexual will become historical, capable of revealing the passions of a particular time and place.

So where, in the century before 1391, did Christians fear that their religion was sexually most at risk? Anxiety over the integrity of sexual boundaries can alight in many different places: on children, wives, slaves, widows, even (as in the case of the Spanish Civil War) on nuns. The particular form the anxiety takes depends not so much on the quantitative reality of sexual interaction (anxieties need not correspond to the real) but on far more complicated cultural logics, whose outcomes can be quite surprising. For example, the previous section described how the metaphor of marriage facilitated the convergence of familial and communal honor upon female sexuality in the theological and social imagination of medieval Christians. Given this convergence, we might expect a good deal of concern about the possibility that married or marriageable women might engage in interfaith adultery. In fact, such concern is almost entirely absent from the archival or the literary record. In the few court cases involving such accusations that I have found, the charges end up being dismissed.[31] Acquittal is the theme, as well, in Alfonso the Wise's *Cantigas de Santa María*, where the Virgin intervenes to save a young wife falsely accused by her mother-in-law of intercourse with her Muslim slave: a rare literary example of such concern in a culture where, it should be remembered, the presence of male Muslim slaves in Christian households was common.[32]

Those few texts that do focus on the desire of married Christian women for non-Christians tend to do so playfully, in the context of "frontier adventures." An Aragonese chronicle, for example, tells about one Count Don Rodrigo, who was engaged in a border skirmish with a Muslim king. Before turning his horse to flee, the king dropped his trousers and showed the count his penis: "What do you think of this," he boasted, and disappeared. Hearing the story from her husband at the dinner table, the count's wife conceived a desire for the Muslim and determined to join him, setting in motion an elaborate plot. The tale narrates the count's many travails, which included being locked in a chest by his wife, who had intercourse upon it with the Muslim and then presented it to him as a postcoital present. In the end, the count avenges himself, and the highly literary trickster narrative concludes on a didactic note: not with a moral about the dangers of miscegenation, but with the text of certain prayers the count had found useful in his tribulations.[33] This sense of the sexual fluidity of the frontier is typical of a number of literary sources. "Mi padre era de Ronda y mi madre de Antequera," one poem begins. That is, my father is from a Christian town and my mother from a Muslim one. Romances like "Moriana y el moro Galván" remind us a bit less explicitly that the reverse could also be true. But the possibility of this type of sexual interaction seems to have provoked little anxiety. Even Alfonso the Wise, the author of the law cited above forbidding Christian women from having sex with non-Christians, could be relaxed enough to write a poem about a Christian woman who fights sexual duels with a Muslim knight on the frontier. She exhausts and defeats the brave Muslim, but not before he wounds her with his "little lance."[34]

None of this is meant to suggest that Christian society approved of such intercourse. To the contrary, we know that it could be savagely repressed, and the legal punishment for it was death.[35] The point is only that, regardless of its quantitative reality, such intercourse did not form an important focus of public concern or anchor a rhetoric of anxiety about sexual boundaries between religious communities. Another sexual boundary does, however, emerge as particularly fraught in the medieval Iberian sources before 1391, and that is the one between Christian prostitutes and non-Christian men.

I have written elsewhere at length about the role of prostitutes in regulating relations between Muslims, Christians, and Jews in fourteenth-century Spain and will therefore state the point baldly here.[36] Within this discourse of honor built on analogies of marriage and the family, concern focused on women who were outside the bounds of both those institutions. The archives are full of accusations charging Jewish and Muslim men with breaking the law against sexual intercourse with Christian prostitutes. In essence, prostitutes became the focal point for anxiety about sexual frontiers, the site at which dishonor threatened the Christian community. Prostitutes were the only Christian women routinely burned or strangled for the crime of sexual intercourse across religious boundaries, and they themselves knew that, if accused, they faced the flames unless they could exculpate themselves by proving that the non-Christian appeared Christian. Because markers of identity were for them a matter of life and death, prostitutes came to play the role of specialists in the recognition (and ideally, the rejection) of religious difference.

The story of Alicsend de Tolba and Aytola the Sarracen is a good example of this role. Alicsend was a Christian prostitute who visited a shepherds' camp in 1304. After some time, Lorenç the Shepherd ("Lorenç Pastor") went to the Muslim called Aytola the Sarracen ("Aytola Sarray") and asked him if he wouldn't like to have intercourse with Alicsend. Aytola objected that he was a Muslim and that he had no money, but Lorenç offered to loan Aytola the money, and "told the said moor to say that his name was Johan, to speak in [illegible], and to say that he was from the port." The deception ended when Alicsend "recognized that he was a moor in his member" and screamed for help. Aytola fled, and Alicsend denounced both him and Lorenç for falsity and deviousness "in dishonor of God and of the Catholic faith."[37] In this case, it is Aytola's expulsion from Alicsend that identifies him as alien, an "otherness," which not coincidentally is somatized and recognized in his sexual member by the prostitute in her role as protector of God's honor.

This emphasis on the prostitute as incarnation of the sexual boundary between religions is perhaps the most distinctive feature of pre-1391 sexual moral economy. Insofar as this "social system" focused responsibility for maintaining the sexual integrity of religious boundaries on the prostitute, it construed sexual danger as narrowly as possible and thereby freed a relatively large proportion of public and private space for interaction and exchange across religious boundaries. Before 1391, in other words, the prostitute's discipline (and the disciplining of prostitutes) sufficed to guarantee Christian confidence in the security of sexual frontiers. So long as the prostitute did her job, Christian and non-Christian could work together, gamble and drink together, even sleep in the same house, without triggering sexual panics.

Remaining within this "functionalist mode" for a moment, what is most striking about this system is its stability, or, rather, its ability to respond adequately to social change. I proposed earlier that the discourse of collective sexual honor functioned to stabilize "the cohesion, standing, regularity, and furtherance of the life processes" of the Christian community. We should therefore expect that heightened instability or incoherence in that cohesion would induce, one, a heightening of the language of sexual honor and a sharpening of the sexual boundaries through which that language inscribes itself in social life and, two, a more insistent demarcation of religious difference. This expectation is not disappointed. Consider, for example, the reactions of Iberian Christians to the murderous advent of the bubonic plague in 1348 and to its remorseless return decade after decade over the centuries that followed. Plague was believed to be (among other things) the result of disorder in Christian society, expressed in terms of insufficient attention to the honor of God and of His privileged people.[38] It is therefore not surprising that outbreaks of plague were often greeted with a host of moral reforms, including the heightened seclusion of prostitutes and increased concern with the dangers of interfaith sexuality.[39] At an extreme, Christians' attempts to augment the distance between Christian and non-Christian as a means of assuaging God's anger could lead to outbreaks of extensive violence against the Jews: the massacres of Jews in 1348 are a notorious example. More commonly, Christians might demarcate what they believed to be "proper boundaries" through more stylized violence. Hence the Jews complained in 1354 that "without any reason they injure, harass, stone, and even kill the Jews living in the said kingdoms and lands, the said Christians declaring that because of the sins of the Jews there come mortalities and famines, and committing the said harms against the Jews so that the said pestilences might cease."[40]

This logic quickly lost its violent force as the plague became familiar, another of a number of routine calamities. But the link between crisis and heightened concerns with interfaith sexuality did not disappear. We see it, for example, during the civil war that consumed Castile in the 1360s and culminated in the murder of King Pedro "the Cruel" by his half-brother Enrique of Trastamara. According to the propagandists of his rivals, Pedro was a "cuckoo," a Jewish baby snuck into the royal cradle by the queen, who had supposedly given birth to a girl and feared being dismissed for failure to produce an heir. This explained Pedro's cruelty and his bad government. For complex reasons, such "hybridity" stories tended to collect around nodes of violent resistance to monarchy.[41] But the point here is a simpler one. As we have seen in several of the preceding chapters, this was a society in which complaints about disorder, the subversion of hierarchy, or the erosion of privilege were often written in the shorthand of interfaith sex. It is in such crises of status, and not in the furtive meetings of star-crossed lovers, that we should locate the occasional outbursts of moral indignation (such as Seville's complaint in 1371 that the law of witness made it virtually impossible to convict Jews caught in adultery with Christians, or the plea of the cities assembled in parliament in 1385 about the proper protection of Christian women) that punctuate the century before 1391.[42]

Despite these crises, what is most characteristic of the system is its equilibrium. Heightened fears about pollution and the coherence of the body social might momentarily sharpen attention to possible lapses in the enforcement of sexual boundaries or result in changes like the one of 1371 in Seville that altered the laws concerning the witnessing of interfaith adultery. But such episodes did not cause Christian society to question its basic confidence in the integrity of those sexual boundaries or to propose their dramatic reconstruction. The massacres and mass conversions of 1391 did.

Throughout that year, Christian rioters attacked Jews in town after town across the Iberian Peninsula. Thousands of Jews were killed; many thousands more converted to Christianity. As we saw in the previous chapter, their conversion could at first be understood as miraculous, but this sense of wonder was eventually replaced by a very different reaction. By the late fifteenth century, many Christians considered the conversions a disaster that threatened the spiritual health of the entire Christian community. The converts and their descendants were now seen as insincere Christians, as clandestine Jews, or even as hybrid monsters, neither Jew nor Christian. They converted merely to gain power over Christians, to degrade, even poison, Christian men and to have sex with Christian women. Some went so far as to see this insincerity as a product of nature. Baptism could not alter the fact that the Jews' blood was corrupted by millennia of mixture and debasement, indelibly saturated with a hatred of everything Christian. Hence purity of blood laws were needed to bar the descendants of converts from any position of power or privilege, and "natural Christians" were encouraged not to intermarry with them. Further, the danger of secret Judaizing warranted the establishment of institutions (such as the Inquisition) to identify, reform, or extirpate those at risk and eventually justified the expulsion of the Jews in 1492.[43]

Beneath the setting sun of Iberian Jewry, these later events cast a long backward shadow. Historians of medieval Iberia have therefore tended, like students of so many other "failed emancipations," to take continuities of hatred for granted. In their writings, new discriminations arise refurbished from the ashes of the old, rendered immortal either by the unchanging character of the persecutor (the anti-Semite remains at heart an anti-Semite) or of the persecuted (the convert remains at heart a Jew).[44] I do not propose to confront the full force of that historiography here but to chip away—in this chapter and those that follow—at its foundations with a series of blunt questions. First, how did the generation of Christians that came of age in 1391 and the quarter century following imagine the consequences of the massacres and conversions they had wrought? Why, as it turns out, were they so unconcerned with convert religiosity and so concerned about sex with Jews? Were their sexual concerns the same as those of their ancestors and descendants? If not, what can such differences teach us about, specifically, the emergence of Old Christian enmity toward converts and, more generally, about the function of sexual boundaries in systems of discrimination and classification?

The mass conversions of 1391 did provoke an important Christian "identity crisis," one that would sharply constrict the space available for religious diversity in the Iberian Peninsula. But this was a very different crisis from the later ones that would transform Iberia into a land of inquisitors and pure blood statutes. The concern of Christians in the years immediately after 1391 was not that religious identity was unchanging but rather the opposite, that the disappearance of the Jews and the emergence of the conversos would undermine the distinctive value and meaning of Christian identity. Correspondingly, their attention was not focused on the religious practices of the converts or on establishing differences between Old Christian and New but on reinforcing the still more fundamental boundary between Christian and Jew.

Listen, for example, to King Joan I of Aragon in 1393. Writing to a number of his most important cities, he informed them that it had become impossible for "natural Christians," that is, not the converts, to tell who was a convert to Christianity and who was still a Jew. Henceforth, converts were to be forbidden to live, dine, or have conversation with Jews. The Jews were to be made to wear more conspicuous badges and Jewish hats, so "that they appear to be Jews." The king ended the letter with his most emphatic point: "And we order and desire that if any of these said Jews are found with a Christian woman in a suspicious place, in order to have carnal copulation with her, let them both be burned without mercy."[45] Similar admonitions would be continually repeated in the decade that followed.

King Joan's letters were probably triggered by the case of Saltell Gracìa, a Jew of Barcelona who was that week being tried for "promenading in Christian dress and under guise of that dress having sex with many Christian women."[46] The case resonated, however, with preexisting concerns, which helps to explain the quite extraordinary fact that, from this particular, the king and his advisers hurried to articulate a general collapse of the normal processes of identification and classification in the wake of the mass conversions. The king stipulated a number of solutions to the problem, and their differential reception is interesting. First, he ordered that the social and physical distance between convert and Jew be increased through segregation. The order was roundly ignored. (In fact, the clearest attempt to increase residential segregation at this time, by the Archbishop of Zaragoza, actually predates the king's letters and was strongly opposed by the monarchy.)[47] Second, the king demanded that the Jews be marked even more visibly. Authorities took to this option with gusto, "hyper-marking" the remaining Jews by forcing them to dress in more distinctive clothes and increasing the size of the badge they were obliged to wear. Within a month of the king's edict, the queen had to issue another, ordering that no additional distinctions be imposed upon the Jews of Valencia, since they were already "sufficiently marked," and additional clothing regulations would lead them to abandon the city.[48] Finally, the more fundamental point from which the others drew their power: the king demanded greater vigilance toward and punishment of sex between Christian women and Jewish men.

Such letters make clear that concern with sexual boundaries rose to the forefront of Christian consciousness in the very first moments of mass conversion. But the practical implications of that concern, and the political uses to which it could be put in ordering society, were very much open to negotiation. The problem of segregation provides a good example. Since the Fourth Lateran

Council, if not earlier, church and (less frequently) secular authorities had preached and legislated the ideal of complete residential segregation of Christians and Jews, often invoking the danger of sexual mixing as justification. But throughout this period, the ideal, though frequently invoked, remained unimplemented.[49] As the example of Zaragoza and other cities suggests, the necessity of sharp spatial or residential segregation did not become more obvious to most Christians in the generation after 1391, despite heightened concerns about sex.[50] In 1403, the town council of Lleida even revoked its statute banning converts from the Jewish quarter, claiming that it had been issued at the request of the Jews in order to inconvenience Christians.[51]

This still relatively permeable religious topography was transformed by the preaching of Saint Vincent. He was the most important evangelist of the day and the impresario of the massive effort undertaken by papacy and monarchy in the early fifteenth century to reform Christian spirituality and to achieve the conversion of all the Jews of the peninsula. His sermons were heard by tens, perhaps hundreds of thousands, Christian and infidel alike, and thousands of Jews converted at his exhortation.[52] His motivations were multiple, ranging from apocalypticism to the politics of papal schism and do not concern us here. For our purposes, it is enough to note that in and through his preaching the logic of segregation was transformed from a marginal and often contested strategy into the central metaphor of a well-ordered Christian polity. Beginning with his first preaching campaign in Murcia, Saint Vincent urged the separation of Jews and Muslims from Christians so as to avoid the deadly sin of "conversation," by which he generally meant sexual intercourse. The Murcian council issued statutes to implement his plans (although they later exempted the Muslims from their prohibitions), and these were approved by King Ferdinand as a way of eliminating the "many pimpings and adulteries between Christians and Jews."[53]

It is a symptom of the sway later events hold over our imagination that we have not been struck by the highly specific contours of the concerns expressed by Saint Vincent's sermons. Like King Joan's letters of twenty years earlier, they focus not so much on the beliefs or religious identity of the converts but on the physical and social proximity of Jew to Christian, a proximity that threatens the very process of religious identification and classification. Moreover, the perils of that proximity are not expressed in terms of sincerity of belief or confessional allegiance but in terms of dangerous social and sexual intimacy. Unlike the solution of the later period, the one proposed here has little to do with the policing of converso orthodoxy. What is advocated is a prophylactic heightening, through marking and segregation, of the physical distance between Christian and Jew.

Like kings Joan and Martí, Saint Vincent was clearly concerned that the converts were not being properly educated as Christians, but such an explicit focus on the religiosity of the converts was as rare in his sermons as it was elsewhere during this period.[54] Much more often, he stressed not the integration of the convert but the segregation of the Jew, and this in explicitly sexual terms. Of course, Saint Vincent was very much concerned with sexual offenses of any kind, and he was convinced that sexual appetites were becoming increasingly deviant in his day. Nowadays, he complained, Christian men "want to taste everything: Muslims and Jews, animals, men with men; there is no limit."[55] But he was especially concerned about what he perceived to be an explosion of sex between Christians and Jews. In 1415, he told a Zaragozan audience that "many Christian men believe their wife's children to be their own, when they are actually by Muslim and Jewish [fathers]." If the citizens did not put a stop to such interfaith adultery, he warned, God would do so through plague. His sermon provoked a sexual panic. Christian patrols searched the streets, on the lookout for predatory Jews or Muslims in search of Christian women. One Muslim was seized, found with "iron tools for . . . forcing open doors" in order to obtain Christian women for Muslim men. Another was arrested after witnesses claimed to have seen him fleeing a Christian woman's room by the flat rooftops one night. So many charges were brought that the responsible judicial official was accused of fomenting a riot against the Muslims and the Jews.[56]

According to Saint Vincent, the problem was one of ambiguous identities. Jews and Muslims were living among Christians, dressing like Christians, even adopting Christian names, so that "by their appearance they are taken and reputed by many to be Christians."[57] The solution he advocated was one of heightened marking and segregation. So powerful was his reasoning that it convinced the pope, the kings of Castile and Aragon, and innumerable town councils and municipal officers to attempt the most extensive efforts at segregation in the Middle Ages. We have already encountered the example of Murcia, where sexual danger was used to justify the segregation of Jew from Christian. Within six months, the strategy had spread across the Iberian Peninsula. In Castile, late in 1411,

the queen [regent] . . . reached Valladolid with the king her son, and found there Friar Vincent, who preached every day his marvelous sermons, and

criticized frequently the living of Muslims and Jew among Christians, saying that they should be separated, both from conversation with Christians,
and from their dwellings, because this was said to be the cause of very great
and very ugly sins. And the queen, taking this upon her conscience, issued a
proclamation throughout her province, that wherever they were, [Jews and
Muslims] should be given places apart.[58]

Similar actions were taken in the Crown of Aragon, where King Fernando I
implemented measures virtually identical to those of Queen Catherine in
Castile.

The architects of these measures expressed themselves in traditional terms.
King Ferdinand, for example, stipulated that respectable Christian women
found in the Jewish quarter would be fined. Christian prostitutes, on the other
hand, would be whipped one hundred lashes, the rough equivalent in Iberian
jurisprudence of the death penalty.[59] But although the form was traditional, its
intent and effect were revolutionary. No matter how heavily she was whipped,
the prostitute no longer sufficed as a boundary between Christian and Jew:
total segregation was necessary. The ideal was to prohibit all exchange:

> Jews and Muslims should be separate, not among Christians. Do not toler-
> ate infidel doctors, do not buy victuals from them, let them be walled up
> and enclosed, for we have no greater enemies. Christian women may not
> be their wet nurses, nor should [you] eat with them. If they send you bread,
> throw it to the dogs. If they send you live meat, accept it, but not dead, for
> Holy Scripture says of these sins: "Do you not know that a little leaven cor-
> rupts the entire dough?" (I Cor. 5). And say of the whore of Corinth . . .[60]

Note again how here the powers of corruption and plague that Saint Paul
attributed to the whore of Corinth are used to represent the dangers of all
forms of exchange with infidels. If authorities fail in preventing such exchange, Saint Vincent warned, the wrath of God would fall upon them and
their cities.

In the interest of separating Christian from non-Christian, Jews were to be
moved to segregated neighborhoods and severely restricted in their market
and economic activities.[61] Trade between Jew and Christian was forbidden:
in some towns, Christians even refused to sell Jews food. Because few Jewish neighborhoods were completely segregated, entire communities were
evicted from their homes, "with boys and girls dying from exposure to the

cold and the snow." A later Jewish chronicler called the discriminations of 1412–16 "the greatest persecution that had ever occurred." And as in 1391, one of the consequences of this persecution was the mass conversion of (tens of?) thousands of Jews to Christianity.[62]

My emphasis in the preceding narrative is highly selective. I have stressed, for example, sexual sensibilities, while ignoring millenarian impulses, papal politics, the spiritual inclinations of kings, and many other topics of tremendous importance in structuring Jewish-Christian relations in the period 1391–1416. But the goal of my narrative is not to provide an adequate causal explanation of the period's events. I am not arguing, for example, that sexual concerns were the "primary reason" for the campaigns of segregation and evangelization. I seek only to demonstrate two much simpler points: that Saint Vincent and his contemporaries chose to express in sexual terms their sense that they were living through a crisis of religious identification, and that their choice is meaningful. The language of sexual danger was invoked both as a symptom of the crisis and as a potent cure for it, simultaneously and somewhat paradoxically fortifying boundaries (through, for example, segregation) and marking them as breached. But even though sex may have been both symptom and cure of the crisis, it was not its cause. The new anxieties were not the result of any increase in the amount of sexual contact between Christians and Jews. Accusations of sexual intercourse involving Christians and Jews were actually much more rare in the period 1391–1416 than they were during the two decades preceding the massacres. Apart from that of Saltell Gracia, the only significant case I know involved a convert who put his wife to work as a prostitute in the Jewish brothel of Zaragoza.[63] An interesting story, but not sufficient stimulus for interfaith sexual panic.

What, then, provoked this sense of sexual crisis? Modern commentators have tended to ignore this question, assuming either that the language of crisis and of sex was a pretext for discriminatory pressure intended to further evangelization or (more frequently), that if there was a real crisis, converso Judaizing was its cause. Saint Vincent and his sponsors certainly hoped and anticipated that their program of sexually justified segregation would result in the conversion of many Jews and Muslims to Christianity.[64] But treating such a powerful aspect of a culture's imagination as merely strategic teaches us little about how it gains its power or functions within society. As for the second and more important point, what is most striking about the generation of 1391 is its relative disinterest in converso orthodoxy and orthopraxis, the very issues that would come to characterize the later period. Certainly, officials did patrol the boundaries of faith. In Morvedre, for example, royal officials entered the Jewish quarter during Passover, 1393, and fined the (few) converts they found participating in "Jewish Easter" with their relatives.[65] But from 1391 to 1410, their chief concern seems to have been the prevention of converso emigration to non-Christian lands where they might return to Judaism.[66] In other words, officials were more concerned with open apostasy than with what we might understand as Judaizing and tended not to equate the two. To the extent that there was concern about Judaizing, it was often projected upon the Jews themselves, not upon the converts. The Jew Jacob Façan, for example, was accused of encouraging his converso son to emigrate to North Africa, and of delivering *matzah* to converts in Sogorb. The converts who allegedly received the *matzah*, on the other hand, were not charged.[67] Christian authorities did worry that converts lingered in their old sensibilities, but voiced those worries relatively rarely.[68] This is in striking contrast with the litany of complaints about Judaizing that would arise in the 1440s, especially when we consider the fact that in the 1390s the thousands of converts who had entered Christianity by force and without catechism almost certainly had little sense of how to practice their new religion.

The perception of crisis was provoked not by the converts' "Jewish" practices but by a much more complex phenomenon: the mass conversion's destabilization of an oppositional process of identification by which generations of Christians had defined themselves theologically and sociologically against Jews and Judaism. It is well known that Christianity had since its earliest days used the Jew to represent the anti-Christian, mapping polarized dualities, such as spiritual-material, allegorical-literal, sighted-blind, redemptive-damning, godly-satanic, good-evil, onto the pairing Christian-Jew.[69] As Rosemary Ruether, one of the most mordant historians of this process, described it: "It was virtually impossible for the Christian preacher or exegete to teach scripturally at all without alluding to the anti-Judaic theses. Christian scriptural teaching and preaching per se is based on a method in which anti-Judaic polemic exists as the left hand of its christological hermeneutic."[70] Ruether was primarily concerned with the first, formative centuries of Pauline Christianity, but her observation holds true for later periods as well. Indeed, in the Middle Ages, the phenomenon is so pervasive as to pass almost unperceived. The polarized pair Christian-Jew provided medieval theologians and their audiences a powerful hermeneutic through which to comprehend and classify their constantly changing world, with phenomena perceived as dangerous mapped onto the negative pole of the opposition. Issues as diverse as the rise of universities, the shift from parchment to paper, the increasing emphasis on the apostolic poverty of clergy, a perceived increase in simony, reliance on lawyers: these "innovations" and many more were characterized as "Judaizing." Perhaps the most fateful (and well-known) of these characterizations were economic. Theologians reacted to what they perceived to be dangerous aspects of the new profit economy by labeling them as materialist and "Jewish." In Sara Lipton's words, "Moneylending . . . is not condemned because it is exclusively or even primarily a 'Jewish' activity; rather, because moneylending is condemned, it becomes in the sign system . . . a 'Jewish' activity."[71]

Again Saint Vincent provides us with examples. He "Judaized" those who sought secular learning, who "for the sake of a little knowledge want to be called Rabbis."[72] He translated Christian spiritual dangers into Jewish idioms in order to sharpen the point for his audiences, as here, on the perils of infrequent confession: "just as the Jews took great care to wash the vessels [taques], so you also take great care to wash the vessels before you drink, but often you take no care to wash the soul and the conscience through confession. And therefore in this way you are similar to the Jews."[73] And he stressed the "Jewishness" of usury and avarice in order simultaneously to reinforce the carnal materialism of the Jews and to criticize Christians who lend at interest as "Judaizers":[74] "Today, nearly everything is avarice, for almost everyone commits usury, which used not to be done except by Jews. But today Christians do it too, as if they were Jews."[75]

Ruether argued that the projection of all carnality onto the Jews made Christianity blind to its own "bodiliness." "Christian spiritualization becomes false consciousness about its own reality, fantasizing its own perfection and unable to cope with its own hypocrisy."[76] As we have just seen, the opposite is also true. The negative pole of "Judaism" provided a powerful diagnostic tool for Christians to identify and condemn "carnal tendencies" within their society and themselves. It thereby threatened to "Judaize" any Christian who, for example, practiced usury, confessed infrequently, or enjoyed secular learning.[77] Nevertheless, it is certainly the case that the projection of carnality upon the Jews facilitated the repression (to echo Ruether's psychologizing language) of Christian anxiety about a great deal of "materialism" and "carnality" in their own beliefs and practices.[78] It is thanks to the power of such projection, for example, that neither Saint Vincent nor his audience were confused when in one breath he derided what he described as the Jews' "carnal" belief that proper piety brings reward in the form of health and good harvests and in the next threatened Christians with famine and plague if they did not enforce segregation.[79] Of course, these projections had little to do with "real Jews" or "real Judaism," and the hermeneutic they were part of did not require the presence of living Jews to function (of this, late medieval England and France are proof). But the existence of living Jews gave foreign flesh to these negations of the Christian and thereby heightened Christian society's sense of its own coherent identity.

In the Iberian Peninsula more than in many other regions of Europe, medieval Christians defined themselves sociologically, as well as theologically, against the Jews. Individually and collectively, they asserted their honor as members of God's privileged people by contrasting themselves to the dishonored Jew.[80] Theologically, as Saint Augustine had put it, the Jews' abjection in comparison with Christians was witness to the truth of the latter's faith.[81] But the performance of this contrast also became fundamental to the representation of Christian political and social privilege. The logic of sexual privilege and sexual boundaries discussed above provides a particularly important example of such sociological differentiation.[82] There were, however, countless others. At a political level, for example, community privilege could be asserted through juxtaposition with Jews. When King Pere the Ceremonious attempted to raise funds for his expedition to Sardinia and Sicily in 1378, the town council of Valencia replied that the imposition of arbitrary taxation "is nothing other than to make a jewry out of each of his municipalities . . . , and we will not give way to such a demand, for we would rather die than be made similar to Jews."[83] And just as the erosion of corporate privilege could threaten to turn municipality into Jewry, so the erosion of honor could Judaize the individual Christian. Saint Vincent himself frequently complained of Christians who believed that failure to avenge an injury "would be a dishonor to me, for they would say of me 'Oh, the madman! Oh, the Jew!'"[84] To withdraw from the economy of violence was tantamount to withdrawing from the fraternity of honorable Christian males. It was, in other words, to become "Jewish."

Christian identity and Christian privilege were defined by insisting on their distance from the Jew (and the Muslim). The performance of that distance could take place in countless venues: in the taking of vengeance or the paying of taxes, in the choice of foods or sexual partners, in law (as in the preferential treatment of Christian witnesses) and in ritual (as in the enclosure and stoning of Jews during Holy Week), to list but a few.[85] It is through the repeated performance of this essential distance that the symbolic capital of Christian honor and privilege was amassed.

The mass conversions of 1391 threatened the performance of Christian identity because they raised the possibility of a world without Jews. Many in the generation after 1391 worked to make that world a reality: a few by urging the slaughter of the unconverted;[86] others, such as the citizens of Barcelona and Valencia, by banning Jews from their cities in perpetuity; still others, like Saint Vincent and his supporters, by mounting a program of evangelization intended to achieve the full conversion of the infidels.[87] These were exhilarating times for a Christian society trained to see the advent of the Messiah in the conversion of the Jews.[88] But they were also unsettling, destabilizing Christian identity in two important ways. First, the messianic "disappearance of the Jews" promised to eliminate the living representatives of a negative pole vital to the coherence of Christian self-understanding. Second, the emergence of the converts as an intermediate class produced a rapid narrowing of the social space that had previously separated Christian from Jew and a consequent perception of the erosion of Christian privilege.

When the converts of 1391 emerged from the baptismal waters, they immediately occupied a good deal of the cultural "no man's land" that had hitherto divided Christian and Jew. On the one hand, they enjoyed all the privileges of the Christian. The convert Francesc de Sant Jordi put it a bit hyperbolically in a letter to the Jew Shaltiel Bonafos: "Those who have emerged from the waters of baptism, from the fountains of salvation, are firmly established upon golden pedestals. They are all personages. In their courts and in their palaces there are ivories and monkeys and peacocks and dwarves; they divested themselves of their soiled attire . . . and donned the garments of salvation."[89] Of course, we know that the vast majority of converts remained poor, without peacock or dwarf. But their status had improved in the sense that even the lowliest could now throw rocks at Jews during Holy Week, have sex with Christian prostitutes, or marry Christian women, and many of them did. In the early sixteenth century, after the forced conversion of many Muslims to Christianity, the town council of Valencia complained that the Christian brothel was so crowded with Moriscos seeking to exercise their new sexual privileges that Old Christians could not get in the door. We have no such official record from the Jewish conversions a century before, but we do have plenty of complaints from individuals such as the Valencian Jaume Roig, who wrote a poem denouncing his former concubine for allowing herself to be penetrated by the "hatless rod" of his converso rival.[90]

Yet at the same time that converts enjoyed the privileges of the Christian, many of them still lived in close social, cultural, and physical proximity to their former coreligionists. The converts often occupied, as they had before their conversion, houses in or near the Jewish quarter. For many years (and certainly throughout the period that concerns us here), their financial affairs remained hopelessly entangled with those of their earlier communities of faith. And of course, they had Jewish relatives with whom they might need to communicate for any number of reasons. Some even had Jewish spouses to whom they remained legally married.[91] Such proximity undercut the radical distinction between the two groups and thereby destabilized the foundations of Christian privilege and identity. It was this destabilization, this narrowing of the gap between Christian and Jew, that Old Christians were reacting to when they complained that it was now impossible to distinguish Christian from Jew. Many converts perceived the problem as well. When a handful of Zaragozan conversos living in a Jewish neighborhood evoked the orders of segregation in the hope of having their much more numerous Jewish neighbors evicted, they were seeking to heighten the distance on which their new privileges depended.[92] The same logic motivated their invasion, together with other Christians, of the Jewish quarter. When, in the course of that invasion, the son of Jerónimo de Santa Fe stabbed a Jew, he was not merely acting out the excessive zeal of a convert. He was performing his claims to Christian honor and privilege in the idioms of his new religion.[93]

Once again, the point was most succinctly articulated by Saint Vincent himself: "For he will never be a good Christian who is neighbor of a Jew." Such "neighborliness," he went on to say, dishonored God and put Christian society at risk of famine, plague, and other manifestations of divine displeasure.[94] Saint Vincent and his sponsors sought to reinstate the necessary distance between Christian and Jew in three ways. One focused on the religiosity of the conversos, seeking to integrate them as fully as possible into "Old Christian" society and thereby distance them from "Jewishness." A second strategy was to sharpen the boundaries between all Christians and Jews through a massive program of segregation. The third possibility was that of eliminating the Jewish antithesis to Christianity altogether, by achieving the conversion of all remaining Jews to Christianity. The least important of these, if the surviving evidence is any guide, is the first. It is not with the conversos but with the segregation of Jews, and with their elimination through evangelization, that the generation after 1391 was most concerned. Both these responses, segregation and evangelization, were nourished by the fertile imagination of a society confronted for the first time by the possibility that the differences by which it defined itself might actually disappear. The evangelizing millenarianism of the age is a vital symptom of this imagination, and its study can teach us a great deal about the crisis of identification that I have been describing. But the period's sexually charged segregationism is equally vital and equally instructive.

These "sexualized" attempts to stabilize Christian identity completely reversed one of the fundamental attributes of the pre-1391 interfaith sexual economy. Instead of narrowing the region of sexual risk in the interest of freeing space for other forms of interaction, they generalized that risk in order to achieve segregation. But in light of the future, there is an important negative observation to be made. The worries of Saint Vincent's generation were sexual, but they had little to do with reproduction and even less to do with race. They do not seem to have feared that mixed intercourse would compromise the transmission of Christian identity or result in offspring that inadequately reproduced Christian values. Christian law codes, for example, clearly stipulated that children born of a mixed union were fully Christian and were to be raised as such.[95] These laws were confidently enforced. In 1401, for example, the Christian Antoni Safàbrega declared on his deathbed that he had once had an adulterous relationship with a Muslim woman named Axa, who had been married to a Muslim named Adambacaix. She was now deceased, but on the strength of Antoni's confession Christian authorities seized Adambacaix's son Mahomet and sent him away to be raised Christian.[96] A similar confidence underlay Saint Vincent's reproach to Christian men for having sex with Muslim prostitutes. Under such circumstances, the father's obligation to baptize the child could not be fulfilled, and the offspring's damned soul would clamor against its Christian progenitor on Judgment Day.[97] These are not the actions of a society anxious about the biological reproduction of religious identity.

In other words, Saint Vincent and his contemporaries drew on the language of sex to widen the separation between Christian and Jew. But they did not invoke it in order to sharpen the line between Old Christian and New, even though a sharp distinction between what quickly came to be called "natural" Christians and converts might have helped to render the converts' proximity to Jews less threatening. The point is worth emphasizing. In the mid-1430s, as we will see in chapters 7 and 8, a number of people began to articulate the view that converts and their descendants were essentially different from (that is, worse than) "natural" Christians and therefore (among many other things) unmarriageable. Such a view represented a profound shift from the anxieties about intercourse that I have been describing up to this point. This new taboo was based not on the fear that sexual proximity to "Jewishness" endangered the present by offending God but that it endangered the future by corrupting the "breeding stock."

These "reproductive strategies" for stabilizing the privileges of Old Christian identity acquired a great deal of influence in the later fifteenth century. It is therefore all the more important to point out that, in the years following the mass conversions of 1391, they were virtually unknown. We can find a few documented examples of attempts at discrimination.[98] One of the more interesting comes from a sermon Saint Vincent preached in 1414, against the great sin of those Christian women who "disdain the Jewess who has become Christian, and refuse to go with her to Church. . . . And there are others who do not wish to give [the converts] their daughters and sons in marriage, because they had once been Jews." He urged these women not only to associate with the converts but also to marry them, for they were "brothers in Christ."[99] These are interesting, but rare, exceptions among a mass of documentation. Such complaints would suddenly become widespread in the 1430s. But they were not characteristic of the long generation that came of age in the aftermath of the massacres of 1391.

These contrasts are significant. We have traced the development of a system of group differentiation based on a logic of displaceable sexual boundaries: a logic capable of representing the myriad distinctions that Christians (as well as Muslims and Jews) held sacred in this multireligious society and of responding with hydraulic power to the slightest change in pressure on these distinctions. Even across half a century of dramatic religious and social change, that sexual logic was sufficient to the task of convincing Christians that their most basic classifications remained vital and stable. From this perspective, the disappearance of that confidence in the middle of the fifteenth century suddenly requires a great deal of explanation. Why, beginning in the 1430s and 1440s, was a sexual logic replaced by a reproductive one? This is a difficult question, not least because the language of reproduction abounds in "false friends" and deceptive continuities with the language of sex. I will leave it for chapters to come. But at least we can now see that the answer will not be found in any easy continuity. The eventual sexual segregation and "re-Judaization" of the conversos through an ideology of reproduction was not the result of a straightforward extrapolation of earlier sexual discriminations and identities, or of some ineluctable process by which societies always recreate their essential "other." It was, rather, the outcome of a highly creative historical transformation. Sexual danger provided the mortar for the new barriers that this society would erect between its most vital categories, as it had for the old. But the substance, location, and meaning of these boundaries were radically different than before. Our conclusion is simple, if not particularly uplifting: the walls with which societies divide themselves need rebuilding by each generation's hands.

[6]

Figures of Thought and Figures of Flesh

Judaism was not only a real religion with real adherents (Jews) and attributes ("Jewishness"). It was also a category within Christian, Muslim, and Jewish thought, as were Christianity and "Christian-ness," Islam and "Muslim-ness." As we have seen over and over again in the previous chapters, the cognitive work people could do with these categories depended as much upon the shape of these concepts in their systems of thought as it did on the "real" attributes of these religions or their adherents. Already in the first chapter we saw, for example, that Christian ideas about Islam did not necessarily correspond to the "real" and that they were not necessarily made more accurate by contact with or knowledge of living adherents to Islam. And in all of the previous chapters we have seen how these concepts could be applied not only to confessed members of a given community but also to those who in no way recognized themselves in the label. Jews might accuse other Jews of behaving like a Christian or a Muslim; Muslims might reproach other Muslims with "Jewishness" or "Christian-ness." And within Christianity, the charge of "Judaizing" was an ancient and powerful one, first invoked by Saint Paul against Saint Peter (in Gal. 2:14), when it already referred to the actions, not of Jews, but of Gentile followers of Jesus.[1]

There were of course living Jews in Christian Spain, but the presence of the "real" in no way diminished the power of "Judaism" as a concept in Christian thought that could be used to make sense of many aspects of the world (such as the administrative politics of chap. 3) that had no obvious relation to "real" Judaism. We need to focus on this power if we want to understand why the mass conversions at the cusp of the fourteenth and fifteenth century had such wide-reaching effects. What kinds of cognitive work did "Judaism" and "Judaizing" do in Christian thought? How did this work depend upon or relate to "real" Judaism or living Jews? And how did the disappearance of so many Jews in the flesh affect the kinds of work that "Jewish" concepts of thought could do? By asking such questions we can approach the immense power that these concepts had in the production of communities and identities. We can become suspicious of too easy an equation between the figural and the real, between the work that concepts like "Jew," "Muslim," and "Christian" do in a society and the living exemplars of those faiths (if there are any) in that society. And finally, we can reinforce our sense that there was nothing simple or inevitable about the ways in which Christians, Jews, and Muslims living in the society we are calling (for the sake of convenience) medieval Spain rebuilt and reproduced themselves after the catastrophic collapse of their co-existence.

* * *

"Who is a Jew?" The question has been asked countless times and by diverse peoples, ranging from ancient prophets to modern politicians. There was even a time, a short century ago, when tourists to certain European cities were exhorted by their guidebooks to wonder of each stranger that passed them in the streets: "Could he be Jewish?" The query was not innocent, the acts of inclusion or exclusion it precipitated rarely without purpose or consequence. Within the medieval lands we now call Spain, its tremendous power was most famously displayed in the discriminations of the Inquisition. Modernity did not attenuate that power. "I determine who is a Jew": the claim, coined by the Austrian politician Karl Lueger in the late1890s and later adopted by Hermann Goering, makes clear the stakes. It makes clear, as well, that the relationship of the question to its object is not simple. As Max Horkheimer and Theodor Adorno put it in their *Dialectic of Enlightenment*, "[To] call someone a Jew amounts to an instigation to work him over until he resembles the image."[2]

"What is Jewish?" This second question, the adjectival form of the first, was also a question of power in the Middle Ages as well as in modernity. Both eras found it easy to imagine their histories in terms of a struggle for emancipation from "Jewishness"; both classified any number of religious, aesthetic, economic, philosophical, and political positions as "Jewish." Even as medievalists, we are, of course, all familiar with the important role that polemical questions about "Jewish literature," "Jewish atheism," "Jewish socialism," "Jewish modernity," and "Jewish materialism" played in producing the twentieth century's turbulent history. We think less often of the complex relationships these modern questions have to the medieval ones we study. And we are often barely conscious of the ways in which the long history of these two questions, "Who is a Jew" and "What is Jewish," has animated the practices of scholars.

A century ago few scholars questioned the possibility of determining the degree of "Jewishness" of a given person or phenomenon, though they may have disagreed on the determination itself. Max Weber, for example, was as convinced of his ability to prove that European capitalism was not the product of "Jewish rationality" as Werner Sombart was convinced of his ability to prove that it was.[3] The murderousness facilitated by this logic eventually gave reason for pause. Some tools for the detection of Jews and Jewishness (racial theories, for example) were felt to be contaminated and cast aside. Others were scanned and rescanned for traces of "essentialism." In the First World (though not in the Second or Third) it became unfashionable to talk of the "Jewishness" of ideas like capitalism or socialism. But "cherchez le juif" remains a scholarly maxim, in the study of Spanish histories as in many others. What relationship is there between the questions we ask as modern students of Spanish (and other) histories and cultures and those that produced the "Jewishness" of Christian converts in the fifteenth century? The following pages will crash those two inquiries together with exaggerated violence. From the wreckage I hope to rescue (if there are any survivors) only a scarred methodological self-consciousness about the questions "Who is a Jew" and "What is Jewish."

Let us return to the mass conversions of 1391 and the decades that followed. As we saw in chapter 4, many saw the conversions themselves as miraculous. "Consider for yourself," the city council of Valencia wrote the king in 1391, "whether these things can have a natural cause. We believe that they cannot, but can only be the work of the Almighty."[4] In chapter 5 we saw that the Almighty did not cease his labors. In the second decade of the fifteenth century tens of thousands more Iberian Jews were baptized, inspired this time by the marvelous eloquence of Saint Vincent Ferrer, as well as by a campaign of total segregation, forced disputation, and compulsory attendance at Christian sermons. Many Christians, including Saint Vincent, saw in these conversions more miraculous proof that messianic times were at hand.[5]

By the end of that century the mood was very different. Many now believed that the converts and their descendants were not Christians but hybrid monsters, motivated only by ambition and a hatred of Christians. The converts' goal was to poison true Christians in order to marry their spouses and stain their "clean lineages" with Jewish traits. These traits were genetic, encoded in blood, the product of natural history: not even God's miraculous grace working through baptism could wash them away.[6] Intermarriage between Old Christian and New was thought to have spread these traits throughout the noble houses of Castile and Aragon. In this sense the converts seemed to pose a far greater danger to Christianity than the Jews had done before them. Because "Jewishness" was now linked to blood, Christian society could fear the spread of "Jewish" tendencies long after the Jews themselves were expelled in 1492. Hence Spanish Christians established the Inquisition to root out Judaizers, and they filled vast archives with apotropaic genealogies. Yet each of these prophylactics only increased the conviction that shades of Judaism lurked in every corner of Spanish society and culture.

What are some of the "Jewish" attributes the converts (sometimes called Marranos, conversos, or "New Christians") are said to have brought into Christian culture? "Inquisitorial fanaticism and recourse to slandering informants . . . , frantic greed and plundering, the concern over purity of blood . . . , the concern with public reputation . . . , the desire of everyone to be a nobleman . . . , somber asceticism . . . , the negative view of the world . . . , disillusionment, and the flight from human values," all of these were the "poisons . . . that seeped into Spanish life, Spanish Christendom, in the increment of forced converts."[7] This list was produced in the mid-twentieth century by Américo Castro, perhaps the most influential advocate for the study of Jewish and Islamic influences on Spanish culture. Not all scholars concurred with every item on it, but even Castro's most famous opponent agreed with him on the more negative: "The Jewish contributed to the forging of the Hispanic not along avenues of light, but by dark and shadowy paths . . . , and it can claim no debt against us, since the inheritance it transmitted to us was to such a degree one of deformations and decadences, and damaged our potential development and our historical credibility."[8]

Many in the generation after Castro dedicated themselves to the uncovering of these hidden currents of Judaism, haunting Spanish archives in search of lineages that might tie a given literary style or innovation to a Jewish ancestry. If, for example, Inquisition records preserve the trace of a suspicion that a given author "Judaized," descended from converts, or even merely dined with people suspected of such faults, then scholars felt justified in positing a "Jewish" or "converso" flavor to his style. Of course, this "Inquisitorial" approach to cultural production has always had its critics, and the voices of these critics have become louder over the past decades. Such criticisms, however, do not quite break free of the "essentializations" they decry, even as they assign to them an alternative history or a different name.[9] As is the case with many "Jewish questions," the difficulty stems from the fact that in medieval Spain (as in our own age) "Judaism" was not only a religion practiced by living adherents but also a basic epistemological and ontological category in the thought of non-Jews. We therefore need to focus upon the bonds between these "Jewish" figures of thought and figures of flesh, if we wish to understand the tensely productive relationship between the two.

Empirically, these two figures are inseparable: the ways in which our sources and their authors represent the "Jewishness" of their world cannot be emancipated from the concepts through which they (or we) think about that world.[10] Within a laboratory setting, however, we can cultivate an analytical distinction, albeit one that is highly artificial. My experiment requires two stages. The first stresses with exaggerated clarity the importance of the Jew as a figure of thought rather than flesh in the creation of Christian literary culture in late medieval Castile. The goal of this exaggeration is not polemical but therapeutic: an Aristotelian corrective to ingrained habits by inclination toward their contraries. The second stage of my experiment will aim more for the mean: it is a brief exploration of how the interpenetration of "Jewish thought" and "Jewish flesh" produced a politics of "purity of blood" that bound "Jewish" culture ever more tightly to "Jewish" genealogy. The end product of my analysis will not be a new certainty about what or who is "Jewish" in medieval, modern, or postmodern cultures. It will rather be a heightened sense of why these questions are so difficult to answer, and so dangerous to ask.

For the first stage of the experiment we could ask for no better subject than the *Cancionero de Baena*, a work sometimes called the "first critical anthology" of Castilian poetry and often interrogated for Jewish origins. This collection of poetry, compiled by Juan Alfonso de Baena, contains some six hundred poems composed in the courts of four Castilian kings, ranging from the late fourteenth century to roughly 1430, when it was presented to King Juan II. The anthology is critical, in the sense that each poem is preceded by a short editorial introduction noting merits and demerits, and the whole is prefaced with a meditation on the function of poetry and the nature of the poet's art.[11]

Baena's collection dates to a period well before Spain's genealogical treasuries were so enriched by the establishment of the Inquisition, but this has not slowed the search for "Jews" in its pages. In the absence of trials and autos-da-fé, the lineages of its poets have been exhumed from the rich loam of the poems themselves. The task is seemingly easy, for Juan Alfonso clearly agreed with Aristotle on the importance of insult and invective as a function of poetry.[12] The *Cancionero*'s poets, nearly all Christian, are constantly defaming one another, and the accusation of Jewishness is prominent among the charges they hurl. Indeed the collection includes many poems that insult Juan Alfonso himself. His birthplace of Baena is impugned in one poem as a land where "much good eggplant" is grown; another mocks him for having "eyes of eggplant," yet another of eating "adefyna," these being dishes associated with Jews. Other poets refer to his "bath in the water of holy baptism" or to his sexual encounters with Jews both male and female (the Mariscal Íñigo de Astuñiga, for example, states that he is stuffed full of Jewish sperm). Even Juan Alfonso's dedication of the anthology to the royal family has been read as a marker. Did he sign himself "el jndino Johan Alfon[so] de Baena" or "el judino Johan Alfon[so] de Baena"? The "unworthy" Johan Alfonso or the "Jew" Johan Alfonso? The grapheme in the manuscript can be read either way, as *n* or as *u*, and generations of critics opted for the second reading, though current philology agrees with the first.[13]

Juan Alfonso and his colleagues in the *Cancionero* accused each other of Jewish ancestry, of having too small a foreskin or too big a nose, of heterosexual and homosexual intercourse with Jews. They also accused each other of sexual intercourse with Muslims and prostitutes, of cowardice, ignorance, greed, and mendacity, of letting themselves be sodomized by shepherds and Muslim slaves, and even of renouncing their Christianity in favor of Islam. Critics often fasten, however, upon claims of Jewishness. If a poet is attacked as Judaizing, then he must be a converso. And if the attacker himself betrays knowledge of Judaism (for example, by drawing on Hebrew vocabulary, such as *meshumad* for apostate), then he, too, may be presumed to have a Jewish past. The result of such logic was the conviction that, as one critic put it already in 1871, the *Cancionero* is full of "half-converted Jews."[14] From there it was but a short step to find in their poetry all the ideas that "Judaism" encodes in the critical discourses of modernity: "Averroism," "irony," "hybridity," "rationalism," "skepticism."[15]

There is, in short, a long tradition of reading the *Cancionero* after the fashion of Inquisitors. In order to rescue poetry from genealogy, I will take a heuristically exaggerated step away from lineage and argue that converso Judaism in Baena's *Cancionero* needs to be treated as a literary product, not as the result of insincere conversion or clandestine Judaism. It is not about prosopography but about poetics, and we cannot understand why the accusation of Judaizing appeared so precociously in poetry, or what poets meant by it, unless we take seriously the problems of poetic language they confronted.

This is true at a number of levels of analysis. At a formal one, it is well known that the *Cancionero* poets drew on earlier genres of competitive poetic defamation such as the Provençal *tenso* and the Galician-Portuguese *cantiga d'escarnho e de mal dizer*.[16] In this earlier poetry of insult, religious identity could be portrayed as ambiguous, as in the late thirteenth-century Galician verses maligning the knight Joan Fernández. "Joan Fernandes, how badly you were cut" ("que mal vos talharon"), one poem mocks, simultaneously criticizing the cut of his clothes and of his penis, suggesting that he is circumcised. Another charges that he is committing the crime of interfaith intercourse whenever he lies with his (Christian) wife: "Joan Fernández, a Muslim is screwing your wife, at the same time that you are screwing her" ("fode-a tal como a fodedes vós").[17] Fifteenth-century poets were engaged in a similar practice. Like their predecessors, they wrote entire poems punning items of clothing with foreskins, though the meaning of allusion was now a different one.[18] The vanishing power of Muslim Granada and the increasing importance of converts from Judaism in Christian Spain had combined to make "Judaism," not "Islam," the preferred language of their mockery, but continuity of genre certainly contributed to the precocity and enthusiasm with which these poets took up the derogatory theme of Jewishness.

At a more materialistic level of literary analysis, we can also see how the theme of Jewishness became useful within the shifting context of poetic production. The *Cancionero de Baena* has fruitfully been read as a staging ground for the competition between three classes of poet: the "full time professionals" or "hired pens," like Alfonso Álvarez de Villasandino (d. ca. 1420), whose verses scramble for patronage and who offer their employers marketable words ("palabras de buen mercado") to aim against their enemies; the *letrados*, members of an expanding class of scribes, bureaucrats, and other non-nobles engaged in the administrative business of the court (Juan Alfonso de Baena was himself of this class), for whom poetizing is something of an alternative career; and the aristocrat, whose poetics presents itself both as a morally edifying practice in the education of the nobility and as an index of that nobility's achievement.[19] To Julian Weiss's elegant exposition of this extraordinarily complex contest I would only add the obvious: that the traditional language of "Jewish" materialism provided a weapon with which to deprecate "careerist" poets. The (admittedly later) attack by the noble Gómez Manrique against Juan Poeta provides a nice example: "You are a novice poet, / which is to say a convert. / I am anciently professed, / an hidalgo from the beginning /. . . / And because your rhymes are store bought, / as I say, . . . / they can do no harm to mine, / for yours are gross, and cold, / and of base metal."[20]

For our purposes, however, the most productive explanation for the early rise and importance of "Jewishness" in Baena's *Cancionero* has to do with even more fundamental questions about the nature of language and of poetry, questions as old as criticism itself. Juan Alfonso's project should be seen as an important and uncharted tributary of a debate which flows mightily through the history of aesthetics, a debate over the nature of poetic mimesis. What is the status of poetry within a system of thought that distinguishes hierarchically between the life of the body and that of the soul, between the confusion of carnal perception and the clarity of spiritual cognition? For Plato and Aristotle, poetry was above all a mimetic genre: its first principle, as Aristotle puts it in the *Poetics* (1447a), is the imitation of the forms of nature, and its appeal is to the bodily senses. This is why Socrates and Phaedrus agree in their dialogue that poets are incapable of perceiving the higher reaches of truth (*Phaedrus* 247C).[21] And it is why Socrates, in his hierarchy of reincarnations, assigns to the poet a soul just above that of the lowly farmer, whose job it is to extract bodily nourishment from the earth (248E). It is this very materialism that makes poetry politically and morally dangerous. As Socrates puts it at the end of his discussion of poetry in the *Republic* (595A–608B): "At all events we are well aware that poetry being such as we have described is not to be regarded seriously as attaining to the truth; and he who listens to her, fearing for the safety of the city which is within him, should be on his guard against her seductions and make our words his law."

Of course, the problem was not simply a poetic one. It afflicted all language, insofar as the same words through which philosophers mounted to incorporeal truth also pointed literally to material things in the world. Hellenistic philosophers, Jewish as well as gentile, developed an anthropomorphic reading practice as one way of addressing the problem. Word and meaning were arrayed against each other in a hierarchy explicitly parallel to that of flesh and spirit. The task of a reader was to penetrate beyond the outer body (Greek *soma*) or literal meaning of a text and into its inner or spiritual meaning. The Hellenistic Jew Philo, for example, stressed the need to read scripture for "the hidden meaning that appeals to the few who study soul characteristics rather than bodily forms" (*On Abraham* 147).[22]

At much the same time that Philo was writing in Alexandria, the first Christians were recasting these problems of language into their own distinctive terms. Many have studied this process.[23] Without repeating the insights of these scholars, I can extend their import by suggesting that the apostle Paul and his successors reconceived the challenges of language in terms of the passage from Judaism to Christianity. They did so, at least in part, because of the challenges posed by questions of conversion in their own day.

As is well known, many among the first generations of Christians were Jews, their flesh and their habits marked by Judaism and Jewish law. It is not surprising, therefore, that questions quickly arose about the Christian's proper relationship to Jewish law. The Acts of the Apostles suggest that, in the case of those who came to Christ from Judaism, early answers to these questions were relatively flexible. So far as we know, all the disciples, even Paul, continued at times to observe Jewish ritual law as followers of Jesus's gospel. Much more conflictual were questions involving the increasingly numerous non-Jewish proselytes. Should gentile converts observe the laws of Judaism? We know that there were communities of gentile converts who advocated at least a minimum of ritual observance (for example, circumcision). Paul saw such views as a horrifying symptom of literalism and incomplete conversion. It was in part to counter them that he developed the tension so predominant in his writings (particularly Galatians and Romans) between outer shell and inner meaning, letter and spirit, literal and allegorical. To give but one example from Romans 2:25: "Being a Jew is not only having the outward appearance of a Jew, and circumcision is not only a visible physical operation. The real Jew is one who is inwardly a Jew, and real circumcision is in the heart, a thing not of the letter but of the spirit." When Christians circumcised themselves, they placed significance in the Jewish outer "letter of the law" rather than in its inner spiritual significance and thereby revealed themselves as "severed from Christ" by the "desires of the flesh" (Gal. 5:4, 16–18; cf. Rom. 8:6–8).

The style of reading through which Paul achieved this translation from promise in the flesh to promise in the spirit was not a novel one.[24] Like Philo and many other Hellenistic exegetes, he mapped word and meaning onto the hierarchy of flesh and spirit.[25] Paul's conclusions, however, could be surprising, as when he suggested that once the inner meaning was understood, the literal meaning could be dispensed with: "For when we were still in the flesh, our sinful passions, stirred up by the law, were at work in our members to bear fruit for death. But now we are fully freed from the law, dead to that in which we lay captive. We can thus serve in the new being of the Spirit and not the old one of the letter" (Rom. 7:5–6). Here (though not everywhere in Paul's writings) it is not just the law that is left behind by the spiritual believer and reader but also the companions that Paul associates with it: the letter, and even flesh itself.

In his attempts to dissuade gentile converts from Mosaic practice, Paul sometimes drew sharp distinctions between Judaism and Christianity. He aligned the former with captivity, law, letter, and flesh; the latter with freedom, grace, inner meaning, and spirit; and he coined a new verb, "to Judaize" (Gal. 2:14, *Judaizare*), in order to characterize the dangerous slippage that could occur between them. For Paul this danger applied primarily to gentile converts, but it quickly shifted its focus to converts from Judaism. Already for the next generations of Christians, those who produced the Gospels, it was Jewish and not gentile converts (and particularly Pharisees like Paul himself) who symbolized the difficulties of true conversion. As in Paul, the problem of conversion manifested itself as a reading disability. Thus Jesus complains in the Sermon on the Mount that even those Jews and Pharisees sympathetic to him incessantly confuse outer appearance with inner truth. They are like tombs (Greek *sema*, punning with *soma*, body), attractive on the outside, repulsive within (Matt. 23:25–32). There is a complex historical movement from the frustrations expressed by the authors of Mark, Matthew, Luke, and John (writing roughly in the period from 70–100 CE)[26] over the pace and nature of Jewish conversion to later opinions like that of Gregory of Nicaea in the ninth century that "no Jew has yet lifted the veil [from his eyes], insofar as not one among them has converted legitimately."[27] That movement cannot concern us here. We need only note a point so obvious that it has become invisible: the passage between Judaism and Christianity came to serve very early as an analogy for other passages, especially those between letter and spirit, body and soul. It was this analogical function that made questions surrounding conversion so productive in all sorts of arguments, like those about the nature of language, which had nothing to do with living converts from Judaism.

A particularly important example was the argument over the relative weight of literal versus spiritual or nonliteral (that is, metaphorical, allegorical, figurative, etc.) readings of the Bible. Many early Christian exegetes like Origen, Chrysostom, and Jerome believed that conversion from Judaism to Christianity required a complete transformation of the convert. Any continuity of practice was dangerous insofar as it constituted Judaizing. But if this was true, then how should Christians read the many New Testament passages attesting to ongoing observance of Judaism by the apostles? Following Origen (ca. 185–252/3), many theologians argued that such biblical passages could not be understood literally but should only be read as allegories. Indeed these passages became very important in debates over biblical hermeneutics precisely because they served allegorists like Origen as the clearest evidence that some parts of the New Testament (and many parts of the Old) were literally untrue. Such a position struck other theologians as heretical, insofar as it stressed spirit excessively over flesh and came perilously close to the critical style of Gnostic exegetes.[28] It is for this reason that Augustine focused on the question when he argued against Jerome that every word of the Bible has a literal truth in addition to a figurative one. According to Augustine, the apostles and their generation of converts from Judaism to Christianity had "retained the ceremonies which by the law they had learned from their fathers." Jerome responded violently. Augustine was "reintroducing within the Church the pestilential heresy" of the Ebionites and other Judaizing sects. Such opinions, Jerome warned, would destroy the Church: "If . . . it shall be declared lawful for [the Jews] to continue in the Churches of Christ what they have been accustomed to practice in the Synagogues of Satan, I will tell you my opinion in the matter: they will not become Christian, but will make us Jews" (*Epistolae* 75.4.13).

Of course, Augustine was not arguing that the Law was binding on the apostolic or any other generation of converts from Judaism. What he did say, most clearly in the treatise *Against Faustus the Manichee* of 398 as well as in his correspondence with Jerome, was that such observance was not prohibited to the apostolic generation, that it was understandable as the product of habit and custom, and that the apostles had favored it as a theologically advisable approach toward the Torah, "lest by compulsory abandonment it should seem to be condemned rather than closed" (*Contra Faustum* 19.17). His was a thoroughly historical response to dualist readings of these biblical passages about apostolic Judaism, one that articulated the legitimacy of Law and Judaism for converts in generational terms. Augustine developed a similar "conversionary" method of thinking, not only about specific passages like these but also about the nature of language itself. As he put it in

De doctrina Christiana (3.5.9): "The ambiguities of metaphorical words . . . demand extraordinary care and diligence. What the Apostle says pertains to this problem. 'For the letter killeth, but the spirit quickeneth.' That is, when that which is said figuratively is taken as though it were literal, it is understood carnally. Nothing can more appropriately be called the death of the soul than that condition in which the thing that distinguishes man from beasts, which is the understanding, is subjected to the flesh in pursuit of the letter." To read carnally, "to be unable to lift the eye of the mind above what is corporeal and created," was "a miserable slavery of the soul." This was in fact, as Augustine went on to say, the slavery of the Jews. But no Christian, at least none who utilized language, was immune to the potential slavery of reading carnally, with all its attendant risks of hermeneutic "Judaization."

This compressed outline of patristic thought should make plausible a basic point. Thinking about conversion from Judaism was for Christians an important way to think about the incompleteness of their own linguistic conversion from letter to spirit, an incompleteness that was as dangerous as it was unavoidable in this pre-apocalyptic world of flesh. The danger assailed all language, but because of poetry's heightened association with sensual mimesis, it confronted Christian poetry in concentrated form. The view of nonbiblical poetry as lie or dangerous fiction was voiced by theologians across the Middle Ages, from Augustine to Thomas Aquinas.[29] Saints fanned the fear of secular poetry in the Spain of Juan Alfonso de Baena as well: Vincent Ferrer and Alonso de Cartagena (the converso bishop of Burgos) both preached about its dangers.[30] Of course, poetic fictions also had their defenders: Lactantius, Macrobius, and Isidore in late antiquity;[31] Bernard Sylvester and the Neoplatonists in the twelfth century;[32] Dante's defense of the spiritual truth-value of poetry (sometimes known as "theological poetics") at the cusp of the thirteenth and fourteenth;[33] Petrarch's and Boccaccio's rebuttal of the theologians at the end of the Middle Ages.[34] It is within the context of this long struggle over the ontological status of poetry that we should read Baena's *Cancionero* and the poems it contains.[35]

Like Dante, Baena and some of his colleagues claimed that secular poetry provided access to spiritual truth. They did so through a theory of "poetic grace" articulated in the prologue to the *Cancionero* as well as in its poetry. Two lines of Latin verse scrawled at the top of the first manuscript folio capture the general theme: "Unicuique gratia est data / secundum Paulum relata" ("To each one grace is given / according to Saint Paul," a paraphrase of Eph. 4.7).[36] This "infused grace of God" was the prerequisite for and the inspiration of good poetry, and therefore good poetry could potentially provide knowledge of divine grace. These poets explored this potential for a "theological poetics" through various competitive exchanges. Theologians like the Friar Pedro de Colunga or the Bachelor of Salamanca, for example, challenged lay poets like Alfonso Álvarez de Villasandino (who often boasted of his lack of learning and elevated inspired poetry above "book knowledge") to answer obscure questions of biblical exegesis.[37] Lay poets, on the other hand, might elevate their inspired simplicity above the sophisticated learning of the theologian, as Ferrán Manuel de Lando did in his challenge to Friar Lope del Monte: "For God chose to reveal his secrets / to simple innocents, heavy and rude, / while he left the learned nude, / and hid from them his glory, / as Our Savior makes clear / in the subtle texts of His Gospel story."[38]

Ferrán Manuel's charge provides a good example of the strategic deployment of accusations of Judaism within these debates insofar as it implicitly aligns the theologian with the negative example of the seemingly learned, but actually blind, rabbis and Pharisees in the Gospels. Friar Lope responds in kind. Christians are not obliged to study poetry, for there are no divine secrets to be found in it. Indeed the poet is associated with those who have never achieved knowledge of divine deeds: "the gentile, the Jew, and the tax collector." In his final riposte Friar Lope turns Lando's "pharisaization" of theologians (that is, his accusation that those who seem clothed in learning are in reality naked and blind) on its head: "God makes bears with furry skins, / and makes the ignorant wise. / But few are the wise and truly learned, / who have hairy chests and thighs." Whatever the ontological uncertainties in this world, Lope implies, one thing is clear: in theological matters his rival Lando, a mere poet, belongs not only with pagans and Jews but with the ignorant beasts.[39]

Beyond such questions of the spiritual truth-value of poetry, the usefulness of accusation of Judaizing extended more generally to the development of a critical poetics itself. The aggrieved sense that bad poetry was often mistaken for good, and good poetry maligned as bad, could be powerfully expressed in terms of a "pharisaic poetics." Villasandino did so, for example, when he characterized graceless "metrificadores" as tax collectors, "arrendadores," and mockingly described the king rewarding them with "ropas con señales (clothes with badges)."[40] This sense of an ontological crisis of poetry approaches the apocalyptic in Villasandino's extended attack on the bad poetic form of Fernán Manuel de Lando: "According to the signs it seems that this world, / base and deceptive, is about to perish / . . . / for truth no longer has any power, / and lies are everywhere pushed up to honor."[41] Poetically as in so many other ways, it seemed that Castile was slouching toward the millennium.

The poets did not give language up for lost. Instead they developed a critical framework within which to argue about its relative merits. The prologue to Juan Alfonso de Baena's *Cancionero* is in this sense an explicit poetic manifesto. I have already mentioned the "infused grace of God" as the primary prerequisite for good poetry. Insofar as Baena's colleagues understood the poet's state of grace as legible in the poetry itself, the poem became a literary marker of its author's place on the continuum between letter and spirit, with the bad poet, the misuser of language, understood as (among other things) a "Jew." Beyond divine grace there were, of course, other prerequisites for poetry: knowledge of rules of meter and form; subtle inventiveness; exquisite discretion and judgment; broad reading; knowledge of all languages; familiarity with court life; nobility, "fydalguía," and courtesy; and "always seeming" to be ("siempre se finja") a good lover, loving whom one should, as one should, where one should. The pages of Juan Alfonso's *Cancionero* were the lists in which the mettle of each poet and each poem were put to the test of this complex standard.

Juan Alfonso himself put this wittily in his poetic challenge to the poet Ferrán Manuel de Lando: "Ferrand Manuel, for the public display / of your marvelous skill / in this great court of the King of Castile / someone must give you a sting." It is out of provocation, according to Baena, that good poetry is born. But the substance of the provocation itself should not be taken too much to heart: "Ferrand Manuel, since to each / is given [poetic] grace doubled or simple, / don't let your face turn yellow / because my tongue splashes or stains you." Insult is only a picador's prod, meant to stimulate the revelation of a poet's virtues.[42] In this case Ferrán responds with accusations, not about Baena's insufficient "Christianity," but about his deficiencies as a lover. Ferrán will, he claims, soften the womb of Baena's girlfriend. The exchange escalates along these lines, ending with Baena's (no. 363) infamous assertion that Ferrán's asshole is full of a shepherd's sperm. In the face of this response, reports the *Cancionero*, Ferrán abandoned the field to Baena.[43]

Here the idiom of poetic criticism is primarily sexual. In the contest that follows, between Baena and Villasandino, the idioms are more diverse. Baena opens by challenging this "rotten old man, whose ribs are made of phlegm" to a contest of poetry. I quote Villasandino's response in full:

Sir, this vile ass with a branded face
twisted and stuffed with wine and garlic
I consider on account of his foolish frenzy
and crazed works a fine troubadour.
This swells the head of the dirty Jew-pig,
he presumes to pick fights with his betters.
Whoever heeds the words of this grackle
must himself be blacker than a sea-faring crow.

He who is unworthy and incapable
of this knowledge and art that we pursue:
his arguments are not worth a straw
nor a lousy cucumber, not even a gherkin.[44]

Far from being the poet he pretends and presumes ("enfinge") to be, Baena is a donkey whose "villainy" is marked on his face and in his diet of wine and garlic. He is a "suzio cohino," a dirty Jew-pig (the word plays with the proximity between Cohen and *cochino*), with the voice of a cormorant, not a poet. He knows, in short, nothing of "this science [of poetry]," and his words are worthless.

"Cohino" here is redolent with poetic and ontological significance, but it is no more genealogical than any of the other assertions made in the course of this contest. Baena will respond by calling Villasandino (among other things) "swine sputum," a drunk, an apostate gambler ("tahur renegado"); Villasandino by calling Baena a bastard ("forniçino") and a pig ("tuerto chazino, gruniente cochino"). These charges drew their meaning and usefulness, not from the biography of their target, but from the rules of the poetic agon in which they were deployed, in which provocation stimulated vulgar poetry and that poetry revealed "state of grace" of the competing poets.

It is this very vulgarity that made it difficult for early generations of modern critics to see much "grace" in the poetry.[45] That vulgarity was itself, however, the critical by-product of our poets' theology, a way of representing the lack in their rivals of any one of their multiple prerequisites for poetry. Judaism, poetic incompetence, ignorance, rudeness, sexual deviance, even animality were the negative poles of poetic virtues: divine grace, good meter and form, learning, courtesy, love, etcetera. Each of these virtues was, as the patristic examples suggested, closely related to its companions and expressible almost interchangeably in their terms. The same is true of their attendant vices. The overlapping of these variables made possible a space of play in which claims to poetic or theological "çiençia" could be both made and criticized in a language of extreme carnality (indeed, from the poets' point of view, the greater the contrast the greater the poem).[46]

Judaism was, as I hope the patristic examples made clear, a key metaphor in this system of thought, a governing insult that carried with it a host of theological, linguistic, and physical implications. The same could be said of other idioms of opprobrium in the *Cancionero*, such as the frequent charges of homosexuality and sodomy, meant to imply of a poet that, as Villasandino put it, "you never served love, / nor were in its company."[47] Indeed these idioms were often combined. To the charge just cited, Alfonso Álvarez added that the target of his poem was an apostate Jew with a prominent nose, a *meshumad*. The Franciscan monk and theologian Diego de Valencia strove for the same derisive combination when he wrote a poem whose rhyme scheme was made up almost entirely of Hebrew words, accusing Juan de Espanha of having no testicles. Those critics who have focused on the poem's Hebrew vocabulary in order to argue that Fray Diego was a converso have missed the point.[48] In the world of Baena's *Cancionero* the discourse of Judaism, like that of sexuality or animality, was as much a language of literary criticism as that of meter and form. As such it was separable from the genealogy and religious orthodoxy of its object. It was even possible for a real Jew to possess the qualities of a poet, as when the same Friar Diego praised the Jew Symuel Dios-Auda for his charity, his courtesy, and his "fydalguía": "For your word never changes or wavers /. . . / these are the markers of a noble man / to say things and do them without any doubt."[49]

In short, we could interpret the critical accusation of Judaism developed by the poets of Baena's circle in the years following the mass conversions as being about language, not lineage. Some of these poets may in fact have been converts, or descended from converts, but it is not at all clear that their "Jewishness" in poetry had anything to do with their "Jewishness" in life. Nor was theirs a "Jewish poetics," except in the sense that it was the product of a Christian theological linguistics that had long understood certain aspects of language (ranging from letter and literalism to mimesis and hypocrisy) in terms of Judaism and Judaizing. We should not doubt that the social and political consequences of the mass conversions lent new urgency and power to this linguistics. But neither should we ignore the extent to which these poets built both their "Jewishness" and their literary criticism out of the terms of Christian aesthetics, epistemology, and ontology.

Many readers, particularly historians of my generation who have been raised from infancy to be suspicious of the high history of ideas, will object that the previous pages pay too much attention to the conceptual tools of Christian linguistics and theology and too little to the social transformations wrought by the mass conversions. Am I suggesting, they will ask, that the fate of the conversos was governed by ancient and unchanging laws of Christian hermeneutics? Nothing could be further from my intent. The migration of thousands of Jews into Christianity destabilized many of the social and religious distinctions through which both groups distinguished themselves from the other. These "identity crises" catalyzed on both sides the reconstruction of distinctions and discriminations in terms that proclaimed their continuity with the old but were also decidedly different. Briefly put, the transformation of the convert from Christian back into "Jew" required a century of vast sociological and theological change. Indeed chapters 5, 7, and 8 of this book are concerned with less "literary" aspects of those transformations.

We are, however, sometimes too eager to forget that these changes were simultaneously achieved and apprehended through available categories or forms of thought. These forms were not shattered by the convulsions of 1391 and after. Rather, they were put to new kinds of work, filled with (and giving meaningful shape to) new kinds of content. If I have stressed excessively the power of certain forms (like that of "Jew" as a container for specific hermeneutic and ontological positions), it is because the work they did in building the "Jewishness" of late medieval Spain has been generally ignored in favor of more genealogical, sociological, and political causalities. I do not mean to imply, however, that these "figures" of thought were independent or determinative of the social world in which they were deployed. Quite the contrary, the two are so intertwined as to be empirically inseparable. The emergence of thousands of real converts in 1391, for example, breathed fresh energy into "Judaism" as a form for linguistic critique (hence its importance for Baena's generation of poets, and not earlier ones). At the same time, the new uses of that form, in poetry and elsewhere, created new types of "Jews," refigured the potential meanings of both "Jew" and "Christian," and thereby transformed the uses to which the linguistic figure of "Jew" could be put.

I can demonstrate this by moving a few years forward and to a form of competition other than verse, for poets were not the only ones to put the language of Judaizing to serious work in the generations following the mass conversions. The royal courts of Castile and Aragon were settings of concentrated factionalism and struggles for power. It is well known that all parties in these struggles sought to blacken their rivals (and not only those descended from converts) as "Jewish" and therefore politically corrupt.[50] In the 1430s and 1440s, as factionalism matured into civil war, this "Judaism" became increasingly linked to genealogy. Alfonso Martínez de Toledo provides a nice example of this logic in his *Arcipreste de Talavera o Corbacho*, written circa 1438. "Thus you will see every day in the places where you live, that the good man of good race (*raça*) always returns to his origins, whereas the miserable man, of bad race or lineage, no matter how powerful or how rich, will always return to the villainy from which he descends. . . . That is why when such men or women have power they do not use it as they should."[51]

Literature here paralleled legislation. Within the increasingly polarized political context of the 1430s, prominent factions in the town councils of Seville, Lleida, Barcelona, Calatayud, and other places attempted to move against their competitors by arguing that those who were converts or descended from converts, that is, those who were not "Christians by nature," should be barred from holding any public office. This sharpening of the somatic limits to conversion was sharply opposed by the monarchy, and it was condemned both by the council of Basel in 1434 and by Pope Eugenius IV in 1437. As the council put it, "Since regeneration of the spirit is much more important than birth in the flesh . . . , [the converts] enjoy the privileges, liberties and immunities of those cities and towns where they were regenerated through sacred baptism to the same extent as the natives and other Christians do." But these genealogical arguments became broadly useful during the civil wars against King Juan II of Castile and his minister Álvaro de Luna, whose attempts to strengthen the monarchy aroused fierce opposition. It was during those wars, and most explicitly during the rebellion of 1449, that the rebel government of the city of Toledo issued the first "statute of purity of blood." Jewish hatred of Christianity and of Christians ran indelibly in the veins of descendants of converts, the rebels argued, and through their actions it was Judaizing society. Once these descendants were barred from ever holding office or exercising power over Christians, the corruption would end and Christian society would be purified.[52]

These political arguments certainly transformed the potential meanings of "Jew," "convert," and "Christian," as we shall see. But neither the genealogical truth claims of these assertions nor the obvious sociopolitical consequences of the statutes they spawned bring us any closer to a world of "real Jews" and "real Jewishness." Scholars have devoted themselves to family trees and prosopographies, counting conversos in public office in order to uncover genealogical and sociopolitical realities underlying Old Christian claims about the dangers of Jewish government.[53] Such research is to my mind one-sided. There were, of course, converso politicians, just as there were converso poets, but their existence does not suffice to explain the rise of "Judaizing" as a language of political critique. The roots of this language lie not only in sociology but also in the same dialectical tension that I discussed so briefly earlier: the tension in Christian thought between the visible, carnal, and literal, on the one hand, and the invisible, spiritual, and nonliteral, on the other. Jews and Judaism could play as crucial a role in the politics generated by this dialectic as they did in the semiotics. This should not be surprising, given that Hellenistic political thought was fashioned out of the same distinctions of body and soul as Hellenistic hermeneutics.

Aristotle articulated a key distinction between the corporeal politics of bare life and the higher politics of the good: "Men form states to secure a bare subsistence; but the ultimate object of the state is the good life."[54] The "natural" relationship of soul to body as ruler to subject provided a powerful political analogy: "Although in bad or corrupted natures the body will often appear to rule over the soul, because they are in an evil and unnatural condition . . . , it is clear that the rule of the soul over the body . . . is natural and expedient" (*Politics* 1254b). For Aristotle and the tradition that followed him, the chief function of the sovereign was to guide politics away from the demands of body and bare life toward those of the immortal soul. As Aristotle put it in the *Nicomachean Ethics*: "We must not follow those who advise us, being men, to think of human things, and being mortal, of mortal things, but must, so far as we can, make ourselves immortal" (1177b). He realized, of course, that many rulers did indeed reverse these priorities, placing worldly gain ahead of a common and immaterial good, and he represented this reversal not as sovereignty but as its most basic distortion, tyranny. Tyranny, in other words, consisted of a perverted preference for self-interest over the commonwealth, for the mortal over the immortal, for flesh over spirit.[55]

These distinctions could be translated into Christian terms, and the relationship in early Christianity between the politics of flesh and the politics of spirit proved every bit as dialectically tense as that between carnal and spiritual hermeneutics. The energy released by this tension, like its hermeneutic analogue, had a tendency to seek ground in the Jew. We can see how great the potential force of this tension was by focusing on the important early Christian debate about the relationship of secular to divine power. There were many apostolic positions available in this debate. Paul, in Romans 13:1–6, had refused to distinguish between the two, treating secular magistrates as God's appointees and agents: "Let every soul be subject to the governing authorities. . . ."[56] The author of Matthew 22:21 drew a clearer distinction: "Render unto Caesar the things that are Caesar's, but unto God the things which are God's." The Gospel of John went further and imagined sharp conflict between the power of the Word and the "prince of this world," which would be resolved only with the defeat and disappearance of the latter (12:31, 14:30, 15:18). Early Christian exegetes developed all of these positions and many others.[57] At one extreme were those who emphasized a futuristic eschatology like that articulated in the Revelation of John. They understood the relationship between Christian Church and pagan Roman Empire as analogous to the struggle between Christ and Satan and tended toward antithesis rather than dialectic: Caesar became Antichrist, empire became Babylon (Rev. 18:1–20, 1 Pet. 5:13). At the other extreme were those who emphasized the "realized" triumph of Christ and understood the relationship in terms of incarnational dialectics, with the empire as fleshy body and the Church as inner spirit.[58] All, however, had a tendency to think of the princes and principalities of this world in carnal terms. And all mapped their distinctions onto the same dualities of flesh and spirit, Old Dispensation and New, which had pointed hermeneutics so fatefully toward the Jew.

Origen, for example, adapted the same distinctions that informed his exegesis to the question of politics, dividing mankind into three classes: the hylics (from *hylē*, matter), or materialists, who were pagans and Jews; the psychics (from *psychē*, soul), who corresponded to the average Christian; and the pneumatics (from *pneuma*, spirit), who included only the most spiritual and ascetic of Christians. Since Caesar's claims were only on the body, only those who were of the body had to render unto him: Jews, pagans, and average Christians, but not pneumatics, not those who dwelt truly in the Spirit. Hence Peter and John had nothing to render unto Caesar ("Gold and silver have I none," Acts 3:6), for they had no business in the world.[59]

It has been justly said of Origen that "in his politics the 'state' is related to the Church, very much as in his exegesis the letter is related to the spirit." The same general point could be made of many a theologian, whether Latin or Greek, that came after him. One seldom noted consequence of this relation is the possibility of characterizing political error (that is, an improper balance between secular and spiritual) in the same terms used to assess hermeneutical error: that is, in terms of Judaism and Judaizing. Origen himself occasionally did so.[60] But the most famous example of such slippage in late antiquity, and the most revealing, comes from more than a century later, when the emperors' conversion to Christianity had sharpened the stakes involved in questions about the relationship between princely and episcopal power. I refer, of course, to the famous altercation between Saint Ambrose of Milan and the emperor Theodosius after some monks, at the instigation of a bishop, burned down a synagogue. The emperor's officials saw this as a violation of imperial law, and the emperor endorsed their order compelling the bishop to pay for the synagogue's reconstruction. In letter and sermon Ambrose responded by insisting upon the superiority of divine over public law and claiming that in this case neither the bishop (as God's priest) nor his victims (as God's enemies) fell under the laws of the state. Most pointedly, he presents the emperor's insistence on upholding the letter of the law as itself Judaizing, and he reminds the emperor of his predecessor's unhappy fate: "Maximus . . . , hearing that a synagogue had been burnt in Rome, had sent an edict to Rome, as if he were the upholder of public order. Wherefore the Christian people said, No good is in store for him. That king has become a Jew."[61]

Ambrose's fusion of politics and hermeneutics here implies a "resistance theory": the monarch who reads literally, upholding the letter of the law over the demands of spirit, deserves deposition as a Jew. The rebellious potential inherent in this "Jewish" figure of political thought surfaced only rarely in late antiquity and the early Middle Ages, but it became a coherent discourse in Latin Christianity after the year 1000, when newly robust monarchies began to extend their power throughout western Europe, in part by establishing their prerogatives over Jews.[62] The history of medieval rebellions is peopled with "Jew-loving" rulers. In Castile alone the list is revealing. The rebels against both Alfonso X "the Wise" and King Pedro "the Cruel" justified their actions by portraying those monarchs as favorers of Jews. Prince Enrique (IV) rebelled against his father Juan II claiming the same. He himself would later be ritually deposed, accused of favoring Jews, of living like a Muslim, and of homosexuality. Even the Catholic monarchs Fernando and Isabel, conquerors of Granada, founders of the Inquisition, expellers of the Jews, were said by some of their subjects to be descended from Jews and to favor them in their policies.[63]

This breathless page or two is not intended as a history of political thought. It is meant only to sketch some associations that might make plausible a potential politics related to the poetics upon which the bulk of this essay has focused. We need not insist on the historical accuracy of these associations in order to agree that a logic very much like this one animated the political imagination of mid-fifteenth-century Castile. It was in 1449, during Enrique's revolt against King Juan, that we first encountered the anticonverso polemic of the Toledan rebels, with their precociously articulate statutes of purity of blood. Their politics was concisely explained in an influential treatise written by the revolt's ideologue, the Bachelor Marcos, shortly before the fall of the city and his execution. The difficulty of his position made his opening choice of address a tortured and therefore highly revealing one:

> To the Holy Father . . . , and to the high and powerful king or prince or ad-
> ministrator to whom, according to God, law, reason and right there belongs
> the administration and governance of the realms . . . of Castile and Leon,
> and to all other . . . administrators in the spiritual and temporal [affairs] of
> the universal orb, in the Church militant, which is the congregation and
> university of faithful Christians, [that is, those] truly believing in the birth,
> Passion and Resurrection [etc.] . . . , excluding from this audience those
> who are the unbelieving and the doubtful in the faith, who are outside of
> us and in confederation (*ayuntamiento*) with the synagogue, which is more
> properly to say a congregation of beasts, for since such bind themselves like
> livestock to the letter, they have always given and still give false meaning to
> divine and human scripture. [In short, I address this letter to those] attest-
> ing to the truth and saying: "The letter kills, the spirit vivifies [2 Cor. 3:6]."[64]

In the Bachelor's discriminating salutation we recognize a variant of the Aristotelian distinction between a community that exists for the mere fact of living and the "congregation and university of faithful Christians" that lives with regard to the higher good. We recognize as well Augustine's posi-tion from *De doctrina Christiana*, in which those who read literally become beasts of flesh. The Bachelor's marriage of Aristotle and Augustine produces a literacy test for citizenship. "Administrators" who read like Jews, literally after the flesh, have lost the human right to participate in the *res publica*. They have become creatures of self-interest, and their power is by definition tyrannical not sovereign. We know exactly who he had in mind: the *Privado* (royal favorite) Álvaro de Luna; the king, Juan II, who supported him; and even the pope, if he ended up rejecting the Bachelor's appeal and ruling in favor of the king. If no prince can be found who reads like a Christian, the treatise concludes, then the city should place itself directly under the gover-nance of the Holy Spirit.

Onto the political oppositions of bare life and good life, private body and body politic, tyrant and legitimate magistrate, the Bachelor grafted a hermeneutic one, killing letter and vivifying spirit, and animated both with the distinction between "Jew" and Christian. The resulting political language proved potent, for the charge of "Judaizing" in late medieval Castile drew power from an unusually powerful confusion of bloodlines and hermeneutics produced by mass conversions and intermarriage. Though the rebels of Toledo were defeated and the Bachelor Marcos was executed shortly after writing his treatise, his logic lost none of its political utility in the ongoing struggle over the balance of political power in Castile. That utility propelled his claims about the genealogical nature of convert Judaism to victory. The period after 1449 saw an explosion of treatises that drew upon sciences as diverse as medicine, metallurgy, animal breeding, etcetera, in order to provide Israel with a natural history capable of explaining why the attributes of its children were unchangeable by God (via baptism) or king (through ennoblement). Within a generation or two, the Iberian body politic had produced a thick hedge of inquisition and genealogy in order to protect itself from penetration by the "Jewish race" and its cultural attributes.

In the following chapters we will ask how that victory was won and think through some of its many implications. Suffice it here to say that the genealogical turn was taken and that it transformed the meaning of conversion from "Jewishness." For descendants of converts, the consequences were vast. Just as some theologians had warned in the 1430s and 1440s, the logic of lineage created despair about the possibility of conversion. After the anticonverso riots of 1449 some descendants of converts gave up hope of becoming Christian and circumcised themselves.[65] The same despair took hold of those who had believed in "poetic conversion." Poetry ceased to be, for converso and Old Christian alike, a place in which hermeneutic good faith could be proven. Converts who wrote poetry in the 1460s and 1470s were acutely aware that it could serve them only as a vessel for satire and self-mockery, not as a literary statement of their state of grace or as a forum for assimilation into the Christian body poetic. The pen of the converso poet Antón de Montoro, for example, is mordantly engaged with those who consider him a Jew. In one poem even his horse abuses him as a "killer of Christ." In his youth, Antón de Montoro had moved in poetic circles like those of Juan Alfonso de Baena, full of hope in the emancipatory power of poetry. By the age of seventy he claimed to have lost any such hope. As he wrote in verses addressed to Queen Isabel, despite all his devotion, all his efforts to write and worship like a Christian, he was never "able to kill this trace of the convert," never "able to lose the name of old faggot Jew."[66]

Conversely, nonconverso poets found that the increasingly combustible nature of converso flesh deprived "Judaism" of its playful utility as a critical language. Poets in the generation after Baena continued to criticize poetry as "Jewish," but such attacks were now aimed more exclusively at convert poets and stressed more pointedly the inescapably corrupting effects of Jewish lineage on textual practice. The Old Christian nobleman Frederico Manrique's description of the convert Juan Poeta's pilgrimage to the Cathedral of Valencia is typical, albeit unusually brilliant: "Johan Poeta, when you came / into this sacred space / you converted many consecrated things / from one thing into another / . . . the bull of the holy father / . . . turned with a loud noise / into scripture from the Talmud. / And the devoted Church itself / through the mere fact of your presence / was then contaminated / and at that moment became / a holy house of the Old Testament."[67]

We could not ask for a more vivid expression of the explosive power granted "Jewishness" by the genealogical turn. Both poets, Old Christian and New, were well aware of the dangers of a new world in which right reading and right breeding were in so intimate an embrace. Far from containing "Jewishness" in the blood of converts and their descendants as its early advocates had promised, the union of flesh and thought, lineage and language threatened to infect all of Spanish culture with "Jewishness."

Despite the claims of the logic of lineage, this "Jewishness" of Spain was not the product of "Jewish" ideas spread by "hybrid" lineages of Marranos. It was rather the product of a Christian theology that rooted extremes of spirituality and carnality, of love and enmity, of metaphor and letter, of freedom and tyranny in the one lineage believed to have produced the flesh of God and of his enemies, the lineage of the Jews. Spain was unusual in that the magnitude of its conversions constituted the largest assimilation of European Jews before modernity. These conversions precipitated a precociously self-conscious exploration of the limitations of Christian dialectic to overcome the stubborn particularities of flesh. That exploration focused its anxiety on Judaism and found in Jewish lineages the most powerful expression of the confused heterogeneity of the fallen world. In so doing, it produced the phenomenon it sought to describe.

The scholarship on the history and literature of late medieval Spain has reproduced this confusion. The lineages of Spain's converts have even come to serve as the foundation for any number of genealogies of European modernity. In 1971, for example, Richard Popkin suggested that the Marranos constituted the "beginning of modernization in Europe."[68] By the 1990s the claims had become less modest, with Spain's converts causing the "collapse of ecclesiastical society of the Middle Ages and the rise of secularism and modernity." These arguments nourish and are nourished by the stress on the Spanish roots of Spinoza ("the first secular Jew, and as such the first secular man"),[69] Montaigne, and others. Today it is common, in fields ranging from intellectual history to psychoanalysis, to discover the roots of skepticism, irony, hybridity, and other concepts believed to be constitutive of modernity, in the flesh of the descendants of the converted Jews of late medieval Spain.[70]

"Discover"? As I have shown, the history of the "Jewishness" of each of these terms stretches far out of the sight of those who stumble upon it so innocently with each generation. Indeed these histories were already old when the Marranos were born in the forced conversions of late fourteenth-century Spain.[71] There are, of course, important differences between contemporary searchers after "Jewishness" and those of previous centuries. It is now much more common, for example, to give a positive rather than negative value to supposedly Jewish traits like skepticism or hybridity and to the ontological, epistemological, and phenomenological positions those traits are thought to produce.[72] This difference, however, should not be overdrawn. It stems from radically differing valuations of skepticism, materialism, and secularism, not from radically different understandings of the transmission of "Jewishness" across time and space. When we turn to these lineages in order to explain the history of our own modernity, we merely achieve the reproduction, in a secularized and unreflective form, of a theology that (to paraphrase Marx) "ceaselessly produces the Jew out of its own entrails" as "the alienated essence of man's labor and life."[73]

[7]

Mass Conversion and Genealogical Mentalities

The previous chapter stressed the cultural creativity unleashed by the mass conversions. In doing so it provided a glimpse of just how newly fruitful religious classifications could be within a landscape transformed by the floodwaters of baptism. And it also offered a certain sense of relief—the relief we call contingency—from the relentless continuity stressed by so many historical inquisitors for whom Judaism and Christianity persisted essential and eternal despite cataclysm and conversion. But we know that over time Christians and Jews *did* succeed in re-imagining their religious communities and classifications, and they did so in ways that proclaimed a genealogical continuity with the past. That continuity is so peculiar that some historians have considered it the birth pangs of racism (a characterization we will take up in the next chapter). But even without leaping from the Middle Ages into the sciences of modernity, we can and should ask why and how medieval Christians and Jews created that continuity, and with what tools.

* * *

It is both well known and worthy of note that Sephardim (that is, the descendants of Jews expelled from Spain) and Spaniards shared an unusually heightened concern with lineage and genealogy in the early modern period. The Spanish obsession with *hidalguía*, Gothic descent, and purity of blood has long constituted a stereotype. Think only of Don Juan's father, mockingly portrayed by Lord Byron: "His father's name was José—*Don*, of course, / A true Hidalgo, free from every stain / Of Moor or Hebrew blood, he traced his source / Through the most Gothic gentlemen of Spain."[1]

The Sephardim, too, were criticized on this score almost from the moment of exile. The (Ashkenazic) Italian David ben Judah Messer Leon, for example, ridiculed the eminent exile Don Yitzḥaq Abarbanel's claims to royal pedigree, scoffing that Abarbanel "made of himself a Messiah with his claims to Davidic descent."[2] That the exiles' emphasis on lineage flourished nonetheless is evident, not only in the splendid armorial bearings of Sephardic tombs in Venice or Livorno,[3] but also in the communal statutes of congregations in Italy and the Netherlands.[4] And just as Spaniards asserted that their unstained nobility set them above other nations, so Isaac de Pinto could attempt to counter Voltaire's negative portrayal of Jews by arguing that Sephardic nobility made "[a] Portuguese Jew of Bordeaux and a German Jew of Metz appear two beings of a different nature!"[5]

The historical "origins" of this emphasis on lineage are among the most polemical issues in the scholarly literature on Spanish and Sephardic identity. Rather than multiply examples, consider only that of Marcelino Menéndez y Pelayo, a writer so central to Spanish historiography that the Royal Academy of History is named in his honor. When he wrote in 1887 that "the fanaticism of blood and race, which we probably owe to the Jews . . . was then hideously turned against them,"[6] he was reiterating an already ancient claim: that the Jews were the inventors of the exclusionary logic of lineage that would later be used in Spain to oppress them. Within the context of Spanish history, the opinion has been embraced by writers as diverse as Américo Castro and his archenemy Claudio Sánchez Albornoz.[7] Conversely, an equally diverse group of Jewish scholars (which includes Yitzhak Baer, Cecil Roth, Haim Hillel Ben-Sason, Yosef Yerushalmi, Benzion Netanyahu, and Yosef Kaplan) has strenuously argued the opposite thesis, that these ideas were invented by Gentiles (in this case Iberian Christians) as a way of denying converts from Judaism full membership in the Christian spiritual and social communities they sought to enter. Only later would they be adopted by the same Sephardic Jews who had earlier been their victims.[8]

The debate may seem abstruse, but it draws its heat from a moralizing logic of genealogy that is of vital importance in the long history of Jewish relations with other peoples. If the Jews gave birth to "racism" and the spirit of exclusion according to birth, then is there not a certain exculpatory irony in the fact that their own monstrous children turned so violently against them?

Hence the unceasing efforts of anti-Jewish polemicists, ranging from Appian to Hitler, to comb ancient biblical and rabbinic texts in order to identify the Jews as the inventors of racist exclusivity; and the equally timeless attempts of Jewish apologists from Philo to the present to defend the "chosen people" against the charge.[9]

Both these positions assume that ideas about lineage have a discrete and essential origin in a particular culture or people, whence they are transmitted from donor to recipient cultures across space and time. Both are, in other words, philogenetic, depending on genealogical models of cultural exchange that reproduce, but do not explain, the logic of lineage whose rise they claim to clarify.[10] In this sense, modern historians of the subject remain methodologically very close to their medieval precursors, whose pens worked so diligently to trace the lineages of kingdoms, people, and ideas into the primordial past (by which they generally meant the historical landscape of either the Hebrew Bible or Greek myth).[11]

I will take a different approach and suggest that the emphasis on lineage amongst Spaniards and Sephardim is not a product of the "genetic" transmission of ideas from one culture to another, but rather the outcome of a specific historical process of conflict in which lineage became a newly meaningful way of thinking about religious identity amongst Christians and Jews alike. My specific arguments are threefold: (1) that the conversion to Christianity of many thousands of Jews caused by the massacres, forced disputation, and segregations that marked the period between 1391 and 1415 produced a violent destabilization of traditional categories of religious identity; (2) that in the face of this destabilization Jews, Christians, and conversos created new forms of communal identity by engaging in a dynamic and dialogic process of rereading their own traditions and those of their rivals, and that over the course of the fifteenth century (that is, from the massacres of 1391 to the generation of the expulsion of 1492) this process elevated genealogy to a primary form of communal memory; and (3) that in each of these communities this genealogical form of collective memory gave rise to new forms of historical consciousness and historical writing, some of which continue to characterize the historiography of Spain and its Jews.

By focusing on the social context of the fifteenth-century Iberian Peninsula, I do not mean to imply that this was either the first or the only time that history and genealogy met, wooed, and were wed. On the contrary, theirs is a common romance, with conflict a frequent go-between. Nor am I suggesting that lineage was unimportant to Jews and Christians before the events of

1391. The genealogical genre is represented in the foundational texts of both religions (that is, the Hebrew Bible and the New Testament), and both had long and complex traditions of thinking about the topic. For the Jews, *yḥus*, or lineage, had important ritual implications before the destruction of the Temple, and the issue was treated extensively in early rabbinical texts. More specifically in medieval Sepharad, important rabbinic dynasties had long used genealogies in the struggle amongst themselves for authority and prestige. In his *Book of Tradition*, for example, the twelfth-century scholar Abraham ibn Daud of Toledo gave several important families noble pedigrees. Families like the Albalias and the Ibn Ezras, he assured his readers, "are of royal blood and descended from nobility, as evidenced by their personal traits."[12]

Such strategies, and the genealogies they produced, were common to the entire western diaspora, in Ashkenaz as well as Sepharad.[13] Further, although such claims might lend a patina of prestige, they carried no legal force, and they were also sometimes ridiculed.[14] In the early fourteenth century, Rabbi Shelomo ben Abraham ben Adret of Barcelona, the leading rabbinic authority of his day, made clear just how little *halakhic* (legal) weight genealogical investigations should have. Responding to a case in which litigants attempted to bar two brothers from giving testimony on the grounds that they had a slave ancestor, Adret responded that "all Jewish families must be held as fit and emanating from the children of Israel"; and, he added, "if we take seriously the authors of such libels, there will not remain a single family [in Israel] that will be considered fit from the standpoint of ancestry."[15]

Among the Christian European nobility genealogy had long played a more important role than it did among the Jews, one that for a variety of reasons became critical (as well as better documented) in the fourteenth century. In western Europe this period saw the widespread adoption of armorial bearings, the development of heraldry, the dissemination of the "family tree" as a standard way of representing lineage.[16] Also, within each of the peninsular kingdoms specific pressures contributed to the particular flavor of genealogical concerns. In Aragon, for example, the growing pressure of taxation led to an explosion of *procesos de infanzonía* in the first half of the fourteenth century, by which thousands of people attempted (generally successfully) to show their descent from tax-exempt minor nobility. In Castile, on the other hand, the civil wars of midcentury had resulted in a new royal dynasty that drew its grandees from an (almost) entirely new circle of families. In that kingdom, it was the new high nobility that displayed the greatest genealogical creativity as it attempted to establish its bona fides.[17]

In both religious communities, in other words, ideas about lineage were always present and never stable. But although in both communities lineage was clearly important at the level of the family, the dynasty, and the individual line, in neither, before the fifteenth century, did it emerge as a central form of cultural memory or communal identification establishing a group identity.[18] Genealogy was not yet being put to the task of producing narratives or systems of knowledge around which large-scale political, social, religious, or ethnic entities might cohere.

The fourteenth century drew to a close with a wave of anti-Jewish violence unparalleled in the Middle Ages. In the massacres of 1391, thousands or perhaps tens of thousands were killed, and a much greater number converted. Reuven, son of the famous Rabbi Nissim Gerundi and a survivor of the massacre, described the damage in words he penned in the margins of his father's Torah scroll:

> Wail, holy and glorious Torah, and put on black raiment, for the expounders of your lucid words perished in the flames. For three months the conflagration spread through the holy congregations of the exile of Israel in Sepharad. The fate [of Sodom and Gomorrah] overtook the holy communities of Castile, Toledo, Seville, Mallorca, Córdoba, Valencia, Barcelona, Tàrrega, and Girona, and sixty neighboring cities and villages. . . . The sword, slaughter, destruction, forced conversions, captivity, and spoliation were the order of the day. Many were sold as slaves to the Ishmaelites; 140,000 were unable to resist those who so barbarously forced them and gave themselves up to impurity [that is, converted].[19]

We need not accept the accuracy of his numbers in order to recognize that these killings and conversions transformed the religious demography of the Iberian Peninsula. The Jews vanished from many of the largest cities of both Castile and Aragon. In their place, converted by force and without catechism into Christians, appeared a new, in some sense intermediary, religious class, that of the "New Christians," or conversos.[20]

The migration of such a large number of Jews into the body of Christ catalyzed a series of reactions whose complexity and dynamism are perhaps comparable to those that marked the debates (so fateful for later Jewish-Christian relations) between Jewish and Gentile followers of Jesus in the first formative century of Christianity. Underlying these reactions (of which the turn toward genealogy was only one) was a crisis of classification and identity, whose first symptoms became evident almost immediately. In chapter 5, for example, we found the king of Aragon complaining in 1393 that it had become impossible for "natural Christians" (that is, not converts) to tell who was a convert to Christianity and who was still a Jew. The king proposed segregation and heightened marking of Jews as a solution. Henceforth converts were to be forbidden to live, dine, or have conversation with Jews. The Jews were to be made to wear more conspicuous badges and Jewish hats, so "that they appear to be Jews."[21] But it is in the sermons of Saint Vincent Ferrer that this crisis of classification and identification received its most elegant and powerful formulation and came in due course to justify the second great wave of conversionary pressure that swept the peninsula in the years 1412–15.

Saint Vincent, together with the papal court in Avignon and the monarchs of Castile and Aragon, professed to desire nothing less than the mass conversion of the Jews and Muslims of Spain, a goal he and his allies pursued through a program of preaching, mandatory disputations, and discriminatory legislation.[22] His motivations, as well as those of the popes and monarchs who supported him and of the populace that so warmly embraced his mission, were complex. But there is no doubt that they were all very much concerned by the ways in which the existence of a group of Christians living in proximity (social, cultural, and physical) to Jews undercut the radical distinction between the two groups, a distinction believed to be crucial to the identity of both communities. In the by now familiar words of Saint Vincent, "he will never be a good Christian who is neighbor to a Jew." Proximity destabilized an essential aspect of Christian identity, dishonored God, and put Christian society at risk of famine, plague, and other manifestations of divine displeasure.[23] Furthermore, he warned in a Castilian sermon of 1412, it made accurate identification difficult: "And above all there should be no communication with them in the home, for Christian and infidel should not dwell together in the same house, for it is an evil which is contagious, that is, luxury, for many are thought to be the children of Jews, and are really Christian, and vice versa. And therefore just as Jews and Muslims are different from Christians in law, they should be different from them in habitation."[24]

Saint Vincent Ferrer and his sponsors sought to reinstate the necessary distance between Christian and Jew in two ways: first, by converting as many Jews as possible to Christianity; and second, by sharpening the boundaries between Christians and those (ideally few) Jews who would inevitably remain in Christian society until the end of time. The program, in a word, was segregation.[25] In the name of separating Christian from non-Christian,

Muslims and Jews were to be moved to segregated neighborhoods and severely restricted in their market and economic activities.[26] These measures clearly advanced the goal of evangelization by encouraging beleaguered non-Christians to convert. But we should not forget that they also reflected, and justified themselves by invoking, increased anxiety about the stability of group boundaries after the mass conversions of 1391.

Whatever the motivations of this segregation, its effects were clear. Entire communities converted, and many of those who did not were barred from their trades and expelled from their homes. Shelomo Alami described this as a period when "the sky was covered with a cloud [so heavy] that it blocked the passage of any prayer to God." Both Christian and Jewish sources tell us of the rabbis attempting to penetrate this cloud by praying tearfully in the graveyards: "At the hour when the world requires mercy, the living go and rouse the souls of the righteous, and cry on their graves." But the souls of the righteous did not waken, or if they did, they failed to rouse the intercession of the patriarchs. By 1415, a new generation of conversos had entered Christendom.[27]

It is not the terror of these massacres and segregations, real as it was, nor even their scale that I want to emphasize here, so much as the classificatory dilemmas they created for Jew and Christian alike. The mass conversions raised, for the first time, systemic doubt about who was a Christian and who was a Jew. At their simplest, these were questions about who had actually converted. Particularly when conversion took place in an atmosphere of mob violence, it could be difficult to ascertain who had in fact been baptized, though the classification was obviously a crucial one, given the Inquisition's interest (at least in the Crown of Aragon) in relapsed converts.[28] But the problem of identification extended far beyond doubts about whether an individual had been baptized or not, for ambiguity could arise in any number of settings.

Topographically, for example, converts from Judaism (and Islam) often remained in the same homes and neighborhoods (that is, in Jewish and Muslim quarters) that they had occupied before their conversion. In this sense Saint Vincent was right: the New Christians really were neighbors of Jews.[29] The converts' fiscal status, too, was indeterminate. Because they were made to assume a proportionate share of the debts and tax obligations of the Jewish community they left behind (obligations that often had maturities of several decades), the converts were often lumped into fiscal groupings separate both from Jewish *aljamas* and the "Old Christian" municipalities.[30] The result was not only that the converts would retain close financial ties with their former coreligionists for at least a generation, but also that they would form confraternities and tax collectives quite distinct from those of their adopted brethren in Christ. The meanings of this "interstitiality" were neither clear nor stable. For example, if the formation of converso confraternities seemed at first a laudable and even necessary step in the neophytes' incorporation into the body of Christ, it soon began to seem a dangerous symptom of separatism, and by midcentury it had become a primary locus for violent conflict between Christians Old and New.[31] Whatever the shifting valences of these intermediate statuses, it is clear that these were significant moves in a highly corporate world very much attuned to such distinctions.

Marriage provided another context for the blurring of boundaries, and one central to the formation of any discourse of lineage. What happened, for example, if only one spouse in a marriage converted? To the rabbis, the answer was clear: the sanctified marriage remained valid, even if, in the words of Adret, the Jewish spouse should flee the convert as one "would a serpent" in order to avoid giving birth to a "child of violence" who might oppress the Jews.[32] Under pressure of events, Christian authorities came to permit similar ambiguities. During the 1391 massacres in Girona, for example, a husband who had just converted sent messengers to the tower where his Jewish wife was still being besieged by the mob, asking her to return to him, under the condition that she not interfere with his observing the Christian faith. (She refused.) Conversely, when Samuel Baruch's wife Aldonça converted to Christianity in 1391, her father (also a convert) publicly presented his son-in-law with two possibilities: convert to Christianity and continue the marriage or, alternatively, remain a Jew but still keep her as his wife without prejudicing her Christian faith.[33] By 1415, Pope Benedict XIII had formalized such choices by taking an unprecedented position in canon law, allowing all couples in this situation to continue living together for a year from the date of conversion, so that the Christian spouse might convince the recalcitrant partner.[34]

Of course, concerns about the sincerity of conversion complicated the issue of classification further. For example, the year limit to mixed marriages makes clear that "hybrid" situations were meant to be temporary, but in fact the problem continued for generations, whenever an "insincere" or "judaizing" convert married a "sincere" one. One early sixteenth-century *responsum* (rabbinic legal opinion) tells of a conversa who abandoned her nursing son and her husband in Valencia by escaping through a window. She now wanted to marry a Jew who had repented as she had, and she asked the rabbis if she needed a divorce. On the other hand, Pope Pius II authorized an annulment for the converso Pedro de la Caballería in 1459, on the grounds that his wife was a heretic who had been taught to judaize by her mother. "Pedro, a true Catholic, is prepared to endure . . . every danger of death rather than consummate a marriage of this sort, lest [any] begotten offspring follow the insanity of the mother, and a Jew be created out of a Christian."[35]

Finally, the multiple expulsions, migrations, conversions, and apostasies that marked the fifteenth century made the classification of an individual's belief a central problem for all three of the religious communities of Iberia. And although Jews and Christians are our focus here, it is worth noting in passing that there are plenty of Muslim examples, such as that of Juan de Granada. Born Mahoma Joffre in Aragon in the mid-fifteenth century, he converted to Christianity (and the name Juan) before joining a military troop on its way to fight on the Granadan frontier. He then settled in Granada as a Muslim. Eventually he left Granada, joining another Christian troop on the frontier and again (!) receiving baptism. Later he returned to his village in Aragon as a Muslim, where he lived for several years before being recognized and denounced to the Inquisition. Because Mahoma's long absence made him suspect, his relatives repeatedly interrogated him about his religion and observed his behavior closely: in particular his dress, attendance at mosque, consumption of wine, and fasting during Ramadan.[36]

But Mahoma/Juan is a late and Muslim example. Returning to Jews and to the earlier part of the century, we should stress that even those Jews who most adamantly refused to convert could experience a destabilization of their identities, because they were often forced to move to avoid physical violence, conversionary pressures, or the designation of certain cities (such as Barcelona or Valencia) as *judenrein*. The parents of Abraham Rimoch, for example, fled Barcelona with their young son after the massacres of 1391, taking refuge in Barbastro. Some twenty years later, after being forced to "debate with the pope and his sages" at Tortosa, Abraham fled again to avoid conversion: "I left my house and abandoned my possessions, wealth, and fortune, my sons and daughters, my family, friends, and belongings." Such refugees found themselves needing to reestablish their reputations at a time when Jewish and Christian communities alike were particularly suspicious of newcomers. As Rabbi Shelomo da Piera put it: "When the persons who have escaped the sword . . . wander and go away . . . it would not be believed by mere hearing that these people have not converted, unless it is from scribes or from written testimonies which testify their being just, signed by well-known people who are 'known at the gates.'"[37]

Da Piera's observation suggests that these massive dislocations stimulated the search among Jewish leaders for new ways to document individual identity. Similar processes are evident in Christian communities as well,[38] and the problem would become even more acute with the conversions and expulsions of the later fifteenth century. Consider the autobiography of Luis de la Isla, a thirty-year-old blind converso, as narrated to the Inquisition of Toledo in 1514. As an eight-year-old he had left the town of Illescas (near Toledo) for North Africa in the expulsion of 1492. From there he had traveled to Venice and Genoa, being baptized while in Italy. He returned to Spain in 1496 when converts were still being readmitted and then, again in Italy in 1506, started attending synagogue in Ferrara. From Ferrara he moved to Salonica, Adrianople, and Constantinople, still as a Jew, then to Alexandria, where he lived as a Christian among Catalan merchants. In Alexandria he came into conflict with the local Jewish community, which reproached him for choosing Christianity "when he came from so honorable a lineage as those of Illescas." It was there, too, that he lost his sight and decided to return first to Naples, then to Valencia, and finally to Toledo, where he voluntarily confessed to the Inquisition.[39] Such movement across geographic and religious space would characterize the experience of many Sephardim well into the seventeenth century. The classification of these "travelers," the fixing of their identities, would require new forms of memory and written record.[40]

Confronted by these displacements, problems of intermediacy, and crises of classification, Jews, Christians, and conversos turned more or less simultaneously to lineage as one means of reestablishing the integrity of religious categories of identity. In doing so, each group drew largely upon its own traditions, but each was also aware of, and responding to, the changes taking place in the others' genealogical imaginations. In the interest of narrative clarity I will treat each of these groups separately, beginning with the Jews. But in so doing I do not intend to imply any priority of invention or to give the impression that the responses can be adequately understood independently of each other.

The Sephardic rabbinate responded to the crisis by adapting two tensely related genealogical strands long present, but largely neglected, in rabbinic tradition. Both strands are already evident in a legal opinion written by Adret nearly a century before 1391, responding to a question about why the Talmud had made no provision for divorcing a Jewish woman from an apostate (*meshumad l-'avodah zarah*). Adret emphasized that even in the extreme case where an apostate woman gives birth to a Gentile son, the son is nevertheless *Yisra'el kasher u-mezuham*, that is, kosher, but loathsome.[41] Both the ideas implicit in this ruling, (1) that an apostate's child is still *Yisra'el kasher*, and (2) that the child's lineage is nevertheless in some sense flawed, were amplified in rabbinic reaction to the mass conversions. But both, it should also be stressed, assign a place of vital importance to genealogy.

This importance is easiest to see in the case of post-1391 writers who came to emphasize genealogy as a way of guaranteeing a sound lineage devoid of taint. Thus we see the appearance after 1391 of phrases like "of a family of believers" or "of a good family" in routine documents such as letters of recommendation, meaning that the bearer was of a family that had not converted in the persecutions. Rabbi Shelomo da Piera addressed the issue explicitly in the letter already cited above: "It would not be believed by mere hearing that these people have not converted, unless it is from scribes or from written testimonies which testify their being just." Da Piera therefore developed a formula: "for X, who is from the sons of good residents of this land, from those who are known to be faithful, decent, and untainted (*kasher*)." A letter written in 1412 on behalf of Meir b. R. Todros b. R. Hasdai stated that Meir was "very afraid lest they should think or suspect him to be one of the converts. . . . Therefore he begged us to give evidence of his untaintedness and this is the certificate of purity of this young man."[42]

Meir's anxiety may have been due to the fact that such instruments of "genealogical memory" were clearly being deployed in the interests of asserting the superiority of individual lineages. The *Menorat ha-Ma'or*, an "advice manual" written by Isaac Aboab I at the end of the fourteenth century, reflects this concern:

A man must be very careful not to trip over a woman who is not fitting for him, so that she not be like a leprosy in his flesh, and that he not have children by her, who are not fitting. As we read in the last [*pereq*] of *Qidushin* . . . every man who marries a woman not fitting to his station, it is as if he married in a house of salt, etc. And in the heavens they pray for him and cry: "Woe to him that damages his foundations and introduces a defect in his lineage and marries a woman who is not his equal!"[43]

On the other hand, at the level of the collective rather than that of the individual lineage, the rabbis used genealogical arguments to emphasize the continuing "Jewishness" (and hence, marriageability) of the converts. Their arguments were based upon a distinction between '*anusim*, forced converts, and willing apostates. Maimonides had famously ruled that, under certain conditions, there was no guilt in renouncing Judaism under threat of force, so long as one intended to continue carrying out the commandments and fled the land of oppression at the first opportunity. The convert remained a Jew, for God forgave the *'anus*.[44] The crucial variable here was the convert's intention.

Sephardic rabbis writing after 1391 followed this tradition but came to rely less on intention and more on lineage. We can trace this transformation across their *responsa* on the subject. Rabbi Yitzḥaq ben Sheshet Perfet (b. 1326), who fled Valencia for North Africa in 1391, upheld the Jewishness of the forced converts, on the grounds that (1) "God forgives the forced convert," (2) "Israel, although he has sinned, is still Israel,"[45] and (3) as Maimonides had said, it is better to live for the commandments than to die for them. But for Yitzḥaq their status as Jews and *'anusim*, rather than apostates, depended on their secret observance of the commandments and upon their willingness to flee the land of their oppression whenever flight was possible. In other words, it still depended upon individual intention.[46] For his successor, R. Shim'on ben Tzemaḥ Duran (RaShBaTz, 1361–1444), a Mallorcan rabbi who had also fled the massacres of 1391, individual volition was of less importance. R. Shim'on argued that it was impossible to know the secrets of the human heart, and so the conversos should not be judged negatively for their seeming unwillingness to emigrate from Spain.[47] His son, Rabbi Shelomo ben Shim'on Duran (RaShBaSh, ca. 1400–1467), ruled further that even the "uncircumcised sons" of converts, that is, second- or third-generation converts who knew nothing of Judaism, remained Jews unless, knowing their origin, they deliberately chose to forget it.[48] Shelomo's son Tzemaḥ agreed in turn, coining the phrase "Israel, even uncircumcised, is circumcised [*mahul*]."[49] And Tzemaḥ's brother, Shim'on II (1438–after 1510), again agreed, supplying the necessary genealogical logic: "For these converts, during their sojourn in the lands of the gentiles, contracted the majority of their marriages amongst themselves. Only a minority contracted marriage with the sons of Edom." Further, Shim'on II argued, the conversos kept good track of their lineages. Therefore not only are they to be considered Jews, but those who claim to be Kohanim, that is, of priestly lineage, are to be considered such.[50] These rulings were of critical importance in answering questions about marriage law, inheritance, and ritual, and they come up again and again in *responsa*. Generally (though not always) the emphasis on lineage in these *responsa* is inclusionary: that is, the rulings affirm the continued Jewishness of the converts, stressing their strict endogamy and their clear genealogical memories, even though we know from other sources that many conversos who escaped to Muslim lands and returned to Judaism could not, for example, remember their family's Hebrew name.[51]

To summarize, over the course of the fifteenth century we can speak of two emerging genealogical emphases among the Sephardic rabbinate, the one stressing the purity of certain lineages, the other insisting on the genealogical integrity and continued Jewishness of the converts and their descendants. These were substantial shifts of emphasis, requiring a rereading of rabbinic legal traditions. At times their advocates even found it necessary to draw on nonlegal traditions in order to make their points, as when Tzemaḥ ben Shelomo borrowed from Qabbalah in order to argue that the offspring of a Gentile and a female apostate from Judaism is still a Jew.[52] But important as these developments were, neither of them necessarily leads to the positions (like those of Isaac de Pinto about the genealogical superiority of Sephardim as a class over other Jews) with which this chapter began. Indeed, the new emphasis upon genealogy among Iberian Jews might have been limited to the sphere of *halakhah*, to be applied only to specific legal questions arising within Jewish communities, were it not for its resonance with the debate that arose in *Christian* society over the proper classification of the conversos. Where did they fit within the then crucial polarity between Christian and Jew?

During the first generation after 1391 the Christian establishment was relatively tolerant of ambiguity, perhaps out of the conviction that it would resolve itself through catechism and acculturation. But toward midcentury, Christians began to characterize the converts in increasingly genealogical terms. This turn to lineage may well have been a reaction to the much more competitive landscape confronting Old Christians as the floodwaters of baptism receded, for the converts took advantage of many opportunities that had been forbidden to them as Jews. To give but one Aragonese example, Fernando de la Cavallería, a prominent Jew of Zaragoza, emerged from the baptismal font in 1414 to occupy the position of royal treasurer, one of the most important in the court. Two of his kindred baptized with him ascended to only slightly less prestigious posts; all three had offices forbidden to Jews in the Crown of Aragon since the late thirteenth century. In Castile, Jewish access to positions in the world of royal finance endured longer, but conversion nevertheless opened entirely new avenues for office holding and advancement.[53] Pablo de Santa María, who had converted in 1390, became not only bishop of Burgos (a position in which his son succeeded him) but chancellor of Castile and León and tutor of the Crown Prince Juan II, as well as executor of King Enrique III's last will and testament. Old and New Christians competed not only for office but also for marriage alliances at the highest level. The conversa Estenza Coneso, for example, married Alfonso de Aragón, the (illegitimate) son of the king.[54] On a less exalted plane, the Valencian poet Jaume Roig penned a bitter poem denouncing his lover Caldesa for allowing herself to be "penetrated by the hatless rod" of his (circumcised) converso rival.[55]

These famous examples could be multiplied at great length. They are cited here merely to give a sense of the rapid ascension of converts to positions of power and influence within the Spanish kingdoms, positions from which, as Jews, they had been officially barred for the past hundred years. Their ascensions took place in the fiercely factional and competitive world of court. The flavor of this world is perhaps best captured in the poetic agon of the day, which produced anthologies of verse packed with genealogical maledictions like those addressed to Pedro Méndez, whose ancestry was said to be "one quarter *marrano* [that is, convert] / and three quarters sodomite." More specific were the Jewish ancestors attributed by Rodrigo Cota to Diego Arias: "by one grandfather Avenzuzén / by the other Abenamías, / by the mother Sophomías, / by the father all Cohen."[56] Translated from poetic to practical diction, lineage became an even sharper weapon. In 1434 King Juan II of Castile suppressed a plot to rob and murder the conversos of Seville.[57] In Aragon the tactics were less violent, the evidence more abundant, but the picture was the same. In 1433 Queen Mary decreed on behalf of the converts of Barcelona that no legal distinction should be made between "natural" Christians on the one hand and neophytes and their descendants on the other.[58] The following year King Alfonso had to bar efforts in Calatayud to impose disabilities on neophytes; in 1436, the councilors of Barcelona moved to bar converts and those whose parents were not both "Christians by nature" from holding the office of notary; in 1437 the town council of Lleida attempted to strip all brokers who could not demonstrate at least four generations of "natural Christian" lineage of their office and license.[59]

In attempting to counter such stratagems, the converts and their allies turned to the highest levels of the Church as well as to the king. The Council of Basel made its position clear in 1434: "Since [the converts] became by the grace of baptism fellow citizens of the saints and members of the house of God, and since regeneration of the spirit is much more important than birth in the flesh . . . they enjoy the privileges, liberties, and immunities of those cities and towns where they were regenerated through sacred baptism to the same extent as the natives and other Christians do."[60] And again in 1437, responding to an appeal from the converts of Catalonia and Valencia, Pope Eugenius IV condemned those "sons of iniquity . . . Christians only in name," who suggested that recent converts be barred from public office and who "refuse to enter into matrimony with them."[61]

The arguments of these "sons of iniquity" ran sharply counter to a long theological tradition that saw in the Pauline epistles a clear statement that in the body of Christ there was neither "Jew nor Greek." Instead they based themselves on a logic that claimed for itself the testimony of nature. In chapter 6 we have already encountered the example of Alfonso Martínez de Toledo, writing circa 1438, whose arguments depended upon the naturalization of cultural characteristics. You could always tell a person's roots, he explained, for those who descended from good stock were incapable of deviating from it, whereas those of base stock could not transcend their origins, regardless of whatever money, wealth, or power they might have obtained. This could be proven, he suggested, by an experiment. If one were to take two babies, the one a son of a laborer, the other of a knight, and rear them together on a mountain in isolation from their parents, one would find that the son of the laborer would delight in agricultural pursuits, while the son of the knight would take pleasure only in feats of arms and equestrianship: "This nature procures." The problem was one of *raça*, race (on the meaning of this word see chap. 8), but its consequences were political: "The miserable man, of bad race or lineage, no matter how powerful or how rich, will always return to the villainy from which he descends. . . .That is why when such men or women have power they do not use it as they should."[62]

The first surviving theorizations about the negative nature of the conversos' Jewish lineage were made in Toledo, during a rebellion against the Castilian monarchy in 1449. The Toledans and their sympathizers claimed that converts were motivated only by ambition for office and "carnal lust for nuns and [Christian] virgins" and that converso physicians poisoned their Christian patients in order to get hold of their inheritance and offices, "marry the wives of the Old Christians they kill," and stain their "clean blood" (*sangre limpia*).[63] They argued that Jewish ancestry (that is, Jewish blood) conveyed canniness and an unusual talent for enriching oneself at the expense of non-Jews and predisposed one to corruption and viciousness in positions of power.[64] To counter this "genetic" tendency the Toledans proposed what later would come to be called a purity of blood statute: descendants of converts were to be banned from holding public office.[65]

Although these arguments were aimed at the conversos, it was upon the Jews that they focused, for it was by mapping a set of "Jewish" cultural characteristics (enmity toward Christians, "subtlety," financial acumen) onto a genealogy said to reproduce them that they sought to disenfranchise the converts as "Judaizing Christians." To that end, they turned to biblical genealogies and to arguments from later history, in order to represent the Jews as a lineage corrupted through hybridity.

Some writers, such as Alonso de Espina, verged on a polygenetic approach, putting the corruption at the very origins of human history. Espina related the lineage of Jews to the offspring of (1) Adam with animals, and (2) Adam with the demon Lilith. As a result of these unions, he wrote, Jews were of the lineage of demons and of monsters, the mule and the sow their adoptive mothers.[66] Others, like the author of a treatise called the *Alborayque* (ca. 1455–65), used biblical accounts of Israelite migration to make similar arguments. The Jews are a mixed lineage, an amalgam of Edom, Moab, Amon, Egypt, and more. The author employed the Alborayque, the composite Qur'anic beast (part horse, part lion, part snake, etc.) who carried Muhammad to heaven, as a symbol of the conversos' monstrously hybrid nature. The converts are not only Alborayques. They are bats, unclassifiable as animal (wings) or bird (teeth); they are a weak alloy rather than pure metal. These unnatural mixtures support the conclusion that, as heirs of the Jews, the conversos and their descendants could never be classified as Christian.[67] Other scholars placed the corruption even later. One influential tradition maintained that since the Roman Emperor Titus had put no Jewish women aboard the ships that carried the survivors of the siege of Jerusalem into the Diaspora, the males had taken Muslim or pagan women to wife, so that their descendants were not real Jews but bastards, without claim to the covenant.[68] These "natural histories" sought to explain why the reproduction of Jewish cultural attributes should be understood as embedded in the reproduction of the flesh. In this sense, they provided the theoretical underpinning for the new genealogical boundaries, such as the doctrine of purity of blood, being established between Christian and "Jew."

Jews and conversos responded to these polemics in a variety of ways, many of which centered on the production of "counter-genealogies." To begin with the Jews, we can speak of an even greater emphasis on lineage at the level of the individual and the family, much along the lines described above in da

Piera and Aboab. Thus, while Alami could still protest against differentiating lineages in 1415, by 1480 Shem Tov ben Joseph ibn Shem Tov's position may have been more typical:

> If a person is of pure blood and has a noble lineage, he will give birth to a son like himself, and he who is ugly and stained [of blood?] will give birth to a son who is similar to him, for gold will give birth to gold and silver will give birth to silver and copper to copper, and if you find some rare instances that from lesser people sprang out greater ones, nevertheless in most cases what I have said is correct, and as you know, a science is not built on exceptions.[69]

We need not attribute Shem Tov's metallurgically flavored brand of Aristotelian *Naturgeschichte* directly to the influence of Christian treatises like the *Alborayque*, for such arguments had a very long history, but their rise to prominence among Iberian Jews in the mid-fifteenth century is doubtless not a coincidence.

Even more marked is the rise of a "national" genealogy among the Sephardim that sought to counter a number of the claims of the Old Christian polemics. Expanding upon traditions that traced the origins of certain families to the nobility of Jerusalem, Sephardic polemicists began to insist upon the noble Judaean origins of the entire Iberian diaspora. The claims were not entirely new. Moses ibn Ezra, for example, had invoked them centuries before in order to explain why Spanish Jews excelled all others in poetry, and Ibn Daud mentioned them as well. During the Maimonidean controversy David Qimḥi had suggested that Iberian Jews were all descended from Judaean nobility, whereas Ashkenazic Jews came from less distinguished provinces of Palestine.

Fifteenth-century Iberian Jews took up these hitherto relatively peripheral arguments, repeated them with more urgency, and extended them further. For example, a letter supposedly written by Toledan Jews at the time of Jesus's mission was produced in Toledo at roughly the same time as the anticonverso riots. The letter (which was claimed to have been translated from the Aramaic at the command of Alfonso X "the Learned") sought to establish that the Toledan Jews had been settled in Spain long before the Diaspora, and had in fact opposed the execution of Jesus by their coreligionists in the Holy Land.[70] Efforts to bolster such claims continued right up to the expulsion. In Murviedro, for example, a tombstone was discovered purporting to be that of Adoniram, a high official of King Solomon. On the eve of the expulsion the grammarian Moses ben Shem Tov ibn Ḥabib visited the same cemetery and deciphered an inscription for the minister of war of the biblical King Amatzya of Judah.[71]

These attempts to free the Sephardim from the charge of corrupt lineage, as well as deicide, and to claim for them a lineage superior to that of other Jews, reached their peak in the aftermath of the expulsion of 1492. The exiles Yitzḥaq Abarbanel (in his 1493 commentary on the Book of Kings) and Shelomo ibn Verga both incorporated forms of the legend into their works. In the apologetic history of Jewish persecution, the *Shevet Yehudah*, Ibn Verga has his fictional "Friar Thomas" explain to "King Alfonso" that when Nebuchadnezzar (605–562 BCE) conquered Jerusalem, he allotted the precinct of Jerusalem that contained the nobility "of royal lineage" to his allies Hispano and Pirro. The latter shipped the inhabitants back to Sepharad, "with the consequence that the Jews who are today in your kingdom are of royal lineage, and a great majority of them, from the lineage of Judah. . . . There is no other recognizable lineage, and only among these unfortunate Jews is their origin recognizable. . . . Is it not an honorable thing that, because they have not mixed with other gentile peoples, their origin and lineage is recognizable?"[72]

Such a lineage, King Alfonso exclaims, was greater even than that of the Goths, for it alone could know its origins. Upon the polemical stage Ibn Verga has constructed for them his characters perform for us the fusion of Iberian and Jewish myths of origin, the competitive comparison of genealogical memories.[73] These characters, moreover, are not Jews, but a friar and a "Gothic" king of Spain whose dynasty's claims to expertise in such matters were frequently and loudly asserted throughout Europe.[74] What better dramatization of the dynamics behind the formation of Sephardic genealogical pretensions and of the interdependence between the genealogical imagination of Christian and Jew?

For the conversos, the confrontation with the exclusionary genealogical arguments of the Old Christians was rather more complicated. Some converso writers, for example, objected that nobility was to be found more in an individual's deeds than in his ancestry. Others, like the leading expert in chivalry and heraldry of the age, Mosén Diego de Valera, asserted that non-Christians too (whether pagan, Muslim, or Jew) had their noble lineages, and that a non-Christian aristocrat's nobility only increased when he accepted the true faith. In the specific case of converts from Judaism, Valera was prepared to add a further argument: they could stress the collective honor of their lineage and boast of descent from God's chosen people.[75] As he wrote in his *Mirror of True Nobility* (1441): "God chose this lineage for His own as the most noble," by which he meant both that God had chosen the Jews as His people and that Christ had chosen this lineage to provide His flesh.[76] The offspring of mixed marriages (like Valera himself) could go so far as to maintain both Christian and Jewish nobility. In the struggle for prestige no claim was too far-fetched, not even that of the famous convert Pablo de Santa María, bishop of Burgos, who was rumored (by his descendants?) to stem on his father's side from King David and on his mother's from the most Gothic kings of Spain.[77]

Fantastic claims aside, the central contention here was that the conversos' Jewish lineage was what distinguished them, for that lineage had provided God and His mother with their own genealogy. Proconverso authors returned constantly to the theme and argued that to cast aspersions on the Jewish lineage of Jesus and Mary was tantamount to dishonoring God.[78] Such an argument, however, was a double-edged sword, for it opened the conversos to the charge of "judaizing." Christian theologians had long agreed, if not from the days of Saint Paul then from shortly thereafter, that to emphasize the merits of descent according to the flesh, and especially of descent from the Chosen People, was an error characteristic of the carnally minded and spiritually blind Jews. In Christ Jesus there is neither Jew nor Greek. This is what Alonso de Oropesa, the General of the Jeronimite order and director of the proto-Inquisition established in Toledo in 1462, meant when he wrote that "to pretend to introduce . . . difference or preference between one nation or another in the faith of Christ would be to diminish the perfect unity of Christendom . . . to the imperfection, yoke, and servitude that characterized the Old Testament, and therefore constitutes judaizing."[79] Oropesa was in fact writing a defense of the conversos, and his point was aimed at those who advocated discrimination against them, but the logic proved much more influential in the other direction.

Nearly every treatise written to defend the conversos from discrimination on the basis of descent (and there were many) manifests this tension, tacking constantly between the seemingly contradictory positions that the origins of the converts should be forgotten and that they descend from a distinguished lineage. But the problem is most starkly visible in the records of that terrifying arbiter of judaizing, the Inquisition, where conversos were frequently accused of the error of glorying in their lineage. Occasionally the charges concern some positive belief, such as being of the opinion that those who descended from the tribes of Israel could not die poor, because "that blessing remained to them from God when He spoke with Moses" (referring to the Deuteronomic blessings); or of interpreting Paul's "First the Jew and then the Greek" as meaning that New Christians should be preferred over Old in the distribution of offices and honors. But frequently the accusations stemmed from "street polemics," that is, from converso responses to insults aimed at their ancestry. Aldonza Romeu, for example, was reported for having replied to an insult with "we come from a better lineage [*generación*] than you do, for we descend from the lineage of the Virgin Mary and you descend from the lineage of the gentiles."[80] The converso retort crystallized into an aphorism: "Cristiano de natura, cristiano de mala ventura" (a Christian by nature is an unfortunate Christian). According to the (rather tortured) logic of defense lawyers, such words, if indeed uttered by the accused, were merely spoken in "melancholy" at the insults to which the convert was being subjected. The accused were only reminding their tormentors that "there is no difference between Jew and Greek . . . for both are men [sic] in Christ Jesus our lord," and that before the ancestors of "cristianos de natura" were converted in antiquity, they had been idol worshipers of "mala ventura," just as much in need of the cleansing waters of baptism as any Jew.[81] They had not, in other words, intended to judaize by implying the superiority of converso lineages over Old Christian ones.

Like the Jews, the conversos reacted to Old Christian genealogical strategies of polemic by responding in genealogical terms, emphasizing the nobility of their lineage. In the case of the conversos, however, this response facilitated the projection upon them of Old Christian anxiety about the "Jewishness" of the genealogical turn. The Jewishness of the converts was said to be nowhere more evident than in their emphasis on lineage. In the words of one of their enemies, "they had the presumption of pride, that there was no better people in the world, nor more discreet, nor more intelligent, nor more honored than they, because they were of the lineage of the tribes of Israel." By locating the origins of the logic of lineage in the conversos' Jewish roots, Old Christian writers like the author of these lines (Andrés Bernáldez) sought to justify the institution of genealogical discriminations in the form of the Inquisition and purity of blood statutes and at the same time to project responsibility for these innovations upon their victims.[82] Such genealogical displacements were a central aspect of Christian anti-Jewish and anticonverso apologetics. A century before, Saint Vincent had attributed the invention of his segregationist measures to the Jews themselves: "And if I say this, Jews, it should not be burdensome to you, for that is what your own law desires, and ours, and it is good logic that since you want to be separate from the Christians in faith, you should be separate from them in conversation."[83] The Toledan rebels of 1449 made similar claims, arguing that Moses had originated the prohibition on the descendants of converts occupying positions of power.[84] The strategies of some of the modern historians invoked in the opening of this chapter are not significantly different.

This is of course ironic, but it is also entirely systemic, part and parcel of the long-established hermeneutic strategies by which Christians categorized not only people but also ideas as Christian or Jewish. Alonso de Oropesa's claim that an emphasis on genealogy was Jewish is but one example of the techniques by which theologians since Paul had used dualities such as Christian-Jew, spiritual-carnal, allegorical-literal, redemptive-damning, sighted-blind, in order to map the negation of the Christian onto the Jew. The space in between these poles was a space of danger and heresy, a "judaizing" middle ground no good Christian should occupy. By essentializing the anti-Christian and projecting it onto what has come to be called "the hermeneutic Jew," Christian exegetes developed a powerful method of theological critique.[85] Within this discourse, "incorrect" Christian belief or deficient Christian practice was understood as "Judaism," and the (Christian) adherents of these beliefs or practices described as judaizing. Thus (to choose an example from our period) Saint Vincent could argue that infrequent confession made Christians "similar to Jews": "Just as the Jews took great care to wash the vessels, so you also take great care to wash the vessels before you drink, but often you take no care to wash the soul and the conscience through confession. And therefore in this way you are similar to the Jews."[86] But such discursive techniques had, for the previous thousand years at least, been deployed in a universe in which the boundaries between Christian and Jew were relatively clear. Their consequences were very different in the genealogically "judaized" world patrolled by the Inquisition in the late fifteenth century. There, ideas that had previously been projected onto an unreal "hermeneutic Jew" now found a lineage and a name in the combustible flesh of the converso.

The result was a mapping of "Jewish ideas" onto the "Jewish" lineages of individuals through genealogical investigation and inquisitional accusation. "Jewish" lineages were plentiful. Responding in 1449 to the purity of blood statutes of the Toledan rebels, Fernán Díaz, the relator of Juan II, had pointed out that there was scarcely a noble house in Spain that had no converso in its family tree. If Jewishness were attached to blood, the relator warned, genealogy would become a weapon of the weak and the nobility of Iberia would be destroyed.[87] Non-Spaniards were more than willing to agree. "Spain is not pleasing," Erasmus wrote in 1517, "because it is full of Jews" (though Germany and Italy also had too many Jews for Erasmus's taste, and England too many riots). One French pamphleteer claimed in the 1590s that "the Catalans, those of Castile and Portugal are Jews, those of Galicia and Granada Muslims, their prince is an atheist." Another called Philip II a "demi-More, demi-Juif, demi-Sarrazin." A French dictionary from 1680 defined *Marrano* ("Marrane") as "an insult we apply to Spaniards, which means a Muslim."[88]

Nor were "Jewish ideas" wanting. Since the classification of a practice or "idea" as Jewish or Christian was determined largely by relating it to the lineage of the person who held it, almost any practice or position could be presented as Jewish if the accused could be shown to have descended from Jews. Returning to the example above, pride in one's lineage could be evidence of judaizing if that lineage contained Jews, or appear perfectly orthodox if not. The classification of practices and ideas and the logic of genealogy depended upon each other. When the two did not coincide, the tension is revealing. One confused Muslim witness to the Inquisition said he had heard two Christians swear "by the law of Moses," but since he knew them to be "cristianos lindos" (that is, "Old Christians") he did not know if they did so "burlando o de veras" (in mockery or sincerely).[89]

Such tension was also productive, for "Jewish" classifications could break free of their genealogical moorings and attach themselves to formerly orthodox "Old Christian" activities. This logic was applied by the Inquisitors not only to vestiges of what they viewed as Jewish religious ceremonial but also to a range of philological, historical, and hermeneutic practices, many of them associated with the new humanism. (The Inquisition's attack on the use of Hebrew philology in biblical criticism is a particularly obvious and well-studied example.) Hence those oft-quoted lines that the son of the then Inquisitor General, Rodrigo Manrique, wrote to the self-exiled humanist Luis Vives in 1533: "You are right. Our country is a land of envy, pride, and . . . barbarism. For now it is clear that no one can possess a smattering of letters without being suspect of heresy, error, and Judaism."[90]

One might say that the genealogical definitions of community that Spain had constructed had turned her into an inescapably hybrid land. To deal with this paradox Spaniards filled vast archives with documents designed to free one's lineage of Judaism (such as proofs of purity of blood and of *hidalguía*) and to Judaize those of others (such as inquisitional records and genealogical pamphlets like the *Tizón de la nobleza* and the *Libro verde de Aragón*).[91] At the level of ideas, the same anxiety produced a genealogical type of cultural history that sought to separate "Jewish" from "Christian" ideas. The products of this type of history were typically lists of supposedly Jewish cultural attributes. According to the bishop of Córdoba in 1530, for example, Jewish attributes included heresy, apostasy, love of novelty and dissension, ambition, presumption, and hatred of peace. These lists sound as fantastic as Borges's Chinese encyclopedia, but they too were the product of a systematic historical method, one that sought in genealogy the secret to an understanding of the origins and transmission of ideas.

Of course this "genealogization" of history was not only a Christian (or even an "Old Christian") phenomenon.[92] Jews, too, produced an explosion of historical and apologetic writing in the fifteenth century, much of which seems to draw on very similar genealogically inflected strategies of historical and philological argumentation. Indeed this tendency is so marked that it may provide us with yet another perspective from which to understand the rapid development of Jewish historiography in the period. Yosef Yerushalmi has famously argued that the trauma of the Spanish expulsion was the principal factor in stimulating the writing of history, a genre until then largely neglected in the Jewish Diaspora. It is certainly true that history streamed from the pens of first-generation Sephardic exiles like Shelomo ibn Verga, Abraham Zacuto, Elijah Capsali, Abraham ben Salomon de Torrutiel Ardutiel, Yosef ben Tzadiq of Arévalo, and others.[93] But the historical sensibilities of these Sephardic writers owed as much to their genealogical mentalities as to their exilic experience, and in this sense the creation of a "Sephardic historiographic mentality" predated the expulsion by several generations.

The importance of genealogy as a template for postexilic Jewish historical narrative is evident, for example, in Abraham Zacuto's adaptation for historiographic purposes of preexisting genealogical genres such as *shalshalaot ha-qabbalah*, "chains of tradition," a genre whose task it was to assign a lineage to ideas—hence the title of his most innovative work, the *Sefer Yuḥasin ha-Shalem*, the "sound book of genealogies" (1504).[94] But it is equally evident in a good deal of writing from throughout the fifteenth century, for writers such as Zacuto and Ibn Verga were inheritors of a genealogical approach to culture developed in Jewish apologetics (and we must remember that history and apologetics were inseparable in this period) a century before the expulsion, in response to heightened Christian (and Muslim) polemical insistence on Jewish cultural hybridity and corruption. Fifteenth-century Sephardic apologists sought to turn the tables upon their attackers by adopting modes of historical argument that stressed the purity of Jewish belief and practice in contrast to the corruption of originally Jewish concepts in their rivals' culture. To do so, they drew on traditional genres (like the "chains of tradition" mentioned above) that Jews had long ago developed to "guarantee" the authoritative origins and stable transmission of their traditions. But they also drew on the most up-to-date methods of their opponents.

In his *Kelimat ha-Goyim* (Reproach of the Gentiles, ca. 1397), for example, Profiat Duran borrowed extensively from Christian humanist strategies for establishing pure archetypes of texts and concepts through critical study of manuscript transmission and corruption. In the hands of Christian polemicists, these strategies supported arguments that rabbinic Judaism represented a corruption of biblical religion and a forfeiture of the biblical covenant. Duran used the same tools to demonstrate the Jewish origins of Christian practices such as baptism in order to present these Christian practices as corruptions of a pure Jewish archetype. Shim'on Ben Tzemah Duran's *Qeshet u-Magen* (Bow and Shield) employed similar techniques against Islam, arguing for the Jewish origins of Muslim dietary and purity laws, circumcision, prayer, and pilgrimage practices. (This is, incidentally, an argument also common to fifteenth-century Iberian Christian anti-Muslim polemic, which presents Islam as a judaizing heresy.) More traditionally, both employed historical philology to demonstrate the textual, as well as cultural, corruption of the pristine Jewish forms in the sacred writings of these later religions. Here too we are witnessing the formation of a genealogical type of cultural history, one whose polemical importance is reflected in Hayyim ibn Musa's advice, in his *Magen va-Romah* (Shield and Spear, ca. 1456), that the primary mode of commentary in religious disputation should be the historical.[95]

Again, it should be stressed that I am not arguing for precedence or priority of invention here. On the contrary, I am suggesting that the question of "origin" or "invention" in this case is a false one, itself a product of the essentializing strategies of our sources. In their attempts to respond to circumstances of mass assimilation, classificatory crises, and heightened polemical pressure, members of each religious community had available to them long and complex traditions that could sustain any number of genealogical reinterpretations. They could also draw upon those of their rivals: here the author of the *Alborayque*'s awareness of rabbinic *responsa* about 'anusim is just as instructive as (albeit much cruder than) Profiat Duran's appropriation of humanist hermeneutics. As a result of these attempts, and over the course of little more than a century, previously marginal logics of lineage had moved to the center of Jewish, converso, and Old Christian communal identity and memory in Iberia. This transformation was achieved, not by the implacable migration of ideas from one culture to another, but by the jostling of countless individuals, Jew and Christian, reorienting themselves in the strangely unfamiliar religious landscape that emerged as the floodwaters of baptism receded.

The genealogical turn was itself an attempt to conceal this unfamiliarity, this rupture, by establishing new continuities, new links to family, faith, "race," and "nation." This chapter has touched upon some symptoms of this genealogical turn, and many more could be added. But it is fitting to end with the rise of history, because of all the products of the genealogical turn in Sepharad, it alone retains its power to convince. We now, for example, treat as so much fiction the richly illuminated *ketubbot* (marriage contracts) that Sephardic families began to produce in the fifteenth century in order to celebrate their Davidic ancestry.[96] Yet we rarely quarrel with historiography, Christian and Jewish, that has in its quest for origins long adopted the genealogical methods of the fifteenth-century polemicist. Like the "Antiquarian historian" of Nietzsche's second "Untimely Meditation," the historian of Spain and its Jews too often "greets the soul of his nation across the long dark centuries of confusion as his own soul."[97] The preceding pages are about the history of lineage and the history of history in fifteenth-century Sepharad. But they are just as much about these shades of genealogy that have proven so difficult to exorcise from our own historical practices.

[8]

Was There Race before Modernity?

The Example of "Jewish" Blood in Late Medieval Spain

> What is known as the history of concepts is really a history
> either of our knowledge of concepts or of the meaning of words.
> Gottlob Frege, *Die Grundlagen der Arithmetik*, vii.

Thus far our inquiries have been focused on the coproduction of diverse communities in the distant past. But like religious communities at any given moment in time, the past and the present are also mutually and dynamically constituted. "The past," as T. S. Eliot put it, may be "altered by the present as much as the present is directed by the past." (Marc Bloch said something very similar at much the same time.) In many of the previous chapters, we watched as medieval people reinterpreted their past in light of their present needs, rereading not only their histories but also their scriptures in order to re-order their world. But our historical subjects are not the only ones who reread the past for the present. Modern historians and philologists, too, feed the past (in the words of Walter Benjamin) with the blood of the living. This nourishment is vital, but it is also dangerous. To quote Benjamin once more: "Just as a man lying sick with fever transforms all the words that he hears into the extravagant images of delirium, so it is that the spirit of the present age seizes on the manifestations of past or distant spiritual worlds, in order to take possession of them and unfeelingly incorporate them into its own self-absorbed fantasizing."[1]

In this and the remaining chapter we will focus on the opportunities for critical reflection that past and present offer each other, as well as on the dangers of fantasy. In this one, we take up a question directly from the previous: how did the genealogical tools taken up by Christians and Jews in medieval

Spain transform the future? And how did the future alter the ways in which that medieval past could be perceived and put to work? In order to sharpen the point, I will ask those questions through the history of "race," a word that burst into Castilian and Catalan at more or less the same time as the converts and their descendants did, and that—like them—has wandered across vast stretches of European (and not only European) thought.

* * *

Less than a lifetime ago many scholars agreed that racial concepts offered reasonable explanations for the differences they perceived between certain human populations. That consensus extended, not only to such "color" distinctions as those between "white" European and "black" sub-Saharan African, but also to less chromatic classifications such as "Indo-European" and "Semite." It extended backward in time, as well. In the nineteenth century, for example, the most eminent historians did not hesitate to describe medieval and early modern conflicts between Christians, Jews, and Muslims as racial. Today the situation has so reversed itself that no scholar of any stripe or period can strip the word "race" of its scare-quotes without inviting polemic.

It is not difficult to find the turning point in the fate of race as theory. It came at mid-twentieth century, with the German National Socialists' implementation of an explicitly racial ideology that culminated in the extermination of millions of members of those races deemed most dangerous or degenerate. Opponents of fascism often pointed critically to the brutality of Nazi racial policies, even if they made relatively little effort to help the victims of those policies, and this critique in turn strengthened the arguments of those who sought to challenge the authority of racial ideologies in the countries and colonies of the eventual Allies. Throughout the 1930s and 1940s in the United States, for example, African American journalists drew frequent comparisons between the treatment of Jews in Germany and blacks at home. In those same decades, social scientists like Ruth Benedict and Ashley Montague took up Franz Boas's invitation to demonstrate the arbitrariness of any definition of "race." In *Man's Most Dangerous Myth: The Fallacy of Race* (1942), Montague made the point through the then timely example of the Jews. For centuries, he claimed, the persecution of Jews "was always done on social, cultural, or religious grounds. . . .Whatever was held against them was never attributed to clearly defined biological reasons. The 'racial' interpretation is a modern 'discovery.' That is the important point to grasp. The objection to any people on 'racial' or biological grounds is virtually a purely modern innovation." The goal of arguments like Montague's was to demolish the scientific grounds upon which racial regimes justified their discriminations between human populations, thereby unmasking those discriminations as the contingent product of the workings of power in modernity. So great was the success of such arguments that by 1950 race was discredited as a mode of discourse in the biological and social sciences, if not in more regional or popular dialects. For evidence of the impact of this discursive shift, we need look no further than the United Nation's postwar declarations on human rights or the deliberations of the United States Supreme Court about the constitutionality of segregation.[2]

The dismantling of racism's claims to provide a natural explanation for the existence of cultural, economic, and social difference, or for the persistence of such difference through time, was one of the most important achievements of the mid-twentieth-century social sciences. Since that time, those sciences have been struggling with mixed success to find new terms and theories with which to describe and explain the persistence of group identity and group difference across time and space.[3] Historians too are struggling with the consequences of the dismantling of race, but theirs is a slightly different problem, for their task is not only that of criticizing the ontological status of key words and concepts such as race but also that of understanding the concepts and categories that their historical subjects used to make sensible (at least to them) claims about the formation and reproduction of group identities in their own societies.

These two goals are not always compatible. When, for example, scholars make use of the word "race" in their analyses of nineteenth- and twentieth-century United States history, as they so often do, they are deploying what they know to be a "myth" incapable of definition. But if they were to follow the injunctions of the more radical among them to erase such fictions from their vocabulary, they would lose purchase on the language of their subjects. (Besides, such a logic would require us to expunge many other words from our analyses, among them "God.")[4] It is for this reason, among others, that modernists, insofar as they are describing the thought-world of their subjects rather than their own, continue to write about "race" and "racism" with relatively little controversy. But the further we move toward the premodern, the more controversial such usage becomes. Why should we apply words denoting concepts that we ourselves believe have no value as explanations of difference to societies whose protagonists were not only ignorant (except, as we shall see, in Romance-speaking lands) of the word "race" itself but also untutored by the scientists (Lamarck, Mendel, Darwin, Huxley, etc.) who would give that word teeth? On both sides of the chronological divide between the modern and the premodern (wherever it may lie), there is today a remarkable consensus that the earlier vocabularies of difference are innocent of race.

Like every consensus, this one has costs as well as benefits. But before exploring those, it is worth pointing out the more or less mutual disinterest upon which the consensus is based. Among advocates of premodern innocence, the dismissal of race too often relies on the most cursory engagement with the complex history of the modern racial concepts whose relevance is at issue.[5] Some take refuge in lexicography, arguing (for example) that because the word *Rasse* did not enter German until the eighteenth century and the word *Anti-Semitismus* until the nineteenth, we need not look for these concepts in the earlier history of German-speaking lands. Others embrace narrow definitional strategies that succeed not in solving the problem but in rendering it uninteresting. It is not surprising, for example, that those who define race as the application of eighteenth- and nineteenth-century vocabularies of biological classification to human populations differentiated by skin color are certain that it cannot be found in earlier periods.[6] Such definitions cannot tell us much about the premodern, since they fail to make sense even of modern racial ideologies against which they define themselves, ideologies which are themselves not only tremendously diverse but also changing a great deal over time.

Perhaps the most widespread and intuitively persuasive argument against the relevance of race for the premodern period is the common view that medieval (for example) classifications of peoples were not sufficiently biological to qualify as racism, no matter how much they might smack of natural history. Robert Bartlett put this consensus particularly well: "While the language of race [in medieval sources]—gens, natio, 'blood,' 'stock,' etc.—is *biological*, its medieval reality was almost entirely *cultural*."[7] Although it is not absolutely clear what "reality" of language means here—perhaps the reality of the differences described by the language?—, what is clear is that the procedure of establishing a difference between the terms of a distinction (biological) and the reality of that distinction (cultural) is meant to relieve the Middle Ages of the charge of racism.

We need not pronounce judgment on the charge in order to wonder if this defense is adequate. All racisms are attempts to ground discriminations, whether social, economic, or religious, in biology and reproduction. All claim a congruence of "cultural" categories with "natural" ones. None of these claims, not even the most "scientific" ones of the twentieth century, reflects biological reality. Modern population genetics has of course discovered some real differences between, say, sub-Saharan African populations and Swedish ones, or between Jewish and non-Jewish populations (as any student of breast cancer or Tay-Sachs disease knows).[8] But these real biological differences have no obvious or natural relationship to the cultural work they are asked to do in systems of racial discrimination, systems which are products of culture, not of nature. If this lack of congruence does not suffice to make modern racist ideologies less "racial," then it cannot suffice to excuse premodern discriminations from the charge.[9]

We can generalize this objection: rather than engage in a systematic comparison of the discursive power of natural histories deployed in specific premodern and modern arguments about the reproduction of group difference, we premodernists too often rely on the questionable axiom that modern racial theories depend upon evolutionary biology and genetics, in order to leap to the demonstrably false conclusion that there exists a truly biological modern racism against which earlier forms of discrimination can be measured and judged innocent.[10] But the certainties of modernists about the origins of race are equally partial, and equally questionable. In one of a series of lectures at the Collège de France in 1976, Michel Foucault (to pick a prominent example) insisted that racism was a uniquely modern phenomenon, the product of a European struggle for sovereignty that did not occur before the seventeenth century. According to Foucault, medieval sovereignty had been organic and corporatist. It was of course hierarchical and therefore often conflictual, but that conflict was always contained by a ritual regime and a historical discourse that were celebratory and inclusive. Even warring nations never forgot their common ancestry, going back, if not to Rome, then to Troy. And from this memory sprang as well a common historiography. "What is there in [medieval] history," Foucault asked, quoting Petrarch, "that is not in praise of Rome?"[11]

Race arose out of the collapse of this system. By the early seventeenth century, society was no longer thought of as an organic system, but as a binary. The governing metaphor was no longer that of society as a harmonious body, but of society as a war between two irreconcilable groups or bodies. And although those groups could be characterized and classified in a number of ways (as classes, for example), the symbolic logic underlying these classifications was always racial, in that it imagined one group as polluting and the other pure, one to be isolated or exterminated, the other to be protected and reproduced. The emerging nation-state was at first the venue for this struggle between groups, then eventually its arbiter, the chief guarantor of racial purity. This final nineteenth-century stage Foucault referred to as "state racism." And just as history in the Middle Ages had been a reflection of the symbolic order that articulated power in terms of organic unity, in modernity history became a battlefield, an accounting of losses and victories in the eternal war of the races.

Even if we were to grant (as many would not)[12] that the struggle for sovereignty within Europe was the key conflict in the emergence of race, we could easily object that Foucault's arguments for the modern origins of race depend upon a falsely organic view of the Middle Ages. Have not R. I. Moore, Dominique Iogna-Prat, Tomaž Mastnak, and many other medievalists (including the author of this volume) shown us the dependence of medieval arguments about sovereignty on the identification of Jewish, Muslim, or heretical threats to Christian society, and on claims to defend Christian society against those threats? It is relatively easy to demonstrate the importance of such religious "enmities" to the formation of western European notions of a Christendom threatened from without and within by impurity and pollution.[13] Why should these enmities not be considered a sufficient stimulus to the symbolic logic Foucault associated with the origins of race? Clearly Foucault's audience shared some of these doubts, for he began his next lecture (of February 4) by addressing them. "During the last week or two, people have sent me a number of objections, both oral and written," asking in particular "what does it mean to have racism originate in the sixteenth or seventeenth century, to attach it only to problems of state sovereignty, when we well know, after all, that religious racism (anti-Semitic racism in particular) has existed since the Middle Ages?" Foucault did not respond to these objections. He merely restated his conviction and concluded with the greatest evasion available to a professor: "come see me during office hours."

The proceedings of Foucault's office hours, unlike those of his lectures, have not been transcribed and published, so we cannot say whether or how he engaged these questions. It is unlikely that he was sympathetic, given that history was for him a scythe, to be swung against the giant stalks of genealogical fantasy with which Europeans attempted (according to Nietzsche) to climb down into their distant past. "History," Foucault insisted in an essay on Nietzsche's genealogies, "is for cutting." When it comes to the question of race, nearly an entire generation of historians—most of whom share neither Foucault's general program for the writing of history nor his specific sense of the struggle for sovereignty as the driving force of race—seems to agree, forgetting that a history that cuts too often or too deep is just as fantastic as one whose filiations are too thick.[14] Hence Nietzsche had insisted on an element of formal continuity to the ideas whose history interested him: a "terrifying mask" that these ideas wore across time, impressing them upon generations of human memory and concealing their transformations behind features of unchanging horror. For Nietzsche (unlike Foucault), the history of ideas consisted less in stripping the "mask" from the "actor" than in developing a dramaturgy appropriate to their interplay.

Be that as it may, the snipping of several generations of historians has by now separated race from whatever masks it may once have worn. Precisely for this reason it seems to me useful to stroll through some more ancient museums of natural history and imagine race placed among their exhibits. What if, for example, we treat race as but one chapter in the long history of the conviction that culture is produced and reproduced in the same way as the species procreates itself? I cannot, in the pages that follow, pretend to provide anything as cosmopolitan as a critical history of this conviction. Nor do I aspire to anything as provincial as a proof that late medieval discriminations were racial. My goal is only to demonstrate that too easy a certainty about where each chapter in a "natural history" of culture begins and ends represses the very processes of contextualization, comparison, and analogy out of which a critical understanding of such histories should emerge. To shift metaphors: it is painfully clear why for the last half-century it has been so important to cut a modern straitjacket for histories of race. Perhaps our analyses have reached the point where we may loosen the sleeves and begin comparing the mad certainties of different times and places. I have chosen one example of what such comparison might look like, the same example with which Ashley Montague confronted his readers, and with which Foucault's audience confronted him—I mean, of course, the venerable debate over the nature of Christian attitudes toward the Jews—and will focus within that example on the Crowns of Aragon and of Castile in the Middle Ages: the polities that we today call Spain.

Like the more general questions of race with which we began, the debate over the racial nature of anti-Semitism was taken up with new urgency after the rise of National Socialism. Some historians, such as Cecil Roth, saw real affinities between premodern ideologies of discrimination (particularly those of late medieval Spain toward Christians descended from Jews) and modern (particularly German) ones, affinities which Roth explored in an essay

published in 1940, entitled "Marranos and Racial Anti-Semitism: A Study in
Parallels." Others, like Guido Kisch, categorically denied any racial element
in premodern anti-Judaism and criticized those who thought otherwise for
"reading modern racist conceptions into medieval sources."[15]

The extermination of nearly all the Jews of Europe during the Second
World War raised the ethical stakes of these debates to heights far greater
than those that historical argument generally affords. For some, the gravi-
tational pull of Auschwitz is so strong that all earlier ideologies about Jews
become coordinates in a trajectory clearly spiraling toward destruction. Historians of this school (Benzion Netanyahu is an example) make relatively free
use of the words "race" and "racism" to describe discriminations against Jews,
whether they occurred in Hellenistic Egypt, fifteenth-century Spain, Nazi
Germany, or the present.[16] For others, indeed the vast majority, such stakes
are unbearably high. They prefer to understand modern racial anti-Semitism
as the specific and contingent product of the intersection of capitalism, imperialism, and post-Enlightenment natural science, a phenomenon radically
discontinuous with other and earlier histories. The deep cuts of this historicism are (at least in part) designed to relieve more distant pasts from responsibility for an ideology that has come to stand for all that is evil in Europe.
Thus Heiko Oberman can reassure us that the Reformation is untainted by
racism, because the many negative comments that Reuchlin, Erasmus, and
Luther made about Jews, about converts from Judaism, and about their descendants, were based on a purely theological understanding, not a biological
one, which we might term anti-Judaism but not anti-Semitism.[17]

This distinction between a "biological" anti-Semitism associated with
modernity and a "cultural" anti-Judaism associated with premodernity did
not, of course, originate with Oberman. It is what we might call the "Jewish
corollary" to the broader axiom about the modernity of race.[18] Every bit as
widespread as that axiom, the corollary has itself assumed in most historical
circles the status of article of faith, even if a few heretics remain.[19] But there
is room for doubt, and the scholarly expression of that doubt tends to cluster
around Spain in the late Middle Ages.[20]

Iberian history has long served as a focal point for arguments about premodern race because, as is well known, large populations of Muslims and
Jews made the peninsular kingdoms the most religiously diverse in medieval
western Europe. The late fourteenth and fifteenth centuries witnessed massive attempts to eliminate that diversity through massacre, segregation, conversion, Inquisition, and expulsion. In one sense these efforts toward homo-

geneity were successful. Over the course of the hundred years from 1391 to 1492, for example, all the Jews of Spain either converted or were expelled.[21]

But the conversion of a large number of people whom Christians had perceived as profoundly different transformed the old boundaries and systems of discrimination rather than abolished them, as categories that had previously seemed primarily legal and religious were replaced by the genealogical notion that Christians descended from Jewish converts (*Cristianos nuevos, confessos, conversos, Marranos*) were essentially different from "Christians by nature" (*Cristianos de natura, cristianos viejos, lindos, limpios*). Moreover, the ideological underpinning of these new discriminations claimed explicitly to be rooted in natural realities, as is most evident in what came to be called the doctrine of "limpieza de sangre." According to this doctrine, Jewish and Muslim blood was inferior to Christian; the possession of any amount of such blood made one liable to heresy and moral corruption; and therefore any descendant of Jews and Muslims, no matter how distant, should be barred from church and secular office, from any number of guilds and professions, and especially from marrying Old Christians.

The debate over the utility of concepts such as race and racism in explaining these conflicts, discriminations, and ideologies has been quite heated. It has remained, however, bedeviled by the fiction of true race. In the early years of history as *Wissenschaft*, of course, this fiction enabled racial analysis, because historians themselves believed in the racial logic they were attributing to their historical subjects. In writing of conflict between Christians, Muslims, and Jews, historians constantly employed the vocabulary of race, although they meant very different things by it.[22] An early example is that of Leopold von Ranke, who believed that the Old Christian refusal to intermarry with New Christians was an extension of the ancient abhorrence that the "Germanic" and "Romanic" races felt toward amalgamation with "Semitic" Jews and Muslims.[23] Half a century later (ca. 1882) the great historian Marcelino Menéndez y Pelayo, in whose honor Spain's Real Academia de la Historia is named, could echo Darwin unself-consciously: "It is madness to believe that battles for existence, bloody and century long struggles between races, could end in any way other than with expulsions and exterminations. The inferior race always succumbs." Elsewhere he opined that "the matter of race [by which he meant the existence of "Semitic" Jews and Muslims] explains many phenomena and resolves many enigmas in our history," and "is the principal cause of decadence for the [Iberian] Peninsula." At much the same time, though an ocean and an ideology away, Henry Charles Lea also accepted racial categories in order to make the argument that the Spanish Inquisition was an instrument of racism.[24]

But as we have already seen from the debate between Cecil Roth and Guido Kisch, such certainties began to fade in the mid-twentieth century. Within the ambit of Spanish historiography, Américo Castro became perhaps the most influential critic of racial vocabulary. Castro was interested in debunking not just notions of Jewish or Muslim racial identity, but the idea of a "raza hispánica" as well. As he put it in one of his later works, "faith in the temporally uncertain biological continuity of the Spaniard has inspired the works both of respected men of wisdom and of superficial scholars."[25] His task, as he saw it, was to demonstrate the falsity of any model of Spanish identity based on such a faith. To this end, Castro began nearly all of his books with an attack upon the relevance of the concept of race to Spanish history.[26] In the opening of *The Spaniards*, for example, he explains that he speaks of Muslim, Jewish, and Christian "castes," not races, "for in that Spain of three religions everyone was light-skinned, with horizontal eyes, except for a few black slaves brought in from Africa" (p. v). Similarly in the introduction to the 1965 edition of *La realidad* he writes: "A much wider detour will be necessary in order to include in future historiography the positive and decisive presence of the Moorish and Jewish castes (not races!). Because the resistance is notable to the acceptance that the Spanish problem was of castes, and not of races, [a term] today only applicable to those distinguished, as the Dictionary of the Academy has it, 'by the color of their skin and other characteristics.'"[27] This repudiation of race depends upon familiar strategies: the focus on the *Diccionario*'s definition of race as referring only to skin color (he ignored the ominous "Y otros caracteres"); and the conjuration of an easily dismissed "true" biological racism based solely on external physical characteristics.[28]

Castro's approach to race is the one point of his oeuvre with which nearly all Spanish and French scholars of peninsular history concur. In the words of a devoted "Castrista," F. Márquez Villanueva: "The problem of the New Christians was by no means a racial one; it was social and in the second line religious. The *converso* did not carry in any moment an indelible biological stigma." Historians with less enthusiasm for many of Castro's broader arguments agree. The fact that the few dissenting voices are mostly North American has perhaps contributed to the polarization, as Spanish scholars have sought to distance themselves from what they perceive to be an excessive willingness of "Anglo-Saxon" scholars to replicate the "Black Legend" by projecting the racial histories of their own lands onto that of Spain.[29]

Each of these repudiations of race has been of undoubted strategic importance. There were, for example, many Spanish scholars who did maintain that
Jews and Muslims were members of races inferior to the "raza hispánica," and
Américo Castro's attack against that vocabulary helped bring these groups
back into the mainstream of Spanish history and culture. But such strategic
skirmishes cannot alone conquer the vast complex of ideas about the reproduction of cultural characteristics that they claim to aim at. Indeed unless
they open a path for heavier engagements, they risk being stranded behind
enemy lines. Castro's easy isolation of race in the epidermis, for example,
blinded him to the ways in which his methodology simply displaced many of
the naturalizing and essentializing functions of "race" into the less charged
term of "caste" (much as many speakers today use "ethnicity"). There is in fact
a close kinship between Castro's "Semitic caste" and "Semitic culture" and
Ernest Renan's "Semitic race."[30] Both posited stable, essential, and inescapable forms of group identity continuously reproduced across time. Castro, like
Renan, combed "Jewish" texts beginning with the Old Testament for Semitic
characteristics whose entrance into Spain he then attributed to Jews and conversos. He found a number of them. "Inquisitorial fanaticism and recourse to
slandering informants—what one might call in Spanish 'malsinismo'—frantic
greed and plundering, the concern over purity of blood . . . the concern with
public reputation . . . , the desire of everyone to be a nobleman . . . somber
asceticism . . . , the negative view of the world . . . , disillusionment, and the
flight from human values," all of these were the "poisons . . . that seeped into
Spanish life, Spanish Christendom, in the increment of forced converts."[31]

These "cultural" traits of Jews and converts are startlingly similar, not only
to those "racial" ones listed by Renan or his disciples (which on this score
included the champion of the "raza hispánica" and Castro's arch-rival, Claudio Sánchez Albornoz),[32] but also to those of fifteenth- and sixteenth-century
anticonverso tracts advocating limpieza. Nor are the means of their reproduction so very different, for though Castro and his students reject biological
explanations for cultural transmission, they rely heavily on genealogical ones,
frequently mapping a particular intellectual position or literary style onto a
family tree in order to prove the "Semiticness" of either the idea or of its exponent, a type of logic that has turned many Iberianists into methodological
disciples of Inquisitors.[33] Like many other historians and philologists, Castro
fled from the horrifying embrace of race straight into the arms of another
genetic fantasy. Small wonder that, far from having banished race and racism,
he found himself accused of replicating it under another name.[34]

Thus far my argument has been entirely "negative," first criticizing the terms in which questions about race in the premodern period have been asked by others; then suggesting that, at the rather gross level of historiography, those terms are much the same whether we are talking of race generally, of the Jewish case more specifically, or of the singular example of Spain. But of course each case differs a great deal in its particulars, and it is through a focus on those particulars in the Spanish case that I will attempt to provide a more "positive" example of the cognitive benefits that may flow from emphasizing, rather than eliding, the medieval vocabularies through which "naturalizations" of difference were expressed. The history of the Romance word *raza*, from whence the English "race," provides an obvious starting point. The Castilian word does cover a broad semantic field,[35] yet certain corners of that field deserve closer cultivation than they have received. Castro's invocation of the Real Academia's modern definition of *raza* in order to dismiss the possibility of premodern "Spanish" racism is in fact a startling procedure, given that Castro was a philologist who had elsewhere, for example, deployed the history of the word *Español* to suggest that the concept of "Spanishness" was a late import to Spanish culture. Had he been willing to apply the same technique to the word *raza*, he would have found that it too is a word with a suggestive history in the various Romances of the peninsula.

Already in the early fifteenth century *raza, casta,* and *linaje* (race, caste, lineage) were part of a complex of closely associated terms that linked both behavior and appearance to nature and reproduction. Some of these words, like the word "lineage" itself, had long been used to tie character to genealogy, and the history of that usage was largely independent of "Jewish" questions, although it could easily be extended to them. Writing around 1435, for example, the chronicler/historian Gutierre Díez de Games explained all treason in terms of Jewish "linaje": "From the days of Alexander up till now, there has never been a treasonous act that did not involve a Jew or his descendants."[36]

The Castilian word *raza*, however, was much newer, and it seems to have come into broad usage as a term in the animal and the human sciences more or less simultaneously. Although the earliest use I know of in Castilian deploys the term to refer to a hoof disease in horses, among breeders the word *raza* quickly came to mean, in the first quarter of the fifteenth century, something like "pedigree."[37] Thus Manuel Dies's popular manual on equine care (written ca. 1430) admonished breeders to be careful in their selection of stock: "For there is no animal that so resembles or takes after the father in virtues and beauties, nor in size, or coat, and similarly for their contraries. So that it is advised that he who wishes to have good race and caste of horses that above all he seek out the horse or stallion that he be good and beautiful and of good coat, and the mare that she be large and well formed and of good coat."[38]

At more or less the same time in Castilian poetry, *raza* emerged as a way of describing a variety of defects linked to poetic speech, to sexuality, and especially to Judaism.[39] Francisco Imperial, whose Italianate verse had an important impact on the Castilian lyric tradition, addressed an exhortatory poem to the king in 1407 which provides an ambiguous but early example of this last. The poet praised, as an exemplary mirror for all the king's successors, his "shining knife/that cuts wherever it discovers race." Scholars have not seen in this early use an association of "raza" to "lineage of Jews." But the poet's condemnation of the "bestia Juderra" a few lines before (line 321) suggests otherwise, as does his echo of the exhortation, commonly addressed to Trastamaran kings of Castile, that they defeat that Jewish beast.[40]

In any event, the "Jewishness" of the defects encoded in "raza" soon became more obvious, and as they did so they were enriched with meanings drawn from the more agricultural corners of the word's semantic field. You will recall from the previous chapter the arguments of Alfonso Martínez de Toledo, writing around 1438 in the midst of an evolving conflict over *converso* office-holding in Toledo: the son of an ass must bray. That is why "the good man of good raça always returns to his origins, whereas the miserable man, of bad raça or lineage, no matter how powerful or how rich, will always return to the villainy from which he descends. . . . When such men or women have power they do not use it as they should."[41]

I will return in a moment to the strenuous debate that developed over this incipient claim that political rights should be dependent on proper "race." But first it is worth insisting that the language of this claim was already saturated with resonance to what contemporaries held to be "common sense" knowledge about the reproductive systems of the natural world.[42] It is the marriage of these two domains, of political disability and of reproductive fitness, which is so well reflected in the famous definition of the word *raza* that Sebastián de Covarrubias provided in his Spanish dictionary of 1611: "the caste of purebred horses, which are marked by a brand so that they can be recognized. . . . Race in [human] lineages is meant negatively, as in having some race of Moor or Jew."[43]

The natural science upon which such wisdom was based was not that of the nineteenth century, but it was nonetheless capable of generating conclusions startlingly similar to those of a later age.[44] Nor, I hasten to add, was this logic in any way peculiar to Spain. Writing in 1538, in praise of the king of France, the Italian Jacobus Sadoletus would urge the readers of his child-rearing manual "that what is done with horses and dogs should also be done with men . . . so that out of good parents there might be born a progeny useful to both the king and the fatherland." Joachim du Bellay (c.1559) admonished the French parliament in a similar vein:

> For if we are so careful to preserve the race
> Of good horses and good hounds for chase
> How much more carefully should a king provide
> For the race, which is his principal power?[45]

The point, in short, is that words like *raza, casta,* and *linaje* (and their cognates in the various Iberian romance languages) were already embedded in identifiably biological ideas about animal breeding and reproduction in the first half of the fifteenth century. Moreover, the sudden and explicit application of this vocabulary to Jews coincides chronologically (the 1430s) with the appearance of an anticonverso ideology (already encountered in the example of Alfonso Martínez de Toledo) that sought to establish new religious categories and discriminations and legitimate these by naturalizing their reproduction. One of the earliest legislative examples comes from 1433. It was on the tenth of January of that year that Queen María decreed on behalf of the converts of Barcelona that no legal distinction could be made between "natural" Christians on the one hand and neophytes and their descendants on the other, a decree which implies that some people were attempting to make precisely those distinctions.[46] A year later a decree of the Council of Basel took particular pains to reject those distinctions: "since [the converts] became by the grace of baptism fellow citizens of the saints and members of the house of God, and since regeneration of the spirit is much more important than birth in the flesh, . . . they enjoy the privileges, liberties, and immunities of those cities and towns where they were regenerated through sacred baptism to the same extent as the natives and other Christians do." We saw in chapter 6 both how necessary and how ineffectual the decree proved to be. A few months after it was issued, King Alfonso of Aragon rejected attempts in Calatayud to impose disabilities on neophytes; in 1436, the councilors of Barcelona moved to bar converts and those whose parents were not both "cristianos de natura" from holding the office of notary; in 1437 the town council of Lleida attempted to strip conversos of broker's licenses. The converts of Catalonia and Valencia appealed to the pope, and in 1437 Eugenius IV condemned as "sons of iniquity . . . Christians only in name" those who suggested that recent converts be barred from public office and who "refuse to enter into matrimony with them." Similarly in Castile, an antimonarchical rebellion may have planned to murder the converso population of Seville in 1433–34, and ten years later, still in the midst of civil war, King Juan II was obliged to instruct the cities of his kingdom that the conversos were to be treated "as if they were born Christians" and to be admitted to "any honorable office of the Republic."[47]

The vocabulary of race evolved under the pressure of this conflict, as words like *raza, casta, linaje,* and even *natura* herself were applied to converts and their descendants. By 1470 the word "race" was so common in poetry that Pero Guillén included it (along with other useful words like "Marrano") in his *Gaya ciencia,* a handbook of rhymes for poets.[48] The "cristiano de natura" mentioned by Queen María became a common (though by no means exclusive) term of reference for "Old Christians." The exclusionary genealogical logic of the term was perfectly clear to conversos, some of whom coined a rebuttal: "cristianos de natura, cristianos de mala ventura" ("Christians by nature are Christians of bad fortune"). By this they meant (or at least so they told the Inquisition decades later) that conversos shared the lineage of the Virgin Mary, whereas old Christians were descended from idol-worshiping Gentiles.[49] Such remarks encode histories that are too complicated to address here, but they suggest that the converts responded to the *Naturgeschichte* of "clean Christians" with genealogies of their own.[50] In any event the wide extension of such vocabulary in the 1430s and following decades makes clear that the role of lineage in determining character, which had become an increasingly important aspect of chivalric and aristocratic ideology in Iberia in the decades following the Trastamaran civil war, was now becoming more explicitly biological and being applied extensively to converts from Judaism.[51] This logic of lineage was not a priori prejudicial to converts: some writers on nobility and genealogy even argued, as did Diego de Valera circa 1441, that descent from the "chosen people" ennobled rather than debased the "New Christians."[52] But in fact throughout the middle decades of the fifteenth century, these naturalizations came increasingly to be deployed against them.

The Toledan revolt of 1449 against the monarchy and the conversos as its perceived agents provides a good example of such deployment. The Toledans and their sympathizers were clearly anxious that the converts posed a threat to the reproduction of social and political status. They saw in "baptized Jews and those proceeding from their damaged line" the implacable and cruel enemies of Christianity and of Christians. Arguing that all those "descended from the perverse lineage of the Jews" were, like their ancestors in ancient times, "enemies" who sought above all "to destroy all the Old Christians," the Toledans set about confronting the danger, first with violence and then with a "Sentencia-Estatuto" banning descendants of converts from holding public office for at least four generations: the first of what would soon be many Spanish statutes of "purity of blood."[53]

The texts produced by the rebels and their allies in defense of their position, and by opponents like Alonso de Cartagena, Juan de Torquemada, Lope de Barrientos, and Fernán Díaz de Toledo against it, became central texts in the Spanish debate over the "Jewishness" of converts and their descendants. The eventual victory of the anticonverso genealogical arguments in the debate was not obvious or easy, for medieval people had a great many ways of thinking about the transmission of cultural characteristics across generations, such as pedagogy and nurture, which did not necessarily invoke nature, inheritance, or sexual reproduction.[54]

Yet as we saw in the previous chapter, the genealogical turn was taken. The reasons for its success are many and complex, but one that should not be underestimated is the power of its appeal to medieval "common knowledge" about nature. It was this type of "common knowledge" that underpinned (to reiterate an example from the previous chapter) the anonymous treatise called the *Alborayque*, composed circa. 1455–65. The Alborayque was an animal from the Qur'an, a composite beast (part horse, part lion, part snake, etc.) who carried Muhammad to heaven. The treatise mapped supposed moral attributes and cultural practices of the conversos onto diverse body parts of this monstrous beast. The use of this hybrid to stand for the converts, though often treated by modern critics as a mere conceit, is in fact a systematic strategy of argument from nature. The converts are not only Alborayques. They are bats, unclassifiable as animal (wings) or bird (teeth); they are a weak alloy rather than pure metal; and above all, they are a mixed lineage. These unnatural mixtures support the conclusion (and here is the leap to culture) that the conversos can never be classified as Christian, for "si los metales son muchos . . . segun la carne, quanto mas de metales de tantas heregias."[55] Similarly the negative imagery of mixed species in the treatise leads ineluctably to its conclusion: a prayer that the "clean" lineages of the old Christians not be corrupted through marriage with the new.[56]

Like a number of polemicists before him, the author of the *Alborayque* chose to focus on the corruption of the Jewish lineage in historical time, but other approaches were possible.[57] We have already seen Alonso de Espina adopt a polygenetic approach, relating the lineage of Jews to the offspring of, first, Adam with animals and, second, Adam with the demon Lilith. As a result of these unions, he wrote, Jews are of the lineage of demons and of monsters, the mule and the sow their adoptive mother.[58] Such genealogies doubtless seemed as fantastic to many medieval readers as they do to us. They provided an important theoretical underpinning, however, for the doctrine of "limpieza de sangre," or purity of blood: the idea that the reproduction of culture is embedded in the reproduction of the flesh.

It is upon this logic that new boundaries would be built between Christian and "Jew" in Spain. These new boundaries were enormously controversial.[59] I know of no more extensive premodern discussion about the relationship between biology and culture than that in the literature produced in the debate over converso exclusion between 1449 and 1550.[60] But the logic of the *Alborayque*, with its mapping of "Judaizing" corruption onto reproductive hybridity, was eventually victorious. The victory of this logic was due, in part, to the fact that resonated so well with other registers of cultural reproduction in late medieval Iberian society. Defenders of the conversos could insist, as they all did, that the reproduction of the flesh could not limit the miraculously transforming power of God working through the sacrament of baptism: it was, after all, dogma that in Christ there is neither Jew nor Greek. But when it came to other areas of culture in which behavior and lineage were traditionally tightly linked, even the most eloquent among them could not attempt to dissociate the two.

Perhaps the most important of such questions was whether or not descendants of Jews could form part of the nobility. A negative answer like that of the Toledan rebels (according to whom not even the king's grace could make descendants of such a debased lineage noble) would effectively bar the New Christians from any number of rights and privileges. But a positive one seemed to require the discovery among them of either an aristocratic lineage or an aptitude for heroism—since military valor was generally understood as the causal foundation of nobility in fifteenth-century peninsular society. Thus advocates for the New Christians found themselves simultaneously preaching "woe to those who build a city on blood" (Habbakuk 2:12) and insisting through genealogies of extremely "longue durée" that the converts recuperated the nobility of the Israelites—which had lain dormant within the Jews for the millennium and a half that they had denied Jesus—and shared the same blood as God and His virgin mother.[61]

Similarly with the question of courage: the Bachelor Marcos deployed a common prejudice when he wrote that the "ruinous lineage" of the Jews conveyed cowardice to their Christian descendants, for the timidity of the Jews was proverbial in the Middle Ages. In the words of Alonso de Cartagena, "when we want to express excessive timidity, we call it Jewishness, and we usually call a man who is excessively fearful a Jew."[62] Again, Alonso de Cartagena's counter-argument did not entirely reject his opponent's theses about the biological reproduction of culture, but argued rather for a different starting point. The Old Testament had famously chronicled the courage of the ancient Israelites, and,

> as Aristotle would have it, among dispositions toward virtue none is more derived among descendants through propagation of the blood than the disposition that tends toward fortitude. . . . Therefore since, considering their small number, proportionally more from among these [descendants of Jews] rise to investiture in the orders of knighthood, than from among those who descend from some rustic family of ignoble commoners, . . . it follows that we should presume that the nobility that some of them had in ancient times, lies latent enclosed within their breasts.

Once the Jewish vessel is baptized, the fortitude encoded in its ancient blood is free to shine once more, like a bright light whose concealing bushel is removed.[63]

Alonso de Cartagena's claims about the "deep heritability" of courage and nobility, like those of other proconverso writers, are based on a reading of Aristotelian natural science that is very similar to that of Manuel Dies's horse breeding manual, or indeed to that of those anticonverso writers who emphasized the "ruinous lineages" of the Jews.[64] This congruence is not evidence of the proconverso party's hypocrisy (as many of their opponents claimed at the time, and some scholars still do today), but rather of the differential densities of reproductive logics across the many registers of a complex culture. The victory of the anticonverso movement consisted in extending the power of ideas about heritability from certain areas where they were already thickly rooted (such as in discourses of animal breeding and of aristocratic genealogy) to previously inhospitable soil (such as sacramental theology). To the degree that this victory extended the cultivation of *raza* into new corners of culture and society, we can literally say that it made fifteenth-century Spain more "racial."

The consequences of this victory were momentous. The argument that converso morals were habitually corrupt, for example, led to the establishment of the first "proto-Inquisition" under Alonso de Oropesa in the 1460s. Oropesa, a prominent opponent of discrimination against descendants of conversos, believed that rooting out the heresies of the few would prove the innocence of the majority. Indeed he found little evidence for the charges against the converts, but their increasingly effective reiteration was used to justify the establishment of the Inquisition itself in 1481. And this Inquisition operated according to a logic strikingly similar to that of the *Alborayque*. Judaizers were to be identified by their behavior, but that behavior gained meaning only in light of their flesh's genealogy.

Already in 1449 Fernán Díaz, the relator of Juan II, had pointed out the dangers of such a system in a society in which there was scarcely a noble house without a converso in its family tree.[65] Moreover, since the effects of genealogy were primarily expressed culturally, the religio-racial classification of cultural practice became an important part of the accusational economy. Virtually any negative cultural trait could be presented as "Judaizing." We have seen the *Alborayque*'s list, and there were many others. The characteristics encoded in Jewish blood, according to the bishop of Cordoba in 1530, included heresy, apostasy, love of novelty and dissension, ambition, presumption, and hatred of peace. (Note the similarity with the list produced by Américo Castro.) The effectiveness of such claims in attracting the attention of Inquisitional courts made them strategically useful and thereby judaized ever more extensive cultural practices. Recall once more the words of Rodrigo Manrique: "No one can possess any culture without being suspect of heresy, error, and Judaism."[66]

It would be a mistake to see, in this attachment of "Jewishness" to culture, evidence that these late medieval discriminations were not "racial." On the contrary, this "judaization" of Spanish culture was the direct result of the increasingly widespread use of ideas about the biological reproduction of somatic and behavioral traits in order to create and legitimate hierarchies and discriminations, within a society where extensive intermarriage (as well as strategic practices like the falsification of genealogies and proofs of purity of blood) made the reproductive segregation of "Judaism" impossible.

It would, however, be just as great an error to conclude that we have shown these discriminations, and the theories of cultural reproduction that underlay them, to be "racial." All we have done is demonstrate the inadequacy of some influential arguments for dismissing the relevance of race to the premodern by finding in medieval Spain some of the attributes of race that various scholars have located in modernity (such as theories of selection in animal breeding, Foucault's binary enmities, and of course the word "race" itself). From this we can conclude only that the vocabularies of difference and the natural histories available to the residents of the Iberian Peninsula in the fifteenth and sixteenth centuries can be fruitfully compared to those of other times and places. We have barely begun the process of comparison itself. We have not explored, for example, the robustness of the binary opposition between "Christian" and "Jew" posited by the enemies of the conversos, or asked how the cultural work of such a binary within the state structures of the late Middle Ages differed or was similar to the work Foucault had in mind in the Modern. We noted some broad similarities in the theoretical underpinnings of Toledo's purity of blood statutes and the "racial anti-Semitism" of later periods, but we did not note how different the uses, applications, functions, and effects of these medieval theories were from those more modern ones. We have, in other words, only arrived at the most provisional and banal of conclusions: more work needs to be done.

This, it seems to me, is the most that can be expected of any history of race, and I would like to end by defending the humility of this conclusion. It is an ancient tendency of the historical imagination to think of ideas and concepts as having a discrete origin in a particular people, whence they are transmitted from donor to recipient cultures across space and time.[67] There may be some concepts whose histories are well described by such etymological and genealogical approaches.[68] Here, however, we are concerned with the history of an idea—the conviction that culture is produced and reproduced in the same way as the species procreates itself—so venerable and widespread that Giambattista Vico elevated it to a universal in his *Principles of the New Science*. It is, moreover, an idea that has produced so heterogeneous a set of discourses and outcomes—even when limited to its most modern forms, such as "race" and "racism"—that these can scarcely be subsumed into a "concept" or a "theory." The history of this idea is not the history of a train of thought, whose wagons can be ordered by class and whose itinerary may be mapped across time and space, but that of a principle of locomotion so general that any account of its origins, applications, and transmission will always be constrained by our ignorance (or to put it more charitably, by what we recognize as significant). We cannot solve this difficulty by cutting ("race did not exist before modernity"), by stitching ("race has always already existed"), or by refusing to talk about what cannot be clearly defined ("races do not exist, and race does not have a history").

None of this means that we should paralyze history with the cautions of a logician—"What is known as the history of concepts is really a history either of our knowledge of concepts or of the meaning of words"—only that we should keep such cautions in mind. There will always be strategic reasons for choosing to represent the relationship of ideas about the natural reproduction of culture that are scattered across time and space in terms of filiations or, conversely, in terms of disjuncture (or even to refuse the possibility of such an idea at all). Yet the choice can only be situational and polemical, in the sense that its recognition of significance springs from the needs and struggles (theological, political, philosophical, professional, etc.) of a specific moment. The polemics produced by such choices are invaluable when they stimulate us to comparison and self-consciousness. If, however, we treat them as anything but strategic, we simply exchange one lack of consciousness for another.

Race demands a history, both because it is a subject urgent and vast and because its own logic is so closely akin to that of the disciplines (etymology, genealogy, history) with which we study the persistence of humanity in time. For these same reasons, any history of race will be at best provocative and limited; at worst a reproduction of racial logic itself, in the form of a genealogy of ideas. In either case, histories of race are best read by premodernist and modernist alike not as prescriptive but as polemical stimuli to comparison. We can each draw energy from the collision of such polemics with our own particles of history and find new elements of both past and present in the wreckage. Put another way, we might read such histories as metaphors. I mean metaphor not in the sense of model or map, as some anthropologists and scholars of comparative religion have recently championed, but in the medieval sense articulated in the eleventh century by Albert of Monte Casino: "It is the function of metaphor to twist, so to speak, its mode of speech from its property; by twisting, to make some innovation; by innovating, to clothe, as it were, in nuptial garb; and by clothing, to sell, apparently at a decent price."[69] As in Albert's understanding of good metaphor, good histories and theorizations of race are a source of productive deceit. The associations they provoke are seductive, communicative, startlingly revealing, but also in some sense fraudulent. We cannot reject their power without impoverishment, but neither can we accept their suggestions without suspicion.

The same is true, of course, in reverse. Just as modernity provokes the medievalist, so should medieval encounters disturb the troubled certitudes of the modernist. The latter will, however, not travel without guides: yet another reason why it is important that premodernists (or at least those interested in specific problems, such as the transformations of religious categories in fifteenth-century Spain) confront their subjects' natural histories, rather than hiding behind over-easy rejections of race. But it is equally important that we not confuse the strategic comparisons and heuristic polemics produced by such confrontations with a history of "race" or "racism." The suggestion that we can benefit from the systematic juxtaposition of various strategies of naturalization need not imply that these strategies can be arranged into an evolutionary history of race, just as the argument that we can learn from the similarities we discover between, say, fifteenth-century ideologies and twentieth-century ones need not suggest that one followed from the other.[70] Admittedly, the danger of such a fallacy is great, for the subject of race tends to bewitch its historians with the same philogenetic fantasies and teleological visions that underwrite racial ideologies themselves. But if we wish to study how medieval people sought to naturalize their own histories, while at the same time attempt to denaturalize our own, it is a risk worth taking.

Islam and the West

Two Dialectical Fantasies

> As, then, these oppositions of contraries lend beauty to
> the language, so the beauty of the course of this world is
> achieved by the opposition of contraries, arranged, as it
> were, by an eloquence not of words, but of things. . . . "So
> look upon all the works of the Most High, and these are two
> and two, one against another."
>
> Saint Augustine, *The City of God*, XI.18

> Is [dialectic] not based at times on an interpretation of signs
> in nature and in history which the interpreter carefully
> placed there himself?
>
> Czesław Miłosz, *The Captive Mind*, 49

This book began (chap. 1) by asking how medieval Christendom constituted itself by thinking about Islam, and it is only fitting that it conclude with a similar meditation about modernity. Today it is almost too fashionable to point out that modern Muslim, Christian, Jewish, and even secular societies have been shaped through their encounters with each other, and it is only slightly less obvious (but more often forgotten) that those encounters have also been shaped by their habits of thought. We know, for example, a great deal about the "Orientalism" through which European scholarship approached and represented the Islamic world in the nineteenth century. And we could (or should) know just as much about the cognitive lenses through which Muslim thinkers perceived their colonizers in the same period. Nor need we be scholars to realize that today much of the Islamic world thinks a great deal in terms of "Judaism," even in the vast reaches of that world that are without living exemplars of that faith. And of course Jews too have spent much ink and thought on Christianity and Islam and have deployed the histories of both in their attempts to make sense of and reform their worlds. From the early nineteenth-century "Wissenschaft des Judentums" ("Sciences of Judaism") to the early twentieth-century Zionists and beyond, thinking about the possibilities of Jewish community and nation has often taken the form of thinking about Christianity and Islam.

The subject is both far too large and too important to be confined within the bounds of one chapter. Nevertheless, and by way of conclusion, I propose to sketch two influential and roughly opposed examples of how we moderns approach questions about the inter-relation of "Islam" and "the West" (as if each were monolithic) and of the work that the past is asked to do in the construction of our present.

1. Islam and the West: Clash or Alliance?

In 2005, at the suggestion of the prime minister of Spain (seconded by Turkey), the United Nations established a new "Secretariat for the Alliance of Civilizations" with the mandate (I am quoting from the Secretariat's concept paper) "to overcome prejudice, misconceptions, misperceptions, and polarization . . . that foment violence." To quote that concept paper just a little bit further, the Secretariat was meant as "a call to all of those who believe in building rather than destroying, who embrace diversity as a means of progress rather than as a threat, and who believe in the dignity of humankind across religion, ethnicity, race, and culture." The Secretariat hosted a series of working groups and then, for reasons that are unknown to me (but presumably not because its mission was accomplished), closed its doors less than a year after it opened them.

The one line I have quoted from the United Nation's concept paper suffices to make clear a contradiction at the Secretariat's very foundation: this "Alliance" of all who are for diversity and deplore polarization defines itself through a series of oppositions and exclusions. It is against those who would (apparently) rather destroy than build, strive to eliminate diversity rather than embrace it, and who do not believe in the dignity of mankind. We know, of course, who the drafters of this constitution had in mind: all followers of that rival paradigm the "Clash of Civilizations." Such people are destroyers, eliminators, misanthropes: in short, barbarians. They are excluded from the

"Alliance of Civilizations" because they are not civilized themselves. In this sense, the "Alliance" is itself also already a "Clash," and a good example of Walter Benjamin's dictum that "there is never a document of civilization that is not at the same time a document of barbarism."[1]

The blitheness with which the Secretariat sailed into aporia is far from unique. On the contrary, it is characteristic of the two most popular models we have available for understanding the historical relationship between the Christian West and Islam (I will begin with Islam, but will suggest below structural analogies between Islam and Judaism in this regard). Models that posit a history of synthesis or "alliance" between Islam and the West quickly reproduce the "clashes" or oppositions that they pretend to overcome. But bipolar models that insist on Islam's exclusion from or irreducible opposition to the triumphs of Europe and the West fare no better and not only because they have difficulty accounting for the many complex particularities of Christianity and Islam's relationships with each other. Perhaps more important, insofar as the oppositions they insist upon are—as they so often are—the building blocks of a teleological dialectic (Christian, Hegelian, Marxist, neo-liberal, or what have you) about the course of history, the enduring persistence of those oppositions itself threatens the overarching truth-claims of the dialectics that they were meant to sustain.[2]

In short, and despite their seeming political differences, to the extent that our two major modes—clash and alliance, opposition and synthesis—for understanding the Christian West's relationship to Islam (or Judaism) are equally dialectical, they are equally fantastic. The meaning of "dialectical" here should become clearer in the pages that follow. By "fantastic," I mean committed to ignoring the gaps between the visions they generate and the complex world. Further: these dialectical models of history are themselves the children of Church fathers impregnated by Christological syntheses and teleologies—fathers like Eusebius, Augustine, or Hegel—and therefore the more dialectical the model the more studied its lack of consciousness, and the more fantastic the visions of the past, present, and future that it produces.

This claim is both too polemical and too large to allow for the pretence of rigorous demonstration. I propose instead to pursue two representative case studies, the first an exclusion of Islam from Europe, the second an inclusion, in order to show their participation in a common dialectical fantasy. My emphasis on the dialectical here should explain what may otherwise surprise some readers: namely, that I will not include Samuel Huntington's (in)famous "Clash of Civilizations" thesis among my example of exclusion. This thesis has provoked exceptional umbrage and much splattering of ink, but it does not interest us here, because it is neither dialectical nor teleological, nor in the least historical.[3]

A brief detour can legitimate this disinterest. Huntington argued that the key conflicts confronting the world order in this and the coming generation are "civilizational," by which he meant that they were produced not so much by rival ideologies or economic systems as was the case during the Cold War, but by deep and long-standing differences of culture, language, and religion. He saw the "clashes" of the "Judeo-Christian" West with Islam, on the one hand, and with the "Confucian" civilization (i.e., China) on the other, as the most dangerous challenges to the current world order. But he did not pretend to explain the long history of Muslim-Christian relations or to claim that the "clashes" he sees at work in the present are the same as those that have structured previous "world orders."[4] Nor do his "civilizations" represent successive stages along some evolutionary road toward truth. They all have the same goal—the power and prosperity associated with modernity—and differ only in their visions of how that power and prosperity should be distributed. Huntington seems interested in marking the strategic implications of these differences, not in making ontological discriminations between the visions. In this sense he remains what in political science is somewhat naively called a "realist."

2. Pope Benedict XVI: The Dialectics of Exclusion

Compare this restraint, by way of contrast, with Pope Benedict XVI's speech at the University of Regensburg on September 12, 2006, which will serve as my first example of a dialectics of exclusion.[5] In "Faith, Reason, and the University: Memories and Reflections" the learned pontiff asserted a long history of struggle between "rational" Christianity and "irrational" Islam and used medieval Christian sources to characterize the violent intolerance of Muhammad and his followers. The speech triggered protests, even violence, across large parts of the Muslim world and was condemned by an unlikely coalition that included the deputy leader of Turkey's governing Islamic party, the parliament of Pakistan, protesters in India, Iraq's Sunni leadership, the top Shiite cleric of Lebanon, and the prime ministers of Indonesia and Malaysia, among many others. At the center of the storm were a few short but pregnant lines of the pope's remarks, quoted from a "Dialogue" that the Byzantine emperor Manuel II Paleologus claimed to have had with a learned

Muslim in the winter of 1391, when he was himself a soldier fighting in the armies of the Muslim Sultan.

> Show me just what Muhammad brought that was new, and there you will find things only evil and inhuman, such as his command to spread by the sword the faith he preached. . . . God is not pleased by blood. . . . Faith is born of the soul, not the body. Whoever would lead someone to faith needs the ability to speak well and reason properly, without violence and threats. . . .To convince a reasonable soul, one does not need a strong arm, or weapons of any kind, or any other means of threatening a person with death.[6]

In response to Muslim furor, the papal palace insisted that the line was incidental to the pope's broader point and that he was not endorsing the medieval emperor's views but simply quoting a historical text to make a historical point. On September 17, the pope himself took the extraordinary step of expressing regret, stating that his quotations from a medieval text did not express his personal thoughts and that his address had been intended as a respectful invitation to frank and sincere dialogue. Many will be inclined to accept the pope's clarification. And though few will say it openly, many among these will presumably see the Muslim world's response to Benedict's comment as a violent over-reaction that only confirms the pope's characterization of Islam and its prophet.

The violence, which ranged from the burning of churches in the West Bank to the murder of a nun in Somalia, is certainly a troubling symptom of a contemporary Muslim political culture that imports far too much of its energy from the insults, whether perceived or real, of Western "Zionists" and "Crusaders." But Muslims were right to perceive hostility to Islam in the pope's speech, and that hostility would remain even if the speech were purged of its medieval quotations. For it was not Manuel's characterization of Muhammad's violence or his lack of originality that was central to the pope's arguments, but his claim about the proper relationship of faith and reason, a subject that was not incidental to the speech, but central to it, as its title makes clear. Like the medieval emperor, the pope was contending that Islam has embraced throughout its history one pole of an opposition that was meant instead to be transcended: the opposition between "Jewish" obedience to God (faith) and "Greek" philosophy (reason). Islam (according to Benedict) has always opted for "Judaism," that is, for faith, obedience, and absolute submission to God's law.[7]

It was in order to make this point that Benedict quoted Manuel—who had also, it is worth noting, in lines just beyond those with which the pope ended his citation, gone on to characterize Islam as a corrupt and particularly violent form of Judaism. Benedict then "corroborated" Paleologus's view by referring to the teachings of the one Muslim to be found in his speech, the eleventh-century Andalusian Ibn Ḥazm (systematically misspelled as Hazn in the Vatican's first posting of the text), who claimed that God is not bound by reason. Benedict's conclusion: because Islam commits itself entirely to faith rather than synthesizing faith with reason, it is a fanatical rather than a rational religion.[8]

Many of the pope's defenders pointed out that his argument was not aimed at Muslims alone, and this is certainly true, though scarcely comforting. Within Benedict's schema it is of course Judaism that plays, as "faith," the role of fundamental antipode to Hellenistic "reason," a role in which it has served European (and particularly German) culture for several centuries. But even within Christianity Benedict found much to criticize, for the marriage of faith and reason has often been strained by attempts at what he called "dehellenization." Luther's move toward faith, for example, occasioned his attack on Catholic rationalism, and particularly on the Aristotelian theological movement we know as Scholasticism. This meant that much of Protestant Christianity became unbalanced, inclining too far away from "Greek" reason and toward "Jewish" faith, while the Catholic Church of the Counter-Reformation strove to safeguard the proper balance. And of course the proper Catholic synthesis was also threatened by movements inclining too far in the opposite direction, the most important of these being the triumphant "scientific" or "practical" reason of the Enlightenment and modernity, with its militant opposition to "faith" in any form.

The pope's basic point was that all of these systems of thought fail to make sense of man's place in the world insofar as they fail to achieve the necessary synthesis of faith and reason. This synthesis was born in the New Testament, which "bears the imprint of the Greek spirit, which had already come to maturity as the Old Testament developed."[9] It was disseminated and preserved through the Catholic Church in western Europe. Indeed for Benedict the "inner rapprochement between Biblical faith and Greek philosophical inquiry" was really a European phenomenon: "Christianity, despite its origins and some significant developments in the East, finally took on its historically decisive character in Europe. We can also express this the other way around: this convergence . . . created Europe and remains the foundation of what can rightly be called Europe."

It will not surprise anyone familiar with his thought that Pope Benedict, like Paleologus half a millennium before, understood himself as a defender of a distinctly Christian Europe against Islam: recall the then-Cardinal Ratzinger's comment to *Le Figaro* (August 13, 2004) that Turkey should not be admitted to the European Union "on the grounds that it is a Muslim nation." What may be more surprising to readers in this third millennium are the oppositions through which Benedict chose to articulate Europe's distinctiveness—faith and reason, Judaism and Hellenism. If we nowadays recognize the importance of these terms in the politics of European culture, it is generally in the context of divorce rather than dialectic. (Think, for example, of the nineteenth- and twentieth-century ideological program to purify Europe's Hellenic legacy from the Hebraic with which it had become contaminated: a process that came to be known in German as *Entjudaisierung*.) But we need only open a page of Matthew Arnold's *Culture and Anarchy* in order to remember a long strand of criticism that thought of the "harmonious fusion" of the Hebraic and the Hellenic—the words are Heinrich Heine's, from 1841—as "the task of all European civilization."[10]

Neither the pope's defense of "Europe" against "Islam" nor the categories with which he carried out that defense (Jew and Greek, faith and reason) are so surprising, but his conclusions are nevertheless shocking. For what begins as a marriage of faith and reason brokered in the particular culture of Greco-Roman Palestine and consummated in that of Catholic Europe, climaxes in a synthesis that (according to Benedict) needs to be "integrated into all cultures." It is now universal, fundamental to "the nature of faith itself." Yet was not the bulk of "Faith, Reason, and the University" explicitly dedicated to the task of demonstrating that only European Catholicism has successfully mixed faith and reason in the *logos* and that other religions and cultures have not? Insofar as the pope was claiming that a uniquely Catholic and European synthesis is a prerequisite for every faith, he was in effect calling all cultures (including the academic one) and all religions (most pointedly Islam) to European Catholicism. The call is not full-throated, but rather muffled in "dialogue," as befits the tolerant politics of our progressive age: "Only through [this rationality of faith] do we become capable of that genuine dialogue of cultures and religions so urgently needed today." The pope's message is certainly not the "convert or die" of medieval crusaders, but rather "convert or be left out of the dialogue of cultures and the European Union." We are reassured that the feast of Catholic reason is open to all: "It is to this great *logos*, to this breadth of reason, that we invite our partners in the dialogue of cultures." But just as in those great banquets for the reconciliation of enemies that pepper the chronicles of our barbarian past, the cultural "others" who accept the papal invitation had best be on their guard, lest they find their differences extinguished by poison in the cups.[11]

Why does the pope's exclusion of all non-Euro-Catholic cultures from the feast of human reason seem reasonable to so many Europeans? When we are told that Islam (for example) is not a religion of "reason," why do we not ask ourselves what such a statement might mean? (Are Muslims incapable of thinking causally? Of applying the principle of induction? Of understanding Euclidean geometry or assessing economic risk and reward?) To the extent that Benedict's audience does not feel a need to ask these questions, it is at least in part because it shares a tendency to believe that the peaks of human reason are not reached by everyday attempts to move in the high-gravity environment of a crowded and complex world, nor even by the great leaps for freedom made by certain minds into the weightless realms of rule-bound mathematics. Reason resides rather in the overcoming of those contraries that centuries of Christian schooling have helped us to recognize as significant.

Benedict's Jew and Greek, faith and reason, are two sets of such contraries, but we know many others, each pair intimately related to the others: slavery and freedom, law and grace, body and soul, perishable and eternal, particular and universal, apparent and real, sign and signified, to name just a few. A venerable pedagogy has taught us to heighten these oppositions, to see chasms in the deepening shadows between them, and to build slender bridges of prophecy and dialectic across the seeming void. Because this pedagogy is so venerable and vast, we cannot comprehend its power by focusing our critical attention on only one pair of the contraries it claims to reconcile—such as Jew and Greek. Nor is it enough to explore this or that chapter in its early history—such as the efforts of those remarkable Alexandrines (Philo, Clement, and Origen) to apply Greek philosophy toward the exegesis of Hebrew scripture, or the attempts of Christian historians (like Eusebius, Rufinus, and the young Augustine) to align the progressive triumphs of prophecy with those of imperial Rome. But for the same reason of scale, it would be equally vain to attempt to deconstruct this education by providing it with an *histoire totale* stretching from Ur or ancient Egypt to our contemporary schools of piety and philosophy. Vain and—if previous efforts are any indication—also dangerous, for such efforts often end up colonizing the past with the contraries of the present, thereby re-orienting the entire history of humankind toward future knowledge or salvation. When historians of the *longue durée* discover difference in the past, it is usually (like the pope) with synthesis aforethought.

3. Hegel's Marriage of Faith and Reason: The "Consummate Religion"

We can put the difficulty in its starkest terms by focusing briefly on the most influential modern attempt at a "total history" of the dialectic of Judaism and Hellenism, faith and reason: that of G. F. W. Hegel. Already in his early writings, such as "The Spirit of Christianity and Its Fate" (1799), Hegel understood the history of reason in terms of the gradual overcoming of the oppositions created by Judaism's radical submission of the will to God.[12] His essay, like that of many Church historians before him, took the form of a renarration of the entire history of revelation, beginning with the great flood of Genesis. Its first section was called "The Spirit of Judaism," a spirit which begins with the patriarch Abraham, who abandoned family and fatherland in order to make himself "a stranger on earth, a stranger to soil and men alike," in order to worship a distant divinity, a "perfect Object on High," an "Ideal."

> The whole world Abraham regarded as simply his opposite. If he did not take it to be a nullity, he looked on it as sustained by the God who was alien to it. Nothing in nature was supposed to have any part in God; everything was simply under God's mastery. . . . Moreover it was through God alone that Abraham came into a mediate relation with the world, the only kind of link with the world possible for him. His Ideal subjugated the world to him, gave him as much as he needed, and put him in security against the rest. Love alone was beyond his power.[13]

The rest of sacred history is for Hegel an attempt to overcome this rupture created by the extreme faith of Abraham and his progeny. According to his section ii—"The Sermon on the Mount Contrasted with the Mosaic Law and with Kant's Ethics"—it is Jesus's teaching to "love God above everything and your neighbor as yourself" that has the power to reunite faith with reason, submission to God with an immediate relation to the things of this world. Jesus wanted to "strip the laws of legality,"[14] to achieve freedom through a synthesis of love and law, subject and object, universal and particular. Hegel adopts Jesus's phrase, the "fulfillment of the law," to describe this synthesis.[15] Sections iii and iv of his essay ("The Moral Teachings of Jesus: Love as the Transcendence of Penal Justice and the Reconciliation of Fate," and "The

Religious Teachings of Jesus") are devoted to expounding Jesus's instructions—drawn largely from the Gospel of John—for how to achieve it. But
section v ("The Fate of Jesus and His Church") outlines why these teachings
have never before been correctly understood or completely implemented.
Jesus addressed a people—the Jews—whose "loveless nature" had entirely
alienated all "love, spirit, and life."[16] In order to reach "the impure attention"
of even the most receptive among them—namely, the apostles—Jesus had
to adulterate his message and speak to them in terms and oppositions that
they could understand, thereby perpetuating the very contraries he died to
overcome.[17]

No evangelist managed to escape this poverty of Jewish culture, not even
John, whom Hegel cites constantly as the most spiritual of them all. "However sublime the idea of God may be made [in John], there yet always remains
the Jewish principle of opposing thought to reality, reason to sense; this
principle involves the rending of life and a lifeless connection between God
and the World."[18] Hence "in all forms of the Christian religion which have
been developed in the advancing fate of the ages, there lies this fundamental
characteristic of opposition." In other words, all the progress of Christianity—from the "servitude" of Catholicism to the various relationships between
God and the world envisioned in different Protestant sects—has not yet sufficed to overcome the Judaism at work within it, so that until now (Hegel
concludes the essay) "church and state, worship and life, piety and virtue,
spiritual and worldly action, can never dissolve into one."[19]

From this point on, nearly everything Hegel wrote was meant to show the
way toward the overcoming of these oppositions and to chart the process of
that overcoming across human history. By writing the man-God union across
all the fundamental oppositions of religion and philosophy, Hegel attempted
to "sublate" all of them in the movement of the Mind and Spirit (*Geist*) over
the ages. Insofar as for Hegel the dialectical evolution of human reason is
itself Trinitarian, world history became a form of "imitatio Christi," an imitation of Christ. As he put it in the *Lectures on the Philosophy of Religion*: "It is in
connection with a true understanding of the death of Christ that the relation
of the subject as such in this way comes into view. . . . The highest knowledge
of the nature of the Idea of Spirit is contained in this thought."[20]

The *Lectures on the Philosophy of Religion* and the *Lectures on the Philosophy
of History* were Hegel's attempts at an *histoire totale* of human reason. As befits
an author of world history, he no longer begins with Abraham, as he had in
"The Spirit of Christianity," nor does he focus so relentlessly on Judaism, but

makes room instead for the ancient religions of Egypt, Asia, and Africa. He now calls Judaism "the religion of sublimity" and puts its radical subjection of the material world to an ideal God in the middle of his history, as a necessary step in the dialectical evolution of the spirit across the ages, rather than an alienation from all that is human. Nevertheless the *telos* of all this history remains the same: the synthesis of Hebrew and Hellenes into the Trinitarian reason of "the Consummate Religion," Christianity.

And what of Islam? In the *Philosophy of History* Islam is merely the transposition of Jewish submission from a tribal God to a universal one, producing a pure "fanaticism" entirely disinterested in the world. Islam's complete submission to the One God once made it capable of exemplary martyrdoms, conquest, and flights of poetic fancy, but its rejection of the world meant that nothing it achieved could be enduring. Its initial fanaticism spent, Islam became a religion of mere sensuality, and it was then driven back to the Asia and Africa from whence it had come, surrendering even its poetry into Goethe's more capable hands.[21]

Given Hegel's teleology, it is not surprising that Islam scarcely fits into his dialectical model of history. Coming as it did after the Christian consummation, it could play only a belated part in the evolution of the human mind and spirit. Like some lineage of australopithecines flourishing in the world of Homo sapiens, Islam was a living fossil, a threatening remnant of oppositions already transcended by the spirit of the age. This was in fact its only role in the *Lectures on the Philosophy of Religion* of 1824, where the Islamic "fanaticism" of faith and its dialectical antipode, the Enlightenment's fanaticism of reason, were arrayed together as exemplary enemies of the Christian synthesis: precisely the role resurrected for both science and Islam by Benedict at Regensburg.[22]

I have juxtaposed Benedict's lecture with Hegel's in order to highlight the logic behind the Vatican's invitation to a "dialogue of cultures." Within the pope's (and Hegel's) dialectic of faith and reason, "faithful" Islam can only meet Europe's "reasonable" conditions for dialogue by stepping into synthesis, thereby—in the terms of the dialectic itself—ceasing to be Islam and becoming Christianity. And what if it refuses? The historical march of the human spirit makes no provision for conscientious objectors. The Jews were for Hegel "the most despicable" (*Verworfenste*) of peoples precisely because they resisted "sublation" and supersession. They had been the first to arrive at the portals of sublimity, but they had balked at passing through "the door to salvation" back into the beauty of the world. The pope was setting similar conditions for the entry of the "Sublime Port" into the dialogue of cultures (and the European Union). Was the same reproach implied should they refuse?[23]

Of course the climax of Hegel's ecclesiology was not Catholicism (which he frequently stigmatized as excessively "slavish" and irrational, i.e., as too "Jewish") but Lutheranism, which he understood as Europe's springboard to the next stage in the human spirit's unfolding, the age of German philosophy. Benedict turned back the dials on Hegel's dialectic, locating Europe's essential ends not in its Idealist future but in its Catholic past. The move may not do justice to Hegel's intentions, but it points to an important truth: the targets of a dialectical teleology are moveable, and it makes a great deal of difference where one places them. If in a genealogy it is the point of origin that is the crucial choice (there are, for example, very different worldviews contained in the choice between Noah, Abraham, or Jacob as spiritual progenitor), the choice that matters for dialectical teleology are what contraries to recognize as significant and where to locate their overcoming. The target need not be in the future, for the end of history may well be in the past. For the pope, for example, Catholic Christology was the key moment of synthesis for Europe. Those who—like Jews and Muslims—missed the target altogether, or who—like Protestants, and scientists—cut right through it and flew off into new contraries, have deviated from Europe's essential course.[24]

The pope—along with other members of our first family of dialectical fantasies about Islam and the West—set the targets so as to justify exclusion (in our example: the exclusion of Judaism and Islam from sufficient reason, of Protestantism and science from sufficient faith). We could, however, choose different targets in order to produce histories that are just as dialectical and just as teleological as Hegel's or Benedict's but that include rather than exclude Islam within whatever syntheses they proclaim as sacred to the Occident. This is precisely the strategy of our second family of fantasies, those that claim an essential identity between Islam and the West and seek to replace dialectical "clash" with synthesis or "alliance."

4. Arabic Poetry and the Dialectics of Inclusion

What are the targets favored by those who would make *The Case for Islamo-Christian Civilization* (to borrow the title of a recent attempt by Richard Bulliet)? Since a frequent argument is that the perceived gulf between Islam and the West is itself a product of Europe and of modernity, it should not be

a surprise that most of these targets lay in the ages before European hegemony. Some scholars focus on the common core of prophetic material that
the Christianity and Islam share as "Abrahamic" religions. Others point to the
importance of Arabic translations of and commentaries upon Greek scientific
and philosophical texts in order to remind us, as al-Jahiz already did in the
ninth century, that the Abbasid Caliphate's claim to be the legitimate inheri-
tor of Greek wisdom rivaled that of Byzantium.[25] Still others (like Bulliet)
stress the similar solutions that the two faiths found to the similar problems
they encountered as universalizing monotheisms that came to rule over vast
polities. Finally, there are those, like María Rosa Menocal, who point to specific cultural forms considered central to the emergence of European subjectivity and argue for their Arabic origins.

We will take up this last example, because the issue that interests Menocal
is the same one we saw troubling Hegel in his *Philosophy of History*: Arabic
poetry. It is easy for us postmoderns to forget that vernacular poetry was once
the heart of many accounts of the emergence of a specifically "European"
subjectivity. The choice to compose in the language of the people rather than
in clerical Latin, to sing of earthly beauty rather than of sacred scripture, to
fashion from romantic love wings for the human soul's migration: these were
understood by many (including Hegel) as key choices in Europe's transformation from a benighted culture enslaved to faith and superstition into one
reaching once more toward human reason. Indeed almost from its origins,
vernacular poetry justified itself in terms of these oppositions and their synthesis. Already in the fourteenth century Petrarch defended secular poetry
against the criticism of the theologians by deriving his poetic practice from
the verse traditions of ancient Greece and aligning the methodologies of his
scholastic opponents with the supposedly blind formalism of Islam and Judaism.[26] Over the centuries that followed an increasingly thick line of scholarly
ink traced an itinerary from vernacular love poetry of the medieval troubadours and through Petrarch's "humanism" before flowing on to encompass
nearly every monument of European literary culture.

But what would the European subject look like if that line began, not in
Provence nor in the ancient colonies of Greek Italy (as Petrarch had proposed), but in Muslim Spain? In *The Arabic Role in Medieval Literary History* (1987), Menocal argued that the emergence of rhyme (as distinct from
rhythm) in the vernacular poetry of Catholic Europe, specifically in the Provençal poetry of the troubadours in southern France, is a borrowing from the
Arabic poets of Muslim al-Andalus. Hence, she suggested, a key aspect of the

poetic subjectivity that Petrarch celebrated as the essence of a Christian humanist aesthetic recovered from ancient Greece and Rome was in fact neither Christian, nor European, nor Greco-Roman, but Arabic and Islamic. As she put it in an essay entitled "Pride and Prejudice in Medieval Studies: European and Oriental": "The segregation of European . . . from Arabic . . . is . . . anachronistic and . . . misleading."[27] But for Europeans, according to Menocal, the acknowledgment of this "indebtedness" became "taboo" for both political reasons (colonialism) and psycho-aesthetic ones (which, borrowing from Harold Bloom, she termed "anxiety of influence"). Her more recent book, *The Ornament of the World*, takes up once more the theme of Arabic influence and its repression, expanding her account of Andalusian cultural interactions like the poetic one into a series of "forgotten" stories which she hopes will provide the post-9/11 world with a new way of thinking about Islam.[28]

It is beyond my competence to contribute to the debate about whether or not the troubadours really learned to sing in Arabic—a debate that has been ongoing, as we shall see, for some five hundred years. I intend only to suggest that the cultural logic of arguments like Menocal's for the inclusion of Islam in the history of Europe is in some ways startlingly similar to the pope's, though oriented toward a very different politics. It too traces the genealogy of a cultural practice up to a moment of idealized synthesis, then moves on to trace the history of that synthesis's betrayal. In this case the union of Latin vernacular rhythm and Arabic rhyme stands for the loving marriage of Christianity and Islam, whereas the divorce that followed, and the subsequent repression of any happy memories of married life, is blamed on Europe's infidelity to her own history.

A different essay might focus on the shared genealogical strategies of arguments for and against the participation of Islam in Europe. For all their inclusiveness, arguments like Menocal's depend on pre-Foucauldian genealogical methodologies generally associated with colonialism in contemporary cultural studies, even if in this case they escape the charge because they locate innovation outside of European hegemony. My point here is best made through a thought experiment. Imagine what we would think if an Arabist today claimed that contemporary Arabic poetry is essentially European, because the mid-twentieth-century poets (for example, Nazik al-Malaika) who broke the monopoly of classical Arabic metrical forms and rhyme schemes did so under the influence of Shakespeare and Shelley?

My goal is not to diminish these important contributions to the history of medieval poetics. I want only to highlight the extent to which cultural histories of inclusion, like those of exclusion, proceed by splitting the strands of interwoven and coproduced histories of identity and difference, in order to rewire them along more polarized lines.[29] One way to make this point is simply by reiterating a fact that María Rosa Menocal and other readers of European literary histories already know: that arguments over the "Jewishness" and "Muslimness" of Christian vernacular poetry are as old as that poetry itself. There have always been some in those arguments who fought to segregate European poetry from a "Jewish" or "Islamic" poetics cast as insufficiently dialectical (for example, Petrarch).[30] And there have always been others for whom Arabic (and Hebrew) letters, far from being an antithesis to the Hellenes, were in fact the key ingredient in the synthesis of a "modern" Europe.

Giammaria Barbieri (1519–75) provides a good example of this latter school. He began to study Provençal in 1538, inspired by his reading of a recently published edition of Dante's *De vulgari eloquentia* (1529). After years of study and tribulation (according to his biographer), Barbieri mastered the Provençal poetic tradition and was much struck by its precocious use of rhyme. The explanation he produced for this precocity explicitly contradicted Petrarch (as Bembo, Castelvetro, and others had already done), who had argued that rhyme had been practiced long before the troubadours, in the Greek poetry of ancient Sicily and other parts of *magna Grecia*. But it also disagreed with Dante, who had attributed the invention to the troubadours themselves. According to Barbieri, Sicily and Provence were both precocious in European rhyme "because they learned it from others, namely from the method of the nation of the Arabs."[31] The Qur'an (as Barbieri had learned from a late medieval anti-Qur'anic polemic, the *Improbatio Alchorani*, by the missionary Ricoldo da Montecroce) already contained examples of rhymed prose (*saj'*). Barbieri also knew that even before the Qur'an, pre-Islamic Arabic poetry had often ended lines with the homophony of "one or two last letters" (as he learned from Averroes's commentaries on Aristotle's *Poetics*). With the help of the Hebraist Mosè Finzio, Barbieri even buttressed his arguments with examples from a number of Andalusian Hebrew treatises on the writing of poetry, whose medieval authors had been quite self-conscious of the Arabic influence on their art.[32]

Barbieri's writings were not published in his lifetime, and even if they had been, they would not have met with unanimous approval. Plenty of Italians continued the Petrarchine privileging of Italian antiquity as the birthplace of poetry. French authors, meanwhile, like Joachim du Bellay in his *Deffence et illustration de la langue françoyse* (1549), ridiculed Italian pretensions and claimed for Bardus V, king of the ancient Gauls, the honor of rhyme's invention. Champions of other "nations" looked in other directions, including Teutonic "*Volk*" singers, Celtic bards, latinate clergy, or any of many other possibilities. But throughout the seventeenth and eighteenth century one can find European proponents of the Arabic origins of rhyme, ranging from the French bishop Pierre Daniel Huet in 1670 to the Jesuit Juan Andrés (1740–1817), whose eight-volume history *Dell'origine, progressi e stato attuale d'ogni letteratura* (1782–85) was devoted to disproving France's claims about the importance of its language, and suggesting Arabic (and hence Spain) as the source, not only of rhyme, but of the entire "risorgimento della moderna letteratura."[33]

Of course, such theories were not unopposed: precisely the opposite. Andrés's treatise, for example, was energetically rebutted at least twice by a fellow Jesuit, Esteban de Arteaga (1747–99). In a twenty-one-page footnote to his second rebuttal of Andrés's thesis, Arteaga sought to demonstrate that much of what Andrés claimed was particular to Arabic poetry was, if not universal, then at least widespread in the poetries of many different peoples. "Therefore I conclude, using the dialectic of the lord abbot Andrés, that Provençal poetry has a Cretan-Greek-Orcadic-Danish-Norwegian-Icelandic-Scottish-Peruvian-Chinese origin."[34] Yet despite the existence of such controversy, or indeed, precisely because of it, it is fair to say that the question of Europe's debts to Arabic letters were far from forgotten or repressed in the West. On the contrary, the earliest histories of modern European literature are filled with its debate.

The question was an important one, for example, in the literary circle orbiting around the exiled French noblewoman Anne-Louise Germaine Necker, Madame de Staël, in the Swiss town of Coppet. Her own *De la littérature considérée dans ses rapports avec les institutions sociales* (1800) was one of the first works to focus on the relationship between literature and social structures. Its stated goal was to observe "the progress of the human spirit" in a millennium-long literary dialectic. Madame de Staël may well have known of Andrés's theories about the Arabic origins of rhyme, but she did not choose to give Islam any place in her dialectic, which was between the Greeks and the Germans, the southern shores of Mediterranean Europe and the frozen forests of the north, nature and sentimental art, male and female. All these were melted together in the Middle Ages by Christianity, creating what was, according to de Staël, a uniquely European vernacular literary culture of love.[35]

Yet on the topic of love lyrics as on so many others, opinion in the salon was not monolithic. Sismonde de Sismondi, for example, took more seriously than Madame de Staël the suggestions of writers like Thomas Warton (whose *History of English Poetry* had appeared in 1774) and Juan Andrés that lyric poetry of love was an Islamic discovery, not a European one. Indeed, in his own *De la littérature du midi de l'Europe* of 1813, Sismondi borrowed liberally from Andrés's *Dell'origine* and granted that southern Europe had indeed imported a great deal (paper, numbers, Greek philosophy, poetic rhyme, and much else) from Islam. Even Madame de Staël's "enivrement d'amour" was, according to Sismondi, of Islamic vintage. But this influence extended only to the Romance languages and the southern climes. The modernity of Europe arose (and here Sismondi followed de Staël) out of the encounter of the German north with these southern sensibilities. So although it could be said that as a child Europe had gone to school in Arabic, she had matured dialectically into modernity. The schoolhouse, meanwhile, had remained frozen in sentiment and decayed into ruin. There was no longer any literature or science to be found "in any Arab country, nor in any country where Muslims have dominated."[36] With Sismondi we have arrived more or less at the same dialectical judgment that Hegel would utter some three years later in his *Lectures on the Philosophy of History*: whatever powers of invention Islamic faith might once have yielded were now in the hands of Goethe.

5. The Inseparability of Exclusion and Inclusion

Of course my use of Hegel as a hinge between the history of Benedict's exclusions and of Menocal's inclusions is artificial, but I hope it helps make recognizable how much dialectical ground is shared by these two seemingly opposed fantasies of Europe's relationship to Islam. Rather than write "fantasy," I should perhaps follow Johann Gottfried von Herder (1744–1803) and use "fairy tale": "Spain was the fortunate region where the first spark of a returning culture struck Europe, which then had to adapt itself to the place and the time in which it came alive. The history of these events reads like a comforting fairy-tale." In Herder's *Märchen*, the influence of Arabic poetry on Provençal lyric shattered Latin's despotism and made possible a vernacular (and hence potentially secular) literature, "producing freedom of thought for all of Europe" and the first Enlightenment (*"die erste Aufklärung"*). "Do we not therefore owe the Provençals, and the Arabs who awakened them, a great debt?"[37] But if for Herder the fairy tale was a happy one, for others, like

August Wilhelm von Schlegel, it was grim. Schlegel was willing to concede that the Arabs might have invented rhyme, but he insisted that they were too "cruel" to have discovered its highest use, the love lyric. Like that of Benedict or Paleologus, his was an adamant defense of Europe from any hint of Islamic influence: "Muhammad's sect never had the slightest influence on anything that constitutes the original genius of the Middle Ages."[38]

We could choose to collect examples of one version of this fairy tale or another, in order to make a case for a Europe engaged either in "anti-semitic" repression of the Islamic role in its culture (as Menéndez Pidal charged in the 1940s) or in a "philo-semitic" celebration of its Arabic origins. Both of these approaches would miss what I think is the more important conclusion: that both exclusion and inclusion are inseparable faces of a debate over Islam that appears in tandem with the idea of Europe itself. The emergence of the one is cognitively related to the emergence of the other, so much so that we might even say that the debate about Europe's relationship to Islam is both a constitutive attribute of Europe and a distinctively European product.[39]

It is worth insisting upon this "European-ness" of both versions of the fantasy, because there is a tendency to split the exclusion of Islam from its inclusion, to see only the former as a child of Europe and to reiterate the latter as evidence of the West's repression of the importance of Islam.[40] This strategy, pioneered in Europe itself, has since been adopted by Muslim critics of Occidental histories. Consider the massive project, funded by the Trust for Culture of the Aga Khan and edited by Salma Khadra Jayyusi, that published two encyclopaedic volumes called *The Legacy of Muslim Spain* in 1992, on the five-hundredth anniversary of the Christian conquest of Muslim Granada.[41] In both acknowledgments and foreword, its editor made the project's object clear: "What greater cause can a Muslim intellectual have at the present time than to help put the history of the illustrious Islamic civilization back in its rightful place on the map of the world?"[42] The project was, in other words, to recover (given Jayyusi's geographic metaphor we might even say reconquer) some of the history of civilization for Islam, at a time (1992) when Islam's "civilizing" role was being unjustly denigrated.

As Jayyusi states a little elliptically, this denigration of Islamic civilization has everything to do with the civilizational politics of the European conquest and colonization of the Muslim world: "The Arabs and Muslims have all silently . . . selected al-Andalus as an ever abiding memory in their hearts. . . . All think of it as . . . an abiding witness to a great civilization that filled, with Baghdad, the civilizational semi-vacuum of earlier medieval times. Many of them, too, think of it as a lost paradise, and the persistent sense of grief at its loss has been greatly augmented by the recent loss of Palestine."[43]

The mention of Palestine reminds us of the present-day conflict within which much of the writing about Islamic Spain is inscribed.[44] It reminds us as well of the colonial logic within which the word "civilization" is being deployed. According to that logic, civilized peoples ought not to be colonized, though they may, of course, be colonizers (remember the *mission civilisatrice*). Like many scholars, Jayyusi sees in the recovery of the "civilization" of al-Andalus an act of resistance, restitution, and decolonization: "The old, wilful avoidance of a vast and shining historical presence of Arabs and Arabised Muslims . . . throughout the Middle Ages, who not only kept the line of human intellectuality and creativity alive, but greatly enhanced it, has, to put it in the mildest terms, been a historical crime long unrecognised. It gives me great happiness to see the increasing number of Western scholars now dedicated to the truth."[45]

Such a project may be morally attractive, but it has little to do with "historical truth." The idea of al-Andalus as a paradise of civilization providing light to a darkened humanity, far from being an eternal memory of the Arabs, as Jayyusi would have it, is itself a European product. From the expulsion of the Moriscos and the chronicles of al-Maqqarī (d. 1632) to the beginning of the twentieth century, al-Andalus seldom appeared in Arabic letters. When it was invoked, it was not in visions of a civilized paradise of tolerant cultural exchange, but in pious wishes that it should be reconquered from the unbelievers.[46]

It was only with the colonial translations of European works like Louis Viardot's two-volume *Essai sur l'histoire des arabes et des maures d'Espagne* (Paris, 1833) into Turkish (Istanbul, 1863–64, with a new edition in 1886–87) or Chateaubriand's *Le dernier Abencerage* into Arabic (Algiers, 1864), that al-Andalus became a politically active "memory" in Islam.[47] It was this memory that Ahmad Shauki, exiled from the British Mandate during World War I because of his nationalist activities, celebrated in his poems on al-Andalus; this memory that, by the end of that war, was becoming a standard part of school curricula in many areas of the Arab world; this memory that served M. Kurd Ali as evidence in 1922 that the West's claims about the Arabs' incapacity for civilization were lies: that in fact, "Arab and Islamic Spain was the schoolhouse of the Christian West."[48]

In short, if anyone forgot "the legacy of al-Andalus," it was Islam and not the West, as Jayyusi claimed. On the contrary, in the West that legacy has been more or less constantly cultivated from the sixteenth century to the present by those who would include Islam in countless registers of European culture: art and architecture, literature and music, history, philology, philosophy and theology, to name a few. Indeed when it comes to the recognition of al-Andalus as a key stage in the "dialogue of civilizations," the most important contribution may well be that of a historiography that would be least congenial to Jayyusi's colonial teleology. The idea that the Muslims of Spain provided the cultural light that illuminated a darkened Europe was widespread among Western writers of the nineteenth century.[49] But it was the writers of the Haskalah, or Jewish Enlightenment, who developed the concept of a "golden age" of tolerance in which religious minorities, especially Jews, had flourished under and been educated by Andalusian Islam.[50] Of course they developed this concept as a polemical foil to the politics of their own time and place, just as advocates of "exclusion" or "inclusion" do today. The cultural achievements of the Arabized Jews of Sepharad helped the *Maskilim* in their arguments with their anti-assimilationist orthodox coreligionists. But above all, they held up the example of a tolerant medieval Islam against the anti-emancipationist and anti-Semitic politics of the modern Christian nations (particularly Germany and the Austro-Hungarian empire) in which they lived.

The pleasant "fairy tale" of a golden age of inter-religious tolerance and cultural exchange in al-Andalus (modern scholarship prefers the word "myth")[51] was of obvious utility to the cultural and political project of European Jews in the nineteenth century. It became a double-edged sword in the changing political and cultural context of the twentieth, when it was increasingly adopted by Arab nationalists in the face of European colonialism in general, and intensified Jewish settlement within the Mandate in particular. In 1946, on the eve of the Palestinian Naqba and the dawn of the State of Israel, Cecil Roth warned his fellow Jewish historians that their cultivation of this exemplary past would be used against them in the coming struggle.[52]

Since then both sides have sought to deploy their own versions of history against the other. And though stories of the "lost paradise" of al-Andalus (a genre known in Arabic as *al-firdaus al-mafqūd*) have played a role in the cultural politics of some Israelis (particularly those whose families immigrated from Muslim lands), they have achieved much greater power in the hands of those who, like M. Kurd Ali in the 1920s, enlist the "tolerance" and "civilization" these stories encode on behalf of Arab nationalism or Islamism. In the words of article 31 of the Hamas Charter of 1988: "The Islamic Resistance Movement is a humanistic movement. . . . Under the wing of Islam it is possible for the followers of the three religions—Islam, Christianity, and Judaism—to coexist in peace and quiet with each other. Peace and quiet are not possible except under the wing of Islam. Past and present history are the best witness to that."[53]

Like Pope Benedict, the drafters of the Hamas Charter seized on one strand—albeit a very different strand—of a dialectical European story about the history of tolerance and dialogue in order to make their claims about the humanism of Islam. Their charter has brought us full circle, to the point with which I began: every "document of civilization" is also one of "barbarism," every dialectical fantasy of inclusion is simultaneously one of exclusion as well. Insofar as both inclusion and exclusion pursue their histories of civilization, reason, love, or poetry in order to invoke the authority of the past on behalf of their own vision of the future, both are claims to power. Given the vast asymmetries in the distribution of that power in our manifestly imperfect world, it is too easy to forget this. We thirst for "comforting fairy tales" of synthesis, alliance, and inclusion, thinking that these might be antidotes to the nightmarish narratives of antithesis, clash, and exclusion that we associate with the ascension to empire of the West. But we should not forget that the active ingredient of both nightmare and fairy tale is the same. Synthesized in soteriologies, compounded in philosophies, as soluble in Marxism, Zionism, or Islamism as in Catholicism or "Occidentalism," dialectical teleologies can be lethal in whatever form we imbibe them.

ACKNOWLEDGMENTS

With the exception of the Introduction and chapter 4, the chapters in this volume have appeared in similar form as essays in journals and edited collections over the past decade or so. They have all been reframed and rewritten in order to make clear their relation to one another and to eliminate redundancy, though with few exceptions I have not attempted to revise their arguments or augment their bibliographies. I am grateful to the publishers of the journals and books in which these essays appeared for allowing me to rehearse the ideas in this book first in their pages.

Chapter 1 appeared in *The Cambridge History of Christianity: Christianity in Western Europe c. 1100–c. 1500*, ed. M. Rubin and W. Simons (Cambridge: Cambridge University Press, 2009). Chapter 2 first appeared under the title "Love between Muslim and Jew in Medieval Spain: A Triangular Affair," in *Jews, Muslims, and Christians in and around the Crown of Aragon: Essays in Honour of Professor Elena Lourie*, ed. Harvey J. Hames (Leiden: Brill, 2004). Chapter 3 first appeared as "Deviant Politics and Jewish Love: Alfonso VIII and the Jewess of Toledo," in *Jewish History* 21 (2007): 15–41, © Springer Science+Business Media B.V. 2007, with kind permission from Springer Science+Business Media B.V. Chapter 5 first appeared with the subtitle "Jews and Christians in Medieval Spain," in *American Historical Review* 107, no. 4 (2002): 1065–93, doi:10.1086/ahr/107.4.1065, ©American Historical Association 2002, by permission of Oxford University Press. Chapter 6 first

appeared with the subtitle "'Jews' and 'Judaism' in Late-Medieval Spanish Poetry and Politics," in *Speculum* 81, no. 2 (2006). Chapter 7 first appeared with
the subtitle "Jews and Christians in Fifteenth-Century Spain," in *Past and
Present: A Journal of Historical Studies* 174, no. 1 (2002): 3–14, doi:10.1093
/past/174.1, © World Copyright: The Past and Present Society, 2002, by permission of Oxford University Press. Chapter 8 appeared in *The Origins of Racism in the West*, ed. Miriam Eliav-Feldon, Benjamin Isaac, and Joseph Ziegler
(Cambridge: Cambridge University Press, 2009). And chapter 9 appeared in
Journal of Religion in Europe 1 (2008): 3–33, © 2008 by Koninklijke Brill NV.

My thanks as well to Mohamad Ballan and Natalie Levin for their help in
preparing the manuscript and to Randolph Petilos, Teófilo Ruiz, and Mercedes García-Arenal for their confidence in the work. This book I dedicate,
along with so much else, to my Sofía.

NOTES

Abbreviations

ACA:C   Archivo de la Corona de Aragón, Cancillería (followed by register and folio)

AHCB   Arxiu Històric de la Ciutat de Barcelona

AMV   Archivo Municipal de Valencia

Baer, no.   Yitzhak Baer, *Die Juden im christlichen Spanien*, 2 vols. (Berlin: Akademie-Verlag, 1936), followed by document number

BT   Babylonian Talmud

Hinojosa, no.   José Hinojosa Montalvo, *The Jews of the Kingdom of Valencia* (Jerusalem, 1993), followed by document number

LM   Lletres Missives

MC   Manuals de Consells

PG   Patrologia Graeca, ed. J.-P. Migne, 161 vols. (Paris: Imprimerie Catholique, 1857–66)

PL   Patrologia Latina, ed. J.-P. Migne, 217 vols. (Paris: Imprimerie Catholique, 1844–55)

Introduction

1. For one example of an interpretation that relies on these verses to draw out multiple Islamic teachings on the treatment of non-Muslims, see Mahmoud Muhammad Taha, *The Second Message of Islam*, trans. Abdullahi Ahmed An-Na'im (Syracuse, NY: Syracuse University Press, 1987), 166.

2. For an early Islamic tradition about the occasion for revelation of Surah 5:56, see the life of the Prophet by Muḥammad Ibn Isḥāq (died in AH 150/768 CE), translated by A. Guillaume, *The Life of Muhammad: A Translation of Ishāq's Sīrat Rasūl Allāh* (Karachi: Oxford University Press, 2000), 364.

3. The words are Moses Maimonides's, from the introduction to his *Mishneh Torah*.

4. See Jonathan Riley-Smith, "Crusading as an Act of Love," *History* 65, no. 214 (June 1980): 177–92; John Connelly, *From Enemy to Brother: The Revolution in Catholic Teaching on the Jews, 1933–1965* (Cambridge, MA: Harvard University Press, 2012), 37–39.

5. For Luther's "sharp mercies" (which he also called "utter mercilessness"), see his "On the Jews and Their Lies," vol. 53 in the Weimar Edition (*Weimarer Ausgabe* [of his *Werke*]) published by Hermann Böhlaus Nachfolger (henceforth WA), pp. 522.34–35, 531.6–7. The "mercies" included the burning of the Jews' synagogues, the destruction of their houses, their segregation and concentration into one place, the confiscation of their wealth and their religious books, the prohibition of their teaching and their money-lending, forced manual labor for the young, and, if all this still failed to contain their blasphemy, then "away with them."

6. Compare the Targum's Aramaic: *ṭūrā de-sīnai*. Alternatively, the language may be Syriac, utilized by Christians in the region, for the word is the same in both. The citation from the Talmud that follows, however, makes Aramaic the more likely source. It is curious that the Qur'an consistently refers (with one exception) to the site of revelation in Aramaic (or Syriac), not Arabic, as in the opening of Surah 52: "By the Mount [*Ṭūr*] (of revelation)! By a decree inscribed in a scroll unfolded!"

7. Babylonian Talmud, Shabbat 88a. See also BT Avoda Zara 2b.

8. Though grammatically in the past tense, the phrase can be taken in the future and the present tense. The Qur'anic transformation of this phrase, however, was itself deeply influenced by rabbinic Jewish commentaries, as Julian Obermann brilliantly demonstrated in "Koran and Agada: The Events at Mount Sinai," *American Journal of Semitic Languages and Literatures* 58 (1941): 23–48. See also G. D. Newby, "Arabian Jewish history in the Sīrah," *Jerusalem Studies in Arabic and Islam* 7 (1986): 136–38; and Ignazio di Mateo, "Il Tahrīf od alterazione della Bibbia secondo i musulmani," *Bessarione* 38 (1922): 64–111, 223–360.

9. The multilingual pun thus underwrites the Islamic doctrine of "*tahrīf*"—the charge of Jewish and Christian alteration and falsification of previous scriptures—that allows the Islamic community both to honor the previous scriptures and to set them aside as tampered with. Compare Surah 4:46: "Of the Jews there are those who displace words from their (right) places and say 'We hear and we disobey' . . . with a twist of their tongues and a slander to the faith."

10. I do not propose the term coproduction as a competitor to "convivencia" and other terms of art, but only as a metaphor. Although I stumbled upon the word on my own, it is a concept very much in the air, and I have since discovered it also in the work of three kindred spirits, Mercedes García-Arenal, Galit Hasan-Rokem, and Uri Shachar.

11. The term Spain is anachronistic, since in the Middle Ages the Iberian Peninsula was made up of multiple polities. I use it here for convenience but will often refer throughout the text to those polities themselves: Castile, Catalonia, Valencia, Aragon, Navarre, Mallorca, etc.

12. Judaize: the Greek term (*ioudaizein*, tr. into Latin as *judaizare*) appears already in the Septuagint (e.g., in Esther 8:17), where it is not, however, negative. Paul's use of it is in the long run transformative. On the verb's history see Michele Murray, *Playing a Jewish Game: Gentile Christian Judaizing in the First and Second Centuries CE* (Ontario: Wilfred Laurier University Press, 2004), esp. 3–4; Róbert Dán, "Judaizare—the Career of a Term," in *Antitrinitarianism in the Second Half of the Sixteenth Century*, ed. R. Dán and A. Pirnát (Budapest and Leiden: Akadémiai Kiadó and Brill, 1982), 25–34; Gilbert Dagron, "Judäiser," in *Travaux et Mémoires* 11 (1991): 359–80.

13. This example and others are found in Uri Rubin, *Between Bible and Qur'an: The Children of Israel and the Islamic Self-Image* (Princeton, NJ: Darwin, 1999), 168ff.; and in Steven M. Wasserstrom, "'The Shi'is are the Jews of Our Community:' An Interreligious Comparison within Sunni Thought," *Israel Oriental Studies (IOS)* 14 (1994): 297–324. On the "Jewish

lineages" of all sects, see Wasserstrom, *Between Muslim and Jew*, (Princeton, NJ: Princeton University Press, 1995), 157–58. His use of the word "heresy" is a bit misleading here, since the denomination is relative to the observer. The Khawārij, for example, probably considered their (eventually victorious and therefore "orthodox") opponents a "Judaizing heresy."

14. For an overview of this process, see David Nirenberg, *Anti-Judaism: The Western Tradition* (New York: W. W. Norton, 2013), 135–82.

15. Ibn Ḥazm, "Al-Radd ʿalā ibn al-naghrīla al yahūdī" [The Refutation of Ibn Naghrila the Jew], in *Rasāʾil ibn ḥazm al-andalusi*, ed. Iḥsān ʿAbbās (Beirut, 1980–83), 3:67. Translated in Moshe Perlmann, "Eleventh-Century Andalusian Authors on the Jews of Granada," *Proceedings of the American Academy for Jewish Research* 18 (1948–49): 281–83. On this treatise see Ross Brann, *Power in the Portrayal: Representations of Jews and Muslims in Tenth- and Twelfth-Century Islamic Spain* (Princeton, NJ: Princeton University Press, 2009), 78–79.

16. *Lamentations Rabbah*, cited (with minimal alteration) from Galit Hasan-Rokem, *Tales of the Neighborhood: Jewish Narrative Dialogues in Late Antiquity* (Berkeley: University of California Press, 2003), 40. The translation is by David Stern, *Parables in Midrash: Narrative and Exegesis in Rabbinic Literature* (Cambridge, MA: Harvard University Press, 1991), 57.

17. For a striking example from early modern central Europe, see Paweł Maciejko's *The Mixed Multitude: Jacob Frank and the Frankist Movement, 1755–1816* (Philadelphia: University of Pennsylvania Press, 2011).

18. Samuel Huntington, "The Clash of Civilizations?" *Foreign Affairs* 72, no. 3 (Summer 1993): 35. For "bloody borders," see Huntington, *The Clash of Civilizations and the Remaking of World Order* (New York: Simon & Schuster, 1996), 258.

19. *The Joint Declaration of the Paris Summit of the Mediterranean*, July 13, 2008, *Union for the Mediterranean*, http://www.ufmsecretariat.org/en/institutional-documents.

20. I am referring here to Sylvain Gouguenheim's *Aristote au Mont-Saint-Michel: Les racines grecques de l'Europe chrétienne* (Paris: Seuil, 2008), and the ensuing controversy.

21. For novelists who have written on themes of medieval neighborliness between the three religions, see, e.g., Salman Rushdie, *The Moor's Last Sigh* (New York: Pantheon, 1995); Amin Maalouf, *Leo Africanus*, trans. Peter Sluglett (New York: New Amsterdam Press, 1992); A. B. Yehoshua, *A Journey to the End of the Millennium*, trans. Nicholas de Lange (New York: Doubleday, 1999); as well as Emile Habibi, Juan Goytisolo, and many others. There are also countless politicians who have voiced views on such questions.

22. Walter Benjamin, "Delirium," in *The Origins of German Tragic Drama*, trans. John Osborne (London: Verso, 1977), 53–54.

23. Compare Walter Benjamin, *Gesammelte Schriften*, ed. Rolf Tiedemann and Hermann Schweppenhäuser (Frankfurt: Suhrkamp, 1972–92) vol. 1, pt. 3, p. 1245.

24. Compare John 21:25: "But there are also many other things which Jesus did; were every one of them to be written, I suppose that the world itself could not contain the books that would be written."

Chapter 1

1. "Christmas Sermon," trans. Walter Kaegi, in "Initial Byzantine Reactions to the Arab Conquest," *Church History* 38 (1969): 139–49.

2. Theophanes the Confessor, *The Chronicle of Theophanes the Confessor*, trans. Cyril Mango and Roger Scott (Oxford: Clarendon Press, 1997), 471.

3. Maximus the Confessor's complaint in *PG* 91, col. 540, is translated in John Lamoreaux, "Early Christian Responses to Islam," in *Medieval Christian Perceptions of Islam: A Book*

of Essays, ed. John Tolan (New York: Garland, 1996), 14–15. For some more positive early Christian appraisals of Islam, see John Tolan, *Saracens: Islam in the Medieval European Imagination* (New York: Columbia University Press, 2002), 45–46. Robert Hoyland collected many of the early references in his *Islam as Others Saw It: A Survey and Evaluation of Christian, Jewish and Zoroastrian Writings on Early Islam* (Princeton, NJ: Darwin Press, 1997).

4. "Doctrina Jacobi nuper baptizati" [The Doctrine of Jacob Recently Baptized], trans. Walter Kaegi, in "Initial Byzantine Reactions," 141. On the interdependence of Christian and Islamic ideas about sacred violence, see Thomas Sizgorich, *Violence and Belief in Late Antiquity: Militant Devotion in Christianity and Islam* (Philadelphia: University of Pennsylvania Press, 2008).

5. John of Damascus, *Liber de haeresibus*, in *Die Schriften des Johannes von Damaskos*, ed. P. Bonafatius Kotter (Berlin: De Gruyter, 1969–81), 4:60. See also Daniel Sahas, *John of Damascus on Islam: The "Heresy" of the Ishmaelites* (Leiden: Brill, 1972). Later Christian polemics against Islam written in Arabic, like the ninth-century *Risâlat al-Kindî*, display even greater knowledge both of Qur'an and of Sirah (the biography of the Prophet) but deploy that greater knowledge to the same goals of characterizing Islam as sexual and as derivative of Judaism and heretical Christianity. On this polemical tradition, see Samir Khalil Samir and Jørgen S. Nielsen, eds., *Christian Arabic Apologetics during the Abbasid Period: 750–1258* (Leiden: Brill, 1994). On the circulation of such polemics in Christian Spain, see Peter Sjoerd van Koningsveld, "La Apología de Al-Kindí en la España del siglo XII: Huellas toledanas de un 'animal disputax'" in *Estudios sobre Alfonso VI y la reconquista de Toledo: Actas del II congreso internacional de estudios mozárabes* (Toledo: Instituto de Estudios, 1989), 107–29.

6. Thomas Burman, ed., *Liber denudationis* §9.20, in *Religious Polemic and the Intellectual History of the Mozarabs* (Leiden: Brill, 1994). On Christian study of Islamic Qur'an exegesis in the Latin West, see also Thomas Burman, "Tafsīr and Translation: Robert of Ketton, Mark of Toledo, and traditional Arabic Qur'ān Exegesis," *Speculum* 73 (1998): 703–32. For a recent survey of the medieval western European literature on Muhammad, see Michelina Di Cesare, "The Prophet in the Book: Images of Muhammad in Western Medieval Book Culture," in *Constructing the Image of Muhammad in Europe*, ed. Avinoam Shalem (Berlin: Walter de Gruyter, 2013), 9–32.

7. Maimonides, *Letters and Essays of Moses Maimonides*, ed. and trans. Isaac Shailat (Jerusalem: Maliyot Press of Yeshivat Birkat Moshe Maaleh Adumim, 1987), 238–39.

8. John Tolan, "Peter the Venerable, on the 'Diabolical Heresy of the Saracens,'" in *The Devil, Heresy, and Witchcraft in the Middle Ages: Essays in Honor of Jeffrey B. Russell*, ed. Alberto Ferreiro (Leiden: Brill, 1998), 345–67; Marie-Thérèse d'Alverny, "Deux traductions latines du Coran au Moyen-Âge," *Archives d'histoire doctrinale et littéraire du Moyen Âge* 16 (1947–48), 69–131.

9. Peter of Cluny, *Summa totius haeresis Saracenorum*, in *Schriften zum Islam*, ed. Rheinhold Glei, Corpus Islamo-Christianum, series latina 1 (Alternberg: CIS-Verlag, 1985), §18.

10. Recounted in Guibert of Nogent's account of the First Crusade, *Dei gesta per Francos*, ed. R. B. C. Huygens, Corpus Christianorum, Coninuatio Mediaevalis 127A (Turnhout: Brepols, 1996), 94, and *The Deeds of God through the Franks*, trans. Robert Levine (Woodbridge: Boydell Press, 1997), 32. See also Jean Flori, "La caricature de l'Islam dans l'Occident médiéval: Origine et signification de quelques stéréotypes concernant l'Islam," *Aevum* 2 (1992): 245–56.

11. The episode involving Abbot Maiolus is particularly interesting. It is related in Syrus, *Vita Sancti Maioli* (PL 137, cols.763D–768D), translated and discussed in Benjamin Z. Kedar, *Crusade and Mission: European Approaches towards the Muslims* (Princeton, NJ: Princeton University Press, 1984), 42–43.

12. *Epistolae et diplomata*, no. 101 (PL 146, cols.1386–1387).

13. Two recent studies of this role, from quite different but complementary points of view, are Dominique Iogna-Prat, *Order and Exclusion: Cluny and Christendom Face Heresy, Judaism, and Islam (1000–1150)*, trans. G. R. Edwards (Ithaca, NY: Cornell University Press, 2002); and Tomaž Mastnak, *Crusading Peace: Christendom, the Muslim World, and Western Political Order* (Berkeley: University of California Press, 2002).

14. On Islamic reactions to the crusades, see Emmanuel Sivan, *L'Islam et la Croisade: Idéologie et propagande dans les réactions musulmanes aux Croisades* (Paris: Librairie d'Amérique et d'Orient, 1968), and *Interpretations of Islam Past and Present* (Princeton, NJ: Darwin Press, 1985), chap. 1; Carole Hillenbrand, *Crusades: Islamic Perspectives* (Edinburgh: Edinburgh University Press, 2008). On the term "Frank," see the *Encyclopedia of Islam*, 2nd ed., under "Ifrandj."

15. Baldric of Dol, *Historia Jerosolimitana* I.iv, 14–15, trans. Mastnak in *Crusading Peace*, 51–52; see also Edward Peters, *The First Crusade: The Chronicle of Fulcher of Chartres and Other Source Materials* (Philadelphia: University of Pennsylvania Press, 1989), 31–32. See also Jonathan Riley-Smith, *The First Crusade and the Idea of Crusading* (London: Athlone, 1993), 149.

16. *Roberti monachi historia Iherosolimitana* I.1–2, 727–29, trans. Peters, *The First Crusade*, 2–4.

17. Otto of Freising, *The Deeds of Frederick Barbarossa*, trans. Charles Christopher Mierow (Toronto: University of Toronto Press, 1994), 1:xliv.

18. Hence Joseph Strayer called the First Crusade "a spectacular advance toward European peace and unity": see "The First Western Union," in his *Medieval Statecraft and the Perspectives of History* (Princeton, NJ: Princeton University Press, 1971), 334. On the emergence of the terms *christianitas* and *christianissimus* in this period, see Jean Rupp, *L'idée de chrétienté dans la pensée pontificale des origines à Innocent III* (Paris: Les Presses Modernes, 1939); Paul Rousset, "La notion de chrétienté aux XIe et XIIe siècles," *Le Moyen Âge* 69 (1963), 195ff. "Intus pax, foris terrores" is cited without attribution by Étienne Delaruelle, "Paix de Dieu et croisade dans la chrétienté du XIIe siècle," in *Paix de Dieu et guerre sainte en Languedoc au XIIIe siècle*, Cahiers de Fanjeaux 4 (Toulouse: Édouard Privat, 1969), 61.

19. On the development of these terms, see Mastnak, *Crusading Peace*, 91–99, 144–46; Agostino Paravicini-Bagliani, *The Pope's Body* (Chicago: Chicago University Press, 2000), 58; Jane E. Sayers, *Innocent III: Leader of Europe (1198–1216)* (London: Longman, 1994), 16. Bernard's uses are in *On Consideration* II.viii.16, IV.vii.23.

20. *Gesta Francorum* VI.xiii: "Turci inimici Dei et sanctae christianitatis." The citation is from Alphonse Dupront's conclusion to the volume of Paul Alphandéry's lectures that he edited: Paul Alphandéry, *La chrétienté et l'idée de croisade*, ed. Alphonse Dupront (Paris: Éditions Albin Michel, 1959), 2:274.

21. Sayers, *Innocent III*, 73–74, 188; Ludovico Gatto, *Il pontificato di Gregorio X (1271–1276)* (Rome: Istituto Storico Italiano per il Medio Evo, 1959), 87–88; Jonathan Riley-Smith, *The Crusades: A Short History* (London: Athlone, 1992), 171, 176; William Chester Jordan, *Louis IX and the Challenge of the Crusade: A Study in Rulership* (Princeton, NJ: Princeton University Press, 1979), chap. 4.

22. For an example of this self-consciousness, see Suzanne Duparc-Quioc, ed., *La chanson d'Antioche* (Paris: Académie des Inscriptions et Belles-Lettres, 1977), 26, IX, lines 170–82, where Jesus predicts on the cross the future birth of the people who will avenge his death, reconquer his land, and restore "sainte Crestïentés."

23. On the use of these expressions, specific to the Holy Land, in the preaching of crusade, see Ursula Schwerin, *Die Aufrufe der Päpste zur Befreiung des Heiligen Landes von*

den Anfängen bis zum Ausgang Innozenz IV: Ein Beitrag zur Geschichte der kurialen Kreuzzugspropaganda und der päpstlichen Epistolographie (Berlin: Ebering, 1937), 51–54. Though the importance of the destination for the early crusading movement is undeniable, some recent historians of the broader crusading movement prefer to stress papal *auctoritas principalis* as a defining principle, since it allows the incorporation into the concept of those many later crusades whose goal was not the Levant. See above all the introduction to Norman Housley, *The Later Crusades: From Lyons to Alcazar 1274–1580* (Oxford: Oxford University Press, 1992). See also Jonathan Riley-Smith, "History, the Crusades, and the Latin East: A Personal View," in *Crusaders and Muslims in Twelfth-Century Syria*, ed. Maya Shatzmiller (Leiden: Brill, 1993), 9–10; and, more generally, Christopher J. Tyerman, *The Invention of the Crusades* (Toronto: University of Toronto Press, 1998).

24. For these phrases, see Paul Rousset, *Les origines et les caractères de la première croisade* (Neuchâtel: Baconnière, 1945), 100–101, and his "La notion de chrétienté," 199; Mastnak, *Crusading Peace*, 123.

25. On the Normans as "Agareni," see Carl Erdmann, *Die Entstehung des Kreuzzugsgedankens* (Stuttgart: W. Kohlhammer, 1935), 110. For a few thirteenth-century Middle English sources that call Danes, Irish, Saxons, and Scots "Sarazins," see Joseph Hall, ed., *King Horn: A Middle English Romance* (Oxford: Clarendon Press, 1901), 96–97; Diane Speed, "The Saracens of King Horn," *Speculum* 65 (1990), 566–67. In 1149 Pope Eugenius III spoke of the unheard-of and inhuman invasion of Christian territory in eastern Europe by "L. dux Poloniae, collecta sarracenorum multitudine." See his letter to Bishop Henry of Moravia: *Epistolae et privilegia* no. 351 (*PL* 180, col. 1385).

26. There is an endless bibliography on the subject of diplomatic and economic connections between Christian polities and Islamic ones. An interesting recent study of institutions for trade and travel is Olivia Remie Constable, *Housing the Stranger in the Mediterranean World: Lodging, Trade, and Travel in Late Antiquity and the Middle Ages* (Cambridge: Cambridge University Press, 2003). On diplomatic contacts, see, inter alia, Michael A. Köhler, *Allianzen und Verträge zwischen fränkischen und islamischen Herrschern im Vorderen Orient: Eine Studie über das zwischenstaatliche Zusammenleben vom 12. bis ins 13. Jahrhundert* (Berlin: Walter de Gruyter, 1991).

27. Carmen Barceló, ed., *Un tratado Catalán medieval de derecho islámico: El libre de la çuna e xara de los moros* (Córdoba: University of Córdoba, 1989).

28. Wolfram of Eschenbach, *Parzival*, ed. Karl Lachmann (Berlin: Walter de Gruyter, 1926), lines 57:15–22. Cf. Stephanie Cain van D'Elden, "Black and White: Contact with the Mediterranean World in Medieval German Narrative," in Marilyn J. Chiat and Kathryn L. Reyerson, eds., *The Medieval Mediterranean: Cross-Cultural Contacts*, Medieval Studies at Minnesota 3 (Minneapolis: University of Minnesota Press, 1988), 112–18. For Chaucer's knight, see *The Canterbury Tales*, the General Prologue, lines 64–67.

29. The cleric's claim is in J. Banogh, ed., *Libellus de institutione morum*, Scriptores rerum Hungaricarum 2 (Budapest: Academia Litter. Hungarica, 1938), 625. King Béla's letter is discussed by Nora Berend, *At the Gates of Christendom: Jews, Muslims, and Pagans in Medieval Hungary, c. 1000–c. 1300* (Cambridge: Cambridge University Press, 2001), 166ff. Chapter 5 provides an illuminating analysis of the conflict between papal and monarchical visions of what a Christian Hungarian kingdom should look like. For Clement's letter to James, see Santiago Dominguez Sánchez, *Documentos de Clemente IV (1265–1268) referentes a España* (León: Universidad de León, 1996), 224–27.

30. *Breve compendio de las Crónicas de los Reyes de España*, Bibliothèque Nationale de France, Paris, Ms. Espagnole 110, folios 4r, 21v, 30r–31v.

31. For other regions a good beginning can be made with James Powell, ed., *Muslims under Latin Rule, 1100–1300* (Princeton, NJ: Princeton University Press, 1990).

32. Cf., for example, the treaty of Xivert (1234), in *Cartas Pueblas de las Morerias Valencianas y documentación complementaria*, ed. M. V. Febrer Romaguera (Zaragoza: Anubar, 1991), 1:10–16, and the treaty of Granada (1491) summarized in L. P. Harvey, *Islamic Spain, 1250–1500* (Chicago: University of Chicago Press, 1990), 314–23.

33. One fourteenth-century Andalusi imam, Ibn Rabīʿ, wrote explicitly about this danger. See Peter Sjoerd van Koningsveld and Gerard Albert Wiegers, "The Islamic Statute of the Mudejars in the Light of a New Source," *Al-Qantara* 17 (1996): 19–59.

34. Hossain Buzineb, "Respuestas de jurisconsultos maghrebies en torno a la inmigración de musulmanes hispánicos," *Hespéris Tamuda* 26–27 (1988): 59, 63.

35. The Maliki school of law, dominant in the Maghreb and al-Andalus, was in fact the most severe on the issue of Muslim minorities living in non-Islamic polities. Khaled Abou el-Fadl, "Islamic Law and Muslim Minorities," *Islamic Law and Society* 1, no. 2 (1994): 141–87.

36. Harvey, *Islamic Spain*, 58.

37. Buzineb, "Respuestas," 65, lines 1–2.

38. Cf. David Nirenberg, *Communities of Violence: Persecution of Minorities in the Middle Ages* (Princeton, NJ: Princeton University Press, 1996), 139.

39. Here and in the following pages I am reiterating my argument in "Varieties of Mudejar Experience: Muslims in Christian Iberia, 1000–1526," in *The Medieval World*, ed. Peter Linehan and Janet L. Nelson (New York: Routledge, 2001), 60–76.

40. The fatwa was discovered by Kathryn Miller. See her path-breaking "Guardians of Islam: Muslim Communities in Medieval Aragon" (PhD Dissertation, Yale University, 1998), 51 and 57. Many of her insights inform my argument here and in "Varieties of Mudejar Experience." And see also, by the same author, *Religious Authority and Muslim Communities of Late Medieval Spain* (New York: Columbia University Press, 2008), 129.

41. Peter Sjoerd van Koningsveld and Gerard Albert Wiegers, "The Polemical Works of Muhammad al-Qaysī (fl. 1309) and Their Circulation in Arabic and Aljamiado among the Mudejars in the Fourteenth Century," *Al-Qanṭara* 15 (1994): 163–99.

42. Nirenberg, *Communities of Violence*, 196–98.

Chapter 2

1. It seems superfluous to footnote something so well known and so widely attested. Those who favor scripture may look to the *Song of Songs*, those who prefer anthropology to Claude Lévi-Strauss, *The Elementary Structures of Kinship*, ed. Rodney Needham, trans. James Harle Bell, John Richard von Sturmer, and R. Needham (Boston: Beacon Press, 1969), for example 67–68.

2. Babylonian Talmud, Tractate ʿAvoda Zarah 36b.

3. This drive toward endogamy struck a number of ancient non-Jewish observers, the most prominent of which was Tacitus: "They eat and sell apart from others . . . , they do not make unions with alien women" (*Histories*, V.5).

4. Maimonides, *Mishneh Torah*, introduction (see n. 5). Though for some purposes (and after much debate) the rabbis chose to define Muslims and Christians as nonheathens (for example, for business purposes such as the lending of money or the selling of cattle), within the context of miscegenation there was no such relaxation. See also Jacob Katz, *Exclusiveness and Tolerance: Studies in Jewish-Gentile Relations in Medieval and Modern Times* (Oxford: Oxford University Press, 1961), 32–36 and chap. 4.

5. Maimonides, *Mishneh Torah*, Sefer Kedushah [SK] XII.1–10 (Louis Rabinowitz and Philip Grossman, trans., *The Code of Maimonides, Book Five: The Book of Holiness*, Yale Judaica Series 16 [New Haven, CT: Yale University Press, 1965], 80–83). The quote is from XII.2.

6. For Maimonides's approval of the zealots, see SK XII.4–6, 14. For early rabbinic discomfort with Pinehas's actions, see Jerusalem Talmud, Tractate Sanhedrin 27b.

7. R. Yehuda ben Asher, *Zikhron Yehuda* (Berlin: D. Fridlender, 1846), no. 91. In no. 63 he invokes the zealots against such men. For Nahmanides's "Whoever goes astray with a Gentile woman desecrates the covenant of Abraham," see H. D. Chavel, *Kitvei Rabenu Moshe ben Nahman* (Jerusalem: Mosad ha-Rav Kook, 1964), 1:370. Cf. *The Zohar*, II, 3a-b (cited in Yitzhak Baer, *A History of the Jews in Christian Spain* [Philadelphia: Jewish Publication Society of America, 1978], 1:262), and II, 87b. For additional citations, see Ben Zion Dinur, *Yisrael ba-Golah*, vol. II, 4 (Tel Aviv: Devir, 1969), 291–92; Louis Epstein, *Sex Laws and Customs in Judaism* (New York: Bloch, 1948), 172–73. See especially Yom Tov Assis, "Sexual Behavior in Mediaeval Hispano-Jewish Society," in *Jewish History: Essays in Honour of Chimen Abramsky*, ed. Ada Rapaport-Albert and Steven Zipperstein (London: Peter Halban, 1988), 38–41. See also Marc Saperstein, *Decoding the Rabbis: a Thirteenth-Century Commentary on the Aggadah* (Cambridge, MA: Harvard University Press, 1980), 96, 246; and Isidore Epstein, *Studies in the Communal Life of the Jews of Spain*, 2nd ed. (New York: Hermon Press, 1968), 88, citing Rabbi Shelomo ben Adret of Barcelona.

8. For a summary of these rules, see Joseph Schacht, *An Introduction to Islamic Law* (Oxford: Clarendon Press, 1964), 131–32. For specifically Maliki law on the subject (the school of law most influential in Muslim Iberia and North Africa), see David Santillana, *Istituzioni di diritto musulmano malichita con riguardo anche al sistema sciafiita* (Rome: Instituto per l'Oriente, 1925–38), 1:207–8. The Maliki school was perhaps the strictest on the question of mixed marriages, especially if they occurred in lands not ruled by Muslims. See especially Khaled, "Islamic Law and Muslim Minorities." There is plenty of evidence that such marriages, even when they were entirely legal, could underwrite a great deal of anxiety in Muslim Spain. A number of Nasrid kings of Granada, for example, were killed by rebels alleging that their Christian maternal ancestry made their loyalty suspect.

9. See, for example, the fourteenth-century Castilian Mudejar law code transcribed as *Leyes de moros del siglo XIV*, in *Memorial Histórico Español*, ed. Pascual de Gayangos (Madrid: Real Academia de la Historia, 1853), title 14, 5:20. The late fourteenth-century Valencian *Llibre de la çuna e xara*, ed. by Carmen Barceló in *Un tratado Catalán medieval de derecho islámico: El llibre de la çuna e xara de los moros* (Córdoba: Universidad de Córdoba, 1989), 90, assigns the death penalty to married Muslim males who commit adultery, no matter what the religion of their accomplices. Similarly, unmarried males who sleep with unmarried females receive the same number of lashes regardless of the religion of the women.

10. *Suma de los principales mandamientos y devedamientos de la ley y çunna por don Içe de Gebir . . . (=Breviario sunni)*: "Ni duerman, ni casen con ynfieles, asi hombres como mugeres." See de Gayangos, *Memorial Histórico Español*, 5:341. The most recent study of the *Breviario* is that of Gerard Albert Wiegers, *Islamic Literature in Spanish and Aljamiado: Yça of Segovia (fl. 1450), His Antecedents and Successors* (Leiden: Brill, 1994), 115–33 and passim.

11. Note that this is a polemic in which Yehuda had the upper hand. On Todros's precarious position, see Ross Brann, *The Compunctious Poet: Cultural Ambiguity and Hebrew Poetry in Muslim Spain* (Baltimore: Johns Hopkins University Press, 1991), chap. 5. The translation of Todros's poem is from Brann, *The Compunctious Poet*, 145.

12. It may be that, as Américo Castro suggested, there was a literary culture of the erotic in Arabic (and later Hebrew) that was generally lacking in the Latin and vernaculars of pen-

insular Christians. See his *The Structure of Spanish History*, trans. Edmund L. King (Princeton, NJ: Princeton University Press, 1954), 318–22.

13. For some of the issues involved in sexual intercourse between members of minority and majority communities, see my *Communities of Violence*, chap. 5, and chap. 5 of this volume.

14. For a very general treatment of this issue, see Richard Trexler, *Sex and Conquest: Gendered Violence, Political Order, and the European Conquest of the Americas* (Cambridge: Polity Press, 1995).

15. Buzineb, "Respuestas de jurisconsultos maghrebies," 59, 63.

16. Cf. John Boswell, *The Royal Treasure: Muslim Communities under the Crown of Aragon in the Fourteenth Century* (New Haven, CT: Yale University Press, 1977), 50–51; Robert Burns, *Islam under the Crusaders* (Princeton, NJ: Princeton University Press, 1973), 252; Elena Lourie, "Anatomy of Ambivalence: Muslims under the Crown of Aragon in the Late Thirteenth Century," in her *Crusade and Colonisation: Muslims, Christians, and Jews in Medieval Aragon* (Aldershot: Variorum, 1990), 62–68. Charles Verlinden, *L'esclavage dans l'Europe Médiévale* (Bruges: De Tempel, 1955), vol. 1, and María-Teresa Ferrer i Mallol, *Els sarraïns de la Corona Catalano-Aragonesa en el segle XIV: Segregació i discriminació* (Barcelona: Consell Superior d'Investigacions Cientifiques, 1987), provide many other examples.

17. The Muslim aljama of Valencia, for example, purchased from King Pere the ceremonious confirmation of its privilege that whenever a Muslim woman was found guilty of sexual intercourse with a non-Muslim she would be condemned to death without possibility of monetary remission. For the edict of 1347 confirming the execution of Muslim adulteresses, see ACA:C 884:167r–v, published in M-T Ferrer, *Els sarraïns*, 271. For an earlier example, see ACA:C 61:101 v (1283/4/23), in which the Muslims of Xàtiva ask that the prohibition on adultery between Christian and Jewish men on the one hand and Muslim women on the other be enforced. The death penalty was almost always commuted in such cases to enslavement.

18. When sex with slaves involved only people from within the household, it did not usually result in disputes at law. Cases involving outsiders to the household were much more conflictual. Hence James II's edict, issued at the request of the city of Valencia and other towns of that kingdom, forbidding anyone from having sex with an owner's slave unless they were of the owner's "parentela" (ACA:C 219:321r [1321/5/1]). On sex with slaves more generally see James A. Brundage, *Law, Sex, and Christian Society in Medieval Europe* (Chicago: Univerity of Chicago Press, 1987), 518. Of course the relationships expressed and established through such sex varied greatly within and across the three religious communities we are discussing.

19. For a broader treatment of this competition see my *Communities of Violence*, chap. 6.

20. Ibn 'Idhārī al-Marrākushī, *Al-Bayān al Mughrib*, trans. Ambrosio Huici Miranda, in *Al-Bayan . . . Nuevos Fragmentos Almorávides y Almohades* (Valencia: Anubar Ediciones, 1963), 99–100. The translation is from Norman Roth, *Jews, Visigoths and Muslims in Medieval Spain* (Leiden: Brill, 1994), 134.

21. On the role of Jews in the thirteenth-century admininstration of Valencia, see Robert Ignatius Burns, *Medieval Colonialism: Postcrusade Exploitation of Islamic Valencia* (Princeton, NJ: Princeton University Press, 1975), passim.

22. The most recent treatment of this grant (and of a very interesting fourteenth-century case) is by Heather Ecker, "The Conversion of Mosques to Synagogues in Seville: The Case of the Mezquita de la Judería," *Gesta* 36, no. 2 (1997): 190–207.

23. The queen's advice is from ACA:C 1582:107r–108r (1374/11/1). The tax contributions are from a war subsidy request of 1363, ACA:C 1185:219v–221r and 1187:212v–214r. See

Jaume Riera i Sans, "Jafudà Alatzar, jueu de València (segle XIV)," *Revista d'Història Medieval* 4 (1993): 76, 79.

24. R. Asher ben Yeḥiel, *Sefer She'elot w-teshuvot le-ha-Rab Rabbenu 'Asher* (Zolkiew, 1602), no. 32, 6. See the discussion in Moisés Orfali, *Los conversos españoles en la literatura rabínica*, (Salamanca: Universidad Pontificia de Salamanca, 1982), 23.

25. For the case of Oro de Par, which occurred in 1356, see ACA:C 691:127r–v. Circa 1319 a correspondent wrote to Rabbi Asher asking permission to punish by disfigurement a Jewish woman from the region of Segovia who had borne two children (twins?) to a Christian. (The son had died, and the daughter had been seized by Christian authorities.) The punishment was proposed so that the Torah not be dishonored in the eyes of the Gentiles. See Yitzhak Baer, *Die Juden im christlichen Spanien* (Berlin: Akademie-Verlag, 1936), 2:138–39. In both cases the proposed punishment involved cutting off the nose.

26. Thus in 1277 the Jews of Calatayud obtained a charter fining any Christian male caught by witnesses in bed with a Jewish woman 300 maravedis and giving the Jewish community the right to arrest him. See ACA:C 39:155r–v, published in Jean Régné, *History of the Jews in the Crown of Aragon*, ed. Yom Tov Assis and Adam Gruzman (Jerusalem: The Magnes Press, 1978), document X. No Muslim community could have consistently enforced such a privilege.

27. See above, note 17.

28. For the case of Amiri, which occurred in 1301, see Carmen Orcástegui and Esteban Sarasa, "El libro-registro de Miguel Royo, merino de Zaragoza en 1301: Una fuente para el estudio de la sociedad y economía Zaragozana a comienzos del siglo XIV," *Aragón en la Edad Media* 4 (1981): 111–12. See also Lourie, "Anatomy," 71.

29. The role of Muslims in the world of prostitution is well documented, though relatively unstudied. The richest treatment is that for the fifteenth century of Mark Meyerson, "Prostitution of Muslim Women in the Kingdom of Valencia: Religious and Sexual Discrimination in a Medieval Plural Society," in *The Medieval Mediterranean: Cross-Cultural Contacts*, ed. Marilyn J. Chiat and Kathryn L. Ryerson (Minneapolis: University of Minnesota Press, 1988), 87–95. On the fourteenth century see Boswell, *Royal Treasure*, 348–51. On the numerical prominence of Muslim prostitutes in thirteenth-century Valencia, see Francisco Roca Traver, "Un siglo de vida mudéjar en la Valencia medieval (1238–1338)," *Estudios de Edad Media de la Corona de Aragón* 5 (1952): 161.

30. The case, recorded in Archivo Histórico Provincial de Huesca Pr. 83, ff. 264v–265v (1444), is cited by Angel Conte Cazcarro, *La aljama de moros de Huesca* (Huesca: Instituto de Estudios Altoaragoneses, 1992), 41. The religion of the prostitute is not mentioned, but she is unlikely to have been a Christian, since if she were the Jew would not have dared go to the authorities with his complaint.

31. Vincent Ferrer, *Sermons*, ed. Josep Sanchis Sivera and Gret Schib (Barcelona: Editorial Barcino, 1932–88), 5:250.

32. See Nirenberg, *Communities*, chap. 5, 141; and Lourie, "Anatomy," 71. On Jewish attitudes toward Muslim concubines in Aragon, see especially Assis, "Sexual Behaviour," 36–40.

33. ACA:C cr. Jaume II, box 30, no. 3804 (1311/2/15), a similar version of which is published in Baer, *Die Juden*, 1:201–3, from ACA:C 239:18v–19r. Conflicts between father and son over intercourse with a slave had an ancient Mediterranean pedigree and were often addressed, for example, in Islamic hadith collections. See, for example, the *Muwaṭṭā' of Imam Mālik*, book XIV, chap. 324, nos. 1096–99.

34. For the circumcision, see ACA:C 385:19r: "concedimus de gracia sp[ecialiter] vobis . . . possitis in civitate predicta, videlicet in calle judayco ipsius civitatis, quandam filium

cuiusdam sarracene serve et captive vestre facere judeum et ad ritum pervertere judeorum et ipsum facere circumscidi, iuxta legem et consuetudinem ebreorum" (1321/12/17). For the suffocation, see ACA:C 62:136v–137r (1285/3/15), published in Régné, *History*, 428–30: "Item quod tu, dictus Abraham, sufocasti duos infantes natos de quadam sarracena, que a te ipsos suscepit. Item quod tenebas publice in domo tua quandam sarracenam de Palia nomine Axian in tuo contubernio, cum qua habebas rem, quociens volebas et que a te suscepit plures partus."

35. ACA:C 67:1r (1286/5/1) [=Régné no. 1543]: "Cecrim Abnabe (?), judeus Osce, genuit genuit (sic) ex quadam sarracena sua quendam prole, et quod fecit ipsam sarracenam converti ad legem judaycam, et quod est consuetudo civitate Osce si aliquis judeus generat prole ex sarracena captiva sua . . . proles quam ex ea habeat pertenuit ad . . ." The conversion may well have enfranchised the mother. Cf. Assis, "Sexual Behaviour," 39.

36. Adret, vol. 5, no. 245. The concubine involved in this incident was probably not a free Muslim, at least not before the marriage. For more general comments on Jewish attitudes toward concubinage, see Assis, "Sexual Behavior," 62.

37. ACA:C 110:34v (1298/3/26): "Unde cum supradicte persone alienni [?] sint a lege nostra et non videamus causam propter quod vos de facto huiusmodi intromitere debeatis." My thanks to M. T. Ferrer for the reference.

38. The purchase of such licenses was not rare. Perfet Gravei of Barcelona bought one in 1292 in order to convert a Muslim slave called Hauha (ACA:C 260:97r [1292/6/25]), as did the community of Barcelona collectively for the conversion of the Muslim Lopello de Serrah Mahomet in 1361 (ACA:C 905:68 [1361/1/4]). That the practice was standard is suggested by a fine levied in 1386 against two women of Alicant for "conversion without license" from Islam to Judaism. They apparently received no other punishment. (ACA:RP, MR 1722:49r, cited in Ferrer, *Els sarraïns*, 82–83.)

39. María's case was first noted, and partially documented, by Boswell, *Royal Treasure*, 351–52. See also David Nirenberg, "María's Conversion to Judaism," *Orim: A Jewish Journal at Yale* 2 (1984): 38–44; Nirenberg, *Communities of Violence*, 185–87.

40. ACA:C 690:31v (1356/8/12).

41. ACA:C 899:60r (1356/8/22), published and translated in Boswell, *Royal Treasure*, 351–52, 442. Adultery here may refer to the practice of prostitution without royal license.

42. ACA:C 691:232r (1358/5/18). See Nirenberg, *Communities of Violence*, 185–86, and cf. Boswell, *Royal Treasure*, 380.

43. On Oldradus, see William Stalls, "Jewish Conversion to Islam: The Perspective of a *Quaestio*," *Revista Española de Teología* 43 (1983): 235–51; Norman Zacour, *Jews and Saracens in the Consilia of Oldradus de Ponte* (Toronto: Pontifical Institute of Medieval Studies, 1990), 21–22, 42–43, 77. The translation here is by Zacour, 42–43. The biblical reference is to Matthew 11:24.

44. See the reference in note 39, above.

45. See Biblioteca Nacional, Madrid (BNM), Ms. Res. 35, ff. 101r(b)-112v(b), which preserves the arguments against the conversion made by the dean of Talavera, the prior of Santa Catalina, and Fernando Alonso, a canon of the town; and those in favor of it by the Jews of Talavera and their lawyer. My thanks to Kathryn Miller for telling me of the manuscript and providing me with a microfilm. On this disputation see Nirenberg, *Communities of Violence*, 191–95, and (appearing simultaneously) Angel Gómez Moreno, "An unknown Jewish-Christian Controversy in Fifteenth-Century Talavera de la Reina: Towards the End of Spanish Jewry," in *Nunca fue pena mayor (estudios de literatura Española en homenaje a Brian Dutton)*, ed. Ana Menéndez Collera and Victoriano Roncero López (Cuenca: Ediciones de la

Universidad de Castilla – La Mancha, 1996), 285–92. The manuscript was apparently copied (at the request of Alfonso de Cartagena?) from the original records of the proceso held in the Archbishop of Toledo's court (f. 101r(b): "Recibi una letra . . . en que me enbiava pedir aquel proceso . . . sobre el judio que avia tornado la mora judia . . . sobre la qual fue nacido aquella grande discordia." On the scandal, see f. 101r(b); 101v(a). For a brief description of BNM Res. 35, see Horacio Santiago-Otero and Klaus Reinhardt, "Escritos de polémica antijudía en lengua vernácula," *Medievalia* 2 (1993): 193–94; and, with less detail, Horacio Santiago-Otero, "The *Libro declarante*: An Anonymous Work in the Anti-Jewish Polemic in Spain," in *Proceedings of the Tenth World Congress of Jewish Studies*, Division B, *The History of the Jewish People* (Jerusalem: World Union of Jewish Studies, 1990), 77.

46. BNM, Ms. Res. 35, fol. 101v(b): "Saco una moça mora de casa de su padre e la torno judia, lo qual ser de consentimiento de ella o non no curamos." If rape or abduction was involved, it is not explicitly stated. That the Jew, "contra Dios e contra su ley, aya seydo mesclado, segund se dize ser notorio, mucho tiempo ante de esta muger . . . ," is mentioned only as a further abomination.

47. That Christian clerics are pleading on behalf of the Muslims is explicit throughout the document. For Christian participation on behalf of the Jews, see, inter alia, the signature of the *letrado* for the Jews on BNM, Ms. Res. 35, fol. 105r(b), and the reference in the rebutal on 105v(a) to "un escripto que por parte de los judios, non sabemos si por algun xristiano."

48. University of Salamanca Ms. 70, fols. 86ra-111vb. The treatise was not included in his *Opera Omnia* (Venice, 1507–30). See Pablo Luis Suárez, "Los manuscritos de Alfonso Tostado de Madrigal conservados en la Biblioteca Universitaria de Salamanca," *Salamanticensis* 4 (1957): 3–50; Antonio García y García, "La Canonística ibérica medieval posterior al Decreto de Graciano," *Repertorio de Historia de las Ciencias Eclesiásticas en España* 5 (1976): 354.

49. Translation of the treaty from Harvey, *Islamic Spain*, 317.

50. Arch. Mun. Murcia, Lib. Actas, 1469–70, fols. 73–74, dated December 11, 1469. Doc. no. 764 in Luis Rubio García, *Los judíos de Murcia en la Baja Edad Media (1350–1500)*, colección documental II (Murcia: Universidad de Murcia, 1997), 14–15.

51. See chaps. 4–8 of this book.

52. The Sampson text was published in volume 10 of the *Opera Omnia*, 248–49, but I have seen it only in the version given by Pedro M. Cátedra, *Amor y pedagogía en la edad media. Estudios de doctrina amorosa y práctica literaria* (Salamanca: Universidad de Salamanca, 1989), 189–90.

53. Ludovicus Pontanus died of the plague at the council of Basel. Many of his *concilia* and *singularia* survive in fifteenth- and sixteenth-century editions, but I have not been able to locate the reference.

54. University of Salamanca Ms. 70, fol. 107r(a): "Ca los judios en los ritos de la su obser-vaçio que agora biven son de peor condiçion e mas damnables e al señor mas aborrecidos e a nos mas infestos e enpeçibles en mucho grado que non sean los moros que entre nos biven."

55. University of Salamanca Ms. 70, fol. 107r(a-b). The key reference is to Saint Augustine, Sermons on Saint John the Baptist: "By denying Christ they denied Moses and the Prophets. Destroying him they destroyed them and lost the law." 107v(a): "Avemos de dezir que estos malditos de dios e obstinados non son judios ni pueblo de dios mas sinoga de sathanas." (Cf. *Apocalypse* 2.9: "ab his, qui se dicunt Iudaeos esse, et non sunt, sed sunt synagoga Satanae.")

56. The frequency of the Christian accusation that the Jews influenced Muhammad has often been noted, e.g. by Thomas Burman, *Religious Polemic and the Intellectual History of the Mozarabs* (Leiden: Brill, 1994), 42, 271–73.

57. 108vb-109ra. "Vaniloqui e seductores": the reference is to *Titus* 1.10: "For there are many insubordinate men, empty talkers and decievers, especially of the circumcision party." The verse became an important anticonverso proof-text.

58. Alonso de Cartagena, *Defensorium unitatis christianae*, ed. P. Manuel Alonso (Madrid: Escuela de Estudios Hebraicos, 1943) was one of a number of treatises arguing that this type of anticonverso discourse was itself heretical.

59. The *Cantigas* emphasize Muslim respect for the Virgin. Cf. Alfonso X, el Sabio, *Cantigas de Santa María, de Don Alfonso el Sabio* (Madrid: Real Academia Española, 1889), henceforth *Cantigas*, 165, 169, 181, 329, 344. For the Virgin's explicit preference of Muslims to Jews, see *Cantiga* 348 "dos iudeus, seus enemigos, a que quer peor ca mouros." (She sometimes prefers Muslims to Catalans as well, as in *Cantiga* 379.) See Mercedes García-Arenal, "Los moros en las Cantigas de Alfonso X el Sabio," *Al-Qantara* 6 (1985): 133–51; and the articles of Albert Bagby, "The Moslem in the *Cantigas* of Alfonso X el Sabio," *Kentucky Romance Quarterly* 20 (1973): 173–207, "The Jew in the *Cantigas* of Alfonso X el Sabio," *Speculum* 46 (1971): 670–88, and "Alfonso X el Sabio compara moros y judíos," *Romanische Forschungen* 82 (1970): 578–83.

60. See, for example, Qur'an, Surah 21 ("The Prophets") 91: "And she who was chaste, therefor We breathed into her (something) of Our spirit and made her and her son a token for (all) peoples" [Pickthall translation]; Surah 19 ("Mary"), 27–34; Surah 4 ("Women"), 155. Christian polemicists could, of course, exaggerate such affinities, as when the clerics of Talavera stated that Muslims believed that Mary remained a virgin after giving birth, a point not generally accepted among Mudejars. On Iberian Muslim beliefs concerning Mary's virginity, cf. Mikel de Epalza, *Jésus otage: Juifs, chrétiens et musulmans en Espagne (VIe-XVIIe s.)* (Paris: Éditions du Cerf, 1987), 179, 182. Epalza provides an excellent survey of Muslim attitudes toward Jesus and Mary, though he does not ask how such material might be used by Muslims against Jews in a Christian context.

61. Surah 4 ("Women"), 156: "And because of their disbelief and of their speaking against Mary a tremendous calumny."

62. The case is preserved in the Archivo General de Simancas [AGS], Registro General del Sello, 1489/11/12, fol. 146. The document is published in Enrique Cantera Montenegro, "Conflictos entre el concejo y la aljama de los judíos de Soria en el último tercio del siglo XV," *Anuario de estudios medievales* 13 (1983): 597–98. The case is also discussed in Carlos Carrete Parrondo, "Judería soriana y morería burgalesa: Una historia de amor," *Estudios Mirandenses* 8 (1988): 57–61. Marien is the convert's Muslim name. Her Jewish name is not recorded.

63. AGS, Registro del Sello, 1490-V, fol. 400, 1490/5/15. The document, along with two others related to the case, is published by Luis Suárez Fernández, *Documentos acerca de la expulsion de los judíos* (Valladolid: Ediciones Aldecoa, 1964), 335–38, 340–41. The quote is from 341.

64. For a fourteenth-century example, see the *Ta'yīd al-milla*, Arabic Ms., Colección Gayangos 31, Real Academia de Historia de Madrid, also available in an edition by Leon Kassin, "A Study of a Fourteenth-Century Polemical Treatise *Adversus judaeos*" (PhD dissertation, Columbia University, New York, 1969). One of the boldest examples is much later, from the Granada of Phillip II, where Moriscos (descendants of Muslim forced converts to Christianity) forged Arabic texts purportedly written by Arab disciples of Saint James the Apostle and hidden in Granada, so that they might be revealed near the end of days as correctives to the corruption and sectionalism of Christianity. The forgeries sought to create a foundational role for Arabs in Christianity and to represent Muslims and Moriscos as the guardians of true Christian religion and uncorrupted gospel. (On the forgeries see especially Mercedes

García-Arenal and Fernando R. Mediano, *Un Oriente español: Los moriscos y el Sacromonte en tiempos de Contrarreforma* [Madrid: Marcial Pons, 2010.]) Aiming perhaps at the conversos (descendants of converts from Judaism), the texts explicitly denigrated Jews as deniers of Christ and invented a prophecy for Saint Peter that Jerusalem would be destroyed because of this denial. See Miguel Hagerty, *Los libros plúmbeos del Sacromonte* (Madrid: Editora Nacional, 1980), 123–24, 208.

Chapter 3

1. Ramón Martí, *Pugio fidei adversus mauros et judaeos* (1687; repr. Farnborough: Gregg Press, 1967) 2:24–27, and trans. by Jeremy Cohen in *Living Letters of the Law: Ideas of the Jew in Medieval Christianity* (Berkeley: University of California Press, 1999), 348–49. Guibert of Nogent's condemnation of John, count of Soissons, is in his *De Vita Sua* III.16. See the edition by Edmond-René Labande, *Autobiographie*, Les Classiques de l'Histoire de France au Moyen Age 34 (Paris, Belles Lettres, 1981), 422–29. For an English translation, see John F. Benton, *Self and Society in Medieval France: The Memoirs of Abbot Guibert of Nogent* (New York: Harper & Row, 1970), 209–11. The Jewess may have been a hypostasis of Guibert's more general claim here and elsewhere in his work that the count was a Judaizer and heretic. On Guibert and the count more generally, see Jay Rubinstein, *Guibert of Nogent: Portrait of a Medieval Mind* (New York: Routledge, 2002), 116–24; and Jan M. Ziolkowski, "Put in No-Man's Land: Guibert of Nogent's Accusations against a Judaizing and Jew-Supporting Christian," in *Jews and Christians in Twelfth-Century Europe*, ed. Michael A. Signer and John Van Engen (Notre Dame, IN: University of Notre Dame Press, 2001). On Pucellina see most recently Susan Einbinder, "Pucellina of Blois: Romantic Myths and Narrative Conventions," *Jewish History* 12 (1998): 29–46. The Estherka legend appears in Polish, Yiddish, and Hebrew sources, of which the earliest one known to me is David Ganz's sixteenth-century *Zemaḥ David*. On Estherka see Haya Bar-Itzhak, *Jewish Poland: Legends of Origin* (Detroit: Wayne State University Press, 2001), 113–32; Chone Shmeruk, *The Esterke Story in Yiddish and Polish Literature: A Case Study in the Mutual Relations of Two Cultural Traditions* (Jerusalem: Zalman Shazar Center for the Furtherance of the Study of Jewish History, 1985). (My thanks to Magda Teter for this last reference.)

2. "Otrosi para mientes, mio fijo, e toma ende mio castigo de lo que contesçio al rey don Alfonso de Castilla, el que vençio la batalla de Hubeda, por siete annos que visco mala vida con vna judia de Toledo diole Dios grand llaga e grand majamiento en la batalla de Alarcos [1195], en que fue vençido e fuxo, e fue mal andante el e todos los de su regno. . . . E demas matol los fijos varones e houo el regno el rey don Fernando, su nieto, fijo de su fija. E se repintio de tan mal pecado commo este que auia fecho, por el qual pecado, por emienda, fizo despues el monasterio de las Huelgas de Burgos de monjas de Cistel e el Espital, e Dios diole despues buena andança contra los moros en la batalla. E commo quier que y buena andança houo, muy mejor la ouiera si la desauentura de la batalla de Alarcos non le ouiera contesçido primero, en la qual desauentura el cayo por su pecado." Agapito Rey, ed., *Castigos e documentos para bien vivir* (Bloomington: Indiana University Press, 1952), 133. I have not used the new edition of Hugo Oscar Bizzarri, *Castigos del rey don Sancho IV* (Madrid: Iberiamericana, 2001) or compared the telling of the story across manuscript families. María Jesús Lacarra notes, however, no variation. See her "Los Exempla en los Castigos de Sancho IV: Divergencias en la transmisión manuscrita," in *La literatura en la época de Sancho IV*, ed. Carlos Alvar and José Manuel Lucía Megías (Alcalá: Universidad de Alcalá, 1996), 201–12. The work was completed in 1292–93. On the debate over dating, see the summary in Fernando Gutiérrez

Baños, *Las empresas artísticas de Sancho IV el Bravo* (Burgos: Junta de Castilla y León, 1997), 205–6.

3. For surveys of the many early modern and modern works that expand upon the story, see the pioneering essay by Elie Lambert, "Alphonse de Castille et la juive de Tolède," *Bulletin Hispanique* 25 (1923): 371–97; and, more recently, James Castañeda, *A Critical Edition of Lope de Vega's "Las paces de los reyes y judía de Toledo"* (Chapel Hill: University of North Carolina Press, 1962), 37–124.

4. Search for historical traces of this Jewess has been thorough but inconclusive. Because the *Crónica Docampo* named the Jewess "Fermosa" (almost certainly a misreading of the adjective "fermosa" in the *Crónica de 1344* and in many manuscripts of the *Crónica de Castilla*), attention has focused on locating the name in Toledan records from the 1180s. In his argument against the truth of the story (see below), P. Fita noted that the name was not to be found in among the seventy-six Hebrew epitaphs from Toledo published by Luzzato. Later generations of scholars have found a Fermosa, the wife of Tomé Saturnino, in Arabic documents. She is, however, almost certainly a Christian. See Angel González Palencia, *Los mozárabes de Toledo en los siglos XII y XIII* (Madrid: Instituto de Valencia de Don Juan, 1926–30), 2:116–17, 127, 165–66, 175–76; J. Gómez Salazar, "Alphonse VIII de Castille et doña Fermosa," *Evidences* 22 (1951): 42; Julio González, *El reino de Castilla en la época de Alfonso VIII* (Madrid: Consejo Superior de Investigaciones Científicas, 1960), 1:37; Pilar León Tello, *Judíos de Toledo* (Madrid: Consejo Superior de Investigaciones Científicas, 1979), 1:40–42; Gerold Hilty, "Die Jüdin von Toledo: Entstehung und Frühgeschichte des Motivs in der spanischen Literatur," in *Verlust und Ursprung, Festschrift für Werner Weber*, ed. Angelika Maass and Bernhard Heinser (Zürich: Ammann, 1989), 261–63, and, most recently, "¿Tiene raíces históricas el motivo de la judía de Toledo?" in *Actas del IX Congreso de la Asociación Hispánica de Literatura Medieval* (Noia: Toxosuoutos, 2005), 505–16 (my thanks to Rafael Mérida for this last).

5. *Crónica de Castilla*, chap. 491, "conta o arçebispo dõ Rrodrigo." See the edition by Ramón Lorenzo, *La traducción gallega de la Crónica General y de la Crónica de Castilla* (Orense: Instituto de Estudios Oresanos Padre Feijóo, 1975), and on the dating, 1:xlii–xlvi. Florian Docampo's *Tercera Crónica General* or *Crónica Ocampiana* (1541) relies heavily on the *Crónica de Castilla* for its account of the story but deletes the reference to Rodrigo, presumably out of familiarity with the archbishop's work. On this point, and more generally on the redaction history of the tale, see above all Hilty, "Die Jüdin."

6. On the chronology and methodology of the Alfonsine historical project, see Diego Catalán, *De Alfonso X al Conde de Barcelos: Cuatro estudios sobre el nacimiento de la historiografía romance en Castilla y Portugal* (Madrid: Gredos, 1962), 70–76, 88–93 specifically, on the dating of the section on Alfonso VIII in the *Primera Crónica*, and "El taller historiográfico alfonsí: Métodos y problemas en el trabajo compilatorio," *Romania* 84 (1963): 354–75. The story of Zaida is told in the *Primera Crónica General*, chap. 883. See the edition by Ramón Menéndez Pidal (Madrid: Gredos, 1955), 552–54. On Zaida, see Bernard F. Reilly, *The Kingdom of León-Castilla under King Alfonso VI, 1065–1109* (Princeton, NJ: Princeton University Press, 1988), 234–35, 248, 328, 339–40.

7. My translation is from the Castilian version preserved in BNM Ms. 10815, fol. 145r, transcribed in Castañeda, *A Critical Edition of Lope de Vega's "Las paces . . . ,"* p. 18, which is almost identical to the Gallician-Portuguese *Crónica de 1344*. The latter, however, does not call the Jewess "muy fermosa" or attribute her power to "fechiços y esperamiento quele ella sabia façer." Like the *Crónica de Castilla*, the *Crónica de 1344* attributes the report to Rodrigo Jiménez de Rada and describes the affair as lasting seven months, not seven years. On the

dating of the various manuscripts (Portuguese and Castilian) of this last chronicle, see Diego Catalán and María Soledad de Andrés, *Crónica General de España de 1344* (Madrid: Gredos, 1971), xvff.; and Catalán, *De Alfonso X al Conde de Barcelos*, 299–302.

8. The first summary of these debates, still invaluable, is that of Georges Cirot, "Alphonse le noble et la juive de Tolède," *Bulletin hispanique* 24 (1922): 289–306.

9. "lo que hay de más inverosímil y de más afrentoso en el cuento, no es que el Rey se prendase de una judía muy hermosa, sino que los ricos hombres de Castilla se conjurasen para asesinar a una infeliz mujer." The quote is from Marcelino Menéndez y Pelayo, *Estudios sobre el teatro de Lope de Vega IV*, in *Obras Completas*, ed. Enrique Sánchez Reyes, vol. 32 (Santander: Consejo Superior de Investigaciones Científicas, 1949), 89. Cf. Cirot, "Alphonse et la juive," 293–94. Cirot (p. 305) argued for the reality of the affair, as does (most recently) Hilty, "Die Jüdin," 251, who believes that the author of the *Castigos* drew upon historical material assembled by the Alfonsine workshop but doubts the murder.

10. Edna Aizenberg, "Una judía muy fermosa: The Jewess as Sex Object in Medieval Spanish Literature and Lore," *La Corónica* 12 (1984): 188. For a more recent reading of a (different) sexual discourse, that of sodomy, as "deeply conservative," see Barbara Weissberger, "'¡A tierra, puto!' Alfonso de Palencia's Discourse of Effeminacy," in *Queer Iberia: Sexualities, Cultures, and Crossings from the Middle Ages to the Renaissance*, ed. Josiah Blackmore and Gregory S. Hutcheson (Durham, NC: Duke University Press, 1999), 294.

11. *Proverbs* 1:20–21, 5:1–23, 6:24–35, 7:1–27, 8:1–9:18, 23:27–28, 31:1–3 (addressed to King Lemuel of Massa by his mother: "Do not give your strength to women, your vigor to those who destroy kings"). On *Proverbs* as court and wisdom literature, see the various essays in Patrick W. Skehan, *Studies in Israelite Poetry and Wisdom* (Washington, DC: Catholic Biblical Association of America, 1971), as well as W. Lee Humphreys, "The Motif of the Wise Courtier in the Book of Proverbs," in *Israelite Wisdom: Theological and Literary Essays in Honor of Samuel Terrien*, ed. John G. Gammie (Missoula, MT: Scholars Press, 1978), 177–90. *Proverbs* forms part of an ancient genre of wisdom addressed from fathers to sons. The "Instructions of Onkhsheshonq," purporting to be written in prison by the pharaoh's chief physician and counselor after his fall from favor, provide an Egyptian example. The relevance of this text for the study of biblical court legends such as those of the Book of Daniel has been noted by John J. Collins, *The Apocalyptic Vision of the Book of Daniel* (Missoula: Scholars Press, 1977), 33, and by Jürgen-Christian Lebram, *Das Buch Daniel* (Zurich: Theologischer Verlag, 1984), 10. Its relevance for the Book of Esther (on which more below) was noted by Lawrence M. Wills, *The Jew in the Court of the Foreign King: Ancient Jewish Court Legends* (Minneapolis: Fortress Press, 1990), 43. On the dating of "Onkhsheshonq" see Miriam Lichtheim, *Ancient Egyptian Literature* (Berkeley: University of California Press, 1973–80), 3:159. Indeed so well worn was the genre of proverbs as paternal pedagogy that it was satirized already in Ancient Egypt, as when the son in the "Instructions of Any" responds to his father's wisdom with the words "It is worthless" (Lichtheim, *Egyptian Literature*, 2:135).

12. Excerpted from Proverbs 7:1–27.

13. The list differs from that given by Alfonso X, who counseled kings only against intercourse with relatives and vile, religious, or married women but made no mention of non-Christians. See his *Siete Partidas* 2.5.3 (following the edition in *Siete Partidas del Rey Don Alfonso el Sabio* [Madrid: Real Academia de la Historia, 1807]). These injunctions for sexual restraint, royal or otherwise, were commonplace. For one among numerous contemporaneous examples see that of Sancho IV's own tutor, Juan Gil de Zamora, *De preconiis Hispaniae*, ed. Manuel de Castro y Castro (Madrid: Universidad de Madrid, 1955), 188–90 (which includes sodomy). Sancho's emphasis on the Jewess is, however, unusual.

14. *Castigos*, 117–23. The proverb: "En juego nin en veras, con tu sennor non partas peras." Cf. *Siete Partidas* 1.5.49.

15. *Castigos*, 127: "Otrosi non deues en afazimiento llegar el tu rostro a la cara de la judia, que es de aquella generaçion de los que escupieron a Jesu Cristo, tu sennor, en la faz."

16. For the importance of the theme in general, see Moshe Halbertal and Avishai Margalit, *Idolatry* (Cambridge, MA: Harvard University Press, 1992), chap. 1. On its importance in medieval Iberia, see chaps. 2 and 5 of this book.

17. *Castigos*, 31–32: "E en pena de aquesto ha querido Nuestro Sennor Dios que si el omne da sennoria a la muger sobre sy mesmo, que ela le sera todos tienpos contraria."

18. On the role of Rodrigo's sexual sin in late medieval ideologies of Castilian kingship, see most recently Barbara Weissberger, *Isabel Rules: Constructing Queenship; Wielding Power* (Minneapolis: University of Minnesota Press, 2004), 103–12. See also Alan Deyermond, "The Death and Rebirth of Visigothic Spain in the Estoria de España," *Revista canadiense de estudios hispánicos* 9, no. 3 (1985): 345–67; and John R. Burt, "The Motif of the Fall of Man in the 'Romancero del Rey Rodrigo,'" *Hispania* 61 (1978): 435–42. The idea that the Islamic conquest of the Visigothic monarchy was the product of a sexual turning away from God is, however, a much older one. In the year 746–47 Boniface explained to King Ethelbald of Mercia that the "peoples of Spain, Provence, and Burgundy" turned "away from God and lived in harlotry until the almighty judge let the penalties for such crimes fall upon them through . . . the coming of the Saracens." Ephraim Emerton, ed. and trans., *The Letters of St. Boniface* (New York: W. W. Norton, 1976), 128.

19. On the much-studied María de Molina, see especially Mercedes Gaibrois de Ballesteros, *María de Molina* (Madrid: Espasa-Calpe, 1936), and most recently, María Jesús Fuente, *Reinas medievales en los reinos hispánicos* (Madrid: La Esfera de los Libros, 2003), 243–68. On the forged bulls, Elsbeth Jaffé and Heinrich Finke, "La dispensa de matrimonio falsificada para le rey Sancho IV y María de Molina," *Anuario de Historia del Derecho Español* 4 (1927): 298–318.

20. In addition to the text in the *Primera Crónica* cited above, see also Rosa Castillo, ed., *Leyendas épicas Españolas* (Madrid: Editorial Castalia, 1956), 151–55. Muslim writers also understood relationships between Christian lords and Muslim women in Iberia in terms of domination: see chap. 1. Sancho himself translated the tombs of Alfonso VI and his wives Isabel and Zaida: see the *Crónica de Sancho IV*, in *Crónicas de los reyes de Castilla*, ed. Cayetano Rosell, Biblioteca de Autores Castellanos 66 (Madrid: M. Rivadeneyra, 1875), 73–74.

21. Jordi Bruguera, ed., *Llibre dels fets del rei en Jaume* (Barcelona: Barcino, 1991) 2:13. See more broadly Sara Lipton, "'Tanquam effeminatum': Pedro II of Aragon and the Gendering of Heresy in the Albigensian Crusade," in Blackmore and Hutcheson, *Queer Iberia*, 107–29.

22. As Alfonso X put it sometime in the 1250s: "Si por ventura acaeciere que el rey tuviese otra mujer que no fuese de bendición . . . decimos que debe ser guardada por honra del rey." Gonzalo Martínez Díez, ed., *Leyes de Alfonso X*, vol. 1, *Espéculo* (Avila: Fundación Sánchez-Albornoz, 1985), Libro II, título III, 1. Arturo R. Firpo, "Los Reyes Sexuales," parts I (*Mélanges de la Casa de Velázquez* 20 [1984], pp. 217–227) and II (21 [1985], pp. 145–58), is one of many commentators who treat the extramarital sexual activities of kings as "la representación misma de los valores de la virilidad." He suggests that sexual corruption became a revolutionary charge against kings as a consequence of increasingly powerful aristocratic attempts to decrease the prestige of monarchy (I, p. 220), but that this did not occur until Enrique IV (II, p. 147, though at I, p. 226, he treats Pedro I as an earlier example).

23. BNM, Ms. 10,815, fol. 145 v. Cf. Ms. Escorial V.II.10 and 11, Diego Rodríguez de Almela, *Compendio de las crónicas de España*, cap. cccclxii (fols. 81v–82v): "De como el rey

don alfonso de castilla caso con la reyna doña leonor fija del rey don enrrique de ynglaterra e
de como estouo ençerrado en toledo con una judía e loque sobre aquello de la judía acaesçio."
At fol. 82r: "a ti e al tu reyno por que telo consintio."

24. On the politics surrounding Alfonso's (and later Sancho's) use of Jewish administrators, and on the controversy over Isaac/Çag, the best narrative is still Baer, *A History of the
Jews in Christian Spain*, 1:120–37. See also José Manuel Nieto Soria, "Los judíos de Toledo
en sus relaciones financieras con la monarquía y la Iglesia (1252–1312)," *Sefarad* 41 (1981):
301–19; 42 (1982): 79–102. On the episcopal complaints and on Sancho's role in investigat-
ing and amplifying them, see Peter Linehan, "The Spanish Church Revisited: The Episcopal *gravamina* of 1279," in *Authority and Power: Studies on Medieval Law and Government
Presented to Walter Ullmann on his Seventieth Birthday*, ed. Brian Tierney and Peter Linehan
(Cambridge: Cambridge University Press, 1980), 127–47. The quote is from p. 137. One
of the bishops' complaints, transcribed on p. 146, is that "los judios son puestos sobre los
cristianos en los offiçios . . . , dela qual cosa vienen muchos males entre los quales es mayor
mal quelos cristianos son subiectos a ellos e son corrumpidos por sus costumbres e por sus
malos husos." For examples of Sancho's anti-Jewish measures during the rebellion in 1282
see p. 136, n. 37.

25. The most detailed study of Sancho's reign remains that of Mercedes Gaibrois de
Ballesteros, *Historia del Reinado de Sancho IV de Castilla*, 3 vols. (Madrid: Revista de Archivos,
Bibliotecas y Museos, 1922–28). On the Haro lineage, see Luis de Salazar y Castro, *Historia
genealógica de la Casa de Haro* (Madrid: Real Academia de la Historia, 1966).

26. For a summary of these events, see José Manuel Nieto Soria, *Sancho IV, 1284–1295*
(Palencia: Diputación Provincial de Palencia, 1994), 83–98. The Cortes of 1288 are
published in Manuel Danvila y Collado, ed., *Cortes de los antiguos reinos de León y de Castilla*
(Madrid: Real Academia de la Historia, 1861–1903), 1:99–106. The count's murder is described in the *Crónica de Sancho IV*, chap. 5, 78–81. For the fifteenth-century bishop Gonzalo
de Hinojosa, author of the *Continuación de la Crónica de España*, the affair of Don Lope was so
noteworthy that it fills the entire section devoted to Sancho's reign. *Colección de Documentos
inéditos para la historia de España* (Madrid: Real Academia de la Historia, 1893), 106:37–46.

27. See especially Miguel Angel Ladero Quesada, *Fiscalidad y poder real en Castilla (1252–
1369)* (Madrid: Editorial Complutense, 1993), and Francisco J. Hernández, *Las rentas del rey.
Sociedad y fisco en el reino castellano en el siglo XIII* (Madrid: Fundación Ramón Areces, 1993).
Some scholars have argued for the expanding role of Jews through the financial administra-
tions of Alfonso XI and Pedro I. See, for example, Maurice Kriegel, *Les Juifs à la fin du Moyen
Age dans l'europe mediterranéene* (Paris: Hachette, 1979), who presents these monarchs' use
of Jews in administrative posts as an effort to build "'l'état de finance' moderne" (pp. 59–69).
It is commonplace to speak of Pedro I's "política filojudía," as does Julio Valdeón Baruque,
Los judíos de Castilla y la revolución Trastámara (Valladolid: Universidad de Valladolid, 1968),
25–38.

28. *Castigos*, 35. For my attempts to make this point convincing, see, besides the present
book: "Christian Sovereignty and Jewish Flesh," in *Rethinking the Medieval Senses*, ed. Steven G. Nichols, Andreas Kablitz, and Alison Calhoun (Baltimore: Johns Hopkins University
Press, 2008), 154–85; "Warum der König die Juden beschützen musste, und warum er sie
verfolgen musste," in *Die Macht des Königs: Herrschaft in Europa vom Frühmittelalter bis in die
Neuzeit*, ed. Bernhard Jussen (Munich: C. H. Beck, 2005), 226–41.

29. On complaints about Peter's favor toward Jews, see Clara Estow, *Pedro the Cruel of
Castile: 1350–69* (Leiden: Brill, 1995), 154–79; and on his Jewish mother, Maurice Kriegel,
"Histoire sociale et ragots: Sur l' 'ascendance juive' de Ferdinand le Catholique," in *Movimien-*

tos migratorios y expulsiones en la diáspora occidental, ed. Fermín Miranda García (Pamplona: Universidad Pública de Navarra, 2000), 95–100. The cases of Juan II and Enrique IV are discussed further below, but for the latter see generally Luis Suárez Fernández, *Enrique IV de Castilla: La difamación como arma política* (Barcelona: Editorial Ariel, 2001). On Isabel as "protector of the Jews and daughter of a Jewess," see the account of the Polish traveler Nicolas Popplau, in Javier Liske, *Viajes de extranjeros por España y Portugal en los siglos XV, XVI, y XVII:Colección* (Madrid: Casa Editorial de Medina, 1878).

30. Both advised repudiating María in favor of a legitimate marriage. The *Crónica de Sancho IV*, 75, understood well the fragility of her situation throughout these negotiations: "commo era mujer de grande entendimiento, é que veia commo el rey andava en poder del Conde é de aquellos sus privados . . . é que era amenguamiento del Rey é daño della é de sus hijos, non ovo á quien tornar, salvo á Dios." On Abbot Gómez see Pilar Lorenzo Gradín "Gómez García, Abade de Valadolide," in Carlos Alvar Ezquerra et al., *La literatura en la época de Sancho IV*, 213–26.

31. Surprisingly little has been written on royal concubinage in Castile. See, for example, Arturo Firpo, "Las concubinas reales en la Baja Edad Media castellana," in *La condición de la mujer en la Edad Media*, ed. Yves-René Fonquerne (Madrid: Editorial de la Universidad Complutense, 1986), 334–41. On queenship, see Jesús Fuente, *Reinas medievales*. For the later period Weissberger's *Isabel Rules* is very useful.

32. Estow, *Pedro the Cruel*, chap. 6, here p. 149. One of the chief complaints of the magnates was that Pedro preferred his concubine's family to candidates from the nobility. The practice of favoring blood relations for office was an ancient practice, recommended as well by the *Siete Partidas* 2.8.1.

33. Antonio Pérez de Gómez, ed., *Romancero del rey Don Pedro, 1368–1800* (Valencia: La fonte que mana y corre, 1954), Romance IX, 134. Recall that some versions of the Jewess's story also attributed her power over Alfonso VIII to "fechiços y esperamientos quele ella sabia façer." On the Romancero tradition about Pedro see Louise Mirrer-Singer, *The Language of Evaluation: A Sociolinguistic Approach to the Story of Pedro el Cruel in Ballad and Chronicle* (Philadelphia: John Benjamins Publishing, 1986); Anne J. Cruz, "The Female Figure as Political Propaganda in the 'Pedro el Cruel' Romancero," in *Spanish Women in the Golden Age, Images and Realities*, ed. Magdalena S. Sánchez and Alain Saint-Saëns (Westport, CT: Greenwood Press, 1996), 69–89.

34. Cf. *Siete Partidas* 2.8.1. Similarly Don Juan Manuel advises in the early fourteenth century that lords fill the important office of chancellor with a "privado," selected from "sus criados." *Libro de los Estados*, chap. 95. For a more extensive discussion and bibliography, see David Nirenberg, "Christian Love, Jewish 'Privacy,' and Medieval Kingship," in *Center and Periphery: Studies on Power in the Medieval World in Honor of William Chester Jordan*, ed. Katherine L. Jansen, G. Geltner, and Anne E. Lester (Leiden: E. J. Brill, 2013), 25–37.

35. Gonzalo de Berceo, *Milagros de Nuestra Señora*, ed. Antonio García Solalinde (Madrid: Espasa-Calpe, 1978), Milagro 25, 791b.

36. In the context of clerical private life, however, the word *privanza* was easily sexualized. Alfonso X, for example, used it to designate the danger zone confronting clerics whose domestic needs were tended to by female relatives. *Siete Partidas* 1.6.38: "pero con todo esto guardarse deben ellos que non hayan con ellas grant privanza nin grant afazimiento, ca por engaño ó por descibimiento del diablo algunos clérigos cayeron."

37. The Jewess's resemblance to the biblical Esther, and also to the Estherka of Poland's King Casimir (see n. 1, above), was noted early by Lambert, "Alphonse de Castille," 371–72, citing Longinus's *Historia Polonica*.

38. See, for example, the coronation formulas in Reinhard Elze, ed., *Ordines coronationis imperialis: Die Ordines für die Weihe und Krönung des Kaisers und der Kaiserin*, MGH Fontes iuris Germanici antiqui in usum scholarum vol. 9 (Hannover: Hahnsche Buchhandlung, 1960). The first (p. 8) is ca. 900 CE: "ineffabilem misericordiam tuam supplices exoramus, ut sicut Esther reginam Israelis causa salutis de captivitatis suae compede solutam ad regis Assueri thalamum regnique sui consortium transire fecisti, ita hanc famulam tuam N." My thanks to Claudius Sieber-Lehmann for the reference.

39. For an excellent beginning focused on Jewish exegesis, see Barry D .Walfish, *Esther in Medieval Garb: Jewish Interpretations of the Book of Esther in the Middle Ages* (Albany: State University of New York Press, 1993).

40. Medieval Jewish commentaries on Esther seem aware of the potential for negative Christian readings of the book. Some defend Ahasueros as a good king, while others put Christian anti-Jewish arguments in the mouth of Haman (as when Abraham Shalom has Haman warn Ahasueros that if the king tolerates the Jews in his lands he will be suspected of heresy by some of his subjects [la-ḥashov 'al ha-melekh toah]. Rabbi Shemeriah b. Elijah of Crete even stressed that Esther had kept her Judaism a secret from the king, because "if it became known that she was Jewish, everyone would think that she was behind the king's actions and that the king acted unjustly out of love for his wife. It would make matters very difficult for the king's officers to say that the king chose as his queen a Jewish woman, a member of a people who hated all other peoples, and out of love for her ordered that his best officers . . . be hanged." These examples are from Walfish, *Esther in Medieval Garb*, 148–49, 164.

41. Later authors tended to bring the story's details into ever-greater conformity with the Esther narrative. In his *Raquel, tragedia española en tres jornadas* (1783), for example, Vicente García de la Huerta added a "Reuben" to parallel Esther's Mordechai and inserted the theme of an anti-Jewish decree that the concubine seeks to overturn and avenge. Joseph G. Fucilla's edition of *Raquel* (Madrid: Ediciones Catedra, 1974) is, it should be noted, preceded by a helpful survey of the history of Alfonso's Jewess in Castilian drama.

42. According to one chronicle tradition, for example, Don Diego López de Haro advised Alfonso VIII to impose the *pecha* tax on the hidalgos of his realm. The hidalgos rebelled under the leadership of the house of Lara, and Don Diego was exiled. See Georges Cirot, "Anecdotes ou légendes sur l'époque d'Alphonse VIII," *Bulletin Hispanique* 28 (1926): 246–59; and Juan Salvador Paredes Núñez, "Sancho IV y su tiempo en la literatura genealógica peninsular," in Alvar and Lucía Megías, *La literatura en la época de Sancho IV*, 235–43. It has already been noted by González, *El reino de Castilla en la época de Alfonso VIII*, 40ff., and Hilty, "Die Jüdin von Toledo," 251–55, that the story of the Jewess bears some traces of this conflict between lineages. The *Crónica de Castilla* explicitly names Don Diego as leader of the tepid faction at Alarcos, while the *Primera Crónica General* (chap. 1006; ed. Menéndez Pidal, p. 685) attributes to the advice of this same Don Diego the expiatory foundation of Las Huelgas. On the rise of the lineage in the reign of Alfonso VIII, see González, *El reino de Castilla en la época de Alfonso VIII*, 300–307.

43. Cf. Louis A. Montrose: "To speak of the social production of 'literature' or of any particular text is to signify not only that it is socially produced but also that it is socially productive—that it is the product of work and that it performs work in the process of being written, enacted, or read." "Professing the Renaissance: The Poetics and Politics of Culture," in *The New Historicism*, ed. H. Aram Vesser (New York: Routledge, 1989), 20.

44. Pedro López de Ayala, *"Libro de Poemas" o "Rimado de Palacio,"* ed. Michel García (Madrid: Gredos, 1978), especially strophes 234–97, 422–534. On the difficulty of choosing the right *privado* to love, see strophe 289.

45. The quote is from Lorenzo Galíndez de Caravajal, *Crónica de Don Juan II*, in *Cróni-cas de los Reyes de Castilla*, vol. 2, ed. Cayetano Rosell, Biblioteca de Autores Españoles 68 (Madrid: M. Rivadeneyra, 1877), year 1416, chap. x, p. 372. The poems addressed by Ferrant Manuel de Lando to both exiles are preserved in Brian Dutton and Joaquín González Cuenca, eds., *Cancionero de Baena* (Madrid: Visor Libros, 1993), nos. 277 and 278 (pp. 477–79). No. 277 (to Inés) is a meditation on Fortune and *privanza*. A humanistic funeral oration for Inés by Giannozzo Manetti has been edited by Jeremy Lawrance, *Un episodio del proto-humanismo Español: Tres opúsculos de Nuño de Guzmán y Giannozzo Manetti* (Salamanca: Biblioteca Espa-ñola del Siglo XV, 1989), 129–92. The exile is mentioned at p. 170.

46. On the extent to which Luna's administrative reforms laid the groundwork for the "state" of the Catholic monarchs, see Nicholas Round, *The Greatest Man Uncrowned: A Study of the Fall of Don Alvaro de Luna* (Dover, NH: Tamesis Books, 1986), 21. On Luna as favorer of Jews and conversos, see, inter alia, Benzion Netanyahu, *The Origins of the Inquisition in Fifteenth Century Spain* (New York: Random House, 1995), 236ff. For discussions about the erotics of Luna's relationship with Juan II, see Gregory S. Hutcheson, "Desperately Seeking Sodom: Queerness in the Chronicles of Alvaro de Luna," in Blackmore and Hutcheson, *Queer Iberia*, 222–49. Alfonso de Palencia's claim about Luna's pedagogy of Juan Pacheco is in his *Gesta Hispaniensia*, ed. Robert Brian Tate and Jeremy Lawrence (Madrid: Real Academia de la Historia, 1998), I.1, pp. 3–4. On sexual representations of Enrique IV, see Barbara Weiss-berger, "A tierra puto." Though more interested in Palencia's discourse of effeminacy than in Judaism, Weissberger remarks helpfully on the intersection of the two in the compound insult "faggot Jew" (*puto judío*), at p. 294. On Pacheco's survival of the many plots of his en-emies against him, see Fernando del Pulgar, *Claros Varones de Castilla*, ed. Robert Brian Tate (Oxford: Clarendon Press, 1971), 29–33: "And though they sometimes came near to having him executed, he was freed by unexpected and admirable twists of fortune from the chains of death that they had placed upon him."

47. For the Coplas, see Marcella Ciceri, "Las Coplas del Provincial," *Cultura Neolatina* 35 (1975): 39–210. See also Julio Rodríguez-Puértolas, ed., *Poesía de protesta en la Edad Media castellana*, Biblioteca Románica Hispánica 25 (Madrid: Gredos, 1968). Diego Rodríguez de Almela spoke of "la gran priuanca que en aquel tiempo tenian los judios con los Reyes & grandes señores asi ecclesiasticos commo seglares destos regnos despaña." *Valerio de las historias eclesiásticas y de España* (Murcia, 1487), fol. 20v.

48. Though clearly the sixteenth- and seventeenth-century dramatists who staged and restaged her story did so in order to make critical sense of contemporary politics. See, for example, D. Luis de Ulloa y Pereyra's adaptation of the theme in a poetic reproach addressed to the king in 1650, after the disgrace of the *privado* Count-Duke of Olivares: "Alfonso Octavo Rey de Castilla, Príncipe perfecto, detenido en Toledo por los amores de Hermosa o Raquel, Hebrea, muerta por el furor de los Vasallos," in his *Versos* (Madrid: Diego Diaz, 1659). Jacques Basnage, who first encountered the story of Alfonso VIII in Mariana's *Histoire gé-nérale d'Espagne*, underlined its political implications in his *Histoire des juifs* as neither Mari-ana nor any other Spanish historian previous had done; see Jacques Basnage, *Histoire des juifs, nouvelle edition augmentée* (The Hague: Henri Scheurleer, 1716), vol. 13, book 9, ch.xii.4–5, pp. 318–21. The importance of the theme needs to be understood in the wider context of the staging of kings and *privados* in early modern politics and drama, for which there is an extensive bibliography. For a beginning, John H. Elliott and Laurence W. B. Brockliss, eds., *The World of the Favorite* (New Haven, CT: Yale University Press, 1999). See also Antonio Feros, "Almas gemelas: Monarcas y favoritos en la primera mitad del siglo XVII," in *España, Europa y el mundo Atlántico: Homenage a John H. Elliott*, ed. Richard L. Kagan and Geoffrey

Parker (Madrid: Marcial Pons, 2001) 49–81, and "'Vicedioses, pero humanos,' el drama del Rey," *Cuadernos de Historia Moderna* 14 (1993): 103–31.

49. "In toto morali negotio modus procedendi, secundum Philosophum, est figuralis et grossus." Aegidius Romanus [Giles of Rome], *De regimine principum libri III*, I.i.1 (Rome, 1607; repr., Aalen, 1967), p. 2. Giles is referring here to Aristotle's *Nichomachean Ethics*, book 2, 11042. "Figuralis" is his translation of Aristotle's *tupô*: a difference that seems to me of vast significance for medieval political theology. On the *De regimine*, see (among many other titles) Charles F. Briggs, *Giles of Rome's De regimine principum: Reading and Writing Politics at Court and University, c. 1275–c. 1525* (Cambridge: Cambridge University Press, 1999).

50. This seems to me one of the many insights toward which Erich Auerbach was gesturing in his "Figura," *Neue Dantestudien*, Instabuler Schriften 5 (Istanbul: Ibrahim Horoz Basımevi, 1944), 11–71, though it is one he chose not to make explicit. English translation by Ralph Mannheim in Erich Auerbach, *Scenes from the Drama of European Literature* (New York: Meridian Books, 1959; repr., Minneapolis: University of Minnesota Press, 1984), 11–76.

51. *De civ. dei*, 15.4–5, 7. Cain's politics give priority to flesh, "that part which the philosophers call vicious, and which ought not to lead the mind, but which the mind ought to rule and restrain by reason." Augustine's proof-texts here come significantly from Galatians (5:17) and Romans (7:17, 6:13).

Chapter 4

1. See David Abulafia, "Nam iudei servi regis sunt, et semper fisco regio deputati: The Jews in the Municipal Fuero of Teruel (1176–7)," in *Jews, Muslims, and Christians in and around the Crown of Aragon: Essays in Honour of Professor Elena Lourie*, ed. Harvey J. Hames (Boston: Brill, 2004). For formulations like "tanquam suum proprium," "sicut res nostre proprie," and "sicut nostrum proprium catallum," all drawn from English law, see John A. Watt, "The Jews, the Law, and the Church: The Concept of Jewish Serfdom in Thirteenth-Century England," in *The Church and Sovereignty c.590–1918: Essays in Honour of Michael Wilks*, ed. Diana Wood (Oxford: Blackwell, 1991), 153–72. King Joan of Catalonia often used similar language, as in a letter of April 5, 1391, describing the Jews as "in nostro dominio populatos velut camere nostre servos ac proprium patrimonium" (ACA:C 2018:17r).

2. For a Capetian example, see William Chester Jordan, "Jews, Regalian Rights, and the Constitution in Medieval France," *Association of Jewish Studies Review* 23 (1998): 1–16.

3. ACA:C 1940:58v–59v (1391/4/13), to Joan de Montbui, governor of Sardinia: "Al .v. dupte del juheus, si seran per Cathalan o Aragoneses reputats, és nostra intenció que los juheus, qui són nostre patrimoni e no han nació certa, poden e deuen ésser jutgats a nostra voluntat, per què remetem a vos la conexença que jaquiscats habitar aquells en lo dit Castell, que conexerets ésser profitosos e necessaris al ben públich e conservació de nostre patrimoni e del dit Castell."

4. On lions, see most recently Anna M. Adroer i Tasis, "La possessio de lleons, simbol de poder," in *XV Congreso de Historia de la Corona de Aragon (Jaca, 20–25 Sept. 1993)* (Zaragoza: Gobierno de Aragón, 1996), vol. 1, pt. 3, 257–68; Asunción Blasco Martínez, "La casa de fieras de la Aljaferia de Zaragoza y los judíos," in *XV Congreso de Historia de la Corona de Aragón, I: El poder real en la Corona de Aragón, siglos XIV–XVI* (Zaragoza: Gobierno de Aragón 1996), 3:291–318; Joan de Deu Domenech i Gasul, *Lleons i besties exotiques a les ciutats catalanes, segles XIV–XVIII* (Barcelona: Rafael Dalmau, 1996). The bill for the lithic arms was published

by Francisco Danvila, "Clausura y delimitación de la judería de Valencia en 1390 á 91," *Boletín de la Real Academia de la Historia* 18 (1891): 154.

5. Augustine, *De civ. dei*, 15.4–5, 7, on Cain and earthly city. See his *Contra Faustum* for Cain as a figure for Jewish exile. For medieval developments, see Gilbert Dahan, "L'Exégèse de l'histoire de Caïn et Abel du XIIe au XIVe siècle en Occident," *Recherches de Théologie ancienne et médiévale* 49 (1982): 21–89; 50 (1983): 5–68.

6. In the twentieth century Erik Peterson drew out Augustine's critique in order to criticize Carl Schmitt's political theology as "Judaizing": *Der Monotheismus als politisches Problem* (Leipzig: Hegner, 1935).

7. AMV, LM, g³ 4, 108v (26 octobre 1378): "no és als sinó fer juheria de cascuna de ses universitats . . . a aytal demanda no darem loch, car més amam morir que ésser semblants a juheus," cited in Dolors Bramon, *Contra moros i jueus: Formació i estratègia d'unes discriminacions al País Valencià* (Valencia: Eliseu Climent, 1981), 67. Cf. the council of Tarrega's reaction to new demands ("novitats") of the nobleman Francesch d'Erill: "com per força forçada hi hajam arresistir, si donchs com a juheus no volem viure" ("we will have to resist this by dint of force, if we do not want to live like the Jews"), AHCB, Consell de Cent, Lletres comunes Originals, X:2, n. 38 (November 7, 1403).

8. For a fuller treatment of this large subject, see my "Warum der König die Juden beschützen musste, und warum er sie verfolgen musste," in *Die Macht des Königs: Herrschaft in Europa vom Frühmittelalter bis in die Neuzeit*, ed. Bernhard Jussen (Munich: C. H. Beck, 2005), 226–41. For Peter's letter, see Joaquim Miret y Sans, "El proces de les hosties contra. ls jueus d'Osca en 1377," *Anuari de l'Institut d'Estudis Catalans* 4 (1911–12): 59–80.

9. On Holy Week riots as rituals of political critique, see my *Communities of Violence: Persecution of Minorities in the Middle Ages* (Princeton: Princeton University Press, 1996), 221–23.

10. On the fifteenth of March, 1391. Easter fell on the twenty-sixth. In the Crown of Aragon the Jewish communities of Alcañiz and Teruel both sought special protections against Holy Week stoning that year; see ACA:C 1846:141r-v; ACA:C 1849:40v–41r; (March 6 and 10).

11. For Castile, see, inter alia, Emilio Mitre Fernández, *Los judíos de Castilla en tiempo de Enrique III: El pogrom de 1391* (Valladolid: Universidad de Valladolid, 1994). The judicial whipping in Seville is mentioned by the chronicler Pedro López de Ayala, who adds that the king's authority was everywhere ignored on account of his youth and the discord among the magnates: *Crónica de Enrique III de Castilla*, ed. Cayetano Rosell, Biblioteca de autores españoles 68 (Madrid: M. Rivadeneyra, 1877), 167 and 177. For the Crown of Aragon, Jaume Riera i Sans, "Los tumultos contra las juderías de la Corona de Aragón en 1391," *Cuadernos de Historia* 8 (1977): 213–25; Riera i Sans, "Estrangers participants als avalots contra les jueríes de la Corona d'Aragó el 1391," *Anuario de Estudios Medievales* 10 (1980): 577–83; Riera i Sans, "Els avalots de 1391 a Girona," in *Jornades d'història dels jueus a Catalunya* (Girona: Ajuntament de Girona, 1987), 95–159. On Jewish reaction to the massacres, see R. Ben Shalom, "Sanctification of the Name and Jewish Martyrology in Aragon and Castile in 1391: Between Spain and Ashkenaz" [in Hebrew] *Tarbiz* 70 (2001): 227–82.

12. The queen's letter of June 28: ACA:C 2039:79v–80r. King Joan's commission in ACA:C 1878:54 r (July 3). The prince reports sending town criers and erecting gallows in ACA:C 2093:112r–v (July 9) [=Hinojosa, no. 5] which also provides the first report of the assault on the Jews earlier that day. ACA:C 2093:121r–v (July 22) makes clear that the queen was not impressed by the prince's efforts. For the prince's response to the council's complaints about the "crida," see ACA:C 2093:108 r (July 6). The council's list of preventive measures, more detailed than the prince's, is in AMV, MC A-19, fol. 241r–245v (July 10) [=Hinojosa, no. 7]. Valencia's council does not seem to have deputized citizens to succor

royal officials, as Barcelona later did: AHCB, Consell de Cent, Llibre del Consell, 19-A, n. 25, fol. 33 bis (July 17).

13. I am drawing on ACA:C 2093:112r–v here. See also the prince's further account at ACA:C 2093:119r–120r. The town council's letters—such as AMV, LM 5, ff. 19r–20r (July 9) [=Hinojosa, no. 6]—are more detailed, but also more precociously aware of the need for self-justification. For the testimony of Joan Pérez de Sent Jordi, formerly Juseff Abarim, who witnessed his brother's knifing, the rape of his niece and her wet-nurse, and his own robbery and beating, see Francisco Danvila, "El robo de la judería de Valencia en 1391," *Boletín de la Real Academia de la Historia* 8 (1886): 390, doc. 25.

14. On the twelfth the prince writes to the queen that only two hundred Jews remain unconverted: ACA:C 2093:117 r.

15. "Senyor sobirà après Déu en Cathalunya": Arxiu Històric de la Ciutat de Girona, I.1.2.1, lligal 5, llibre 2, fol 39r (1342).

16. ACA:C 1878:66 v (1391/07/13): "ho tenim per orrible e per fort enorme, majorment que vos fossets present en tant que deu esser fet tal castich e tan cruel per nos, si ja donchs no es fet o comencat, que sia pena e castich a aquells qui aço han assajat e als altres sobira exempli, com nos e vos e tots altres princeps e officials semblants concitacions e avolots ultra lo dapnatge qui s'ens seguit deiam fortment corregir e castigar . . . vos . . . manam que les coses dessus dites vullats ab sobirana diligencia entendre e aquelles corregir e castigar, en tal manera que vostra punicio e castich sia divulgada e anomenada, no tan solament per nostres regnes e terres mes encara per los altres, passant hi ultra tota justicia, car certificam vos que si aço es punit e castigat e greument axi com se pertany, la temeritat e desenfrenament dels malignants paria tant crexer e punir que seria incorregible e gens maior dapnatge no poria passar." The king writes the same day to the city (ACA:C 1878:66v–67r) telling them to support the prince, but without the instruction he gave the prince on the need to maintain sovereignty. He writes as well (ACA:C 1878:67v) to a jurist in Valencia, urging him to insistently press the prince to devise an especially horrible punishment.

17. ACA:C 1961:41v–42v (July 16) [=Hinojosa, no. 14; Baer I, 409]. See also ACA:C 1961:43r (July 17) [=Hinojosa, no. 20].

18. On royal claims to judicial power, see, for example, Flocel Sabaté, "Discurs i estratègies del poder reial a Catalunya al segle XIV," *Anuario de Estudios Medievales* 9 (1995): 143–51; Francesc Eiximenis, *Dotze llibre del Crestià* (Girona: Collegi Universitari de Girona, 1986), 177: "Com pot príncep dar licència a negun de matar altre si, donchs, no y ha al mig procés jurídich, com lo príncep no sea senyor de la ley mas servidor, execudor, e minister." Eiximenis seems to have been shocked by the events of 1391 into moderating his millennialist republicanism; see Robert Lerner, *The Feast of Saint Abraham: Medieval Millenarians and the Jews* (Philadelphia: University of Pennsylvania Press, 2001), 107–9.

19. AMV, MC A-19, fol. 241r–245v, [=Hinojosa, no. 7].

20. Even if the spark came from sailors, the tinder was indigenous. As Prince Martí put it: "Trobarets senyor que tots los christians comunament estan fort comoguts contra los juheus." Hence (the prince concludes) he cannot apply "aquell castich que·s pertany": ACA:C 2093:96v–97r (July 18) (similar language in 2093:119r–120r: "Tota esta terra está fort comoguda contra aquells qui romanen"). For special worries about sailors, see ACA:C 2039:89r–v (August 8); Riera i Sans, "Estrangers."

21. The Valencians' first letter speaks (like the prince) of a "disposicio divinal" and uses the curious phrase "fortunal pertilencia" to describe the riots: AMV, LM, g3–5, fol. 19r–20r (July 9). Less than a week later (fol. 20v–22v, July 14) they speak of a "misteri divinal," evidenced "per los miracles e maravelles qui dejus veurets." The admission of adult leadership is at fols. 23r–24r.

22. AMV, LM, g3–5, fol. 20v–22v (July 14). The city council writes a similar letter to the king on the 17th (AMV, LM g3–5, fol. 23r–24r) professing its willingness to pursue punishment of the guilty despite the miracles but reminding the king that no Christian can be displeased by the conversion of the Jews: "a tots feels christians deu plaure, empero, senyor, la imquisicio e punicio dels principals malfeytors no romandra." Similarly it writes to the council of Barcelona on July 20 (AMV, LM g3–5, fol. 27r–28r) stating that it will inquire and punish, "com no deia cessar per tot lo be seguit dels dits babtismes e sguardada la intencio e qualitat del dit primer mal." Hasdai Crescas's "Letter to the community of Avignon" is included in Shelomo Ibn Verga, *Das Buch Schevet Jehuda*, ed. Meir Wiener (Hannover: Orient-Buchhandlung H. Lafaire, 1924), 128.

23. On July 16 the king complains that "some people" are trying to convert the few Jews that survived the massacre hidden in the houses of Christians (ACA:C 1961:41v–42v). Similar efforts after the massacre in Barcelona were decreed by the town council itself: AHCB, Consell de Cent, Llibre del Consell, 19-A, n. 25, fols. 37r, 47r (August 23 and August 27). In ACA:C 1878:91r–v (August 1) [=Hinojosa, no. 35] the king instructs his brother to force episcopal officials to revoke their prohibition on aiding Jews. If any refuse, "fets li dar a beure per que no haja set."

24. ACA:C 2093:119r–120r (July 20). The prince describes "very large" groups of armed men leaving Valencia to attack the Jews of Morvedre. By August 19 the council was informing the king (in defiance of his stated desire to rebuild the community) of its plans to transfer Valencia's surviving Jews to Morvedre and tear down the walls of the Jewish quarter See AMV, LM g3–5, fol. 44r [=Hinojosa, no. 42]. The reasons it gave were strategically self-serving but unimpeachable: the better security of the Jews and the spiritual purity of the New Christians.

25. King Joan acknowledges a complaint from the council of Morvedre about "alguns de la ciutat de València" who are trying to incite riots in Morvedre in ACA:C 1961:41 v (July 16) [=Baer, p. 657–58, doc. 410]. On the miracle of the reluctant Chrism, see Josef Teixidor, *Antigüedades de Valencia*, ed. Roque Chabás (Valencia: Francisco Vives Mora, 1895), 2:196. For the council's claim about the converts, AMV, LM g3–5, fol. 20v–22v.

26. AMV, LM g3–5, fol. 34v: "escusar la culpa del esvaiment o approvar aquell per alleviar la punicio dels culpables" (July 21?, 29?). Cf. 30r.

27. AMV, LM, 30v–31r (for the miracles), 34v; 37r–v.

28. ACA:C 1961:43r (July 17) [=Hinojosa, no. 20] to the Jews of Morvedre: "de aquells que trobara esser en lo dit avalot culpables faça correccio corporal, no esperant que proces algu sobre aço se'n faça." In a different letter written the same day, he blames the riot in Morvedre on the tepid punishment administered in Valencia: ACA:C 1961:41v–42v. [=Hinojosa, p. 334, no. 14; Baer, no. 409].

29. ACA:C 2093:120v–121r (July 21) "Que de feyt volia enantar en fer execució en les persones de molts de aquells; e los jurats d'esta ciutat e tots los de mon consell, per la gran comoció del poble qui ací era, e per les noves qui eren vengudes ajust e aplech del rey de Granada, de que ja·us he scrit, supplicaren me, e enquera consellaren, que per res no procehís ni enantàs en la dita execució, com fos cosa de que·s poria seguir en tal cas irreparable dampnatge. Per la qual rahó jo sobreseguí en lo dit feyt." Cf. AMV, LM g3–5, fol. 30r, where the council protests to the king that it is all for severe punishment but that the rumor of the attack from Granada makes action impossible.

30. The letter to Barcelona is in AHCB, Consell de Cent, Lletres closes, VI-2 (1383–1393), fol. 28r–29r. Cf. ACA:C 1961:50v–51v (July 26) [=Baer, no. 414].

31. See ACA:C 1961:63v–64r (August 9) for the king's decision to travel to Barcelona instead of Valencia. Cf. ACA:C 1961:64r, 64v–65r, and 65, which include some of his efforts to raise the military force necessary for "an exemplary punishment" in Barcelona.

32. It is true that despite his admission of suspension and his request for the king's presence, the prince continued to promise that he would carry out the punishments. See ACA:C 2093:72v–73r (July 30).

33. Hence, writes Augustine, "no emperor or monarch who finds under his government the people with this mark [of Cain] kills them, that is to say, makes them cease to be Jews, separate in their observance and unlike the rest of the world" (*Contra Faustum* XII.13).

34. Ambrose, Ep. 74 and Ep. 1a *extra collectionem*. I quote from the latter, in *Epistulae et acta*, ed. Otto Faller and Michaela Zelzer, CSEL 82.1–4 (Vienna: F. Tempsky, 1968–96), 3:162–77.

35. Robert Chazan, *Medieval Jewry in Northern France* (Baltimore: Johns Hopkins University Press, 1973), 186. Cf. David Abulafia, "Monarchies and Minorities in the Christian Western Mediterranean around 1300: Lucera and Its Analogues," in *Christendom and Its Discontents: Exclusion, Persecution, and Rebellion, 1000–1500*, ed. Scott L. Waugh and Peter D. Diehl (Cambridge: Cambridge University Press, 1996), 234–63.

36. Robert Stacey, "Parliamentary Negotiation and the Expulsion of the Jews from England," in *Thirteenth-Century England, VI: Proceedings of the Durham Conference*, ed. Michael Prestwich, Richard Britnell, and Robin Frame (Woodbridge: Boydell Press, 1997), 77–101.

37. It remains to be seen whether or not we are speaking of an "event" in the sense intended by Alain Badiou, *L'Être et l'événement* (Paris: Éditions du Seuil, 1988).

38. Like his brother, he was aware of the extent of popular unrest: "videamus populum irritatum in judeos ipsos" (ACA:C 1949:153v, a letter reserving all jurisdiction over the attacks for himself personally).

39. Cf. Giorgio Agamben, *Stato di Eccezione: Homo Sacer II, 1* (Turin: Bollati Boringhieri, 2003), 55–67.

40. ACA:C 2054:126v–127r: "a nos és cert que·l senyor rey no condescendria a la dita supplicació nostra, e hauríem gran vergonya de començar cosa que veem clarament que no vendria a perfecció." On queenly intercession in 1391 see also ACA:C 2054:115v–116r, 2054:128v–129r, 2054:129v, and 2041:75v–77v.

41. ACA:C 1880:191v (1392/11/09): "a intercessio e humil suplicacio de nostra molt cara companyera la reyna desijant que nos e ella, qui encara com a rey e a reyna no eren e no som entrats en la dita ciutat vers la qual tenim ajudant Deu nostre dret cami entrem en aquella pacifichs e benignes." The council designates the twenty to be condemned in AMV, MC A20, fol. 37v (1392/11/15) [=Hinojosa, no. 103]. For all of its representation as a spontaneous "grace," the settlement followed a year of intense political and financial negotiation that, in Valencia as in the other cities of the Crown, monetized most of the king's claims to justice, producing only a very few executions. These few, however, were as "exemplary" as possible. When a participant in the Mallorcan riots was executed in Barcelona, his head was mounted on the mast of a ship sailing to the island. See Frederic Schwarz and Frances Carreras, *Manual de novells ardits vulgarment apellat dietari del antich consell barcelonia* (Barcelona: Henrich y Companyia, 1893), 1:25. And in Lleida, the corpses of the condemned still hung on the gallows in midsummer of 1393 (ACA:C 1881:174r, July 21).

42. For the council's letter of July 28 (addressed to the councilors of Lleida), see Teixidor, *Antigüedades*, 2:171. For the king's order, see ACA:C 1961:41v–42v (July 16): "alguns volen fer esgleya de ls sinagoga de la dita aljama . . . no soffrats que la dita sinagoga sie deffeta, car nos volem e entenem reparar la dita aljama." On November 8, 1392, he endows and declares himself patron of Saint Christopher (ACA:C 1904:163v–165r, 1927:133v–134r [=Hinojosa, no. 96]). For his continued patronage, see ACA:C 1942:8v (October 5, 1393).

43. Both Joan and Martí I abandoned efforts to have the remaining Jews of Morvedre maintain the lions. For Martí's attempt, see ACA:C 2230:44v–45r (January 13, 1398), revoked in ACA:C 2116:16r–v (March 1). By 1424 the Jews were contributing money to the task [see Hinojosa, no. 330]. In Barcelona the lion keeper remained Jucef Tovi, now converted as Juan de Verdejo: ACA:C 1963:17v–18r (January 18, 1392), and (for his former name) ACA:C 2041:63v–65r (March 1, 1392). Only in the kingdom of Aragon, relatively unscathed by the riots, did the lions remain in the care of Jews: ACA:C 1911:70r (April 6, 1396).

44. Carl Schmitt, *Politische Theologie*, 2nd ed. (Berlin: Duncker & Humblot, 1934–2004), 13, 43.

45. Walter Benjamin, *Ursprung des deutschen Trauerspiels*, in *Gesammelte Schriften* (Frankfurt: Suhrkamp Verlag, 1974), 1:250; Schmitt, *Politische Theologie*, 13.

46. Giorgio Agamben, *Homo Sacer: Il potere sovrano e la nuda vita* (Turin: Einaudi, 1995), and *Stato di Eccezione*.

47. I say "a starting point" because there are many others. I think, for example, of Franz Rosenzweig's introduction to Part II of his *The Star of Redemption*; and Jacques Lacan's essay on "Logical Time and the Assertion of Anticipated Certainty: A New Sophism," tr. from the *Écrits* by B. Fink and M. Silver, *Newsletter of the Freudian Field* 2 (1988).

48. Eric L. Santner, "Miracles Happen: Benjamin, Rosenzweig, Freud, and the Matter of the Neighbor," in *The Neighbor: Three Inquiries in Political Theology*, ed. Slavoj Žižek, Eric L. Santner, and Kenneth Reinhard (Chicago: University of Chicago Press, 2005), 103.

49. Slavoj Žižek, *Welcome to the Desert of the Real* (London: Verso, 2002), 116, quoted in Santner, "Miracles Happen," 105.

50. Medievalists are familiar with specific instances of such arguments. Particularly well studied is the relationship between miraculous judgments and communal consensus in the trials by ordeal—fire, water, battle—that were prominent in the early medieval juridical order. See, inter alia, Peter Brown, "Society and the Supernatural, a Medieval Change," *Daedalus* 104 (1975): 133–51; Paul Hyams, "Trial by Ordeal: The Key to Proof in the Early Commonlaw," in *On the Laws and Customs of England: Essays in Honor of Samuel E. Thorne*, ed. Morris S. Arnold, Thomas A. Green, Sally A. Scully, and Stephen D. White (Chapel Hill: University of North Carolina Press, 1981), 90–126; Robert Bartlett, *Trial by Fire and Water: The Medieval Judicial Ordeal* (Oxford: Clarendon Press, 1986). For an important argument about medieval ritual more generally, see Philippe Buc, *The Dangers of Ritual* (Princeton, NJ: Princeton University Press, 2001).

51. Of course I recognize that this functional tension takes many different forms in different times and places (and even in the same time and place, as in Valencia in 1391), as well as in different "political theologies" (Saint Augustine's version of the tension is very different from that of Thomas Hobbes). My point is not that it is always the same, but only that it is never suspended.

52. We could, for example, agree instead with Hans Kelsen, who quipped contra Schmitt in 1925 that "there is no lawlessness, even the worst dictatorship is law." The quote is from Jacob Taubes, *The Political Theology of Paul* (Palo Alto, CA: Stanford University Press, 2004), 105, who attributes the quotation to Gerhard Anschütz and Hans Kelsen but cites only the 1925 edition of Kelsen's *General Theory of the State*, without giving bibliographical or page reference. I offer Kelsen as an alternative, not a solution: his monism is as problematic for my purposes as Schmitt's decisionism. We could draw as well on the "Grundnormen" of another Weimar legal theorist, Hermann Kantorowicz. See, for example, Stanley Paulson, ed., *Hans Kelsen und die Rechtssoziologie: Auseinandersetzung mit Hermann U. Kantorowicz, Eugen Ehrlich, und Max Weber* (Aalen: Scientia, 1992).

53. To my mind the framing of the choice in these terms is itself a particular historical instantiation of a Pauline theology, but that is yet another argument.

Chapter 5

1. See Homi Bhabha, "Difference, Discrimination and the Discourse of Colonialism," in *The Politics of Theory: Proceedings of the Essex Conference on the Sociology of Literature*, ed. Francis Barker et al. (Colchester: University of Essex, 1983), 194: "The body is always simultaneously inscribed in both the economy of pleasure and desire and the economy of discourse, domination and power. . . . It follows that the epithets racial or sexual come to be seen as modes of differentiation." Cf. Judith Butler, *Bodies That Matter: On the Discursive Limits of "Sex"* (New York: Routledge, 1993), 167–68; and Ronald Hyam, *Empire and Sexuality: The British Experience* (Manchester: Manchester University Press, 1990), 203, "sex is at the very heart of racism."

2. The quote is from Marcelino Menéndez y Pelayo, *Historia de los heterodoxos Españoles* (1882; repr., Mexico City: Editorial Porrúa, 1982), 1:410.

3. On which see chap. 8 of this volume.

4. For an early fifteenth-century example of such a metaphor from Iberia, see Saint Vincent Ferrer, *Sermons*, 1:140. For a later (1449), richer, and more systematic use of the metaphor, see Alonso de Cartagena, *Defensorium unitatis christianae*, for example at 150–51.

5. The organic imagery may also have attenuated the negative valence of sexuality by presenting it as a necessary function of the natural body. Thus prostitutes, when they are explicitly included in such imagery, are assigned a vital role as "drains" of excess male lust. See Jacques Rossiaud, *Medieval Prostitution* (Oxford: Basil Blackwell, 1988), 81, 103; Francesc Eiximenis, *Lo Crestià*, ed. Albert Hauf (Barcelona: Edicions 62, 1983), chap. 574, 155ff.

6. See Sara Lipton, "The Temple Is My Body: Gender, Carnality, and *Synagoga* in the Bible Moralisée," in *Imaging the Self, Imaging the Other: Representations of Jews in Medieval Visual Culture*, ed. Eva Frojmovic (Leiden: Brill, 2002), 129–63 and the bibliography contained therein.

7. Compare the delightful analysis of Halbertal and Margalit, *Idolatry*, chap. 1. The bibliography on the erotic imagery of the Song of Songs is enormous. See, for example, E. Ann Matter, "Il matrimonio mistico," in *Donne e fede: Santità e vita religiosa in Italia*, ed. Lucetta Scaraffia and Gabriella Zarri (Bari: Laterza, 1994), 43–60; Judith S. Neaman, "The Harlot Bride: From Biblical Code to Mystical Topos," *Vox benedictina* 4, no. 4 (1987): 277–306; Gerson D. Cohen, "The Song of Songs and the Jewish Religious Mentality," in *The Samuel Friedland Lectures, 1960–1966* (New York: Jewish Theological Seminary of America, 1966), 1–21. A number of Muslim thinkers, including Ibn Hazm, saw in the erotics of the Song of Songs proof that the Jews had corrupted the scriptures. See Camilla Adang, *Muslim Writers on Judaism and the Hebrew Bible: From Ibn Rabban to Ibn Hazm* (New York: E. J. Brill, 1996), 247, citing his *Kitāb al-fiṣal fī al-milal wal-ahwā' wal-niḥal* (The Book of Distinguishing between Religions, Heresies, and Sects).

8. Epistle to the Ephesians 5:25–33.

9. *Siete Partidas* 7.24.9. The translation is Dwayne E. Carpenter's, *Alfonso X and the Jews: An Edition and Commentary on Siete Partidas 7.24 "De los judíos"* (Berkeley: University of California Press, 1986), 35. For the punishment of Muslims, see *Siete Partidas* 7.25.10, briefly discussed in Dwayne E. Carpenter, "Minorities in Medieval Spain: The Legal Status of Jews and Muslims in the *Siete Partidas*," *Romance Quarterly* 33 (1986): 283.

10. Vincent, *Sermons*, 1:190–91, Feria V; 2:18, In die sancti Iohannis.

11. Vincent, *Sermons*, 1:121, Feria VI. In 3:263, Sabbato [post dominicam XIV post Trinitatem], he uses the same image to explain why Jews and Muslims, who are not baptized, are not children of God.

12. Vincent, *Sermons* 2:231–32. A similar analogy is used in 2:153.

13. Vincent, *Sermons* 3:179, urges all Christians to be attracted by God's beauty and to seek to lie with Him, just as they would seek to lie with a beautiful woman.

14. See, for example, his sermon on "In omnibus honorificetur Deus," in Vincent, *Sermons*, 1:111–22.

15. Vincent, *Sermons*, 3:263.

16. There were other analogies available that were less "sexualized" than the family analogy, but these too were generally implicated in the same logic of honor. Consider, for example, the analogy of baptism as an oath of fealty, requiring the Christian's loyalty and willingness to uphold the honor of his lord (Vincent, *Sermons*, 3:111).

17. Ute Frevert, *Men of Honor: A Social and Cultural History of the Duel* (Cambridge, MA: Blackwell, 1995), 47; Georg Simmel, *Soziologie*, 5th ed. (Berlin: Duncker & Humblot, 1968), 403–6.

18. Museo de Arte de Catalunya, inv. no. 15916, attributed to Jaume Serra. See José Gudiol and Santiago Alcolea i Blanch, *Pintura gótica catalana* (Barcelona: Polígrafa, 1986), 51, no. 110 (illustration on p. 224).

19. Hence the municipal governments of Valencia worried, in 1335, about the public health implications of sins taking place within their jurisdiction, "for which sins, so enormous and grave . . . our lord God . . . gives great whippings, even canings." See AMV, Lletres Missives (Ll.M.), g3–1, f. 51v (November 1335).

20. Vincent, *Sermons*, 3:111–13. The Pauline citation is from 1 Cor. 5. Elsewhere, Saint Vincent draws on different analogies from the world of fermentation: "Corruption of the populace: for if there is a woman, concubine, or [sexual] friend of someone in the town, the entire town is corrupted . . . , and one such person can corrupt more than all the others can cure." He goes on: "If you have 1,000 apples in a bin, and one is rotten, all the others will rot . . . thus one bad person corrupts the good ones." Such corruption angers God, so that he sends us plague (*Sermons*, 2:217–19). Similarly, *Sermons*, 3:140: one bad apple can corrupt the whole container, and even all the good apples together cannot cure the one that is rotten.

21. "In habitacione sancta coram ipso ministravi." The reference is to Ecclesiasticus 24.10–11: "In the holy tent I ministered before Him / and thus became established in Zion. In the beloved city he has given me rest, / and in Jerusalem I wield my authority."

22. The quote is from Mary Douglas, *Natural Symbols: Explorations in Cosmology* (New York: Pantheon Books, 1982), viii. Her work is of obvious relevance here, although I believe it is quite significant that the metaphors I have described are not those preferred by her theory, of Christian society as a body. Rather, the emphasis in my sources is on society as an aggregate of individual units bound together by the intimately related forces of kinship, common honor, and a shared vulnerability to each other's disease. See also Douglas, *Purity and Danger: An Analysis of the Concepts of Pollution and Taboo* (Boston: Routledge, 1966), 122–28; and her more recent "Rightness of Categories," in *How Classification Works: Nelson Goodman among the Social Sciences*, ed. Douglas and David L. Hull (Edinburgh: Edinburgh University Press, 1992), 239–71.

23. Vincent, *Sermons*, 1:190–91, Feria V.

24. BT, 'Avoda Zahra 36b (Soncino translation).

25. BT, 'Avoda Zahra 36b. Cf. *Sifrei on Numbers*, sec. 131, where the Israelite descent into the worship of Ba'al begins with the search for bargains in Gentiles' shops, continues

through a shared cup of wine during negotiation, and culminates in sex with the young shopwoman.

26. Moses Maimonides, *Mishneh Torah*, Sefer Kedushah XII.2; Lévi-Strauss, *The Elementary Structures of Kinship*, 67–68.

27. See Johannes's gloss to Gratian's *Decretum*, C.28 q.1 c.14 (Omnes deinceps clerici), s.v. Iudeorum: "Sed quare loquimur cum eis cum nec comedamus cum eis? Sed de hoc redditur ratio: quia maior familiaritas est in cibo sumendo quam in colloquio, et facilius quis decipitur inter epulas, ut xxii. q.iiii. Unusquisque [C.22 q.4 c.8]." My thanks to Ken Pennington for help with this reference. There are a number of studies on the status of non-Christians in canon law pertaining to marriage. See Paul Mikat, *Die Judengesetzgebung der merowingisch-fränkischen Konzilien* (Opladen: Westdeutscher Verlag, 1995); James A. Brundage, "Intermarriage between Christians and Jews in Medieval Canon Law," *Jewish History* 3 (1988): 25–40; Walter Pakter, *Medieval Canon Law and the Jews* (Ebelsbach am Main: R. Gremer, 1988), 263–91.

28. The frequency of miscegenation between Christian and Jew would be cited, for example, to justify the expulsion of Jews from Anjou and Maine in 1289 and from the French royal domains in 1308 and 1322. See William Chester Jordan, *The French Monarchy and the Jews from Philip Augustus to the Last Capetians* (Philadelphia: University of Pennsylvania Press, 1989), 182; Nirenberg, *Communities of Violence*, 53.

29. *Siete Partidas* 7.24.11; Carpenter, *Alfonso X*, 36.

30. 1 Cor. 6:16–17. The relationship between sexual and spiritual kinship could be explored further through the literature on consanguinity. See the material collected by Brundage, *Law, Sex, and Christian Society in Medieval Europe*, 356 nn. 155–56; James A. Brundage, "Marriage and Sexuality in the Decretals of Pope Alexander III," in *Miscellanea Rolando Bandinelli Papa Alessandro III*, ed. Filippo Liotta and Roberto Tofanini (Sienna: Accademia senese degli intronati, 1986), 71. Cf., for example, Gratian's ambiguity on whether a prostitute can marry a former client (James A. Brundage, "Prostitution in the Medieval Canon Law," *Signs: Journal of Women in Culture and Society* 1 [1976]: 844) to Thomas Aquinas's ruling that a Christian who sponsored a non-Christian for baptism was barred on grounds of consanguinity from marriage with the convert. Thomas Aquinas, *Quaestiones quodlibetales* 6.3.2, ed. Raimondo Spiazzi, 8th ed. (Rome, 1949), 120–21. My thanks to Mark Jordan for this last reference.

31. For example, when the Muslim Çalema Abinhumen was accused of sexual relations with Arnaldona, the wife of Ramon d'Aguilar, of Lleida, Ramon denied any knowledge or suspicion of the deed, and the charges were dismissed. ACA:C 876: 60v–62r (April 2, 1344), cited by Ferrer i Mallol, *Els sarraïns de la corona catalano-aragonesa en el segle XIV*, 31; published by Josefa Mutgé Vives, *L'aljama sarraïna de Lleida a l'edtat mitjana: aproximació a la seva història* (Barcelona: Consell Superior d'Investigacions Científiques, 1992), 298–302. Of course, the motives for such denials need have little to do with innocence or guilt. The Jew who struggled with a naked Gentile he found hiding under his wife's bed chose to believe his wife's story that the man had given her his pants and shirt to repair, since if he doubted her she would be forbidden him by Jewish law. Solomon ben Adret (RaShbA), *She'elot u-Teshuvot* 1: no. 1187, cited by Assis, "Sexual Behavior in Mediaeval Hispano-Jewish Society," 47. There are exceptions. Samuel Bon Aloor, a Jew of Tafailla in Navarre, was killed by the Christian Pere Xemeniz in 1376 when he found the Jew in bed with his wife. See Béatrice Leroy, "Les difficultés de la communauté juive navarraise, observées par les officiers du royaume, au xive siècle," in *Exile and Diaspora: Studies of the Jewish People Presented to Professor Haim Beinart*, ed. Aaron Mirsky, Avraham Grossman, and Yosef Kaplan (Jerusalem: Ben-Zvi Institute;

Madrid: Consejo Superior de Investigaciones Científicas, 1991), 54. Leroy calls the case "unique."

32. *Cantigas*, 2:262–64.

33. Biblioteca de Catalunya (Barcelona), Ms. 353, fols. 29v–32r. The manuscript is from the fifteenth century and has been noted (for very different purposes) only by Martín de Riquer, "Una versión aragonesa de la leyenda de la enterrada viva," *Revista de Bibliografía Nacional* 6 (1945): 241–48.

34. For examples of such romances (which are admittedly fifteenth-century), see *Romancero viejo (antología)*, ed. María Cruz García de Enterría (Madrid: Castalia, 1987), nos. 41, 54, 56. There is much recent work on the literary image of the Muslim. For a panoramic view, María Soledad Carrasco Urgoiti, *El moro de Granada en la literatura (del siglo XV al XX)* (Madrid: Revista de Occidente, 1956) remains useful. For Alfonso's poem, Manuel Rodrigues Lapa, ed., *Cantigas d'Escarnho e de mal dezir dos cancioneiros medievais galego-portugueses*, 3rd ed. (Lisbon: Edições J. Sá da Costa, 1995), 36, no. 25. See also David Ashurst, "Masculine Postures and Poetic Gambits: The Treatment of the Soldadeira in the *Cantigas d'Escarnho e de mal dezir*," *Bulletin of Hispanic Studies* 74 (1997): 1–6.

35. The risks were more theoretical than real in that, apart from prostitutes, virtually no Christian women were executed for the crime. I know of only one case, involving a nun and a Jew in Mallorca. Nevertheless, the punishments were feared. In 1311, Prima Garsón fled her home in Daroca when rumors implicated her in an affair with a Muslim named Ali, burned at the stake in her absence. After her capture, a medical exam proved her virginity and therefore her innocence (as well as the unfortunate Ali's), none of which had served to assuage her initial terror. See ACA:C 239: 32v, 95r, 125r, 205v; ACA:C 241: 117r.

36. The next two pages summarize material from my *Communities of Violence*, chap. 5, to which the reader is referred for references.

37. ACA:C Procesos, new numeration 12/14 (1304), fol. 2v, testimony of Pedro, "fil d'en Enegot Saragoça." Unfortunately, the advice as to how Aytola should speak is illegible. For another case of a Muslim using the name "John" to pass as a Christian, see ACA:C 528: 285r–v, February 28, 1334. The formula about dishonor of God is used often in cases of blasphemy or interfaith sexuality.

38. For more extended discussion, see the epilogue to Nirenberg, *Communities of Violence*. Cf. René Girard's claim that in primitive societies "contagious disease is not clearly distinguished from acute internal discord," in "Generative Scapegoating," in *Violent Origins: Ritual Killing and Cultural Formations*, ed. Robert G. Hamerton-Kelly (Stanford, CA: Stanford University Press, 1987), 84, 90.

39. Rafael Narbona Vizcaíno has shown that prohibitions on such intercourse were almost invariably reissued during times of famine and plague. See *Pueblo, poder y sexo: Valencia medieval (1306–1420)* (Valencia: Diputació de Valencia, 1992), 75. Contemporaries were quite explicit about the association. For example, the bishop of Valencia wrote to the town council in 1351 condemning the presence of Christians in the Muslim and Jewish neighborhoods of the city lest "by their sins, our lord God all-powerful might wish to send pestilences about the land." AMV Manuals de Consells, A-10, fol. 25 (October 7, 1351). Such arguments are frequent in the documentation.

40. See the texts mentioned in Nirenberg, *Communities of Violence*, 239 n. 29. Add to those Real Biblioteca de El Escorial Ms. ç.III.18, fol. 35r–v, where Prince Pere of Ribagorça writes to the pope in 1354 that "whenever God's omnipotent hand afflicts the people with some pestilence, mortality, famine, or poor harvest, many of the country folk hold the ignorant opinion that this happens because of the sins of the Jews," and indiscreet men exploit

this belief in order to foment riots against the Jews, "deducing what is infamous, that once the Jews are banished, these pestilences, deaths, famines, and poverty will cease."

41. See generally chap. 3, and for Pedro specifically, n. 29.

42. In 1371, the municipal council of Seville complained of a law that they claimed allowed a Jew to be convicted of adultery with a Christian woman only if a Jew witnessed the crime and stipulated that the accusing husband be executed if he could not thus prove his accusation. The king responded by granting that Jews could be convicted of adultery on the basis of only Christian witnesses, if those witnesses were unimpeachable. See Isabel Montes Romero-Camacho, "El antijudaismo o antisemitismo sevillano hacia la minoría hebrea," in *Los caminos del exilio*, ed. Juan Carrasco (Tudela: Gobierno de Navarra, 1996), 106. For the Cortes of Valladolid in 1385, see Danvila y Collado, *Cortes de los antiguos reinos de León y de Castilla*, 2:322, law 3, against Christian women who live with Jews and Muslims.

43. We will take up these later claims in chaps. 7 and 8.

44. For an example of the first position, see Netanyahu, *The Origins of the Inquisition*. For the second, see Jaume Riera i Sans, "Judíos y conversos en los reinos de la Corona de Aragón durante el siglo XV," in *La Expulsión de los judíos de España: Conferencias pronunciadas en el II Curso de Cultura Hispano-Judía y Sefardí de la Universidad de Castilla-la Mancha*, ed. Ricardo Izquierdo Benito (Toledo: Caja de Castilla-La Mancha, 1993): 82–83: "Está claro, para cualquiera que sea sensato, que los judíos bautizados masivamente en 1391 no podían sentirse integrados en la sociedad cristiana."

45. ACA:C 1964: 108v–109v, August 18, 1393, addressed to Tortosa, published in Baer, *Die Juden im Christlichen Spanien*, 1:716–18, no. 456. The Tortosa letter should be viewed together with those to Barcelona (see José-María Madurell Marimón, "La cofradía de la Santa Trinidad, de los conversos de Barcelona," *Sefarad* 18 [1958]: 72–77) and Girona (unedited, ACA:C 1960: 120v–121v). A similar letter to Morvedre is dated April 4, 1396 (ACA:C 1911: 46r–v, 2d numeration). See also Riera, "Judíos y conversos," 83.

46. ACA:C 2030: 80r–v (August 23, 1393): "quod ambulans in habitu christianorum et sub ipsis habitus velamine habuit rem carnalem cum pluribus mulieribus christianis."

47. In early 1393, the archbishop of Zaragoza claimed that Christians could not "be well" near Jews, and he began excommunicating those who lived (as they always had) near the streets of the Jewish quarter. His position was not popular and threatened to foment a riot, or at least such was the pretext with which the queen ordered him to desist. See ACA:C 2030: 47r–v (March 14, 1393).

48. ACA:C 2030: 136v–137r (September 3, 1393): "prou son senyalats," published in José Hinojosa Montalvo, *Jews of the Kingdom of Valencia* (Jerusalem: Magnes Press, 1992), 440, no. 191, see also nos. 218, 231, 235. In 1397 the tables would be turned, with King Martí revoking Queen María's severe statutes concerning Jewish dress: ACA:C 2190: 30r–31v (July 10, 1397).

49. For Castile, the best evidence for this comes from complaints in Cortes. See José María Monsalvo Antón, "Cortes de Castilla y León y minorías," in *Las Cortes de Castilla y León en La Edad Media: Actas de la primera etapa del Congreso Científico sobre la Historia de las Cortes de Castilla y León* (Valladolid: Simancas Ediciones, 1988), 2: 145–91; Pilar León Tello, "Legislación sobre judíos en las Cortes de los antiguos reinos de León y Castilla," in *Fourth World Congress of Jewish Studies* (Jerusalem: World Union of Jewish Studies, 1968), 2:55–63. For the Crown of Aragon, the archives allow us to witness the negotiation in much closer detail. Cf., for example, King Alfonso's edicts stipulating the need to create separate Jewish neighborhoods in Cervera (for instance, ACA:C 519: 98v–99r [May 9, 1328], 475: 116v [June 21, 1328]) with his issuing of licenses to Jews allowing them to live in Christian neighborhoods (see ACA:C 433: 24r–v [October 14, 1328], 462: 201r–v [June 9, 1333]).

50. In Mallorca, for example, converts were allowed to choose whether to remain living in their old homes in the Jewish quarter among Jews or to rent them out and move into traditionally Christian neighborhoods. A notary recorded the choices immediately after the mass conversions. See José María Quadrado, "La judería de la ciudad de Mallorca en 1391," *Boletín de la Real Academia de la Historia* 9 (1886): 294–312. A short time later the city received a letter from King Joan urging that conversos not cohabit with Jews, "car lur conversació a present no poria esser sens perill e gran dampnatge." ACA:C 1994: 186v–187r, cited in Riera, "Judíos y conversos," 83.

51. Arxiu Municipal de Lleida, Llibre d'Actes no. 404 (1402–1403), fol. 91r. In Castile, the lull in segregatory legislation between 1391 and 1405 has been noted. The 1405 ordinances of Valladolid reiterated the demand from the Cortes of Palencia (1313), Toro (1371), and elsewhere that Jews wear badges, complaining that Jews "wear clothes and go about as Christians." See Emilio Mitre Fernández, "Notas en torno a las disposiciones anti-judías de las cortes de Valladolid de 1405," in *Proceedings of the Seventh World Congress of Jewish Studies* (Jerusalem: World Union of Jewish Studies, 1981), 4:115–22.

52. The bibliography on Saint Vincent is vast. On the specific topic of his mission to the Jews, see Vicente Beltrán de Heredia, "San Vicente Ferrer, predicador de las sinagogas," in *Miscelánea Beltrán de Heredia* (Salamanca: Editorial OPE, 1972), 225–33; Antonio C. Floriano, "San Vicente Ferrer y las aljamas turolenses," *Boletín de la Real Academia de la Historia* 84 (1924): 558–80; Juan Torres Fontes, "Moros, judíos y conversos en la regencia de Don Fernando de Antequera," *Cuadernos de Historia de España* 31–32 (1960): 60–97; Francisca Vendrell de Millás, "La actividad proselitista de San Vicente Ferrer durante el reinado de Fernando I de Aragón," *Sefarad* 13 (1953): 87–104; Vendrell de Millás, "La política proselitista del Rey D. Fernando I," *Sefarad* 10 (1950): 349–66; José María Millás Vallicrosa, "En torno a la predicación judaica de San Vicente Ferrer," *Boletín de la Real Academia de la Historia* 147 (1958): 189–98; and especially Pedro M. Cátedra, *Sermón, sociedad y literatura en la edad media: San Vicente Ferrer en Castilla (1411–1412)* (Salamanca: Junta de Castilla y León, 1994).

53. The widely imitated Murcian statutes were issued on March 24, 1411: "Friar Vincent . . . has opened our eyes to the errors in which we live, and especially to the dealings and gatherings [*congregaciones*] that we . . . make with the Jews and the Moors, through which we sinned mortally each day against God." The second clause of the ordinance bars Christian women from Muslim and Jewish neighborhoods. Royal confirmation of the ordinance stressed the danger posed by the presence of Christian women in Jewish neighborhoods. See Torres Fontes, "Moros, judíos y conversos," 95–96. On Vincent's preaching in Murcia, see Julián Zarco Cuevas, "Sermón predicado en Murcia por S. Vicente Ferrer," *La Ciudad de Dios* 148 (1927): 122–47.

54. For one example, see AMV Manuals de Consells, A-25, fol. 79r, published in Hinojosa, *Jews of the Kingdom of Valencia*, 487–88, no. 288 (April 12, 1413). There, Saint Vincent exhorts the town council to force the dispersal of the many conversos whose homes were clustered in the old Jewish quarter and resettle them in Old Christian neighborhoods, so that they might learn proper conduct from Old Christians. The councilors do adopt the plan, but the extent of its implementation is unclear. Note that there were virtually no Jews living in Valencia, so that the difference between Christian and Jew could not be heightened merely through the Jews' more stringent segregation.

55. Vincent, *Sermons*, 1:224, "Sabbato [post pentecostes]."

56. ACA:C cr. Fernando I, box 22, no. 2764: "That he knew for certain that Jewish and Muslim men were having relations with Christian women, to such an extent that many Christian men thought that they had sons by their wives who were theirs, when [in fact]

they were by Moors and by Jews." Dated the last day of April [1415?], by Nicholau Burgés, procurator and syndic of Zaragoza. We have the text of a similar sermon given in Castile in 1412: "And first, there is no conversing with them in their homes, for Christians and infidels should not dwell in the same house, for luxury is an infectious evil, and many think they are sons of Jews but are [sons] of Christians, and vice versa. And just as Jews and Muslims are different from Christians in their law, so they should be different in their habitations." Colegio del Corpus Christi de Valencia, Ms. 139, fol. 113, cited in Cátedra, "Fray Vicente Ferrer y la predicación antijudaica en la campaña castellana (1411–1412)," in *"Qu'un sang impur . . ."*: *Les Conversos et le pouvoir en Espagne à la fin du moyen âge: Actes du 2ème colloque d'Aix-en-Provence*, ed. Jeanne Battesti- Pelegrin (Aix-en-Provence: Université de Provence Service des publications, 1997), 30–31.

57. The original: "por su aspecto son havidos e reputados por muytos seyer cristianos, senyaladament entre qui no son conoscidos." From a letter written by the sworn men of Zaragoza after hearing a sermon by Saint Vincent, dated January 28, 1415. ACA:C, cr. Fernando I, box 8, no. 919.

58. *Crónica de Juan II*, Ms. of the Biblioteca Colombina (Seville), 85–5-14, fol. 176r. See also Cátedra, *Sermón, sociedad, y literatura*, 134–35.

59. ACA:C 2416: 60v–63v (March 20, 1413). The fine for married women was fifty florins, for single women loss of their clothes. I have found relatively few instances of Muslims and Jews involved with Christian prostitutes in the fifteenth century. One case involved a Muslim from Zaragoza (1451), another a Jew from the same city (1484) who apparently quoted Saint Jerome when apprehended. Both are reported in María del Carmen García Herrero, "Prostitución y amancebamiento en Zaragoza a fines de la Edad Media," *En la España Medieval* 12 (1989): 311–12.

60. Vincent, *Sermons*, 3:13–14.

61. Although some have sought to minimize the impact of these policies by claiming that they were rarely implemented, the ACA preserves plenty of evidence of their implementation vis-à-vis the Jews and of the violence and dislocation that this implementation caused. Muslims, on the other hand, though often named in the edicts, were apparently often exempted, sometimes formally (as in the case of Murcia), sometimes informally. The evidence for Castile, as in all things having to do with governance in this period, is much sparser than that of Aragon, but what there is suggests that the decrees involving Jews were enforced. See, for example, the document from the Archivo Municipal de Alba de Tormes published by Carlos Carrete Parrondo in *Fontes Iudaeorum Regni Castellae* (Salamanca: Universidad Pontificia de Salamanca / Granada: Universidad de Granada, 1981–98), 1:30–31.

62. Solomon Alami, *Iggeret Musar*, ed. Adolf Jellinek (Vienna, 1872), 10b; Abraham Zacuto, *Sefer Yuhasim ha-Shalem*, ed. Herschell Filipowski (London, 1857), 225b; Heinrich Graetz, *Geschichte der Juden* (Leipzig: Leiner, 1890), 8:111 n. 2. For a Christian (converso) chronicler's report of hardship and conversions by both Muslims and Jews, see Alvar García de Santa María, *Crónica de Juan II*, cited above in n. 58 (see also the edition in the Colección de Documentos Inéditos para la Historia de España, vols. 99–100).

63. ACA:C 2237: 39r–v (July 6, 1408). The king complained that this not only dishonored God but was also against nature, for even animals protect their mates from the sexual advances of others. ACA:C 2312: 113v–114r (July 14, 1408), apparently concerns a number of Jews of Calatayud who had been imprisoned for having sexual intercourse with this woman.

64. For a rare recognition of the strategic function of the legislation against Jews and Muslims, see the words of the child-king Juan II in 1411, "The goal for which these penalties

were imposed is reached when the said infidels convert to the holy faith." Baer, *Die Juden*, 2: no. 277. See also Riera, "Judíos y conversos," 72.

65. "Pascha judahica," that is, Passover. See ACA: Mestre Ractional 393: 36v, 38r–v.

66. The concern here was partly with apostasy, partly with the fact that the converts took their wealth with them. There is a great deal of documentation concerning such emigration. On emigration to North Africa, see Haim Zeev Hirschberg, *A History of the Jews of North Africa* (Leiden, 1974–81), 1:384–88. For emigration to the Holy Land, Ben Zion Dinur, "A Wave of Emigration from Spain to the Land of Israel after the Persecutions of 1391" [In Hebrew], *Zion* 32 (1967): 161–74; Joseph Hacker, "Links between Spanish Jewry and Palestine, 1391–1492," in *Vision and Conflict in the Holy Land*, ed. Richard I. Cohen (New York: St. Martin's Press, 1985), 114–25.

67. ACA:C 1906: 64r–66r (May 10, 1393). Published by Baer, *Die Juden*, 1:705–11, no. 451; Hinojosa, *Jews of the Kingdom of Valencia*, 423–25, no. 164. See also Mark Meyerson, "The Jewish Community of Murviedro (1391–1492)," in *The Jews of Spain and the Expulsion of 1492*, ed. Moshe Lazar and Stephen Haliczer (Lancaster, CA: Labyrinthos, 1997), 132–33. In a related case, however, Joan did order his subjects to cooperate with the inquisitor Barthomeu Gaçó, who was inquiring against necromancers and "malicious converts who hold the erroneous sect in their depraved hearts." ACA:C 1927: 101r–v (November 7, 1393), published by Johannes Vincke, *Zur Vorgeschichte der Spanischen Inquisition* (Bonn, 1941), no. 144.

68. In 1398 King Martí expressed concern that converts met with Jews to observe the Sabbath and that "many frequently Judaize [*judaytzant*]." He ordered all officials to aid the inquisitors "to extirpate the aforesaid errors." ACA:C 2229: 60r (February 4, 1398). In 1400, he decreed that converso observance of any Jewish holiday would be punishable by a fine of one hundred sous and encouraged the inquisitors in their search for such practices. ACA:C 2173: 115r (August 12, 1400).

69. For an example from Saint Vincent, see *Sermons*, 3:311.

70. Rosemary Radford Ruether, *Faith and Fratricide: The Theological Roots of Anti-Semitism* (New York: Seabury Press, 1974), 121.

71. Sara Lipton, *Images of Intolerance: The Representation of Jews and Judaism in the Bible Moralisée* (Berkeley: University of California Press, 1999), 45.

72. Vincent, *Sermons*, 6:104. The allusion is to Matthew 23:7–12.

73. Vincent, *Sermons*, 5:221. The allusion is to Matthew 23:25–26.

74. This particular projection flourished into modernity. It is only "since Auschwitz," to quote Dan Diner, that "common linguistic usages such as the description of phenomena from the sphere of circulation as Jewish have forfeited their dubious claim to reality." (The claim may prove unduly optimistic.) See Diner "Reason and the 'Other': Horkheimer's Reflections on Anti-Semitism and Mass Annihilation," in *On Max Horkheimer: New Perspectives*, ed. Seyla Benhabib, Wolfgang Bonss, and John McCole (Cambridge, MA: MIT Press, 1993), 337.

75. Vincent, *Sermons*, 5:147.

76. Ruether, *Faith and Fratricide*, 160.

77. "[To] call someone a Jew amounts to an instigation to work him over until he resembles the image." Max Horkheimer and Theodore W. Adorno, *Dialectic of Enlightenment*, trans. John Cumming (New York: Herder & Herder, 1972), 186.

78. Cf. Horkheimer and Adorno, *Dialectic of Enlightenment*, 187: "What is pathological about anti-Semitism is not projective behavior as such, but the absence of reflection in it."

79. As he did in a sermon from 1414, Biblioteca de Catalunya, Ms. 476, fols. 136v–153v, in Josep Perarnau i Espelt, ed., "Els quatre sermons catalans de sant Vicent Ferrer en el manuscrit 476 de la Biblioteca de Catalunya," *Arxiu de Textos Catalans Antics* 15 (1996): 109–340.

80. The Muslim played an important role in this process as well, but that is a subject for another day.

81. The literature on the point is vast, but see most recently the chapter on Augustine in Cohen, *Living Letters of the Law*.

82. Particularly important in that so many other distinctions were mapped onto the sexual one. For a formulation of the point derived from Lévi-Strauss, see Stanley Tambiah, "Animals Are Good to Think and Good to Prohibit," in *Culture, Thought, and Social Action: An Anthropological Perspective* (Cambridge, MA: Harvard University Press, 1985), 169–70.

83. AMV, Ll.M., g³⁻4, 108v (October 26, 1378), cited in Dolors Bramon, *Contra moros y judíos* (Barcelona: Península, 1986), 67.

84. Vincent, *Sermons*, 1:42: "It would be a dishonor to me, for they would say of me: 'Oh, the madman! Oh, the Jew! He isn't up to avenging the death of his father!'"; 1:93: "You aren't up to avenging yourself, for you have the heart of a Jew"; 1:155: "Oo, they will say that you are a Jew!"; 3:16: "'Why didn't he kill him?' They will say: 'because he has the heart of a Jew!'"; 5:190: "Oo, the Jew!" "Oo, the others will insult me."

85. For an extended treatment of the Holy Week example, see my *Communities of Violence*, chap. 7, and "Les juifs, la violence, et le sacré," *Annales: Histoire, sciences sociales* 50 (1995): 109–31.

86. See, for example, the charges made circa 1393 against Antoni Rieri of Lleida, who was accused, among other things, of preaching that the prophecied time had arrived "in which all the Jews should be killed, so that henceforth no Jew should remain in the world." Jaume De Puig i Oliver, "La *Incantatio studii ilerdensis* de Nicolau Eimeric, O.P.," *Arxiu de Textos Catalans Antics* 15 (1996): 47. Lleida was the scene of anti-Jewish violence just a few years later, perpetrated by "some children of iniquity seeking the destruction of the Jewry of that city, which . . . we have just established." ACA:C 2232: 95v–96r (October 25, 1400).

87. Vincent's messianic inspiration is well known. On apocalyptic currents in the peninsula, see Guadalajara Medina, *Las profecías del anticristo en la Edad Media*, 232–47; José María Pou y Martí, *Visionarios, beguinos, y fraticelos catalanes (siglos XIII-XV)* (Madrid: Ed. Colegio "Cardenal Cisneros," 1991).

88. See Lerner, *The Feast of Saint Abraham*, especially chap. 7, on 1391 and Francesc Eiximenis's millenarian ideas.

89. Hebrew text in Frank Talmage, "The Francesc de Sant Jordi-Solomon Bonafed Letters," in *Studies in Medieval Jewish History and Literature*, ed. Isadore Twersky, (Cambridge, MA: Harvard University Press, 1979), 345. The biblical allusion is to 1 Kings 10:22. The translation is from Eleazar Gutwirth, "Habitat and Ideology: The Organization of Private Space in Late Medieval *Juderías*," *Mediterranean Historical Review* 9, no. 2 (1994): 208.

90. I know of the complaint about Moriscos through conversation with L. P. Harvey. For Jaume Roig's lament ("[V]os calà lo seu pern descapolat"), see Joan Roís de Corella, *Obres completes*, vol. 1: *Obra profana*, ed. Jordi Carbonell (Valencia, 1973), 57. The poem is also cited in Bramon, *Contra moros y judíos*, 167. The poet is admittedly of a later generation than the one that concerns us here.

91. For examples of these and other ambiguities of status, see chap. 7.

92. The case is discussed in Francisca Vendrell de Millás, "En torno a la confirmación real, en Aragón, de la pragmática de Benedicto XIII," *Sefarad* 20 (1960): 1–33. Less dramatic but equally meaningful are the "distancing" actions of converts like Gil Roiz Najarí, who succesfully petitioned to have an entrance to the Jewish quarter of Teruel moved so that he would have no contact with Jews. See ACA:C 2391: 102r–v (March 16, 1416).

93. ACA:C 2389: 111r–v (November 20, 1415): "We have just heard with displeasure how a few days ago, entering into one of the Jewries of the city of Zaragoza, called Barrio Nuevo, Master Gerónimo de Sancta Fe and some other converts and Christians . . . provoked in the said Jewry great rumor and scandal, causing riot and scandal against the Jews of the said aljama, and a son of the said Master Gerónimo stabbed a Jew." Cf. ACA:C 2389: 110r–v, 112r–v (November 20, 1415).

94. The original is: "car nunqua será bon christià, lo qui és vehí de juheu." Biblioteca de Catalunya, Ms. 476, fols. 136v–153v, in Perarnau i Espelt, "Els quatre sermons," 231–32.

95. For a Castilian example, see *Fuero Real*, Book III, 8.3. For a Catalan one, *Costums de Tortosa*, VI.1, paragraphs 12, 14, 17, 18.

96. For a description of the case, see Ferrer i Mallol, *Els sarraïns*, 27–28, citing ACA:C 2132: 114v–115r, 121r–v, 139v–140r. For an example involving children born of a Jewish woman, see the question addressed by Yehuda ben Wakar, personal physician to the regent of Castile Don Juan Manuel, to Rabbi Asher ben Yeḥiel of Toledo circa 1320 (Responsa 18.13). See Baer, *Die Juden*, 1.2:138–39.

97. Vincent, *Sermons*, 5:250.

98. See, for example, Enrique III of Castile's exhortation to the town council and citizens of Burgos in 1392 "that you should treat [the conversos] like brothers, and they should partake of your privileges and liberties and good usages and costumes." Mitre Fernández, *Los judíos de Castilla*, 83. The town council of Valencia claimed in 1402 that a convert's accusation against a Valencian Old Christian was not to be believed, given that the converts "retain the accustomed calumnies of their ancient infidelity, which they have not yet purged from their character." See Agustín Rubio Vela, *Epistolari de la València Medieval* (Valencia: Institut de Filologia Valenciana, 1985), 279–80.

99. Perarnau i Espelt, "Els quatre sermons," 257–59, lines 2380–2455.

Chapter 6

1. See Introduction.

2. Horkheimer and Adorno, *Dialectic of Enlightenment*, 186. On Karl Lueger's (1844–1910) political use of the claim, see Carl E. Schorske, "Politics in a New Key: An Austrian Trio," in *Fin-de-Siècle Vienna: Politics and Culture* (New York: Knopf, 1979), 133–69.

3. This particular example is developed in David Nirenberg, "The Birth of the Pariah: Jews, Christian Dualism, and Social Science," *Social Research* 70 (2003): 201–36.

4. See chap. 4.

5. See chap. 5.

6. Many of these claims were first put forth explicitly in the polemics surrounding a revolt in Toledo in 1449. They were edited by Eloy Benito Ruano, "El memorial contra los conversos del bachiller Marcos García de Mora ('Marquillos de Mazarambroz')," in *Los orígenes del problema converso* (Barcelona: El Albir, 1976), 95–132; and Benito Ruano, "La Sentencia-Estatuto de Pero Sarmiento contra los conversos toledanos," *Revista de la Universidad de Madrid* 6 (1957): 277–306. The first of these texts will be discussed further below. These and many other texts produced in the event are now gathered in a new edition by Tomás González Rolán and Pilar Saquero Suárez-Somonte, *De la Sentencia-Estatuto de Pero Sarmiento a la Instrucción del Relator* (Madrid: Aben Ezra Ediciones, 2012), which came to my attention too late for its findings to be incorporated into this volume.

7. The quotations are from Castro, *The Structure of Spanish History*, 542–43 and 569. In a review of the Spanish version of the work (*España en su historia*) Yakov Malkiel observed

that Castro's approach resembled theories of cultural transmission discredited by association with National Socialism. In 1965, on the other hand, Francisco Márquez Villanueva praised these pages as "the most acute and fruitful of [Castro's] oeuvre"; see the revised version of his essay "El problema de los conversos: Cuatro puntos cardinales," in *Hispania Judaica: Studies on the History, Language and Literature of the Jews in the Hispanic World,* ed. Josep Solà-Solé, Samuel G. Armistead, and Joseph H. Silverman (Barcelona: Puvill, 1982), 1:69.

8. Claudio Sánchez-Albornoz, *España. Un enigma histórico,* 4th ed. (Barcelona: Edhasa, 1973), 284: "Lo judío contribuyó a la forja de lo hispano no por caminos de luz, sino por sendas tenebrosas . . . , y ningún crédito puede alegar contra nosotros, a tal punto nos legó deformaciones y desdichas y dañó nuestro despliegue potencial y nuestro crédito histórico." Cf. José Luis Abellán, "Función cultural de la presencia judía en España," in *Judíos, sefarditas, conversos: La expulsión de 1492 y sus consecuencias,* ed. Ángel Alcalá (Valladolid: Ambito, 1995), 395–407. In the same work Sánchez-Albornoz endorsed Castro's theory on the Jewishness of the Inquisition. On this convergence of opinion see also Benzion Netanyahu, *Toward the Inquisition: Essays on Jewish and Converso History in Late Medieval Spain* (Ithaca, NY: Cornell University Press, 1997), chaps. 1 and 5.

9. Early critical voices include Peter E. Russell, "La historia de España, túnica de Neso," in *Temas de La Celestina y otros estudios, del Cid al Quijote,* Letras e Ideas, Maior, 14 (Barcelona: Editorial Ariel, 1978), 481–91; Nicasio Salvador Miguel, "El presunto judaísmo de La Celestina," in *The Age of the Catholic Monarchs, 1474–1516: Literary Studies in Memory of Keith Whinnom,* ed. Alan Deyermond and Ian Macpherson (Liverpool: Liverpool University Press, 1989), 162–77; and Paul Julian Smith, *Representing the Other: "Race," Text, and Gender in Spanish and Spanish American Narrative* (Oxford: Clarendon Press, 1992), 29. More recent is the "Critical Cluster" of articles under the rubric "Inflecting the Converso Voice" gathered in *La Corónica* 25 (1996), together with a "forum" of responses in *La Corónica* 26 (1997) and a further flurry of debate in *La Corónica* 28 (1999). See also Gregory B. Kaplan, *The Evolution of Converso Literature: The Writings of the Converted Jews of Medieval Spain* (Gainesville: University Press of Florida, 2002), 33, which elaborates a specific converso "code" and "semiotics" produced by the "unhomeliness" (the term is borrowed from Freud via Homi Bhabha) of "the boundaries of a marginal condition imposed by an oppressive majority."

10. This is partly why I do not here adopt the helpful but somewhat misleading distinction between "hermeneutic" or "discursive" and "real" or "sociological" Judaism that has developed in some fields of Jewish studies.

11. All references are from Dutton and González Cuenca, *Cancionero de Juan Alfonso de Baena,* henceforth *Cancionero,* and are cited by poem and page numbers, with line numbers where needed. Poems from *cancioneros* other than that of Baena are cited according to the numbering system in Brian Dutton's *El cancionero del siglo XV, c. 1360–1520,* Biblioteca Española del Siglo XV, serie maior, 1–7 (Salamanca: Universidad de Salamanca, 1990–91), henceforth Dutton; see vol. 7 for an index of the poems. On the dating of Baena's life and composition, see Alberto Blecua, "'Perdióse un quaderno . . .': Sobre los cancioneros de Baena," *Anuario de estudios medievales* 9 (1974–79): 229–66; Manuel Nieto Cumplido, "Aportación histórica al Cancionero de Baena," *Historia, instituciones, documentos* 6 (1979): 197–218; and Nieto Cumplido, "Juan Alfonso de Baena y su Cancionero: Nueva aportación histórica," *Boletín de la Real Academia de Córdoba* 52 (1982): 35–57. Two recent collections may serve as a starting point for the vast bibliography on the *Cancionero:* E. Michael Gerli and Julian Weiss, eds., *Poetry at Court in Trastamaran Spain: From the Cancionero de Baena to the Cancionero general,* Medieval and Renaissance Texts and Studies 181 (Tempe, AZ: Medieval and Renaissance Texts and Studies, 1998); and José Luis Serrano Reyes and Juan Fernán-

dez Jiménez, eds., *Juan Alfonso de Baena y su Cancionero: Actas del I Congreso Internacional sobre el Cancionero de Baena* (Córdoba: M.I. Ayuntamiento de Baena, Delegación de Cultura, 2001). Those interested in attitudes toward Jews and converts in the *Cancionero* may begin with (in addition to the works cited below) Stanley Rose, "Anti-Semitism in the 'Cancioneros' of the Fifteenth Century: The Accusation of Sexual Indiscretions," *Hispanofila* 26 (1983): 1–11, and "Poesía antijudía y anticonversa en la poesía artística del siglo XV en España" (PhD dissertation, Catholic University of America, 1975); and Gregory S. Hutcheson, "Marginality and Empowerment in Baena's *Cancionero*" (PhD dissertation, Harvard University, 1993).

12. Aristotle, *Poetics* 1448b.

13. It is entirely on the evidence of these poems that Baena's status as converso rests. The eggplant quotations are from poems by Diego de Estúñiga (no. 424, pp. 687–88) and Juan García (no. 384, p. 655). The reference to *adefyna* is by Juan de Guzmán (no. 404, p. 676), and the baptismal allusion by Ferrán Manuel (no. 370, p. 644). For allusions to Juan Alfonso de Baena's sexual encounters with Jewesses, see, inter alia, the same poem by Juan Garçia: "Con judía Aben Xuxena / o Cohena / bien me plaze que burledes" (no. 386, pp. 656–57, lines 10–12). For the Mariscal's insult, see no. 418 (p. 684). Allusions to interfaith sexual dalliance are very common in the *Cancionero*. Thus Juan Alfonso de Baena asks Gonçalo de Quadros: "nunca nombrastes la vuestra señora, / sy era cristiana, judía nin mora" (no. 449, p. 704, lines 14–15). Most beautiful is the love poem by Alfonso Álvarez de Villasandino (no. 31 bis, p. 48, lines 1–3): "Quien de linda se enamora / atender deve perdón / en caso que sea mora." For the debate over "indino"/"judino," see the commentary in José María Azáceta, *Cancionero*, Clásicos Hispánicos 2/10, 3 vols. (Madrid: Consejo superior de investigaciones científicas, 1966), vol. 1, pages v, 4, and accompanying notes. Gregory S. Hutcheson surprisingly takes "judino" for granted in "'Pinning Him to the Wall': The Poetics of Self-Destruction in the Court of Juan II," *Disputatio: An International Transdisciplinary Journal of the Late Middle Ages* 5 (2002): 92. Juan Bautista Avalle Arce considered the possibility of a Morisco as well as a converso background for Juan Alfonso in "Sobre Juan Alfonso de Baena," *Revista de filología hispánica* 8 (1946): 141–47. Dutton and González Cuenca begin by accepting such poetic evidence of Baena's converso status only "provisionalmente" but end by treating them as certainty: *Cancionero*, xv and xviii.

14. Examples of this underlying logic are legion. In addition to the works already cited, see Francisco Cantera Burgos, "El Cancionero de Baena: Judíos y conversos en él," *Sefarad* 27 (1967): 71–111; Rodríguez-Puértolas, *Poesía de protesta en la Edad Media castellana*, 216–24; and Cristina Arbós, "Los cancioneros castellanos del siglo xv como fuente para la historia de los judíos españoles," in *Jews and Conversos: Studies in Society and the Inquisition*, ed. Yosef Kaplan (Jerusalem: World Union of Jewish Studies, 1985), 77–78. The quotation is from Théodore de Puymaigre, *La cour littéraire de don Juan II, roi de Castille* (Paris: Franck, 1871), 131. Cf. José Amador de los Ríos, *Estudios históricos, políticos y literarios sobre los judíos en España* (Madrid: D. M. Diaz, 1848), 425–27. In the nineteenth and early twentieth century this ethnic judgment usually coincided with the aesthetic one that the poems were unrefined, vulgar, and unworthy of literary analysis (see below, n. 45).

15. See, for example, the work of Charles F. Fraker Jr., *Studies on the Cancionero de Baena* (Chapel Hill: University of North Carolina Press, 1966), 9–62, "Judaism in the Cancionero de Baena"; Hutcheson, "Marginality and Empowerment," 141 ("highly sophisticated blending of moralism and irony . . . points to possible Jewish ancestry"), and "Pinning Him to the Wall," 92–95. See also the pages dedicated to Baena in Kaplan, *The Evolution of Converso Literature*.

16. John Cummins, "The Survival in the Spanish Cancioneros of the Form and Themes of Provençal and Old French Poetic Debates," *Bulletin of Hispanic Studies* 42 (1965): 9–17; Cum-

mins, "Methods and Conventions in the Fifteenth-Century Poetic Debate," *Hispanic Review* 31 (1963): 307–23; Kenneth Scholberg, *Sátira e invectiva en la España Medieval* (Madrid: Gredos, 1971); Julio Rodríguez Puértolas, *Poesía crítica y satírica del siglo XV* (Madrid: Castalia, 1981). The *recuesta* of Baena's *Cancionero*, however, cannot quite be reduced to any of these forms, as Hutcheson points out in "Pinning Him to the Wall," 89–90 and 97.

17. Manuel Rodrigues Lapa, ed., *Cantigas d'escarnho e de mal dizer*, rev. ed. (Coimbra: Galaxia, 1970), nos. 300, 229 and 51. On these poems see Benjamin Liu, "'Affined to Love the Moor': Sexual Misalliance and Cultural Mixing in the *Cantigas d'escarnho e de mal dizer*," in Blackmore and Hutcheson, *Queer Iberia*, 61.

18. Villasandino's attack against Alfonso Ferrández Semuel in no. 141 (p. 165, lines 1–2) provides an early and lapidary example: "Alfonso, capón corrido, / tajarte quiero un vestido." The association of items of clothing with circumcision recurs constantly in the *cancionero* genre, with terms like *capirote* (little cape) becoming key words. Perhaps the wittiest example is the much later ditty by Juan Poeta in the *Cancionero General*, written upon receiving the gift of a small cape from a nobleman: "Vos no soys sayo ni saya / tajo frances ni morisco / ni soys funda dazagaya / ni ropa de san francisco / Soys beca de capirote / no se como soys cortada / soys embiada por mote / pese atal que no soys nada" (Dutton, ID6768, 11CG-996). For a dictionary of clothing vocabulary in the *Cancionero,* see Alicia Puigvert Ocal, "El léxico de la indumentaria en el *Cancionero de Baena*," *Boletín de la Real Academia Española* 67 (1987): 171–206.

19. See especially the study of Julian Weiss, *The Poet's Art: Literary Theory in Castile c. 1400–60*, Medium Aevum Monographs, n.s., 14 (Oxford: Society for the Study of Medieval Languages and Literature, 1990), 25–40. For "palabras de buen mercado," see no. 177, pp. 201–2, line 22.

20. Dutton, ID3377, MP3–94. Among the many examples of poems awarded cash payment, see Villasandino's nos. 28–30 (pp. 44–46). The metallic metaphor as a measure of quality occurs in Baena as well (for example, in no. 218, pp. 246–47, written in 1422).

21. "The place beyond heaven—none of our earthly poets has ever sung or will ever sing its praises enough! . . . What is in this place is without color and without shape and without solidity, a being that really is what it is, the subject of all true knowledge, visible only to the intelligence, the soul's steersman." To the passages cited here add *Phaedrus* 245A. For a useful summary of the issue and compendium of texts (which slights, however, the *Phaedrus*), see Penelope Murray, ed., *Plato on Poetry* (Cambridge: Cambridge University Press, 1996).

22. On Philo's (and later Origen's) Neoplatonic use of the analogy of body and soul for text and meaning I have found especially helpful David Dawson, "Plato's Soul and the Body of the Text in Philo and Origen," in *Interpretation and Allegory: Antiquity to Modern Period*, ed. Jon Whitman, Brill's Studies in Intellectual History 101 (Leiden: Brill, 2000), 89–107. I do not mean to imply here that this "spiritualization" of the word is in its origins a Greek phenomenon. It has deep roots as well in Hebrew biblical traditions, and for Ernst Cassirer it was even a fundamental characteristic of "all great cultural religions": *Language and Myth*, trans. Susanne K. Langer (New York: Dover, 1946), 45–46.

23. Most notable among them, for my purposes, is Auerbach, "Figura."

24. See A. J. M. Wedderburn, *Baptism and Resurrection: Studies in Pauline Theology against Its Graeco-Roman Background*, Wissenschaftliche Untersuchungen zum Neuen Testament 44 (Tübingen: J. C. B. Mohr, 1987), 127.

25. For Philo spiritual meaning increased, rather than lessened, the necessity of the bodily practice. See, for example, *On the Migration of Abraham* 92–93: "We should look on all these [outward observances] as resembling the body, and [these inner meanings as resem-

bling] the soul. It follows that, exactly as we have to take thought for the body, because it is the abode of the soul, so we must pay heed to the written laws. If we keep and observe these, we shall gain a clearer conception of those things of which these are the symbols."

26. As with all things related to the New Testament, the dating of its books is much debated, but there is a scholarly consensus at which all revisions aim. That consensus has long placed the genuine writings of Paul first, circa 45–60 C.E. The Gospel of Mark is thought to be the earliest Gospel, written shortly before or after the destruction of the Temple in 70 C.E., followed by Matthew later in the first century. Luke is sometimes treated as contemporaneous with Matthew but is probably later, since Acts, generally held to be written by the same author, is dated to circa 100 C.E. John has almost universally been treated as coming last and latest, though some revisionists argue instead for its priority.

27. Gilbert Dagron, "Le traité de Grégoire de Nicée sur le baptème des juifs," *Travaux et mémoires* 11 (1991): 314–57.

28. On Origen I have especially depended on Gerard E. Caspary, *Politics and Exegesis: Origen and the Two Swords* (Berkeley: University of California Press, 1979); Elizabeth A. Clark, *The Origenist Controversy: The Cultural Construction of an Early Christian Debate* (Princeton, NJ: Princeton University Press, 1992); Karen Jo Torjesen, *Hermeneutical Procedure and Theological Method in Origen's Exegesis*, Patristische Texte und Studien 28 (Berlin: De Gruyter, 1985).

29. On Augustine's aesthetics see recently Joachim Küpper, "'Uti' und 'frui' bei Augustinus und die Problematik des Genießens in der ästhetischen Theorie des Okzidents," in *Genuß und Egoismus: Zur Kritik ihrer geschichtlichen Verknüpfung*, ed. Wolfgang Klein and Ernst Müller (Berlin: Akademie Verlag, 2002), 3–29, and *De Civitate Dei* 11.18; *De doctrina Christiana* 2.6 (7, 8) and 4.11 (26). Closer to the period of our poets discussed here, see Thomas Aquinas's assertion, in his *Quodlibetal Questions*, that "poetic fictions have no purpose except to signify; and such signification does not go beyond the literal sense" (7.6.16). Elsewhere Aquinas attempted to distinguish between poetic fictions and other, more salvific ones. See in particular his discussion in *Summa theologiae* I.I.9, "Utrum sacra scriptura debeat uti metaphoris": "Procedere autem per similitudines varias, et repraesentationes, est proprium Poeticae." Here Aquinas concludes that, because mankind can achieve knowledge only through the senses, "unde convenienter in sacra Scriptura traduntur nobis spiritualia sub metaphoris corporalium." See also I.II.101 on the dependence of the ritual of the Mass on "aliquibus sensibilibus figuris." There his conclusion is that "sicut poetica non capiuntur a ratione humana propter defectum veritatis, qui est in eis, ita etiam ratio humana perfecte capere non potest divina propter excedentem ipsorum veritatem, et ideo utrobique opus est repraesentatione per sensibiles figuras."

30. On these themes see especially Karl Kohut, "Zur Vorgeschichte der Diskussion um das Verhältnis von Christentum und antiker Kultur im spanischen Humanismus: Die Rolle des *Decretum Gratiani* in der Übermittlung patristischer Gedankengutes," *Archiv für Kulturgeschichte* 55 (1973): 80–106, and "Der Beitrag der Theologie zum Literaturbegriff in der Zeit Juans II von Kastilien: Alonso de Cartagena (1384–1456) und Alonso de Madrigal, genannt el Tostado (1400?-1455)," *Romanische Forschungen* 89 (1977): 183–226, and more generally *Las teorías literarias en España y Portugal durante los siglos XV y XVI*, Anejos de Revista de Literatura 36 (Madrid: Consejo Superior de Investigaciones Científicas, 1973). On Saint Vincent Ferrer, and on responses by *cancionero* poets to his preaching in Castile, see Cátedra, *Sermón, sociedad y literatura*, 251–68. For Ferrer's Thomistic opposition to the allegorization of poetry, see Cátedra, "La predicación castellana de San Vicente Ferrer," *Boletín de la Real Academia de Buenas Letras de Barcelona* 39 (1983–84): 235–309, especially 278, citing Biblioteca Nacional, Madrid, Ms. 9433, fols. 33r–43r.

31. Lactantius, *Epitome Divinarum Institutionum* 11 and 12; Macrobius, *Commentum ad Somnium Scipionis*, 1.2.11; Isidore of Seville, *Etymologiae* 8.7.10.

32. See especially the work attributed to Bernard Sylvester, *Commentary on the First Six Books of Virgil's Aeneid*, trans. Earl G. Schreiber and Thomas E. Maresca (Lincoln: University of Nebraska Press, 1979).

33. Dante's poetics is articulated not only in his poetry but also in treatises such as the "Letter to Cangrande della Scala" (in Dante Alighieri, *Tutte le opere*, ed. Luigi Blasucci, 2nd ed. [Florence: Sansoni, 1965], 341–52), where Dante draws a parallel between the multiple levels of meaning of biblical and nonbiblical poetry. (The example Dante uses is that of Ps. 113:1–2: "Qui modus tractandi, ut melius pateat, potest considerari in hiis versibus: 'In exitu Israel de Egipto, domus Iacob de populo barbaro, facta est Iudea sanctificatio eius, Israel potestas eius.'") On these issues, see August Buck, *Italienische Dichtungslehren vom Mittelalter bis zum Ausgang der Renaissance*, Beihefte zur Zeitschrift für romanische Philologie 94 (Tübingen: M. Niemeyer, 1952), 33–53; and Otfried Lieberknecht, *Allegorese und Philologie: Überlegungen zum Problem des mehrfachen Schriftsinns in Dantes Commedia*, Text und Kontext 14 (Stuttgart: Franz Steiner Verlag, 1999), who discusses the debate over Dante's authorship of the letter on pp. 4–5. On the more general topic of the "fourfold meaning" of scripture, Henri de Lubac remains fundamental: *Exégèse médiévale: Les quatre sens de l'Écriture*, Théologie 41, 42, and 49 (Paris, 1959–64).

34. Giovanni Boccaccio's *Geneologia deorum gentilium libri*, ed. Vincenzo Romano, Scrittore d'Italia 200–201 (Bari: Laterza, 1951), especially the preface and books 14–15; Petrarch, *Invective contra medicum*, in *Opere latine di Francesco Petrarca*, ed. Antonietta Bufano, Classici Italiani 4, (Turin: Unione Tipografico-Editrice Torinese, 1975) 2:818–981; Petrarch, *Familiares* 10.4, "de proportione inter theologiam et poetriam," in *Le familiari*, ed. Vittorio Rossi, Edizione Nazionale delle Opere di Francesco Petrarca 11 (Florence: Casa Editrice Le Lettere, 1997), 2:301–10; Petrarch, *Collatio laureationis*, ed. Carlo Godi, in "La *Collatio laureationis* del Petrarca nelle due redazioni," *Studi petrarcheschi*, 5 (1988): 1–58. On the relationship between these defenses of poetry, see Alastair J. Minnis's introduction to the chapter "The Transformation of Critical Tradition: Dante, Petrarch, and Boccaccio," in *Medieval Literary Theory and Criticism, c. 1000–c. 1375*, ed. Alastair J. Minnis and A. B. Scott, rev. ed. (Oxford: Clarendon Press, 1991), 373–94; and Joachim Küpper, "Zu einigen Aspekten der Dichtungstheorie in der Frührenaissance," in *Genuß und Egoismus: Zur Kritik ihrer geschichtlichen Verknüpfung*, ed. Wolfgang Klein and Ernst Müller (Berlin: Akademie Verlag, 2002), 3–29. On the Castilian career of these texts, see, inter alia, Jules Piccus, "El traductor español de *De genealogia deorum*," in *Homenaje a Rodríguez-Moñino: Estudios de erudición que le ofrecen sus amigos o discípulos hispanistas norteamericanos* (Madrid: Castalia, 1966), 2:59–75; Hernando de Talavera, "Invectivas contra el médico rudo e parlero," ed. Pedro M. Cátedra, in *Petrarca: Obras*, 1: *Prosa*, ed. Francisco Rico et al., Clásicos Alfaguara 12 (Madrid: Alfaguara, 1978), 369–410.

35. An influential master narrative of this struggle was penned by Ernst Robert Curtius, "Poesie und Theologie," in *Europäische Literatur und lateinisches Mittelalter* (Bern: A. Francke A.G. Verlag, 1948), 219–32. For revisions to it, see the works of Minnis and Küpper cited in the previous note, as well as *The Cambridge History of Literary Criticism, 2: The Middle Ages*, ed. Alastair Minnis and Ian Johnson (Cambridge: Cambridge University Press, 2005). So far as I know, the only works to treat the *Cancionero de Baena* in this context are that of Karl Kohut, "La teoría de la poesía cortesana en el Prólogo de Juan Alfonso de Baena," in *Actas del coloquio hispano-alemán Ramón Menéndez Pidal* (Tübingen, Niemeyer, 1982) 131, n. 27; and Wolf-Dieter Lange, *El fraile trobador. Zeit, Leben, und Werk des Diego Valencia de León*, Analecta Romanica 28 (Frankfurt: V. Klostermann, 1971), 101–2.

36. *Cancionero*, p. 1. The rubric is discussed in a number of poems, most notably by Baena (no. 359, p. 639, lines 9–10) and Manuel de Lando (no. 253, pp. 451–52, lines 17–24; and no. 257, pp. 456–58, lines 81–88). For a good summary and revision of the scholarly debates over the meaning of this theme of *gracia* in the *Cancionero*, see Weiss, *Poet's Art*, 25–40.

37. For the exchange between Villasandino and Fray Pedro, see nos. 80–83 (pp. 107–13). Pedro challenges Villasandino, as "grant sabio perfeto / en todo fablar de linda poetría, / estrenuo en armas e en cavallería" (no. 82, pp. 109–11, lines 1–3), to explain obscurities in the Apocalypse. In no. 136 (pp. 161–62, lines 1–2) he does the same again, referring ironically to Villasandino as "Poeta eçelente, profundo, poético / e clarificador de toda escureza." Villasandino's response comes in no. 137 (p. 162). For the Bachelor from Salamanca, see nos. 92–93 (pp. 119–20).

38. "Aunque vos seades famoso jurista, / sabed que delante de sabios sotiles / ya fize yo prosas por actos gentiles, / maguer non só alto nin lindo partista. // Mas por aquesto non deven tomar / embidia los grandes dotores sesudos, / que Dios sus secretos quiso revelar / a párvulos simples, pesados e rudos, / e a los prudentes dexólos desnudos, / escondiendo d'ellos el su resplandor, / segunt verifica Nuestro Salvador / en su Evangelio de testos agudos" (no. 272, pp. 472–74, lines 21–32). The reference is to Matthew 11:25. For the moment I am concerned only with "Judaization" in debates about the relative value of secular poetry and theology. Accusations of Judaism are also made, however, in contests where both sides claim explicitly theological authority. In a debate (nos. 323–28, pp. 567–83) between Franciscans and Dominicans over the immaculate conception of the Virgin Mary, for example, Fray Lope accuses Diego Martínez de Medina of misreading (no. 324, pp. 568–74, lines 137–38: "La palavra mal entendida / mata e non da consuelo," a paraphrase of 2 Cor. 3.6), calls him a hypocritical Pharisee (lines 209–11), and suggests that "bueno vos será juntar / con essos de Moisén / e parientes de Cohén" (no. 326, pp. 575–77, lines 61–63). These strategies are revealingly similar to those used in Martin Luther's debate with the "Scholastics" over the same issue.

39. "Nunca vi secretos de Dios en ditar / nin al tal saber non somos tenudos. / Los fechos divinos son a nos escudos / que non alcançó el flaco armador, / gentil nin judío nin arrendador, / que tiene tristeza con gestos çejudos. // Él faze los ossos con cueros lanudos / e al que poco sabe ser grant sabidor; / pocos son los sabios de sabio valor / que tengan los pechos e lomos peludos" (no. 273, pp. 473–74, lines 27–35). Ferrán responds in no. 274 (pp. 474–75). Friar Lope attacks Villasandino on similar grounds in no. 117 (pp. 150–52, line 9), criticizing "Quien troba parlando, non seyendo letrado." The poem is an attack on political as well as poetic falsity, ending with a curse on those "hypocrites" who sow discord among the magnates and with the exhortation that princes "abhor Jews" and "honor good men" (lines 89–96). Even here Maestro Lope may be taking aim at the poets, whose inflammatory role in royal courts seems already a literary commonplace. See, for example, the first lines of Diego de Valencia's poem no. 227 (pp. 266–75) on the birth of Juan II (1405), regarding the "contiendas, roídos e daño muy farto" (line 6) that arise every day over the interpretation of figurative poetry. From a somewhat earlier period, see Alfonso X's condemnation of the violence occasioned by poetry in his *Siete Partidas*, 2.9.30, and Ramon Llull's complaint in his *Libre de contemplació en Deu*, ed. Mn. Antoni Ma. Alcover (Palma de Mallorca: Comissió Editora Lulliana, 1910), 3:98: "Los malvats juglas veem, Sènyer, esser maldígols e malmescaldors enfre un príncep e altre, e enfre un baro e altre; e per la mala fama que sembren los juglars, e per loy e la mala volentat que engenren enfrels alts barons, per so veem destruir emperis e regnats e comdats e terres, viles e castells."

40. No. 96, pp. 122–23, lines 28–45.

41. No. 255, pp. 453–55: "Si el mundo mirades bien en derredor / veredes las gentes ser ledas e tristes, / e muchos que enfingen segunt enfengistes / e otros que comen su pan con dolor; / alguno se piensa ser grant doctor / que en toda su vida non es bachiller, / aquí se demuestra que es bien menester / la graçia devina del grant Senador. // . . . // mas pues van las cosas de mal en peor, / . . . / por qué en España suele conteşçer / vençer el rectado a su rectador. // Quiçá este mundo, vil, engañador, / segunt las señales se va pereşçer, / pues ya la verdat non tiene poder / e es la mentira pujada en onor" (lines 35–44).

42. No. 359, p. 639, lines 1–4 and 9–12: "Ferrand Manuel, por que se publique / la vuestra çiençia de grant maravilla, / en esta grant corte del Rey de Castilla / conviene forçado que alguno vos pique; / . . . / Fernand Manuel, pues unicuique / data est graçia doblada e senzilla, / non se vos torne la cara amarilla / por que mi lengua vos unte o salpique." Or as Baena puts it in the challenge he issued to Villasandino and Lando in 1423: "que pierdan malenconía / e tomen plazentería, / sin enojo e sin zizaña, / ca la burla non rascaña" (no. 357, pp. 637–38, lines 27–30). The function of insult in poetry deserves to be studied in the light of Jean-Claude Milner's *De la syntaxe à l'interprétation: Quantités, insultes, exclamations* (Paris: Seuil, 1978), 174–223, but I have not been able to undertake the project (my thanks to G. Agamben for drawing my attention to this aspect of Milner's work).

43. Lando to Baena, no. 360, pp. 639–40, here lines 6–8: "que yo nunca tenga la novia muy presta, / si a vuestra amiga non punço en la cresta / fasta que la madre se le molifique." Baena to Lando, no. 363, pp. 641–42, lines 1–8: "Ferrand Manuel, boz mala vos gique / diz' que vos dexó en la culcasilla / un chato pastor toda rezmilla / e fuese fuyendo al campo d'Orique. / Por ende /. . . / medio puto vos queda el taxbique." Note Baena's assertion in this poem that insult specifically enables good poetry: "Fernand Manuel, por que versefique / donaires mi lengua sin raça e polilla, / sabed que vos mando de mula pardilla / dozena de festes en el quadruplique" (lines 9–12; *festes* 'horse turdlets'). On the use of the word *raça* (race) to signify (poetic) defect see Chapter 8.

44. Baena's challenge is no. 364, Villasandino's response no. 365; the exchange continues with Baena's no. 366, Villasandino's no. 367, and Baena's no. 368, to which Villasandino does not reply (pp. 642–44 for the entire exchange). The translation is of no. 365 (pp. 642–43): "Señor, este vil borrico frontino, / torçino e relleno de vino e de ajos, / sus neçios afanes e locos trabajos / es porque l'tengo por trobador fino; / en esto se enfinge el suzio cohino / e con muchos buenos levanta baraja; / e quien reçelasse su parlar de graja / más negro sería que cuervo marino. // Quien non es capaz bastante nin dino / de aquesta çiençia de que se trabaja, / su argumentar non vale una paja, / nin un mal cogombro, tampoco un pepino."

45. See, for example, Marcelino Menéndez y Pelayo, *Antología de poetas líricos castellanos*, ed. Enrique Sánchez Reyes, Edición Nacional de las Obras Completas de Menéndez Pelayo 17–26 (Santander: Aldus, 1944–45), 1:372–73: "En el *Cancionero de Baena*, como en todos los de su clase, hay mucho verso y muy poca poesía. . . . Ni una sola vez vienen a refrescarnos en las áridas y monótonas páginas del *Cancionero* de Baena, aquellas ráfagas de poesía que nos sorprenden en las *cantigas de amigo* o en las *de ledino*." Even Azáceta (above, n. 13), who dedicated himself to an edition of Baena, was upset by the poetry: "la bella forma de sus estrofas y el buen acabado de sus versos, a veces sirven para envolver pensamientos burdos, insultos groseros, palabras chabacanas. El Baena de los 'debates' resulta pendenciero, burlón y de baja calidad humana, y hasta presume la facilidad de su lengua para el mal hablar" (p. ix).

46. See, for example, no. 270, pp. 470–71, Alfonso de Moraña against Ferrán Manuel de Lando. The latter had written a love poem that placed his beloved among the heavenly spheres, the work of the Moon, Mars, and Venus. Alfonso responds by telling him that the

planets and fortune are not enough to produce such beauty, that he will be loved (i.e., sodom-ized) only by Alfonso's Moor, and that he sins.

47. No. 140, pp. 164–65, lines 31–32, Alfonso Álvarez de Villasandino against Alfonso Ferrández Semuel: "Nunca serviste Amor / nin fuste en su conpañía." For a suggestive study on the place of love in the production of poetry and nobility in Castile during this period, see Julian Weiss, "Alvaro de Luna, Juan de Mena and the Power of Courtly Love," *Modern Language Notes* 106 (1991): 241–56.

48. No. 501, p. 343. Cantera Burgos is among those who move from vocabulary to sociol-ogy: "Ya adelantamos que se ignora la ascendencia de Fray Diego y desde luego sorprende en él el amplio conocimiento que del vocabulario hebreo hace gala. Nada nos chocaría, pues, que . . . poseyera amplios contactos judaicos, quizá incluso familiares" ("El Cancionero de Baena" [above, n. 14], 103). Fraker's phrasing and conclusion are almost identical: *Studies on the Cancionero*, 9–10, n. 2.

49. No. 511, pp. 355–56, lines 13–16: "ca vuestra palabra jamás non se muda / . . . / Éstas son señales de omne fidalgo: / dezir e fazer las cosas sin dubda." Of course the possibility of an ironic allusion to Jewish "literal" understanding should not be dismissed here. Cf., how-ever, the Marqués de Santillana's comment on the writings of Rabbi Shem Tov de Carrion: "No vale el açor menos / por nasçer en víl nío, / ni los exemplos buenos / por los dezir iudío," Iñigo López de Mendoza (Marqués de Santillana), "Proemio," in *Obras Completas*, ed. Ángel Gómez Moreno and Maximilian P. A. M. Kerkhof (Barcelona: Planeta, 1988), 451.

50. The "Jewishness" of bad governance is a topos in the *Cancionero de Baena* as in Castilian literature both earlier and later (on which see chap. 3). For examples in Baena's collection, see the already cited no. 117 of Lope del Monte against Villasandino (ca. 1405) or Villasandino's own verses addressed to King Enrique (no. 57, pp. 78–81, lines 73–80, ca. 1391–93): "Vuestro padre, que heredado / con Dios sea en Paraíso, / en su vida siempre quiso / servidor noble, esmerado; / en lo tal fue su cuidado: / buscar ombre sin boliçio, / ca non vender el ofiçio / como judío renegado." Baena attributes the poem to Alfonso but doubts himself, "por quanto va errado en algunos consonantes, non embargante qu'el dezir es muy bueno e pica en lo bivo" (p. 78).

51. Alfonso Martínez de Toledo, *Arcipreste de Talavera o Corbacho*, ed. E. Michael Gerli, Letras Hispánicas 92, 4th ed. (Madrid: Cátedra, 1992), 108–9.

52. On the shift described here, and on the debates that accompanied it, see chap. 7.

53. See, for example, the many works on this topic by Francisco Márquez Villanueva, be-ginning with his "Conversos y cargos concejiles en el siglo XV," *Revista de archivos, bibliotecas, y museos* 63 (1957): 503–40.

54. *Politics* 1252b, 30. See also *Politics* 1278b, 23–31; and 1252a, 26–35.

55. For example, *Politics* 1279b.

56. Elsewhere Paul seems less monistic: cf. 1 Thess. 5:1–11; 1 Cor. 3:5–4:5, 15:24; and 2 Thess. 1:1–12.

57. I have relied on Caspary, *Politics and Exegesis* (especially chap. 4), and Lester K. Field Jr., *Liberty, Dominion, and the Two Swords: On the Origins of Western Political Theology (180–398)*, Publications in Medieval Studies 28 (Notre Dame, IN: University of Notre Dame Press, 1998), to clarify the issues treated in the paragraphs that follow.

58. For Tertullian, for example, church and empire are opposed as castle of light to castle of darkness, banner of Christ and banner of demons: *De idolatria* 19.1. Similarly for Hippoly-tus of Rome "the kingdom of this world" "rules through the power of Satan," and Rome is equated with *anomia*, lawlessness (*On Daniel* 2:27, 3:23, and 4:5–6). A more neutral position was that of kingdoms as "exterae potestates," natural powers appointed for those who were

not of God. The phrase is from the council of Antioch (341), canon 5, but the argument that earthly kingdoms are godly institutions for the utility of the pagan ungodly emerges first (I believe) in the second-century author Irenaeus, *Adversus haereseos* 5.24.2. Caspary, *Politics and Exegesis*, uses the term "fleshly envelope" to refer to Origen's view of the relationship of state to church (p. 181). Eusebius will more famously articulate this penumbral theology as a way of integrating Christianity and empire.

59. See Caspary, *Politics and Exegesis*, 142–43, and the bibliography cited there. This position is less antinomian than it sounds. Elsewhere in his commentary on Romans Origen stressed (tropologically) that since all men must care for their bodies, and since all bodily things "bear the bodily image of the Prince of Bodies," all men must pay "tribute to Caesar" (ibid., 155).

60. The quotation is from Caspary, *Politics and Exegesis*, 9. For examples of Origen's "Judaizing" political error, see his *Commentary on Matthew* 17:27 (quoted and discussed ibid., 155–56), where he calls those Christians who err by refusing to acknowledge the debts of the flesh "Pharisaei," or his characterization, in his *Commentary on Romans*, of pneumatics who resist the earthly powers with material force as Judaizing Zealots (ibid., 149).

61. Ambrose, *Sancti Ambrosi Opera*, ed. Michaela Zelzer, Corpus Scriptorum Ecclesiasticorum Latinorum 82/3 (Vienna: Hoelder-Pichler-Tempsky, 1982), letters 40 and 41, pp. 145–77; letter 40.23: "Nil boni huic imminet, rex iste Iudaeus factus est" (p. 173).

62. For an example of this process, see Jordan, "Jews, Regalian Rights, and the Constitution in Medieval France."

63. See chap. 3.

64. Text in Benito Ruano, "El memorial" (above, n. 6), 320–21; González Rolán and Saquero Suárez-Somonte, *De la Sentencia-Estatuto*, 199–200.

65. See, for example, Haim Beinart's discussion of Ciudad Real in *Conversos on Trial: The Inquisition in Ciudad Real* (Jerusalem: Magnes Press, 1981), 55–58.

66. Montoro to his horse: Dutton, ID6767, 11CG-995, and 14CG-1074; to Queen Isabel: ID1933, MP2–81. In ID0181 PN10–33, Montoro deploys the "killers of Christ motif" to threaten the Corregidor of Córdoba: "Ca el linaje que es ya visto / de grandeza y de valor / que pudo con ihesu xpisto / Podra con corregidor." On converso self-mockery, see, inter alia, Francisco Márquez Villanueva, "Jewish 'Fools' of the Spanish Fifteenth Century," *Hispanic Review* 50 (1982): 385–409. On Montoro's poem to Isabel see most recently Barbara F. Weissberger's "'Deceitful Sects': The Debate about Women in the Age of Isabel the Catholic," in *Gender in Debate from the Early Middle Ages to the Renaissance*, ed. Thelma S. Fenster and Clare A. Lees (New York: Palgrave, 2002), 214–19. See also the valuable review essay of E. Michael Gerli, "Antón de Montoro and the Wages of Eloquence: Poverty, Patronage, and Poetry in Fifteenth-Century Castile," *Romance Philology* 48 (1994–95): 265–76.

67. Dutton, ID0219, PM1–15, ca. 1472.

68. Richard H. Popkin, "Epicureanism and Skepticism in the Early Seventeenth Century," in *Philomathes: Studies and Essays in the Humanities in Memory of Philip Merlan*, ed. Robert B. Palmer and Robert Hamerton-Kelly (The Hague: Martinus Nijhoff, 1971), 346–57.

69. José Faur, *In the Shadow of History: Jews and Conversos at the Dawn of Modernity* (Albany: State University of New York Press, 1992), 142. Cf. Yirmiyahu Yovel on the "special hybrid phenomenon—perhaps even sui generis," of the Marranos: *Spinoza and Other Heretics*, vol. 1, *The Marrano of Reason* (Princeton, NJ: Princeton University Press, 1989), 23. Much more discrete are Yosef Hayim Yerushalmi's arguments about the non-normative nature of Marrano Judaism in *From Spanish Court to Italian Ghetto: Isaac Cardoso. A Study in Seventeenth-Century Marranism and Jewish Apologetics*, Columbia University Studies in Jewish

History, Culture, and Institutions 1 (New York: Columbia University Press, 1971), for example, p. 44. On the "Jewishness" of Spinoza see, more generally, Manfred Walther, "Spinoza und das Problem einer jüdischen Philosophie," in *Die philosophische Aktualität der jüdischen Tradition*, ed. Werner Stegmaier, Suhrkamp Taschenbuch Wissenschaft 1499 (Frankfurt: Suhrkamp, 2000), 281–330; and more recently Willi Goetschel, *Spinoza's Modernity: Mendelssohn, Lessing, and Heine* (Madison: University of Wisconsin Press, 2004).

70. See, for example, the special issue of *Pardes* 29 (1999): "Le juif caché." For other arguments that find the origin and transmission of modern subjectivities in Marrano lineages, see, for example, Jean-Pierre Winter, *Les errants de le chair: Études sur l'hystérie masculine* (Paris: Calmann-Lévy, 1998); and Elaine Marks, *Marrano as Metaphor: The Jewish Presence in French Writing* (New York: Columbia University Press, 1996). A different juxtaposition of converts and modernity, although equally problematic, is Geoffrey Galt Harpham's "So . . . What *Is* Enlightenment? An Inquisition into Modernity," *Critical Inquiry* 20 (1994): 524–56.

71. See, for example, Aitor García Moreno, ed., *Coloquio entre un cristiano y un judío*, Papers of the Medieval Hispanic Research Seminar 40 (London: Queen Mary, University of London, 2003), 148–49, on the Jews as rationalist skeptics; 154–55, on the Jews as a hybrid people; and 85, on the Talmud as an ironic joke by the rabbis that the Jews later confused with truth. All of these polemical topoi occur in other Christian sources, but this one (first produced ca. 1370 and copied in the mid-fifteenth century) spans the period that concerns me here.

72. Arguments for the philosophical importance of converso hybridity in the development of modernity also have a distinguished scholarly pedigree. Carl Gebhardt provides an early example: "Wenn wir der Geschichte der Marranen einen Sinn geben wollen, so kann er nicht darin gefunden werden, dass sie in einer im ganzen wenig eigenartigen Weise fremde Religionen reproduzierten. Ihr Erlebnis war, ihre Einmaligkeit in der Geschichte, dass sie zwischen den Welten, zwischen den Glauben standen, in der Spaltung ihres Bewusstseins die ersten Menschen ohne eingeborene Kategorien": *Die Schriften des Uriel da Costa*, Bibliotheca Spinozana 2 (Amsterdam: Menno Hertzberger, 1922), xxxix (my thanks to Benjamin Lazier for the reference). For a contemporary example, see Klaus W. Hempfer's discussion of "Ambiguität," "Hybridität," and "Komplexitätspotenzierung" in *Möglichkeiten des Dialogs: Struktur und Funktion einer literarischen Gattung zwischen Mittelalter und Renaissance in Italien*, Text und Kontext 15 (Stuttgart: F. Steiner, 2002), 1–38.

73. Karl Marx, "Zur Judenfrage," in *Karl Marx, Friedrich Engels, Werke* (Berlin: Dietz, 1957; repr. 1981), 1:374.

Chapter 7

1. Lord Byron, *Don Juan*, I.v.9.

2. On Abarbanel (1437–1508), see Benzion Netanyahu, *Don Isaac Abravanel: Statesman and Philosopher*, 5th ed. (Ithaca, NY: Cornell University Press, 1998); the Davidic claims are discussed at p. 3 and p. 266, n. 6. On David, see Hava Tirosh-Rothschild, *Between Worlds: The Life and Thought of Rabbi David ben Judah Messer Leon* (Albany: State University of New York Press, 1991). For this passage, see *Israelitische Letterbode* xii (1886–87): 88; Tirosh-Rothschild, *Between Worlds*, 269. Lawee's recent study of Abarbanel has a thoughtful discussion of the issue of lineage in Abarbanel's thought: Eric Lawee, *Isaac Abarbanel's Stance toward Tradition: Defense, Dissent, and Dialogue* (Albany: State University of New York Press, 2001), chaps. 1–2.

3. On the tombs, see Mair J. Bernardete, *Hispanic Culture and Character of the Sephardic Jews* (New York: Hispanic Institute, 1953), 44, 79, 82. Not all Sephardic tombs, however,

were so ornate: those of Salonica are relatively unadorned. And tomb style may owe as much to local Christian practice (the tombstone carvers were often Christian) as to any "Sephardic style."

4. In Amsterdam, for example, offspring of mixed Sephardic-Ashkenazic marriages were barred from burial in the communal Sephardic cemetery. The burial statutes are discussed in Miriam Bodian, "'Men of the Nation': The Shaping of *Converso* Identity in Early Modern Europe," *Past and Present*, no. 143 (May 1994): 69; and in Yosef Kaplan, "The Self-Definition of the Sephardic Jews of Western Europe and Their Relation to the Alien and the Stranger," in *Crisis and Creativity in the Sephardic World, 1391–1648*, ed. Benjamin Gampel (New York: Columbia University Press, 1997), 126, 143.

5. Isaac de Pinto, *Apologie pour la nation juive, ou réflexions critiques sur le premier chapitre du VIIe tome des oeuvres de M. de Voltaire au sujet des juifs* (Amsterdam, 1762). De Pinto pointed out that the Sephardim were "scrupulous not to intermingle . . . by marriage, nor by covenant, nor by any other means with the Jews of other nations." Translations from Philip Lefanu, trans., *Letters of Certain Jews to Monsieur Voltaire, Concerning an Apology for Their Own People and for the Old Testament*, 2nd ed. (Covington, KY: G. G. Moore, Rector of St. Peter's Church, 1845), 26. See also Kaplan, "Self-Definition of the Sephardic Jews," 140; Bodian, "Men of the Nation," 48; and especially Arthur Hertzberg, *The French Enlightenment and the Jews* (New York: Schocken Books, 1970), 180ff. For prohibitions on intermarriage, see Kaplan, "Self-Definition of the Sephardic Jews," 142. Examples of similar sentiments (though with different underlying logics) could be multiplied: see, for example, B. N. Teensma, "Fragmenten uit het Amsterdamse convolut van Abraham Idaña, alias Gaspar Mendez del Arroyo (1623–1690)," *Studia Rosenthaliana* 11 (1977): 149; Bodian, "Men of the Nation," 73; Yosef Kaplan, "The Sephardim in North-Western Europe and the New World," in Beinart, *Moreshet Sepharad: the Sephardi Legacy*, 2:252, n. 42.

6. The quotation is from his letter to Valera, October 17, 1887: *Epistolario de Valera y Menéndez Pelayo*, ed. Miguel Artigas Ferrnado (Madrid: Espasa-Calpe, 1946), 408. See also Menéndez y Pelayo, *Historia de los heterodoxos Españoles*, 1:410, 2:381.

7. A convergence pointed out by Netanyahu, *Toward the Inquisition*, chaps. 1, 5. Sánchez-Albornoz, for example, cited approvingly Castro's arguments about the Jewish origins of the Inquisition before invoking the vocabulary of race and of nineteenth-century racial theory in order to arrive at very similar conclusions about other Jewish and converso attributes: see Sánchez-Albornoz, *España: un enigma histórico*, 2:16, 255.

8. Kaplan, in a number of his articles, is only the latest to suggest that the Sephardic diaspora drew these ideas from the "repertory of concepts . . . that had been used against them by their [Iberian] oppressors": Kaplan, "Self-Definition of the Sephardic Jews," 128. He offers no justification, however, for this position. For a less pointed intervention on related themes, see Henri Méchoulan, "The Importance of Hispanicity in Jewish Orthodoxy and Heterodoxy in Seventeenth-Century Amsterdam," in *In Iberia and Beyond: Hispanic Jews Between Cultures*, ed. Bernard Dov Cooperman (Newark: University of Delaware Press, 1998), 353–72.

9. Some twentieth-century eugenicists and racists went so far as to praise the Jews as the inventors of racism, at the same time, of course, that they advocated discrimination against them: see, for example, Alfred Schultz, *Race or Mongrel: A Brief History of the Rise and Fall of the Ancient Races of Earth* (Boston: L. C. Page, 1908). The insistence on the Jewish invention of racism continues in contemporary historical writing: see, for example, Ivan Hannaford, *Race: The History of an Idea in the West* (Baltimore: Johns Hopkins University Press, 1996), 100–115. Less systematic, but equally wrongheaded on this score, is Winthrop Jordan, *White over Black* (New York: Norton, 1977), where he attempts to place ancient Jewish exegesis of

the curse of Ham at the origins of a genealogic history of racism. For criticism of Jordan, see the bibliography in Benjamin Braude, "The Sons of Noah and the Construction of Ethnic and Geographical Identities in the Medieval and Early Modern Periods," *William and Mary Quarterly* 54 (1997): 129–30.

10. Given Nietzsche's and Foucault's success in redefining the meaning of the term "genealogy," it is important to note that here, and throughout, I am using the term "genealogical" in its traditional, non-Foucauldian, sense. Indeed the philogenetic historiographies this article describes are very much of the type against which they were reacting. Following Nietzsche, Foucault (somewhat confusingly) used the term "genealogy" to describe his antithetical alternative to such historiographies, history as an "anti-genealogy" that does not "go back in time to restore an unbroken continuity that operates beyond the dispersion of forgotten things . . . [that] does not resemble the evolution of a species or map the destiny of a people": see Michel Foucault, "Nietzsche, Genealogy, History," in *Language, Counter-Memory, Practice*, ed. Donald Bouchard, trans. Bouchard and Sherry Simon (Ithaca, NY: Cornell University Press, 1977), 154, 162; Michel Foucault, *Il faut défendre la société: Cours au Collège de France, 1976* (Paris: Seuil, 1997), 10.

11. Cf. Alfonso de Toledo, *Invencionario*, ed. Philip Gericke (Madison, WI: Hispanic Seminary of Medieval Studies, 1992), which confidently identifies the inventors of technical innovations like the mule and the fork and of cultural ones like heresy. The genre was not specifically a late medieval one: see, for example, the writings of Isidore of Seville.

12. Gerson D. Cohen, *The Book of Tradition by Abraham ibn Daud* (Philadelphia: Jewish Publication Society, 1967), 79, 98. See also Joseph Shatzmiller, "Politics and the Myth of Origins: The Case of the Medieval Jews," in *Les Juifs au regard de l'histoire: Mélanges en l'honneur de Bernhard Blumenkranz*, ed. Gilbert Dahan (Paris: Picard, 1985), 49–61. Ibn Daud rooted this nobility in an account of the Diaspora: "When Titus overpowered Jerusalem, his lieutenant in charge of Spain requested him to send some of the nobles of Jerusalem": Cohen, *Ibn Daud*, 59.

13. Similar stories were told about the Kalonymos family, for example, whose influence underlies the Ashkenazic collection known as the *Sefer Hasidim*.

14. As a descendant of the Kalonymide dynasty wrote ca. 1320 in Catalonia, about a man who boasted of his lineage, "yet perhaps his family was the youngest from among those of whom it is written: 'they ravished the women in Zion' on the bitter day, in the time of oppression": R. Kalonymos, *Even Bohan* (Lemberg: J. M. Stand, 1865), 24ff., 35ff., cited in Baer, *A History of the Jews in Christian Spain*, 2:19. The cite is from Lam. 5:11; BT Kiddushin 71b.

15. Benzion Netanyahu, "The Racial Attack on the *Conversos*: Américo Castro's View of its Origin," in Netanyahu, *Towards the Inquisition*, 34, citing RaShbA, *responsum*, no. 386. RaShbA may have been alluding to Maimonides, who went further, suggesting ironically that anyone given to making such accusations was himself suspect of mixed ancestry, because a true Jew would not make such a charge: see Mishneh Torah, Sefer Qedushah, chap. 19 (V.17).

16. The literature on all these topics is vast. For a recent and particularly illuminating example, see Christiane Klapisch-Zuber, *L'Ombre des ancêtres* (Paris: Fayard Press, 2000).

17. For Castile the classic work is Salvador de Moxó, "De la nobleza vieja a la nobleza nueva: La transformación nobiliaria castellana en la baja Edad Media," *Cuadernos de historia* 3 (1969): 1–210. See also Adeline Rucquoi, "Être noble en Espagne aux XIVe-XVIe siècles," in *Nobilitas: Funktion und Repräsentation des Adels in Alteuropa*, ed. Otto Gerhard Oexle and Werner Paravicini (Göttingen: Vandenhoeck & Ruprecht, 1997), 273–98. For Infanzones in Aragon, see Elena Lourie, "Seigneurial Pressure and the *salva de infanzonía*: Larués, Marcuello and Yeste (1300–1329)," *15 Congreso de Historia de la Corona de Aragón* (Zaragoza: Gobierno de Aragón, Departamento de educación y cultura, 1996), 5:197–208.

18. I am here using the term "cultural memory" in more or less the sense elaborated by Jan and Aleida Assmann, whose work builds upon the studies of collective memory by Aby Warburg and Maurice Halbwachs: see Aby Warburg. *Ausgewählte Schriften und Würdigungen*, ed. D. Wuttke and C. G. Heise (Baden-Baden: Verlag V. Koerner, 1979); Maurice Halbwachs, *Les Cadres sociaux de la mémoire* (Paris: Félix Alcan, 1925). See also Jan Assmann, *Das kulturelle Gedächtnis: Schrift, Erinnerung und politische Identität in frühen Hochkulturen* (Munich: C. H. Beck, 1992); Aleida Assmann, *Erinnerungsräume: Formen und Wandlungen des kulturellen Gedächtnisses* (Munich: C. H. Beck, 1999).

19. In Abraham Hershman, *Rabbi Isaac Perfet and His Times* (New York: Jewish Theological Seminary, 1943), 194–96. I have altered the translation in several places and accepted the emendations offered (along with a Catalan translation) by Riera i Sans in his "Els avalots del 1391 a Girona," 156. See also the letter of the prominent rabbi and courtier Ḥasdai Crescas included in the much later work Shelomo Ibn Verga, *Shevet Yehudah*, ed. Me'ir ben David ha-Kohen Wiener (1854; repr. Hanover: K Rimpler, 1924), 128. Not even contemporaries of the events attempted to determine the exact proportion of Jews killed or converted. In the case of Girona, for example, the royal chancery limited itself to stating that the majority converted while another portion was killed ("major pars aljame sive habitantium in eadem ad fidem catholicam sunt conversi, et alii ex eis fuerunt gladio interempti"): see ACA:C 1902:16v–17r (July 16, 1392), cited in Riera, "Els avalots del 1391," 135. In his "Letter to the Community of Avignon," Ḥasdai Crescas wrote of Valencia that no Jews remained there except in Murviedro.

20. On the events of 1391 see chap. 4.

21. See chap. 5.

22. On the disputation, see Antonio Pacios López, *La disputa de Tortosa* (Madrid: Consejo Superior de Investigaciones Científicas, 1957); Jaume Riera i Sans, *La crònica en Hebreu de la disputa de Tortosa* (Barcelona: Fundació Salvador Vives Casajuana, 1974). The literature on Ferrer is too vast to summarize. For his activities in Castile, see, most recently, Cátedra, "Fray Vicente Ferrer y la predicación antijudaica en la campaña castellana," and *Sermón, sociedad y literatura en la edad media*. On his activities in the Crown of Aragon, the various articles of Vendrell de Millás remain important: see especially Vendrell de Millás, "La actividad proselitista de San Vicente Ferrer durante el reinado de Fernando I de Aragón."

23. The quotation is from a sermon given in 1414, cited in chap. 5, n. 94. There is some irony in the fact that earlier in the sermon Vincent chastises the Jews for what he describes as their materialistic belief that proper piety brings reward in the form of health and good harvests.

24. Colegio del Corpus Christi de Valencia, Ms. 139, fol. 113, in Cátedra, "Fray Vicente Ferrer y la predicación antijudaica," 30–31.

25. Contemporaries understood themselves to be responding to Saint Vincent's call for heightened segregation. The *Crónica de Juan II* (Biblioteca Colombina, Ms. 85–5-14, fol. 176r), for example, presents the edict of Valladolid as Queen Catherine's response to his preaching on the subject. At a more local level, numerous surviving letters from municipal authorities allow us to perceive how the sermons stimulated segregation in the towns Saint Vincent visited: see, for example, Floriano, "San Vicente Ferrer y las aljamas turolenses."

26. Royal edicts ordering the segregatory measures can be found in, for Castile: Baer, *Die Juden im christlichen Spanien*, 2:263–70, from Escorial, Ms. Z.1.6, fos. 139v–141v; and for Aragon: ACA:C 2416:60v–63v (March 20, 1413). See also Pope Benedict XIII's bull of May 11, 1415, and its confirmation (for the Crown of Aragon): ACA:C 2395:122r–176v, published in Francisca Vendrell de Millás, "En torno a la confirmación real, en Aragón, de la pragmatica

de Benedicto XIII," *Sefarad* 20 (1960): 22–33. For a Castilian example of the implementation of residential segregation, see *Fontes Iudaeorum Regni Castellae*, ed. Carlos Carrete Parrondo (Salamanca: Universidad Pontificia de Salamanca, 1981–98), 1:30–1, on Alba de Tormes. For an Aragonese example, see ACA:C 2370:109r–v (June 12, 1414), where the violence of the process is acknowledged (and reprimanded) by the king.

27. See the sources listed in chap. 5, n. 65. For practices of prayer among the rabbis, see the discussion of *Zohar* III 70b in Moses ben Jacob Cordovero, *Or Yakar*, XIII, 64, where he describes the digging of trenches over the bodies of the righteous. The text is transcribed and analysed in J. H. Chajes, "Spirit Possession in Early Modern Jewish Culture" (PhD dissertation, Yale University, 1999), 49, 52. Such a practice seems to be described in Diego de Colmenares, *Historia de la insigne ciudad de Segovia y compendio de las históras de Castilla* (Segovia: Diego Diez, 1637), 2:134–35, when he refers to the "miserable people, who threw themselves on the graves of their dead" when the edict of expulsion's deadline arrived in 1492.

28. Even the queen of Aragon had trouble interceding with the Inquisitors on behalf of her servant Mira, arrested in 1401. The Jewess had never been baptized, the queen explained, because the priest did not show up to carry out the ceremony. Besides, Mira's accusers now confessed to having lied. Nevertheless, much time and several stern letters passed before she was freed: see ACA:C 2338:1v (September 30, 1401); 2174:26r–v [= Baer, *Die Juden im christlichen Spanien*, 1:772–74].

29. Quadrado published an example of an early stage in this process, where shortly after the massacre the converts were asked whether they wished to remain in their old homes or move to Christian neighborhoods; the majority opted to stay: see Quadrado, "La judería de la ciudad de Mallorca en 1391." Authorities soon sought to segregate converts from Jews, but distinctively converso parishes remained a feature of urban topography in many Iberian cities (Barcelona, Córdoba, Seville, Toledo, Valencia) up to the sixteenth century.

30. In the Aragonese archives, documents concerning the creation of institutions for converso self-government are legion. To cite but two examples, see ACA:C 2186:55r–v (1408), giving the converso leadership of Barcelona the right to call all conversos together for the purposes of community business; and ACA:C 2193:116v–117r (1400), which establishes the procedure by which the conversos of Montblanc are to contribute to their outstanding share of the Jewish *aljama's* tax burden. Numerous individual complaints about indeterminate fiscal identity can be found in the archives as well.

31. In Valencia the confraternity of Saint Christopher was founded in 1399 (ACA:C 2191:143v ff. = Próspero de Borafull y Mascaró, Manuel de Borafull y de Sartorio and Francisco de Asís de Borafull y Sans, eds., *Colección de documentos inéditos del Archivo General de la Corona de Aragón* (Barcelona: J. E. Montfort, 1847–1910), vol. 41, no. 92, pp. 117–28); in Barcelona that of the Holy Trinity in 1405 (ACA:C 2915:47r ff. = Borafull y Mascaró et al., *Colección de documentos inéditos*, vol. 41, no. 93, pp. 129–40); in Mallorca that of Saint Michael in 1410 (ACA:C 2271:54r–57v; 2416:120v–126v). See, for example, Madurell Marimón, "La cofradía de la Santa Trinidad, de los conversos de Barcelona." In 1419 King Martí dissolved the Valencian confraternity, on the grounds that it perpetuated a dangerous division between Old and New Christians and fomented heterodoxy, though he rescinded the order shortly thereafter: see Archivo del Reino de Valencia, Bailía Ms. 1145, fol. 211r–v (April 12, 1419); Jaime Castillo Sainz, "De solidaritats jueves a confraries de conversos: Entre la fossilització i la integració d'una minoria religiosa," *Revista d'història medieval* 4 (1993): 197–98. We know less about the establishment of such confraternities in Castile, but more about the later conflicts they engendered, most spectacularly in Toledo. In a particularly vivid anecdote from 1465, for example, King Enrique tried to "bring about friendship be-

tween two confraternities [of Toledo], one of converts, the other of Old Christians, who were at odds with one another. And he turned them into one, and joined the brethren himself as a member, in order to make peace between them": see José de Mata Carriazo, ed., "Los Anales de Garci Sánchez, jurado de Sevilla," *Anales de la Universidad Hispalense* 14 (1953): 50. The attempt failed, and violence in Toledo continued into the 1470s.

32. Shelomo ben Abraham ben Adret, *She'elot u-teshuvot*, no. 1162. "Child of violence" is my translation of the phrase *ben paritz*, an allusion to Dan. 11:14.

33. Luis Batlle y Prats, "Un episodio de la persecución judía de 1391," in *Per a una història de la Girona jueva*, ed. David Romano (Girona: Ajuntament de Girona, 1988), 2:614–17 (the article was originally published in 1948); Gabriel Secall i Güell, *La comunitat hebrea de Santa Coloma de Queralt* (Tarragona: Diputació Provincial de Tarragona, 1986), 118–19.

34. See, for example, ACA:C 2374:77r–v (February 5, 1415).

35. *Responsa Yakin u-Bo'az* (Jerusalem, 1782), vol. 2, no. 19; ASV, Reg. Vat. 470, fo. 201r–v [= Shlomo Simonsohn, *The Apostolic See and the Jews* (Toronto: Pontifical Institute of Medieval Studies, 1988–91), vol. 2, 1051, doc. no. 856]. Although Pius's letter has been interpreted as exhibiting a sense of hereditary Jewishness, its logic appears quite different once we realize that Pedro de la Caballería was himself a converso. The problem here is one of pedagogy and nurture, not inheritance. Cf. the very different reading of Steven F. Kruger, "Conversion and Medieval Sexual, Religious, and Racial Categories," in *Constructing Medieval Sexuality*, ed. Karma Lochrie, Peggy McCracken, and James Alfred Schultz (Minneapolis: University of Minnesota Press, 1997), 169ff.

36. See María Luisa Ledesma Rubio, *Vidas mudéjares: Aspectos sociales de una minoría religiosa en Aragón* (Zaragoza: Mira Editores, 1994), 63–103.

37. On Rimoch, see Frank Talmage, "Trauma at Tortosa: The Testimony of Abraham Rimoch," *Medieval Studies* 47 (1985): 383. For Shelomo da Piera, see below, n. 42.

38. In the early fifteenth century, for example, some parishes began keeping special records of Jewish baptisms.

39. Fidel Fita, "El judío errante de Illescas," *Boletín de la Real Academia de la Historia* 6 (1885): 130–40.

40. The Inquisition archives from which accounts such as that of Luis de la Isla are drawn were themselves a response to that challenge.

41. Adret, *She'elot u-teshuvot*, no. 1162.

42. The examples are drawn from Gutwirth's invaluable article: Eleazar Gutwirth, "Lineage in XVth Century Hispano-Jewish Thought," *Miscelánea de estudios árabes y hebraicos* 34 (1985): 86–87. Gutwirth is translating from Heinrich Brody, *R. Salomon da Pieras Leben und Werken* (Frankfurt: J. Kauffman, 1893), 18, 22, 24–25.

43. Isaac Aboab, *Menorat ha-Ma'or* (Jerusalem: Mossad Harav Kook, 1961). I cite from the sixth treatise, "on marriage," which also describes how the origin and conclusion of each lineage are sealed by the name of God. For a seventeenth-century Ladino translation of the passage, see the "Almenara de la Luz," in *Antología Sefardí 1492–1700*, ed. María del Carmen Artigas (Madrid: Verbum, 1997), 283.

44. Citing BT Nedarim 27a, 'Avoda Zarah 54a, Yoma 85a.

45. Citing BT Sanhedrin 44a, *'Af-'al-pi she-hata' Yisra'el hu'*. See Ya'aqov Katz's article of the same title in *Tarbiz* 27 (1958), 203–17.

46. RIBaS, *She'elot u-teshuvot* (Constantinople, 1546–47; repr. Vilna, 1839), no. 4, 11. See, on this subject, M. Slae, "References to Marranos in the Responsa of R. Isaac Bar Sheshet," *Annual of Bar-Ilan University* 7–8 (1970): 397–419.

47. TaShBeTz, 3 vols. (Amsterdam, 1738–41), i, no. 63, ii, no. 63.

48. RaSBaS, *She'elot u-teshuvot* (Livorno: A. Ben Rafa,, 1742), no. 29. See especially Moisés Orfali, "La cuestión de la identidad judía en el *Maamar ha-Anusim* (Tratado de los conversos forzados) de RaShBaSh," in *Pensamiento medieval hispano: Homenaje a Horacio Santiago-Otero*, ed. José María Soto Rábanos (Madrid: Consejo Superior de Investigaciones Científicas, 1998), 2:1267–1287.

49. *Responsa Yakin u-Bo'az*, vol. 1, no. 107. Cf. BT Nedarim 31b.

50. *Responsa Yakin u-Bo'az*, vol. 2, no. 31, no. 3.

51. For an example of such reaffirmation from the late sixteenth century, see Moshe di Trani, *Teshuvot MaBIT*, ii, no. 40. For a more negative view, see Joseph Trani's *responsum* of 1604. This *responsum* and a number of others are discussed in Simon Schwarzfuchs, "Le retour des marranes au judaïsme dans la littérature rabbinique," in *Xudeus e Conversos na historia*, ed. Carlos Barros (Santiago de Compostela: Editorial de la Historia, 1994), 1:339–48. We know, from *responsa* asking whether a Hebrew name is necessary for a *get* (divorce) or a *ketubbah* (marriage contract), that onomastic memory was not always good.

52. *Responsa Yakin u-Bo'az*, vol. 1, no. 107: "The merciful one changes the seed of the gentile [to Jewish seed] in the womb of the daughter of Israel, as it says [Ezek. 23:20], 'the flow of horses you have caused to flow.' In accord with their saying there that the son that comes from your daughter is your son."

53. A great deal has been written on the converts' immigration into political, administrative, and ecclesiastical offices. For Castile, an influential article is Márquez Villanueva, "Conversos y cargos concejiles en el siglo xv." María del Pilar Rábade Obradó studies a number of converso office-holding families in *Una elite de poder en la corte de los Reyes Católicos: Los judeoconversos* (Madrid: Sigilo, 1993). Manuel Serrano y Sanz, *Orígenes de la dominación española en América*, vol. 1, *Los amigos y protectores de Cristóbal Colón* (Madrid: Bailly-Baillère, 1918), remains useful for Aragon. On the persistence of Jewish office holding in Castile, see Estow, *Pedro the Cruel of Castile*, 158.

54. *Libro verde de Aragón*, ed. Isidro de las Cagigas (Madrid: Compañía Ibero-Americana de Publicaciones, 1929), 14–16.

55. The Cavallería clan still awaits its monograph, but see the bibliography in Baer, *A History of the Jews in Christian Spain*, 2: 464–65. On the Santa María family, see Francisco Cantera Burgos, *Alvar García de Santa María y su familia de conversos* (Madrid: Instituto Arias Montano, 1952). For Jaume Roig's lament, see chap. 5, n. 90.

56. These and other examples quoted in Arbós, "Los cancioneros castellanos del siglo xv como fuente para la historia de los judíos españoles," 77–78. See also Francisco Cantera Burgos, "El cancionero de Baena."

57. *Crónica del Halconero de Juan II*, ed. José de Mata Carriazo (Madrid: Espasa-Calpe, 1946), 152. For additional sources, and a characteristically conspiratorial account of the events, see Netanyahu, *Origins of the Inquisition*, 284–92.

58. ACA:C 3124:157r–v: "separatio aut differentia nulla fiat inter christianos a progenie seu natura et neophytos . . . et ex eis descendentes."

59. ACA:C 2592:21r–22v; *Privilegios y ordenanzas históricos de los notarios de Barcelona*, ed. Raimundo Noguera de Guzmán and José María Madurell Marimón (Barcelona: Seix y Barral Hermanos, 1965), doc. 57; Pedro Sanahuja, *Lérida en sus luchas por la fe (judíos, moros, conversos, Inquisición, moriscos)* (Lleida: Instituto de Estudios Ilerdenses, 1946), 103–10 (105 for the text of the ordinance). See especially Riera i Sans, "Judíos y conversos en los reinos de la Corona de Aragón," 86–87.

60. J. D. Mansi, *Sacrorum conciliorum nova et amplissima collectio* (Florence, 1759–93; repr. Graz: Akademische Druck- und Verlagsanstalt, 1961), 29:100.

61. Vicente Beltrán de Heredia, "Las bulas de Nicolás V acerca de los conversos de Castilla," *Sefarad* 21 (1961): 37–38. Recall that the Council of Basel (quoted in the reference in n. 60 above) had included an exhortation to the *conversos* that they marry Old Christians: "curent & studeant neophytos ipsos cum originariis Christianis matrimonio copulare."

62. Alfonso Martínez de Toledo, *Arcipreste de Talavera o Corbacho*, 108ff. For a fuller citation see chap. 6, n. 51. Jews and conversos are nowhere mentioned here, but given the conflict over converso office holding developing in Toledo at about this time, Alfonso Martínez doubtless had them very much in mind.

63. These accusations are taken from a fifteenth-century manuscript by an anonymous author whose relationship to the Toledan rebels is unclear. See "Privilegio de Don Juan II en favor de un Hidalgo": Biblioteca Nacional, Madrid, Ms. 13043, fols. 172–77; and the edited text in *Sales españolas; o, Agudezas del ingenio nacional. Recogidas por Antonio Paz y Media*, Biblioteca de Autores Españoles 176 (Madrid: Ediciones Atlas, 1964), 26. (The "Privilegio" is newly edited in González Rolán and Saquero Suárez-Somonte, *De la Sentencia-Estatuto*, 82–92.)

64. The view that Jewish blood conveyed enmity to Christians was not exclusively Spanish, but was rather pan-European. Compare, for example, Martin Luther's argument that the Jews' poisonous hatred of Christians "has penetrated through blood and flesh, through marrow and bone, and has become their entire life and nature. And as little as they can alter flesh and blood, marrow and bone, just so little can they alter such haughtiness and envy: they must remain thus"; with Francisco de Vitoria's view in *Relectio de Indis*, ed. L. Pereña and J. M. Peres Prendes (Madrid: Consejo Superior de Investigaciones Científicas, 1967), 30. The Luther quote is from his "On the Jews and Their Lies," *Weimarer Ausgabe* 53:481.

65. The statute is published in Baer, *Die Juden im christlichen Spanien*, 2:315–17. On these texts, see Benito Ruano, "La 'Sentencia-Estatuto' de Pero Sarmiento contra los conversos Toledanos," "D. Pero Sarmiento, repostero mayor de Juan II de Castilla," *Hispania* 17 (1957): 483–504, and "El Memorial del bachiller Marcos García de Mora contra los conversos"; and now González Rolán and Saquero Suárez-Somonte, *De la Sentencia-Estatuto*.

66. Alonso de Espina, *Fortalitium fidei*, *Consideratio* (Nuremberg: Antonius Koberger, 1494), vol. 2, fo. 79, col. d. See Alisa Meyuhas Ginio, *De bello iudaeorum: Fray Alonso de Espina y su "Fortalitium fidei,"* Fontes Iudaeorum Regni Castellae 8 (Salamanca: Universidad de Pontifícia de Salamanca, 1998), 16–17. See also Netanyahu, *Origins of the Inquisition*, 83; Ana Echevarría, *The Fortress of Faith: The Attitude towards Muslims in Fifteenth-Century Spain* (Leiden: Brill, 1999), 167.

67. "Tratado del *Alborayque*," Biblioteca Nacional, Madrid, Ms. 17567: "si los metales son muchos . . . segun la carne, quanto mas de metales de tantas heregias." The quotation is from fo. 11r. The negative imagery of mixed species in the treatise leads ineluctably to its conclusion: a prayer that the "clean" lineages of the Old Christians not be corrupted through marriage with the New. For editions of the text, see Moshe Lazar, "Anti-Jewish and Anti-*Converso* Propaganda: Confutatio libri Talmud and Alboraique," in Lazar and Haliczer, *The Jews of Spain and the Expulsion of 1492*, 153–236 (based on Bibliothèque Nationale, Paris, Ms. Esp. 356); and Dwayne Carpenter, *Alborayque* (Mérida: Editorial Regional de Extremadura, 2005).

68. A number of fourteenth-century polemics stressed the hybrid nature of the Jewish people: see Josep Hernando i Delgado, "Un tractat anònim *Adversus iudaeos* en català," in *Paraula i història. Miscellània P. Basili Rubí* (Barcelona: Edicions Franciscanes, 1986), 730; José María Millás Vallicrosa, "Un tratado anónimo de polémica contra los judíos," *Sefarad* 13 (1953): 28. These can almost be read as a deliberate inversion of Jewish narratives such as Abraham ibn Daud's "story of the four captives."

69. Shem Tov ben Joseph ibn Shem Tov, *Derashot* (Salonika, 1525; repr. Jerusalem: Hebrew University, 1973), 14a col. b; cited in Gutwirth, "Lineage in XVth Century Hispano-Jewish Thought," 88. Cf. Shelomo Alami's attack upon those who emphasize lineage: Alami, *Igeret musar* (ca. 1415).

70. Biblioteca Nacional, Madrid, Ms. 838, fol. 3r–v: "Carta que fiz traducir de caldeo en latin e romance el noble rey don Alfonso que la vila de Toledo conquiro e yaze en el armario del aiuntamiento de Toledo."

71. Francisco Cantera Burgos and José María Millas Vallicrosa, *Las inscripciones hebraicas de España* (Madrid: C. Bermejo, 1956), 297–98, 303–5. These are also discussed in Shatzmiller, "Politics and the Myth of Origins," 59.

72. Shelomo ibn Verga, *Shevet Yehuda*, ed. 'Azri'el Shohet and Yitzhak Baer (Jerusalem: Mosad Bi'alik, 1946), 33–35. See also Enrique Cantera Montenegro, "Negación de la 'imagen del judío' en la intelectualidad hispano-hebrea medieval: el ejemplo del *shebet yehuda*," *Aragón en la Edad Media* 14–15 (1999): 270. Capsali, too, stresses that the Jews of Toledo "had not been present in the land of Israel at the time of Jesus": Elijah Capsali, *Seder Eliyahu Zuta*, ed. Aryeh Shmuelevitz, Shlomo Simonsohn and Meir Benayahu (Jerusalem: Makhon Ben Tsvi, 1975–83), chap. 60. A number of Christian chronicles accept the claim as true (for example Bibliothèque Nationale, Paris, Ms. Esp. 110, "Breve compendio de las crónicas de los reyes de España," fol. 2v). Even the anti-*converso* polemicist Bernáldez cited approvingly the ancient origins of Toledan Jews: Andrés Bernáldez, *Historia de los Reyes Católicos don Fernando y doña Isabel*, in *Crónicas de los reyes de Castilla desde don Alfonso el Sabio, hasta los católicos don Fernando y doña Isabel*, Biblioteca de Autores Españoles, 70 (Madrid: M. Rivadeneyra, 1878), chap. 93, though elsewhere (chap. 90) he stresses that the Jews "in this age are derived, both in lineage as in contumacy," from the Jews enslaved by Titus.

73. The exclamation of "Alfonso" is quite revealing in that it represents an explicit moment of comparison of the two evolving claims (Gothic and Sephardic) to distinguished lineage. Other writers attempted to derive one from the other. Thus the Christian author of BN Paris Ms. Esp. 110, "Breve compendio de las crónicas de los reyes de España," could write to King Ferrante I of Naples in 1492 that the Goths (*Godos*) were brave in battle because they were descended from the tribe of Gad (fol. 4v). The fictional Spanish king in Shelomo ibn Verga's *Shevet Yehudah* had made the same claim (see previous note). On Ferrante, see David Abulafia, "The Crown and the Economy under Ferrante I of Naples," in his *Commerce and Conquest in the Mediterranean, 1100–1500* (Aldershot: Variorum, 1993); Abulafia, "The Role of the Jews in the Cultural Life of the Kingdom of Naples," in *Gli Ebrei in Sicilia dal tardoantico al medioevo: Studi in onore di Mons. Benedetto Rocco*, ed. Nicolò Bucaria (Palermo: Flaccovio, 1998), 35–53. Ferrante's policies were characterized as philo-Semitic by some contemporaries: see Alexander Marx, "The Expulsion of the Jews from Spain: Two New Accounts," *Jewish Quarterly Review*, original ser., 20 (1908): 251.

74. See, for example, the claims made by the converso Bishop Alonso de Cartagena on behalf of the king of Spain at the Council of Basel: Alonso de Cartagena, *Discurso sobre la preeminencia*, Biblioteca de Autores Españoles 116 (Madrid: M. Rivadeneyra, 1959), 208. By the sixteenth century similar claims were made not just about the king's lineage but about that of the entire "nation." Cf. the king's words in *Shevet Yehudah* with those of Gonzalo Fernández de Oviedo, who wrote that, thanks to Spain's purity of blood laws, there was no Christian nation "where it was easier to recognize who was noble, and of good and clean caste [that is, without Muslim or Jewish ancestry], and those who were of suspect faith, which in other nations is obscured": Gonzalo Fernández de Oviedo, *Quinquagenas de la nobleza de España*

(Madrid: Real Academia de la Historia, 1880), 281, cited in Américo Castro, *Los Españoles: Cómo llegaron a serlo* (Madrid: Taurus, 1965), 105.

75. See, for example, the words attributed to Alonso de Cartagena by Juan de Lucena, *De vita beata*, in *Opúsculos literarios de los siglos XIV–XVI*, ed. Antonio Paz y Melía (Madrid: Sociedad de Bibliófilos Españoles, 1892), 147–48. Antonio Domínguez Ortiz, *La clase social de los conversos en Castilla en la edad moderna* (Madrid: Instituto Balmes de Sociología, 1955), 159, and Castro, *The Structure of Spanish History*, 558, quote the same passage. Castro, of course, uses the passage as evidence for the Jewish origins of purity of blood and the obsession with genealogy, "something different from the Castilian Christian's awareness of seigniorial grandeur and the urge to attain it."

76. Mosén Diego de Valera, *Espejo de la verdadera nobleza*, in *Prosistas castellanos del siglo xv*, ed. Mario Penna, Biblioteca de Autores Españoles 116 (Madrid: M. Rivadeneyra, 1959), 103: "este linaje escogió para sí por el más noble." The literature on converso ideas about nobility, and particularly about Diego de Valera, is considerable: see most recently E. Michael Gerli, "Performing Nobility: Mosén Diego de Valera and the Poetics of *Converso* Identity," *La Corónica* 15 (1996): 19–36; Jesús D. Rodríguez Velasco, *El debate sobre la caballería en el siglo XV* (Valladolid: Junta de Castilla y León, Consejería de Educación y Cultura, 1996); Ottavio di Camillo, "Las teorías de la nobleza en el pensamiento ético de Mosén Diego de Valera," in Menéndez Collera and Roncero López, *Nunca fue pena mayor*, 223–37.

77. The story derived from Trastamaran propaganda during the civil war against King Pedro "the Cruel," according to which Alfonso XI's wife, Maria of Portugal, unable to produce a male heir, had exchanged her newborn daughter with a Jewish couple for their baby boy, the future Pedro the Cruel. The girl, brought up Jewish, then gave birth to Pablo. On this legend, see Kriegel, "Histoire social et ragots," 96.

78. See, inter alia, Fernán Díaz (relator of Juan II), "Instrucción," in Alonso de Cartagena, *Defensorium unitatis christianae*, appendix II, 351–55. The converts' possession of the blood of Jesus and Mary remained a standard argument in defense of converso rights well into the modern era: see, for example, Juan Antonio Llorente, *Histoire critique de l'Inquisition depuis l'époque de son établissement par Ferdinand V, jusqu'au règne de Ferdinand VII, tirée des pieces originales des archives du Conseil de la Supreme, et de celles des tribunaux subalternes du Saint-office* (Paris: Treuttel & Wurtz, 1817), 1:24.

79. Alonso de Oropesa, *Luz para conocimiento de los gentiles*, ed. Luis A. Díaz y Díaz (Madrid: Universidad Pontificia de Salamanca, 1979), 628ff., 649. See also Moshe Orfali, "Oropesa and Judaism" [in Hebrew], *Zion* 51 (1986): 411–32; Maurice Kriegel, "Alonso de Oropesa devant la question des conversos: Une stratégie d'intégration hiéronymite?" in Battesti-Pelegrin, *"Qu'un sang impur. . . ,"* 14.

80. Encarnación Marín Padilla, *Relación judeoconversa durante la segunda mitad del siglo XV en Aragón: La Ley* (Madrid: printed by author, 1988), 14–15. See also Haim Beinart, ed., *Records of the Trials of the Spanish Inquisition in Ciudad Real I (1483–85)* (Jerusalem: Israel National Academy of Sciences and Humanities, 1974–85), 1:391; Yolanda Moreno Koch, "La comunidad judaizante de Castillo de Garcimuñoz, 1489–1492," *Sefarad* 37 (1977): 370. The Deuteronomic blessing is only one example of the biblical warrant for robbing Christians in which conversos were suspected of believing. Another was the charge made by Bernáldez, *Historia de los Reyes Católicos*, chap. 44, that the command to rob the Egyptians during the Exodus was believed by conversos to apply to them. For an example of apparently converso devotional poetry which refers to "Christians of Israel," and stresses the shared lineage of the converts and the Virgin Mary, see Pierre Vidal, "Mélanges d'histoire, de littèrature et de philologie catalane," *Revue des langues romanes*, 4th ser., 2 (1888): 333–59, 354–57; and the

commentary in Jaume Riera i Sans, "Contribució a l'estudi del conflicte religiós dels conversos jueus (segle xv)," in *IX Congresso di Storia della Corona d'Aragona: La Corona d'Aragona e il Mediterraneo* (Naples: Società Napoletana di Storia Patria, 1978–82), 2:411–14.

81. "Non est diferencia judey e greu . . . que omnes virii sunt in Christo Ihesu domino nostro" (a strained conflation of Rom. 10:12 and Gal. 3:28): Marín Padilla, *Relación judeoconversa*, 60–67.

82. Bernáldez, *Historia de los Reyes Católicos*, 600: partial translation in David Raphael, *The Expulsion 1492 Chronicles* (North Hollywood, CA: Carmi House Press, 1992), 61–81, here 65. The charge was extremely common. Cf. Alfonso de Palencia, on the conversos as "a nation apart, which everywhere refuses contact with the Old Christians": *Crónica de Enrique IV*, Biblioteca de Autores Españoles 228 (Madrid: M. Rivadeneyra, 1973–75), 2:93–94. The constant use of the word *nación* to describe the conversos is evidence of the widespread nature of the idea. See, for example, *Records of the Trials of the Spanish Inquisition in Ciudad Real I*, ed. Beinart, 2:30; Beinart, *Conversos on Trial*, 168.

83. Colegio del Corpus Christi de Valencia, Ms. 139, fol. 113, cited in Cátedra, "Fray Vicente Ferrer y la predicación antijudaica," 30–31. This last point, that Christian proposals were motivated by the same goals as the Jews' Mosaic laws, is similar to Innocent III's justification for the Jewish badge at the Fourth Lateran Council: that it enforces Moses's ruling about fringes on garments.

84. Thus in 1449 the "Bachiller Marquillos" defended the exclusion from office of the descendants of converts, writing that "in the time when the Mosaic law and its ceremonies were kept by God's command, the Jews made an ordinance that if people of other nations or laws should convert to the Mosaic Law they should have no property or office until a certain generation . . . and it is true that anyone who obtains a law against another, however unjust it might be, is bound to receive it against himself." See an edition of the treatise in Eloy Benito Ruano, *Los orígenes del problema converso* (Barcelona: El Albir, 1976), 116. Cf. Fernando del Pulgar's comment to Pedro González de Mendoza: "Now [the converts] are paying for the prohibition Moses made for his people that they not marry gentiles," cited by Américo Castro, *La realidad histórica de España*, 3rd ed. (Mexico City: Editorial Porrúa, 1966), 54.

85. Here, too, there is a vast literature. For a particularly mordant presentation of the thesis, see Ruether, *Faith and Fratricide*.

86. Saint Vincent Ferrer, *Sermons*, 5:221.

87. For the relator's text, see Alonso de Cartagena, *Defensorium unitatis christianae*, appendix II, 343–56 (here 351–55), and González Rolán and Saquero Suárez-Somonte, *De la Sentencia-Estatuto*, 93–120. Note that, although the relator condemns the anticonverso aspects of this genealogical approach, he nevertheless utilizes genealogical arguments as well, referring constantly to the converts as of the lineage of Christ. This seemingly contradictory strategy is common in proconverso texts. On the relator, see, inter alia, Nicholas Round, "Politics, Style and Group Attitudes in the *Instrucción del Relator*," *Bulletin of Hispanic Studies* 46 (1969): 289–319.

88. Arturo Farinelli, *Marrano (Storia di un vituperio)* (Biblioteca del Archivum Romanicum, 2nd ser., x [Geneva, 1925]), 53, 56, 66–67; Marcel Bataillon, *Erasmo y España* (Mexico City: Fondo de Cultura Económica, 1950), 1:90; 2:74ff.; Desiderius Erasmus, *Opus epistolarum*, ed. Percy Stafford Allen et al. (Oxford: Clarendon Press, 1906–58), 3:6, 52. On these and other views of Spaniards, see J. N. Hillgarth, *The Mirror of Spain* (Ann Arbor: University of Michigan Press, 2000), 236–40. "Portuguese," too, would eventually become a synonym for "Jew" throughout western Europe.

89. Marín Padilla, *Relación judeoconversa*, 109.

90. Henry de Vocht, "Rodrigo Manrique's Letter to Vives," in *Monumenta Humanistica Lovaniensia: Texts and Studies about Louvain Humanists in the First Half of the Sixteenth Century*, Humanistica Lovaniensia 4 (Louvain: Charles Uystpruyst, 1934), 427–58, here p. 435. See also Enrique González González, "Vives: Un humanista judeoconverso en el exilio de Flandes," in *The Expulsion of the Jews and Their Emigration to the Southern Low Countries (15th-16th C.)*, ed. L. Dequeker and Werner Verbeke, Mediaevalia Lovaniensia 1/26 (Louvain: Leuven University Press, 1998), 35–81, here p. 77.

91. The "libros verdes" (Green Books), in particular, were a popular genre of genealogical aspersion that often combined genealogies of supposedly converso families with lists of those condemned by the Inquisition and with anti-Jewish polemical texts. They were banned in Aragon as "pessimarum detractionum originem" in 1623, presumably to little effect. For an edition, see n. 54. For the ban, see *Consultationis resolutio grauissimorum doctorum . . . condemnans Auctorem libelli famosi nuncupati el Verde* (Zaragoza: Caesaraugustae apud Iannem a Lanaje et Quartanet, 1623). The *Tizón*, on the other hand, was a more stable text, written (presumably by the Cardinal Archbishop of Valencia Francisco Mendoza y Bovadilla) as part of the polemic over the implementation of purity of blood in the mid-sixteenth century. For a recent edition, see *El tizón de la nobleza* (Madrid: Colegio Heráldico de España y de las Indias, 1992).

92. Although a number of conversos (most famously Pablo de Santa María, Alonso de Cartagena, and Álvar García de Santa María) wrote history, the task of identifying a New Christian "historiographic voice" tends too easily to turn into precisely the kind of genealogical fetishism criticized in these pages. For that reason, and because much of their work is still in need of editing, converso historiography will not be discussed here.

93. Yosef Haim Yerushalmi, *Zakhor: Jewish History and Jewish Memory* (Seattle: University of Washington Press, 1982), 58–59: "In effect, the primary stimulus to the rise of Jewish historiography in the sixteenth century was the great catastrophe that had put an abrupt end to open Jewish life in the Iberian peninsula at the end of the fifteenth."

94. Abraham Zacuto, *Sefer Yuḥasin ha-Shalem*, ed. Herschell Filipowski and Abraham Hayyim Freimann (Frankfurt: Wahrmann Verlag, 1924).

95. Profiat Duran, *Kelimat ha-Goyim*, in *Kitvei Pulmos le-Profet Duran* [The Polemical Writings of Profiat Duran], ed. Frank Talmage (Jerusalem: Zalman Shazar Center and Dinur Center, 1981), 29 for example; Shim'on Ben Tzemaḥ Duran, *Qeshet u-Magen* (Jerusalem, 1970); Hayyim ibn Musa, *Magen va-Romaḥ* (Jerusalem, 1971). Here I am adapting the views of a number of scholars who have suggested ways in which the Yerushalmi thesis needs to be reconceived. See, in particular, Eleazar Gutwirth, "History and Apologetics in XVth-Century Hispano-Jewish Thought," *Helmantica* 35 (1984): 231–42, and "The Expulsion from Spain and Jewish Historiography," in *Jewish History: Essays in Honour of Chimen Abramsky*, ed. Ada Rapaport-Albert and Steven J. Zipperstein (London: P. Halban, 1988), 141–61; Robert Bonfil, "Jewish Attitudes toward History and Historical Writing in Pre-Modern Times," *Jewish History* 11 (1997): 7–40; David Berger, "On the Uses of History in Medieval Jewish Polemic against Christianity: The Quest for the Historical Jesus," in *Jewish History and Jewish Memory: Essays in Honor of Yosef Hayim Yerushalmi*, ed. Elisheva Carlebach, John M. Efron, and David N. Myers (Hanover, NH: University Press of New England for Brandeis University Press, 1998), 25–39; R. Ben-Shalom, "Dimmui ha-tarbut ha-noṣerit be-toda'ah ha-hisṭorit shel yehudei sefarad u-provens (ha-me'ot ha-shtem-'esrei 'ad ha-ḥamesh-'esrei)" (PhD dissertation, University of Tel Aviv, 1996). Lawee discusses the place of some of these precursors in Abarbanel's historical thought: Eric Lawee, "The Messianism of Isaac Abarbanel, 'Father of the Messianic Movements of the Sixteenth and Seventeenth Centuries'," in *Jewish Messian-*

ism in the Early Modern Period, ed. R. Popkin and M. Goldish (Dordrecht: Kluwer Academic Publishers, 2010), 1–40.

96. The custom of illuminating *ketubbot* seems to originate in late fourteenth-century Spain, before spreading throughout the Sephardic diaspora: see Robert Bonfil, "The History of the Spanish and Portuguese Jews in Italy," in *Moreshet Sepharad: The Sephardi Legacy*, ed. Haim Beinart 2:237; Shalom Sabar, "The beginnings of *Ketubbah* Decoration in Italy: Venice in the Late Sixteenth to the Early Seventeenth Centuries," *Jewish Art* 12–13 (1987): 96–110.

97. Friedrich Nietzsche, *Unzeitgemässe Betrachtungen, Zweites Stück: Vom Nutzen und Nachteil der Historie*, sec. 3, in his *Werke in drei Bänden* (Cologne: Könemann, 1994), 1:175. Thus Márquez Villanueva praises Américo Castro for his "dialogue with Fernando de Rojas, Cervantes, Sem Tob, Quevedo, Ibn Hazm, and so many other Spaniards with something to teach us about the common womb from which all were born." He also remarks, "His ultimate *telos* was nothing other than to understand dispassionately his own roots and to contribute to a collective *nosce te ipsum*." See Francisco Márquez Villanueva, "Presencia judía en la literatura española: releyendo a Américo Castro," in *La sociedad medieval a través de la literatura hispanojudía*, ed. Ricardo Izquierdo Benito and Ángel Sáenz-Badillos (Cuenca: Ediciones de la Universidad de Castilla – La Mancha, 1998), 27.

Chapter 8

1. Benjamin, "Delirium," in *The Origins of German Tragic Drama*, 53–54.

2. Ashley Montague, *Man's Most Dangerous Myth: The Fallacy of Race*, rev. ed. (New York: Oxford University Press, 1974), 21–22. At p. 56 he quotes Boas, "We talk all the time glibly of races and nobody can give us a definite answer to the question what constitutes a race" (quoted from Franz Boas, "History and Science in Anthropology: A Reply," *American Anthropologist* 38 [1936]: 140). Thurgood Marshall's successful arguments before the Supreme Court in the case of Sweatt v. Texas (1950) provide a good example of some of the legal consequences of the delegitimization of racial theory in academic circles. Marshall called on Robert Redfield, chair of the anthropology department at the University of Chicago, to explain to the justices that "there is no understandable factual basis for classification by race." See Richard Kluger, *Simple Justice* (New York: Vintage Books, 1977), 264. My thanks to Jane Dailey for these last references.

3. See, inter alia, Michael Banton, *Racial Theories*, 2nd ed. (Cambridge: Cambridge University Press, 1998), ix. On the struggle for a vocabulary to apply to the case of Jews and Judaism specifically, see Gavin Langmuir, "Prolegomena to any present analysis of hostility against Jews," *Social Science Information = Information sur les sciences sociales* 15 (1976): 691.

4. "The more radical among them": for Barbara Fields's argument against the explanatory value of race in American history, see her "Ideology and Race in American History," in *Region, Race, and Reconstruction: Essays in Honor of C. Vann Woodward*, ed. Joseph M. Kousser and James MacPherson (New York: Oxford University Press, 1982), 143–77.

5. Rainer Walz, "Der vormoderne Antisemitismus: Religiöser Fanatismus oder Rassenwahn?," *Historische Zeitschrift* 260 (1995): 719–48, offers an excellent review of some of the definitions of race proposed in the debate, as well as some new suggestions.

6. A criticism I would make also of Walz. This tendency is manifest even in the otherwise excellent article "Rasse," in *Geschichtliche Grundbegriffe: Historisches Lexicon zur politisch-sozialen Sprache in Deutschland*, ed. Otto Brunner, Werner Conze, and Reinhart Koselleck (Stuttgart: E. Klett, 1984), 5:135–78. On the other hand, neither is it very helpful to describe as racial every ideology that assigns to lineage a role in the production of identity,

as many proponents of premodern "racism" do. Thus for Arlette Jouanna, race is an idea "according to which the qualities that classify an individual within society are hereditarily transmittable through blood." Arlette Jouanna, *L'idee de Race en France au XVIème siècle et au Début du XVIIème Siècle (1498–1614)*, 3 vols. (Lille/Paris: Université Lille III, 1976), 1:1.

7. Robert Bartlett, *The Making of Europe: Conquest, Colonization, and Cultural Change, 950–1350* (Princeton, NJ: Princeton University Press, 1993), 197 [emphasis added]. Bartlett's insights on the topic are very helpfully expanded in his "Medieval and Modern Concepts of Race and Identity," *Journal of Medieval and Early Modern Studies* 31 (2001): 39–56, which, however, largely avoids both Jews and the Romance languages.

8. The possibility of identifying genetic markers whose relative frequency varies markedly between specific populations has long been known. See, for one example of such variation, Surinder S. Papiha, "Genetic Variation and Disease Susceptibility in NCWP (New Commonwealth with Pakistani) Groups in Britain," *New Community* 13 (1987): 373–83, on the genetic causes of the varying susceptibility to specific diseases in Britain of Anglo-Saxon populations and populations of immigrants from the Asian subcontinent.

9. For similar reasons, arguments like that of David Romano, who insists that "els antropòlegs seriosos . . . estableixen clarament que no hi ha races" and that therefore there was complete racial equality of Christians and Jews in medieval Catalonia, seem to me beside the point. On that argument, there can have been no racial inequality in 1930s Germany, either. See David Romano, "Característiques dels jueus en relació amb els cristians en els estats hispànics," in *Jornades d'història dels jueus a Catalunya* (Girona: Ajuntament de Girona, 1987), here 15–16.

10. I call the axiom questionable on two grounds. First, the late eighteenth-century efflorescence of racial theory (for example, in Immanuel Kant's 1775 "Von den vershiedenen Rassen der Menschen," in *Gesammelte Schriften, Akademie-Ausgabe* [Berlin: Georg Reimer, 1902], 2:429–43, and Johann Friedrich Blumenbach, *De generis humani varietate nativa* [On the Natural Varieties of Mankind] [Gottingen: Vandenhoek and Ruprecht, 1795]) depended much more on Montesquieu's updated version of climate theory than on genetic arguments. (For an early example of the impact of such theories on writing about Jews, see Johann David Michaelis's critique of Christian Wilhelm Dohm, *Ueber die bürgerliche Verbesserung der Juden* [Berlin and Stettin: Friedrich Nicolai, 1781–83], 2:51, 63.) Second, even after the widespread dissemination of Darwinian evolution, many of the examples of hybridity and its dangers most favored by nineteenth- and twentieth-century racist writers (like Schultz, *Race or Mongrel*) were drawn from an agricultural domain of animal breeding that was already well known in the ancient and medieval worlds. I know of no comparative study on this topic and will myself no more than gesture toward one below.

11. Foucault, *Il faut défendre la société*, 65.

12. Although my conclusion here is not quantitative, my sense is that scholars of the emergence of race and racism are generally more interested in the external challenges of European exploration, expansion, and colonialism than in internal European conflicts over sovereignty.

13. John Marshall's *John Locke, Toleration and Early Enlightenment Culture*, Cambridge Studies in Early Modern British History (Cambridge: Cambridge University Press, 2006), is, among many other things, a masterful demonstration of the ongoing power of these religious models of enmity and pollution in the very age where Foucault sees the emergence of his binaries.

14. On Foucault's use of Nietzsche's term "genealogy" see chap. 7, n. 10. Numerous scholars have castigated Foucault for some of his periodizations, most notably his argument for a

transition from premodern "blood" regimes to modern "sexual" ones. Kathleen Biddick, for example, finds in medieval texts a simultaneous insistence on the importance of blood and of pedagogy, and she concludes that Foucault's insistence on the modernity of blood regimes and disciplinarity is therefore incorrect. "Disciplinarity (pedagogy) was always already folded within this colonial symbolics of blood." See Kathleen Biddick, "The Cut of Genealogy: Pedagogy in the Blood," *Journal of Medieval and Early Modern Studies* 30 (Fall, 2000): 453. Biddick's "always already" may, however, obscure as much as it reveals.

15. Salo Baron took an intermediate position, agreeing that medieval people did not have a conscious concept of race in its modern form but seeing real similarities between the ideologies. See Salo Baron, *Modern Nationalism and Religion* (New York: Harper, 1947), 276, n. 26, and p. 15, reformulated in Baron, *A Social and Religious History of the Jews* (New York: Columbia University Press, 1969), 13:84ff. Kisch rejected this approach as well, in Guido Kisch, *The Jews of Medieval Germany* (Chicago: University of Chicago Press, 1949), 314–16 and 531, n. 60. The debate is summarized in Yosef Haim Yerushalmi's classic pamphlet on the topic, *Assimilation and Racial Anti-Semitism: The Iberian and the German Models* (New York: Leo Baeck Institute, 1982), 29.

16. On this tendency in Netanyahu's *The Origins of the Inquisition in Fifteenth-Century Spain*, see David Nirenberg, "El sentido de la historia judía," *Revista de libros* 28 (April 1999): 3–5.

17. Heiko Oberman, *Wurzeln des Antisemitismus. Christenangst und Judenplage im Zeitalter von Humanismus und Reformation*, 2nd ed. (Berlin: Severin & Siedler, 1983), 63. Oberman's work is also characteristic of this scholarship in that it makes no attempt to demonstrate assumed differences in the biological knowledge that underlay modern racist anti-Semitism and that which was encoded in comments like Martin Luther's, that the Jews' poisonous hatred of Christians was unalterably impregnated in their blood, flesh, and bone (see chap. 7, n. 64).

18. The bibliography on the question of anti-Judaism (nonracial) vs. anti-Semitism (racial) is vast. In addition to the works already cited (for example, Walz), see, inter alia, Peter Herde, "Von der mittelalterlichen Judenfeindschaft zum modernen Antisemitismus," in *Geschichte und Kultur des Judentums*, ed. Karlheinz Müller and Klaus Wittstadt (Würzburg: Kommissionsverlag F. Schoningh, 1988), 11–69; Christhard Hoffmann, "Christlicher Antijudaismus und moderner Antisemitismus. Zusammenhänge und Differenzen als Problem der historischen Antisemitismusforschung," in *Christlicher Antijudaismus und Antisemitismus. Theologische und kirchliche Programme Deutscher Christen*, ed. Leonore Siegele-Wenschkewitz. (Frankfurt: Haag & Herchen, 1994), 293–317; Winfried Frey, "Vom Antijudaismus zum Antisemitismus. Ein antijüdisches Pasquill von 1606 und seine Quellen," *Daphnis* 18 (1989): 251–79; Johannes Heil, "'Antijudaismus' und 'Antisemitismus'—Begriffe als Bedeutungsträger," *Jahrbuch für Antisemitismusforschung* 6 (1997): 91–114. Gavin Langmuir divided the vocabulary differently in *History, Religion, and Antisemitism* (Berkeley: University of California Press, 1990), positing a (medieval) shift from rational anti-Judaism to irrational anti-Semitism.

19. Jonathan Elukin, for example, argued for an "incipient racial ideology" evident in the Christian treatment of converts from Judaism in the Middle Ages. See Jonathan Elukin, "From Jew to Christian? Conversion and Immutability in Medieval Europe," in *Varieties of Religious Conversion in the Middle Ages*, ed. James Muldoon (Gainesville: University Press of Florida, 1997), 171. One of the best-known cases was addressed by Aryeh Grabois, "From 'Theological' to 'Racial' Anti-Semitism: The Controversy over the 'Jewish' Pope in the Twelfth Century" [in Hebrew], *Zion* 47 (1982): 1–16. Such arguments tend to see evidence of racial thought in medieval assertions about the ongoing Jewishness (or "immutability") of converts

or their descendants, but do not engage in the comparative exploration of medieval theories of immutability with modern racial ones that would seem to me to be a prerequisite for such a claim. For an important survey of medieval Christian attitudes toward converts from Judaism in the eleventh- and twelfth-century Rhineland, see Alfred Haverkamp, "Baptized Jews in German Lands during the Twelfth Century," in *Jews and Christians in Twelfth Century Europe*, ed. Michael Signer and John van Engen (Notre Dame, IN: University of Notre Dame Press, 2001), 255–310 (who does not, however, engage the question of "racial anti-Semitism").

20. This case was of course implicit in the question posed to Foucault, and explicit in the debates between Roth, Kisch, et al. Yosef Haim Yerushalmi took up the debate in 1982 (*Assimilation and Racial Anti-Semitism*), comparing late medieval Spanish ideologies that understood Jewishness as carried in the blood with nineteenth-century German anti-Semitic ideologies, and understanding both as recognizably racial. The line of argument was pursued further by Jerome Friedman, "Jewish Conversion, the Spanish Pure Blood Laws, and Reformation: A Revisionist View of Racial and Religious Antisemitism," *Sixteenth-Century Journal* 18 (1987): 3–31.

21. The population of Jews in the Crown of Aragon dropped from a high of twenty-seven to fifty thousand just before the massacres of 1391 to approximately nine thousand at the time of the expulsion of 1492 (and thereafter, of course, to zero). These figures, which are far below those offered by many historians, are meant primarily to illustrate the scale of the decline. They are taken from Riera i Sans, "Judíos y conversos en los reinos de la Corona de Aragón, 78, who, however, provides no evidence for them. Henry Kamen, in his self-consciously revisionist "The Mediterranean and the Expulsion of Spanish Jews in 1492," *Past and Present* 119 (1988): 30–55, provides very similar numbers but also adduces no evidence.

22. Though in this chapter I will be focusing on the Jewish case, the same phenomenon applies to the historiography of Muslims in the Iberian Peninsula. Examples of racial language in the description of Christian-Muslim relations abound in José María Perceval, *Todos son uno. Arquetipos, xenofobia y racismo. La imagen del morisco en la Monarquía Española durante los siglos XVI y XVII* (Almería: Instituto de Estudios Almerienses, 1997), passim but see, for example, 63.

23. See Leopold von Ranke, *Fürsten und Völker von Süd-Europa im sechzehnten und siebzehnten Jahrhundert* (Berlin: Duncker & Humbolt, 1837), 1:246.

24. "Locura es pensar que *batallas por la existencia*, luchas encarnizadas y seculares de razas, terminen de otro modo que con expulsiones o exterminios. La raza inferior sucumbe siempre y acaba por triunfar el principio de nacionalidad más fuerte y vigoroso." Menéndez y Pelayo, *Historia de los heterodoxos Españoles*, 2:379. Cf. 1:410; 2:381. Despite the Darwinian overtones of this passage, and though he everywhere utilizes the vocabulary of race, Menéndez Pelayo nevertheless also claims to reject some of the racial theories of his day (cf. 1:249: "Sin asentir en manera alguna a la teoría fatalista de las razas . . . los árabes . . . han sido y son muy poco dados a la filosofía"). Cf. Henry Charles Lea, *A History of the Inquisition of Spain* (1906; repr., New York: AMS Press, 1966), 1:126.

25. Américo Castro, *The Spaniards: An Introduction to Their History* (Berkeley: University of California Press, 1971), 20. If such a faith lasted longer in Spain than it did in the rest of western Europe, this is partly because Franco's triumph allowed Falangist historians to continue celebrating the achievements of the "raza hispánica" for many years. But it should be added that the "faith . . . in biology continuity" of Spanish fascists had its own distinctive flavor. Primo de Rivera, for example, could proclaim: "España no se justifica por tener una lengua, ni por ser una raza, ni por ser un acervo de costumbres, sino que España se justifica

por una vocación imperial para unir lenguas, para unir razas, para unir pueblos y para unir costumbres en un destino universal." Cited in Eduardo González Calleja and Fredes Limón Nevado, *La hispanidad como instrumento de combate: Raza e imperio en la prensa franquista durante la guerra civil española* (Madrid: Consejo Superior de Investigaciones Científicas, 1988), 27–28. Can we imagine a similar statement from a German fascist?

26. An approach common to Américo Castro's *España en su historia: Cristianos, moros y judíos* (Buenos Aires: Editorial Losada, 1948), *La realidad histórica de España*, De la edad conflictiva, Colección Persiles 18 (Madrid: Taurus, 1963), *"Español," palabra extranjera: Razones y motivos* (Madrid: Taurus, 1970), and *The Spaniards*.

27. Castro, *La realidad histórica*, p. 5 of the 1966 introduction. In this context it is worth pointing out that the *Diccionario* itself actually uses the word *raza* in its definition of the word *antisemita*: "enemigo de la raza hebrea, de su cultura, o de su influencia" (my thanks to Daniel Waissbein for bringing this to my attention). Writing at much the same time as Castro, Nicolás López Martínez, "Teología española de la convivencia a mediados del siglo XV," *Repertorio de las Ciencias Eclesiásticas de España 1 (Siglos III–XVI)* (Salamanca, 1967), 465–76, embraced the vocabulary Castro rejected. He saw the fifteenth-century drive toward assimilation as "un fenómeno casi biológico" (p. 466), and did not hesitate to speak of race: "Si añadimos la notoria eficacia de la raza hebrea para hacerse con las claves económicas del país, comprenderemos . . . que, a veces, por motivos inmediatos aparentemente fútiles, se haga guerra sin cuartel" (p. 467). "Como se ve, pretendía una discriminación semejante a la que, todavía en nuestros tiempos, se basa exclusivamente en motivos de raza o del color de la piel" (p. 468).

28. One might further complain that late medieval and early modern Spaniards were perfectly capable of believing that Jews and conversos actually *were* distinguished by physical characteristics, such as large noses. Lope de Vega pokes fun at precisely this belief in Vega, *Amar sin saber a quién*, ed. Carmen Bravo-Villasante (Salamanca: Anaya, 1967), 10: "Largas hay con hidalguía / y muchas cortas sin ella." See María Rosa Lida de Malkiel, "Lope de Vega y los judíos," *Bulletin Hispanique* 75 (1973): 88.

29. Francisco Márquez Villanueva, "El problema de los conversos: Cuatro puntos cardinales," in *Hispania Judaica: Studies on the History, Language, and Literature of Jews in the Hispanic World*, ed. Joseph Sola-Solé et al., vol. 1, *History* (Barcelona: Puvill, 1982), 61. For a less "Castrista" example, see Adeline Rucquoi, "Noblesse des conversos?" in Battesti-Pelegrin, *"Qu'un Sang Impur . . ."* 89–108. For a representative critique of "Anglo-Saxon" historiography on these grounds, albeit on a slightly different issue, see Mercedes García-Arenal and Béatrice Leroy, *Moros y judíos en Navarra en la baja Edad Media* (Madrid: Hiperion, 1984), 13–14. In *Inquisición y moriscos, los procesos del Tribunal de Cuenca*, 2nd ed. (Madrid: Siglo Veintiuno, 1983), 116, Mercedes García-Arenal suggests that although today anti-Muslim attitudes are racial, four centuries ago they were religious. On the question of an Anglo-American vision of Spanish history, see Ángel Galán Sánchez, *Una visión de la 'decadencia española': La historiografía anglosajona sobre mudéjares y moriscos, siglos XVIII–XX*, Colección "Monografías" 4 (Málaga: Servicio de Publicaciones, Diputación Provincial de Málaga, 1991). Nevertheless the word *raza* is still sometimes applied to the Jews by Spanish historians writing today, for example Ramón Gonzálvez Ruiz, "El Bachiller Palma y su obra de polémica proconversa," in Battesti-Pelegrin, *"Qu'un Sang Impur . . ."*, 48: "Palma . . . guarda una natural vinculación con los hombres de su raza convertidos al cristianismo."

30. On the racial nature of Renan's categories, see Shmuel Almog, "The Racial Motif to Renan's Attitude to Jews and Judaism," in *Antisemitism through the Ages* (Oxford: Pergamon Press, 1988), 255–78.

31. The quotes are from Américo Castro, *The Structure of Spanish History*, 542–43, 569. In a review of the Spanish version of the work (Castro, *España en su historia*) Yakov Malkiel rather mildly observed that Castro's approach resembled theories of cultural transmission discredited by association with National Socialism. Márquez Villanueva, on the other hand, praised precisely these pages as "the most acute and fruitful of [Castro's] oeuvre." See his "El problema de los conversos," 69. (The piece originally appeared in a Castro Festschrift in 1965.)

32. A convergence pointed out by Netanyahu in his *Toward the Inquisition*, chaps. 1 and 5. For a good example of Sánchez-Albornoz's agreement with Castro on this score, see Claudio Sánchez-Albornoz, *España: Un enigma histórico* (Buenos Aires: Editorial Sudamericana, 1962), 2:16, 255.

33. Thus Márquez Villanueva, seeking to prove that (*pace* Horace) the literary figure of the procuress or go-between is a "semitic" trope, writes of one author (Feliciano de Silva) that, although his ancestry is not certain, he "looks highly suspicious, given his marriage to a lady of known Jewish lineage and his life-long affinity with the *converso* literary milieu." See Francisco Márquez Villanueva, "*La Celestina* as Hispano-Semitic Anthropology," *Revue de Littérature Comparée* 61 (1987): 452, n. 2. The association of particular intellectual positions or literary interests with "judaizing," so prominent a feature of the Inquisition, has also become a prominent strategy of essentialization among a particular school of Spanish philologists in the United States.

34. Castro expressed surprise at this in his introduction to *The Spaniards*.

35. Ricardo del Arco Garay, for example, could speak of a "raza Aragonesa," and José Plá of a "raza hispánica" which encompassed all of Spain and Latin America. See Ricardo del Arco Garay, *Figuras Aragonesas: El genio de la raza* (Zaragoza: Tip. Heraldo de Aragón, 1923–26), and José Plá, ed., *La misión internacional de la raza hispánica* (Madrid: Javier Morata, 1928), just two among countless examples.

36. Juan de Mata Carriazo, ed., *El Victorial: Crónica de don Pero Niño, Conde de Buelna, por su alférez Gutierre Díez de Games* (Madrid: Espasa-Calpe, 1940), 17: "desde la muerte de Alexandre acá nunca traición se hizo que no fuese judío o su linaxe." For the dating of these lines, see p. xiii.

37. See Teodorico Borgognoni, "Libro de los Caballos," Ms. Escorial b-IV-31, in *Electronic Texts and Concordances, Madison Corpus of Early Spanish Manuscripts and Printings*, ed. John O'Neill (Madison, WI: Hispanic Seminary of Medieval Studies, 1999), CD-ROM: "La.x. titulo dela enfermedat. que dizen raza. // Faze se alos cauallos una malautia quel dizen Raça. Et faze se de sequedat dela unna." Gianfranco Contini gave a related etymology for *raza* in his "*Tombeau* de Leo Spitzer," in *Varianti e altra linguistica. Una raccolta di saggi (1938–1968)* (Turin: Einaudi, 1970), 651–60. There he argued that Spitzer's derivation of Romance *raza* from Latin *ratio* was incorrect, and drew the etymology instead from *haraz/haras*, the breeding of horses, the stallion's deposit.

38. Manuel Dies, "Libre de la menescalia," ca. 1424–36, Biblioteca General i Històrica de la Universitat de València, Ms. 631, llib. I (Libre de cavalls), cap. 1 (Com deu ésser engendrat cavall): "car no ha animal nengú [que] tant semble ne retraga al pare en les bondats hi en les bellees, ni en la talla, ni en lo pèl, e axí per lo contrari. Axí que cové qui vol haver bona raça o casta de cavalls que sobretot cerch lo guarà o stalló que sia bo e bell e de bon pèl, e la egua gran e ben formada e de bon pèl." There is a forthcoming edition by Lluís Cifuentes in the series *Els Nostres Clàssics*. For the Castilian translation, see Manuel Dies, *Libro de albeytería*, trans. Martín Martínez de Ampiés (1495; repr. Zaragoza: Pablo Hurus, 1499). There is a transcription of the 1499 edition by Antonio Cortijo and Ángel Gómez Moreno in the

Archivo digital de manuscritos y textos españoles [= ADMYTE] (Madrid, 1992), disc I, no. 32: lib. I (Libro de los cavallos), cap. 1 (En qué manera deve el cavallo ser engendrado): "El cavallo deve ser engendrado de garañón que haya buen pelo, y sea bien sano y muy enxuto de manos, canillas, rodillas y piedes. Y deve mirar en ésto mucho, que en él no haya mal vicio alguno, porque entre todos los animales no se falla otro que al padre tanto sea semejante en las bondades, belleza ni talle, ni en el pelo, y por el contrario en todo lo malo. Por ende, es muy necessario a qualquier persona que haver codicia raça o casta buena y fermosa cercar garañón muy escogido en pelo, tamaño y en la bondad, y la yegua creçida y bien formada y de buen pelo."

39. For an example of *raça* as referring to a defect in poetic performance, see Dutton and González Cuenca, *Cancionero*, Baena to Lando, no. 363, pp. 641–42: "Fernand manuel, por que versefique / donaires mi lengua sin raça e polilla, / sabed que vos mando de mula pardilla / dozena de festes en el quadruplique" (ll. 9–12. festes: horse turdlets). In early usages the word seems also to have designated sexual defects and was in this sense used to refer to procuresses and prostitutes. Cf. in the same *Cancionero*, no. 496 (p. 339, line 17) and (perhaps the earliest usage) no. 100, by Alfonso Álvarez de Villasandino (p. 127, line 10).

40. "Dezir de miçer Francisco a las syete virtudes," lines 393–400, in Dutton and González Cuenca, *Cancionero*, 316: "A los tus suçessores claro espejo / sera mira el golpe de la maça. / sera miral el cuchillo bermejo / que cortara doquier que falle Raza / . . . / biua el Rey do justiçia ensalça." Writing ca. 1432, Juan Alfonso de Baena also linked good kingship to the elimination of "raza": "quitastes / del reyno todas las raças." See his "Desir que fiso Juan Alfonso de Baena," 766, lines 1183–84. Against my view of this early association between *raza* and Judaism see María Rosa Lida, "Un decir más de Francisco Imperial: Respuesta a Fernán Pérez de Guzmán," *Nueva Revista de Filología Hispánica* 1 (1947): 170–77, and Leo Spitzer, "Ratio>Race," in *Essays in Historical Semantics* (New York: Russell & Russell, 1948), 47–69, cited therein. See also Joan Corominas and J. A. Pascual, *Diccionario crítico etimológico castellano e hispánico* (Madrid: Gredos, 1981), 4:800–802, sub "raza."

41. Alfonso Martínez de Toledo, *Arcipreste de Talavera o Corbacho*, chap. 18, 108–9. Cf. chap. 6 and chap. 7.

42. Of course much of this knowledge predated the Middle Ages, as a glance at Aristotle's *History of Animals* (7.6 on the resemblance of children to their parents, and cf. his *On the Generation of Animals* I.17–18), or Xenophon's *On Hunting* (III, VII on breeding of dogs), makes clear.

43. Sebastián de Covarrubias, *Tesoro de la lengua castellana o española* (Madrid: Por L. Sánchez, impressor del rey n.s., 1611) sub "raza": "La casta de cavallos castizos, a los quales señalan con hierro para que sean conocidos. . . . Raza, en los linages se toma en mala parte, como tener alguna raza de moro o judío." Examples of such usage are legion. A particularly famous one is that of Juan de Pineda, *Diálogos Familiares de la Agricultura Cristiana* (Salamanca: P. de Adurça y Diego López, 1589), vol. 2, xxi, sec. 14: "Ningún cuerdo quiere muger con raza de judía ni de marrana."

44. The topic of medieval knowledge about animal breeding is only now beginning to be studied. See, for example, Charles Gladitz, *Horse Breeding in the Medieval World* (Dublin: Four Courts Press, 1997). The well-known contribution of knowledge about animal breeding to the development of biological discourses about evolution in the eighteenth and nineteenth centuries suggests that for our purposes the topic would repay further research.

45. Jacobus Sadoletus, *De pueris recte ac liberaliter instituendis* (Basel, 1538), 2: "Maxime autem in hoc laudanda Francisci Regis nostri sapientia est, et consilium summo principe dignum, qui quod caeteri fere in equis et canibus, ipse praecipue in uiris facit, ut prouiden-

tiam omnem adhibeat, quo ex spectatis utrinque generibus electi in hoc sanctum foedus matrimonii conueniant, ut ex bonis parentibus nascatur progenies, que postea et Regi, et patriae possit esse utilis." Cited in Walz, "Der vormoderne Antisemitismus," 727. Joachim du Bellay, "Ample Discours au Roy sur le Faict des quatre Estats du Royaume de France," in *Oeuvres poétiques*, ed. Henry Chamard (Paris: Droz, 1931), 11:205, and Jouanna, *L'Idee de Race en France*, 3:1323: "Car si des bons chevaux et des bons chiens de chasse / Nous sommes si soigneux de conserver la race, / Combien plus doit un Roy soigneusement pourvoir / A la race, qui est son principal pouvoir?" I cite nonpeninsular texts in order to stress that, *pace* the Black Legend, there is nothing specifically Iberian about these strategies of naturalization. They are pan-European, as much Protestant as Catholic. See, for example, the citation from Martin Luther above.

46. ACA:C 3124:157r–v: "separatio aut differentia nulla fiat inter christianos a progenie seu natura et neophytos . . . et ex eis descendentes." The use of the word "by nature" to distinguish Old Christians was already common by this date.

47. See chap. 6.

48. See José María Casas Homs, ed., *La gaya ciencia de P. Guillén de Segovia* (Madrid: CSIC, 1962), sub "raça."

49. Marín Padilla, *Relación judeoconversa durante la segunda mitad del siglo XV en Aragón*, 60–67.

50. For a fuller exploration of the dialogic evolution of genealogical thinking among Jews, Christians, and converts, see chap. 7.

51. On these changing notions of nobility, see Rucquoi, "Noblesse des conversos?," 89–108, and "Etre noble en Espagne aux XIVᵉ-XVIᵉ siècles." On evolving chivalric ideology, see Jesús D. Rodríguez Velasco, *El debate sobre la caballería en el siglo xv: La tratadística caballeresca castellana en su marco europeo*, Colección de estudios de historia (Valladolid: Junta de Castilla y León, Consejería de Educación y Cultura, 1996).

52. Diego de Valera, *Espejo de la verdadera nobleza*, 102–3: "si los convertidos . . . retienen la nobleza de su linaje después de cristianos . . . en quál nasción tantos nobles fallarse pueden . . . Dios . . . el qual este linaje escogió para sí por el más noble?" The converts' possession of the blood of Jesus and Mary remained a standard argument in defense of converso rights well into the sixteenth century (more on this below). Apologizing for any embarrassment he might cause to the descendants of conversos, Joan Antonio Llorente, the author of the first critical history of the Inquisition, used the same argument to insist that such descent was cause not for shame but for pride. See Llorente, *Histoire critique de l'Inquisition*, 24.

53. On these events see chaps. 6 and 7.

54. The lines of difference between these various ways are, however, not always easy to establish. For the example of Pedro de la Caballería in 1459, see chap. 7, n. 35.

55. "Tratado del Alborayque," BNM Ms. 17567. The quote is from fol. 11r. For editions of this treatise, see chap. 7, note 67.

56. Once again these argumentative strategies seem to be quickly mirrored in Jewish sources. Shem Tov ben Joseph ibn Sem Tov, writing in the 1480s, made a similarly "metallurgical" argument: "If a person is of pure blood and has a noble lineage, he will give birth to a son like himself, and he who is ugly and stained (of blood?) will give birth to a son who is similar to him, for gold will give birth to gold and silver will give birth to silver and copper to copper, and if you find some rare instances that from lesser people sprang out greater ones, nevertheless in most cases what I have said is correct, and as you know, a science is not built on exceptions." Shem Tov, *Derashot*, 14a col. b, cited in Gutwirth, "Lineage in XVth Century Hispano-Jewish Thought," 88.

57. A number of polemics stressed the hybrid nature of the Jewish people. To the examples in chap. 7, n. 68, add the Castilian polemic written ca. 1370 but preserved in a fifteenth-century manuscript: "Coloquio entre un Cristiano y un Judío," Biblioteca del Palacio, Ms. 1344, fols. 106r–v (in the recent edition by García Moreno, pages, 154–55).

58. For Alonso de Espina, see chap. 7.

59. The arrival of the *Tratado del Alborayque* in Guadalupe, for example, provoked a bitter schism that was later remembered by the friars as the defining moment in relations between Old and New Christians in the monastery. See Gretchen Starr-Lebeau, *In the Shadow of the Virgin: Inquisitors, Friars, and Conversos in Guadalupe, Spain* (Princeton, NJ: Princeton University Press, 2003).

60. The scholarship on purity of blood statutes is too large to summarize here. Early and foundational contributions include Albert Sicroff, *Les controverses des statuts de "pureté de sang" en Espagne du xvᵉ au xviiᵉ siècle* (Paris: Didier, 1960); Domínguez Ortiz, *La clase social de los conversos en Castilla en la Edad Moderna*; I. S. Revah, "La controverse sur les statuts de pureté de sang," *Bulletin Hispanique* 63 (1971): 263–316.

61. Diego de Valera, "Espejo de la verdadera nobleza," 102–3, is an early example of such an argument. Alonso de Cartagena, *Defensorium unitatis christianae*, is another prominent example. The citation of Habakkuk is from Cardinal Juan de Torquemada, who then goes on to suggest that the converts deserve special honor because of the genealogy they share with Jesus. See Juan de Torquemada, *Tractatus contra Madianitas et Ismaelitas*, ed. Nicolás López Martínez and Vicente Proaño Gil Burgos (Burgos: Seminario Metropolitano de Burgos, 1957), 123.

62. Proverbially timorous: Alonso de Cartagena, *Defensorium unitatis christianae*, II.iv. 20, p. 215. This passage (as well as the next I will quote from Cartagena) is helpfully discussed (toward a different conclusion) in Bruce Rosenstock, *New Men: Conversos, Christian Theology, and Society in Fifteenth-Century Castile* (London: Queen Mary and Westfield College, 2002), 47–49. Marcos on "ruin linaxe": "El Memorial del bachiller Marcos García de Mora," 112. A few decades earlier, Saint Vincent Ferrer bemoaned that Christians would insult as "Jews" other Christians who refused to participate in violence or vengeance. See Saint Vincent Ferrer, *Sermons*, 1:42, 93, 155; 3:16; 5:190.

63. Alonso de Cartagena, *Defensorium unitatis christianae*, II.iv.20, p. 217.

64. There were other readings available, since Aristotle had said diverse things on the subject. In Politics 7.7, for example, he (like Hippocrates) put forward a more climatological model of courage according to which the cold regions of Europe produce fortitude (and therefore comparatively free peoples), whereas those who live in the warmth of Asia are more fearful and therefore "ruled and enslaved." Alonso de Cartagena, however, could not embrace such a climatological reading (*avant* Montesquieu) without calling into question crucial axioms of fifteenth-century Castilian aristocratic culture. On knowledge of Aristotle's politics in the fifteenth century, see Christoph Flüeler, *Rezeption und Interpretation der aristotelischen Politica im späten Mittelalter* (Amsterdam-Philadelphie: B. R. Grüner-J. Benjamins, 1992); and Anthony R. D. Pagden, "The diffusion of Aristotle's moral philosophy in Spain, ca. 1400-ca.1600," *Traditio* 31 (1975): 287–313.

65. On the relator and his warning, see chap. 7.

66. De Vocht, "Rodrigo Manrique's Letter to Vives," 435, and chap. 7.

67. A tendency as well represented in fifteenth-century Castile as in other times and places: see, for example, the "Invencionario of Alfonso de Toledo," BNP Ms. Esp. 204, fol. 1–105v.

68. Given Foucault's success in redefining the meaning of the term "genealogy," it is important to reiterate that here and throughout I am using the term "genealogical" in its traditional, non-Foucauldian sense.

69. "Suum autem est metaphorae modum locutionis a proprietate sui quasi detorquere, detorquando quadammodo innovare, innovando quasi nuptiali amictu tegere, tegendo quasi praecio dignitatis vendere." Mauro Inguanez and Henry M. Willard, eds., *Alberici Casinensis Flores rhetorici* (Montecassino: Miscellanea Cassinese, 1938), 45. For a modern statement of a similar epistemology, see Fitz John Porter Poole, "Metaphors and Maps: Towards Comparison in the Anthropology of Religion," *Journal of the American Academy of Religion* 54 (1986): 411–57.

70. As George Fredrikson implicitly suggests by beginning his *Racism: A Short History* (Princeton, NJ: Princeton University Press, 2002) with a treatment of "limpieza de sangre."

Chapter 9

1. Walter Benjamin, "Über den Begriff der Geschichte," thesis VII, in *Gesammelte Schriften*, ed. Rolf Tiedemann and Hermann Schweppenhäuser (Frankfurt: Suhrkamp, 1991), vol. 1 ("Abhandlungen"), 691–704.

2. In this chapter my focus is on triumphant dialectical teleologies that are European and Christian, but similar critiques could be made of, for example, many forms of Islamism today.

3. Huntington's thesis was first articulated in his "The Clash of Civilizations?" and subsequently expanded into Samuel Huntington, *The Clash of Civilizations and the Remaking of World Order* (New York: Simon & Schuster, 1996). For one of countless examples of anti-Huntingtonian arguments, see Edward Said, "The Clash of Definitions: On Samuel Huntington," in *Reflections on Exile and Other Essays* (Cambridge, MA: Harvard University Press, 2000), 569–92. Richard Bulliet takes a different tack in *The Case for Islamo-Christian Civilization* (New York: Columbia University Press, 2004).

4. When, for example, he asserted that "Islam has bloody borders" (Huntington, *Clash of Civilizations,* 262), he invoked statistics about contemporary conflicts, rather than making claims about Islam's historical propensity for violence.

5. This analysis of Pope Benedict's address proceeds from and expands my "What Benedict Really Said. Paleologus and Us," *New Republic*, October 10, 2006.

6. Benedict XVI, "Faith, Reason and the University: Memories and Reflections" (lecture, University of Regensburg, Regensburg, September 12, 2006), accessed September 16, 2006, http://www.vatican.va/holy_father/benedict_xvi/speeches/2006/september/documents/hf_ben-xvi_spe_20060912_university-regensburg_en.html. All references to the pope's Regensburg speech are to the version on the Vatican Web site. The current version on the site has been expanded, primarily by the addition of footnotes. There are no page divisions in the text, hence none in my citations from it.

7. Footnote 3 of the speech, added after the outbreak of the controversy and intended to absolve the pope from accusations of disrespect toward Islam, gives no ground on this essential point: "In the Muslim world, this quotation has unfortunately been taken as an expression of my personal position, thus arousing understandable indignation. I hope that the reader of my text can see immediately that this sentence does not express my personal view of the Qur'an, for which I have the respect due the holy book of a great religion. In quoting the text of the Emperor Manuel II, I intended solely to draw out the essential relationship between faith and reason. On this point I am in agreement with Manuel II, but without endorsing his polemic."

8. Adel Theodore Khoury, the editor of the translation of Paleologus used by the pope (*Manuel II Paléologue, Entretiens avec un Musulman, 7ᵉ Controverse*, Sources Chrétiennes 115 [Paris: Les Editions du Cerf, 1966], 144), also adduces Ibn Ḥazm as evidence for the truth of Paleologus's indictment, and it seems to be from Khoury's notes that the pope's knowledge of

the Muslim scholar derives. Of course from a historian's point of view it seems absurd to attempt to confirm a fourteenth-century Orthodox Christian's characterization of Islam by citing one eleventh-century Muslim, and even more absurd to choose Ibn Ḥazm, whose Zahiri school of literalist exegesis was extreme within Islam. We might as well choose the words of a Cathar scholar with which to characterize Counter-Reformation Catholicism!

9. Note that Ratzinger is not arguing, as Kant had, that Jesus's teachings were not Jewish but Greek: occidental wisdom merely clothed in Jewish garb (see *Reflexionen Kants zur Anthropologie, Aus Kants handschriftlichen Aufzeichnungen*, ed. Benno Erdmann [Leipzig: Fues' Verlag, 1882], 213–14). Rather he is claiming, as the mature Hegel did, that the Gospels were a synthesis of the two cultures. We will briefly trace Hegel's position below.

10. Matthew Arnold, *Culture and Anarchy* (London: Smith, Elder & Co., 1869). On this strand see Lionel Gossman, "Philhellenism and Antisemitism: Matthew Arnold and His German Models," *Comparative Literature* 46 (1994): 1–39. Heine's words are cited by Gossman at p. 17, from "Ludwig Börne. Eine Denkschrift." For Heine's awareness that this "fusion" might be anything but "harmonious," see David Nirenberg, *Anti-Judaism: the Western Tradition* (New York: W. W. Norton, 2013), chap. 12. I will use Hegel's example to demonstrate some of the potential violence below.

11. It may be unnecessary to note that Benedict's "logos" is not the entire "breadth of reason," but a specifically Christian form of reason that from its very first articulation in the Gospel of John 1:1–13 was already very much concerned with identifying its "Jewish" enemies. (Although the word "Jew" appears in John more than sixty times, Jews were not that gospel's only targets. For others, see, inter alia, Elaine Pagels, *Beyond Belief: The Secret Gospel of Thomas* [New York: Random House, 2003].) As for my simile of deceitful banquets, I hasten to add that we find these in the annals of Islamic as well as Germanic civilizations, and indeed in many others.

12. Georg Wilhelm Friedrich Hegel, "The Spirit of Christianity and Its Fate" was first published by Herman Nohl in *Hegels theologische Jugendschriften* (Tübingen: J. C. B. Mohr, 1907), and translated into English by T. J. Knox in *Early Theological Writings* (Chicago: University of Chicago Press, 1948; repr., Philadelphia: University of Pennsylvania Press, 1975), 182–301. All citations are from the Knox translation.

13. Hegel, *Early Theological Writings*, 185–87; see also pp. 194, 196, 199, 202, and passim. Hegel's interpretation of Abraham's self-sufficient isolation was no doubt conditioned by his reading of Aristotle's *Politics*, 1253a, 25ff. As for "love," it played an important role in Hegel's philosophy, and his frequent stress on the "lovelessness" of the Jews is therefore significant. Readers interested in exploring that significance can turn to Joseph Cohen, *Le spectre juif de Hegel* (Paris: Galilée, 2005).

14. Hegel, *Early Theological Writings*, 212.

15. "Fulfillment" = Gk. *pleroma*: 214, 253.

16. Hegel, *Early Theological Writings*, 240–41, citing John 2:25.

17. Ibid., 282.

18. Ibid., 259.

19. Ibid., 301. Hegel makes a related point in the last section of his *Lectures on the Philosophy of History*, "The Modern Time," where he asserts that once it becomes established, every "Ecclesiastical principle" contains within its bosom the negative principles of "slavish deference to Authority," the "adamantine bondage" of the Spirit to what is "alien to itself," "hypocrisy," etc. (413). He goes on to argue, however, that some peoples are more given to this alienation than others, namely the "Romanic nations": "Italy, Spain, Portugal, and in part France" (420).

20. *"Imitatio Christi"*: Cf. Werner Hamacher, *Pleroma: Reading in Hegel. The Genesis and Structure of a Dialectical Hermeneutics in Hegel*, trans. Nicholas Walker and Simon Jarvis (London: Athlone Press, 1998), 199–200, which concludes on the basis of the *Encyclopedia* and the *Philosophy of Religion* that for Hegel "all of world history is an *imitatio Christi*." "It is in connection . . .": Hegel, *Lectures on the Philosophy of Religion*, ed. and trans. Peter C. Hodgson (Berkeley: University of California Press, 1984), 325–26. Cf. Hegel, *Phenomenology of Spirit*, ed. and trans. A.V. Miller (Oxford: Clarendon Press, 1977), 470–78. Hegel's attempt in the *Philosophy of Religion* to demonstrate the rational structure of all reality can also be understood as his demonstration of reality's Trinitarian structure, since for Hegel reason was dialectical, and dialectic was Trinitarian. See, for example, Peter C. Hodgson's "Editorial Introduction," to the Lectures of 1827, 63.

21. Hegel, G.W.F. *Hegel: The Philosophy of History*, trans. J. Sibree, from the 2nd edition (New York: Collier & Son, 1902), 355–60 (Goethe's *West-östlicher Divan* is mentioned as the heir to Arabic poetry on p. 360).

22. Hegel, *Lectures on the Philosophy of Religion*, 3:35, 242–44. These pages from the 1824 lectures were not carried over into those of 1827, which have virtually nothing to say about Islam.

23. *"Verworfenste"*: the term occurs both in Hegel, *Phenomenology of Spirit*, 206; Hegel, *Phänomenologie des Geistes*, ed. J. Hoffmeister (Hamburg: Felix Meiner, 1952), 257, and in the *Lectures* (see Hegel, *Lectures on the Philosophy of Religion*, 2:15). For debate over its meaning, cf. Yirmiyahu Yovel, *Dark Riddle: Hegel, Nietzsche, and the Jews* (Cambridge: Polity Press, 1998), 55, and Michael Mack, *German Idealism and the Jew* (Chicago: University of Chicago Press, 2002), 53–54. It should be clear that I do not think, as Yovel does, that because the Berlin lectures on religion "recognize Judaism's essential contributions" and "thereby, do dialectical justice to it," the mature Hegel has "overcome the principal bias of his youth" (ibid., 80). He has simply brought the place of Judaism in his dialectic into closer conformity with its place in Lutheran Christology and thereby done "justice" to Lutheran Christianity, not to Judaism.

24. I pick on the pope because he has been a particularly articulate advocate of this type of ontologically and teleologically laden "clash" paradigm, but I do not mean to imply that this type is exclusive to Catholicism, to Christianity, or to the West. On the contrary, there are plenty of variants within contemporary Islam, Hinduism, Judaism, and other religions, and even within secular movements ranging from neoliberalism to antiglobalization.

25. On al-Jahiz, see Dmitri Gutas, *Greek Thought, Arabic Culture: The Graeco-Arabic Translation Movement in Baghdad and Early 'Abbasid Society* (London: Routledge, 1998), 84–87.

26. Petrarch, *Invective contra medicum*. For an introduction to these early defenses of vernacular poetry, see Minnis, "The Transformation of Critical Tradition: Dante, Petrarch, and Boccaccio." On humanistic associations of certain medical traditions with Islam, see Peter Dilig, "Anti-Arabism in the Medicine of Humanism," in *La diffusione delle scienze islamiche nel Medio Evo europeo*, ed. Biancamaria Scarcia (Rome: Accademia nazionale dei Lincei, 1987), 269–89.

27. María Rosa Menocal, "Pride and Prejudice in Medieval Studies: European and Oriental," *Hispanic Review* 53 (1985): 61.

28. María Rosa Menocal, *The Arabic Role in Medieval Literary History: A Forgotten Heritage* (Philadelphia: University of Pennsylvania Press, 1987), and *The Ornament of the World: How Muslims, Jews and Christians Created a Culture of Tolerance in Medieval Spain* (Boston: Little, Brown, 2002).

29. The claim that this dialectic of identity and difference is peculiarly European seems to animate Roberto M. Dainotto's *Europe (in Theory)* (Durham, NC: Duke University Press, 2007).

30. It is worth reiterating here that the paradigm for medieval Christian poetic theory was the "dialectic" of Trinity, Logos, and Incarnation, not that of Hegelian philosophy. For my own quite different version of the importance of Judaism as a foil for Christian vernacular poetics, see chap. 6.

31. Giammaria Barbieri, *Dell'origine della poesia rimata*, ed. Girolamo Tiraboschi (Modena: Società tipografica, 1790), 41. On Barbieri's thesis see most recently Roberto M. Dainotto, "Of the Arab Origins of Modern Europe: Giammaria Barbieri, Juan Andrés, and the Origin of Rhyme," *Comparative Literature* 58 (2006): 271–92, whose arguments I am adapting here.

32. Barbieri, *Dell'origine*, 40–44. Barbieri's mention of the writings of Jews from al-Andalus points to an important and seldom-noted analogue to discussions of Arabic poetics in early modern Christian sources, because the Jews of al-Andalus were acutely aware of their poetry's debt to Arabic poetics. On their writings see Esperanza Alfonso, *Islamic Culture through Jewish Eyes: Al-Andalus from the Tenth to the Twelfth Century* (London: Routledge, 2007).

33. Joachim du Bellay, *Deffence et illustration de la langue françoyse*, ed. Henri Chamard (Paris: M. Didier, 1997), 151. Pierre-Daniel Huet, *Traité de l'origine des romans* (Stuttgart: Metzler, 1966), 15. "Risorgimento": Juan Andrés, *Dell'origine, progressi e stato attuale d'ogni letteratura*, 2nd ed. (Parma: Stamperia reale 1785–1822), 1:261. On the debate between Andrés and Arteaga see Dainotto, "Of the Arab Origins of Modern Europe," 280–86.

34. Esteban de Arteaga, *Le rivoluzioni del teatro musicale italiano dalla sua origine fino al presente*, 2nd ed. (Venice: Stamperia di C. Palese, 1785), 1:168, cited by Dainotto, "Of the Arab Origins," 284–85.

35. Madame de Staël, *De la littérature considérée dans ses rapports avec les institutions sociales*, ed. Gérard Gengembre and Jean Goldink (Paris: Flammarion, 1991): "progress of the human spirit," 120; "Christian religion . . . has melted, so to speak, two opposed customs into one opinion," 168–69. De Staël's distinction between mimetic (Greek) and sentimental (German) poetry was very much in the air. See, by way of comparison, Friedrich Schiller's essay of 1800, "Über naive und sentimentalische Dichtung." Her view of Christianity as the synthesizing element of Europe was also shared by, among others, Novalis (Friedrich Leopold von Hardenberg), whose "Die Christenheit oder Europe: Ein Fragment" appeared in 1799.

36. Sismonde de Sismondi, *De la littérature du midi de l'Europe* (Paris: Treuttel & Wurtz, 1819), 1:10, 40–77. "Enivrement d'amour" is at p. 66.

37. Johann Gottfried Herder, *Briefe zu Berförderung der Humanität*, ed. Hans Dietrich Irmscher, *Johann Gottfried Herder: Werke 7* (Frankfurt: Deutscher Klassiker Verlag, 1991), 470: "Spanien war die glückliche Gegend, wo für Europa der erste Funke einer wiederkommenden Kultur schlug, die sich denn auch nach dem Ort und der Zeit gestalten mußte, in denen sie auflebte. Die Geschichte davon lautet wie ein angenehmes Märchen." See also 475.

38. August Wilhelm von Schlegel, *Observations sur la langue et la littérature provençales* (Paris: Librairie grecque-latine-allemande, 1818), 67–69.

39. The literature on the development of the concept of Europe is vast. A recent work, whose chapter 4 ("Mme de Staël to Hegel: the End of French Europe") covers much of the ground retraced here is Dainotto's *Europe (in Theory)*. Although I only encountered this book after drafting this chapter, I have attempted to incorporate its observations on the Coppet circle into my analysis. Among many other works, see Denys Hay, *Europe: The Emergence of an Idea* (Edinburgh: Edinburgh University Press, 1957); and Anthony Pagden, "Europe: Conceptualizing a Continent," in *The Idea of Europe: From Antiquity to the European Union*, ed. Anthony Pagden (Washington: Woodrow Wilson Centre Press, 2002), 33–54.

40. Thus Menocal believes that the Arab theory of the origin of rhyme was regnant in Europe until the beginning of the nineteenth century, when it became "inconceivable" to Europeans and was repressed. See Menocal, "Pride and Prejudice," as well as her "Close Encounters in Medieval Provence: Spain's Role in the Birth of Troubadour Poetry," *Hispanic Review* 49 (1981): 43–64. This last was an extended review of Roger Boase's *The Origins and Meaning of Courtly Love: A Critical Study of European Scholarship* (Manchester: Manchester University Press, 1977). It may well be that, as Boase argued, the second half of the nineteenth century saw a decline in popularity for the Arab thesis, but there was never a period in which it lacked some distinguished proponent, such as Julián Ribera in the early twentieth century, or Ramón Menéndez Pidal and A. R. Nykl in the 1930s and 1940s. For some additional examples, see the bibliography in Nykl's *Hispano-Arabic Poetry and Its Relations with the Old Provençal Troubadours* (Baltimore: Johns Hopkins University Press, 1946).

41. Salma Khadra Jayyusi, ed., *The Legacy of Muslim Spain* (1992; repr. Leiden: Brill, 1994).

42. Ibid., xi.

43. Ibid., xvii.

44. References to the present political situation seem irresistible to those attracted to "the wonders" of al-Andalus. Thus Georg Bossong writes in the introduction to his recent collection of poetry from Al-Andalus: "Die Symbiose von arabischer und hebräischer Sprachkultur, von muslimischem und jüdischem Geist bringt Wunder hervor - ihre Konfrontation kann nur Ungeheuer gebären." Georg Bossong, ed. and trans., *"Das Wunder von al-Andalus": Die schönsten Gedichte aus dem Maurischen Spanien* (Munich: C. H. Beck, 2005).

45. Jayyusi, *The Legacy of Muslim Spain*, xix.

46. This, at least, was the conclusion of Henri Pérès, *L'Espagne vue par les voyageurs musulmans de 1610 à 1930* (Paris: Librairie d'Amérique et d'Orient, 1937). Pérès published in the same year a book that suggested the Arabic origins of troubadour poetry: *La poésie andalouse en arabe classique du XIe siècle* (Paris: Librairie d'Amérique et d'Orient, Adrien-Maisonneuve, 1937). Pérès's conclusions are noteworthy, but there were also important Arabic literary traditions about al-Andalus that deserve attention. See, for example, Alexander E. Elinson, *Looking Back at al-Andalus: The Poetics of Loss and Nostalgia in Medieval Arabic and Hebrew Literature* (Leiden: Brill, 2009). Within post-1492 Arabic letters Aḥmad ibn Muḥammad al-Maqqarī was the key figure in the compilation and transmission of material on al-Andalus, most notably in his *Nafḥ al-ṭīb: Min ghuṣn al-Andalus al-raṭīb* (Beirut: Dār Ṣādir, 1968).

47. On these translations see Bernard Lewis, *Islam in History: Ideas, Men, and Events in the Middle East* (London: Alcove Press, 1973), and *History: Remembered, Recovered, Invented* (Princeton, NJ: Princeton University Press, 1975).

48. I have benefited a good deal from a similar argument made by Siegfried Kohlhammer, "'Ein angenehmes Märchen': Die Wiederentdeckung und Neugestaltung des muslimischen Spanien," *Merkur: Deutsche Zeitschrift für europäisches Denken* 57 (2003): 595–608. On the recovery of the theme of al-Andalus in Arabic poetry of the early twentieth century, see Yaseen Noorani, "The Lost Garden of al-Andalus: Islamic Spain and the Poetic Inversion of Colonialism," *International Journal of Middle East Studies* 31 (1999): 237–54; and Pedro Martínez Montavez, *Al-Andalus, España, en la literatura árabe contemporánea: La casa del pasado* (Madrid: Editorial Mapfre, 1992).

49. On this subject, see, inter alia, Michael Scholz-Hänsel, "'Antigüedades Arabes de España': Wie die einst vertriebenen Mauren Spanien zu einer Wiederentdeckung im 19. Jahrhundert verhalfen," in *Europa und der Orient: 800–1900*, ed. Gereon Sievernich and Hendrik Budde (Berlin: Berliner Festspiele, 1989), 368–82. On the shifting interest of Europe in Spanish history more generally, see Hans Hinterhäuser, ed., *Spanien und Europa:*

Texte zu ihrem Verhältnis von der Aufklärung bis zur Gegenwart (Munich: Deutscher Taschenbuch Verlag, 1979); W. Brüggemann, *Die Spanienberichte des 18. und 19. Jahrhunderts und ihre Bedeutung für die Formung und Wandlung des deutschen Spanienbildes* (Münster: Aschendorff, 1956). For Spanish scholarship on Islam, see the invaluable book of James T. Monroe, *Islam and the Arabs in Spanish Scholarship (Sixteenth Century to the Present)* (Leiden: Brill, 1970). A more general approach to these questions can also be found in Siegfried Kohlhammer, *Die Feinde und die Freunde des Islam* (Göttingen: Steidl, 1996).

50. Two caveats: first, the Christians were not numerically a minority in the first century of Muslim domination. Second, the term "golden age" was not a monopoly of Jewish writers (the Protestant Franz Delitzch, for example, used it in his *Zur Geschichte der jüdischen Poesie* [Leipzig: Karl Tauchnitz, 1836]). The idea saw its greatest development, however, in Jewish historiography.

51. Norman Stillman, "Myth, Countermyth, and Distortion," *Tikkun* 6, no. 3 (May–June, 1991): 60–64. Stillman's essay is part of a debate with Mark Cohen, whose fullest response can be found in Cohen, *Under Crescent and Cross: The Jews in the Middle Ages* (Princeton, NJ: Princeton University Press, 1994). See also Ismar Schorsch, "The Myth of Sephardic Supremacy," *Leo Baeck Institute Year Book* 34 (1989): 47–66.

52. For the publication history of Roth's essay, which first appeared in the Zionist Organization of America's *New Palestine* on October 4, 1946, and was reprinted in the 1967 *Near East Report* and repeatedly thereafter, see Cohen, *Under Crescent and Cross*, 9–10.

53. "The Covenant of the Islamic Resistance Movement," August 18, 1988, *The Avalon Project: Documents in Law, History and Diplomacy*, http://www.yale.edu/lawweb/avalon/mideast/hamas.htm. For a slightly different translation see "The Charter of Allah: The Platform of the Islamic Resistance Movement (Hamas)," *The Jerusalem Fund*, http://www.palestinecenter.org/cpap/documents/charter.html.

BIBLIOGRAPHY OF WORKS CITED

Abellán, José Luis. "Función cultural de la presencia judía en España." In Judíos, sefarditas, conversos: La expulsión de 1492 y sus consecuencias, edited by Ángel Alcalá, 395–407. Valladolid: Ambito, 1995.

Aboab, Isaac. "Almenara de la Luz." In Antología Sefardí, 1492–1700, edited by María del Carmen Artigas, 272–94. Madrid: Verbum, 1997.

———. Menorat ha-Ma'or. Jerusalem: Mossad Harav Kook, 1961.

Abou el-Fadl, Khaled. "Islamic Law and Muslim Minorities." Islamic Law and Society 1, no. 2 (1994): 141–87.

Abulafia, David. "The Crown and the Economy under Ferrante I of Naples." In Commerce and Conquest in the Mediterranean, 1100–1500, 125–46. Aldershot: Variorum, 1993.

———. "Monarchies and Minorities in the Christian Western Mediterranean around 1300: Lucera and Its Analogues." In Christendom and Its Discontents: Exclusion, Persecution, and Rebellion, 1000–1500, edited by Scott L. Waugh and Peter D. Diehl, 234–63. Cambridge: Cambridge University Press, 1996.

———. "Nam iudei servi regis sunt, et semper fisco regio deputati: The Jews in the Municipal Fuero of Teruel (1176–7)." In Jews, Muslims, and Christians in and around the Crown of Aragon: Essays in Honour of Professor Elena Lourie, edited by Harvey J. Hames, 97–123. Leiden: Brill, 2004.

———. "The Role of the Jews in the Cultural Life of the Kingdom of Naples." In Gli Ebrei in Sicilia dal tardoantico al medioevo: Studi in onore di Mons. Benedetto Rocco, edited by Nicolò Bucaria, 35–53. Palermo: Flaccovio, 1998.

Adang, Camilla. Muslim Writers on Judaism and the Hebrew Bible: From Ibn Rabban to Ibn Hazm. New York: E. J. Brill, 1996.

Adroer i Tasis, Anna M. "La possessio de lleons, simbol de poder." In XV Congreso de Historia de la Corona de Aragon (Jaca, September 20–25, 1993), vol. 1, pt. 3, 257–68. Zaragoza: Gobierno de Aragón, 1996.

Aegidius Romanus. De regimine principum libri III. Rome, 1607. Reprint, Aalen, 1967.

Aizenberg, Edna. "Una judía muy fermosa: The Jewess as Sex Object in Medieval Spanish Literature and Lore." La Corónica 12 (1984): 187–94.

Alfonso, Esperanza. Islamic Culture through Jewish Eyes: Al-Andalus from the Tenth to the Twelfth Century. London: Routledge, 2007.

Alfonso de Madrigal. Opera Omnia. 15 vols. Venice, 1507–30.

Alfonso de Palencia. Crónica de Enrique IV. 3 vols. Biblioteca de autores españoles 228. Madrid: M. Rivadeneyra, 1973–75.

Alfonso X, el Sabio. Cantigas de Santa María, de Don Alfonso el Sabio. 2 vols. Madrid: Real Academia Española, 1889.

———. Siete Partidas del Rey Don Alfonso el Sabio. 3 vols. Madrid: Real Academia de la Historia, 1807.

Almog, Shmuel. "The Racial Motif to Renan's Attitude to Jews and Judaism." In Antisemitism through the Ages, 255–78. Oxford: Pergamon Press, 1988.

Alonso de Cartagena. Defensorium unitatis christianae. Edited by P. Manuel Alonso. Madrid: Escuela de Estudios Hebraicos, 1943.

———. Discurso sobre la preeminencia. Biblioteca de Autores Españoles 116. Madrid: M. Rivadeneyra, 1959.

Alonso de Espina, Fortalitium fidei, Consideratio. Nuremberg: Antonius Koberger, 1494.

Alphandéry, Paul. La chrétienté et l'idée de croisade. Edited by Alphonse Dupront. 2 vols. Paris: Éditions Albin Michel, 1959.

Amador de los Ríos, José. Estudios históricos, políticos y literarios sobre los judíos en España. Madrid: D. M. Diaz, 1848.

Ambrose. Epistulae et acta, vol. 3. Edited by Otto Faller and Michaela Zelzer. Corpus Scriptorum Ecclesiasticorum Latinorum 82.1–4. Vienna: F. Tempsky, 1968–96.

———. Sancti Ambrosi Opera. Edited by Michaela Zelzer. Corpus Scriptorum Ecclesiasticorum Latinorum 82.3. Vienna: Hoelder-Pichler-Tempsky, 1982.

Andrés, Juan. Dell'origine, progressi e stato attuale d'ogni letteratura. 2nd ed. 8 vols. Parma: Stamperia reale, 1785–1822.

Arbós, Cristina. "Los cancioneros castellanos del siglo xv como fuente para la historia de los judíos españoles." In Jews and Conversos: Studies in Society and the Inquisition, edited by Yosef Kaplan, 74–82. Jerusalem: World Union of Jewish Studies, 1985.

Arco Garay, Ricardo del. Figuras Aragonesas: El genio de la raza. Zaragoza: Tip. Heraldo de Aragón, 1923–26.

Arnold, Matthew. Culture and Anarchy. London: Smith, Elder & Co., 1869.

Arteaga, Esteban de. Le rivoluzioni del teatro musicale italiano dalla sua origine fino al presente. 2nd ed. 3 vols. Venice: Stamperia di C. Palese, 1785.

Ashurst, David. "Masculine Postures and Poetic Gambits: The Treatment of the Soldadeira in the Cantigas d'Escarnho e de mal dezir." Bulletin of Hispanic Studies 74 (1997): 1–6.

Assis, Yom Tov. "Sexual Behavior in Mediaeval Hispano-Jewish Society." In Jewish History: Essays in Honour of Chimen Abramsky, edited by Ada Rapaport-Albert and Steven Zipperstein, 25–59. London: Peter Halban, 1988.

Assmann, Aleida. Erinnerungsräume: Formen und Wandlungen des kulturellen Gedächtnisses. Munich: C. H. Beck, 1999.

Assmann, Jan. Das kulturelle Gedächtnis: Schrift, Erinnerung und politische Identität in frühen Hochkulturen. Munich: C. H. Beck, 1992.

Assmann, Jan, and Aleida Assmann. Aby Warburg. Ausgewählte Schriften und Würdigungen. Edited by D. Wuttke and C. G. Heise. Baden-Baden: Verlag V. Koerner, 1979.

Auerbach, Erich. "Figura." In Neue Dantestudien, 11–71. Instabuler Schriften 5. Istanbul: Ibrahim Horoz Basımevi, 1944.

———. Scenes from the Drama of European Literature. Trans. Ralph Mannheim. New York: Meridian Books, 1959. Reprint, Minneapolis: University of Minnesota Press, 1984.

Avalle Arce, Juan Bautista. "Sobre Juan Alfonso de Baena." Revista de filología hispánica 8 (1946): 141–47.

Azáceta, José María. Cancionero. Clásicos Hispánicos 2/10. 3 vols. Madrid: Consejo Superior de Investigaciones Científicas, 1966.

Badiou, Alain. L'Être et l'événement. Paris: Éditions du Seuil, 1988.

Baer, Yitzhak. A History of the Jews in Christian Spain. 2 vols. Philadelphia: Jewish Publication Society of America, 1978.

———. Die Juden im christlichen Spanien. 2 vols. Berlin: Akademie-Verlag, 1936.

Bagby, Albert. "Alfonso X el Sabio compara moros y judíos." Romanische Forschungen 82 (1970): 578–83.

———. "The Jew in the Cantigas of Alfonso X el Sabio." Speculum 46 (1971): 670–88.

———. "The Moslem in the Cantigas of Alfonso X el Sabio." Kentucky Romance Quarterly 20 (1973): 173–207.

Banogh, J., ed. Libellus de institutione morum. Scriptores rerum Hungaricarum 2. Budapest: Academia Litter. Hungarica, 1938.

Banton, Michael. Racial Theories. 2nd ed. Cambridge: Cambridge University Press, 1998.

Barbieri, Giammaria. Dell'origine della poesia rimata. Edited by Girolamo Tiraboschi. Modena: Società tipografica, 1790.

Barceló, Carmen, ed. Un tratado Catalán medieval de derecho islámico: El llibre de la çuna e xara de los moros. Córdoba: Universidad de Córdoba, 1989.

Bar-Itzhak, Haya. Jewish Poland: Legends of Origin. Detroit: Wayne State University Press, 2001.

Baron, Salo. Modern Nationalism and Religion. New York: Harper, 1947.

———. A Social and Religious History of the Jews. 18 vols. New York: Columbia University Press, 1969.

Bartlett, Robert. The Making of Europe: Conquest, Colonization, and Cultural Change, 950–1350. Princeton, NJ: Princeton University Press, 1993.

———. "Medieval and Modern Concepts of Race and Identity." Journal of Medieval and Early Modern Studies 31 (2001): 39–56.

———. Trial by Fire and Water: The Medieval Judicial Ordeal. Oxford: Clarendon Press, 1986.

Basnage, Jacques. Historie des juifs, nouvelle edition augmentée. 15 vols. The Hague: Henri Scheurleer, 1716.

Bataillon, Marcel. Erasmo y España. 2 vols. Mexico City: Fondo de Cultura Económica, 1950.

Batlle y Prats, Luis. "Un episodio de la persecución judía de 1391." In Per a una història de la Girona jueva, vol. 2, edited by David Romano, 614–17. Girona: Ajuntament de Girona, 1988.

Battesti-Pelegrin, Jeanne. "Qu'un sang impur . . .": Les Conversos et le pouvoir en Espagne à la fin du moyen âge; actes du 2ème colloque d'Aix-en-Provence, 18–19–20 novembre 1994. Aix-en-Provence: Publications de l'Université de Provence, 1997.

Beinart, Haim. Conversos on Trial. Jerusalem: Magnes Press, 1981.

———, ed. Moreshet Sepharad: The Sephardi Legacy. 2 vols. Jerusalem: Magnes Press, 1992.

———, ed. Records of the Trials of the Spanish Inquisition in Ciudad Real I (1483–85). 4 vols. Jerusalem: Israel National Academy of Sciences and Humanities, 1974–85.

Beltrán de Heredia, Vicente. "Las bulas de Nicolás V acerca de los conversos de Castilla." Sefarad 21 (1961): 22–47.

———. "San Vicente Ferrer, predicador de las sinagogas." In Miscelánea Beltrán de Heredia, 225–233. Salamanca: Editorial OPE, 1972.

Benedict XVI. "Faith, Reason and the University: Memories and Reflections." Lecture, University of Regensburg, Regensburg, September 12, 2006. http://www.vatican.va/holy_father/benedict_xvi/speeches/2006/september/documents/hf_ben-xvi_spe_20060912_university-regensburg_en.html.

Benito Ruano, Eloy. "D. Pero Sarmiento, repostero mayor de Juan II de Castilla." Hispania 17 (1957): 483–504.

———. "El Memorial del bachiller Marcos García de Mora contra los conversos." In Los orígenes del problema converso, 95–132. Barcelona: El Albir, 1976.

———. Los orígenes del problema converso. Barcelona: El Albir, 1976.

———. "La Sentencia-Estatuto de Pero Sarmiento contra los conversos toledanos." Revista de la Universidad de Madrid 6 (1957): 277–306.

Benjamin, Walter. "Delirium." In The Origins of German Tragic Drama, translated by John Osborne, 53–54. London: Verso, 1977.

———. Gesammelte Schriften. Edited by Rolf Tiedemann and Hermann Schweppenhäuser. 7 vols. Frankfurt: Suhrkamp, 1972–92.

———. "Über den Begriff der Geschichte." In Gesammelte Schriften, edited by Rolf Tiedemann and Hermann Schweppenhäuser, vol. 1, 691–704. Frankfurt: Suhrkamp, 1991.

———. Ursprung des deutschen Trauerspiels. In Gesammelte Schriften, vol. 1, 203–430. Frankfurt: Suhrkamp Verlag, 1974.

Benton, John F. Self and Society in Medieval France. The Memoirs of Abbot Guibert of Nogent. New York: Harper & Row, 1970.

Berend, Nora. At the Gates of Christendom: Jews, Muslims, and Pagans in Medieval Hungary, c. 1000–c. 1300. Cambridge: Cambridge University Press, 2001.

Berger, David. "On the Uses of History in Medieval Jewish Polemic against Christianity: The Quest for the Historical Jesus." In Jewish History and Jewish Memory: Essays in Honor of Yosef Hayim Yerushalmi, edited by Elisheva Carlebach, John M. Efron, and David N. Myers, 25–39. Hanover: University Press of New England for Brandeis University Press, 1998.

Bernáldez, Andrés. Historia de los Reyes Católicos don Fernando y doña Isabel. In Crónicas de los reyes de Castilla desde don Alfonso el Sabio, hasta los católicos don Fernando y doña Isabel. Biblioteca de Autores Españoles 70. Madrid: M. Rivadeneyra, 1878.

Bernardete, Mair J. Hispanic Culture and Character of the Sephardic Jews. New York: Hispanic Institute, 1953.

Bhabha, Homi K. "Difference, Discrimination and the Discourse of Colonialism." In The Politics of Theory: Proceedings of the Essex Conference on the Sociology of Literature, edited by Francis Barker Peter Hulme, Margaret Iverson, and Dianna Loxley, 194–211. Colchester: University of Essex, 1983.

Biddick, Kathleen. "The Cut of Genealogy: Pedagogy in the Blood." Journal of Medieval and Early Modern Studies 30 (Fall, 2000): 449–62.

Bizzarri, Hugo Oscar, ed. Castigos del rey don Sancho IV. Madrid: Iberiamericana, 2001.

Blackmore, Josiah, and Gregory S. Hutcheson, eds. Queer Iberia: Sexualities, Cultures, and Crossings from the Middle Ages to the Renaissance. Durham, NC: Duke University Press, 1999.

Blasco Martínez, Asunción. "La casa de fieras de la Aljafería de Zaragoza y los judíos." In XV Congreso de Historia de la Corona de Aragón, I: El poder real en la Corona de Aragón, siglos XIV–XVI. 5 vols. Zaragoza: Gobierno de Aragón, 1996.

Blecua, Alberto. "'Perdióse un quaderno . . .': Sobre los cancioneros de Baena." Anuario de estudios medievales 9 (1974–79): 229–66.

Blumenbach, Johann Friedrich. De generis humani varietate nativa [On the Natural Varieties of Mankind]. Gottingen: Vandenhoek & Ruprecht, 1795.

Boas, Franz. "History and Science in Anthropology: A Reply." American Anthropologist 38 (1936): 137–41.

Boase, Roger. The Origins and Meaning of Courtly Love: A Critical Study of European Scholarship. Manchester: Manchester University Press, 1977.

Boccaccio, Giovanni. Geneologia deorum gentilium libri. Edited by Vincenzo Romano. Scrittore d'Italia, 200–201. Bari: Laterza, 1951.

Bodian, Miriam. "'Men of the Nation': The Shaping of Converso Identity in Early Modern Europe." Past and Present, no. 143 (May 1994): 48–76.

Bonfil, Robert. "The History of the Spanish and Portuguese Jews in Italy." In Moreshet Sepharad: The Sephardi Legacy, edited by Haim Beinart, 2:217–39. Jerusalem: Magnes Press, 1992.

———. "Jewish Attitudes toward History and Historical Writing in Pre-Modern Times." Jewish History 11 (1997): 7–40.

Borafull y Mascaró, Próspero de, Manuel de Borafull y de Sartorio, and Francisco de Asís de Borafull y Sans, eds. Colección de documentos inéditos del Archivo General de la Corona de Aragón. 41 vols. Barcelona: J. E. Montfort, 1847–1910.

Borgognoni, Teodorico. "Libro de los Caballos." Ms. Escorial b-IV-31. In Electronic Texts and Concordances, Madison Corpus of Early Spanish Manuscripts and Printings, edited by John O'Neill. Madison, WI: Hispanic Seminary of Medieval Studies, 1999. CD-ROM.

Bossong, Georg, ed. and trans. "Das Wunder von al-Andalus": Die schönsten Gedichte aus dem Maurischen Spanien. Munich: C. H. Beck, 2005.

Boswell, John. The Royal Treasure: Muslim Communities under the Crown of Aragon in the Fourteenth Century. New Haven, CT: Yale University Press, 1977.

Bramon, Dolors. Contra moros i jueus: Formació i estratègia d'unes discriminacions al País Valencià. Valencia: Eliseu Climent, 1981.

———. Contra moros y judíos. Barcelona: Península, 1986.

Brann, Ross. The Compunctious Poet: Cultural Ambiguity and Hebrew Poetry in Muslim Spain. Baltimore: Johns Hopkins University Press, 1991.

———. Power in the Portrayal: Representations of Jews and Muslims in Tenth- and Twelfth-Century Islamic Spain. Princeton, NJ: Princeton University Press, 2009.

Braude, Benjamin. "The Sons of Noah and the Construction of Ethnic and Geographical Identities in the Medieval and Early Modern Periods." William and Mary Quarterly 54 (1997): 103–34.

Briggs, Charles F. Giles of Rome's De regimine principum. Reading and Writing Politics at Court and University, c. 1275–c.1525. Cambridge: Cambridge University Press, 1999.

Brody, Heinrich. R. Salomon da Pieras Leben und Werken. Frankfurt: J. Kauffman, 1893.

Brown, Peter. "Society and the Supernatural, a Medieval Change." Daedalus 104 (1975): 133–51.

Brüggemann, W. Die Spanienberichte des 18. und 19. Jahrhunderts und ihre Bedeutung für die Formung und Wandlung des deutschen Spanienbildes. Münster: Aschendorff, 1956.

Bruguera, Jordi, ed. Llibre dels fets del rei en Jaume. 2 vols. Barcelona: Barcino, 1991.

Brundage, James A. "Intermarriage between Christians and Jews in Medieval Canon Law." Jewish History 3 (1988): 25–40.

———. Law, Sex, and Christian Society in Medieval Europe. Chicago: University of Chicago Press, 1987.

────. "Marriage and Sexuality in the Decretals of Pope Alexander III." In Miscellanea Rolando Bandinelli Papa Alessandro III, edited by Filippo Liotta and Roberto Tofanini, 57–83. Sienna: Accademia senese degli intronati, 1986.

────. "Prostitution in the Medieval Canon Law." Signs: Journal of Women in Culture and Society 1 (1976): 824–45.

Buc, Philippe. The Dangers of Ritual. Princeton, NJ: Princeton University Press, 2001.

Buck, August. Italienische Dichtungslehren vom Mittelalter bis zum Ausgang der Renaissance. Beihefte zur Zeitschrift für romanische Philologie 94. Tübingen: M. Niemeyer, 1952.

Bulliet, Richard. The Case for Islamo-Christian Civilization. New York: Columbia University Press, 2004.

Burman, Thomas. Religious Polemic and the Intellectual History of the Mozarabs. Leiden: Brill, 1994.

────. "Tafsīr and Translation: Robert of Ketton, Mark of Toledo, and Traditional Arabic Qur'ān Exegesis." Speculum 73 (1998): 703–32.

────, ed. Liber denudationis. In Religious Polemic and the Intellectual History of the Mozarabs, 213–386. Leiden: Brill, 1994.

Burns, Robert. Islam under the Crusaders. Princeton, NJ: Princeton University Press, 1973.

Burns, Robert Ignatius. Medieval Colonialism: Postcrusade Exploitation of Islamic Valencia. Princeton, NJ: Princeton University Press, 1975.

Burt, John R. "The Motif of the Fall of Man in the 'Romancero del Rey Rodrigo." Hispania 61 (1978): 435–42.

Butler, Judith. Bodies That Matter: On the Discursive Limits of "Sex." New York: Routledge, 1993.

Buzineb, Hossain. "Respuestas de jurisconsultos maghrebies en torno a la inmigración de musulmanes hispánicos." Hespéris Tamuda 26–27 (1988): 53–65.

Camillo, Ottavio di. "Las teorías de la nobleza en el pensamiento ético de Mosén Diego de Valera." In Menéndez Collera and Roncero López, Nunca fue pena mayor, 223–37.

Cantera Burgos, Francisco. Alvar García de Santa María y su familia de conversos. Madrid: Instituto Arias Montano, 1952.

────. "El Cancionero de Baena: Judíos y conversos en él." Sefarad 27 (1967): 71–111.

Cantera Burgos, Francisco, and José María Millas Vallicrosa. Las inscripciones hebraicas de España. Madrid: C. Bermejo, 1956.

Cantera Montenegro, Enrique. "Conflictos entre el concejo y la aljama de los judíos de Soria en el último tercio del siglo XV." Anuario de estudios medievales 13 (1983): 583–99.

────. "Negación de la 'imagen del judío' en la intelectualidad hispano-hebrea medieval: El ejemplo del shebet yehuda." Aragón en la Edad Media 14–15 (1999): 263–74.

Capsali, Elijah. Seder Eliyahu Zuta. Edited by Aryeh Shmuelevitz, Shlomo Simonsohn, and Meir Benayahu. Jerusalem: Makhon Ben Tsvi, 1975–83.

Carpenter, Dwayne E. Alfonso X and the Jews: An Edition and Commentary on Siete Partidas 7.24 "De los judíos." Berkeley: University of California Press, 1986.

────. "Minorities in Medieval Spain: The Legal Status of Jews and Muslims in the Siete Partidas." Romance Quarterly 33 (1986): 275–83.

Carrasco Urgoiti, María Soledad. El moro de Granada en la literatura (del siglo XV al XX). Madrid: Revista de Occidente, 1956.

Carrete Parrondo, Carlos. "Judería soriana y morería burgalesa: una historia de amor." Estudios Mirandenses 8 (1988): 57–61.

────, ed. Fontes Iudaeorum Regni Castellae. 6 vols. Salamanca: Universidad Pontificia de Salamanca / Granada: Universidad de Granada, 1981–98.

Casas Homs, José María, ed. La gaya ciencia de P. Guillén de Segovia. 2 vols. Madrid: Consejo Superior de Investigaciones Científicas, 1962.

Caspary, Gerard E. Politics and Exegesis: Origen and the Two Swords. Berkeley: University of California Press, 1979.

Cassirer, Ernst. Language and Myth. Translated by Susanne K. Langer. New York: Dover, 1946.

Castañeda, James. A Critical Edition of Lope de Vega's Las paces de los reyes y judía de Toledo. Chapel Hill: University of North Carolina Press, 1962.

Castillo, Rosa, ed. Leyendas épicas Españolas. Madrid: Editorial Castalia, 1956.

Castillo Sainz, Jaime. "De solidaritats Jueves a confraries de conversos: Entre la fossilització i la integració d'una minoria religiosa." Revista d'història medieval 4 (1993): 183–206.

Castro, Américo. De la edad conflictiva. Colección Persiles 18. Madrid: Taurus, 1963.

———. España en su historia: Cristianos, moros y judíos. Buenos Aires: Editorial Losada, 1948.

———. Los Españoles: Cómo llegaron a serlo. Madrid: Taurus, 1965.

———. La realidad histórica de España. 3rd ed. Mexico City: Editorial Porrúa, 1966.

———. The Spaniards: An Introduction to Their History. Berkeley: University of California Press, 1971.

———. The Structure of Spanish History. Translated by Edmund L. King. Princeton, NJ: Princeton University Press, 1954.

Catalán, Diego. De Alfonso X al Conde de Barcelos. Cuatro Estudios sobre el nacimiento de la historiografía romance en Castilla y Portugal. Madrid: Gredos, 1962.

———. "El taller historiográfico alfonsí: Métodos y problemas en el trabajo compilatorio." Romania 84 (1963): 354–75.

Catalán, Diego, and María Soledad de Andrés. Crónica General de España de 1344. Madrid: Gredos, 1971.

Cátedra, Pedro M. Amor y pedagogía en la edad media. Estudios de doctrina amorosa y práctica literaria. Salamanca: Universidad de Salamanca, 1989.

———. "Fray Vicente Ferrer y la predicación antijudaica en la campaña castellana (1411–1412)." In "Qu'un sang impur . . .": Les Conversos et le pouvoir en Espagne à la fin du moyen âge; actes du 2ème colloque d'Aix-en-Provence, 18–19–20 novembre 1994, edited by Jeanne Battesti-Pelegrin, 19–46. Aix-en-Provence: Publications de l'Université de Provence, 1997.

———. "La predicación castellana de San Vicente Ferrer." Boletín de la Real Academia de Buenas Letras de Barcelona 39 (1983–84): 235–309.

———. Sermón, sociedad y literatura en la edad media. San Vicente Ferrer en Castilla (1411–1412). Salamanca: Junta de Castilla y León, 1994.

Cesare, Michelina di. "The Prophet in the Book: Images of Muhammad in Western Medieval Book Culture." In Constructing the Image of Muhammad in Europe, edited by Avinoam Shalem, 9–32. Berlin: Walter de Gruyter, 2013.

Chajes, J. H. "Spirit Possession in Early Modern Jewish Culture." PhD dissertation, Yale University, New Haven, CT, 1999.

"The Charter of Allah: The Platform of the Islamic Resistance Movement (Hamas)." August 18, 1988. The Jerusalem Fund. http://www.palestinecenter.org/cpap/documents/charter.html.

Chavel, H. D. Kitvei Rabenu Moshe ben Nahman. Jerusalem: Mosad ha-Rav Kook, 1964.

Chazan, Robert. Medieval Jewry in Northern France. Baltimore: Johns Hopkins University Press, 1973.

Ciceri, Marcella. "Las Coplas del Provincial." Cultura Neolatina 35 (1975): 39–210.

Cirot, Georges. "Alphonse le noble et la juive de Tolède." Bulletin hispanique 24 (1922): 289–306.

———. "Anecdotes ou légendes sur l'époque d'Alphonse VIII." Bulletin Hispanique 28 (1926): 246–59.

Clark, Elizabeth A. The Origenist Controversy: The Cultural Construction of an Early Christian Debate. Princeton, NJ: Princeton University Press, 1992.

Cohen, Gerson D. The Book of Tradition by Abraham ibn Daud. Philadelphia: Jewish Publication Society, 1967.

———. "The Song of Songs and the Jewish Religious Mentality." In The Samuel Friedland Lectures, 1960–1966, 1–21. New York: Jewish Theological Seminary of America, 1966.

Cohen, Jeremy. Living Letters of the Law: Ideas of the Jew in Medieval Christianity. Berkeley: University of California Press, 1999.

Cohen, Joseph. Le spectre juif de Hegel. Paris: Galilée, 2005.

Cohen, Mark. Under Crescent and Cross: The Jews in the Middle Ages. Princeton, NJ: Princeton University Press, 1994.

Colección de Documentos inéditos para la historia de España. Madrid: Real Academia de la Historia, 1893.

Collins, John J. The Apocalyptic Vision of the Book of Daniel. Missoula, MT: Scholars Press, 1977.

Connelly, John. From Enemy to Brother: The Revolution in Catholic Teaching on the Jews, 1933–1965. Cambridge, MA: Harvard University Press, 2012.

Constable, Olivia Remie. Housing the Stranger in the Mediterranean World: Lodging, Trade, and Travel in Late Antiquity and the Middle Ages. Cambridge: Cambridge University Press, 2003.

Consultationis resolutio grauissimorum doctorum . . . condemnans Auctorem libelli famosi nuncupati el Verde. Zaragoza: Caesaraugustae apud Iannem a Lanaje et Quartanet, 1623.

Conte Cazcarro, Anchel. La aljama de moros de Huesca. Huesca: Instituto de Estudios Altoaragoneses, 1992.

Contini, Gianfranco. "Tombeau de Leo Spitzer." In Varianti e altra linguistica: Una raccolta di saggi (1938–1968), 651–60. Turin: Einaudi, 1970.

Corominas, Joan, and J. A. Pascual. Diccionario crítico etimológico castellano e hispánico. 6 vols. Madrid: Gredos, 1980–1991.

Cortes de los antiguos reinos de León y de Castilla. 5 vols. Madrid: Real Academia de la Historia, 1861–1903.

Las Cortes de Castilla y León en La Edad Media: Actas de la primera etapa del Congreso Científico sobre la Historia de las Cortes de Castilla y León. 2 vols. Valladolid: Simancas Ediciones, 1988.

"The Covenant of the Islamic Resistance Movement." August 18, 1988. The Avalon Project: Documents in Law, History and Diplomacy. http://www.yale.edu/lawweb/avalon/mideast/hamas.htm.

Cruz, Anne J. "The Female Figure as Political Propaganda in the 'Pedro el Cruel' Romancero." In Spanish Women in the Golden Age, Images and Realities, edited by Magdalena S. Sánchez and Alain Saint-Saëns, 69–89. Westport, CT: Greenwood Press, 1996.

Cummins, John. "Methods and Conventions in the Fifteenth-Century Poetic Debate." Hispanic Review 31 (1963): 307–23.

———. "The Survival in the Spanish Cancioneros of the Form and Themes of Provençal and Old French Poetic Debates." Bulletin of Hispanic Studies 42 (1965): 9–17.

Curtius, Ernst Robert. "Poesie und Theologie." In Europäische Literatur und lateinisches Mittelalter, 219–32. Bern: A. Francke A.G. Verlag, 1948.

Dagron, Gilbert. "Judäiser." In Travaux et Mémoires 11 (1991): 359–80.

———. "Le traité de Grégoire de Nicée sur le baptème des juifs." Travaux et mémoires 11 (1991): 314–57.

Dahan, Gilbert. "L'Exégèse de l'histoire de Caïn et Abel du XIIe au XIVe siècle en Occident." Recherches de Théologie ancienne et médiévale 49 (1982): 21–89; 50 (1983): 5–68.

Dainotto, Roberto M. Europe (in Theory). Durham, NC: Duke University Press, 2007.

———. "Of the Arab Origins of Modern Europe: Giammaria Barbieri, Juan Andrés, and the Origin of Rhyme." Comparative Literature 58 (2006): 271–92.

D'Alverny, Marie-Thérèse. "Deux traductions latines du Coran au Moyen-Âge." Archives d'histoire doctrinale et littéraire du Moyen Âge 16 (1947–48): 69–131.

Dán, Róbert. "Judaizare—the Career of a Term." In Antitrinitarianism in the Second Half of the 16th Century, edited by R. Dán and A. Pirnát, 25–34. Budapest and Leiden: Akadémiai Kiadó and Brill, 1982.

Dante Alighieri. "Letter to Cangrande della Scala." In Tutte le opere, edited by Luigi Blasucci, 341–52. 2nd ed. Florence: Sansoni, 1965.

Danvila, Francisco. "Clausura y delimitación de la judería de Valencia en 1390 á 91." Boletín de la Real Academia de la Historia 18 (1891): 142–59.

———. "El robo de la judería de Valencia en 1391." Boletín de la Real Academia de la Historia 8 (1886): 358–96.

Dawson, David. "Plato's Soul and the Body of the Text in Philo and Origen." In Interpretation and Allegory: Antiquity to Modern Period, ed. Jon Whitman. Brill's Studies in Intellectual History 101, 89–107. Leiden: Brill, 2000.

Delaruelle, Étienne. "Paix de Dieu et croisade dans la chrétienté du XIIe siècle." In Paix de Dieu et guerre sainte en Languedoc au XIIIe siècle. Cahiers de Fanjeaux 4, 51–71. Toulouse: Édouard Privat, 1969.

D'Elden, Stephanie Cain van. "Black and White: Contact with the Mediterranean World in Medieval German Narrative." In The Medieval Mediterranean: Cross-Cultural Contacts, edited by Marilyn J. Chiat and Kathryn L. Reyerson, 112–18. Medieval Studies at Minnesota 3. Minneapolis: University of Minnesota Press, 1988.

Delitzch, Franz. Zur Geschichte der jüdischen Poesie. Leipzig: Karl Tauchnitz, 1836.

De Puig i Oliver, Jaume. "La Incantatio studii ilerdensis de Nicolau Eimeric, O.P." Arxiu de Textos Catalans Antics 15 (1996): 7–108.

De Riquer, Martín. "Una versión aragonesa de la leyenda de la enterrada viva." Revista de Bibliografía Nacional 6 (1945): 241–48.

Deu Domenech i Gasul, Joan de. Lleons i besties exotiques a les ciutats catalanes, segles XIV–XVIII. Barcelona: Rafael Dalmau, 1996.

Deyermond, Alan. "The Death and Rebirth of Visigothic Spain in the Estoria de España." Revista canadiense de estudios hispánicos 9, no. 3 (1985): 345–67.

Dies, Manuel. Libro de albeytería. [In Spanish.] Trans. Martín Martínez de Ampiés. 1495. Reprint, Zaragoza: Pablo Hurus, 1499.

Dilig, Peter. "Anti-Arabism in the Medicine of Humanism." In La diffusione delle scienze islamiche nel Medio Evo europeo, edited by Biancamaria Scarcia, 269–89. Rome: Accademia nationale dei Lincei, 1987.

Diner, Dan. "Reason and the 'Other': Horkheimer's Reflections on Anti-Semitism and Mass Annihilation." In On Max Horkheimer: New Perspectives, edited by Seyla Benhabib, Wolfgang Bonss, and John McCole, 335–63. Cambridge, MA: MIT Press, 1993.

Dinur, Ben Zion. "A Wave of Emigration from Spain to the Land of Israel after the Persecutions of 1391." [In Hebrew.] Zion 32 (1967): 161–74.

———. Yisrael ba-Golah. 2 vols. Tel Aviv: Devir, 1969.

Domínguez Ortiz, Antonio. La clase social de los conversos en Castilla en la edad moderna. Madrid: Consejo Superior de Investigaciones Científicas, 1955.

Dominguez Sánchez, Santiago. Documentos de Clemente IV (1265–1268) referentes a España. León: Universidad de León, 1996.

Douglas, Mary. Natural Symbols: Explorations in Cosmology. New York: Pantheon Books, 1982.

———. Purity and Danger: An Analysis of the Concepts of Pollution and Taboo. Boston: Routledge, 1966.

———. "Rightness of Categories." In How Classification Works: Nelson Goodman among the Social Sciences, edited by Douglas and David L. Hull, 239–71. Edinburgh: Edinburgh University Press, 1992.

Du Bellay, Joachim. "Ample Discours au Roy sur le Faict des quatre Estats du Royaume de France." In Oeuvres poétiques, vol. 11, edited by Henry Chamard, 205. Paris: Droz, 1931.

———. Deffence et illustration de la langue françoyse. Edited by Henri Chamard. Paris: M. Didier, 1997.

Duparc-Quioc, Suzanne, ed. La chanson d'Antioche. Paris: Académie des Inscriptions et Belles-Lettres, 1977.

Duran, Profiat. Kelimat ha-Goyim. In Kitvei Pulmos le-Profet Duran [The Polemical Writings of Profiat Duran], edited by Frank Talmage, 3–67. Jerusalem: Zalman Shazar Center and Dinur Center, 1981.

Dutton, Brian. El cancionero del siglo XV, c. 1360–1520. Biblioteca Española del Siglo XV, serie maior, 1–7. Salamanca: Universidad de Salamanca, 1990–91.

Dutton, Brian, and Joaquín González Cuenca, eds. Cancionero de Baena. Madrid: Visor Libros, 1993.

Echevarría, Ana. The Fortress of Faith: The Attitude towards Muslims in Fifteenth-Century Spain. Leiden: Brill, 1999.

Ecker, Heather. "The Conversion of Mosques to Synagogues in Seville: The Case of the Mezquita de la Judería." Gesta 36, no. 2 (1997): 190–207.

Einbinder, Susan. "Pucellina of Blois: Romantic Myths and Narrative Conventions." Jewish History 12 (1998): 29–46.

Eiximenis, Francesc. Dotze llibre del Crestià. Girona: Collegi Universitari de Girona, 1986.

———. Lo Crestià. Edited by Albert Hauf. Barcelona: Edicions 62, 1983.

Elinson, Alexander E. Looking Back at al-Andalus: The Poetics of Loss and Nostalgia in Medieval Arabic and Hebrew Literature. Leiden: Brill, 2009.

Elliott, John H., and Laurence W. B. Brockliss, eds. The World of the Favorite. New Haven, CT: Yale University Press, 1999.

Elukin, Jonathan. "From Jew to Christian? Conversion and Immutability in Medieval Europe." In Varieties of Religious Conversion in the Middle Ages, edited by James Muldoon, 171–89. Gainesville: University Press of Florida, 1997.

Elze, Reinhard, ed. Ordines coronationis imperialis: Die Ordines für die Weihe und Krönung des Kaisers und der Kaiserin. MGH Fontes iuris Germanici antiqui in usum scholarum 9. Hannover: Hahnsche Buchhandlung, 1960.

Emerton, Ephraim, ed. and trans. The Letters of St. Boniface. New York: W.W. Norton & Co., 1976.

Epalza, Mikel de. Jésus otage: Juifs, chrétiens et musulmans en Espagne (VIe–XVIIe s.). Paris: Éditions du Cerf, 1987.

Epstein, Isidore. Studies in the Communal Life of the Jews of Spain. 2nd ed. New York: Hermon Press, 1968.

Epstein, Louis. Sex Laws and Customs in Judaism. New York: Bloch Publishing Company, 1948.

Erasmus, Desiderius. Opus epistolarum. Edited by Percy Stafford Allen, Helen Mary Allen, Heathcote William Garrod, and Barbara Flower. 12 vols. Oxford: Clarendon Press, 1906–58.

Erdmann, Carl. Die Entstehung des Kreuzzugsgedankens. Stuttgart: W. Kohlhammer, 1935.

Estow, Clara. Pedro the Cruel of Castile: 1350–69. Leiden: Brill, 1995.

Farmer, William R. The Synoptic Problem: A Critical Analysis. Dillsboro: Western North Carolina Press, 1976.

Faur, José. In the Shadow of History: Jews and Conversos at the Dawn of Modernity. Albany: State University of New York Press, 1992.

Febrer Romaguera, M.V., ed. Cartas Pueblas de las Morerias Valencianas y documentación complementaria. Zaragoza: Anubar, 1991.

Fernández de Oviedo, Gonzalo. Quinquagenas de la nobleza de España. Madrid: Real Academia de la Historia, 1880.

Feros, Antonio. "Almas gemelas: monarcas y favoritos en la primera mitad del siglo XVII." In España, Europa y el mundo Atlántico: Homenage a John H. Elliott, edited by Richard L. Kagan and Geoffrey Parker, 49–82. Madrid: Marcial Pons, 2001.

———. "'Vicedioses, pero humanos,' el drama del Rey." Cuadernos de Historia Moderna 14 (1993): 103–31.

Ferrer, Vincent. Sermons. Edited by Josep Sanchis Sivera and Gret Schib. 6 vols. Barcelona: Barcino, 1932–88.

Ferrer i Mallol, María-Teresa. Els sarraïns de la Corona Catalano-Aragonesa en el segle XIV: Segregació i discriminació. Barcelona: Consell Superior d'Investigacions Cientifiques, 1987.

Field, Lester K., Jr., Liberty, Dominion, and the Two Swords: On the Origins of Western Political Theology (180–398). Publications in Medieval Studies 28. Notre Dame, IN: University of Notre Dame Press, 1998.

Fields, Barbara. "Ideology and Race in American History." In Region, Race, and Reconstruction: Essays in Honor of C. Vann Woodward, edited by Joseph M. Kousser and James MacPherson, 143–77. New York: Oxford University Press, 1982.

Firpo, Arturo. "Las concubinas reales en la Baja Edad Media castellana." In La condición de la mujer en la Edad Media, edited by Yves-René Fonquerne, 334–41. Madrid: Universidad Complutense, 1986.

Fita, Fidel. "El judío errante de Illescas." Boletín de la Real Academia de la Historia 6 (1885): 130–40.

Flori, Jean. "La caricature de l'Islam dans l'Occident médiéval: Origine et signification de quelques stéréotypes concernant l'Islam." Aevum 2 (1992): 245–56.

Floriano, Antonio C. "San Vicente Ferrer y las aljamas turolenses." Boletín de la Real Academia de la Historia 84 (1924): 558–80.

Flüeler, Christoph. Rezeption und Interpretation der aristotelischen Politica im späten Mittelalter. 2 vols. Amsterdam-Philadelphie: B. R. Grüner-J. Benjamins, 1992.

Foucault, Michel. Il faut défendre la société: Cours au Collège de France, 1976. Paris: Seuil, 1997.

———. "Nietzsche, Genealogy, History." In Language, Counter-Memory, Practice, edited by Donald Bouchard, translated by Donald Bouchard and Sherry Simon, 139–84. Ithaca, NY: Cornell University Press, 1977.

Fraker, Charles F., Jr. Studies on the Cancionero de Baena. Chapel Hill: University of North Carolina Press, 1966.

Fredrikson, George. Racism: A Short History. Princeton, NJ: Princeton University Press, 2002.

Frevert, Ute. Men of Honor: A Social and Cultural History of the Duel. Cambridge, MA: Blackwell, 1995.

Frey, Winfried. "Vom Antijudaismus zum Antisemitismus: Ein antijüdisches Pasquill von 1606 und seine Quellen." Daphnis 18 (1989): 251–79.

Friedman, Jerome. "Jewish Conversion, the Spanish Pure Blood Laws, and Reformation: A Revisionist View of Racial and Religious Antisemitism." Sixteenth-Century Journal 18 (1987): 3–31.

Fucilla, Joseph G., ed. Raquel. Madrid: Ediciones Catedra, 1974.

Fuente, María Jesús. Reinas medievales en los reinos hispánicos. Madrid: La Esfera de los Libros, 2003.

Gaibrois de Ballesteros, Mercedes. Historia del Reinado de Sancho IV de Castilla. 3 vols. Madrid: Revista de Archivos, Bibliotecas y Museos, 1922–28.

———. María de Molina. Madrid: Espasa-Calpe, 1936.

Galán Sánchez, Ángel. Una visión de la 'decadencia española': La historiografía anglosajona sobre mudéjares y moriscos, siglos XVIII-XX. Colección "Monografías" 4. Málaga: Servicio de Publicaciones, Diputación Provincial de Málaga, 1991.

Galíndez de Caravajal, Lorenzo. Crónica de Don Juan II. In Crónicas de los Reyes de Castilla, vol. 2, edited by Cayetano Rosell. Biblioteca de Autores Españoles 68. Madrid: M. Rivadeneyra, 1877.

García-Arenal, Mercedes. Inquisición y moriscos, los procesos del Tribunal de Cuenca. 2nd ed. Madrid: Siglo Veintiuno, 1983.

———. "Los moros en las Cantigas de Alfonso X el Sabio." Al-Qantara 6 (1985): 133–51.

García-Arenal, Mercedes, and Béatrice Leroy. Moros y judíos en Navarra en la baja Edad Media. Madrid: Hiperión, 1984.

García-Arenal, Mercedes, and Fernando R. Mediano. Un Oriente español: Los moriscos y el Sacromonte en tiempos de Contrarreforma. Madrid: Marcial Pons, 2010.

García de Enterría, María Cruz, ed. Romancero viejo (antología). Madrid: Castalia, 1987.

García Herrero, María del Carmen. "Prostitución y amancebamiento en Zaragoza a fines de la Edad Media." En la España Medieval 12 (1989): 305–22.

García Moreno, Aitor, ed. Coloquio entre un cristiano y un judío. Papers of the Medieval Hispanic Research Seminar 40. London: Queen Mary, University of London, 2003.

García y García, Antonio. "La Canonística ibérica medieval posterior al Decreto de Graciano." Repertorio de Historia de las Ciencias Eclesiásticas en España 5 (1976): 351–402.

Gatto, Ludovico. Il pontificato di Gregorio X (1271–1276). Rome: Istituto Storico Italiano per il Medio Evo, 1959.

Gayangos, Pascual de, ed. Leyes de moros del siglo XIV in Memorial Histórico Español. Madrid: Real Academia de la Historia, 1853.

Gebhardt, Carl. Die Schriften des Uriel da Costa. Bibliotheca Spinozana 2. Amsterdam: Menno Hertzberger, 1922.

Gerli, E. Michael. "Antón de Montoro and the Wages of Eloquence: Poverty, Patronage, and Poetry in 15th-Century Castile." Romance Philology 48 (1994–95): 265–76.

———. "Performing Nobility: Mosén Diego de Valera and the Poetics of Converso Identity." La Corónica 15 (1996): 19–36.

Gerli, E. Michael, and Julian Weiss, eds. Poetry at Court in Trastamaran Spain: From the Cancionero de Baena to the Cancionero General. Medieval and Renaissance Texts and Studies 181. Tempe, AZ: Medieval and Renaissance Texts and Studies, 1998.

Gil de Zamora, Juan. De preconiis Hispaniae. Edited by Manuel de Castro y Castro. Madrid: Universidad de Madrid, 1955.

Girard, René. "Generative Scapegoating." In Violent Origins: Ritual Killing and Cultural Formations, edited by Robert G. Hamerton-Kelly, 73–105. Stanford, CA: Stanford University Press, 1987.

Gladitz, Charles. Horse Breeding in the Medieval World. Dublin: Four Courts Press, 1997.

Goetschel, Willi. Spinoza's Modernity: Mendelssohn, Lessing, and Heine. Madison: University of Wisconsin Press, 2004.

Gómez Moreno, Angel. "An Unknown Jewish-Christian Controversy in Fifteenth-Century Talavera de la Reina: Towards the End of Spanish Jewry." In Menéndez Collera and Roncero López, Nunca fue pena mayor, 285–92.

González, Julio. El reino de Castilla en la época de Alfonso VIII. 3 vols. Madrid: Consejo Superior de Investigaciones Científicas, 1960.

González Calleja, Eduardo, and Fredes Limón Nevado. La hispanidad como instrumento de combate: Raza e imperio en la prensa franquista durante la guerra civil española. Madrid: Consejo Superior de Investigaciones Científicas, 1988.

González González, Enrique. "Vives: Un humanista judeoconverso en el exilio de Flandes." In The Expulsion of the Jews and Their Emigration to the Southern Low Countries (15th–16th Centuries), edited by Luc Dequeker and Werner Verbeke, Mediaevalia Lovaniensia 1/26, 35–82. Louvain: Leuven University Press, 1998.

González Palencia, Angel. Los mozárabes de Toledo en los siglos XII y XIII. 4 vols. Madrid: Instituto de Valencia de Don Juan, 1926–30.

González Ruiz, Ramón. "El Bachiller Palma y su obra de polémica proconversa." In Battesti-Pelegrin, "Qu'un Sang Impur . . . ," 47–59.

González Rolán, Tomás, and Pilar Saquero Suárez-Somonte. De la Sentencia-Estatuto de Pero Sarmiento a la Instrucción del Relator. Madrid: Aben Ezra Ediciones, 2012.

Gonzalo de Berceo. Milagros de Nuestra Señora. Edited by Antonio García Solalinde. Madrid: Espasa-Calpe, 1978.

Gossman, Lionel. "Philhellenism and Antisemitism: Matthew Arnold and His German Models." Comparative Literature 46 (1994): 1–39.

Gouguenheim, Sylvain. Aristote au Mont-Saint-Michel: Les racines grecques de l'Europe chrétienne. Paris: Seuil, 2008.

Grabois, Aryeh. "From 'Theological' to 'Racial' Anti-Semitism: The Controversy over the 'Jewish' Pope in the Twelfth Century." [In Hebrew.] Zion 47 (1982): 1–16.

Graetz, Heinrich. Geschichte der Juden. 11 vols. Leipzig: Leiner, 1890.

Guadalajara Medina, José. Las profecías del anticristo en la edad media. Madrid: Gredos, 1996.

Gudiol, José, and Santiago Alcolea i Blanch. Pintura gótica catalana. Barcelona: Polígrafa, 1986.

Guibert of Nogent. Autobiographie. Edited by Edmond-René Labande. Les Classiques de l'Histoire de France au Moyen Age 34. Paris: Belles Lettres, 1981.

———. The Deeds of God through the Franks. Translated by Robert Levine. Woodbridge: Boydell Press, 1997.

———. Dei gesta per Francos. Edited by R. B. C. Huygens. Corpus Christianorum, Coninuatio Mediaevalis 127A. Turnhout: Brepols, 1996.

Gutas, Dmitri. Greek Thought, Arabic Culture: The Graeco-Arabic Translation Movement in Baghdad and Early 'Abbasid Society. London: Routledge, 1998.

Gutiérrez Baños, Fernando. Las empresas artísticas de Sancho IV el Bravo. Burgos: Junta de Castilla y León, 1997.

Gutwirth, Eleazar. "The Expulsion from Spain and Jewish Historiography." In Jewish History: Essays in Honour of Chimen Abramsky, edited by Ada Rapaport-Albert and Steven J. Zipperstein, 141–61. London: P. Halban, 1988.

———. "History and Apologetics in XVth-Century Hispano-Jewish Thought." Helmantica 35 (1984): 231–42.

———. "Lineage in XVth Century Hispano-Jewish Thought." Miscelánea de estudios árabes y hebraicos 34 (1985): 85–91.

Hacker, Joseph. "Links between Spanish Jewry and Palestine, 1391–1492." In Vision and Conflict in the Holy Land, edited by Richard I. Cohen, 114–25. New York: St. Martin's Press, 1985.

Hagerty, Miguel. Los libros plúmbeos del Sacromonte. Madrid: Editora Nacional, 1980.

Halbertal, Moshe, and Avishai Margalit. Idolatry. Cambridge, MA: Harvard University Press, 1992.

Halbwachs, Maurice. Les Cadres sociaux de la mémoire. Paris: Félix Alcan, 1925.

Hall, Joseph, ed. King Horn: A Middle English Romance. Oxford: Clarendon Press, 1901.

Hamacher, Werner. Pleroma: Reading in Hegel. The Genesis and Structure of a Dialectical Hermeneutics in Hegel. Translated by Nicholas Walker and Simon Jarvis. London: Athlone Press, 1998.

Hannaford, Ivan. Race: The History of an Idea in the West. Baltimore: Johns Hopkins University Press, 1996.

Harpham, Geoffrey Galt. "So . . . What Is Enlightenment? An Inquisition into Modernity." Critical Inquiry 20 (1994): 524–56.

Harvey, L. P. Islamic Spain, 1250–1500. Chicago: University of Chicago Press, 1990.

Hasan-Rokem, Galit. Tales of the Neighborhood: Jewish Narrative Dialogues in Late Antiquity. Berkeley: University of California Press, 2003.

Haverkamp, Alfred. "Baptized Jews in German Lands during the Twelfth Century." In Jews and Christians in Twelfth Century Europe, edited by Michael Signer and John van Engen, 255–310. Notre Dame: University of Notre Dame Press, 2001.

Hay, Denys. Europe: The Emergence of an Idea. Edinburgh: Edinburgh University Press, 1957.

Hegel, Georg Wilhelm Friedrich. G.W.F. Hegel: The Philosophy of History. Translated by J. Sibree from the 2nd edition. New York: Collier & Son, 1902.

———. Hegels theologische Jugendschriften. Edited by Herman Nohl. Tübingen: J. C. B. Mohr, 1907.

———. Lectures on the Philosophy of Religion. 3 vols. Edited and translated by Peter C. Hodgson. Berkeley: University of California Press, 1984.

———. Phänomenologie des Geistes. Edited by J. Hoffmeister. Hamburg: Felix Meiner, 1952.

———. Phenomenology of Spirit. Edited and translated by A.V. Miller. Oxford: Clarendon Press, 1977.

———. "The Spirit of Christianity." In Early Theological Writings, translated by T. J. Knox, 182–301. Chicago: University of Chicago Press, 1948. Reprint, Philadelphia: University of Pennsylvania Press, 1975.

Heil, Johannes. "'Antijudaismus' und 'Antisemitismus'—Begriffe als Bedeutungsträger." Jahrbuch für Antisemitismusforschung 6 (1997): 91–114.

Heine, Heinrich. "Ludwig Börne: Eine Denkschrift." In Sämtliche Schriften, vol. 4, 7–148. Munich: Carl Hanser Verlag, 1978.

Hempfer, Klaus W. Möglichkeiten des Dialogs: Struktur und Funktion einer literarischen Gattung zwischen Mittelalter und Renaissance in Italien. Text und Kontext 15. Stuttgart: F. Steiner, 2002.

Herde, Peter. "Von der mittelalterlichen Judenfeindschaft zum modernen Antisemitismus." In Geschichte und Kultur des Judentums, edited by Karlheinz Müller and Klaus Wittstadt, 11–69. Würzburg: Kommissionsverlag F. Schoningh, 1988.

Herder, Johann Gottfried. Briefe zu Berförderung der Humanität. Edited by Hans Dietrich Irmscher. Johann Gottfried Herder: Werke 7. Frankfurt: Deutscher Klassiker Verlag, 1991.

Hernández, Francisco J. Las rentas del rey. Sociedad y fisco en el reino castellano en el siglo XIII. Madrid: Fundación Ramón Areces, 1993.

Hernando i Delgado, Josep. "Un tractat anònim Adversus iudaeos en català." In Paraula i història, 1013–1024. Miscellània P. Basili Rubí. Barcelona: Edicions Franciscanes, 1986.

Hershman, Abraham. Rabbi Isaac Perfet and His Times. New York: Jewish Theological Seminary, 1943.

Hertzberg, Arthur. The French Enlightenment and the Jews. New York: Schocken Books, 1970.

Hillenbrand, Carole. Crusades: Islamic Perspectives. Edinburgh: Edinburgh University Press, 2008.

Hillgarth, J. N. The Mirror of Spain. Ann Arbor: University of Michigan Press, 2000.

Hilty, Gerold. "Die Jüdin von Toledo: Entstehung und Frühgeschichte des Motivs in der spanischen Literatur." In Verlust und Ursprung, Festschrift für Werner Weber, edited by Angelika Maass and Bernhard Heinser, 241–67. Zürich: Ammann, 1989.

———. "¿Tiene raíces históricas el motivo de la judía de Toledo?" In Actas del IX Congreso de la Asociación Hispánica de Literatura Medieval, 505–16. Noia: Toxosuoutos, 2005.

Hinojosa Montalvo, José. Jews of the Kingdom of Valencia. Jerusalem: Magnes Press, 1992.

Hinterhäuser, Hans, ed. Spanien und Europa: Texte zu ihrem Verhältnis von der Aufklärung bis zur Gegenwart. Munich: Deutscher Taschenbuch Verlag, 1979.

Hirschberg, Haim Zeev. A History of the Jews of North Africa. 2 vols. Leiden: Brill, 1974–81.

Hoffmann, Christhard. "Christlicher Antijudaismus und moderner Antisemitismus. Zusammenhänge und Differenzen als Problem der historischen Antisemitismusforschung." In Christlicher Antijudaismus und Antisemitismus: Theologische und kirchliche Programme Deutscher Christen, edited by Leonore Siegele-Wenschkewitz, 293–317. Frankfurt: Haag & Herchen, 1994.

Horkheimer, Max, and Theodor W. Adorno. "The Birth of the Pariah: Jews, Christian Dualism, and Social Science." Social Research 70 (2003): 201–36.

———. Dialectic of Enlightenment. Translated by John Cumming. New York: Herder & Herder, 1972.

Housley, Norman. The Later Crusades: From Lyons to Alcazar 1274–1580. Oxford: Oxford University Press, 1992.

Hoyland, Robert. Islam as Others Saw It: A Survey and Evaluation of Christian, Jewish and Zoroastrian Writings on Early Islam. Princeton, NJ: Darwin Press, 1997.

Huet, Pierre-Daniel. Traité de l'origine des romans. Stuttgart: Metzler, 1966.

Humphreys, W. Lee. "The Motif of the Wise Courtier in the Book of Proverbs." In Israelite Wisdom: Theological and Literary Essays in Honor of Samuel Terrien, edited by John G. Gammie, 177–90. Missoula: Scholars Press, 1978.

Huntington, Samuel. The Clash of Civilizations and the Remaking of World Order. New York: Simon & Schuster, 1996.

———. "The Clash of Civilizations?" Foreign Affairs 72, no. 3 (Summer 1993): 22–49.

Hutcheson, Gregory S. "Desperately Seeking Sodom: Queerness in the Chronicles of Alvaro de Luna." In Blackmore and Hutcheson, Queer Iberia, 222–49.

———. "Marginality and Empowerment in Baena's Cancionero." PhD dissertation, Harvard University, Cambridge, MA, 1993.

——. "'Pinning Him to the Wall': The Poetics of Self-Destruction in the Court of Juan II." Disputatio: An International Transdisciplinary Journal of the Late Middle Ages 5 (2002): 87–102.

Hyam, Ronald. Empire and Sexuality: The British Experience. Manchester: Manchester University Press, 1990.

Hyams, Paul. "Trial by Ordeal: The Key to Proof in the Early Commonlaw." In On the Laws and Customs of England: Essays in Honor of Samuel E. Thorne, edited by Morris S. Arnold, Thomas A. Green, Sally A. Scully, and Stephen D. White, 90–126. Chapel Hill: University of North Carolina Press, 1981.

Ibn Ḥazm. "Al-Radd ʿalā ibn al-naghrīla al yahūdī." [The Refutation of Ibn Naghrila the Jew.] In Rasāʾil ibn h.azm al-andalusi, vol. 3, edited by Iḥsān ʿAbbās, 39–70. Beirut, 1980–83.

——. "Al-Radd ʿalā ibn al-naghrīla al yahūdī." [The Refutation of Ibn Naghrila the Jew.] Translated by Moshe Perlmann in "Eleventh-Century Andalusian Authors on the Jews of Granada." Proceedings of the American Academy for Jewish Research 18 (1948–49): 269–80.

Ibn ʿIdhārī al-Marrākushī, Al-Bayān al Mughrib, vol. 5, trans. Ambrosio Huici Miranda. In Al-Bayan . . . Nuevos Fragmentos Almorávides y Almohades. Valencia: Anubar Ediciones, 1963.

Ibn Isḥāq, Muḥammad. The Life of Muhammad: A Translation of Ishāq's Sīrat Rasūl Allāh, translated by A. Guillaume. Karachi: Oxford University Press, 2000.

Ibn Muḥammad al-Maqqarī, Aḥmad. Nafḥ al-ṭīb: Min ghuṣn al-Andalus al-raṭīb. 8 vols. Beirut: Dār Ṣādir, 1968.

Ibn Verga, Shelomo. Das Buch Schevet Jehuda. Edited by Meir Wiener. Hannover: Orient-Buchhandlung H. Lafaire, 1854. Reprint, Hannover: K. Rimpler, 1924.

——. Shevet Yehuda. Edited by ʿAzriʾel Shohet and Yitzhak Baer. Jerusalem: Mosad Biʾalik, 1946.

Inguanez, Mauro, and Henry M. Willard, eds. Alberici Casinensis Flores rhetorici. Montecassino: Miscellanea Cassinese, 1938.

Iogna-Prat, Dominique. Order and Exclusion: Cluny and Christendom Face Heresy, Judaism, and Islam (1000–1150). Translated by. G. R. Edwards. Ithaca, NY: Cornell University Press, 2002.

Jaffé, Elsbeth, and Heinrich Finke. "La dispensa de matrimonio falsificada para le rey Sancho IV y María de Molina." Anuario de Historia del Derecho Español 4 (1927): 298–318.

Jayyusi, Salma Khadra, ed. The Legacy of Muslim Spain. 2 vols. 1992. Reprint, Leiden: Brill, 1994.

John of Damascus. Liber de haeresibus. In Die Schriften des Johannes von Damaskos, vol. 4, edited by P. Bonafatius Kotter, 19–67. Berlin: De Gruyter, 1969–81.

The Joint Declaration of the Paris Summit of the Mediterranean. July 13, 2008. Union for the Mediterranean. http://www.ufmsecretariat.org/en/institutional-documents.

Jordan, William Chester. The French Monarchy and the Jews from Philip Augustus to the Last Capetians. Philadelphia: University of Pennsylvania Press, 1989.

——. "Jews, Regalian Rights, and the Constitution in Medieval France." AJS Review 23 (1998): 1–16.

——. Louis IX and the Challenge of the Crusade: A Study in Rulership. Princeton, NJ: Princeton University Press, 1979.

Jordan, Winthrop. White over Black. New York: Norton, 1977.

Jouanna, Arlette. L'idée de Race en France au XVIème siècle et au Début du XVIIème Siècle (1498–1614). 3 vols. Lille/Paris: Université Lille III, 1976.

Juan de Pineda. Diálogos Familiares de la Agricultura Cristiana. 5 vols. Salamanca: P. de Adurça y Diego López, 1589.

Kaegi, Walter. "Initial Byzantine Reactions to the Arab Conquest." Church History 38 (1969): 139–49.

Kamen, Henry. "The Mediterranean and the Expulsion of Spanish Jews in 1492." Past and Present 119 (1988): 30–55.

Kant, Immanuel. Reflexionen Kants zur Anthropologie, Aus Kants handschriftlichen Aufzeichnungen. Edited by Benno Erdmann. Leipzig: Fues' Verlag, 1882.

———. "Von den vershiedenen Rassen der Menschen." In Gesammelte Schriften, Akademie-Ausgabe, vol. 2, 429–43. Berlin: Georg Reimer, 1902.

Kaplan, Gregory B. The Evolution of Converso Literature: The Writings of the Converted Jews of Medieval Spain. Gainesville: University Press of Florida, 2002.

Kaplan, Yosef. "The Self-Definition of the Sephardic Jews of Western Europe and Their Relation to the Alien and the Stranger." In Crisis and Creativity in the Sephardic World, 1391–1648, edited by Benjamin Gampel, 121–45. New York: Columbia University Press, 1997.

———. "The Sephardim in North-Western Europe and the New World." In Beinart, Moreshet Sepharad: The Sephardi Legacy, vol. 2, 240–87.

Kassin, Leon. "A Study of a Fourteenth-Century Polemical Treatise Adversus judaeos." PhD dissertation, Columbia University, New York, 1969.

Katz, Jacob. Exclusiveness and Tolerance: Studies in Jewish-Gentile Relations in Medieval and Modern Times. Oxford: Oxford University Press, 1961.

Kedar, Benjamin Z. Crusade and Mission: European Approaches towards the Muslims. Princeton, NJ: Princeton University Press, 1984.

Khoury, Adel Théodore. Polémique byzantine contre l'Islam (VIIIe–XIIIe s.). Leiden: Brill, 1972.

———. Les théologiens byzantins et l'Islam: Textes et auteurs (VIIIe–XIIIe s.). Paris: Editions Nauwelaerts, 1969.

———, ed. and trans. Manuel II Paléologue, Entretiens avec un Musulman, 7e Controverse. Sources Chrétiennes 115. Paris: Les Editions du Cerf, 1966.

Kisch, Guido. The Jews of Medieval Germany. Chicago: University of Chicago Press, 1949.

Klapisch-Zuber, Christiane. L'Ombre des ancêtres. Paris: Fayard Press, 2000.

Kluger, Richard. Simple Justice. New York: Vintage Books, 1977.

Köhler, Michael A. Allianzen und Verträge zwischen fränkischen und islamischen Herrschern im Vorderen Orient: Eine Studie über das zwischenstaatliche Zusammenleben vom 12. bis ins 13. Jahrhundert. Berlin: Walter de Gruyter, 1991.

Kohlhammer, Siegfried. Die Feinde und die Freunde des Islam. Göttingen: Steidl, 1996.

———. "'Ein angenehmes Märchen': Die Wiederentdeckung und Neugestaltung des muslimischen Spanien." Merkur: Deutsche Zeitschrift für europäisches Denken 57 (2003): 595–608.

Kohut, Karl. "Der Beitrag der Theologie zum Literaturbegriff in der Zeit Juans II von Kastilien: Alonso de Cartagena (1384–1456) und Alonso de Madrigal, genannt el Tostado (1400?-1455)." Romanische Forschungen 89 (1977): 183–226.

———. "La teoría de la poesía cortesana en el Prólogo de Juan Alfonso de Baena." In Actas del coloquio hispano-alemán Ramón Menéndez Pidal, 120–37. Tübingen, Niemeyer, 1982.

———. Las teorías literarias en España y Portugal durante los siglos XV y XVI. Anejos de Revista de Literatura 36. Madrid: Consejo Superior de Investigaciones Científicas, 1973.

———. "Zur Vorgeschichte der Diskussion um das Verhältnis von Christentum und antiker Kultur im spanischen Humanismus: Die Rolle des Decretum Gratiani in der Übermittlung patristischen Gedankengutes." Archiv für Kulturgeschichte 55 (1973): 80–106.

Koningsveld, Peter Sjoerd van. "La Apología de Al-Kindî en la España del siglo XII: Huellas
     toledanas de un 'animal disputax.'" In Estudios sobre Alfonso VI y la reconquista de
     Toledo: Actas del II congreso internacional de estudios mozárabes, 107–29. Toledo:
     Instituto de Estudios, 1989.
Koningsveld, Peter Sjoerd van, and Gerard Albert Wiegers. "The Islamic Statute of the Mude-
     jars in the Light of a New Source." Al-Qantara 17 (1996): 19–59.
———. "The Polemical Works of Muhammad al-Qaysī (fl. 1309) and Their Circulation in
     Arabic and Aljamiado among the Mudejars in the Fourteenth Century." Al-Qanṭara 15
     (1994): 163–99.
Kriegel, Maurice. "Alonso de Oropesa devant la question des conversos: Une stratégie
     d'intégration hiéronymite?" In Battesti-Pelegrin, "Qu'un sang impur . . . ," 9–18.
———. "Histoire sociale et ragots: Sur l''ascendance juive' de Ferdinand le Catholique." In
     Movimientos migratorios y expulsiones en la diáspora occidental, edited by Fermín Mi-
     randa García, 95–100. Pamplona: Universidad Pública de Navarra, 2000.
———. Les Juifs à la fin du Moyen Age dans l'europe mediterranéene. Paris: Hachette, 1979.
Krueger, Stephen. "Conversion and Medieval Sexual, Religious, and Racial Categories."
     In Constructing Medieval Sexuality, edited by Karma Lochrie, Peggy McCracken, and
     James A. Schultz, 158–79. Minneapolis: University of Minnesota Press, 1997.
Kruger, Steven F. "Conversion and Medieval Sexual, Religious, and Racial Categories." In
     Constructing Medieval Sexuality, eds. Karma Lochrie, Peggy McCracken and James Alfred
     Schultz, 158–79. Minneapolis: University of Minnesota Press, 1997.
Kümmel, Werner Georg. Introduction to the New Testament. Translated by Howard Clark
     Kee. Rev. ed. Nashville: Abingdon Press, 1975.
Küpper, Joachim. "'Uti' und 'frui' bei Augustinus und die Problematik des Genießens in
     der ästhetischen Theorie des Okzidents." In Genuß und Egoismus: Zur Kritik ihrer
     geschichtlichen Verknüpfung, edited by Wolfgang Klein and Ernst Müller, 3–29. Berlin:
     Akademie Verlag, 2002.
———. "Zu einigen Aspekten der Dichtungstheorie in der Frührenaissance." In Renaissance:
     Episteme und Agon; für Klaus W. Hempfer anläßlich seines 60. Geburtstages, edited by
     Andreas Kablitz, 47-72. Heidelberg, 2006.
Lacan, Jacques. "Logical Time and the Assertion of Anticipated Certainty: A New Sophism,"
     tr. by B. Fink and M. Silver. Newsletter of the Freudian Field 2 (1988).
Lacarra, María Jesús. "Los Exempla en los Castigos de Sancho IV: Divergencias en la trans-
     misión manuscrita." In La literatura en la época de Sancho IV, edited by Carlos Alvar and
     José Manuel Lucía Megías, 201–12. Alcalá: Universidad de Alcalá, 1996.
Ladero Quesada, Miguel Angel. Fiscalidad y poder real en Castilla (1252–1369). Madrid:
     Editorial Complutense, 1993.
Lambert, Elie. "Alphonse de Castille et la juive de Tolède." Bulletin Hispanique 25 (1923):
     371–97.
Lamoreaux, John. "Early Christian Responses to Islam." In Medieval Christian Perceptions of
     Islam: A Book of Essays, edited by John Tolan, 3–31. New York: Garland, 1996.
Lange, Wolf-Dieter. El fraile trobador. Zeit, Leben, und Werk des Diego Valencia de León.
     Analecta Romanica 28. Frankfurt: V. Klostermann, 1971.
Langmuir, Gavin. "Prolegomena to Any Present Analysis of Hostility against Jews." Social Sci-
     ence Information = Information sur les sciences sociales 15 (1976): 689–727.
———. Religion and Antisemitism. Berkeley: University of California Press, 1990.
Lawee, Eric. Isaac Abarbanel's Stance toward Tradition: Defense, Dissent, and Dialogue.
     Albany: State University of New York Press, 2001.

————. "The Messianism of Isaac Abarbanel, 'Father of the Messianic Movements of the Sixteenth and Seventeenth Centuries.'" In Jewish Messianism in the Early Modern Period, edited by R. Popkin and M. Goldish, 1–40. Dordrecht: Kluwer, 2010.

Lawrance, Jeremy. Un episodio del proto-humanismo Español: Tres opúsculos de Nuño de Guzmán y Giannozzo Manetti. Salamanca: Biblioteca Española del Siglo XV, 1989.

Lazar, Moshe. "Anti-Jewish and Anti-Converso Propaganda: Confutatio libri Talmud and Alboraique." In Lazar and Haliczer, The Jews of Spain and the Expulsion of 1492, 153–236.

Lazar, Moshe, and Stephen Halicer, eds. The Jews of Spain and the Expulsion of 1492. Lancaster, CA: Labyrinthos, 1997.

Lea, Henry Charles. A History of the Inquisition of Spain. 4 vols. 1906. Reprint, New York: AMS Press, 1966.

Lebram, Jürgen-Christian. Das Buch Daniel. Zurich: Theologischer Verlag, 1984.

Ledesma Rubio, María Luisa. Vidas mudéjares: Aspectos sociales de una minoría religiosa en Aragón. Zaragoza: Mira Editores, 1994.

Lefanu, Philip, trans. Letters of Certain Jews to Monsieur Voltaire, Concerning an Apology for Their Own People and for the Old Testament. 2nd ed. Covington, KY: G. G. Moore, Rector of St. Peter's Church, 1845.

León Tello, Pilar. Judíos de Toledo. 2 vols. Madrid: Consejo Superior de Investigaciones Científicas, 1979.

————. "Legislación sobre judíos en las Cortes de los antiguos reinos de León y Castilla." In Fourth World Congress of Jewish Studies, vol. 2, 55–63. Jerusalem: World Union of Jewish Studies, 1968.

Lerner, Robert. The Feast of Saint Abraham: Medieval Millenarians and the Jews. Philadelphia: University of Pennsylvania Press, 2001.

Leroy, Béatrice. "Les difficultés de la communauté juive navarraise, observées par les officiers du royaume, au xive siècle." In Exile and Diaspora: Studies of the Jewish People Presented to Professor Haim Beinart, edited by Aaron Mirsky, Avraham Grossman, and Yosef Kaplan, 44–55. Jerusalem: Ben-Zvi Institute; Madrid: Consejo Superior de Investigaciones Científicas, 1991.

Lévi-Strauss, Claude. The Elementary Structures of Kinship. Edited by Rodney Needham. Translated by James Harle Bell, John Richard von Sturmer, and R. Needham. Boston: Beacon Press, 1969.

Lewis, Bernard. History: Remembered, Recovered, Invented. Princeton, NJ: Princeton University Press, 1975.

————. Islam in History: Ideas, Men, and Events in the Middle East. London: Alcove Press, 1973.

Lichtheim, Miriam. Ancient Egyptian Literature. 3 vols. Berkeley: University of California Press, 1973–80.

Lida, María Rosa. "Un decir más de Francisco Imperial: Respuesta a Fernán Pérez de Guzmán." Nueva Revista de Filología Hispánica 1 (1947): 170–77.

————. "Lope de Vega y los judíos." Bulletin Hispanique 75 (1973): 73–112.

Lieberknecht, Otfried. Allegorese und Philologie: Überlegungen zum Problem des mehrfachen Schriftsinns in Dantes Commedia. Text und Kontext 14. Stuttgart: Franz Steiner Verlag, 1999.

Linehan, Peter. "The Spanish Church Revisited: The Episcopal Gravamina of 1279." In Authority and Power: Studies on Medieval Law and Government Presented to Walter Ullmann on his Seventieth Birthday, edited by Brian Tierney and Peter Linehan, 127–47. Cambridge: Cambridge University Press, 1980.

Lipton, Sara. Images of Intolerance: The Representation of Jews and Judaism in the Bible Moralisée. Berkeley: University of California Press, 1999.

———. "'Tanquam effeminatum': Pedro II of Aragon and the Gendering of Heresy in the Albigensian Crusade." In Blackmore and Hutcheson, Queer Iberia, 107–29.

———. "The Temple Is My Body: Gender, Carnality, and Synagoga in the Bible Moralisée." In Imaging the Self, Imaging the Other: Representations of Jews in Medieval Visual Culture, edited by Eva Frojmovic, 129–63. Leiden: Brill, 2002.

Liske, Javier. Viajes de extranjeros por España y Portugal en los siglos XV, XVI, y XVII: Colección. Madrid: Casa Editorial de Medina, 1878.

Liu, Benjamin. "'Affined to Love the Moor': Sexual Misalliance and Cultural Mixing in the Cantigas d'escarnho e de mal dizer" In Blackmore and Hutcheson, Queer Iberia, 48–72.

Llorente, Juan Antonio. Histoire critique l'Inquisition dupuis l'époque de son établissement par Ferdinand V, jusqu'au règne de Ferdinand VII, tirée des pieces originales des archives du Conseil de la Supreme, et de celles des tribunaux subalternes du Saint-office. 4 vols. Paris: Treuttel & Wurtz, 1817.

Llull, Ramon. Libre de contemplació en Deu. Edited by Mn. Antoni Ma. Alcover. 7 vols. Palma de Mallorca: Comissió Editora Lulliana, 1910.

López de Ayala, Pedro. Crónica de Enrique III de Castilla. Edited by Cayetano Rosell. Biblioteca de Autores Españoles 68. Madrid: M. Rivadeneyra, 1877.

———. "Libro de Poemas" o "Rimado de Palacio." Edited by Michel García. Madrid: Gredos, 1978.

López Martínez, Nicolás. "Teología española de la convivencia a mediados del siglo XV." Repertorio de las Ciencias Eclesiásticas de España 1 (Siglos III–XVI), 465–76. Salamanca, 1967.

López de Mendoza, Iñigo (Marqués de Santillana). "Proemio." In Obras Completas, edited by Ángel Gómez Moreno and Maximilian P. A. M. Kerkhof, 437–54. Barcelona: Planeta, 1988.

Lorenzo, Ramón. La traducción gallega de la Crónica General y de la Crónica de Castilla. 2 vols. Orense: Instituto de Estudios Oresanos Padre Feijóo, 1975.

Lorenzo Gradín, Pilar. "Gómez García, Abade de Valadolide." In La literatura en la época de Sancho IV: Actas del congreso internacional «La Literatura en la Época de Sancho IV», Alcalá de Henares, 21–24 de febrero de 1994, ed. Carlos Alvar Ezquerra et al., 213–26. Alcalá de Henares: Servicio de Publicaciones, Universidad de Alcalá, 1996.

Lourie, Elena. "Anatomy of Ambivalence: Muslims under the Crown of Aragon in the Late Thirteenth Century." In Crusade and Colonisation: Muslims, Christians, and Jews in Medieval Aragon, edited by Elena Lourie, 1–77. Aldershot: Variorum, 1990.

———. "Seigneurial Pressure and the salva de infanzonía: Larués, Marcuello and Yeste (1300–1329)." 15 Congreso de Historia de la Corona de Aragón, vol. 5, 197–208. Zaragoza: Gobierno de Aragón, Departamento de educación y cultura, 1996.

Lubac, Henri de. Exégèse médiévale: Les quatre sens de l'Écriture. Paris: Aubier, 1959–64.

Lucena, Juan de. De vita beata. In Opúsculos literarios de los siglos XIV–XVI, edited by Antonio Paz y Melía. Madrid: Sociedad de Bibliófilos Españoles, 1892.

Luedemann, Gerd. Paul, Apostle to the Gentiles: Studies in Chronology. Philadelphia: Fortress Press, 1984.

Luis Suárez, Pablo. "Los manuscritos de Alfonso Tostado de Madrigal conservados en la Biblioteca Universitaria de Salamanca." Salamanticensis 4 (1957): 3–50.

Luther, Martin. Dr. Martin Luthers Werke. Multiple editors. Weimar: Hermann Böhlaus Nachfolger, 1883–present.

Maalouf, Amin. Leo Africanus. Translated by Peter Sluglett. New York: New Amsterdam Press, 1992.

Maciejko, Paweł. The Mixed Multitude: Jacob Frank and the Frankist Movement, 1755–1816. Philadelphia: University of Pennsylvania Press, 2011.

Mack, Michael. German Idealism and the Jew. Chicago: University of Chicago Press, 2002.

Madurell Marimón, José María. "La cofradía de la Santa Trinidad, de los conversos de Barcelona." Sefarad 18 (1958): 60–82.

Maimonides. The Code of Maimonides, Book Five: The Book of Holiness. Translated by Louis Rabinowitz and Philip Grossman. Yale Judaica Series 16. New Haven, CT: Yale University Press, 1965.

———. Letters and Essays of Moses Maimonides. Edited and translated by Isaac Shailat. Jerusalem: Maliyot Press of Yeshivat Birkat Moshe Maaleh Adumim, 1987.

Mansi, J. D. Sacrorum conciliorum nova et amplissima collectio. 53 vols. Florence, 1759–93. Reprint, Graz: Akademische Druck- und Verlagsanstalt, 1961.

Marín Padilla, Encarnación. Relación judeoconversa durante la segunda mitad del siglo XV en Aragón: La Ley. Madrid: printed by author, 1988.

Marks, Elaine. Marrano as Metaphor: The Jewish Presence in French Writing. New York: Columbia University Press, 1996.

Márquez Villanueva, Francisco. "La Celestina as Hispano-Semitic Anthropology." Revue de Littérature Comparée 61 (1987): 425–53.

———. "Conversos y cargos concejiles en el siglo XV." Revista de archivos, bibliotecas, y museos 63 (1957): 503–40.

———. "Jewish 'Fools' of the Spanish Fifteenth Century." Hispanic Review 50 (1982): 385–409.

———. "Presencia judía en la literatura española: Releyendo a Américo Castro." In La sociedad medieval a través de la literatura hispanojudía, edited by Ricardo Izquierdo Benito and Ángel Sáenz-Badillos, 11–28. Cuenca: Ediciones de la Universidad de Castilla – La Mancha, 1998.

———. "El problema de los conversos: Cuatro puntos cardinales." In Hispania Judaica: Studies on the History, Language and Literature of the Jews in the Hispanic World, vol. 1, edited by Josep Solà-Solé, Samuel G. Armistead, and Joseph H. Silverman, 51–75. Barcelona: Puvill, 1980.

Marshall, John. John Locke, Toleration and Early Enlightenment Culture. Cambridge Studies in Early Modern British History. Cambridge: Cambridge University Press, 2006.

Martí, Ramón. Pugio fidei adversus mauros et judaeos. 1687. Reprint, Farnborough: Gregg Press, 1967.

Martínez de Toledo, Alfonso. Arcipreste de Talavera o Corbacho. Edited by E. Michael Gerli. 4th ed. Madrid: Cátedra, 1992.

Martínez Díez, Gonzalo. ed. Leyes de Alfonso X. Vol. 1, Espéculo. Avila: Fundación Sánchez-Albornoz, 1985.

Martínez Montavez, Pedro. Al-Andalus, España, en la literatura árabe contemporánea: La casa del pasado. Madrid: Editorial Mapfre, 1992.

Mata Carriazo, José de, ed. "Los Anales de Garci Sánchez, jurado de Sevilla." Anales de la Universidad Hispalense 14 (1953): 3–63.

———, ed. Crónica del Halconero de Juan II. Madrid: Espasa-Calpe, 1946.

———, ed. El Victorial: Crónica de don Pero Niño, Conde de Buelna, por su alférez Gutiéerre Díez de Games. Madrid: Espasa-Calpe, 1940.

Marx, Alexander. "The Expulsion of the Jews from Spain: Two New Accounts." Jewish Quarterly Review, original ser., 20 (1908): 240–71.

Marx, Karl. "Zur Judenfrage." In Karl Marx, Friedrich Engels, Werke, vol. 1, 347–77. 1957. Reprint, Berlin: Dietz, 1981.

Mastnak, Tomaž. Crusading Peace: Christendom, the Muslim World, and Western Political Order. Berkeley: University of California Press, 2002.

Mateo, Ignazio di. "Il Tahrīf od alterazione della Bibbia seconodo i musulmani." Bessarione 38 (1922): 64–111, 223–360.

Matter, E. Ann. "Il matrimonio mistico." In Donne e fede: Santità e vita religiosa in Italia, edited by Lucetta Scaraffia and Gabriella Zarri, 43–60. Bari: Laterza, 1994.

Méchoulan, Henri. "The Importance of Hispanicity in Jewish Orthodoxy and Heterodoxy in Seventeenth-Century Amsterdam." In In Iberia and Beyond: Hispanic Jews between Cultures, edited by Bernard Dov Cooperman, 353–72. Newark: University of Delaware Press, 1998.

Mendoza y Bovadilla, Francisco. El tizón de la nobleza. Madrid: Colegio Heráldico de España y de las Indias, 1992.

Menéndez Collera, Ana, and Victoriano Roncero López, eds. Nunca fue pena mayor (estudios de literatura Española en homenaje a Brian Dutton). Cuenca: Ediciones de la Universidad de Castilla – La Mancha, 1996.

Menéndez y Pelayo, Marcelino. Antología de poetas líricos castellanos. Edited by Enrique Sánchez Reyes. 10 vols. Edición Nacional de las Obras Completas de Menéndez Pelayo 17–26. Santander: Aldus, 1944–45.

———. Estudios sobre el teatro de Lope de Vega IV, Obras Completas. 6 vols. Santander: Consejo Superior de Investigaciones Científicas, 1949.

———. Historia de los heterodoxos Españoles. 3 vols. 1882. Reprint, Mexico City: Editorial Porrúa, 1982.

Menocal, María Rosa. The Arabic Role in Medieval Literary History: A Forgotten Heritage. Philadelphia: University of Pennsylvania Press, 1987.

———. "Close Encounters in Medieval Provence: Spain's Role in the Birth of Troubadour Poetry." Hispanic Review 49 (1981): 43–64.

———. The Ornament of the World: How Muslims, Jews and Christians Created a Culture of Tolerance in Medieval Spain. Boston: Little, Brown, 2002.

———. "Pride and Prejudice in Medieval Studies: European and Oriental." Hispanic Review 53 (1985): 61–78.

Meyerson, Mark. "The Jewish Community of Murviedro (1391–1492)." In Lazar and Haliczer, The Jews of Spain and the Expulsion of 1492, 129–52.

———. "Prostitution of Muslim Women in the Kingdom of Valencia: Religious and Sexual Discrimination in a Medieval Plural Society." In The Medieval Mediterranean: Cross-Cultural Contacts, edited by Marilyn J. Chiat and Kathryn L. Ryerson, 87–95. Minnesota: University of Minnesota Press, 1988.

Meyuhas Ginio, Alisa. De bello iudaeorum: Fray Alonso de Espina y su "Fortalitium fidei." Fontes Iudaeorum Regni Castellae 8. Salamanca: Universidad de Pontifícia de Salamanca, 1998.

Michaelis, Johann David. Ueber die bürgerliche Verbesserung der Juden. 2 vols. Berlin: Friedrich Nicolai, 1781–83.

Mikat, Paul. Die Judengesetzgebung der merowingisch-fränkischen Konzilien. Opladen: Westdeutscher Verlag, 1995.

Millás Vallicrosa, José María. "En torno a la predicación judaica de San Vicente Ferrer." Boletín de la Real Academia de la Historia 147 (1958): 189–98.

———. "Un tratado anónimo de polémica contra los judíos." Sefarad 13 (1953): 3–34.

Miller, Kathryn. "Guardians of Islam: Muslim Communities in Medieval Aragon" PhD dissertation, Yale University, New Haven, CT, 1998.

Milner, Jean-Claude. De la syntaxe à l'interprétation: Quantités, insultes, exclamations. Paris: Seuil, 1978.

Minnis, Alastair J. "The Transformation of Critical Tradition: Dante, Petrarch, and Boccaccio." In Medieval Literary Theory and Criticism, c. 1000–c.1375, edited by Alastair J. Minnis and A. B. Scott, 373–94. Rev. ed. Oxford: Clarendon Press, 1991.

Miret y Sans, Joaquim. "El proces de les hosties contra. los jueus d'Osca en 1377." Anuari de l'Institut d'Estudis Catalans 4 (1911–12): 59–80.

Mirrer-Singer, Louise. The Language of Evaluation: A Sociolinguistic Approach to the Story of Pedro el Cruel in Ballad and Chronicle. Amsterdam: John Benjamins Publishing Company, 1986.

Missis, Alastair, and Ian Johnson, eds. The Cambridge History of Literary Criticism, 2: The Middle Ages. Cambridge: Cambridge University Press, 2005.

Mitre Fernández, Emilio. Los judíos de Castilla en tiempo de Enrique III: El pogrom de 1391. Valladolid: Universidad de Valladolid, 1994.

———. "Notas en torno a las disposiciones anti-judías de las cortes de Valladolid de 1405." In Proceedings of the Seventh World Congress of Jewish Studies, vol. 4, 115–22. Jerusalem: World Union of Jewish Studies, 1981.

Monroe, James T. Islam and the Arabs in Spanish Scholarship (Sixteenth Century to the Present). Leiden: Brill, 1970.

Montague, Ashley. Man's Most Dangerous Myth: The Fallacy of Race. Rev. ed. New York: Oxford University Press, 1974.

Montes Romero-Camacho, Isabel. "El antijudaismo o antisemitismo sevillano hacia la minoría hebrea." In Los caminos del exilio, edited by Juan Carrasco, 73–157. Tudela: Gobierno de Navarra, 1996.

Montrose, Louis A. "Professing the Renaissance: The Poetics and Politics of Culture." In The New Historicism, edited by H. Aram Vesser, 15–36. New York: Routledge, 1989.

Moreno Koch, Yolanda. "La comunidad judaizante de Castillo de Garcimuñoz, 1489–1492," Sefarad 37 (1977): 351–72.

Moxó, Salvador de. "De la nobleza vieja a la nobleza nueva: La transformación nobiliaria castellana en la baja Edad Media." Cuadernos de historia 3 (1969): 1–210.

Murray, Michele. Playing a Jewish Game: Gentile Christian Judaizing in the First and Second Centuries CE. Ontario: Wilfred Laurier University Press, 2004.

Murray, Penelope, ed. Plato on Poetry. Cambridge: Cambridge University Press, 1996.

Mutgé Vives, Josefa. L'aljama sarraïna de Lleida a l'edtat mitjana: Aproximació a la seva història. Barcelona: Consell Superior d'Investigacions Científiques, 1992.

Narbona Vizcaíno, Rafael. Pueblo, poder y sexo: Valencia medieval (1306–1420). Valencia: Diputació de Valencia, 1992.

Neaman, Judith S. "The Harlot Bride: From Biblical Code to Mystical Topos." Vox benedictina 4, no. 4 (1987): 277–306.

Netanyahu, Benzion. Don Isaac Abravanel: Statesman and Philosopher. 5th ed. Ithaca, NY: Cornell University Press, 1998.

———. The Origins of the Inquisition in Fifteenth-Century Spain. New York: Random House, 1995.

———. Toward the Inquisition: Essays on Jewish and Converso History in Late Medieval Spain. Ithaca, NY: Cornell University Press, 1997.

Newby, G. D. "Arabian Jewish history in the Sīrah." Jerusalem Studies in Arabic and Islam 7 (1986): 121–38.

Nieto Cumplido, Manuel. "Aportación histórica al Cancionero de Baena." Historia, instituciones, documentos 6 (1979): 197–218.

———. "Juan Alfonso de Baena y su Cancionero: Nueva aportación histórica." Boletín de la Real Academia de Córdoba 52 (1982): 35–57.

Nieto Soria, José Manuel. "Los judíos de Toledo en sus relaciones financieras con la monarquía y la Iglesia (1252–1312)." Sefarad 41 (1981): 301–19; 42 (1982): 79–102.

———. Sancho IV, 1284–1295. Palencia: Diputación Provincial de Palencia, 1994.

Nietzsche, Friedrich. Unzeitgemässe Betrachtungen, Zweites Stück: Vom Nutzen und Nachteil der Historie. In Werke in drei Bänden, vol. 1, 153–244. Cologne: Könemann, 1994.

Nirenberg, David. Anti-Judaism: The Western Tradition. New York: W. W. Norton, 2013.

———. "Christian Sovereignty and Jewish Flesh." In Rethinking the Medieval Senses, edited by Steven G. Nichols, Andreas Kablitz, and Alison Calhoun, 154–85. Baltimore: Johns Hopkins University Press, 2008.

———. Communities of Violence: Persecution of Minorities in the Middle Ages. Princeton, NJ: Princeton University Press, 1996.

———. "Les juifs, la violence, et le sacré." Annales: Histoire, sciences sociales 50 (1995): 109–31.

———. "María's Conversion to Judaism." Orim: A Jewish Journal at Yale 2 (1984): 38–44.

———. "El sentido de la historia judía," Revista de libros 28 (April 1999): 3–5.

———. "Varieties of Mudejar Experience: Muslims in Christian Iberia, 1000–1526." In The Medieval World, edited by Peter Linehan and Janet L. Nelson, 60–76. New York: Routledge, 2001.

———. Violence et minorités au Moyen Age. Paris: Presses Universitaires de France, 2001.

———. "Warum der König die Juden beschützen musste, und warum er sie verfolgen musste." In Die Macht des Königs: Herrschaft in Europa vom Frühmittelalter bis in die Neuzeit, edited by Bernhard Jussen, 226–41. Munich: C. H. Beck, 2005.

———. "What Benedict Really Said: Paleologus and Us." New Republic, October 10, 2006.

Noguera de Guzmán, Raimundo, and José María Madurell Marimón, eds. Privilegios y ordenanzas históricos de los notarios de Barcelona. Barcelona: Seix y Barral Hermanos, 1965.

Noorani, Yaseen. "The Lost Garden of al-Andalus: Islamic Spain and the Poetic Inversion of Colonialism." International Journal of Middle East Studies 31 (1999): 237–54.

Nykl, A. R. Hispano-Arabic Poetry and Its Relations with the Old Provençal Troubadours. Baltimore: Johns Hopkins University Press, 1946.

Oberman, Heiko. Wurzeln des Antisemitismus: Christenangst und Judenplage im Zeitalter von Humanismus und Reformation. 2nd ed. Berlin: Severin & Siedler, 1983.

Obermann, Julian. "Koran and Agada: The Events at Mount Sinai." American Journal of Semitic Languages and Literatures 58 (1941): 23–48.

Orcástegui, Carmen, and Esteban Sarasa. "El libro-registro de Miguel Royo, merino de Zaragoza en 1301: Una fuente para el estudio de la sociedad y economía Zaragozana a comienzos del siglo XIV." Aragón en la Edad Media 4 (1981): 87–156.

Orfali, Moisés. "La cuestión de la identidad judía en el Maamar ha-Anusim (Tratado de los conversos forzados) de RaShBaSh." In Pensamiento medieval hispano: Homenaje a Horacio Santiago-Otero, vol. 2, edited by José María Soto Rábanos, 1267–1287. Madrid: Consejo Superior de Investigaciones Científicas, 1998.

———. Los conversos españoles en la literatura rabínica. Salamanca: Universidad Pontificia de Salamanca, 1982.

Orfali, Moshe. "Oropesa and Judaism." [In Hebrew.] Zion 51 (1986): 411–32.

Oropesa, Alonso de. Luz para conocimiento de los gentiles. Edited by Luis A. Díaz y Díaz. Madrid: Universidad Pontificia de Salamanca, 1979.

Otto of Freising. The Deeds of Frederick Barbarossa. Translated by Charles Christopher Mierow. Toronto: University of Toronto Press, 1994.

Pacios López, Antonio. La disputa de Tortosa. Madrid: Consejo Superior de Investigaciones Científicas, 1957.

Pagden, Anthony. "Europe: Conceptualizing a Continent." In The Idea of Europe: From Antiquity to the European Union, ed. Anthony Pagden, 33–54. Washington: Woodrow Wilson Center Press, 2002.

———. "The diffusion of Aristotle's moral philosophy in Spain, ca. 1400–ca.1600." Traditio 31 (1975): 287–313.

Pagels, Elaine. Beyond Belief: The Secret Gospel of Thomas. New York: Random House, 2003.

Pakter, Walter. Medieval Canon Law and the Jews. Ebelsbach am Main: R. Gremer, 1988.

Papiha, Surinder S. "Genetic Variation and Disease Susceptibility in NCWP (New Commonwealth with Pakistani) Groups in Britain." New Community 13 (1987): 373–83.

Paravicini-Bagliani, Agostino. The Pope's Body. Chicago: Chicago University Press, 2000.

Paredes Núñez, Juan Salvador. "Sancho IV y su tiempo en la literatura genealógica peninsular." In La literatura en la época de Sancho IV, 235–43.

Paulson, Stanley, ed. Hans Kelsen und die Rechstsoziologie: Auseinandersetzung mit Hermann U. Kantorowicz, Eugen Ehrlich, und Max Weber. Aalen: Scientia, 1992.

Perarnau i Espelt, Josep, ed. "Els quatre sermons catalans de sant Vicent Ferrer en el manuscrit 476 de la Biblioteca de Catalunya." Arxiu de textos catalans antics 15 (1996): 231–32.

Perceval, José María. Todos son uno. Arquetipos, xenofobia y racismo. La imagen del morisco en la Monarquía Española durante los siglos XVI y XVII. Almería: Instituto de Estudios Almerienses, 1997.

Pérès, Henri. L'Espagne vue par les voyageurs musulmans de 1610 à 1930. Paris: Librairie d'Amérique et d'Orient, 1937.

———. La poésie andalouse en arabe classique du XIe siècle. Paris: Librairie d'Amérique et d'Orient, Adrien-Maisonneuve, 1937.

Pérez de Gómez, Antonio, ed. Romancero del rey Don Pedro, 1368–1800. Valencia: La fonte que mana y corre, 1954.

Peter of Cluny. Summa totius haeresis Saracenorum. In Schriften zum Islam, edited by Rheinhold Glei, Corpus Islamo-Christianum, series latina 1. Alternberg: CIS-Verlag, 1985.

Peters, Edward. The First Crusade: The Chronicle of Fulcher of Chartres and Other Source Materials. Philadelphia: University of Pennsylvania Press, 1989.

Petrarch. Collatio laureationis. Edited by Carlo Godi, in "La Collatio laureationis del Petrarca nelle due redazioni." Studi petrarcheschi 5 (1988): 1–58.

———. Invective contra medicum. In Opere latine di Francesco Petrarca, vol. 2, edited by Antonietta Bufano, 818–981. Classici Italiani 4. Turin: Unione Tipografico-Editrice Torinese, 1975.

Piccus, Jules. "El traductor español de De genealogia deorum." In Homenaje a Rodríguez-Moñino: Estudios de erudición que le ofrecen sus amigos o discípulos hispanistas norteamericanos, vol. 2, 59–75. Madrid: Castalia, 1966.

Plá, José, ed. La misión internacional de la raza hispánica. Madrid: Javier Morata, 1928.

Poole, Fitz John Porter. "Metaphors and Maps: Towards Comparison in the Anthropology of Religion." Journal of the American Academy of Religion 54 (1986): 411–57.

Popkin, Richard H. "Epicureanism and Skepticism in the Early Seventeenth Century." In Philomathes: Studies and Essays in the Humanities in Memory of Philip Merlan, edited by Robert B. Palmer and Robert Hamerton-Kelly, 346–57. The Hague: Martinus Nijhoff, 1971.

Pou y Martí, José María. Visionarios, beguinos, y fraticelos catalanes (siglos XIII–XV). Madrid: Ed. Colegio "Cardenal Cisneros," 1991.

Powell, James, ed., Muslims under Latin Rule, 1100–1300. Princeton, NJ: Princeton University Press, 1990.

"Privilegio de Don Juan II en favor de un Hidalgo." In Sales españolas; o, Agudezas del ingenio nacional: Recogidas por Antonio Paz y Media, 25–28. Biblioteca de Autores Españoles 176. Madrid: Ediciones Atlas, 1964.

Puigvert Ocal, Alicia. "El léxico de la indumentaria en el Cancionero de Baena." Boletín de la Real Academia Española 67 (1987): 171–206.

Pulgar, Fernando del. Claros Varones de Castilla. Edited by Robert Brian Tate. Oxford: Clarendon Press, 1971.

Puymaigre, Théodore de. La cour littéraire de don Juan II, roi de Castille. Paris: Franck, 1871.

Quadrado, José María. "La judería de la ciudad de Mallorca en 1391." Boletín de la Real Academia de la Historia 9 (1886): 294–312.

Rábade Obradó, María del Pilar. Una elite de poder en la corte de los Reyes Católicos: Los judeoconversos. Madrid: Sigilo, 1993.

Ranke, Leopold von. Fürsten und Völker von Süd-Europa im sechzehnten und siebzehnten Jahrhundert. 2 vols. Berlin: Duncker und Humbolt, 1837.

Raphael, David. The Expulsion 1492 Chronicles. North Hollywood, CA: Carmi House Press, 1992.

Régné, Jean. History of the Jews in the Crown of Aragon. Edited by Yom Tov Assis and Adam Gruzman. Jerusalem: Magnes Press, 1978.

Reilly, Bernard F. The Kingdom of León-Castilla under King Alfonso VI, 1065–1109. Princeton, NJ: Princeton University Press, 1988.

Revah, I. S. "La controverse sur les statuts de pureté de sang," Bulletin Hispanique 63 (1971): 263–316.

Rey, Agapito, ed. Castigos e documentos para bien vivir. Bloomington: Indiana University Press, 1952.

Riera i Sans, Jaume. "Els avalots del 1391 a Girona." In Jornades d'història dels jueus a Catalunya, 95–159. Girona: Ajuntament de Girona, 1987.

———. "Contribució a l'estudi del conflicte religiós dels conversos jueus (segle xv)." In IX Congresso di Storia della Corona D'Aragona: La Corona d'Aragona e il Mediterraneo, vol. 4, 409–25. Naples: Società Napoletana di Storia Patria, 1978–82.

———. La crònica en Hebreu de la disputa de Tortosa. Barcelona: Fundació Salvador Vives Casajuana, 1974.

———. "Estrangers participants als avalots contra les jueríes de la Corona d'Aragó el 1391." Anuario de Estudios Medievales 10 (1980): 577–83.

———. "Jafudà Alatzar, jueu de València (segle XIV)." Revista d'Història Medieval 4 (1993): 65–100.

———. "Judíos y conversos en los reinos de la Corona de Aragón durante el siglo XV." In La Expulsión de los judíos de España: Conferencias pronunciadas en el II Curso de Cultura Hispano-Judía y Sefardí de la Universidad de Castilla-la Mancha, edited by Ricardo Izquierdo Benito, 71–90. Toledo: Caja de Castilla-La Mancha, 1993.

———. "Los tumultos contra las juderías de la Corona de Aragón en 1391." Cuadernos de Historia 8 (1977): 213–25.

Riley-Smith, Jonathan. The Crusades: A Short History. London: Athlone, 1992.

———. "Crusading as an Act of Love." History 65, no. 214 (June 1980): 177–92.

———. The First Crusade and the Idea of Crusading. London: Athlone, 1993.

———. "History, the Crusades, and the Latin East: A Personal View." In Crusaders and Muslims in twelfth-century Syria, edited by Maya Shatzmiller. Leiden: Brill, 1993.

Robinson, John A. T. Redating the New Testament. London: SCM Press, 1976.

Roca Traver, Francisco. "Un siglo de vida mudéjar en la Valencia medieval (1238–1338)." Estudios de Edad Media de la Corona de Aragón 5 (1952): 115–208.

Rodrigues Lapa, Manuel, ed. Cantigas d'escarnho e de mal dizer. Rev. ed. Coimbra: Galaxia, 1970.

———, ed. Cantigas d'Escarnho e de mal dezir dos cancioneiros medievais galego-portugueses. 3rd ed. Lisbon: Edições J. Sá da Costa, 1995.

Rodríguez Puértolas, Julio. Poesía crítica y satírica del siglo XV. Madrid: Castalia, 1981.

———, ed. Poesía de protesta en la Edad Media castellana. Biblioteca Románica Hispánica 25. Madrid: Gredos, 1968.

Rodríguez Velasco, Jesús D. El debate sobre la caballería en el siglo xv: La tratadística caballeresca castellana en su marco europeo. Colección de estudios de historia. Valladolid: Junta de Castilla y León, Consejería de Educación y Cultura, 1996.

Romano, David. "Característiques dels jueus en relació amb els cristians en els estats hispànics." In Jornades d'història dels jueus a Catalunya, 9–27. Girona: Ajuntament de Girona, 1987.

Rose, Stanley. "Anti-Semitism in the 'Cancioneros' of the Fifteenth Century: The Accusation of Sexual Indiscretions." Hispanofila 26 (1983): 1–11.

———. "Poesía antijudía y anticonversa en la poesía artística del siglo XV en España." PhD dissertation, Catholic University of America, Washington, DC, 1975.

Rosell, Cayetano, ed. Crónicas de los reyes de Castilla, Biblioteca de Autores Castellanos 66. Madrid: Rivadeneyra, 1875.

Rosenstock, Bruce. New Men: Conversos, Christian Theology, and Society in Fifteenth-Century Castile. London: Queen Mary and Westfield College, 2002.

Rosenzweig, Franz. The Star of Redemption. Tr. Barbara E. Galli. Madison: University of Wisconsin, 2005.

Rossiaud, Jacques. Medieval Prostitution. Oxford: Basil Blackwell, 1988.

Roth, Norman. Jews, Visigoths and Muslims in Medieval Spain. Leiden: Brill, 1994.

Round, Nicholas. The Greatest Man Uncrowned: A Study of the Fall of Don Alvaro de Luna. Dover, NH: Tamesis Books, 1986.

———. "Politics, Style and Group Attitudes in the Instrucción del Relator." Bulletin of Hispanic Studies 46 (1969): 289–319.

Rousset, Paul. "La notion de chrétienté aux XIe et XIIe siècles." Le Moyen Âge 69 (1963): 191–203.

———. Les origines et les caractères de la première croisade. Neuchâtel: Baconnière, 1945.

Rubinstein, Jay. Guibert of Nogent: Portrait of a Medieval Mind. New York: Routledge, 2002.

Rubio García, Luis. Los judíos de Murcia en la Baja Edad Media (1350–1500). Murcia: Universidad de Murcia, 1997.

Rubio Vela, Agustín. Epistolari de la València Medieval. Valencia: Institut de Filologia Valenciana, 1985.

Rucquoi, Adeline. "Être noble en Espagne aux XIVe–XVIe siècles." In Nobilitas: Funktion und Repräsentation des Adels in Alteuropa, edited by Otto Gerhard Oexle and Werner Paravicini, 273–98. Göttingen: Vandenhoeck & Ruprecht, 1997.

———. "Noblesse des conversos?" In Battesti-Pelegrin, "Qu'un Sang Impur . . . ," 89–108.

Ruether, Rosemary Radford. Faith and Fratricide: The Theological Roots of Anti-Semitism. New York: Seabury Press, 1974.

Rupp, Jean. L'idée de chrétienté dans la pensée pontificale des origines à Innocent III. Paris: Les Presses Modernes, 1939.

Rushdie, Salman. The Moor's Last Sigh. New York: Pantheon, 1995.

Russell, Peter E. "La historia de España, túnica de Neso." In Temas de La Celestina y otros estudios, del Cid al Quijote, 481–91. Letras e Ideas, Maior, 14. Barcelona: Editorial Ariel, 1978.

Sabar, Shalom. "The Beginnings of Ketubbah Decoration in Italy: Venice in the Late Sixteenth to the Early Seventeenth Centuries." Jewish Art 12–13 (1987): 96–110.

Sabaté, Flocel. "Discurs i estratègies del poder reial a Catalunya al segle XIV." Anuario de Estudios Medievales 9 (1995): 143–51.

Sahas, Daniel. John of Damascus on Islam: The "Heresy" of the Ishmaelites. Leiden: Brill, 1972.

Said, Edward. "The Clash of Definitions: On Samuel Huntington." In Reflections on Exile and Other Essays, 569–92. Cambridge, MA: Harvard University Press, 2000.

Salazar, J. Gómez. "Alphonse VIII de Castille et doña Fermosa." Evidences 22 (1951): 37–43.

Salazar y Castro, Luis de. Historia genealógica de la Casa de Haro. Madrid: Real Academia de la Historia, 1966.

Salvador Miguel, Nicasio. "El presunto judaísmo de La Celestina." In The Age of the Catholic Monarchs, 1474–1516: Literary Studies in Memory of Keith Whinnom, edited by Alan Deyermond and Ian Macpherson, 162–77. Liverpool: Liverpool University Press, 1989.

Samir, Samir Khalil, and Jørgen S. Nielsen, eds. Christian Arabic Apologetics during the Abbasid Period: 750–1258. Leiden: Brill, 1994.

Sanahuja, Pedro. Lérida en sus luchas por la fe (judíos, moros, conversos, Inquisición, moriscos). Lleida: Instituto de Estudios Ilerdenses, 1946.

Sánchez-Albornoz, Claudio. España. Un enigma histórico. 2 vols. 4th ed. Barcelona: Edhasa, 1973.

Santiago-Otero, Horacio. "The Libro declarante: An Anonymous Work in the Anti-Jewish Polemic in Spain." In Proceedings of the Tenth World Congress of Jewish Studies, Division B, The History of the Jewish People, 77–82. Jerusalem: World Union of Jewish Studies, 1990.

Santiago-Otero, Horacio, and Klaus Reinhardt, "Escritos de polémica antijudía en lengua vernácula." Medievalia 2 (1993): 185–95.

Santillana, David. Istituzioni di diritto musulmano malichita con riguardo anche al sistema sciafiita. 2 vols. Rome: Instituto per l'Oriente, 1925–38.

Santner, Eric L. "Miracles Happen: Benjamin, Rosenzweig, Freud, and the Matter of the Neighbor." In The Neighbor: Three Inquiries in Political Theology, edited by Slavoj Žižek, Eric L. Santner, and Kenneth Reinhard, 76–133. Chicago: University of Chicago Press, 2005.

Saperstein, Marc. Decoding the Rabbis: A Thirteenth-Century Commentary on the Aggadah. Cambridge, MA: Harvard University Press, 1980.

Sayers, Jane E. Innocent III: Leader of Europe (1198–1216). London: Longman, 1994.

Schacht, Joseph. An Introduction to Islamic Law. Oxford: Clarendon Press, 1964.

Schlegel, August Wilhelm von. Observations sur la langue et la littérature provençales. Paris: Librairie grecque-latine-allemande, 1818.

Schmitt, Carl. Der Monotheismus als politisches Problem. Leipzig: Hegner, 1935.

Scholberg, Kenneth. Sátira e invectiva en la España Medieval. Madrid: Gredos, 1971.

Schorsch, Ismar. "The Myth of Sephardic Supremacy." Leo Baeck Institute Year Book 34 (1989): 47–66.

Schorske, Carl E. "Politics in a New Key: An Austrian Trio." In Fin-de-Siècle Vienna: Politics and Culture, 133–69. New York: Knopf, 1979.

Schultz, Alfred. Race or Mongrel: A Brief History of the Rise and Fall of the Ancient Races of Earth. Boston: L. C. Page, 1908.

Schwarz, Frederic, and Frances Carreras. Manual de novells ardits vulgarment apellat dietari del antich consell barcelonia. 28 vols. Barcelona: Henrich i Companyia, 1893.

Schwarzfuchs, Simon. "Le retour des marranes au judaïsme dans la littérature rabbinique." In Xudeus e Conversos na historia, vol. 1, edited by Carlos Barros, 339–48. Santiago de Compostela: Editorial de la Historia, 1994.

Schwerin, Ursula. Die Aufrufe der Päpste zur Befreiung des Heiligen Landes von den Anfängen bis zum Ausgang Innozenz IV: Ein Beitrag zur Geschichte der kurialen Kreuzzugspropaganda und der päpstlichen Epistolographie. Berlin: Ebering, 1937.

Sebastián de Covarrubias. Tesoro de la lengua castellana o española. Madrid: Por L. Sánchez, impressor del rey n.s., 1611.

Secall i Güell, Gabriel. La comunitat hebrea de Santa Coloma de Queralt. Tarragona: Diputació Provincial de Tarragona, 1986.

Serrano Reyes, José Luis, and Juan Fernández Jiménez, eds., Juan Alfonso de Baena y su Cancionero: Actas del I Congreso Internacional sobre el Cancionero de Baena. Córdoba: M.I. Ayuntamiento de Baena, Delegación de Cultura, 2001.

Serrano y Sanz, Manuel. Orígenes de la dominación española en América. Vol. 1, Los amigos y protectores de Cristóbal Colón. Madrid: Bailly-Baillère, 1918.

Shatzmiller, Joseph. "Politics and the Myth of Origins: The Case of the Medieval Jews." In Les Juifs au regard de l'histoire: Mélanges en l'honneur de Bernhard Blumenkranz, edited by Gilbert Dahan, 49–61. Paris: Picard, 1985.

Shmeruk, Chone. The Esterke Story in Yiddish and Polish Literature: A Case Study in the Mutual Relations of Two Cultural Traditions. Jerusalem: Zalman Shazar Center for the Furtherance of the Study of Jewish History, 1985.

Sicroff, Albert. Les controverses des statuts de "pureté de sang" en Espagne du xve au xviie siècle. Paris: Didier, 1960.

Simmel, Georg. Soziologie. 5th ed. Berlin: Duncker & Humblot, 1968.

Simonsohn, Shlomo. The Apostolic See and the Jews. 8 vols. Toronto: Pontifical Institute of Medieval Studies, 1988–91.

Sismondi, Sismonde de. De la littérature du midi de l'Europe. 4 vols. Paris: Treuttel & Wurtz, 1819.

Sivan, Emmanuel. Interpretations of Islam Past and Present. Princeton, NJ: Darwin Press, 1985.

———. L'Islam et la Croisade: Idéologie et propagande dans les réactions musulmanes aux Croisades. Paris: Librairie d'Amérique et d'Orient, 1968.

Sizgorich, Thomas. Violence and Belief in Late Antiquity: Militant Devotion in Christianity and Islam. Philadelphia: University of Pennsylvania Press, 2008.

Skehan, Patrick W. Studies in Israelite Poetry and Wisdom. Washington, DC: Catholic Biblical Association of America, 1971.

Slae, M. "References to Marranos in the Responsa of R. Isaac Bar Sheshet." Annual of Bar-Ilan University 7–8 (1970): 397–419.

Smith, Paul Julian. Representing the Other: "Race," Text, and Gender in Spanish and Spanish American Narrative. Oxford: Clarendon Press, 1992.

Speed, Diane. "The Saracens of King Horn." Speculum 65 (1990): 564–95.

Spitzer, Leo. "Ratio>Race." In Essays in Historical Semantics, 47–69. New York: Russell & Russell, 1948.

Stacey, Robert. "Parliamentary Negotiation and the Expulsion of the Jews from England." In Thirteenth-Century England VI: Proceedings of the Durham Conference, edited by Michael Prestwich, Richard Britnell, and Robin Frame, 77–101. Woodbridge: Boydell Press, 1997.

Staël, Madame de. De la littérature considérée dans ses rapports avec les institutions socials. Edited by Gérard Gengembre and Jean Goldink. Paris: Flammarion, 1991.

Stalls, William. "Jewish Conversion to Islam: The Perspective of a Quaestio." Revista Española de Teología 43 (1983): 235–51.

Starr-Lebeau, Gretchen. In the Shadow of the Virgin: Inquisitors, Friars, and Conversos in Guadalupe, Spain. Princeton, NJ: Princeton University Press, 2003.

Stern, David, trans. Lamentations Rabbah. In Parables in Midrash: Narrative and Exegesis in Rabbinic Literature, 57. Cambridge, MA: Harvard University Press, 1991.

Stillman, Norman. "Myth, Countermyth, and Distortion." Tikkun 6, no. 3 (May–June, 1991): 60–64.

Strayer, Joseph. Medieval Statecraft and the Perspectives of History. Princeton, NJ: Princeton University Press, 1971.

Suárez Fernández, Luis. Documentos acerca de la expulsion de los judíos. Valladolid: Ediciones Aldecoa, 1964.

———. Enrique IV de Castilla: La difamación como arma política. Barcelona: Ariel, 2001.

Sylvester, Bernard. Commentary on the First Six Books of Virgil's Aeneid. Translated by Earl G. Schreiber and Thomas E. Maresca. Lincoln: University of Nebraska Press, 1979.

Taha, Mahmoud Muhammad. The Second Message of Islam. Translated by Abdullahi Ahmed An-Na'im. Syracuse: Syracuse University Press, 1987.

Talmage, Frank. "The Francesc de Sant Jordi-Solomon Bonafed Letters." In Studies in Medieval Jewish History and Literature, edited by Isadore Twersky, 337–74. Cambridge, MA: Harvard University Press, 1979.

———. "Trauma at Tortosa: The Testimony of Abraham Rimoch." Medieval Studies 47 (1985): 379–415.

Tambiah, Stanley. "Animals Are Good to Think and Good to Prohibit." In Culture, Thought, and Social Action: An Anthropological Perspective, 169–211. Cambridge, MA: Harvard University Press, 1985.

Taubes, Jacob. The Political Theology of Paul. Palo Alto, CA: Stanford University Press, 2004.

Teensma, B. N. "Fragmenten uit het Amsterdamse convolut van Abraham Idaña, alias Gaspar Mendez del Arroyo (1623–1690)." Studia Rosenthaliana 11 (1977): 127–56.

Teixidor, Josef. Antigüedades de Valencia. Edited by Roque Chabás. 2 vols. Valencia: Francisco Vives Mora, 1895.

Theophanes the Confessor. The Chronicle of Theophanes the Confessor, translated by Cyril Mango and Roger Scott (Oxford: Clarendon Press, 1997).

Tirosh-Rothschild, Hava. Between Worlds: The Life and Thought of Rabbi David ben Judah Messer Leon. Albany: State University of New York Press, 1991.

Tolan, John. "Peter the Venerable, on the 'Diabolical Heresy of the Saracens.'" In Devil, Heresy, and Witchcraft in the Middle Ages: Essays in Honor of Jeffrey B. Russell, edited by Alberto Ferreiro, 345–67. Leiden: Brill, 1998.

———. Saracens: Islam in the Medieval European Imagination. New York: Columbia, 2002.

Torjesen, Karen Jo. Hermeneutical Procedure and Theological Method in Origen's Exegesis. Patristische Texte und Studien 28. Berlin: De Gruyter, 1985.

Torquemada, Juan de. Tractatus contra Madianitas et Ismaelitas. Edited by Nicolás López Martínez and Vicente Proaño Gil Burgos. Burgos: Seminario Metropolitano de Burgos, 1957.

Torres Fontes, Juan. "Moros, judíos y conversos en la regencia de Don Fernando de Antequera." Cuadernos de Historia de España 31–32 (1960): 60–97.

Trexler, Richard. Sex and Conquest: Gendered Violence, Political Order, and the European Conquest of the Americas. Cambridge: Polity Press, 1995.

Tyerman, Christopher J. The Invention of the Crusades. Toronto: University of Toronto Press, 1998.

Ulloa y Pereyra, D. Luis de. Versos. Madrid: Diego Diaz, 1659.

Valdeón Baruque, Julio. Los judíos de Castilla y la revolución Trastámara. Valladolid: Universidad de Valladolid, 1968.

Valera, Juan. Epistolario de Valera y Menéndez Pelayo. Madrid: Espasa-Calpe, 1946.

Valera, Mosén Diego de. Espejo de la verdadera nobleza. In Prosistas castellanos del siglo xv, edited by Mario Penna, 89–116. Biblioteca de Autores Españoles 116. Madrid: M. Rivadeneyra, 1959.

Vega, Lope de. Amar sin saber a quién. Edited by Carmen Bravo-Villasante. Salamanca: Anaya, 1967.

Vendrell de Millás, Francisca. "La actividad proselitista de San Vicente Ferrer durante el reinado de Fernando I de Aragón." Sefarad 13 (1953): 87–104.

———. "La política proselitista del Rey D. Fernando I." Sefarad 10 (1950): 349–66.

———. "En torno a la confirmación real, en Aragón, de la pragmatica de Benedicto XIII." Sefarad 20 (1960): 22–33.

Verlinden, Charles. L'esclavage dans l'Europe Médiévale. 2 vols. Bruges: De Tempel, 1955.

Vidal, Pierre. "Mélanges d'histoire, de littèrature et de philologie catalane." Revue des langues romanes, 4th ser., 2 (1888): 333–59.

Vitoria, Francisco de. Relectio de Indis. Edited by L. Pereña and J. M. Peres Prendes. Madrid: Consejo Superior de Investigaciones Científicas, 1967.

Vocht, Henry de. "Rodrigo Manrique's Letter to Vives." In Monumenta Humanistica Lovaniensia: Texts and Studies about Louvain Humanists in the First Half of the Sixteenth Century. Humanistica Lovaniensia 4, 427–58. Louvain: Charles Uystpruyst, 1934.

Walfish, Barry D. Esther in Medieval Garb: Jewish Interpretations of the Book of Esther in the Middle Ages. Albany: State University of New York Press, 1993.

Walther, Manfred. "Spinoza und das Problem einer jüdischen Philosophie." In Die philosophische Aktualität der jüdischen Tradition, edited by Werner Stegmaier, Suhrkamp Taschenbuch Wissenschaft 1499, 281–330. Frankfurt: Suhrkamp, 2000.

Walz, Rainer. "Der vormoderne Antisemitismus: Religiöser Fanatismus oder Rassenwahn?" Historische Zeitschrift 260 (1995): 719–48.

———. "Rasse." in Geschichtliche Grundbegriffe: Historisches Lexicon zur politisch-sozialen Sprache in Deutschland, vol. 5, edited by Otto Brunner, Werner Conze, and Reinhart Koselleck, 135–78. Stuttgart: E. Klett, 1984.

Wasserstrom, Steven M. Between Muslim and Jew. Princeton, NJ: Princeton University Press, 1995.

———. "'The Shi'is Are the Jews of Our Community': An Interreligious Comparison within Sunni Thought." Israel Oriental Studies 14 (1994): 297–324.

Watt, John A. "The Jews, the Law, and the Church: The Concept of Jewish Serfdom in Thirteenth-Century England." In The Church and Sovereignty c.590–1918: Essays in Honour of Michael Wilks, edited by Diana Wood, 153–72. Oxford: Blackwell, 1991.

Wedderburn, A. J. M. Baptism and Resurrection: Studies in Pauline Theology against Its Graeco-Roman Background. Wissenschaftliche Untersuchungen zum Neuen Testament 44. Tübingen: J. C. B. Mohr, 1987.

Weiss, Julian. "Alvaro de Luna, Juan de Mena and the Power of Courtly Love." Modern Language Notes 106 (1991): 241–56.

———. The Poet's Art: Literary Theory in Castile c. 1400–60. Medium Aevum Monographs, n.s., 14. Oxford: Society for the Study of Medieval Languages and Literature, 1990.

Weissberger, Barbara. "'¡A tierra, puto!' Alfonso de Palencia's Discourse of Effeminacy." In Blackmore and Hutcheson, Queer Iberia, 291–324.

———. "'Deceitful Sects': The Debate about Women in the Age of Isabel the Catholic." In Gender in Debate from the Early Middle Ages to the Renaissance, edited by Thelma S. Fenster and Clare A. Lees, 214–19. New York: Palgrave, 2002.

———. Isabel Rules: Constructing Queenship: Wielding Power. Minneapolis: University of Minnesota Press, 2004.

Wiegers, Gerard Albert. Islamic Literature in Spanish and Aljamiado: Yça of Segovia (fl. 1450), His Antecedents and Successors. Leiden: Brill, 1994.

Wills, Lawrence M. The Jew in the Court of the Foreign King: Ancient Jewish Court Legends. Minneapolis: Fortress Press, 1990.

Winter, Jean-Pierre. Les errants de le chair: Études sur l'hystérie masculine. Paris: Calmann-Lévy, 1998.

Wolfram of Eschenbach. Parzival. Edited by Karl Lachmann. Berlin: Walter de Gruyter, 1926.

Yehoshua, A. B. A Journey to the End of the Millennium. Translated by Nicholas de Lange. New York: Doubleday, 1999.

Yehuda R. ben Asher. Zikhron Yehuda. Berlin: D. Fridlender, 1846.

Yerushalmi, Yosef Haim. Assimilation and Racial Anti-Semitism: The Iberian and the German Models. New York: Leo Baeck Institute, 1982.

———. From Spanish Court to Italian Ghetto: Isaac Cardoso. A Study in Seventeenth-Century Marranism and Jewish Apologetics. Columbia University Studies in Jewish History, Culture, and Institutions 1. New York: Columbia University Press, 1971.

———. Zakhor: Jewish History and Jewish Memory. Seattle: University of Washington Press, 1982.

Yovel, Yirmiyahu. Dark Riddle: Hegel, Nietzsche, and the Jews. Cambridge: Polity Press, 1998.

———. Spinoza and Other Heretics. Vol. 1, The Marrano of Reason. Princeton, NJ: Princeton University Press, 1989.

Zacour, Norman. Jews and Saracens in the Consilia of Oldradus de Ponte. Toronto: Pontifical Institute of Medieval Studies, 1990.

Zacuto, Abraham. Sefer Yuḥasin ha-Shalem. Edited by Herschell Filipowski and Abraham Hayyim Freimann. Frankfurt: Wahrmann Verlag, 1924.

Zarco Cuevas, Julián. "Sermón predicado en Murcia por S. Vicente Ferrer." La Ciudad de Dios 148 (1927): 122–47.

Ziolkowski, Jan M. "Put in No-Man's Land: Guibert of Nogent's Accusations against a Judaizing and Jew-Supporting Christian." In Jews and Christians in Twelfth-Century Europe, edited by Michael A. Signer and John Van Engen, 110–22. Notre Dame, IN: University of Notre Dame Press, 2001.

Žižek, Slavoj. Welcome to the Desert of the Real. London: Verso, 2002.

INDEX

Abarbanel, Yitzḥaq, 144, 160, 261n2, 272–73n95
Abarim, Juseff, 238n13
'Abd al-Malik, 17
Abinhumen, Çalema, 244–45n31
Aboab, Isaac, 153, 158–59
Abraham (biblical patriarch), 283n13
Abraham ben Salomon de Torrutiel Ardutiel, 165
Abraham de Barchillon, 64
Abraham de Turri, 42
Abraham ibn Daud of Toledo, 146
Abulfacem (Jew with a concubine), 43, 45
Açan, Çide, 52
Adambacaix (husband of Axa), 113
Adorno, Theodor, 118
Adret, Shelomo ben Abraham ben, of Barcelona, 43, 146, 150, 152–53, 222
Agamben, Giorgio, 86–87
Ahasueros (king), 68
Aizenberg, Edna, 58
Alami, Shelomo, 149, 159
Alatzar, Jafuda, 40, 223–24n23
Albert of Monte Casino, 189
Alborayque, 158, 159, 166, 184, 187, 281n59
Aldonça (wife of Samuel Baruch), 150
Alexander II (pope), 20

Alfonso (fictional king), 160
Alfonso V of Aragon, 156, 246n49
Alfonso VI, 57, 62, 231n20
Alfonso VIII and the Jewess of Toledo: in *Castigos* (Sancho IV of Castile), 60; conflict between lineages and, 234n42; death of Jewess and, 64, 70; dramatization of, 235–36n48; Esther and, 69, 234n41; expansion of story of, 57–58; figural and gross political negotiation and, 72; historical documentation of, 57, 229n4; history of medieval governance and, 66; Jewess of Toledo's textual work and, 62; Jewess's resemblances and, 233n37; Jews and fiscal power and, 66; legitimation of Sancho IV's rebellion and, 64, 66; love of God and love of woman and, 72; many versions of story of, 56, 229n5, 229–30n7; monarchical versus aristocratic power in, 70–71; nature of Alfonso VIII's error and, 64; origins of story and, 229n1; political love as foundation for sovereign power and, 73; politics of consensus and, 69; politics of queens and concubines and, 67, 70; punishment of Alfonso VIII and, 56, 57; rebellion as consequence of, 63; religious loyalties and, 61; representation in

Alfonso VIII and the Jewess of Toledo
(*continued*)
literature about, 58–59, 65; story of, as
fact or fiction, 56–57, 70, 230n9; tax on
hidalgos and, 234n42
Alfonso X "the wise" of Castile: accusations
against, 63; autonomy of administration
from nobility under, 66; execution of
Jewish minister by, 84; expansion of royal
power and, 65; on extramarital affairs of
kings, 231n22; as favorer of Jews, 137;
historical edifice built by, 57; injunctions for sexual restraint and, 230n13;
on interreligious love relationships, 92;
Jewish mark and, 96; mosques converted
to synagogues under, 40; poem about
interreligious sex by, 98; punishments at
hand of, 63–64; rebellion against, 137;
Sancho IV of Castile's war against, 55;
story of Theophilus and, 68; on violence
occasioned by poetry, 257n39. See also
Cantigas de Santa María (Alfonso X)
Alfonso XI, 66–67, 231n27, 270n77
Alfonso de Madrigal "el Tostado," 46, 47,
48–51
Alfonso de Palencia. *See* Palencia, Alfonso de
Alfonso de Toledo, 263n11
Alfonso Martínez de Toledo. *See* Martínez de
Toledo, Alfonso
Alfonso of Aragon, 182
Ali (alleged paramour of Prima Garsón),
245n35
Ali, M. Kurd, 209
Alicsend de Tolba, 99
al-Jahiz, 203
Aljamiado, 31, 32
al-Maqqarī, Aḥmad ibn Muḥammad, 209,
286n46
al-Muʿtamid (emir of Seville), 62
al-Muwwaq, 31
Alonso, Fernando, 225–26n45
Alonso de Cartagena, 48, 51, 128, 184, 186,
227n58, 272n92, 281n64
Alonso de Oropesa. *See* Oropesa, Alonso de
al-Qaysī, 32
Álvarez de Villasandino, Alfonso, 123,
129–31, 132, 254n18, 254n20, 257n37,
257n39
Álvaro de Luna, 65, 71, 134, 138
al-Wansharīsī, 28, 29

Amatzya (king of Judah), 160
Ambrose of Milan, 137
Amiri (woman caught in intercourse), 41–42
Andrés, Juan, 206–7
Anschütz, Gerhard, 241n52
antinomianism, 77–78, 80, 85, 260n59
anti-Semitism: versus anti-Judaism, 176,
275–76nn18–19; continuity of, 102, 109;
Martin Luther and, 176, 216n5; pathol-
ogy of, 249n78; racial, 90–91, 175–76,
275n15, 276n20, 277n27; "sharp mercies"
and, 216n5
Appian, 145
Arab League, 11
Arco y Garay, Ricardo del, 278n35
Arias, Diego, 156
Aristotle: on community, 138; on corporeal
versus higher politics, 135; on courage,
281n64; Hegel and, 283n13; inclination
toward contraries and, 121; insult and
invective in poetry and, 122; natural science and, 186; *Naturgeschichte* and, 159;
Nichomachean Ethics and, 135, 236n49; on
poetry, 124; Scholasticism and, 196; on
tyranny, 135
Arnaldona (wife of Ramon d'Aguilar),
244–45n31
Arnold, Matthew, 197
Arteaga, Esteban de, 206
Asher (rabbi), 224n25
Ashkenazic Jews, 146, 159, 262n4, 263n13
Assmann, Aleida, 264n18
Assmann, Jan, 264n18
Auerbach, Erich, 236n50
Augustine: Christological syntheses and, 193;
conversionary thinking about language
and, 127–28; on earthly city, 73; encounters with Jews by, 72–73; on Jews' abjection, 110; Jews' destruction of Christ and,
83–84, 226n55; law versus miracle and,
241n51; on literal and figurative meanings, 72, 127, 138; on nonbiblical poetry,
128; on observance of Jewish law, 127; on
opposition of contraries, 191; prophecy
and Rome and, 198; sign or mark of Cain
and, 77, 237n6, 240n33
Axa (Muslim woman with Christian lover), 113
Axona (Muslim concubine), 43
Aytola the Sarracen, 99, 245n37
Azáceta, José María, 258n45

Bachelor Marcos, 137–38, 139, 186
Badiou, Alain, 87, 240n37
Baena, Juan Alfonso de: career of, 123; as convert, 253n13; critics of, 258n45; insult and invective in poetry and, 122, 130–31, 258nn42–43; as Jewish, 122, 253n15; mass conversions' importance for, 133. See also *Cancionero de Baena*
Baer, Yitzhak, 144
Baldric of Bourgueil, 21
baptism: Juan Alfonso de Baena and, 122; children of God and, 243n11; of children of interreligious unions, 113; conversion and, 182; forced, 47; fortitude and, 186; identification of converts and, 149, 265n28; as oath of fealty, 166, 243n16; privileges for conversos and, 155–57; records of, 266n38; salvation and, 113; transformation and, 185
Barbieri, Giammaria, 205, 285n32
Bardus V, 206
Baron, Salo, 275n15
Barrientos, Lope de. *See* Lope de Barrientos
Bartlett, Robert, 172
Baruch, Samuel, 150
Basnage, Jacques, 235–36n48
Béla IV (king of Hungary), 26
Bellay, Joachim du, 182, 205–6
Bembo, 205
Benedict XIII (pope), 150
Benedict XVI (pope): clash of civilizations and, 284n24; dialectics of exclusion and, 194–99; European Union and, 197, 201, 202; on Gospels as synthesis of two cultures, 283n9; Islam in European history and, 204; *logos* of, 197–98, 283n11; opposed fantasies of Europe and Islam and, 207–8; before papacy, 197; single strand of European story and, 211; University of Regensburg speech and, 194–97, 201, 282–83nn7–8
Benedict, Ruth, 170
Benjamin, Walter, 86, 87, 88, 169
Ben-Sason, Haim Hillell, 144
Berceo, Gonzalo de. *See* Gonzalo de Berceo
Bernáldez, Andrés, 162, 270–71n80
Bernard of Clairvaux, 22
Bhabha, Homi, 242n1, 252n9
Bible. *See* Hebrew Bible; New Testament
Biddick, Kathleen, 274–75n14

Blanche of France, 67
Bloch, Marc, 169
Bloom, Harold, 204
Blumenbach, Johann Friedrich, 274n10
Boas, Franz, 170, 273n2
Boase, Roger, 286n40
Boccaccio, 128
Bonafos, Shaltiel, 111
Bon Aloor, Samuel, 244–45n31
Boniface, 231n18
Borges, Jorge Luis, 90, 165
Bosson, Georg, 286n44
Breviario Sunni (Gebir), 37
bubonic plague. *See* plague
Buddhists and Buddhism, 10
Bulliet, Richard, 202, 203
Burgos, Cantera, 259n48
Byron, George Gordon, Lord, 143–44

Caballería, Pedro de la, 150–51, 266n35
Caballete, Abrahén, 52
Cain (biblical figure), 73, 236n51, 237n6, 240n33
Caldesa (lover of Jaume Roig), 156
Cancionero de Baena: aesthetic critique of, 253n14; author of, 128; genre of, 123, 253–54n16; homosexuality as idiom of opprobrium in, 132; Jewishness as bad governance in, 259n50; Jewish origins in, 121–24; metaphors in, 123–24, 254n20; poetic grace and, 128, 130; poetic manifesto, 130; standards of good poetry and, 130. *See also* Baena, Juan Alfonso de
Canterbury Tales (Chaucer), 26
Cantigas de Santa María (Alfonso X), 51, 68, 98
Capsali, Elijah, 165
Casimir the Great, 55
Castelvetro, 205
Castigos (Sancho IV of Castile), 57, 59–61, 63–65, 67, 69, 230n9
Castro, Américo: commendation of, 273n97; cultural transmission and, 179, 278n31; on Jewish and Islamic influences on Spanish culture, 120; Jewish cultural traits and, 187; on Jewishness of the Inquisition, 252n8, 262n7; Jews and racism and, 144; on literary culture of the erotic, 222nn11–12; National Socialism and, 251–52n7, 278n31; racial vocabulary and, 178, 179, 180, 277n27

Catherine (queen of Castile), 106, 264n25
Catherine of Lancaster, 71
Cavallería, Fernando de la, 155
Çeano, Salamo, 52
Cecrim Abraham, 43
Charles of Anjou, 84
Chateaubriand, 209
Chaucer, Geoffrey, 26
Chresches de Turri, 42, 43
Christendom: anti-Jewish polemic in, 51;
    Christian thinking about Jews in, 75;
    as created by crusades, 22; enemies of
    Christian kingship and, 65; expansion
    of, via crusades, 23–24; growth of anti-
    Judaism in, 50–51, 52–53; Islam within,
    15–16; Jews and Muslims side-by-side
    under, 35; Jews as figures of supreme
    subjection in, 76–77, 83–84; Jews as focal
    point for expression of sovereignty in, 77;
    justifications of massacres and, 76; king's
    sovereignty in, 79–80; knowledge about
    Islam in, 15, 16–19; love of God and love
    of woman in, 72; Muslims as conquerors
    in, 16–17; Muslims converting to Judaism
    in, 44; Muslims under Christian rule and,
    27–32; New World colonization and,
    24; papal monarchy and, 22; polemics
    of Muslims living in, 32–33; peace at
    home and war abroad for, 22; prohibi-
    tions affecting Jews in, 50; protection
    of Muslim women's chastity under, 38;
    purity and, 174; questions about Islam
    and, 15; religious enmities and, 174; royal
    governance as Jew loving in, 65; services
    of non-Christian peoples, 26; slavery and,
    42; sovereignty and exception in, 88;
    spiritualization versus bodiliness in, 109;
    taxation by church and, 22–23; treaties
    with Muslims and, 27–28. See also Chris-
    tians and Christianity; conversos and
    conversion; crusades; interreligious love
    and sex relationships; reconquest
Christian rule. See Christendom
Christians and Christianity: anti-Islam
    polemics and, 218n5; anti-Jewish polemic
    and, 50, 51, 226nn55–56, 261n71; anti-
    Judaic theses in preaching and teaching
    of, 108; apostles as observant Jews and,
    127; binary opposition between Jews
    and, 188; body of Christ and, 91; body

versus soul and, 135; as caste not race,
    178; Christianizing and, 9; Christian-Jew
    polarization and, 108; Christian-ness and,
    117; Christian readings of Esther and,
    234n40; Christian society as body
    and, 243n22; church and empire and,
    259–60n58; church as bride of Christ
    and, 92; classification of conversos and,
    155; continuity of anti-Semitism among,
    102; conversion of Jews as threat to, 101,
    102–3, 120; conversos allegedly robbing,
    270–71n80; corruption and, 243n20;
    dangers of Jewish government and, 135;
    dualities in, 163; eating with Jews, 96;
    Ecclesia and, 91–92; endogamy and, 93;
    exclusion from, 91; excommunicated for
    living near Jews, 246n47; faith versus
    reason in, 196–98; as falsifiers of scrip-
    ture, 216n9; genealogy and, 145–46, 147;
    God as beautiful woman and, 243n13; as
    heathens for Jews, 221n4; honor among,
    110; ideas as Christian versus Jewish and,
    163, 164–65; identity crisis among, 102,
    103, 108, 111–14, 133, 147–48; Islam in
    thinking of about war, 20; Jewishness
    as concept in thought of, 6–7, 117–18,
    121, 132–33, 137, 140, 163, 284n23;
    Jews' alleged hatred of, 268n64, 275n17;
    Judaism in early days of, 125; Judaizing
    in, 7; law versus miracle in, 88, 241n51,
    242n53; literal versus nonliteral in, 135;
    love and extermination in, 2–3; marginal
    notes in Qur'an by, 18–19; meaning of,
    76; messianic expectations of, 47; military
    reach of, 20; Muslim conversion to Juda-
    ism and, 46, 47–50; under Muslim rule,
    32–33; Muslims and Muslim conversos as
    guardians of, 227–28n64; Muslims versus
    Jews in theological imagination of, 45,
    47–52; neighborliness in scripture of, 2;
    as neighbors of Jews, 1; "neither Jew nor
    Greek" in, 157, 161, 162, 185; patriarchal
    family as metaphor for church in, 92–93,
    243n16; politics of flesh versus spirit
    in, 135; pope as vicar of Christ and, 22;
    as proportion of population in Muslim
    lands, 287n50; purity of blood and, 177,
    269–70n74; Reformation and, 176;
    sacrament of confession in, 163; Saracens
    in imagination of, 24, 220n25, 231n18;

science of Islam and, 19; secular versus divine power and, 135–36; segregation of, from Jews, 103–7; segregation of, from Muslims, 104, 105–6; self-definition of, vis-à-vis Jews and, 108, 110–13, 133, 250n80; self-definition of, vis-à-vis Muslims and, 27, 110; sex and boundaries of, 94; sexual honor among, 93, 98; as shaped by encounters with other groups, 191–92; Torah and, 127; as uninterested in content of Islam, 16–17; Vatican justification of Nazi policy and, 3; Western Civilization as civilizational block and, 10; women as God's daughters and, 92; women as God's wives and, 92. *See also* baptism; Christendom; clash of civilizations; interreligious love and sex relationships; places of worship
Chrysostom, 127
Cid, Rodrigo Díaz de Vivar, 39
circumcision, 51, 123, 125, 154, 254n18
Cirot, Georges, 230n9
clash of civilizations: Abrahamic religions and, 203; versus alliance of civilizations, 192–93, 202–7; Arabic poetry and, 203–5, 208; Benedict XVI and, 194–99, 201–2, 211, 284n24; Christianity as consummate religion and, 201; Christianity in Hegel's thought and, 201; Christians and Jews in opposition and, 195; Christological syntheses and, 193; deceitful banquets and, 197–98, 283n11; demise of Islamic literature and science and, 207; dialectic teleology and, 202; European Catholicism as moment of synthesis and, 202; European conquest of Islamic world and, 208–9; European indebtedness to Islam and, 204; exclusion and inclusion and, 207–11; faith versus reason and, 195–98, 199–202; fantastical understandings and, 193, 207–8, 210–11; golden age of tolerance and, 210–11, 287n50; Hamas Charter and, 210–11; Samuel Huntington's thesis on, 193–94; invention of rhyme and, 205–6, 208; Islam in European history and, 204; Islam in Hegel's thought and, 201; Islamo-Christian civilization and, 202–3; Islam's exclusion from synthesis and, 202; Jewish Enlightenment and, 210;

Judaism in Hegel's thought and, 201, 202; Judaism versus Hellenism and, 196–98, 199; justification of exclusion and, 202; lethal dialectical teleologies and, 211; love lyrics and, 207, 208; Palestine and, 209; paradigm of, in world religions and schools of thought, 284n24; post-9/11 thinking about Islam and, 204; primacy of European Catholicism and, 197–98; "rational" Christianity versus "violent" Islam and, 194–97, 201, 282n4; rejection of Islamic influence and, 207; Spain as paradise of civilization and, 208–10; teleological dialectic and, 193; troubadours and, 203–4; United Nations Secretariat for the Alliance of Civilizations and, 192–93; universalizing monotheisms and, 203; vernacular poetry and, 203–5
Clement IV (pope), 26
Clement of Alexandria, 198
Colmenares, Diego de, 58, 265n27
Colunga, Pedro de, 129, 257n37
community: genealogical definitions and, 164; for mere living versus higher good, 138. *See also* coproduction of religious communities
Comnena, Anna, 20
Coneso, Estenza, 156
confraternities, 149–50, 265–66n31
Constantinople, fall of, 24
conversos and conversion: advent of Messiah and, 111; as Alborayque, 184–85; allegedly robbing Christians, 270–71n80; anticonverso discourse and, 47, 138–39, 157, 163, 183–84, 227n58; anticonverso ideology and racism and, 182; in antiquity, 162; as 'anusim, 153, 154; apostasy concerns and, 108, 249nn66–67; without catechism, 147; character traits associated with, 179, 251n98; Christian identity crisis and, 102, 103, 108, 111–14, 133, 147–48; competition for marriage alliances and, 156; complete transformation and, 127; conflicts with Old Christians and, 150; confraternities and, 149–50, 265–66n31; confusion of bloodlines and, 139; contingency versus continuity and, 143; conversos and "natural" Christians and, 113–14, 156, 161–62, 177, 182, 280n46; conversos as deceivers

conversos and conversion (*continued*)
and, 51, 227n57; conversos as guardians
of gospel and, 227–28n64; conversos
as hybrid monsters and, 120; conversos
as intermediate class and, 111; conversos as Judaizers and, 158; conversos as
threats to Christianity and, 120; converso
self-government and, 265n30; conversos in positions of power and, 155–56;
conversos' separation from Jews and, 103;
Council of Basel on, 156–57; debates over
exclusion of, 185; descendants of, barred
from office holding, 177; destabilization
of religious categories and, 145, 149,
151, 166–67, 177; in development of
modernity, 261n72; as disaster threatening Christian community, 101, 102–3;
discriminations of 1412–16 and, 107; distancing action of conversos and, 250n92;
documentation of identity and, 151–52;
in earliest Christianity, 125, 126; elimination of Jews through evangelization and,
112; elimination of Judaism from Spain
and, 176–77; emigration of conversos
and, 108, 249n66; enfranchisement and,
43, 225n35; erosion of Christian privilege
and, 111; evangelization and, 111; fiscal
status of, 149–50, 265n30; forced, during
massacres, 147; forced, during Valencia
massacre of 1391, 81–82, 101, 102, 111;
forced, in early fifteen century, 119;
forced baptisms and, 47; forced conversos' willingness to emigrate and, 154;
forced converts versus willing apostates
and, 153–54; force versus instruction
and, 108; former coreligionists and, 111–
12; genealogies of European modernity
and, 140–41; heightened sexual boundaries following, 103; historians among,
272n92; history of race and, 170; hybrid
phenomenon of, 260–61n69, 261n72;
illegitimate, 126; immutability of converts
and their descendants and, 275–76n19;
incompleteness of, 128; Inquisition and,
149, 183, 249nn67–68; interreligious
love relationships and, 44–45, 48; invasion of Jewish neighborhood by, 112,
251n93; Jewishness in poetry and, 132;
Jewishness of converts and descendants
and, 153–54, 157, 184; Jewish-to-Muslim,

52–53; Judaism and Judaizing in Christian thought and, 118; Judaizing among
conversos and, 107–8, 162, 249n68;
legislation discriminating against conversos and, 134, 156–58, 182–83; lineage
and possibility of conversion and, 139;
lineage of Jesus and Mary and, 161–62,
183, 186, 270n78, 271n87, 280n52,
281n61; marriage and, 150–55, 157, 177,
183, 267n51, 268n61, 268n67, 271n84;
marriage between convert and sponsor
and, 244n30; Moriscos and, 227–28n64;
motivations for, 53, 148; Muslim
adoption of Christian perspectives on,
54; of Muslims to Christianity, 151; of
Muslims versus Jews to Christianity, 51;
Muslim-to-Jewish, 44–45, 46, 47–50,
225n8, 225n36; as nation apart, 271n82;
new meanings and dangers of, 53; New
Testament and, 125; nobility of, 160–61;
noble lineage of, 185–86; office holding
by, 155–56, 157–58, 183, 268n62; office
holding prohibited for descendants of,
182, 185, 271n84; Old Christian genealogy and, 160–61; orthodoxy of conversos
and, 104–5, 107–8; poetry and, 139–40;
pride versus shame in converso descent
and, 280n52; privileges for conversos
and, 155–56, 182, 251n98; punishment
for conversion and, 46, 48–50; purity of
blood and, 179, 184; religious identity of
children born to, 155, 267n52; residential location of conversos and, 111–12,
149, 247n50, 247n54, 265n29; royal
licenses for, 43, 225n38; second wave of
conversionary pressure and, 148, 149;
segregation preceding, 107, 149; semiotics
of, 252n9; slaughter of unconverted and,
111; social transformations and, 133;
social versus racial difference and, 178;
strategic function of laws against Jews
and Muslims and, 248–49n64; strategies to effect, 148–49; Toledan revolt of
1449 and, 183–84; treatises in defense
of, 161–62; unprecedented number of,
in Spain, 140; Valencia massacre of 1391
and, 119, 238n14, 239n22
"Coplas del Provincial," 71
coproduction of religious communities: as
constant but not smooth, 75; as continu-

ing process, 5, 7–8; coproduction as term and, 216n10; as field of Jewish studies, 9; genealogical reinterpretation of traditions and, 166–67; past and present in, 11, 169; proximity of other faiths and, 33

Cota, Rodrigo, 156

Council of Basel, 134, 156–57, 182, 268n61

Covarrubias, Sebastián, 181

Crescas, Ḥasdai, 81

Crónica de Castilla, 56, 63, 64–65, 229n5

Crónica de 1344, 63, 64–65, 229n30n7

crusades: as act of love, 3; Almoravid's halt of Christian expansion and, 62; Catholic canon law and, 3; as created by Christendom, 22; creation of pan-European institutions and, 23; European peace and unity and, 219n18; expansionary ideology and, 23–24; Holy Land as destination for, 23, 219–20n23; interaction with versus demonization of Muslims and, 25; Jesus's predictions and, 219n22; as most famous example of wider practice, 20; taxation for, 22–23; Thomas Aquinas's justification for, 24

d'Aguilar, Ramon, 244–45n31

Dante, 128, 205, 256n33

da Piera, Shelomo, 151–52, 153, 158–59

Darwin, Charles, 172, 177, 274n10, 276n24

Decretals, 18

De doctrina Christiana (Augustine), 138

Delitzsch, Franz, 287n50

de Staël (Madame), 206, 284n35

Díaz de Haro, Lope, 64, 66, 70, 231n26

Díaz de Toledo, Fernán, 163–64, 184, 187, 271n87

Díaz de Vivar, Rodrigo, 39

Diego de Valencia, 132, 257n39, 259n48

Dies, Manuel, 180–81, 186

Díez de Games, Gutierre, 180

Diner, Dan, 249n74

Docampo, Florian, 229n5

Dominicans, 257n38

Douglas, Mary, 243n22

Duran, Profiat, 166

Durkheim, Émile, 22

Ebionites, 127

edict of Valladolid, 264n25

Eiximenis, Francesc, 80, 238n18

Eiximin, Martí, 44

Elionor of Catalonia-Aragon, 40, 223–24n23

Eliot, T. S., 169

empire: church and state and, 259–60n58; secular versus divine power and, 136

Enrique III, 156, 237n11, 251n98

Enrique IV, 65, 71, 137–38, 139, 265–66n31

Enrique of Trastámara, 84–85, 101

Epalza, Mikel de, 227n60

Erasmus, 164, 176

Espanha, Juan de, 132

Espina, Alonso de, 158

Esther, 68–69, 233n37, 234n40, 234n41

Estherka (wife of Casimir of Poland), 55, 233n37

Ethelbald of Mericia, 231n18

Eugenius III, 220n25

Eugenius IV (pope), 134, 157, 183

European Union, 11

Eusebius, 193, 198, 259–60n58

exception, state of, 86–88

expulsion of Jews: from Anjou and Maine, 84; banning in perpetuity and, 111; cities as *judenrein* and, 151; claims of superior lineage after, 160; Clement IV's command to expel, 26; discriminations of 1412–16 and, 106–7; documentation of identity and, 152; in Iberia versus non-Iberia, 84; Jewish population before and after, 276n21; justifications for, 84, 244n28; versus protection of, 84; Sephardim and, 143, 165, 272n93; from Spain in 1492, 26, 53, 102, 120, 160; taxation and, 84; thoroughness of, 176–77; urged by Jewish conversos, 112

Façan, Jacob, 108

fatwa, 31

Fernández, Joan, 123

Fernández de Oviedo, Gonzalo, 269–70n74

Fernando (grandson of Alfonso VIII), 56

Fernando (heir of Sancho IV of Castile), 56

Fernando III, 40

Fernando IV, 66

Fernando and Isabel, 65–66, 72, 104, 106, 137, 139

Ferrández Semuel, Alfonso, 254n18

Feuchtwanger, Lion, 56

Fields, Barbara, 273n4

Finzio, Mosè, 205

Fita, Fidel, 58
Flórez, Enrique (padre), 58
Foucault, Michel, 173–75, 188, 263n10, 274–75nn13–14, 281n68
Fourth Lateran Council (1215), 96, 103–4, 271n83
Fraker, Charles, 259n48
Francesc de Sant Jordi, 111
Franchesch d'Erill, 237n7
Franciscans, 257n38
Franco, Francisco, 276–77n25
Frege, Gottlob, 169
Freud, Sigmund, 252n9
Fucilla, Joseph G., 234n41

Gaçó, Barthomeu, 249n67
García, Gómez (abbot), 66
García-Arenal, Mercedes, 216n10, 277n29
García de la Huerta, Vicente, 234n41
García de Santa María, Álvar, 272n92
Garsón, Prima, 245n35
Gautier de Compiègne, 19
Gebhardt, Carl, 261n72
Gebir, Yçe de, 37
genealogy and lineage: in accusations of crime, 180; *Alborayque* and, 184–85; anticonverso discourse and, 184, 271n87; Christians descended from conversos and, 177; colonialism and, 204; common knowledge and, 184; corruption through hybridity and, 158; counter-genealogies and, 158–59; courage and nobility and, 186; cultural transmission and, 179, 184, 280n54; definitions of, 263n10, 281n68; determination of character and, 183; European fantasies and, 174; genre of genealogical aspersion and, 271n87, 272n91; historiography and, 165, 166, 167, 263n10, 272n92; of ideas, 165; Inquisition and, 162, 187; of Jesus and Mary, 161; in Jewish and Christian tradition, 145–46, 147; Jewishness attached to blood and, 163–64; Jewishness of conversos and, 154–55; Jewish origins of obsession with, 270n75; Jews' mixed lineage and, 158; Judaizing and, 164–65; Kalonymos family and, 263nn13–14; *libros verdes* and, 272n91; as literary genre, 146, 263n11; literary maledictions and, 156; marriage and, 154–55, 267n51; metallurgical argu-

ment and, 280n56; of New versus Old Christians, 183; obsession with, in Spain, 143–44; Old Christians and, 160–61; origins of emphasis on, 144, 262n8; origins of racism and, 144–45; point of origin and, 202; purity and, 153, 158–59, 162, 185, 187, 268n67, 270n75; of purveyor of ideas, 164; rabbinic dynasties' noble pedigrees and, 146; race and racism and, 187–88, 273–74n6; reestablishment of religious categories of identity and, 152; versus religious identity in communal memory, 145, 147; royal dynasties and, 146; as sealed by name of God, 266n43; Sephardim and, 143–44, 152–53, 154–55, 159–60, 167; street polemics and, 162; tax-exempt nobility and, 146; transformation of the future and, 169–70; treatises in defense of conversos and, 162; vocabulary of race and, 180
Gerundi, Nissim, 147
Gil de Zamora, Juan, 230n13
Giles of Rome, 72, 236n49
Girard, René, 245n38
Goering, Hermann, 118
Goethe, 201
González de Mendoza, Pedro, 271n84
Gonzalo de Berceo, 68, 71
Gracia, Saltell, 103, 107
Gratian, 244n30
Gravei, Perfet, 225n38
Gregory X (pope), 23
Gregory of Nicaea, 126
Grenada, 26, 28
Grillparzer, Franz, 56
Guibert of Nogent, 55
Guillén, Pero, 183
Guzmán, Leonor de, 67

Halbwachs, Maurice, 264n18
Hamas Charter, 210–11
Hasan-Rokem, Galit, 216n10
Hauha (slave convert), 225n38
Hayyim ibn Musa, 166
Hebrew Bible: Adam and Eve and, 61–62; ambivalence about neighborliness in, 1–2; body and soul and, 254n22; David's messianic line in, 1; Deuteronomic blessing and, 270–71n80; Egyptians robbed during Exodus and, 270–71n80; geneal-

ogy in, 146; Greek philosophy versus, 198; Hosea in, 91; Judaizing in, 216n12; medieval literary imagination and, 59–60; ministerial power as female in Esther and, 68; monogamy in, 59; mount of revelation in, 4, 216n6; paternal pedagogy in Proverbs and, 230n11; proverbs about sexuality and, 230n11; in Qur'an, 4–5, 216n8; residents of Promised Land in, 1; restrictions on intermarriage and, 95; Semitic characteristics in, 179; Septuagint version of, 216n12; King Solomon and women in, 61; Song of Songs in, 91, 242n7. *See also* Cain (biblical figure); Esther

Hegel, G. W. F.: on Abraham, 283n13; Arabic poetry and, 203; Christological syntheses and, 193; on deference to authority, 283n19; faith and reason and, 199–202; on Gospels as synthesis of two cultures, 283n9; Judaism in dialectic of, 284n23; opposed fantasies of Europe and Islam and, 207; teleology of, 201; on Trinitarian structure of reality, 284n20

Heine, Heinrich, 197

Herder, Johann Gottfried von, 207

heresy, 216–17n13

Hinojosa, Gonzalo de, 231n26

Hippocrates, 281n64

Hippolytus of Rome, 259–60n58

Hispano (ally of Nebuchadnezzar), 160

history and historiography: Arab thesis in, 286n40; blood versus sexual regimes in, 274–75n14; of concepts, 169; continuity and discontinuity in, 174–75, 176, 189, 198–99; critical approach to, 11–12; cultural memory and, 173; for cutting, 174–75; dismantling of race and, 171–72; Europe's external challenges versus internal conflicts in, 274n12; explanatory value of race in, 273n4; expulsion of Jews as stimulus to, 165, 272n93; Falangists and, 276–77n25; genealogy and, 165, 166, 167, 263n10, 272n92; of human reason, 200–201; as imitation of Christ, 200; intractability of race in, 188–90; metaphors in, 189; of Muslims in Iberian Peninsula, 276n22; organic view of Middle Ages in, 173–74; polemics in, 189; premodern innocence and, 172–74; premodernists and modernists informing

each other in, 190; of race, 170; *telos* of, 201; universal, 90; vocabulary of race and, 177–78, 180, 276n24; as *Wissenschaft*, 177

Hitler, Adolf, 145

Hobbes, Thomas, 241n51

Holocaust, 176

homosexuality: accusations against Enrique IV and, 137; accusations of Jewishness and, 122; as idiom of opprobrium, 132; Jews and, 71–72, 140; in poetic exchanges, 122, 130–31, 132; *privados* and, 71; sodomy versus heterosexual rape and, 49

honor: analogies of marriage and family and, 99; baptism as oath of fealty and, 243n16; bubonic plague and, 100; charges of dishonoring God and, 99, 245n37; children born of interreligious unions and, 224n25; Christian analogies and, 243n16; Christian distancing from Jews and, 110; cohesion of social group and, 93, 94, 100; conversos' acts of violence and, 112; definition of religious communities and, 94, 97, 100; economy of violence and, 110; erosion of, as Judaizing, 110; failure to avenge an injury and, 110, 250n84; of the king, 231n22; for prostitutes, 99

Horkheimer, Max, 118

Huet, Pierre Daniel, 206

Huntington, Samuel, 10, 193–94, 282n4

Huxley, Aldous, 172

Ibn Daud, 159, 263n12, 268n68

Ibn Ḥazm, 8, 31–32, 196, 242n7, 282–83n8

Ibn ʿIdhārī, 39–40

Ibn Miqlash, 28, 38

Ibn Rushd, 28

Imperial, Francisco, 181

Inés de Torres, 71

Innocent III (pope), 22, 23, 271n83

Innocent IV (pope), 26

Inquisition: *Alborayque* and, 187; archives of, 266n40; determination of Jewishness and, 118; genealogy and, 162, 187, 272n91; Hebrew philology and, 164; intercession on behalf of accused in, 265n28; Jewish conversos and, 149, 183, 249nn67–68; Jewishness of, 252n8, 262n7; Judaizing and, 161, 163, 278n33; Muslim converts to Christianity and, 151; proto-Inquisition and, 161, 187; purpose

Inquisition (*continued*)
of, 120; racism and, 177–78; traveling conversos and, 152

interreligious love and sex relationships: administrative importance of queens and concubines and, 66; administrative love and, 67–68; biblical Esther and, 68–69; Castilian court intrigue and, 71; Christian attitudes toward Muslim-Jewish relationships and, 52; Christian conquest of Iberia and, 37; Christian *Ecclesia* as woman and, 91; Christian men and Jewish women and, 40–41; Christian prostitutes and non-Christian men and, 99–100; Christian rulers and Jewish women and, 63–64; Christian woman and male Muslim slave and, 98; Christian women and Jewish men and, 103; with Christian women as adultery, 92; confusion of bloodlines and, 139; continuity of concerns about, 102; continuum of relationships and, 95–97; conversion and, 44, 111, 150–51, 152–54, 225n36; Count Don Rodrigo story and, 98; death as penalty for, 92, 93, 99, 103, 223n17, 245n35, 246n42; death penalty for Muslim women and, 41, 223n17; defeat of kings and, 62–64; deviance and, 105; disease as punishment for, 245n39; disfigurement as punishment for, 224n25; eating versus talking together and, 96; frequency of, 244n28; as frontier adventures, 98; genealogy and, 187; in hierarchy of sexual sins, 95; hybridity stories and, 101; individualized versus corporatist metaphors for, 92; for Israelite men versus women, 95; Jewish-Christian love stories and, 55–56; Jewish generalization of specific biblical prohibitions and, 36; Jewish men and Muslim women versus vice versa, 38, 40–41, 44–46, 52–53; in Jewish scripture and tradition, 1, 36–37; Jewish zealots on, 36–37; Jews' unclear status and, 39; Jews' versus Muslims' ability to enact punishments for, 224n26; Jews with Muslims rather than Christians and, 38; as justification of expulsion of Jews, 244n28; law of witness and, 101; love of Jews as accusation against Christians and, 55; Maliki jurists on, 221n35; versus marriage into nobility, 67; between

married Christian women and non-Christians, 98; mixed-religion households and, 247–48n56; monetary fines for, 224n26; Muslim adoption of Christian perspectives on, 54; Muslim anxiety over, 222n8; Muslim-Jewish apostasy versus miscegenation and, 44–46; Muslim men versus Jewish men and, 37; Muslim men versus Muslim women and, 37; Muslim women prostitutes and, 41–42; negotiations triggered by, 38; nuns and, 60–61; offspring of, 113, 152–53, 155, 161, 222n8, 247–48n56, 267n52; outbursts of moral indignation about, 101; plague outbreaks and, 100–101; poetry about, 37–38; poetry of insult and, 123; political order and, 61; politics of queens and concubines and, 66–67, 68–69, 71, 231n32; power relations and, 38–39, 42, 47, 59, 231n20; *privados* and, 67, 70, 233n34, 235–36n48; *privanza* and, 67–68, 69, 71–72, 233n36; prohibited during famine and plague, 245n39; prostitutes as guardians of sexual frontier and, 100; real and perceived amount of, 107; regularization of, 43; religious loyalties and, 61; segregation to prevent, 247n53; sexual panics and, 105; as shorthand for subversion of hierarchy, 101; slavery and, 38–39, 40, 41–43, 98, 223n18; as subject of study, 35; uxorial expansion and, 59. *See also* Alfonso VIII and the Jewess of Toledo; sex and sexuality; sexual boundaries

Iogna-Pratt, Dominique, 174
Irenaeus, 259–60n58
Isaac ibn Zadok (Çag de la Maleha), 63–64
Isabel. *See* Fernando and Isabel
Isabel (wife of Alfonso VI), 231n20
Isidore, 128, 263n11
Isla, Luis de la, 152
Islam. *See* Muslims and Islam
Israel, 10, 88, 210–11

James I, 40
James II, 42, 45
James the Conqueror (king of Aragon), 26
Jamila (Muslim convert to Judaism), 45
Jaume I of Catalonia-Aragon, 62–63
Jayyusi, Salma Khadra, 208–9, 210
Jerome (saint), 127, 248n59

Jerónimo de Santa Fe, 112

Jesus: Jewishness versus Greekness of teachings of, 283n9; lineage of, 161–62, 186, 270n78, 271n87, 280n52, 281n61

Jewishness: accusations of political corruption and, 133–34; of bad governance, 259n50; as category in thought of non-Jews, 121; character traits associated with, 122, 179, 186; in Christian literature, 122; as concept in Christian thought, 117–18; conversion from, 139; of conversos and descendants, 153–55, 157, 184; cultural attributes and, 120, 139, 141, 158, 165, 187, 251n6; as descriptor of ideas and positions, 118–19; determination of, 118–19, 155; encoding of, in critical discourse, 122; as figure of thought versus flesh, 121; genealogy and, 154–55, 163–64; of ideas, 163, 164–65, 278n33; immutability of converts and descendants and, 275–76n19; of the Inquisition, 252n8, 262n7; of Jesus's teachings, 283n9; letter versus spirit of the law and, 125; personal defects and, 181; poetry and, 123–24, 130–32, 133, 259n49; production of, 141; racial anti-Semitism and, 276n20; as racial category, 120; real, 134–35; search for, in history and culture, 120–23, 141; sexual accusations and, 122. See also Jews and Judaism

Jews and Judaism, 109; abhorrence of, counseled, 257n39; accusations for sexual misconduct and, 105, 244–45n31, 246n42; accusations of mixed ancestry among, 263n15; as administrators in Christian realms, 39–40, 46, 65, 66, 84–85, 231n27; as Alborayque, 184–85; alleged hatred of Christians by, 268n64, 275n17; annihilation of, allegedly prophesied, 250n86; anti-Jewish interpretations of Esther and, 234nn40–41; anti-Jewish polemic and, 50, 51, 108–10, 226nn55–56; anti-Judaism versus anti-Semitism and, 176; attacks on, in Seville, 78, 237n11; Augustine and, 72–73; authority of, over Muslims, 39–40; binary opposition between Christians and, 188; burning of synagogues and, 137; care of royal lions by, 77; as caste not race, 178; chains of tradition genre and, 165–66; Christian

apostles as observant Jews and, 127; Christianizing in, 9; Christian-Jew polarization and, 108; Christians and Muslims and heathens for, 221n4; Christians as neighbors of, 1; in Christian scripture and thought, 6–7, 76, 132, 133, 140, 163; Christians defining selves against, 108, 110, 111, 112; Christian self-definition and, 110, 250n80; Christians excommunicated for living near, 246n47; clothing regulations for, 103, 246n48; competing claims to right to decide fate of, 78; conversion of, as threat to Christianity, 101, 102–3; conversion of, during massacres, 81–82; conversos distancing selves from, 250n92; conversos observing holidays of, 249n68; coproduction of culture with neighbors and, 8–9; as corrupters of scripture, 242n7; crisis of classification and, 90; dangers of Jewish government and, 135; dangers of Jewish power and, 70; as deniers of Christ, 227–28n64; descendants of, barred from office holding, 177; descent into worship of Ba'al and, 243–44n25; disadvantages of mistreating, 26; in earliest Christianity, 125, 127; eating with Christians, 96; effeminacy of, 235n46; elimination of, through evangelization, 112–13; as falsifiers of scripture, 216n9; Fernando and Isabel as descended from, 65–66; as figure of political thought, 137; as figures of supreme subjection, 76–77, 83–84, 87–88; fiscal power and, 65–66; flesh versus spirit and, 136; as focal point for expression of sovereignty, 77; genealogy and, 145–46, 147; growth of anti-Judaism in Spain and, 50–51, 52–53; Hebrew literary culture of the erotic and, 222nn11–12; hermeneutic Jew and, 163; as homosexuals, 140; as hybrid people, 165, 261n71, 268n68; incorrect Christian beliefs and practices and, 163; as influencers of Muhammad, 50; intermarriage in scripture of, 1; as inventors of racism, 262–69; Islamizing in, 9; Jerusalem/Israel as God's spouse and, 91; "Jew" as insult and, 109, 110, 118, 131–32, 249n77, 250n84, 281n62; Jewish badges and, 96, 103, 105, 148, 247n51, 271n83; Jewish historiography and, 165;

Jews and Judaism (*continued*)
Jewish idioms for spiritual dangers and,
109; Judaizing and, 7–8, 216–17nn12–13;
letter versus spirit and, 72; as lion keep-
ers, 241n43; lovelessness of, 283n13; in
Lutheran Christology, 284n23; materialism and, 109, 136, 264n23; mixed lineage
of, 158, 268n67; monogamy and, 59; as
murderers of Jesus, 50, 53, 61, 83–84, 139,
260n66; Muselmänner and, 87; Muslim
polemics against, 32; under Muslim rule,
32–33; Muslims called Jews and, 16–17;
in Muslim scripture, 4–5; versus Muslims
in Christian theological imagination,
47–52; and Muslims under Christendom, 35; Muslim-to-Jewish conversions
and, 44–45, 46, 47–50; neighborhood
of, invaded by conversos, 112, 251n93;
neighborliness in scripture of, 1–2; obsession with genealogy and, 270n75; origins
of racism and, 144; ostracization of, 8; in
patristic thought, 127–28; poetry as Jewish and, 140; political love as foundation
for sovereign power and, 73; politics and,
138; population of, in Aragon, 276n21;
privados and, 138; prohibitions affecting,
50; projection of carnality onto, 109–10;
protection of, as Judaizing, 84; purity of
blood and, 102, 134, 137–38, 157–59, 162,
177, 268n67, 269–70nn74–75; rabbinic
Judaism and, 166; as race, 181, 277n29; as
rationalist skeptics, 261n71; real, 134–35,
252n10; rejection of Mary by, 52; resi-
dency rules for, 246n49; royal governance
as Jew loving and, 65; "ruinous lineage"
of, 186; as scapegoats at times of affliction,
245–46n40; segregation of, from Christians, 103–7; self-definition of, vis-à-vis
Christians and, 133; sign of Cain and, 77;
as slave owners, 46–47; sodomites and,
71–72; as source of Christian and Muslim
traditions, 166; sovereignty and exception
and, 87–88; stoning of, during Holy Week,
77, 110, 111, 237n10; strategic function
of laws against, 248–49n64; *Synagoga* as
personification of, 91; treason and, 180;
as trusted officials in reconquest, 39–40;
as unbaptized and not children of God,
243n11; as usurers, 109, 249n74; Vatican
justification of Nazi policy and, 3; violence

against during plague outbreaks, 100; vocabulary for, 273n3. *See also* anti-Semitism;
clash of civilizations; conversos and conversion; expulsion of Jews; interreligious love
and sex relationships; places of worship;
Sephardim; Valencia massacre of 1391
Jiménez de Rada, Rodrigo, 56–57
Joan I: inquisitor Barthomeu Gaçó and,
249n67; Jewish badges and, 103; Jewish
conversos and, 103, 247n50; Jews of Morvedre and, 241n43; jurisdiction of, 85; on
king's sovereignty, 79–80; on massacre in
Morvedre, 239n28; orthodoxy of conversos and, 105; as patron of Saint Christopher, 240n42; punishment of attackers
and, 239nn28–29, 239–40nn31–32,
239nn28–29; segregation of Christians
from others and, 104; on subjection of
Jews, 76–77, 236n1; Valencia massacre of
1391 and, 78, 79–80, 83, 85–86, 239n24,
240n38
Joffre, Mahoma, 151
John of Damascus, 17
John of Salisbury, 91
Joinville, 25
Juan II: Álvaro de Luna and, 71; birth of,
257n39; *Cancionero de Baena* and, 121;
civil war and, 134; conversos employed by,
156; Fernán Díaz and, 163–64; as favorer
of Jews, 137; protection of conversos by,
156, 183; rebellion against, 137–38, 139;
on strategic function of laws against Jews
and Muslims, 248–49n64
Juan Alfonso de Baena. *See* Baena, Juan
Alfonso de
Juan de Granada, 151
Judaizers and Judaizing: *Alborayque* and, 185,
187; anti-Judaic polemic and, 108–10;
carnal readings of scripture and, 128;
as cause of sexual crisis, 107; continuity of Jewish practice and, 127; among
conversos, 107–8, 158, 249n68; within
conversos' marriages, 150–51; converts
and, 162; critical poetics and, 129–30,
132; danger of secret acts of, 102; in
debates over poetry and theology, 257n38;
erosion of honor and, 110; genealogy and
lineage and, 164–65; ideas as, 278n33;
ideology of reproduction and, 114; incorrect Christian beliefs and practices and,

163; Inquisition and, 120, 161, 163, 187, 278n33; Islam as Judaizing heresy and, 166; Judaizing sects and, 127; as language of political critique, 135; lineage of Jesus and Mary and, 161–62; mass conversions and, 118; middle ground and, 163; in New Testament, 117, 126; Origen and, 260n60; politics and, 136–37, 139; *privanza* and, 71; protection of Jews as, 84; race and, 187–88; re-Judaization of conversos and, 114; Carl Schmitt's political theology and, 237n6; taxation as, 110; territorial sovereignty and, 77; withdrawal from economy of violence and, 110; woman Jewish ministers and, 69; Zealots and, 260n60

Kabbalah, 9
Kant, Immanuel, 274n10, 283n9
Kantorowicz, Hermann, 241n52
Kaplan, Gregory, 252n9
Kaplan, Yosef, 144, 262n8
Kelimat ha-Goyim (Duran), 166
Kelsen, Hans, 241n52
Khoury, Adel Theodore, 282–83n8
Kisch, Guido, 176, 178, 275n15, 276n20

Lactantius, 128
Lamarck, Jean-Baptiste, 172
Lamentations Rabbah (rabbinic text), 8–9
Lando, Ferrán Manuel de, 129–30, 257n38, 258n42, 258–59n46
Langmuir, Gavin, 273n3
law: dictatorship and, 241n52; letter versus spirit of, 1, 125–26; versus miracle, 88, 241n51, 242n53; in New Testament, 199–200
Lawee, Eric, 261n2, 272–73n95
Lea, Henry Charles, 177–78
Leah (apostate woman), 40, 42
Leon, David ben Judah Messer, 143–44
Leonor de Guzmán, 67
Leroy, Béatrice, 244–45n31
Liber denudationis, 18
Lipton, Sara, 109
literature: ambiguous religious identity in, 123; anthropomorphic reading practice and, 124–25; Arabic poetry and, 203–5, 206, 208, 285n32, 286n46; biblical and non-biblical poetry and, 128; chains of tradition genre and, 165–66; competitive poetic ex-

changes and, 123–24, 129–32; contention over interpretation of poetry and, 257n39; demise of Islamic literature and science and, 207; genealogical maledictions and, 156; genealogy as genre in, 146, 263n11; insult in poetry and, 258nn42–43; invention of rhyme and, 205–6, 208; language of Judaizing in, 133–34; literal and allegorical meaning of, 128; literal and spiritual meanings of, 124–26; love lyrics and, 207, 208; mimetic versus sentimental poetry and, 284n35; multiple levels of meaning in, 256n33; opponents and defenders of poetry and, 128; paradigm for medieval Christian poetic theory and, 285n30; poetic and other fictions and, 255n26; poetic falsity and, 257n39; poetic grace and, 128, 130, 131; poetry and conversion and, 139–40; poetry and truth and, 124, 254n21; poetry as Jewish and, 140; politics and poetics and, 137–38; puns related to foreskins, 123, 254n18; representation in, 58–59; search for Judaism in, 122–23; secular poetry versus theology and, 129, 257n38; Semitic tropes in, 278n33; social production of, 234n43; standards of good poetry and, 130; vernacular poetry and, 203–5; violence occasioned by poetry and, 257n39; vocabulary of race in, 181, 183, 279n39
Llorente, Joan Antonio, 280n52
Llull, Ramon, 257n39
Lope de Barrientos, 48, 184
Lope del Monte, 129, 257nn38–39
Lope de Vega, Félix Arturo, 56, 277n28
Lopello de Serrah Mahomet, 225n38
López de Ayala, Pedro, 71, 237n11
López de Haro, Diego, 234n42
Lorenç the Shepherd, 99
Ludovicus Pontanus of Rome, 50
Lueger, Karl, 118
Luna, Álvaro de. *See* Álvaro de Luna
Luther, Martin: anti-Semitism and, 176, 216n5; debate with Scholastics and, 257n38; on Jews' hatred of Christians, 268n64, 275n15; move of, toward faith, 196; on "sharp mercies," 3, 216n5

Macrobius, 128
Magen va-Romaḥ (Hayyim ibn Musa), 166
Mahomet (son of Axa), 113

Maimonides, Moses: on accusations of mixed ancestry, 263n15; on forced converts, 154; on interreligious love relationships, 36–37; Maimonidean controversy and, 159; on Muslims, 18; on sanctification, 2, 216n3; on social interaction between Jews and non-Jews, 95–96
Maiolus of Cluny, 20, 218n11
Malkiel, Yakov, 251–52n7, 278n31
Manrique, Frederico, 140
Manrique, Gómez, 124
Manrique, Rodrigo, 164, 187
María (Muslim convert to Judaism), 43–44
María (queen), 182, 183, 246n49
María de Sixena, 93
Maria of Portugal, 67, 270n77
Marques de Mondéjar, 58
Márquez Villanueva, Francisco, 178, 251–52n7, 273n97, 278n31, 278n33
Marranos. See conversos and conversion
Marshall, John, 274n13
Marshall, Thurgood, 273n2
Martí (king), 105, 241n43, 246n49, 249n68, 265–66n31
Martí (prince), 78–79, 83, 85, 237–38n12, 238n16, 238nn20–21, 239n24, 240n32
Martí, Ramón, 55
Martínez, Ferrant, 78
Martínez de Medina, Diego, 257n38
Martínez de Toledo, Alfonso, 134, 157, 181, 182, 268n62
Martínez López, Nicolás, 277n27
Marx, Karl, 141
Mary (mother of Christ): descent from, 162; immaculate conception of, 257n38; lineage of, 161–62, 183, 186, 270n78, 280n52; redemption of Theophilus and, 68; virginity of, 52, 227n60
Mary (queen), 156
massacres: graves of victims of, 149, 265n27; Jewish population before and after, 276n21; mass conversions and, 75–76, 101, 111, 145, 147, 150, 239nn22–23; numbers killed and converted during, 147, 264n19; during plague outbreaks, 100; punishment for participants in, 240n41; reasons given for, 239n24, 239n28; reconstruction of sexual boundaries and, 101; sales of Jews into slavery and, 147; settlements following, 240n41; transformed

religious demography and, 147. See also Valencia massacre of 1391
Mastnak, Tomaž, 24, 174
Maximus the Confessor, 16–17, 137
Meir b. R. Todros b. R. Hasdai, 153
memory, cultural, 173, 264n18
Mendel, Gregor, 172
Mendoza y Bovadilla, Francisco, 272n91
Menéndez y Pelayo, Marcelino, 58, 144, 177, 276n24
Menocal, María Rosa, 203–4, 205, 207, 286n40
Menorat ha-Ma'or (advice manual), 153
Milner, Jean-Claude, 258n42
Milosz, Czeslaw, 191
miracles: as events, 240n37; versus law, 88, 241n51, 242n53; state of exception and, 87–88; Valencia massacre of 1391 and, 81, 82, 85–86
Mirror of True Nobility (Valera), 161
Molina, María de, 62, 64, 66, 231n30
monarchy, 101
Mondéjar, Marques de, 58
monotheism, 91
Montague, Ashley, 170–71, 175
Montaigne, 141
Montesquieu, 274n10
Montoro, Antón de, 139–40, 260n66
Montrose, Louis A., 234n43
Moore, R. I., 174
Moraña, Alfonso de, 258–59n46
Mordechai (uncle of Esther), 69
Moses (biblical figure), 163, 271nn83–84
Moses ben Jacob Cordovero, 265n27
Moses ben Shem Tov ibn Ḥabib, 160
Moses ibn Ezra, 159
Mudejar, 35
Muhammad, 17
Murcian council, 104, 105, 247n53, 248n61
Muselmänner, 87
Muslim lands: Christians as proportion of population in, 287n50; Christians under, 32–33; conversos in, 155; majority of Jewish-Muslim interactions under, 35; protection of women's chastity under, 38
Muslims and Islam: accusations against, for sexual crimes, 105; accusations of Jewishness and, 122; anti-Jewish polemic among, 53–54; Arabic literary culture of the erotic and, 222nn11–12; avail-

ability of information about, 20; called
Jews, 16–17; as caste not race, 178;
Christendom's self-definition of, vis-à-vis,
27; Christian anti-Jewish polemic and,
51; Christian converts to, 16; Christian
interaction with versus demonization of,
25; Christian lands' treaties with, 27–28;
Christian polemics against, 218n5; under
Christian rule, 27–32; Christians' axioms
about, 17; Christians defining selves
against, 110; Christians' self-definition
vis-à-vis Jews and, 250n80; in Christian
thinking about war and, 20; circumcision and, 51; Clement IV's command to
expel, 26; as conquerors, 16; conquest of
Visigothic monarchy by, 231n18; conversion to Christianity among, 111, 151; in
courtly literature, 25–26; cultural decline
and, 29–30, 31; cultural vulnerability of
under Christian rule, 28; death penalty
for adultery and, 222n9; de pacis versus
de guerra, 27; descendants of, barred
from office holding, 177; devolution of
boundary marking and, 31–32; diaspora
of, 27–28; disadvantages of mistreating,
26; as enemies of God to crusaders, 22,
23; versus expansion as motivation for
crusades, 23–24; fall of Constantinople
and, 24; as false and carnal religion, 17; as
heathens for Jews, 221n4; hostility to, 195;
identity markers for, 29, 30, 31–32; Islam
as Judaizing heresy and, 166; Islamic law
and, 28–29, 37, 221n35, 222n8; Islamic
World as most aggressive civilizational
block and, 10; Islamism and, 282n2;
Islamizing and, 9; Jewish authority over,
39–40; Jewish origins of practices in,
166; on Jews and Christians as falsifiers of
scripture, 216n9; Jews and Jesus's death
in, 53–54; on Jews as corrupters of scripture, 242n7; Jews as influence on Muhammad and, 226nn55–56; versus Jews in
Christian theological imagination, 47–52;
Jews in scripture of, 4–5; and Jews under
Christendom, 35; Judaizing in, 7–8;
knowledge and learning among, 31; love
and extermination in, 2–3; Moses Maimonides on, 18; male bodies in paradise
and, 18; Maliki school of law and, 221n35,
222n8; Marrano as insult and, 164; Mary's

virginity and, 52, 53; medieval Christians'
vilification of, 18–19; military reach of,
20; as most aggressive civilizational block,
10; Muslim-ness and, 117; Muslim prostitutes and, 113; Muslims in non-Islamic
polities and, 221n35; Muslim-to-Jewish
conversions and, 44–45, 46, 47–50;
neighborliness in scripture of, 2; ostracization of Jews by, 8; popular polemics
against Jews and, 32–33; populations of,
in medieval Europe, 27–28; present-day
tropes against, 17–18; purity of blood and,
177, 269–70n74; racial versus religious
anti-Muslimism and, 277n29; reconquest
of Iberian Peninsula from, 26; role of, in
Christian sacred history, 16; role of, in
prostitution, 224n29; as Saracens, 16;
science of Islam and, 19; segregation of,
from Christians, 104, 105–6, 148–49;
segregation policies and, 248n61; as
Semites, 177; sexuality of Muslim women
and, 30; as slaves, 38–39, 42, 46–47,
98; strategic function of laws against,
248–49n64; thought of, about crusades,
20–21; as unbaptized and not children of
God, 243n11; using name "John" to pass as
Christian, 99, 245n37; virginity of Mary
(mother of Christ) and, 227n60; as worshipers of Greek gods, 18. See also clash of
civilizations; conversos and conversion;
interreligious love and sex relationships;
Muslim lands; places of worship; Qur'an

Nahmanides, 36–37, 43
Narbona Vizcaíno, Rafael, 245n39
National Socialism, 170, 175–76, 251–52n7
Nazik al-Malaika, 204
Nazis. See National Socialism
Nebuchadnezzar, 160
Necker, Anne-Louise Germaine (Madame de
    Staël), 206, 284n35
neighborliness, 1–8, 10–11, 217n21
Neoplatonism, 128, 254n22
Netanyahu, Benzion, 144, 176
New Testament: ambivalence about neigh-
    borliness in, 2; body of Christ in, 91;
    corruption in, 94; dating of books in,
    255n26; dualities in, 163; genealogy in,
    146; as incomplete account of Jesus's acts,
    217n24; Judaizing in, 7, 117, 126; law and

New Testament (*continued*)
  legality in, 199–200; letter versus spirit
  of the law in, 125–26, 127–28; literal and
  allegorical meaning in, 125–27; marriage
  in, 91–92; Old and New Christians in,
  162; passage from Judaism to Christianity
  and, 125; patriarchal family as metaphor
  in, 92; secular versus divine power in,
  135–36; spiritual and sexual union in, 97;
  synthesis of faith and reason and, 196;
  whore of Corinth in, 106
Nietzsche, Friedrich, 174–75, 263n10
Nykl, A. R., 286n40

Oberman, Heiko, 176, 275n15
Obermann, Julian, 216n8
Oldradus de Ponte, 44–45, 47, 50, 51
Old Testament. *See* Hebrew Bible
"On Christian Doctrine" (Augustine), 72
"On the Government of Princes" (Giles of
  Rome), 72
Orientalism, 19, 191
Origen: body and soul and, 254n22; church
  and state and, 259–60n58; on conver-
  sion, 127; Greek philosophy and, 198;
  Judaizing error of, 260n60; taxation and,
  260n59; on three classes of people, 136
Oro de Par, 40, 224n25
Oropesa, Alonso de, 161, 163, 187
Ottoman Empire, 24
Otto of Friesing, 19

Pacheco, Juan, 71, 235n46
Padilla, María de, 67
Palencia, Alfonso de, 71, 235n46, 271n82
Paleologus, Manuel II, 194–97, 208,
  282–83nn7–8
Palestine, 10, 88, 209, 210–11
Papiha, Surinder S., 274n8
Parzival, 25
Pedro (friar poet), 257n37
Pedro the Cruel (king of Castile): cruelty and
  downfall of, 26; as favorer of Jews, 137;
  Jewish origins of, 270n77; Jews as admin-
  istrators and, 231n27; murder of, 65, 84,
  101; politics of queens and concubines
  and, 66–67, 231n32; rebellion against,
  137; as son of Jewess, 84, 101
Pere (father of Jaume I of Catalonia-Aragon),
  62–63

Pere of Ribagorça, 245–46n40
Pérès, Henri, 286n46
Pere Xemeniz, 244–45n31
Pérez de Sent Jordi, Joan, 238n13
Peter (saint), 227–28n64
Peterson, Erik, 237n6
Peter the Ceremonious (king of Catalon):
  Muslim converts to Judaism and, 43–44;
  Muslim women in adultery and, 41, 77,
  79, 110, 223n17, 238n16
Peter the Venerable of Cluny, 19, 22
Petrarch, 128, 173, 203, 205
Phaedrus, 124, 254n21
Philo, 124–25, 145, 198, 254n22, 254–55n25
Pidal, Ramón Menéndez, 286n40
Pinehas, 36
Pinto, Isaac de, 144, 262n5
Pirro (ally of Nebuchadnezzar), 160
Pius II (pope), 150–51, 266n35
Plá, José, 278n35
places of worship, 40, 49
plague, 100–101, 105, 106, 245n38, 245n39
Plato, 6, 124
Poeta, Juan, 124, 140
poetry. *See* literature
politics: bare life versus good life and, 139;
  body politic and, 91; church and state
  and, 136–37, 138; conversos excluded
  from, 134; corporeal versus higher politics
  and, 135; of flesh versus spirit, 135;
  hermeneutics and, 136–37; Jewishness
  of bad governance and, 259n50; Jewish
  participation in, 138; Jews as figure of
  political thought and, 137; Jew versus
  Christian in, 138–39; Judaizing and,
  136–37, 139; literacy tests and, 138; poetics and, 137–38; private body versus body
  politic and, 139; of queens and concubines, 66–67, 68–69, 71, 231n32; reading
  like Jew versus Christian in, 138; rebellions against "Jew-loving" rulers and, 137;
  secular versus divine power and, 135–36;
  sovereignty and exception and, 86–88;
  taxation and, 136; versus theology, 88;
  tyranny and, 135
Pontanus, Ludovicus, 226n53
Popkin, Richard, 141
Primera Crónica General, 62
privados, 67, 70, 71, 138, 233n34, 235–
  36n48

prostitution: Christian prostitutes and non-Christian men and, 99, 248n59; conversos' new sexual privileges and, 111; God's punishments and, 92, 94; honor and, 99; husband putting wife to work in, 107, 248n63; marriage of former client and, 244n30; Muslims' role in, 113, 224n29; necessity of, 242n5; punishments for, 106, 248n59; real and perceived amount of, 107; recognition of religious difference by, 99; religion of prostitutes and, 224n30; seclusion of, amid plague outbreaks, 100; security of social frontiers and, 100; vocabulary of race and, 279n39

Pucellina (Jewish woman in relationship with Christian count), 55

Pulgar, Fernando del, 271n84

punishment: of attackers in Valencia massacre of 1391, 79, 83, 239n22, 239nn28–29; for Christian protectors in Valencia massacre of 1391, 81–83; death penalty for adultery and, 222n9, 223n17, 246n42; death penalty for interreligious relationships and, 41, 92, 93, 99, 103, 223n17, 245n35; disease as punishment for interreligious relationships and, 245n39; disfigurement as, 224n25; health implications of sins and, 243n19; individual versus communal, 93, 94; instruments of God's discipline and, 94; Jews' versus Muslims' ability to enact, 224n26; loss of clothes as, 248n59; monetary fines and, 224n26, 248n59; for participants in massacres, 240n41; for prostitution, 106, 248n59; provocations to, 94; trials by ordeal and, 241n50. See also Castigos (Sancho IV of Castile)

Punishments, The (Castigos). See Castigos (Sancho IV of Castile)

Qabbalah, 155

Qeshet u-Magen (Shim'on Ben Tzemaḥ Duran), 166

Qimḥi, David, 159

Quadrado, José María, 265n29

Qur'an: Alborayque beast in, 158, 184; ambivalence about neighborliness in, 2; Christian marginal notes in, 18–19; coproduction of religious communities in, 7–8; generation of meaning and, 12; geographic vocabulary of, 4; Hebrew Bible in,

4–5, 216n8; Mary (mother of Christ) in, 227n60; mount of revelation in, 4, 216n6; poetry and, 205; Talmud in, 4–5

race and racism: agricultural allusions and, 180–82, 188, 274n10, 279n44; anticonverso ideology and, 182; anti-Semitism versus anti-Judaism and, 176, 275–76nn18–19; Aragonese race and, 278n35; axiom of modernity of, 176, 276n20; axiom of race and biology and, 173, 274n10; biology versus culture and, 172–73, 176, 178, 179, 181–82, 185; birth of racism and, 90–91, 143, 144–45; versus caste, 178, 179; chromatic and less chromatic classifications and, 170; confusion of bloodlines and, 139; consequences of dismantling, 171–72, 273n2; cultivation of, in fifteenth-century Spain, 186–87; curse of Ham and, 262–63n9; Darwinian evolution and, 274n10, 276n24; decadence and, 177; definitions of, 172, 178, 181, 273n2, 273n5, 277n27; determination of Jewishness and, 119; discrediting of, 170, 171–72; etymology of, 180–81, 278n37; Europe's external challenges versus internal conflicts in, 274n12; explanatory value of, 273n4; external physical characteristics and, 178, 277n28; fallacy of race and, 170; as fiction, 177; genealogy and, 145, 187–88, 273–74n6; genetic markers and, 274n8; genetic transmission of ideas and, 144–45; German Jews and American blacks and, 170; grounding of discrimination and, 172–73; Hispanic race and, 178, 179, 276–77n25, 278n35; history of, 170; Inquisition and, 177–78; as intractable historical problem, 188–90; Jewish and converso attributes and, 262n7; Jews and origins of, 144; Jews as inventors of, 262–69; Jews as race and, 277n29; Judaization and, 187–88; logic of lineage, 144–45; masks and, 175; medieval theories of immutability and, 275–76n19; modern and premodern uses of terms and, 171–73; as modern innovation, 170–71, 173–74; modes of differentiation and, 242n1; naturalization of difference and, 180, 182, 279–80n45; origins of, 173–74; outcomes of historical processes and, 145; poetic de-

race and racism (*continued*)
fect and, 258n43; premodern innocence and, 172–74, 176, 273–74n6, 274n9; Protestant Reformation and, 176; purity and, 102, 134, 143–44, 157–59, 173–74; racial anti-Semitism and, 90–91, 175–76, 275n15, 275n17, 276n20, 277n27; racial categories and, 90; racial versus religious anti-Muslimism and, 277n29; versus religious differences, 134; replication of, under new name, 179; scientific, 139; Semitic race and, 179; sex as site of production of, 90; sexuality and, 113; state racism and, 173–74; testimony of nature and, 157; vocabulary of, 171–72, 177–78, 179, 180–82, 183, 188, 276n24, 279n39

Ranke, Leopold, 177
Ratzinger, Joseph. *See* Benedict XVI (pope)
Real Academia de la Historia, 177, 180
reconquest, 35, 39–40
Redfield, Robert, 273n2
Reformation, 176
Renan, Ernest, 179
Reuchlin, Johann, 176
Reuven (son of Nissim Gerundi), 147
Rieri, Antoni, 250n86
Rimoch, Abraham, 151
Robert the Monk, 21
Rodrigo (king), 62
Rodríguez de Almela, Diego, 72, 235n47
Roig, Jaume, 111, 156
Rois Najarí, Gil, 250n92
Roman Empire, 136, 259–60n58
Romano, David, 274n9
Romeu, Aldonza, 162
Rosenzweig, Franz, 87
Roth, Cecil, 144, 175–76, 178, 210, 276n20
Ruether, Rosemary, 108, 109
Rufinus, 198

Sadoletus, Jacobus, 182
Safàbrega, Antoni, 113
Saint Vincent. *See* Vincent Ferrer (saint)
Sánchez-Albornoz, Claudio, 144, 252n8, 262n7
Sancho IV of Castile: illegitimate success of, 66; on Jewess of Toledo, 58, 230n13; Lope Díaz de Haro and, 64, 70; love story of, 55–56; María de Molina and, 62, 64, 66, 231n30; marriage of, into nobility, 67; rebellion of, 64; translation of tombs

by, 231n20; wives of, 231n20. See also *Castigos* (Sancho IV of Castile)
Sancta Fe, Gerónimo de, 251n93
Santa María, Pablo de, 155–56, 161, 272n92
Santner, Eric, 87
Sarkozy, Nicolas, 10
Schlegel, August Wilhelm von, 208
Schmitt, Carl, 22, 86, 87, 88, 237n6, 241n52
scripture: body and soul and, 254n22; literal versus figural interpretation of, 72, 236n50; as living record, 9–10; polemic engagement with other faiths' texts and, 18–19; reading for hidden meaning and, 125. *See also* Hebrew Bible; New Testament; Qur'an
Secretariat for the Alliance of Civilizations, 10
Sefer Hasidim (genealogy), 263n13
segregation: of converts from Jews, 265n29; Jewish badges and, 148, 247n51; Jews blamed for, 162–63; limits of, 247n54; mass conversions and, 148–49; Murcian statutes and, 247n53; Muslims and, 248n61; to prevent interreligious relationships, 94, 103–7, 247n53; reasons given for, 148–49; royal edicts and, 264nn25–26; scriptural justification for, 271n83; in United States, 171; Saint Vincent Ferrer and, 104–7, 112, 113, 162–63, 264n25; violence involved in implementation of, 248n61
Sephardim: cemeteries and tombs of, 144, 261–62nn3–4; genealogy and, 143–44, 152–53, 154–55, 159–60, 167; versus Goths, 160, 269n73; historiographic mentality and, 165; intermarriage with other Jews and, 262nn4–5; literature on Sephardic identity and, 144; marriage contracts of, 167, 273n96; offspring of Sephardic-Ashkenazic marriages and, 262n4; origins of emphasis on lineage and, 144, 262n8; records of travels of, 152, 266n40; royal pedigree and, 144, 159–60, 263n12; superiority of, compared to other Jews, 143–44, 155, 159
sex and marriage. *See* interreligious love and sex relationships; sex and sexuality; sexual boundaries
sex and sexuality: accusations for sexual crimes and, 105, 244–45n31, 246n42; accusations of Jewishness and, 122; anach-

ronism and, 90; boundaries of Christianity and, 94; in Christian divine economy, 93; Christian sexual honor and, 93, 98; clerical concubines and, 95; consanguinity and, 244n30; death penalty for adultery and, 222n9, 223n17, 246n42; deviance and, 105; *Ecclesia* as female body and, 91–92; father-son conflict over sex with slaves and, 224n30; God as beautiful woman and, 243n13; hierarchy of sexual sins and, 94–95; images to express dangers of, 94; individual versus communal sin and, 94; integrity of the self and, 97; literary culture of the erotic and, 222nn11–12; location of anxiety about, 97–98; modes of differentiation and, 242n1; as necessary function, 242n5; in poetic exchanges, 130–31; as popular subject of study, 89–90; pretext for evangelization and, 107; prevention of rape and, 94; in Proverbs, 230n11; race and, 90, 113; religious classification and, 90, 91; religious identity and, 91–92; reproduction and, 113; sexual and spiritual kinship and, 244n30; sexual corruption of kings and, 231n22; slavery as punishment for adultery and, 223n17; sodomy and, 230n10; in Song of Songs, 242n7; spiritual union and, 97; universality of, 90. *See also* homosexuality; interreligious love and sex relationships; prostitution; sexual boundaries

sexual boundaries: before and after 1391, 97–98, 99–100, 101–2, 103–7, 113–14; Christian endogamy and, 93, 221n3; Christian identity and, 113, 114; between conversos and "natural" Christians, 113–14; enforcement of, 38; injunctions for sexual restraint and, 230n13; Jewish badges and, 97, 105; protection of lineage and, 153; religious versus racial difference and, 113–14; segregation to prevent interreligious sex and, 94, 103–7, 113; sexual versus reproductive logic and, 114–15; shifting of, 95, 114–15; societal imagination of, 90; sociological differentiation and, 110, 250n82. *See also* interreligious love and sex relationships; sex and sexuality

Shachar, Uri, 216n10

Shalom, Abraham, 234n40

Shauki, Ahmad, 209

Shelomo ben Shim'on Duran, 154

Shelomo ibn Verga, 160, 165

Shemeriah ben Elijah of Crete, 234n40

Shem Tov ben Joseph ibn Shem Tov, 159, 280n56

Sheveṭ Yehudah (ibn Verga), 160

Shim'on II (son of Shelomo ben Shim'on Duran), 154

Shim'on ben Tzemaḥ Duran, 154, 166

Silva, Feliciano de, 278n33

Simfa (Muslim convert to Judaism), 45

Simmel, Georg, 93

Sismondi, Sismonde de, 207

slavery, 38–44, 46–47, 98, 147, 223n18, 224n30

Socrates, 124, 254n21

Soissons, count of, 55

Song of Roland, 18, 25

Song of the Cid, 25

Sophronios, 16

sovereignty and exceptions, 86–88

Spain: as anachronistic term, 216n11; Black Legend and, 178, 279–80n45; civil war in, 97, 101, 276–77n25; fascism in, 276–77n25; fear of Judaization of, 47; 1492 expulsion of Jews from, 26, 53, 102, 120, 160; as full of Jews, 164; Garden of Eden as template for, 62; growth of anti-Judaism in, 50–51, 52–53; as hybrid land, 164; interreligious proximity in, 6; Jewish influences on culture of, 120; Jewishness of, 140–41; kings' autonomy from nobility in, 66–67, 70; as land of three religions, 12–13; obsession with genealogy in, 143–44; as paradise of civilization, 208–10, 286n44; purity of blood laws and, 269–70n74; queens as regents in, 66; racial identity and, 178; religious diversity of, 176–77; Secretariat for the Alliance of Civilizations and, 11; sexual boundaries before and after 1391 in, 97–98; in study of history of race, 175, 176–77, 180

Spinoza, 141

Strayer, Joseph, 219n18

Sweatt v. Texas, 273n2

Sylvester, Bernard, 128

Tacitus, 221n3

Talavera disputation, 46, 47, 50–52, 53, 225–26nn45–47, 227n60

Talmud, 4–5, 95–96, 97, 261n71
Taubes, Jacob, 241n52
taxation, 136, 146, 149–50, 260n59, 265n30
Tay-Sachs disease, 173
Tertullian, 259–60n58
Teutonicus, Johannes, 96
Theodosius (emperor), 137
Theophilus, 68, 71
Thibault of Blois, 55
Thomas Aquinas: justification of crusades by, 24; on law and sovereignty, 80; on marriage between convert and sponsor, 244n30; on nonbiblical poetry, 128; on poetic and other fictions, 255n26
Titus (emperor), 158, 263n12
Tizón (Bovadilla), 272n91
Todros Abulafia, 37–38
Toledan revolt of 1449: anticonverso discourse and, 47, 138, 139, 157, 163, 183–84; anticonverso legislation and, 134; anticonverso violence and, 48, 71; debate over anticonverso discrimination and, 185; purity of blood statutes and, 102, 134, 188
Torah, 127
Torquemada, Juan de, 184
Tostado. See Alfonso de Madrigal "el Tostado"
Tovi, Jucef, 241n43
Trust for Culture of the Aga Khan, 208
Turner, Frederick Jackson, 22
Tzemaḥ (son of Shelomo ben Shim'on Duran), 154, 155

'Umar (caliph), 16
Union for the Mediterranean, 10–11
United Nations Secretariat for the Alliance of Civilizations, 10, 192–93
University of Chicago, 273n2
Urban II (pope), 21–22

Valencia massacre of 1391: as act of God, 80, 81; as antinomian explosion, 77–78; as cataclysm for Jews and Christians, 90; children in, 80–81; Christian and Jewish as categories after, 133; Christian identity crisis and, 102, 103; consequences of, 89; constitutional implications of, 76, 83, 85, 88; as crisis of sovereignty, 78; deputization of citizens and, 237–38n12; forced conversions and, 81–82, 101–2, 111, 119, 238n14, 239n22; forgiveness

of participants in, 85; Jews as figures of supreme subjection and, 76–77, 83–84; Joan I summoned to Valencia and, 82–83; Judaism as form for linguistic critique after, 133; justifications of, 76; miracles and, 81, 82, 85–86, 119, 238–39nn21–22; multiple accounts of, 78–79, 80; number killed in, 79; origins of, 78, 80–81, 238n13, 238nn20–21; outcome of, 75–76; political theology and, 87–88; protection of Jews in, 78–79, 81–82, 84, 237–38n12, 238n16; punishment for Christian protectors and, 81–83; punishment of attackers in, 79, 83, 239n22, 239nn28–29; as quasi-liturgical, 81; remaining Jews in Morvedre and, 241n43; services to crown as Jewish and, 77, 237n7; sexual boundaries before and after, 97–98; sovereign suspension of law and, 79–80, 82; thoroughness of, 86; transfer of surviving Jews and, 239nn24–25
Valera, Mosén Diego de, 160–61, 183
Vashti (queen), 69
Verdejo, Juan de, 241n43
Viardot, Louis, 209
Vincent Ferrer (saint): carnality of Jews and, 109–10; on Christian patrons of Muslim prostitutes, 42; on Christian refusal of violence, 281n62; Christians as neighbors of Jews and, 148, 149; contours of concerns expressed by, 104; on corruption, 243n20; crisis of religious identity and, 148; on dangers of secular poetry, 128; evangelization and, 111; on God as beautiful woman, 243n13; on God's punishment, 94; hierarchy of sexual sins and, 94; importance of, 104; on infrequent confession, 163; Jewish idioms for spiritual dangers and, 109; on Jews and Muslims as not God's children, 243n11; on Jews as neighbors of Christians, 1; on Jews' materialistic beliefs, 264n23; mass conversions and, 119, 148; messianic inspiration of, 119, 250n87; Murcian statutes and, 247n53; orthodoxy of conversos and, 105; on prostitution, 92, 94, 113; residential rules for conversos and, 247n54; segregation and, 104–7, 112, 113, 162–63, 264n25; sex in divine economy of honor and, 93; warnings of, 106, 109–10

Violant (queen), 78, 85
Vives, Luis, 164
Voltaire, 144

Walid I, 17
Walz, Rainer, 273–74nn5–6
Warburg, Aby, 264n18
Warton, Thomas, 207
Weber, Max, 119
Weimar debates, 86–87
Weiss, Julian, 123–24
Weissberger, Barbara, 230n10, 235n46
Werner Sombart, 119

Xerxes (king), 68

Yehuda ben Asher ben Yeḥiel of Toledo, 36–37, 40, 43, 222n11

Yerushalmi, Yosef Hayim, 144, 165, 260–61n69, 272n93, 272–73n95, 275n15, 276n20
Yosef ben Tzadiq of Arévalo, 165
Yovel, Yirmiyahu, 260–61n69, 284n23
Yuda (Jewish man in Talavera disputation), 46
Yuhanna b. Mansur b. Sarjun. See John of Damascus

Zacuto, Abraham, 165
Zaida (wife of Alfonso VI), 57, 62, 231n20
zakāt, 29, 30
Zaragoza, archbishop of, 103, 104
Žižek, Slavoj, 87, 88